The Critical Pedagogy Reader

The Critical Pedagogy Reader

ANTONIA DARDER, MARTA BALTODANO, AND RODOLFO D. TORRES

RoutledgeFalmer
New York • London

Published in 2003 by
RoutledgeFalmer
29 West 35th Street
New York, NY 10001
www.routledge-ny.com

Published in Great Britain by
RoutledgeFalmer
11 New Fetter Lane
London EC4P 4EE
www.routledgefalmer.com

10 9 8 7 6 5 4

Library of Congress Cataloging-in-Publication Data

The critical pedagogy reader / Antonia Darder, Marta Baltodano, and Rodolfo D. Torres [editors].
    p. cm.
    Includes bibliographical references.
    ISBN 0-415-92260-7—ISBN 0-415-92261-5 (pbk.)
    1. Critical pedagogy. I. Darder, Antonia. II. Baltodano, Marta. III. Torres, Rodolfo D.,
1949–

LC196 .C758 2002
370.11′5—dc21

                                                                              2002024903

Dedicated to the memory of
Carmen Francisca Aguilo Rosario
1932–2001

Contents

Part 3 RACE, RACISM, AND EDUCATION

Part 4 GENDER, SEXUALITY, AND SCHOOLING

Part 5 LANGUAGE, LITERACY, AND PEDAGOGY

Part 6 CRITICAL ISSUES IN THE CLASSROOM

Part 7 TEACHING AND SOCIAL TRANSFORMATION

Acknowledgments

ON A PUBLIC NOTE

In pulling together this volume, we discovered that our publisher, Routledge, has been one of the foremost leaders in publishing works by critical education scholars in the country. For their continuing commitment to extend the definition of democracy and freedom through the written word, we would like to extend our deepest appreciation for their addition of this volume to their long list of notable works.

ON A SCHOLARLY NOTE

We want to thank our numerous colleagues and comrades for their sustaining and continuing support, but especially to Peter McLaren, who has been a true and ever-present comrade in the most difficult of times. We love you, Pete!

ON A PEDAGOGICAL NOTE

We want to acknowledge and express our most sincere appreciation to our students who teach and learn with us each day about what it means to live a critical pedagogy.

ON A PERSONAL NOTE

AD: Thank you Gabriel, Kelly, Christy, and Mike for being there for me, no matter what.

MB: Thank you Alberto and Emanuel for your love and patience.

RDT: Thank you Patricia and Jacob for making my life complete.

Critical Pedagogy: An Introduction

ANTONIA DARDER, MARTA BALTODANO, AND RODOLFO D. TORRES

A society which makes provision for participation in its good of all members on equal terms and which secures flexible readjustment of its institutions through interaction of the different forms of associated life is insofar democratic. Such a society must have a type of education which gives individuals a personal interest in social relationships and control, and the habits of mind which secure social changes.

—John Dewey
Education & Democracy, 1916

We believe that Education leads to action.

—Myles Horton
Founder of the Highlander Folk School, 1932

Students live in a historical situation, in a social, political and economic moment. Those things have to be part of what we teach.

—Herbert Kohl
Founder of the Open School Movement, 1964

The dual society, at least in public education, seems in general to be unquestioned.
—Jonathan Kozol
Death at an Early Age, 1967

If situations cannot be created that enable the young to deal with feelings of being manipulated by outside forces, there will be far too little sense of agency among them. Without a sense of agency, young people are unlikely to pose significant questions, the existentially rooted questions in which learning begins.

—Maxine Green
The Dialectics of Freedom, 1988

Many students, especially those who are poor, intuitively know what the schools do for them. They school them to confuse process and substance. Once these become blurred, a new logic is assumed: the more treatment there is, the better are the results; or escalation leads to success. The pupil is thereby "schooled" to confuse teaching with learning, grade advancement with education, a diploma with competence, and fluency with the ability to say something new.

—Ivan Illich
Deschooling Society, 1971

Knowledge emerges only through invention and re-invention, through the restless, impatient continuing, hopeful inquiry [we] pursue in the world, with the world, and with each other.

—Paulo Freire
Pedagogy of the Oppressed, 1971

Our analysis of the repressiveness, inequality, and contradictory objectives of contemporary education in America is not only a critique of schools and educators, but also of the social order of which they are a part.

—Samuel Bowles & Herbert Gintis
Schooling in Capitalist America, 1976

As these words well illustrate, the struggle for public democratic schooling in America has been a multidimensional enterprise that has for over a century occupied the dreams, hearts, and minds of many educators. These educators were not only seriously committed to the ideal and practice of social justice within schools, but to the transformation of those structures and conditions within society that functioned to thwart the democratic participation of all people.

Critical pedagogy loosely evolved out of a yearning to give some shape and coherence to the theoretical landscape of radical principles, beliefs, and practices that contributed to an emancipatory ideal of democratic schooling in the United States during the twentieth century. In many ways, it constituted a significant attempt to bring an array of divergent views and perspectives to the table, in order to invigorate the capacity of radical educators to engage critically with the impact of capitalism and gendered, racialized relations upon the lives of students from historically disenfranchised populations.

The first textbook use of the term *critical pedagogy* is found in Henry Giroux's *Theory and Resistance in Education* published in 1983. During the 1980s and 1990s, Henry Giroux's work, along with that of Paulo Freire, Stanley Aronowitz, Michael Apple, Maxine Greene, Peter McLaren, bell hooks, Donaldo Macedo, Michelle Fine, Jean Anyon, and many others, was, inarguably, one of the most central and potent forces in the revitalization of educational debates regarding democratic schooling in this country. However,

Giroux would be the first to adamantly insist that critical pedagogy emerged from a long historical legacy of radical social thought and progressive educational movements that aspired to link the practice of schooling to democratic principles of society and to transformative social action in the interest of oppressed communities.

MAJOR INFLUENCES ON THE FORMATION OF CRITICAL PEDAGOGY
TWENTIETH-CENTURY EDUCATORS AND ACTIVISTS

The views of the American philosopher and educator John Dewey often referred to as the father of the progressive education movement, had a significant influence on progressive educators concerned with advancing democratic ideals within education. During the early 1900s, Dewey sought to articulate his pragmatic philosophy and expand on the idea of community to explain the purpose of education in a democratic society. His beliefs centered on a variety of basic principles, including the notion that education must engage with and enlarge experience; that thinking and reflection are central to the act of teaching; and that students must freely interact with their environments in the practice of constructing knowledge. Although there are those who have sharply criticized Dewey's faith in creative intelligence as eminently naïve and accused him of underestimating the sociopolitical and economic forces that shape inequality and injustice, Dewey's work is consistent in "his attempt to link the notion of individual and social (cooperative) intelligence with the discourse of democracy and freedom" (McLaren, 1989, p. 199). By so doing, John Dewey provided "a language of possibility"—a philosophical construct that has been of foremost significance to the evolution of critical pedagogy.

Myles Horton, considered by some to be one of the sparks that ignited the civil rights movement in the United States, channeled his belief in the political potential of schooling into the founding of the Highlander Folk School (known today as the Highlander Research and Education Center) in Monteagle, Tennessee. The purpose of the school was to provide a place for the education of blacks and whites in defiance of segregation laws. Over the years, Horton's work resulted in the participation of thousands of people, challenging entrenched social, economic, and political structures of a segregated society. One of the most noted among them was the civil rights activist Rosa Parks, who had attended Highlander just a few months prior to her refusal to move to the back of the bus. Key to Horton's political practice was the notion that in order for education or institutional change to be effective, it had to begin with the people themselves—a particularly significant tenet of critical pedagogical thought.

In the early 1960s, the views of Herbert Kohl provided the impetus for the development of the Open School Movement in the United States. His efforts to challenge and address issues of democratic schooling were fundamentally rooted in a tradition of radical politics and radical history that could counter the structures of oppression at work in public schools. Kohl's deep commitment to community interactions and his tremendous faith in students set a significant example for the practice of teaching diverse students from working-class populations. And although he has been known to take issue with the academic writings of critical educators today, Kohl's uncompromising political views on schooling and activism were significant in helping to lay the groundwork for the development of critical pedagogical practices in the years to come.

Beginning with his first book, *Death at an Early Age,* the work of long-time social activist Jonathan Kozol consistently examined issues related to racism, class, and schooling through his many efforts to ground his conclusions upon the actual stories and experiences of dispossessed populations in the United States. More importantly, he sought to address the material conditions and expose the social consequences of poverty and racism to those children and their families who were relegated to an existence at the margins of American life. For Kozol, as for educators like Paulo Freire, questions of education could not only be engaged in terms of the theoretical, programmatic or technical, they had to also be reconceptualized along human and spiritual, as well as political grounds. In many ways, Kozol (as did Freire) denounced the immorality of human oppression, particularly as these related to the needs of children across the country.

The internationally recognized philosopher and educator Maxine Greene has played a pivotal role in her work with critical educators in the United States. Often referred to as the mother of aesthetic education, Greene was the first woman philosopher to be hired at Columbia University's Teachers College in 1963. In the midst of the hostility she faced as a woman and a Jew, Greene persevered to become a formidable force in the theoretical arena of aesthetics and its relationship to education and society. Many of her views on education and democracy today still echo thoughts and concerns raised by Dewey almost a century ago. For Greene, democracy constitutes a way of life that must be practiced within both social and political arenas, made living through our relationships, our educational experiences, as well as our moments of beauty and enjoyment out in the world. Greene's contribution to critical pedagogy is most evident by the manner in which her reflective theories of knowledge, human nature, learning, curriculum, schooling, and society have influenced the practice of progressive educators for over thirty years

In the arena of schooling and the political economy, the work of such noted theorists as Samuel Bowles and Herbert Gintis, Martin Carnoy, and Michael Apple all contributed greatly to the forging of a critical pedagogical perspective that upheld the centrality of the economy to the configuration of power relations within schools and society. Through their persistent critique of capitalism, these theorists argued in a variety of ways that the problems associated with schooling were actually tied to the reproduction of a system of social relations that perpetuate the existing structures of domination and exploitation. Michael Apple, in particular, linked notions of cultural capital with the school's reproduction of official knowledge—knowledge that primarily functioned to sustain the inequality of class relations within schools and society.

Ivan Illich, who in the 1950s worked as a parish priest among the poor Irish and Puerto Rican communities of New York City, has been considered by many to be one of the most radical political and social thinkers in the second half of the twentieth century. His critical writings, including *Deschooling Society* published in 1971, on schooling and society, sought to analyze the institutional structures of industrialization and to provide both rigorous criticism and an alternative to what he perceived as the crisis of a society that endorses growth economy, political centralization, and unlimited technology. In very important ways, Illich's views on education and the institutionalization of everyday life inspired critical education theorists and activists during the latter half of the twentieth century to rethink their practice in schools and communities. Most notable among these educators was the Brazilian educator Paulo Freire.

THE BRAZILIAN INFLUENCE

While progressive educators and social activists such as Myles Horton, Martin Luther King, Herbert Kohl, Angela Davis, Cesar Chavez, Malcohm X, and many others challenged the disgraceful conditions of oppressed people in the United States, Brazilian educator Paulo Freire and his contemporary Augusto Boal were also involved in challenging the horrendous conditions they found in the cities and countryside of Brazil–a struggle that was historically linked to the emancipatory efforts of many educators and political activists in other countries across Latin America.

Paulo Freire would be forced to live in exile for over fifteen years for his writings on education and the dispossessed members of Brazilian society. In the early 1970s, Paulo Freire was extended an invitation to come to Harvard University as a visiting professor. It was his presence in the United States during that precise historical moment, along with the translation of his book *Pedagogy of the Oppressed* into English, that became a watershed for radical educators within schools, communities, and labor organizations that were struggling to bring about social change to public health, welfare, and educational institutions across the country.

As a consequence, Paulo Freire is considered by many to be the most influential educational philosopher in the development of critical pedagogical thought and practice. From the 1970s until his death in 1997, Freire continued to publish and speak extensively to educators throughout the United States. Although Freire's writings focused on questions of pedagogy, his thought widely influenced postcolonial theory, ethnic studies, cultural studies, adult education, and theories of literacy, language, and human development.

Most importantly, Freire labored consistently to ground the politics of education within the existing framework of a larger societal milieu.

As with so many of the influential educators previously mentioned, Freire's efforts were never simply confined to discussions of methodology or applications of teaching practice. Instead, Freire forthrightly inserted questions of power, culture, and oppression within the context of schooling. In so doing, he reinforced the Frankfurt School's focus on theory and practice as imperative to the political struggles against exploitation and domination. Through his views on emancipatory education, Freire made central pedagogical questions related to social agency, voice, and democratic participation—questions that strongly inform the recurrent philosophical expressions of critical pedagogical writings even today.

Augusto Boal's book *Theatre of the Oppressed* was released in 1971, the same year as Freire's seminal text, *Pedagogy of the Oppressed.* In the 1960s, Boal developed an experimental theater approach whereby the cast would stop a performance and invite members of the audience to provide or demonstrate new suggestions onstage. By so doing, he unexpectedly discovered an effective pedagogical form of praxis that evolved directly from the audience's participation, collective reflection, and the action generated by the participants. Excited and inspired by the process of empowerment he witnessed among the participants, Boal began to develop what was to be known as the "spec-actor" (in contrast to spectator) theater approach.

Seeing the possibilities of his approach as a vehicle for grassroots activism, Boal's work in communities began to give shape to his *Theatre of the Oppressed.* Similar to Freire, Boal's work as cultural activist was repressed by the military coup that came to power during the 1960s. He was arrested, tortured, and eventually exiled for his activities. Boal continued to develop his work in Argentina and later in Paris. He returned to Brazil in 1986, when the military junta was removed from power. Boal's work was first linked to Freire's work in the United States at the Pedagogy and Theatre of the Oppressed Conference in 1994. Boal's contribution was to mark a significant turning point for those critical educators and artists who had become frustrated with what they perceived as, on one hand, the deeply theoretical nature of critical pedagogy and, on the other, the absence of more practical and affective strategies to enliven their work. For these critical educators, Boal's theater of the oppressed provided a new avenue upon which to build and rethink their educational practices in schools and communitites.

GRAMSCI AND FOUCAULT

Although it is impossible to discuss here all the "classical" theorists who influenced the intellectual development of critical pedagogy, the contributions of Antonio Gramsci and Michel Foucault to a critical understanding of education merit some discussion. These philosophers extended the existing understanding of power and its impact on the construction of knowledge. Their writings also strengthen the theoretical foundation upon which to conduct critical readings of culture, consciousness, history, domination, and resistance.

Antonio Gramsci, imprisoned by Mussolini during World War II for his active membership in the Communist Party and public rejection of fascism, was deeply concerned with the manner in which domination was undergoing major shifts and changes within advanced industrial Western societies. With his theory of hegemony, Gramsci sought to explain the manner by which this change was being exercised less and less through brutal physical means and more and more through the moral leaders of society (including teachers) who participated in and reinforced universal "commonsense" notions of what is considered to be truth within a society.

This phenomenon can be understood within the context of schooling in the following way. Through the daily implementation of specific norms, expectations, and behaviors that incidentally conserve the interest of those in power, students are ushered into consensus. Gramsci argued that through nourishing such consensus through personal and institutional rewards, students could be socialized to support the interest of the ruling elite, even when such actions were clearly in contradiction with the student's own class interests. As such, this reproduction of ideological hegemony within schools functioned to sustain the hegemonic processes that reproduced cultural and economic domination within the society. This process of reproduction was then perpetuated through what Gramsci termed "contradictory consciousness." However, for Gramsci this was not a clean and neat act of one-dimensional reproduction. Instead, domination existed here as a complex combination of thought and practices in which could also be found the seeds for resistance.

The French philosopher Michel Foucault deeply questioned what he termed "regimes of truth" that were upheld and perpetuated through the manner in which particular knowledge was legitimated within the context of a variety of power relationships within society. However, for Foucault, power did not represent a static entity, but rather an active process constantly at work on our bodies, and our relationships, and our sexuality, as well as on the ways we construct knowledge and meaning in the world. However, it is important to note that power in Foucault's conceptualization is not solely at play in the context of domination, but also in the context of creative acts of resistance—creative acts that are produced as human beings interact across the dynamic of relationships and shaped by moments of dominance and autonomy. Such a view of power challenged the tendency of radical education theorists to think of power solely from the dichotomized standpoint of either domination or powerlessness. As such, Foucault's writings on knowledge and power shed light on a critical understanding of student resistance within the classroom and opened the door to better understanding power relationships within the context of teaching practice.

THE FRANKFURT SCHOOL

Critical educational thought is fundamentally linked to those critical theories of society that emerged from the members of the Frankfurt School and their contemporaries, as they sought to challenge the traditional forms of rationality that defined the concept of meaning and knowledge in the Western world during a very critical moment in the history of the twentieth century. As such, their work was driven by an underlying commitment to the notion that theory, as well as practice, must inform the work of those who seek to transform the oppressive conditions that exist in the world.

The Institute for Social Research (Das Institut für Sozialforschung) was officially established in Frankfurt in 1923 and was the home of the Frankfurt School. The Institute came under the direction of Max Horkeimer in 1930. Although there were a number of other prominent thinkers who worked under the direction of Horkheimer, those most significant to the development of critical social theory included Theodor Adorno, Walter Benjamin, Leo Lowenthal, Erich Fromm, and Herbert Marcuse. More recently, the work of Jürgen Habermas was also to receive much attention within the arena of critical theory.

The Institute in its early years was primarily concerned with an analysis of bourgeois society's substructure, but with time its interest focused on the cultural superstructures. This change in the Institute's focus was, undoubtedly, a result of the disruptions and certain fragmentation experienced in the process of emigration and repeated relocation in the 1930s and 1940s—a process that was precipitated by the threat of Nazism, the members' avowedly Marxist orientation, and the fact that most of them were Jews.

One cannot attempt to understand the foundations of critical theory without considering the historical context that influenced its development and shaped the minds of its foremost thinkers. The Frankfurt School came into being as a response to the important political and historical transformations taking place in the early part of the twentieth century. The political shifts in Germany's governing structure had a significant impact on its founders. During the early part of the century, Germany had managed to temporarily contain class conflict. But within two years following the end of World War I, the foundations of the German imperial system were undermined and a republic was declared in Berlin (Held, 1980). What followed were thirteen years of chaotic political struggles between the German Communist Party (KPD) and the more conservative forces of the Social Democratic Party (SPD).

As the KPD became increasingly ineffective in its efforts to organize a majority of the working class, the Social Democratic Leadership of the Weimar Republic supervised the destruction of the competing radical and revolutionary movements. In the process, the SDP not only failed to implement the promised democratization and socialization of production in Germany, but also failed to stop the monopolistic trends of German industrialists and the reactionary elements that eventually paved the way for the emergence of Nazism. As the forces of the Nazis, under Hitler's control, seized power in Germany, Italy and Spain came under the fascist leaderships of Mussolini and Franco. A similar fate befell the workers' struggles in these countries, where all independent socialist and liberal organizations were suppressed.

In light of the Marxist orientation shared by the members of the Frankfurt School, "the emergence of an antidemocratic political system in the country of the first socialist revolution" (Warren, 1984, 145), consequently, had a profound impact upon the development of critical theory. Moreover, the Russian Revolution had been systematically weakened by foreign interventions, blockades, and civil war, and Lenin's revolutionary vision was rapidly losing ground. After Lenin's death in 1924, Stalin advanced in Russia with the expansion of centralized control and censorship, a process created to maintain European communist parties under Moscow's leadership. In 1939, the Hitler-Stalin pact was enacted representing an ironic historical moment for those committed to the struggle of the working class and the socialist principles espoused by Marx.

A final event that strongly influenced the thinking of the Frankfurt School theorists was the nature and impact of the unconfined forces of advanced capitalism in the West. The rapid development of science and technology and their persuasive penetration into the political and social systems summoned a new and major transformation in the structure of capitalism. This accelerated development of an advanced industrial-technological society represented a serious area of concern.

The major historical and political developments of capitalist society, as well as the rise of bureaucratic communist orthodoxy, affirmed for the founders of critical theory the necessity of addressing two basic needs: 1) the need to develop a new critical social theory within a Marxist framework that could deal with the complex changes arising in industrial-technological, postliberal, capitalist society; and 2) the need to recover the philosophical dimensions of Marxism that had undergone a major economic and materialistic reduction by a new Marxist orthodoxy (Warren, 1984).

The Frankfurt School intended their findings to become a material force in the struggle against domination of all forms. Based upon the conditions they observed, the following questions were central to the work of the Institute (Held, 1980, 35):

The European labor movements did not develop in a unified struggle of workers. What blocked these developments?

Capitalism was a series of acute crises. How could these better be understood? What was the relationship between the political and the economic? Was that relationship changing?

Authoritarianism and the development of bureaucracy seemed increasingly the order of the day. How could the phenomena be comprehended? Nazism and fascism rose to dominate central and southern Europe. How was this possible? How did these movements attain large-scale support?

Social relationships, for example, those created by the family, appeared to be undergoing radical social change. In what directions? How were these affecting individual development?

The arena of culture appeared open to direct manipulation. Was a new type of ideology being formed? If so, how was this affecting everyday life?

Given the fate of Marxism in Russia and western Europe, was Marxism itself nothing other than a state orthodoxy? Was there a social agent capable of progressive change? What possibilities were there for effective socialist practices?

PHILOSOPHICAL PRINCIPLES OF CRITICAL PEDAGOGY

In response to many of these questions, Horkheimer, Adorno, Marcuse, Fromm, and others wrote seminal essays that were to serve as the building blocks for a critical theory of society. It was this critical perspective that ultimately provided the foundation for the philosophical principles that were to determine the set of *heterogeneous* ideas that were later to be known as critical pedagogy. We highlight the use of heterogeneous here because it is important to emphasize that no formula or homogeneous representation exists for the universal implementation of any form of critical pedagogy. In fact, it is precisely this distinguishing factor that constitutes its critical nature, and therefore its most emancipatory and democratic function.

The philosophical heterogeneity of its array of radical expressions is then consolidated only through an underlying and explicit intent and commitment to the unwavering liberation of oppressed populations. Toward this end, a set of principles tied to the radical belief in the historical possibility of change and social transformation can be tentatively fleshed out for the purpose of teaching and coming to better understand what is implied by a critical perspective of education, society, and the world. The following provides a very brief and general introduction to the principles that inform critical pedagogy. However, it is imperative that the reader bear in mind that the multitude of both specific and complex expressions of these philosophical ideas have been articulated through a variety of intellectual traditions—traditions that have sought to explore the relationship between human beings, schools, and society from a myriad of epistemological, political, economic, cultural, ideological, ethical, historical, and aesthetical, as well as methodological, points of reference.

CULTURAL POLITICS

Critical pedagogy is fundamentally committed to the development and evolvement of a culture of schooling that supports the empowerment of culturally maginalized and economically disenfranchised students. By so doing, this pedagogical perspective seeks to help transform those classroom structures and practices that perpetuate undemocratic life. Of particular importance, then, is a critical analysis and investigation into the manner in which traditional theories and practices of public schooling thwart or influence the development of a politically emancipatory and humanizing culture of participation, voice, and social action within the classroom. The purpose for this is intricately linked to the fulfillment of what Paulo Freire defined as our "vocation"—to be truly humanized social (cultural) agents in the world.

In an effort to strive for an emancipatory culture of schooling, critical pedagogy calls upon teachers to recognize how schools have historically embraced theories and practices that function to unite knowledge and power in ways that sustain asymmetrical relations of power under the guise of neutral and apolitical views of education—views that are intimately linked to ideologies shaped by power, politics, history, culture, and economics. From this vantage point, schools function as a terrain of ongoing cultural struggle over what will be accepted as legitimate knowledge. In accordance with this notion, a critical pedagogy seeks to address the concept of cultural politics by both legitimizing and challenging students' experiences and perceptions that shape the histories and socioeconomic realities that give meaning to how students define their everyday lives and how they construct what they perceive as truth.

POLITICAL ECONOMY

Critical education contends that, contrary to the traditional view, schools actually work against the class interests of those students who are most politically and economically vulnerable within society. The role of competing economic interests of the marketplace in the production of knowledge and in the structural relationships and policies that shape public schools are recognized as significant factors, particularly in the education of disenfranchised students. From the standpoint of economics, public schools serve to position select groups within asymmetrical power relations that serve to replicate the existing values and privileges of the culture of the dominant class. It is this uncontested relationship between schools and society that critical pedagogy seeks to challenge, unmasking traditional claims that education provides equal opportunity and access for all.

Hence, what is at issue here is the question of class reproduction and how schooling practices are deceptively organized to perpetuate racialized inequalities. This is to say that within the context of critical pedagogy, the relationship between culture and class is intricately linked and cannot be separated within the context of daily life in schools. The concept of class here refers to the economic, social, ethical, and political relationships that govern particular sectors of the social order. More importantly, critical pedagogy acknowledges the myriad ways in which material conditions within the lives of students and teachers contribute to their understanding of who they are and how they are perceived within schools and society.

HISTORICITY OF KNOWLEDGE

Critical pedagogy supports the notion that all knowledge is created within a historical context and it is this historical context that gives life and meaning to human experience. Within the context of this principle, schools must be understood not only within the boundaries of their social practice but within the boundaries of the historical events that inform educational practice. Along these lines, students and the knowledge they bring into the classroom must be understood as historical—that is, being constructed and produced within a particular historical moment and under particular historical conditions.

As such, critical pedagogy urges teachers to create opportunities in which students can come to discover that "there is no historical reality which is not human" (Freire, 1970, p. 125). By so doing, students come to understand themselves as subjects of history and to recognize that conditions of injustice, although historically produced by human beings, can also be transformed by human beings. This concept of student social agency is then tied to a process of collective and self-determined activity. This historical view of knowledge also challenges the traditional emphasis on historical continuities and historical development. Instead, it offers a mode of analysis that stresses the break, discontinuities, conflicts, differences, and tensions in history, all of which serve in bringing to light the centrality of human agency as it presently exists, as well as within the possibilities for change (Giroux, 1983).

DIALECTICAL THEORY

In opposition to traditional theories of education that serve to reinforce certainty, conformity, and technical control of knowledge and power, critical pedagogy embraces a dialectical view of knowledge that functions to unmask the connections between objective knowledge and the cultural norms, values, and standards of the society at large. Within this dialectical perspective, all analysis begins first and foremost with human existence and the contradictions and disjunctions that both shape and make its meaning problematic. Hence, the problems of society are not seen as mere random or isolated events, but rather as moments that arise out of the interactive context between the individual and society (McLaren, 1989).

An important emphasis here is that students are encouraged to engage the world within its complexity and fullness, in order to reveal the possibilities of new ways of constructing thought and action beyond how it currently exists. Rooted in a dialectical view of knowledge, critical pedagogy seeks to support the dynamic interactive elements, rather than participate in the formation of dichotomies and polarizations in thought and practice. By so doing, it supports a view of humans and nature that is relational, an objectivity and subjectivity that is interconnected, and an understanding of theory and practice as coexistent. Most importantly, this perspective resurfaces the power of human activity and human knowledge as both a product and a force in shaping the world, whether it be in the interest of domination or liberation.

IDEOLOGY AND CRITIQUE

Ideology can best be understood as the framework of thought that is used in society to give order and meaning to the social and political world in which we live. As important here is the notion that ideology be understood as existing at the deep, embedded psychological structures of the personality. Ideology more often than not manifests itself in the inner histories and experiences that give rise to questions of subjectivity as they are constructed by individual needs, drives, and passions, as well as the changing material conditions and social foundations of society. As such, a critical notion of ideology provides the means for not only a critique of educational curricula, texts, and practices, but the fundamental ethics that inform their production.

As a pedagogical tool, ideology can be used to interrogate and unmask the contradictions that exist between the mainstream culture of the school and the lived experiences and knowledge that students use to mediate the reality of school life. Ideology in this instance provides teachers with the necessary context to examine how their own views about knowledge, human nature, values, and society are mediated through the commonsense assumptions they use to structure classroom experiences. In this way, the principle of ideology in critical pedagogy serves as a starting point for asking questions that will help teachers to evaluate critically their practice and to better recognize how the culture of the dominant class becomes embedded in the hidden curriculum—curriculum that is informed by ideological views that silence students and structurally reproduce the dominant cultural assumptions and practices that thwart democratic education.

HEGEMONY

Hegemony refers to a process of social control that is carried out through the moral and intellectual leadership of a dominant sociocultural class over subordinate groups (Gramsci, 1971). Critical pedagogy incorporates this notion of hegemony in order to demystify the asymmetrical power relations and social arrangements that sustain the interest of the ruling class. Moreover, hegemony points to the powerful connection that exists between politics, economics, culture, and pedagogy. Within this context, teachers are challenged to recognize their responsibility to critique and transform those classroom conditions tied to hegemonic processes that perpetuate the economic and cultural maginalization of subordinate groups.

What is important to recognize here is that the process of critique must be understood as an ongoing process, for hegemony is not a static or absolute state. On the contrary, hegemony must be fought for constantly in order to retain its privileged position as the status quo. As a consequence, each time a radical form threatens the integrity of the status quo, generally this element is appropriated, stripped of its transformative intent, and reified into a palatable form. This process serves to maintain the existing power relations intact. Hence, understanding how hegemony functions in society provides critical educators with the basis for understanding not only how the seeds of domination are produced, but also how they can be challenged and overcome through resistance, critique, and social action.

RESISTANCE AND COUNTER-HEGEMONY

Critical pedagogy incorporates a theory of resistance in an effort to better explain the complex reasons why many students from subordinate groups consistently fail within the educational system. It begins with the assumption that all people have the capacity and ability to produce knowledge and to resist domination. However, how they choose to resist is clearly influenced and limited by the social and material conditions in which they have been forced to survive and the ideological formations that have been internalized in the process.

The principle of resistance seeks to uncover the degree to which student oppositional behavior is associated with their need to struggle against elements of dehumanization or are simply tied to the perpetuation of their own oppression. As in other aspects of critical pedagogy, the notion of emancipatory interests serves here as a central point of reference in determining when oppositional behavior reflects a moment of resistance that can support counter-hegemonic purposes.

The term *counter-hegemony* is used within critical pedagogy to refer to those intellectual and social spaces where power relationships are reconstructed to make central the voices and experiences of those who have historically existed within the margins of mainstream institutions. This is achieved whenever a counter-hegemonic context is forged out of moments of resistance, through establishing alternative structures and practices that democratize relations of power, in the interest of liberatory possibilities. It is significant to note here that given the powerful and overarching hegemonic political apparatus of advanced capitalist society, there is great pressure often placed upon individuals and groups who, rather than simply conform to the status quo, seek counter-hegemonic alternatives to teaching and learning.

PRAXIS: THE ALLIANCE OF THEORY AND PRACTICE

A dialectical view of knowledge supports the notion that theory and practice are inextricably linked to our understanding of the world and the actions we take in our daily lives. In keeping with this view, all theory is considered with respect to the practical intent of transforming asymmetrical relations of power. Unlike deterministic notions of schooling practice that focus primarily on an instrumental/technical application of theory, praxis is conceived of as self-creating and self-generating free human activity. All human activity is understood as emerging from an ongoing interaction of reflection, dialogue, and action—namely praxis—and as praxis, all human activity requires theory to illuminate it and provide a better understanding of the world as we find it and as it might be.

Hence, within critical pedagogy, all theorizing and truth claims are subject to critique, a process that constitutes analysis and questions that are best mediated through human interaction within democratic relations of power. Critical pedagogy places a strong emphasis on this relationship of question-posing within the educational process. Freire argued that a true praxis is impossible in the undialectical vacuum driven by a separation of the individual from the object of their study. For within the context of such a dichotomy, both theory and practice lose their power to transform reality. Cut off from practice, theory becomes abstraction or "simple verbalism." Separated from theory, practice becomes ungrounded activity or "blind activism."

DIALOGUE AND CONSCIENTIZATION

The principle of dialogue as best defined by Freire is one of the most significant aspects of critical pedagogy. It speaks to an emancipatory educational process that is above all committed to the empowerment of students through challenging the dominant educational discourse and illuminating the right and freedom of students to become subjects of their world. Dialogue constitutes an educational strategy that centers on the development of critical social consciousness or what Freire termed *conscientização*.

Within the practice of critical pedagogy, dialogue and analysis serve as the foundation for reflection and action. It is this educational strategy that supports a problem-posing approach to education—an approach in which the relationship of students to teacher is, without question, dialogical, each having something to contribute and receive. Students learn from the teachers; teachers learn from the students. Hence, the actual lived experiences cannot be ignored or relegated to the periphery in the process of coming to know. They must be incorporated as part of the exploration of existing conditions and knowledge in order to understand how these came to be and to consider how they might be different.

Conscientização or conscientization is defined as the process by which students, as empowered subjects, achieve a deepening awareness of the social realities that shape their lives and discover their own capacities to re-create them. This constitutes a recurrent, regenerating process of human interaction that is utilized for constant clarification of the hidden dimensions of reflections and actions, as students and teachers move freely through the world of their experiences and enter into dialogue once more.

CRITIQUES OF CRITICAL PEDAGOGY

There is no question that the fundamental purpose of this volume is to provide a starting place for the study of critical pedagogy. We have done this through providing a short historical overview of those views that have particularly shaped the manner in which we speak of critical pedagogy today, along with a general description of the philosophical principles that inform a critical theory of pedagogy. However, it would be contrary to its philosophical origins and intent for us not to mention, albeit briefly, some of the fundamental critiques that over the last two decades have fueled major debates within the context of critical pedagogical circles—some of which are included in the articles and bibliographic material contained in this volume.

FEMINIST CRITIQUES

Numerous criticisms of critical pedagogy have been rooted in feminist views and articulations of identity, politics, and pedagogy. Some of the most significant critiques have been issued by such notable feminist scholars as Elizabeth Ellsworth, Carmen Luke, Jennifer Gore Patti Lather, and Magda Lewis. As one might instantly recognize in the preceding discussion, the leading recognized scholars considered to have most influenced the development of critical theory and critical pedagogy have all been men, with the exception of Maxine Greene. From this standpoint alone, there has been much suspicion and concern about the failure of critical pedagogy to engage forthrightly questions of women, anchored within the context of female experience and knowledge construction. As such, critical pedagogy has often been accused of challenging the structures and practices of patriarchy in society, solely from a myopic and superficial lens.

Within the context of these critiques, questions have been launched against the underlying carte blanche acceptance of the Enlightenment's emphasis on the emancipatory function of cognitive learning that informs the Marxian perspective of reason—a view that underpins critical philosophical views of human beings, knowledge and the world. Along the same lines, there has been concern with the integration of Freudian analytical views within the work of the Frankfurt School—theories that clearly have served as a guiding light for the evolvement of critical pedagogical thought. Hence, in an effort to challenge the privileging of reason as the ultimate sphere upon which knowledge is constructed, feminists have passionately argued for the inclusion of personal biography, narratives, and the explicit engagement with the historical and political location of the knowing subject—all aspects that feminist theorists believe are essential to understanding the world and transforming the sexual politics that have limited the participation of women as full and equal contributing members of society.

THE LANGUAGE OF CRITICAL PEDAGOGY

In very practical ways, the language of critical pedagogy has often been a serious point of contention not only among feminist scholars but also working-class educators who believed that theoretical language ultimately functioned to create a new form of oppression, rather than to liberate those who historically had found themselves at the margins of classical intellectual discourse. Hence, the language was not only critiqued in the early days for its incessant use of the masculine pronoun in reference to both male and female subjects, but for its elitism and consequent inaccessibility to those whose practice the language was attempting to inform. On one hand, these critiques challenged critical theorists to rethink the direction of their work and reconsider alternative strategies and approaches to the articulation of theoretical concerns. On another, it encouraged critical theorists to engage forthrightly with the deeper questions that were being stirred by the debate in terms of literacy, class, gender, culture, power, and the emancipatory potential of diverse political projects within the context of different traditions of struggle and pedagogy.

CRITIQUES FROM THE BORDERLANDS

As might be expected, similar concerns were raised among those who were intimately involved in the struggle against racialized inequalities within schools and society. Although it cannot be denied that the writings of feminist scholars of color, such as Audre Lorde, Toni Morrison, Gloria Anzaldua, Trinh Minh-Ha, and bell hooks, have had an impact on some of the contemporary perspectives on gender, sexuality, and race in critical pedagogy, the work of these scholars remained primarily linked to ethnic, cultural or feminist studies, except perhaps for the writings of bell hooks.

Hence, another "obvious" characteristic of these men once again provoked some controversy—the fact that most of them are "white." At moments in the history of critical pedagogy, this factor became a major source of contention, as concerns were raised about the failure of critical pedagogy to explicitly treat questions of subordinate cultures from the specific location of racialized populations themselves. When such concerns were raised they were often silenced by accusations of "essentialism." Hence, questions of voice, agency, and identity politics fueled massive debates that often created great suspicion and strife in efforts to work across diverse cultural perspectives.

From such debates sprang the intersectionality argument, grounded in the notion that critical theorists with their link to Marxist analysis and classical European philosophical roots were not only ethnocentric but reductionistic. Feminists and critics of color insisted that questions of race/gender/sexuality be given equal weight in any critical analysis of schooling in the United States, in an effort to not only produce different readings of history but to reclaim power for those groups that had existed historically at the margins of mainstream life.

THE POSTMODERN TWIST

In may ways the impact of such postmodernist notions as intersectionality upon the direction of critical pedagogy have been seen by some as truly a double-edged sword. As postmodernist theories brought into question many of the philosophical "sacred cows" of the western Enlightenment, they also stoked the coals of identity politics. Postmodern theories sought to move away from all-consuming metanarratives, rejecting traditional notions of totality, reason, and universality of absolute knowledge. As a consequence, the boundaries of traditional configurations of power and their impact on what constituted legitimate knowledge were suddenly pushed wide open by new methods of deconstruction and reconstruction in the intellectual act of border crossing.

Although such a view appeared to hold real promise for the serious theoretical engagement of questions of cultural hybridity, racialized subjects, sexualities, and the politics of difference, its intense fragmenting influence on formally effective organizing strategies across communities of difference led to systematic dismantling of former political visions—political visions that could have potentially offered some unifying direction to our diverse political projects. As a consequence, the educational left found itself in a disheartening state of disarray, tension, and befuddlement. What is most unfortunate is that this philosophical shift in our understanding of diversity and the multicultural body politic often failed to acknowledge the deep oppressive or privileging similarities at work among members of the same socioeconomic class—a factor that had functioned historically as a significant common ground for social justice struggles in the United States and around the world.

THE RETREAT FROM CLASS

For almost a decade, postmodernist views dominated much of the debate as post–civil rights education activists attempted to stave off the impact of the rapidly growing conservative trend in the latter decades of the twentieth century. Critical theorists, who were particularly concerned with the totalizing impact of capitalism, its growing internationalization of capital, and its deleterious impact on working-class people in the United States and abroad, lamented the retreat from class in postmodern writings about issues of culture, race, gender, and sexuality. The "postmodern" trend to see "power everywhere and nowhere" (Naiman, 1996) signaled for many a dangerous form of political abstraction that failed to acknowledge forthrightly the manner in which advanced capitalism was very concretely whipping wildly through the global sphere, well-consolidated in its neoliberal efforts to perpetuate the structures of economic domination and exploitation.

Without question, there were critical pedagogical theorists who were also tremendously concerned about the destructive impact that this intensified globalization of the economy was having upon the commercialization of public schooling. In light of these growing concerns, critical theorists such as Michael Apple, Stanley Aronowitz, Jean Anyon, Peter McLaren, Alex Molnar, and others, urged educators to remain ever cognizant to the centrality of class relations in shaping the conditions students experienced within schools and communities. As a consequence, they worked more rigorously to draw attention to the continuing significance of class analysis by challenging the changing nature of the "postindustrial" economy and its consequences on education. However, in the foreground of this concern remained questions of how to engage class as both an analytical and political category, without falling prey to "red-herring" accusations of economic determinism and reductionism. In response, a number of critical educators began to rethink post–civil rights notions of class, race, and gender, in an effort to begin formulating new language for our understanding of gendered and racialized class relations and their impact on education. Hence, at a time in our history when critical educators most needed an economic understanding of schooling, a revived historical materialist approach began to reinvigorate critical educational debates in the age of "globalization."

"CRITICAL PEDAGOGY IS ONLY ABOUT POLITICS"

There are many traditional, as well as liberal, educators and public school administrators who adamantly dismiss the value of critical pedagogy. It is not uncommon to hear such folks rail bitterly against the political nature of critical pedagogy, insisting sarcastically that critical pedagogy has little to no practical value within the classroom. Critical educators would argue that such expressions of opposition are, more often than not, disingenuous proclamations intended to obstruct the establishment of critical approaches to teaching and learning within schools—approaches that seek to transform the oppressive power relations hidden within those educational structures, practices, and relationships that deceptively function to retain control over the majority.

More importantly, this critique is often generated by the fear, confusion, and hysteria generated among school officials, mainstream educators, and scholars within schools, communities, and universities when teachers, students, or parents voice oppositional views and begin to challenge the undemocratic contradictions at work in public schools. The tensions are usually heightened when those in power attempt to obstruct efforts by teachers, students, and parents to integrate their voices and participation within the practice of public schooling—an act that if successful might cause substantive changes to business as usual. Here we must note that what is brought into question by the powerful is the legitimacy of critical social action among subordinated groups. Hence, overtures for people to conduct themselves in reasonable and civilized ways, is too often used to not only truncate the expression of legitimate anger, frustration, and concerns, but to deflect the possibility of any substantive dialogue that might potentially lead to fundamentally new ideas, new language, new practices, and perhaps even new relationships of power within schools.

In response to the political stress and strain faced by many critical educators for their particular perspectives on teaching and learning, Paulo Freire always insisted that it is a political imperative for critical educators to develop a strong command of their particular academic discipline, whether that be within preschool or primary education, the middle or high-school grades, or higher education. By so doing, they can competently teach the "official transcript" of their field, while simultaneously creating the opportunities for students to engage critically in classroom content from the standpoint of their own knowledge and the events and experiences that comprise their living history.

THE FUTURE OF CRITICAL PEDAGOGY

Understanding critical pedagogy within a long tradition of progressive educational movements and ongoing struggles offers a possible safeguard against the temptation to inadvertently reify and reduce critical pedagogy to a teaching "method." This is particularly at issue in the current conservative climate that plagues all educational institutions from preschool to universities. Within this reactionary moment in U.S. history, there are those who, in an effort to protect themselves from the malignant criticism and opposition of conservative administrators, colleagues, students, or parents, are willing to placate the opposition by offering more palatable readings of critical pedagogy. Given the nature of schooling and the current conditions that shape the political landscape, such survival politics of appropriation among progressive educators is to be expected. Hence, we should not be too surprised or become too discouraged when we find an acceleration of such efforts. Rather, in keeping with the tradition of critical pedagogy, it signals the importance of learning to read the formal and informal power relationships at work within schools. But even more importantly, it serves as a reminder that no real political struggle can be waged by one lone voice in the wilderness. Emancipatory efforts within schools must be linked to collective emancipatory efforts within and across communities.

Although we have included the work of many prominent thinkers in the tradition of critical theory, critical pedagogy as a school of thought is very often associated with the work of Paulo Freire. Yet, as we have attempted to illustrate here, critical pedagogy does not begin and end with Freire. Nevertheless, it cannot be denied that Freire's influence as a Brazilian or Latin American, that is to say not "white" or European, played a significant role in the inspiration his writings brought to many radical educators of color in this country and other parts of the world. His presence, consciously or unconsciously, signaled and signified our right to express and define, on our own terms, the educational needs of working-class and racialized students in the United States. But, we also found in Freire a living politics that defied the iconography of his own contribution to the political project of critical pedagogy. As such, his ethics sought to reinforce the necessity for greater solidarity among critical theorists and critical educators in the years to come—a solidarity that must be willing to break with the politics of competitiveness, internalized notions of superiority, tendencies to demonize difference, and our "colonized" dependence and yearning to be recognized or legitimated by those who hold official power. Only through such a politics of solidarity can critical pedagogy potentially inform the building of an effective emancipatory educational and social movement for a new millennium.

And lastly, in light of a long-standing historical tradition of progressive educational efforts in the United States and around the world, we can safely guarantee that the underlying commitment and intent of critical pedagogy will continue as long as there are those who are forced to exist in conditions of suffering and alienation, and those who refuse to accept such conditions as a natural evolution of humankind.

REFERENCES

Boal, A. (1982). *Theatre of the oppressed.* New York: Routledge.

Bowles, S., and Gintis, H. (1976) *Schooling in capitalist America.* New York: Basic Books.

Dewey, J. (1916). *Democracy and education.* New York: The Free Press.

Freire, P. (1971). *Pedagogy of the oppressed.* New York: Seabury.

Giroux, H. (1983). *Theory and Resistance in Education.* South Hadley, Mass.: Bergin & Garvey.

Gramsci, A. (1971). Selection from the Prison Notebooks. New York: International Publishers.

Greene, M. (1988). *The dialectics of freedom.* New York: Teachers College.

Held, D. (1980). *Introduction to Critical Theory: Horkheimer to Habermas.* Berkeley and Los Angeles: University of California Press.

Illich, I. (1971). *Deschooling society.* New York: Harper.

Kozol, J. (1967). *Death at an early age.* Boston: Houghton.

McLaren, P. (1989). *Life in Schools: An Introduction to Critical Pedagogy and the Foundations of Education.* New York: Longman.

Naiman, J. (1996). "Left Feminism and the Return to Class." *Monthly Review* 48, no. 2 (June).

Warren, S. (1984). *The Emergence of Dialectical Theory.* Chicago: University of Chicago Press.

Part 1

FOUNDATIONS OF CRITICAL PEDAGOGY

INTRODUCTION

The first four articles of this collection synthesize the foundations of Critical Pedagogy. "Critical Theory & Educational Practice" by Henry Giroux begins the journey through this volume. Giroux's work is credited with repositioning the education debates of the "New Left" beyond the boundaries of reproduction theories and the hidden curriculum. The analysis found here constitutes a turning point in the development of the progressive educational agenda of the 1980s. In this article, he traces the history and development of critical theory back to the members of the Frankfurt School, examining the major themes that informed their work—rejection of orthodox Marxism, critique of late capitalism, analysis of instrumental reason, deep concerns about the culture industry, and their psychoanalytical view of domination. Giroux's exploration into the historical development of the Frankfurt School provided the analytical basis upon which to develop his conceptualization of one of the most distinctive features of critical pedagogy—the principle of resistance.

The second contribution to this section is a chapter from the internationally acclaimed book, *Pedagogy of the Oppressed,* by the Brazilian educator Paulo Freire. Freire's work provided a solid foundation for the initial development of critical pedagogy. The essay included here truly captures the essence of Freire's contribution to the field. Freire's critique of the traditional banking concept of education along with a discussion of authoritarian teacher-student interaction represents one of the most powerful critiques of schooling. His discussion of the historical nature of knowledge—including the false duality between theory and practice—and the need to transcend the "problem-solving" approach in order to engage students in a "problem-posing" pedagogy became an important point of departure in the articulation of critical pedagogy.

"Critical Pedagogy: A Look at the Major Concepts" by Peter McLaren, a former Canadian schoolteacher and a recognized leader in the critical educational movement, articulates for the reader the theoretical principles that underscore a critical pedagogical perspective. McLaren's analysis focuses on the significance of dialectical theory, the nature of knowledge, the concepts of hegemony and ideology, and the effects of the hidden curriculum on schooling. McLaren's discussion of these concepts is intended to assist teachers in considering more closely what ideas inform their teaching practice.

Maxine Greene, a noted philosopher and remarkable educator, has often been referred to as the mother of aesthetic education. In her essay, "In Search of a Critical Pedagogy," she reflects on the historical traditions of the progressive education movement in the United States. Her purpose is to link the development of critical pedagogy, both historically and philosophically, to the foundations of American social activism. Since many of the philosophical roots of critical theory are linked to the European experience, Greene felt it was important to find an analogous experience from which to relate the project of critical pedagogy to the American struggle for "life, liberty and the pursuit of happiness." She discusses the impact of compulsory public education and "the appearance of utopian communities and socialist societies" in the nineteenth century in the United States. More importantly, Greene takes the reader on a journey of rediscovery to highlight American "rebellious figures," where innumerable names emerge that speak to the struggles for the abolition of slavery, women's rights, antiracism, freedom schools, and the civil rights movement. She argues passionately for reclaiming these struggles—erased from the American psyche—in an effort to invigorate the contribution of critical pedagogy to the struggles in education today.

QUESTIONS FOR REFLECTION AND DIALOGUE

1. Describe the school of thought known as Critical Theory. What is the role of the Frankfurt School in the development of critical theory?
2. Identify the major themes addressed by the Frankfurt School and why these were important to the development of critical theory.
3. Explain how Paulo Freire's vision of education differs from traditional approaches to schooling?
4. What are the fundamental changes that Freire proposes to help teachers counteract the banking approach to education?
5. Explain how Freire defines knowledge and the implications of his view to democratic schooling.
6. What are the major distinctions between a problem-solving and a problem-posing pedagogy? What are the political implications of these approaches for classroom instruction?

7. How does Freire defined *praxis* and how does this concept relate to teaching and learning?
8. How does McLaren define dialectical thinking and its importance to critical pedagogy?
9. Define hegemony. Explain what roles class, culture, and ideology play in the process of hegemony.
10. How do McLaren's concerns about the hidden curriculum and the notion of cultural capital relate to the standardization of knowledge in schools?
11. What is Greene's interpretation of U.S. history? What account of American radical thinkers is found in the K-12 curriculum? Reflect on your own school experience and describe the major historical events and how these influenced your views of yourself, education, and the world.
12. According to Greene, what are the challenges faced by the present generation of Americans? Elaborate in what ways critical pedagogy can help address these challenges.

Critical Theory and Educational Practice

HENRY A. GIROUX

INTRODUCTION

This chapter attempts to contribute to the search for a theoretical foundation upon which to develop a critical theory of education. Within the parameters of this task, the notion of critical theory has a two-fold meaning. First, critical theory refers to the legacy of theoretical work developed by certain members of what can be loosely described as "the Frankfurt School." What this suggests is that critical theory was never a fully articulated philosophy shared unproblematically by all members of the Frankfurt School. But it must be stressed that while one cannot point to a single universally shared critical theory, one can point to the common attempt to assess the newly emerging forms of capitalism along with the changing forms of domination that accompanied them. Similarly, there was an attempt on the part of all the members of the Frankfurt School to rethink and radically reconstruct the meaning of human emancipation, a project that differed considerably from the theoretical baggage of orthodox Marxism. Specifically, I argue in this chapter for the importance of original critical theory and the insights it provides for developing a critical foundation for a theory of radical pedagogy. In doing so, I focus on the work of Adorno, Horkheimer, and Marcuse. This seems to be an important concern, especially since so much of the work on the Frankfurt School being used by educators focuses almost exclusively on the work of Jürgen Habermas.

Second, the concept of critical theory refers to the nature of SELF-CONSCIOUS CRITIQUE and to the need to develop a discourse of social transformation and emancipation that does not cling dogmatically to its own doctrinal assumptions. (In other words, critical theory refers to both a "school of thought" and a process of critique.) It points to a body of thought that is, in my view, invaluable for educational theorists; it also exemplifies a body of work that both demonstrates and simultaneously calls for the necessity of ongoing critique, one in which the claims of any theory must be confronted with the distinction between the world it examines and portrays, and the world as it actually exists.

The Frankfurt School took as one of its central values a commitment to penetrate the world of objective appearances to expose the underlying social relationships they often conceal. In other words, penetrating such appearances meant exposing through critical analysis social relationships that took on the status of things or objects. For instance, by examining notions such as money, consumption, distribution, and production, it becomes clear that none of these represents an objective thing or fact, but rather all are historically contingent contexts mediated by relationships of domination and subordination. In adopting such a perspective, the Frankfurt School not only broke with forms of rationality that wedded science and technology into new forms of domination, it also rejected all forms of rationality that subordinated human consciousness and action to the imperatives of universal laws. Whether it be the legacy of Victorian European positivist intellectual thought or the theoretical edifice developed by Engels, Kautsky, Stalin, and other heirs of Marxism, the Frankfurt School argued against the suppression of "subjectivity, consciousness, and culture in history" (Breines 1979–80). In so doing it articulated a notion of negativity or critique that opposed all theories that celebrated social harmony while leaving unproblematic the basic assumptions of the wider society. In more specific terms, the Frankfurt School stressed the importance of critical thinking by arguing that it is a constitutive feature of the struggle for self-emancipation and social change. Moreover, its members argued that it was in the contradictions of society that one could begin to develop forms of social inquiry that analyzed the distinction between *what is* and *what should be.* Finally, it strongly supported the assumption that the basis for thought and action should be grounded, as Marcuse argued just before his death, "in compassion, [and] in our sense of the sufferings of others" (Habermas 1980).

In general terms, the Frankfurt School provided a number of valuable insights for studying the relationship between theory and society. In so doing, its members developed a dialectical framework by which to understand the mediations that link the institutions and activities of everyday life with the logic and commanding forces that shape the larger social totality. The characteristic nature of the form of social inquiry that emerged from such a framework was articulated by Horkheimer when he suggested that members of the Institute for Social Research explore the question of "the interconnection between the economic life of society, the psychic development of the individual, and transformations in the realm of culture . . . including not only the so-called spiritual contents of science, art, and religion, but also law, ethics, fashion, public opinion, sport, amusement, life style, etc." (Horkheimer 1972).

The issues raised here by Horkheimer have not lost their importance with time; they still represent both a critique and a challenge to many of the theoretical currents that presently characterize theories of social education. The necessity for theoretical renewal in the education field, coupled with the massive number of primary and secondary sources that have been translated or published recently in English, provide the opportunity for American- and English-speaking pedagogues to begin to appropriate the discourse and ideas of the Frankfurt School. Needless to say, such a task will not be easily accomplished, since both the complexity of the language used by members of the School and the diversity of the positions and themes they pursued demand a selective and critical reading of their works. Yet their critique of culture, instrumental rationality, authoritarianism, and ideology, pursued in an interdisciplinary context, generated categories, relationships, and forms of social inquiry that constitute a vital resource for developing a critical theory of social education. Since it will be impossible in the scope of this chapter to analyze the diversity of themes examined by the Frankfurt School, I will limit my analysis to the treatment of *rationality, theory, culture,* and *depth psychology.* Finally, I will discuss the implications of these for educational theory and practice.

HISTORY AND BACKGROUND OF THE FRANKFURT SCHOOL

The Institute for Social Research (*Das Institut für Sozialforschung*), officially created in Frankfurt, Germany, in February, 1923, was the original home of the Frankfurt School. Established by a wealthy grain merchant named Felix Weil, the Institute came under the directorship of Max Horkheimer in 1930. Under Horkheimer's directorship, most of the members who later became famous joined the Institute. These included Erich Fromm, Herbert Marcuse, and Theodor Adorno. As Martin Jay points out in his now-famous history of the Frankfurt School: "If it can be said that in the early years of its history the Institute concerned itself primarily with an analysis of bourgeois society's socio-economic substructure, in the years after 1930 its prime interests lay in its cultural superstructure" (Jay 1973).

The change in the Institute's theoretical focus was soon followed by a shift in its location. Threatened by the Nazis because of the avowedly Marxist orientation of its work and the fact that most of its members were Jews, the Institute was forced to move for a short time in 1933 to Geneva, and then in 1934 to New York City, where it was housed in one of Columbia University's buildings. Emigration to New York was followed by a stay in Los Angeles in 1941, and by 1953 the Institute was re-established in Frankfurt, Germany.

The strengths and weaknesses of the Frankfurt School project become intelligible only if seen as part of the social and historical context in which it developed. In essence, the questions it pursued and the forms of social inquiry it supported represent both a particular moment in the development of Western Marxism and a critique of it. *Reacting to the rise of Fascism and Nazism, on the one hand, and to the failure of orthodox Marxism, on the other, the Frankfurt School had to refashion and rethink the meaning of domination and emancipation.*

The rise of Stalinism, the failure of the European or Western working class to contest capitalist hegemony in a revolutionary manner, and the power of capitalism to reconstitute and reinforce its economic and ideological control forced the Frankfurt School to reject the orthodox reading of Marx and Engels, particularly as developed through the conventional wisdom of the Second and Third Internationals. It is particularly in the rejection of certain doctrinal Marxist assumptions, developed under the historical shadow of totalitarianism and through the rise of the consumer society in the West, that Horkheimer, Adorno, and Marcuse attempted to construct a more sufficient basis for social theory and political action. Certainly, such a basis was not to be found in standard Marxist assumptions such as (a) the notion of historical inevitability, (b) the primacy of the mode of production in shaping history, and (c) the notion that class struggle as well as the mechanisms of domination take place primarily within the confines of the labor process. For the Frankfurt School, orthodox Marxism assumed too much while simultaneously ignoring the benefits of self-criticism. It had failed to develop a theory of consciousness and thus had expelled the human subject from its own theoretical calculus. It is not surprising, then, that the focus of the Frankfurt School's research deemphasized the area of political economy to focus instead on the issues of how subjectivity was constituted and how the spheres of culture and everyday life represented a new terrain of domination. It is against this historical and theoretical landscape that we can begin to abstract categories and modes of analysis that speak to the nature of schooling as it presently exists, and to its inherent potential for developing into a force for social change.

RATIONALITY AND THE CRITIQUE OF INSTRUMENTAL REASON

Fundamental to an understanding of the Frankfurt School's view of theory and of its critique of instrumental reason is its analysis of the heritage of Enlightenment rationality. Echoing Nietzsche's earlier warning about humanity's unbounded faith in reason, Adorno and Horkheimer voiced a trenchant critique of modernity's unswerving faith in the promise of Enlightenment rationality to rescue the world from the chains of superstition, ignorance, and suffering. The problematic nature of such a promise marks the opening lines of *Dialectic of Enlightenment:* "In the most general sense of progressive thought the Enlightenment has always aimed at liberating men from fear and establishing their sovereignty. Yet the fully enlightened earth radiates disaster triumphant" (Adorno & Horkheimer 1972).

Faith in scientific rationality and the principles of practical judgement did not constitute a legacy that developed exclusively in the seventeenth and eighteenth centuries, when people of reason united on a vast intellectual front in order to master the world through an appeal to the claims of reasoned thought. According to the Frankfurt School, the legacy of scientific rationality represented one of the central themes of Western thought and extended as far back as Plato (Horkheimer 1974). Habermas, a later member of the Frankfurt School, argues that the progressive notion of reason reaches its highest point and most complex expression in the work of Karl Marx, after which it is reduced from an all-encompassing concept of rationality to a particular instrument in the service of industrialized society. According to Habermas:

> On the level of the historical self-reflection of a science with critical intent, Marx for the last time identifies reason with a commitment to rationality in its thrust against dogmatism. In the second half of the nineteenth century, during the course of the reduction of science to a productive force in industrial society, positivism, historicism, and pragmatism, each in turn, isolate one part of this all-encompassing concept of rationality. The hitherto undisputed attempts of the great theories to reflect on the complex of life as a whole is henceforth itself discredited as dogma . . . The spontaneity of hope, the art of taking a position, the experience of relevance or indifference, and above all, the response to suffering and oppression, the desire for adult autonomy, the will to emancipation, and the happiness of discovering one's identity—all these are dismissed for all time from the obligating interest of reason. (Habermas 1973)

Marx may have employed reason in the name of critique and emancipation, but it was still a notion of reason limited to an overemphasis on the labor process and on the exchange rationality that was both its driving force and ultimate mystification. Adorno, Horkheimer, and Marcuse, in contrast to Marx, believed that "the fateful process of rationalization" (Wellmer 1974) had penetrated all aspects of everyday life, whether it be the mass media, the school, or the workplace. The crucial point here is that no social sphere was free from the encroachments of a form of reason in which "all theoretical means of transcending reality became metaphysical nonsense" (Horkheimer 1974).

In the Frankfurt School's view, reason has not been permanently stripped of its positive dimensions. Marcuse, for instance, believed that reason contained a critical element and was still capable of reconstituting history. As he put it, "Reason represents the highest potentiality of man and existence; the two belong together" (Marcuse 1968a). But if reason was to preserve its promise of creating a more just society, it would have to demonstrate powers of critique and negativity. According to Adorno (1973), the crisis of reason takes place as society becomes more rationalized; under such historical circumstances, in the quest for social harmony, it loses its critical faculty and becomes an instrument of the existing society. As a result, reason as insight and critique turns into its opposite—irrationality.

For the Frankfurt School, the crisis in reason is linked to the more general crises in science and in society as a whole. Horkheimer argued in 1972 that the starting point for understanding "the crisis of science depends on a correct theory of the present social situation." In essence, this speaks to two crucial aspects of Frankfurt School thought. First, it argues that the only solution to the present crisis lies in developing a more fully self-conscious notion of reason, one that embraces elements of critique as well as of human will and transformative action. Second, it means entrusting to theory the task of rescuing reason from the logic of technocratic rationality or positivism. It was the Frankfurt School's view that positivism had emerged as the final ideological expression of the Enlightenment. The victory of positivism represented not the high point but the low point of Enlightenment thought. Positivism became the enemy of reason rather than its agent, and emerged in the twentieth century as a new form of social administration and domination. Friedman sums up the essence of this position:

> To the Frankfurt School, philosophical and practical positivism constituted the end point of the Enlightenment. The social function of the ideology of positivism was to deny the critical faculty of reason by allowing it only the ground of utter facticity to operate upon. By so doing, they denied reason a critical moment. Reason, under the rule of positivism, stands in awe of the fact. Its function is simply to characterize the fact. Its task ends when it has affirmed and explicated the fact. . . . Under the rule of positivism, reason inevitably stops short of critique. (Friedman 1981)

It is in its critique of positivistic thought that the Frankfurt School makes clear the specific mechanisms of ideological control that permeate the consciousness and practices of advanced capitalist societies. It is also in its critique of positivism that it develops a notion of theory that has major implications for educational critics. But the route to understanding this concept necessitates that one first analyze the Frankfurt School's critique of positivism, particularly since the logic of positivist thought (though in varied forms) represents the major theoretical impetus currently shaping educational theory and practice.

The Frankfurt School defined positivism, in the broad sense, as an amalgam of diverse traditions that included the work of Saint-Simon and Comte, the logical positivism of the Vienna Circle, the early work of Wittgenstein, and the more recent forms of logical empiricism and pragmatism that dominate the social sciences in the West. While the history of these traditions is complex and cluttered with detours and qualifications, each of them has supported the goal of developing forms of social inquiry patterned after the natural sciences and based on the methodological tenets of sense observation and quantification. Marcuse provides both a general definition of positivism as well as a basis for some of the reservations of the Frankfurt School regarding its most basic assumptions:

> Since its first usage, probably in the school of Saint-Simon, the term "positivism" has encompassed (1) the validation of cognitive thought by experience of facts; (2) the orientation of cognitive thought to the physical science as a model of certainty and exactness; (3) the belief that progress in knowledge

depends on this orientation. Consequently, positivism is a struggle against all metaphysics, transcendentalisms, and idealisms as obscurantist and regressive modes of thought. To the degree to which the given reality is scientifically comprehended and transformed, to the degree to which society becomes industrial and technological, positivism finds in the society the medium for the realization (and validation) of its concepts—harmony between theory and practice, truth and facts. Philosophic thought turns into affirmative thought; the philosophic critique criticizes within the societal framework and stigmatizes non-positive notions as mere speculation, dreams or fantasies. (Marcuse 1964)

Positivism, according to Horkheimer, presented a view of knowledge and science that stripped both of their critical possibilities. Knowledge was reduced to the exclusive province of science, and science itself was subsumed within a methodology that limited "scientific activity to the description, classification, and generalization of phenomena, with no care to distinguish the unimportant from the essential" (Horkheimer 1972). Accompanying this view are the ideas that knowledge derives from sense experience and that the ideal it pursues takes place "in the form of a mathematically formulated universe deducible from the smallest possible number of axioms, a system which assures the calculation of the probable occurrence of all events" (ibid).

For the Frankfurt School, positivism did not represent an indictment of science; instead it echoed Nietzsche's insight that "It is not the victory of science that is the distinguishing mark of our nineteenth century, but the victory of the scientific method over science" (Nietzsche 1966). Science, in this perspective, was separated from the question of ends and ethics, which were rendered insignificant because they defied "explication in terms of mathematical structures" (Marcuse 1964). According to the Frankfurt School, the suppression of ethics in positivist rationality precludes the possibility for self-criticism, or, more specifically, for questioning its own normative structure. Facts become separated from values, objectivity undermines critique, and the notion that essence and appearance may not coincide is lost in the positivist view of the world. The latter point becomes particularly clear in the Vienna Circle pronouncement: "The view that thought is a means of knowing more about the world than may be directly observed . . . seems to us entirely mysterious" (Hahn 1933). For Adorno, the idea of value freedom was perfectly suited to a perspective that was to insist on a universal form of knowledge while simultaneously refusing to inquire into its own socio-ideological development and function in society.

According to the Frankfurt School, the *outcome of positivist rationality and its technocratic view of science represented a threat to the notion of subjectivity and critical thinking.* By functioning within an operational context free from ethical commitments, positivism wedded itself to the immediate and "celebrated" world of "facts." The question of essence—the difference between the world as it is and as it could be—is reduced to the merely methodological task of collecting and classifying facts. In this schema, "Knowledge relates solely to what is, and to its recurrence" (Horkheimer 1972). Questions concerning the genesis, development, and normative nature of the conceptual systems that select, organize, and define the facts appear to be outside the concern of positivist rationality.

Since it recognizes no factors behind the "fact," positivism freezes both human beings and history. In the case of these, the issue of historical development is ignored since the historical dimension contains truths that cannot be assigned "to a special fact-gathering branch of science" (Adorno, quoted in Gross 1979). Of course, positivism is not impervious to history, or to the relationship between history and understanding, at any rate. On the contrary, its key notions of objectivity, theory, and values, as well as its modes of inquiry, are paradoxically a consequence of and a force in the shaping of history. In other words, positivism may ignore history but it cannot escape it. What is important to stress is that fundamental categories of socio-historical development are at odds with the positivist emphasis on the immediate, or more specifically with that which can be expressed, measured, and calculated in precise mathematical formulas. Russell Jacoby (1980) points concisely to this issue in his claim that "the natural reality and natural sciences do not know the fundamental historical categories: consciousness and self-consciousness, subjectivity and objectivity, appearance and essence."

By not reflecting on its paradigmatic premises, positivist thought ignores the value of historical consciousness and consequently endangers the nature of critical thinking itself. That is, inherent in the very structure of positivist thought, with its emphasis on objectivity and its lack of theoretical grounding with regard to the setting of tasks (Horkheimer 1972), are a number of assumptions that appear to preclude its ability to judge the complicated interaction of power, knowledge, and values and to reflect critically on the genesis and nature of its own ideological presuppositions. Moreover, by situating itself within a number of false dualisms (facts vs. values, scientific knowledge vs. norms, and description vs. prescription) positivism dissolves the tension between potentiality and actuality in all spheres of social existence. Thus, under the guise of neutrality, scientific knowledge and all theory become rational on the grounds of whether or not they are efficient, economic, or correct. In this case, a notion of methodological correctness subsumes and devalues the complex philosophical concept of truth. As Marcuse points out, "The fact that a judgement can be correct and nevertheless without truth, has been the crux of formal logic from time immemorial" (quoted in Arato & Gebhardt 1978).

For instance, an empirical study that concludes that native workers in a colonized country work at a slower rate than imported workers who perform the same job may provide an answer that is correct, but such an answer tells us little about the notion of domination or the resistance of workers under its sway. That the native workers may slow down their rate as an act of resistance is not considered here. Thus, the notions of intentionality and historical context are dissolved within the confines of a limiting quantifying methodology.

For Adorno, Marcuse, and Horkheimer, the fetishism of facts and the belief in value neutrality represented more than an epistemological error; more importantly, such a stance served as a form of ideological hegemony that infused positivist rationality with a political conservatism that made it an ideological prop of the status quo. This is not to suggest, however, an intentional support for the status quo on the part of all individuals who work within a positivist rationality. Instead, it implies a particular relationship to the status quo; in some situations this relationship is consciously political, in others it is not. In other words, in the latter instance the relationship to the status quo is a conservative one, but it is not self-consciously recognized by those who help to reproduce it.

THE FRANKFURT SCHOOL'S NOTION OF THEORY

According to the Frankfurt School, any understanding of the nature of theory has to begin with a grasp of the relationships that exist in society between the particular and the whole, the specific and the universal. This position appears in direct contradiction to the empiricist claim that theory is primarily a matter of classifying and arranging facts. In rejecting the absolutizing of facts, the Frankfurt School argued that in the relation between theory and the wider society mediations exist that give meaning not only to the constitutive nature of a fact but also to the very nature and substance of theoretical discourse. As Horkheimer writes, "The facts of science and science itself are but segments of the life process of society, and in order to understand the significance of facts or of science, generally one must possess the key to the historical situation, the right social theory" (Horkheimer 1972).

This speaks to a second constitutive element of critical theory. If theory is to move beyond the positivist legacy of neutrality, it must develop the capacity of meta-theory. That is, it must acknowledge the value-laden interests it represents and be able to reflect critically on both the historical development or genesis of such interests and the limitations they may present within certain historical and social contexts. In other words, "methodological correctness" does not provide a guarantee of truth, nor does it raise the fundamental question of why a theory functions in a given way under specific historical conditions to serve some interests and not others. Thus, a notion of self-criticism is essential to a critical theory.

A third constitutive element for a critical theory takes its cue from Nietzsche's dictum that "A great truth wants to be criticized, not idolized" (quoted in Arato & Gebhardt 1978). The Frankfurt School believed that the critical spirit of theory should be represented in its unmasking function. The driving force of such a function was to be found in the Frankfurt School's notions of immanent criticism and dialectical thought. Immanent critique is the assertion of difference, the refusal to collapse appearance and essence, the willingness to analyze the reality of the social object against its possibilities. As Adorno wrote:

> Theory . . . must transform the concepts which it brings, as it were, from outside into those which the object has of itself, into what the object, left to itself, seeks to be, and confront it with what it is. It must dissolve the rigidity of the temporally and spatially fixed object into a field of tension of the possible and the real: each one in order to exist, is dependent upon the other. In other words, theory is indisputably critical. (Adorno et al. 1976)

Dialectical thought, on the other hand, speaks to both critique and theoretical reconstruction (Giroux 1981a). As a mode of critique, it uncovers values that are often negated by the social object under analysis. The notion of dialectics is crucial because it reveals "the insufficiencies and imperfections of 'finished' systems of thought. . . . It reveals incompleteness where completeness is claimed. It embraces that which is in terms of that which is not, and that which is real in terms of potentialities not yet realized" (Held 1980). As a mode of theoretical reconstruction, dialectical thought points to historical analysis in the critique of conformist logic, and traces out the "inner history" of the latter's categories and the way in which these are mediated within a specific historical context. By looking at the social and political constellations stored in the categories of any theory, Adorno (1973) believed their history could be traced and their existing limitations revealed. As such, dialectical thought reveals the power of human activity and human knowledge as both a product of and force in the shaping of social reality. But it does not do so to proclaim simply that humans give meaning to the world. Instead, as a form of critique, dialectical thought argues that there is a link between knowledge, power, and domination. Thus it is acknowledged that some knowledge is false, and that the ultimate purpose of critique should be critical thinking in the interest of social change. For instance, as I mentioned earlier, one can exercise critical thought and not fall into the ideological trap of relativism, in which the notion of critique is negated by the assumption that all ideas should be given equal weight. Marcuse points to the connection between thought and action in dialectical thought:

> Dialectical thought starts with the experience that the world is unfree; that is to say, man and nature exist in conditions of alienation, exist as "other than they are." Any mode of thought which excludes this contradiction from its logic is faulty logic. Thought "corresponds" to reality only as it transforms reality by comprehending its contradictory structure. Here the principle of dialectic drives thought beyond the limits of philosophy. For to comprehend reality means to comprehend what things really are, and this in turn means rejecting their mere factuality. Rejection is the process of thought as well as of action . . . Dialectical thought thus becomes negative in itself. Its function is to break

down the self-assurance and self-contentment of common sense, to undermine the sinister confidence in the power and language of facts, to demonstrate that unfreedom is so much at the core of things that the development of their internal contradictions leads necessarily to qualitative change: the explosion and catastrophe of the established state of affairs. (Marcuse 1960)

According to the Frankfurt School, all thought and theory are tied to a specific interest in the development of a society without injustice. Theory, in this case, becomes a transformative activity that views itself as explicitly political and commits itself to the projection of a future that is as yet unfulfilled. Thus, critical theory contains a transcendent element in which critical thought becomes the precondition for human freedom. Rather than proclaiming a positivist notion of neutrality, critical theory openly takes sides in the interest of struggling for a better world. In one of his most famous early essays comparing traditional and critical theory, Horkheimer spelled out the essential value of theory as a political endeavour:

> It is not just a research hypothesis which shows its value in the ongoing business of men; it is an essential element in the historical effort to create a world which satisfies the needs and powers of men. However extensive the interaction between the critical theory and the special sciences whose progress the theory must respect and on which it has for decades exercized a liberating and stimulating influence, the theory never aims simply at an increase of knowledge as such. Its goal is man's emancipation from slavery. (Horkheimer 1972)

Finally, there is the question of the relationship between critical theory and empirical studies. In the ongoing debate over theory and empirical work, we recognize recycled versions of the same old dualisms in which one presupposes the exclusion of the other. One manifestation of this debate is the criticism that the Frankfurt School rejected the value of empirical work, a criticism that is also being lodged currently against many educational critics who have drawn upon the work of the Frankfurt School. Both sets of criticisms appear to have missed the point. It is certainly true that for the Frankfurt School the issue of empirical work was a problematic one, but what was called into question was its universalization at the expense of a more comprehensive notion of rationality. In writing about his experiences as an American scholar, Adorno spelled out a view of empirical studies that was representative of the Frankfurt School in general:

> My own position in the controversy between empirical and theoretical sociology . . . I may sum up by saying that empirical investigations are not only legitimate but essential, even in the realm of cultural phenomena. But one must not confer autonomy upon them or regard them as a universal key. Above all they must terminate the theoretical knowledge. Theory is no mere vehicle that becomes superfluous as soon as data are in hand. (Adorno 1969)

By insisting on the primacy of theoretical knowledge in the realm of empirical investigations, the Frankfurt School also wanted to highlight the limits of the positivist notion of experience, where research had to confine itself to controlled physical experiences that could be conducted by any researcher. Under such conditions, the research experience is limited to simple observation. As such, abstract methodology follows rules that preclude any understanding of the forces that shape both the object of analysis as well as the subject conducting the research. By contrast, a dialectical notion of society and theory would argue that observation cannot take the place of critical reflection and understanding. That is, one begins not with an observation but with a theoretical framework that situates the observation in rules and conventions that give it meaning while simultaneously acknowledging the limitations of such a perspective or framework. The Frankfurt School's position on the relation between theory and empirical studies thus helps to illuminate its view of theory and practice.

But a further qualification must be made here. While critical theory insists that theory and practice are interrelated, it nonetheless cautions against calling for a specious unity, for as Adorno points out:

> The call for the unity of theory and practice has irresistably degraded theory to the servant's role, removing the very traits it should have brought to that unity. The visa stamp of practice which we demand of all theory became a censor's place. Yet whereas theory succumbed in the vaunted mixture, practice became nonconceptual, a piece of the politics it was supposed to lead out of; it became the prey of power. (Adorno 1973)

Theory, in this case, should have as its goal emancipatory practice, but at the same time it requires a certain distance from such practice. Theory and practice represent a particular alliance, not a unity in which one dissolves into the other. The nature of such an alliance might be better understood by illuminating the drawbacks inherent in the traditional anti-theoretical stance in American education, in which it is argued that concrete experience is the great "teacher."

Experience, whether on the part of the researcher or others, contains no inherent guarantees to generate the insights necessary to make it transparent to the self. In other words, while it is indisputable that experience may provide us with knowledge, it is also indisputable that knowledge may distort rather than illuminate the nature of social reality. The point here is that the value of any experience "will depend not on the experience of the subject but on the struggles around the way that experience is interpreted and defined" (Bennet 1980b). Moreover, theory cannot be reduced to being perceived as the mistress of experience, empowered to provide recipes for pedagogical practice. Its real value lies in its ability to establish possibilities for reflexive thought and practice on the part of those who use it; in the case of teachers, it becomes invaluable as an instrument of critique and understanding. As a mode of critique and analysis, theory functions as a set of tools inextricably affected by the context in which it is brought to bear, but it is never reducible to that context. It has its own distance and purpose, its own element of practice. The crucial element in both its production and use is not the structure at which it is aimed, but the human agents who use it to give meaning to their lives.

In short, Adorno, Horkheimer, and Marcuse provided forms of historical and sociological analysis that pointed to the promise as well as to the limitations of the existing dominant rationality as it developed in the twentieth century. Such an analysis took as a starting-point the conviction that for self-conscious human beings to act collectively against the modes of technocratic rationality that permeated the workplace and other sociocultural spheres, their behaviour would have to be preceded and mediated by a mode of critical analysis. In other words, the pre-condition for such action was a form of critical theory. But it is important to stress that in linking critical theory to the goals of social and political emancipation, the Frankfurt School redefined the very notion of rationality. Rationality was no longer merely the exercise of critical thought, as had been its earlier Enlightenment counterpart. Instead, rationality now became the nexus of thought and action in the interest of liberating the community or society as a whole. As a higher rationality, it contained a transcendent project in which individual freedom merged with social freedom.

THE FRANKFURT SCHOOL'S ANALYSIS OF CULTURE

Central to the Frankfurt School's critique of positivist rationality was its analysis of culture. Rejecting the definition and role of culture found in both traditional sociological accounts and orthodox Marxist theory, Adorno and Horkheimer (1972) were noteworthy in developing a view of culture that assigned it a key place in the development of historical experience and everyday life. On the other hand, the Frankfurt School rejected the mainstream sociological notion that culture existed in an autonomous fashion, unrelated to the political and economic life-processes of society. In their view, such a perspective neutralized culture and in so doing abstracted it from the historical and societal context that gave it meaning. For Adorno the conventional view was shot through with a contradiction that reduced culture to nothing more than a piece of ideological shorthand:

> [The conventional view of culture] overlooks what is decisive: the role of ideology in social conflicts. To suppose, if only methodologically, anything like an independent logic of culture is to collaborate in the hypostasis of culture, the ideological proton pseudos. The substance of culture . . . resides not in culture alone but in relation to something external, to the material life-process. Culture, as Marx observed of juridical and political systems, cannot be fully "understood either in terms of itself . . . or in terms of the so-called universal development of the mind." To ignore this . . . is to make ideology the basic matter and to establish it firmly [Adorno 1967a]

On the other hand, while orthodox Marxist theory established a relationship between culture and the material forces of society, it did so by reducing culture to a mere reflex of the economic realm. In this view, the primacy of economic forces and the logic of scientific laws took precedence over issues concerning the terrain of everyday life, consciousness, or sexuality (Aronowitz 1981a). For the Frankfurt School, changing socioeconomic conditions had made traditional Marxist categories of the 1930s and 1940s untenable. They were no longer adequate for understanding the integration of the working class in the West or the political effects of technocratic rationality in the cultural realm.

Within the Frankfurt School perspective the role of culture in Western society had been modified with the transformation of critical *Enlightenment rationality into repressive forms of positivist rationality.* As a result of the development of new technical capabilities, greater concentrations of economic power, and more sophisticated modes of administration, the rationality of domination increasingly expanded its influence to spheres outside of the locus of economic production. Under the sign of Taylorism and scientific management, instrumental rationality extended its influence from the domination of nature to the domination of human beings. As such, mass-cultural institutions such as schools took on a new role in the first half of the twentieth century as "both a determinant and fundamental component of social consciousness" (Aronowitz 1976). According to the Frankfurt School, this meant that the cultural realm now constitutes a central place in the production and transformation of historical experience. Like Gramsci (1971), Adorno and Horkheimer (1972) argued that domination has assumed a new form. Instead of being exercised primarily through the use of physical force (the army and police), the power of the ruling classes was now reproduced through a form of ideological hegemony; that is, it was established primarily through the rule of consent, and mediated via cultural institutions such as schools, family, mass media, churches, etc. Briefly put, the colonization of the workplace was now supplemented by the colonization of all other cultural spheres (Aronowitz 1973; Enzenberger 1974; Ewen 1976).

According to the Frankfurt School, culture, like everything else in capitalist society, had been turned into an object. Under the dual rationalities of administration and exchange the elements of critique and opposition, which the Frankfurt School believed inherent in traditional culture, had been lost. Moreover, the objectification of culture did not simply result in the repression of the critical elements in its form and content; such objectification also represented the negation of critical thought itself. In Adorno's words: ". . . Culture in the true sense did not simply accommodate itself to human beings; . . . it always simultaneously raised a protest against the petrified relations under which they lived, thereby honoring them. Insofar as culture becomes wholly assimilated to and integrated into those petrified relations, human beings are once more debased" (Adorno 1975).

As far as the Frankfurt School was concerned, the cultural realm had become a new locus of control for that aspect of Enlightenment rationality in which the domination of nature and society proceeded under the guise of technical progress and economic growth. For Adorno and Horkheimer (1972) culture had become another industry, one which not only produced goods but also legitimated the logic of capital and its institutions. The *term "culture industry" was coined by Adorno as a response to the reification of culture, and it had two immediate purposes.* First, it was coined in order to expose the notion that "culture arises spontaneously from the masses themselves" (Lowenthal 1979). Second, it pointed to the concentration of economic and political determinants that control the cultural sphere in the interest of social and political domination. The term "industry" in the metaphor provided a point of critical analysis. That is, it pointed not only to a concentration of political and economic groups who reproduced and legitimated the dominant belief and value system, it also referred to the mechanisms of rationalization and standardization as they permeated everyday life. In other words, "the expression 'industry' is not to be taken literally. It refers to the standardization of the thing itself— such as the Western, familiar to every movie-goer—and to the rationalization of distribution techniques . . . [and] not strictly to the production process" (Adorno 1975).

At the core of the theory of culture advanced by Horkheimer, Adorno, and Marcuse was an attempt to expose, through both a call for and demonstration of critique, how positivist rationality manifested itself in the cultural realm. For instance, they criticised certain cultural products such as art for excluding the principles of resistance and opposition that once informed their relationship with the world while simultaneously helping to expose it (Horkheimer 1972). Likewise, for Marcuse (1978), "the truth of art lies in its power to break the monopoly of established reality (i.e., of those who established it) to define what is real. In this rupture . . . the fictitious world of art appears as true reality." The Frankfurt School argued that in a one-dimensional society art collapses, rather than highlights, the distinction between reality and the possibility of a higher truth or better world. In other words, in the true spirit of positivist harmony, art becomes simply a mirror of the existing reality and an affirmation of it. Thus, both the memory of a historical truth or the image of a better way of life are rendered impotent in the ultra-realism of Warhol's Campbell-soup painting or the Stakhanovite paintings of socialist realism.

Dictates of positivist rationality and the attendant mutilation of the power of imagination are also embodied in the techniques and forms that shape the messages and discourse of the culture industry. Whether it be in the glut of interchangeable plots, gags, or stories, or in the rapid pace of the film's development, the logic of standardization reigns supreme. The message is conformity, and the medium for its attainment is amusement, which proudly packages itself as an escape from the necessity of critical thought. Under the sway of the culture industry, style subsumes substance and thought is banished from the temple of official culture. Marcuse states this argument superbly:

> By becoming components of the aesthetic form, words, sounds, shapes, and colors are insulated against their familiar, ordinary use and function; . . . This is the achievement of style, which is the poem, the novel, the painting, the composition. The style, embodiment of the aesthetic form, in subjecting reality to another order, subjects it to the laws of beauty. True and false, right and wrong, pain and pleasure, calm and violence become aesthetic categories within the framework of the oeuvre. Thus deprived of their [immediate] reality, they enter a different context in which even the ugly, cruel, sick become parts of the aesthetic harmony governing the whole. (Marcuse 1972)

Inherent in the reduction of culture to amusement is a significant message which points to the root of the ethos of positivist rationality—the structural division between work and play. Within that division, work is confined to the imperatives of drudgery, boredom, and powerlessness for the vast majority; culture becomes the vehicle by which to escape from work. The power of the Frankfurt School's analysis lies in its exposure of the ideological fraud that constitutes this division of labor. Rather than being an escape from the mechanized work process, the cultural realm becomes an extension of it. Adorno and Horkheimer write:

> Amusement under late capitalism is the prolongation of work. It is sought-after as an escape from the mechanized work process, and to recruit strength in order to be able to cope with it again. But at the same time mechanization has such power over a man's leisure and happiness and so profoundly determines the manufacture of amusement goods, that his experiences are after-images of the work process itself. The ostensible content is merely a faded background; what sinks in is an automatic succession of standardized operations. (Adorno & Horkheimer 1972)

The most *radical critique of the division of labour* among the three theorists under study finds its expression in the work of *Herbert Marcuse* (1955, 1968b). Marcuse (1968b) claims that Marxism has not been radical enough in its attempt to develop a new sensibility that would develop as "an instinctual barrier against cruelty, brutality, ugliness." Marcuse's (1955) point is that a new rationality taking as its goal the erotization of labour and "the development and fulfillment of human needs" would necessitate new relations of production and organizational structures under which work could take place. This should not suggest that Marcuse abandons all forms of authority or that he equates hierarchical relationships with the realm of domination. On the contrary, he argues that work and play can interpenetrate each other without the loss of either's primary character. As Agger points out:

Marcuse is . . . saying that . . . work and play converge without abandoning the "work" character of work itself. He retains the rational organization of work without abandoning the Marxian goal of creative praxis. As he notes . . . "hierarchical relationships are not unfree per se." That is, it depends upon the kind of hierarchy which informs relationships. . . . Marcuse . . . suggests two things: in the first place, he hints at a theory of work which rests upon the merger of work and play components. His views in this regard are captured in his vision of the "erotization of labor." In the second place, Marcuse hints at a form of organizational rationality which is nondominating. (Agger 1978)

According to Marcuse (1964) science and technology have been integrated under the imprint of a dominating rationality that has penetrated the world of communicative interaction (the public sphere) as well as the world of work. It is worth mentioning, by contrast, Habermas's (1973) argument that science and technology in the sphere of work are necessarily limited to technical considerations, and that the latter organization of work represents the price an advanced industrial order must pay for its material comfort. This position has been challenged by a number of theorists, including Aronowitz (1981), who astutely argues that Habermas separates "communications and normative judgments from the labor process" and thus "cede[s] to technological consciousness the entire sphere of rational purposive action (work)." In further opposition to Habermas, Marcuse (1964) argues that radical change means more than simply the creation of conditions that foster critical thinking and communicative competence. Such change also entails the transformation of the labor process itself and the fusion of science and technology under the guise of a rationality stressing cooperation and self-management in the interest of democratic community and social freedom.

While there are significant differences among Adorno, Horkheimer, and Marcuse in their indictment of positivist rationality and in their respective notions about what constitutes an aesthetic or radical sensibility, their views converge on the existing repressiveness underlying positivist rationality and on the need for the development of a collective critical consciousness and sensibility that would embrace a discourse of opposition and non-identity as a precondition of human freedom. Thus, for them, criticism represents an indispensable element in the struggle for emancipation, and it is precisely in their call for criticism and a new sensibility that one finds an analysis of the nature of domination that contains invaluable insights for a theory of education. The analysis, in this case, includes the Frankfurt School's theory of depth psychology, to which I will now briefly turn.

THE FRANKFURT SCHOOL'S ANALYSIS OF DEPTH PSYCHOLOGY

As I have pointed out previously, the Frankfurt School faced a major contradiction in attempting to develop a critical tradition within Marxist theory. On the one hand, the historical legacy since Marx had witnessed increased material production and the continued conquest of nature in both the advanced industrial countries of the West and the countries of the socialist bloc as well. In both camps, it appeared that despite economic growth the objective conditions that promoted alienation had deepened. For example, in the West the production of goods and the ensuing commodity fetishism made a mockery of the concept of the Good Life, reducing it to the issue of purchasing power. In the socialist bloc, the centralization of political power led to political repression instead of political and economic freedom as had been promised. Yet in both cases the consciousness of the masses failed to keep pace with such conditions.

For the Frankfurt School it became clear that a theory of consciousness and depth psychology was needed to explain the subjective dimension of liberation and domination. Marx had provided the political and economic grammar of domination, but he relegated the psychic dimension to a secondary status, believing that it would follow any significant changes in the economic realm. Thus it was left to the Frankfurt School, especially Marcuse (1955, 1964, 1968b, 1970), to analyse the formal structure of consciousness in order to discover how a dehumanized society could continue to maintain its control over its inhabitants, and how it was possible that human beings could participate willingly at the level of everyday life in the reproduction of their own dehumanization and exploitation. For answers, the Frankfurt School turned to a critical study of Freud.

For the Frankfurt School, Freud's metapsychology provided an important theoretical foundation for revealing the interplay between the individual and society. More specifically, the value of Freudian psychology in this case rested with its illumination of the antagonistic character of social reality. As a theoretician of contradictions, Freud provided a radical insight into the way in which society reproduced its powers both in and over the individual. As Jacoby puts it:

> Psychoanalysis shows its strength; it demystifies the claims to liberated values, sensitivities, emotions, by tracing them to a repressed psychic, social, and biological dimension. . . . It keeps to the pulse of the psychic underground. As such it is more capable of grasping the intensifying social unreason that the conformist psychologies repress and forget: the barbarism of civilization itself, the barely suppressed misery of the living, the madness that haunts society. (Jacoby 1975)

The Frankfurt School theorists believed that it was only in an understanding of the dialectic between the individual and society that the depth and extent of domination as it existed both within and outside of the individual could be open to modification and transformation. Thus, for Adorno, Horkheimer, and Marcuse, Freud's emphasis on the constant struggle between the individual desire for instinctual gratification and the dynamics of social repression provided an indispensable clue to understanding the nature of society and the dynamics of psychic domination and liberation. Adorno points to this in the following comments:

> The only totality the student of society can presume to know is the antagonistic whole, and if he is to attain to totality at all, then only in contradiction. . . . The jarring elements that make up the individual, his "properties," are invariable moments of the social totality. He is, in the strict sense, a monad, representing the whole and its contradictions, without however being at any time conscious of the whole. (Adorno 1967b)

To explore the depth of the conflict between the individual and society, the Frankfurt School accepted with some major modifications most of Freud's most radical assumptions. More specifically, Freud's theoretical schema contained three important elements for developing a depth psychology. First, Freud provided a formal psychological structure for the Frankfurt School theorists to work with. That is, the Freudian outline of the structure of the psyche with its underlying struggle between Eros (the life instinct), Thanatos (the death instinct), and the outside world represented a key conception in the depth psychology developed by the Frankfurt School.

Secondly, Freud's studies on psychopathology, particularly his sensitivity to humanity's capacity for self-destructiveness and his focus on the loss of ego stability and the decline of the influence of the family in contemporary society added significantly to the Frankfurt School analyses of mass society and the rise of the authoritarian personality. For the Frankfurt School, the growing concentration of power in capitalist society, along with the pervasive intervention of the state in the affairs of everyday life, had altered the dialectical role of the traditional family as both a positive and negative site for identity formation. That is, the family had traditionally provided, on the one hand, a sphere of warmth and protection for its members, while, on the other hand, it also functioned as a repository for social and sexual repression. But under the development of advanced industrial capitalism, the dual function of the family was gradually giving way, and it began to function exclusively as a site for social and cultural reproduction.

Finally, by focusing on Freud's theory of instincts and metapsychology, the Frankfurt School devised a theoretical framework for unraveling and exposing the objective and psychological obstacles to social change. This issue is important because it provides significant insights into how depth psychology might be useful for developing a more comprehensive theory of education. Since Adorno shared some major differences with both Horkheimer and Marcuse regarding Freud's theory of instincts and his view of the relationship between the individual and society, I will treat their respective contributions separately.

Adorno (1968) was quick to point out that while Freud's denunciation of "man's unfreedom" over-identified with a particular historical period and thus "petrified into an anthropological constant," it did not seriously detract from his greatness as a theoretician of contradictions. That is, in spite of the limitations in Freudian theory, Adorno—and Horkheimer as well—firmly believed that psychoanalysis provided a strong theoretical bulwark against psychological and social theories that exalted the idea of the "integrated personality" and the "wonders" of social harmony. True to Adorno's (1968) view that "Every image of man is ideology except the negative one," Freud's work appeared to transcend its own shortcomings because at one level it personified the spirit of negation. Adorno (1967b, 1968) clearly exalted the negative and critical features of psychoanalysis and saw them as major theoretical weapons to be used against every form of identity theory. The goals of identity theory and revisionist psychology were both political and ideological in nature, and it was precisely through the use of Freud's metapsychology that they could be exposed as such. As Adorno put it:

> The goal of the well-integrated personality is objectionable because it expects the individual to establish an equilibrium between conflicting forces, which does not obtain in existing society. Nor should it, because these forces are not of equal moral merit. People are taught to forget the objective conflicts which necessarily repeat themselves in every individual instead of helped to grapple with them. (Adorno 1968)

While it was clear to the Frankfurt School that psychoanalysis could not solve the problems of repression and authoritarianism, they believed that it did provide important insights into how "people become accomplices to their own subjugation" (Benjamin, J. 1977). Yet beneath the analyses put forth on psychoanalysis by Adorno (1967b, 1968, 1972, 1973) and Horkheimer (1972) there lurked a disturbing paradox: while both theorists went to great lengths to explain the dynamics of authoritarianism and psychological domination, they said very little about those formal aspects of consciousness that might provide a basis for resistance and rebellion. In other words, Horkheimer and Adorno, while recognizing that Freudian psychology registered a powerful criticism of existing society in exposing its antagonistic character, failed to extend this insight by locating in either individuals or social classes the psychological or political grounds for a self-conscious recognition of such contradictions and the ability of human agents to transform them. Consequently, they provided a view of Freudian psychology that consigned Freud to the ambiguous status of radical as well as prophet of gloom.

If Adorno and Horkheimer viewed Freud as a revolutionary pessimist, Marcuse (1955) read him as a revolutionary utopian. That is, though he accepts most of Freud's most controversial assumptions, his interpretation of them is both unique and provocative. In one sense, Marcuse's (1955,

1968a&b, 1970) analysis contained an original dialectical twist in that it pointed to a utopian integration of Marx and Freud. Marcuse (1955) accepted Freud's view of the antagonistic relations between the individual and society as a fundamental insight, but he nevertheless altered some of Freud's basic categories, and in doing so situated Freud's pessimism within a historical context that revealed its strengths as well as limitations. In doing so, Marcuse was able to illuminate the importance of Freud's metapsychology as a basis for social change. This becomes particularly clear if we examine how Marcuse (1955, 1968a&b, 1970) reworked Freud's basic claims regarding the life and death instincts, the struggle between the individual and society, the relationship between scarcity and social repression, and, finally, the issues of freedom and human emancipation.

Marcuse (1955, 1964) begins with the basic assumption that inherent in Freud's theory of the unconscious and his theory of the instincts could be found the theoretical elements for a more comprehensive view of the nature of individual and social domination. Marcuse points to this possibility when he writes:

> The struggle against freedom reproduces itself in the psyche of man as the self-repression of the repressed individual, and his self-repression in turn sustains his masters and their institutions. It is this mental dynamic which Freud unfolds as the dynamic of civilization. . . . Freud's metapsychology is an ever-renewed attempt to uncover, and to question, the terrible necessity of the inner connection between civilization and barbarism, progress and suffering, freedom and unhappiness—a connection which reveals itself ultimately as that between Eros and Thanatos. (Marcuse 1955)

For Marcuse (1955, 1970) Freudian psychology, as a result of its analysis of the relationship between civilization and instinctual repression, posited the theoretical basis for understanding the distinction between socially necessary authority and authoritarianism. That is, in the interplay between the need for social labor and the equally important need for the sublimation of sexual energy, the dynamic connection between domination and freedom, on the one hand, and authority and authoritarianism, on the other, starts to become discernible. Freud presented the conflict between the individual's instinctual need for pleasure and the society's demand for repression as an insoluble problem rooted in a trans-historical struggle; as a result, he pointed to the continuing repressive transformation of Eros in society, along with the growing propensity for self destruction. Marcuse (1970) believed that the "Freudian conception of the relationship between civilization and the dynamics of the instincts [was] in need of a decisive correction." That is, whereas Freud (1949) saw the increased necessity for social and instinctual repression, Marcuse (1955, 1970) argued that any understanding of social repression had to be situated within a specific historical context and judged as to whether such systems of domination exceeded their bounds. To ignore such a distinction was to forfeit the possibility of analyzing the difference between the exercise of legitimate authority and illegitimate forms of domination. Marcuse (1955) deemed that Freud had failed to capture in his analyses the historical dynamic of organized domination, and thus had given to it the status and dignity of a biological development that was universal rather than merely historically contingent.

While Marcuse (1955) accepts the Freudian notion that the central conflict in society is between the reality principle and the pleasure principle, he rejects the position that the latter had to adjust to the former. In other words, Freud believed that "the price of civilization is paid for in forfeiting happiness through heightening of the sense of guilt" (Freud 1949). This is important because at the core of Freud's notion that humanity was forever condemned to diverting pleasure and sexual energy into alienating labor was an appeal to a trans-historical "truth": that scarcity was inevitable in society, and that labor was inherently alienating. In opposition to Freud, Marcuse argued that the reality principle referred to a particular form of historical existence when scarcity legitimately dictated instinctual repression. But in the contemporary period such conditions had been superceded, and as such abundance, not scarcity, characterized or informed the reality principle governing the advanced industrial countries of the West.

In order to add a more fully historical dimension to Freud's analysis, Marcuse (1955) introduced the concepts of the performance principle and of surplus-repression. By arguing that scarcity was not a universal aspect of the human condition, Marcuse (1955, 1970) claimed that the moment had arrived in the industrial West when it was no longer necessary to submit men and women to the demands of alienating labor. The existing reality principle, which Marcuse (1955) labeled the performance principle, had outstripped its historical function, i.e., the sublimation of Eros in the interest of socially necessary labor. The performance principle, with its emphasis on technocratic reason and exchange rationality, was, in Marcuse's (1955) terms, both historically contingent and socially repressive. As a relatively new mode of domination, it tied people to values, ideas, and social practices that blocked their possibilities for gratification and happiness as ends in themselves.

In short, Marcuse (1955) believed that inherent in Marx's view of societal abundance and in Freud's theory of instincts was the basis for a new performance principle, one that was governed by principles of socially necessary labor and by those aspects of the pleasure principle that integrated work, play, and sexuality. This leads us to Marcuse's second important idea, the concept of surplus-repression. The excessiveness of the existing nature of domination could be measured through what Marcuse labeled as surplus-repression. Distinguishing this from socially useful repression, Marcuse claims that:

> Within the total structure of the repressed personality, surplus-repression is that portion which is the result of specific societal conditions sustained in the spe-

cific act of domination. The extent of this surplus-repression provides the standard of measurement: the smaller it is, the less repressive is the stage of civilization. The distinction is equivalent to that between the biological and the historical sources of human suffering. (Marcuse 1955)

According to Marcuse (1955, 1970), it is within this dialectical interplay of the personality structure and historically conditioned repression that the nexus exists for uncovering the historical and contemporary nature of domination. Domination in this sense is doubly historical: first, it is rooted in the historically developed socio-economic conditions of a given society; further, it is rooted in the sedimented history or personality structure of individuals. In speaking of domination as a psychological as well as a political phenomenon, Marcuse did not give a carte blanche to wholesale gratification. On the contrary, he agreed with Freud that some forms of repression were generally necessary. What he objected to was the unnecessary repression that was embodied in the ethos and social practices that characterized social institutions like school, the workplace, and the family.

For Marcuse (1964), the most penetrating marks of social repression are generated in the inner history of individuals, in the "needs, satisfactions, and values which reproduce the servitude of human existence." Such needs are mediated and reinforced through the patterns and social routines of everyday life, and the "false" needs that perpetuate toil, misery, and aggressiveness become anchored in the personality structure as second nature; that is, their historical character is forgotten, and they become reduced to patterns of habit.

In the end, Marcuse (1955) grounds even Freud's important notion of the death instinct (the autonomous drive that increasingly leads to self-destruction) in a radical problematic. That is, by claiming that the primary drive of humanity is pleasure, Marcuse redefines the death instinct by arguing that it is mediated not by the need for self-destruction—although this is a form it may take—but by the need to resolve tension. Rooted in such a perspective, the death instinct is not only redefined, it is also politicized as Marcuse argues that in a non-repressive society it would be subordinated to the demands of Eros. Thus, Marcuse (1955, 1964) ends up supporting the Frankfurt School's notion of negative thinking, but with an important qualification. He insists on its value as a mode of critique, but maintains equally that it is grounded in socio-economic conditions that can be transformed. It is the promise of a better future, rather than despair over the existing nature of society, that informs both Marcuse's work and its possibilities as a mode of critique for educators.

TOWARDS A CRITICAL THEORY OF EDUCATION

While it is impossible to elaborate in any detail on the implications of the work of the Frankfurt School for a theory of radical pedagogy, I can point briefly to some general considerations. I believe that it is clear that the thought of the

Frankfurt School provides a major challenge and a stimulus to educational theorists who are critical of theories of education tied to functionalist paradigms based on assumptions drawn from a positivist rationality. For instance, against the positivist spirit that infuses existing educational theory and practice, whether it takes the form of the Tyler model or various systems approaches, the Frankfurt School offers an historical analysis and a penetrating philosophical framework that indict the wider culture of positivism, while at the same time providing insight into how the latter becomes incorporated within the ethos and practices of schools. Though there is a growing body of educational literature that is critical of positivist rationality in schools, it lacks the theoretical sophistication characteristic of the work of Horkheimer, Adorno, and Marcuse. Similarly, the importance of historical consciousness as a fundamental dimension of critical thinking in the Frankfurt School perspective creates a valuable epistemological terrain upon which to develop modes of critique that illuminate the interaction of the social and the personal as well as of history and private experience. Through this form of analysis, dialectical thought replaces positivist forms of social inquiry. That is, the logic of predictability, verifiability, transferability, and operationalism is replaced by a dialectical mode of thinking that stresses the historical, relational, and normative dimensions of social inquiry and knowledge. The notion of dialectical thinking as critical thinking, and its implications for pedagogy, become somewhat clear in Jameson's comment that "[D]ialectical thinking is . . . thought about thinking itself, in which the mind must deal with its own thought process just as much as with the material it works on, in which both the particular content involved and the style of thinking suited to it must be held together in the mind at the same time" (Jameson 1971).

What we get here are hints of what a radical view of knowledge might look like. In this case, it would be knowledge that would instruct the oppressed about their situation as a group situated within specific relations of domination and subordination. It would be knowledge that would illuminate how the oppressed could develop a discourse free from the distortions of their own partly mangled cultural inheritance. On the other hand, it would be a form of knowledge that instructed the oppressed in how to appropriate the most progressive dimensions of their own cultural histories, as well as how to restructure and appropriate the most radical aspects of bourgeois culture. Finally, such knowledge would have to provide a motivational connection to action itself; it would have to link a radical decoding of history to a vision of the future that not only exploded the reifications of the existing society, but also reached into those pockets of desires and needs that harbored a longing for a new society and new forms of social relations. It is at this point that the link between history, culture, and psychology becomes important.

It is with regard to the above that the notion of historical understanding in the work of the Frankfurt School makes some important contributions to the notion of radical pedagogy. History, for Adorno and others connected with critical theory, had a two-fold meaning and could not be interpreted as continuous pattern unfolding under the imperatives of "natural" laws. On the contrary, it had to be viewed as an emerging open-ended phenomenon, the significance of which was to be gleaned in the cracks and tensions that separated individuals and social classes from the imperatives of the dominant society. In other words, there were no laws of history that prefigured human progress, that functioned independently of human action. Moreover, history became meaningful not because it provided the present with the fruits of "interesting" or "stimulating" culture, but because it became the present object of analyses aimed at illuminating the revolutionary possibilities that existed in the given society. For the radical educator, this suggests using history in order "to fight against the spirit of the times rather than join it, to look backward at history rather than 'forward' " (Buck-Morss 1977). To put it another way, it meant, as Benjamin claimed "to brush history against the grain" (Benjamin 1974).

Not only does such a position link historical analysis to the notions of critique and emancipation, it also politicizes the notion of knowledge. That is, it argues for looking at knowledge critically, within constellations of suppressed insights (dialectical images) that point to the ways in which historically repressed cultures and struggles could be used to illuminate radical potentialities in the present. Knowledge in this instance becomes an object of analysis in a two-fold sense. On the one hand, it is examined for its social function, the way in which it legitimates the existing society. At the same time it could also be examined to reveal in its arrangement, words, structure, and style those unintentional truths that might contain "fleeting images" of a different society, more radical practices, and new forms of understanding. For instance, almost every cultural text contains a combination of ideological and utopian moments. Inherent in the most overt messages that characterize mass culture are elements of its antithesis. All cultural artifacts have a hidden referent that speaks to the initial basis for repression. Against the image of the barely clad female model selling the new automobile is the latent tension of misplaced and misappropriated sexual desire. Within the most authoritative modes of classroom discipline and control are fleeting images of freedom that speak to very different relationships. It is this dialectical aspect of knowledge that needs to be developed as part of a radical pedagogy.

Unlike traditional and liberal accounts of schooling, with their emphasis on historical continuities and historical development, critical theory points educators toward a mode of analysis that stresses the breaks, discontinuities, and tensions in history, all of which become valuable in that they highlight the centrality of human agency and struggle while simultaneously revealing the gap between society as it presently exists and society as it might be.

The Frankfurt School's theory of culture also offers new concepts and categories for analysing the role that schools play as agents of social and cultural reproduction. By illuminating the relationship between power and culture, the Frankfurt School provides a perspective on the way in which dominant ideologies are constituted and mediated via specific cultural formations. The concept of culture in this view exists in a particular relationship to the material base of society. The explanatory value of such a relationship is to be found in making problematic the specific content of a culture, its relationship to dominant and subordinate groups, as well as the socio-historical genesis of the ethos and practices of legitimating cultures and their role in constituting relations of domination and resistance. For example, by pointing to schools as cultural sites that embody conflicting political values, histories, and practices, it becomes possible to investigate how schools can be analyzed as an expression of the wider organization of society. Marcuse's (1964) study of the ideological nature of language, Adorno's (1975) analysis of the sociology of music, Horkheimer's (1972) method of dialectical critique and W. Benjamin's (1969, 1977) theory of cognition, all provide a number of valuable theoretical constructs through which to investigate the socially produced nature of knowledge and school experience.

The centrality of culture in the work of the Frankfurt School theorists (despite the differing opinions among its members) points to a number of important insights that illuminate how subjectivities get constituted both within and outside of schools. Though their analysis of culture is somewhat undialectical and clearly underdeveloped, it does provide a foundation for a greater elaboration and understanding of the relationship between culture and power, while simultaneously recognizing the latter as important terrain upon which to analyze the nature of domination and of resistance. By urging an attentiveness to the suppressed moments of history, critical theory points to the need to develop an equal sensitivity to certain aspects of culture. For example, working-class students, women, Blacks, and others need to affirm their own histories through the use of a language, a set of social relations, and body of knowledge that critically reconstructs and dignifies the cultural experiences that make up the tissue, texture, and history of their daily lives. This is no small matter, since once the affirmative nature of such a pedagogy is established, it becomes possible for students who have been traditionally voiceless in schools to learn the skills, knowledge, and modes of inquiry that will allow them to critically examine the role society has played in their own self-formation. More specifically, they will have the tools to examine how this society has functioned to shape and thwart their aspirations and goals, or prevented them from even imagining a life outside the one they presently lead. Thus it is important that students come to grips with what a given society has made of them, how it has incorporated them ideologically and materially into its rules and logic, and what it is that they need to affirm and reject in their own histories in order to begin the process of struggling for the conditions that will give them opportunities to lead a self-managed existence.

While it is true that Adorno, Marcuse, and Horkheimer placed heavy emphasis on the notion of domination in their analyses of culture, and in fact appeared to equate mass culture with mass manipulation, the value of their analyses rests with the mode of critique they developed in their attempt to reconstruct the notion of culture as a political force, as a powerful political moment in the process of domination. There is a paradox in their analyses of culture and human agency—that is, a paradox emerged in their emphasis on the overwhelming and one-sided nature of mass culture as a dominating force, on the one hand, and their relentless insistence on the need for critique, negativity, and critical mediation on the other. It is within this seeming contradiction that more dialectical notions of power and resistance have to be developed, positions that recognize wider structural and ideological determinations while recognizing that human beings never represent simply a reflex of such constraints. Human beings not only make history, they also make the constraints; and needless to say, they also unmake them. It needs to be remembered that power is both an enabling as well as a constraining force, as Foucault (1980) is quick to point out.

It must be stressed that the ideological justification of the given social order is not to be found simply in modes of interpretation that view history as a "natural" evolving process, or in the ideologies distributed through the culture industry. It is also found in the material reality of those needs and wants that bear the inscription of history. That is, history is to be found as "second nature" in those concepts and views of the world that make the most dominating aspects of the social order appear to be immune from historical socio-political development. Those aspects of reality that rest on an appeal to the universal and invariant often slip from historical consciousness and become embedded within those historically specific needs and desires that link individuals to the logics of conformity and domination. There is a certain irony in the fact that the personal and political join in the structure of domination precisely at those moments where history functions to tie individuals to a set of assumptions and practices that deny the historical nature of the political. "Second nature" represents history that has hardened into a form of social amnesia (Jacoby 1975), a mode of consciousness that "forgets" its own development. The significance of this perspective for radical pedagogy is that it points to the value of a *depth psychology* that can unravel how the mechanisms of domination and the possible seeds of liberation reach into the very structure of the human psyche. Radical pedagogy is much too cognitive in its orientation, and it needs to develop a theory of domination that incorporates needs and wants. Radical pedagogy lacks a depth psychology as well as appreciation for a sensibility that points to the importance of the sensual and imaginative as central dimensions of the schooling experience. The Frankfurt School's notion of depth psychology, especially Marcuse's work, opens up new terrain for developing a critical pedagogy. It speaks to the need to fashion new categories of analysis that will enable educators to become more knowledgeable about how teachers, students, and other educational workers become part of the system of social and cultural reproduction, particularly as it works through the messages and values that are constituted via the social practices of the hidden curriculum (Giroux 1981). By acknowledging the need for a critical social psychology, educators can begin to identify how ideologies get constituted, and they can then identify and reconstruct social practices and processes that break rather than continue existing forms of social and psychological domination.

The relevance of Marcuse's analysis of depth psychology for educational theory becomes obvious in the more recent work of Pierre Bourdieu (1977a, 1977b). Bourdieu argues that the school and other social institutions legitimate and reinforce through specific sets of practices and discourses class-based systems of behavior and dispositions that reproduce the existing dominant society. Bourdieu extends Marcuse's insights by pointing to a notion of learning in which a child internalizes the cultural messages of the school not only via the latter's official discourse (symbolic mastery), but also through the messages embodied in the "insignificant" practices of daily classroom life. Bourdieu (1977b) is worth quoting at length on this issue:

> [Schools] . . . set such a store on the seemingly most insignificant details of dress, bearing, physical and verbal manners. . . . The principles embodied in this way are placed beyond the grasp of consciousness, and hence cannot be touched by voluntary, deliberate transformation, cannot even be made explicit. . . . The whole trick of pedagogic reason lies precisely in the way it extorts the essential while seeming to demand the insignificant: in obtaining respect for forms and forms of respect which constitute the most visible and at the same time the best hidden manifestations to the established order. (Bourdieu 1977b)

Unlike Bourdieu, Marcuse believes that historically conditioned needs that function in the interest of domination can be changed. That is, in Marcuse's view (1955) any viable form of political action must begin with a notion of political education in which a new language, qualitatively different social relations, and a new set of values would have to operate with the purpose of creating a new environment "in which the nonaggressive, erotic, receptive faculties of man, in harmony with the consciousness of freedom, strive for the pacification of man and nature." (Marcuse 1969). Thus the notion of depth psychology developed by the Frankfurt School not only provides new insights into how subjectivities are formed or how ideology functions as lived experience, it also provides theoretical tools to establish the conditions for new needs, new systems of values, and new social practices that take seriously the imperatives of a critical pedagogy.

CONCLUSION

In conclusion, I have attempted to present selected aspects of the work of critical theorists such as Adorno, Horkheimer, and Marcuse that provide theoretical insights for developing a critical theory of education. Specifically, I have focused on their critique of positivist rationality, their view of theory, their critical reconstruction of a theory of culture, and, finally, on their analysis of depth psychology. It is within the context of these four areas that radical educators can begin the task of reconstructing and applying the insights of critical theory to schooling. Of course, the task of translating the work of the Frankfurt School into terms that inform and enrich radical educational theory and practice will be difficult. This is especially true since any attempt to use such work will have to begin with the understanding that it contains a number of shortcomings and moreover cannot be imposed in grid-like fashion onto a theory of radical pedagogy. For example, the critical theorists I have discussed did not develop a comprehensive theoretical approach for dealing with the patterns of conflict and contradictions that existed in various cultural spheres. To the contrary, they developed an unsatisfactory notion of domination and an exaggerated view of the integrated nature of the American public; they constantly underestimated the radical potential inherent in working-class culture; and they never developed an adequate theory of social consciousness. That is, in spite of their insistence, on the importance of the notion of mediation, they never explored the contradictory modes of thinking that characterize the way most people view the world. Of course, the latter selection does not exhaust the list of criticisms that could be made against the work of the critical theorists under analysis here. The point is that critical theory needs to be reformulated to provide the opportunity to both critique and elaborate its insights beyond the constraints and historical conditions under which they were first generated. It must be stressed that the insights critical theory has provided have not been exhausted. In fact, one may argue that we are just beginning to work out the implications of their analyses. The real issue is to reformulate the central contributions of critical theory in terms of new historical conditions, without sacrificing the emancipatory spirit that generated them.

REFERENCES

Adorno, T. W. 1967a. *Prisms,* trans. Samuel and Shierry Weber. London: Neville Spearman.
———. 1967b. "Sociology and psychology: Part I." *New Left Review,* 46.
———. 1968. "Sociology and psychology: Part II." *New Left Review,* 47.
———. 1969. "Scientific Experiences of a European Scholar in America." In *The Intellectual Migration,* ed. Donald Fleming and Bernard Bailyn. Cambridge, Mass.: Harvard University Press.
Adorno, T. W., and M. Horkheimer, 1972. *Dialectic of Enlightenment,* trans. John Cumming. New York: Seabury Press.
———. 1973. *Negative Dialectics.* New York: Seabury Press.
———. 1975. "The Culture Industry Reconsidered." *New German Critique,* 6 (Fall).
———. 1976. "On the Logic of the Social Sciences." In *The Positivist Dispute in German Sociology,* T. W. Adorno et al. London: Heinemann.
Agger, B. 1978. "Work and Authority in Marcuse and Habermas." *Human Studies,* 2(3) (July).

Aronowitz, S. 1973. *False Promises*. New York: McGraw-Hill.

———. 1976. "Enzenberger on Mass Culture: A Review Essay." *Minnesota Review, 7* (Fall).

———. 1981. *The Crisis in Historical Materialism: Class, Politics, and Culture in Marxist Theory.* New York: Bergin.

———. 1981b. "Redefining Literacy." *Social Policy* (Sept.–Oct.).

Benjamin, J. 1977. "The End of Internationalization: Adorno's Social Psychology." *Telos*, 32 (Summer).

Benjamin, W. 1974. In *Über den Begriff der Geschichte: Gesammelte Schriften,* 1(2), ed. Rolf Tiedemann and Hermann Schweppenhauser, Abhandlungen, Suhrkamp Verlag, Frankfurt am Main.

———. 1969. In *Illuminations*, ed. Hannah Arendt. New York: Schocken.

———. 1977. *The Origin of German Tragic Drama,* trans. John Osborne. London: New Left Books.

Bennett, T. 1980b. "The Not-So-Good, the Bad, and the Ugly." *Screen Education,* 36 (Autumn).

Bourdieu, P., and J. C. Passeron. 1977a. *Reproduction in Education, Society, and Culture.* Beverly Hills, Cal.: Sage.

———. 1977b. *Outline of Theory and Practice.* Cambridge: Cambridge University Press.

Breines, P. 1979/80. "Toward an Uncertain Marxism." *Radical History Review,* 22 (Winter).

Buck-Morss, S. 1977. *The Origins of Negative Dialectics.* New York: Free Press.

Enzenberger, H. M. 1974. *The Consciousness Industry.* New York: Seabury Press.

Ewen, S. 1976. *Captains of Consciousness: Advertising and the Social Roots of the Consumer Culture.* New York: McGraw-Hill.

Foucault, M. 1980. *Power and Knowledge: Selected Interviews and Other Writings,* ed. C. Gordon. New York: Pantheon.

Freud, S. 1949. *Civilization and Its Discontents.* London: Hogarth Press.

Friedman, G. 1981. *The Political Philosophy of the Frankfurt School.* Ithaca, N.Y.: Cornell University Press.

Giroux, H. A. 1981. *Ideology, Culture, and the Process of Schooling.* Philadelphia: Temple University Press.

Gramsci, A. 1971. *Selections from Prison Notebooks,* ed. and trans. Quinten Hoare and Geoffrey Smith. New York: International Publishers.

Gross, H. 1979. "Adorno in Los Angeles: The Intellectual Emigration." *Humanities in Society,* 2(4) (Fall).

Habermas, J. 1973. *Theory and Practice.* Boston: Beacon Press.

———. 1980. "Psychic Thermidor and the Rebirth of Rebellious Subjectivity." *Berkeley Journal of Sociology,* 25.

Hahn, H. 1933. "Logik Mathematik and Naturerkennen." In *Einheitswissenschaft,* ed. Otto Neurath et al. Vienna: n.p.

Held, D. 1980. *Introduction to Critical Theory: Horkheimer to Habermas.* Berkely: University of California Press.

Horkheimer, M. 1972. *Critical Theory.* New York: Seabury Press.

———. 1974. *Eclipse of Reason.* New York: Seabury Press.

Jacoby, R. 1975. *Social Amnesia.* Boston: Beacon Press.

———. 1980. "What Is Conformist Marxism?" *Telos,* 45 (Fall).

Jameson, F. 1971. *Marxism and Form.* Princeton, N.J.: Princeton University Press.

Jay, M. 1973. *The Dialectical Imagination: A History of the Frankfurt School and the Institute of Social Research 1923–1950.* Boston: Little, Brown.

Lowenthal, L. 1979. "Theodor W. Adorno: An Intellectual Memoir." *Humanities in Society,* 2(4) (Fall).

Marcuse, H. 1955. *Eros and Civilization.* Boston: Beacon Press.

———. 1960. *Reason and Revolution.* Boston: Beacon Press.

———. 1964. *One Dimensional Man.* Boston: Beacon Press.

———. 1968a. *Negations: Essays in Critical Theory.* Boston: Beacon Press.

———. 1968b. *An Essay on Liberation.* Boston: Beacon Press.

———. 1970. *Five Lectures,* trans. Jeremy Shapiro and Sheirry Weber. Boston: Beacon Press.

———. 1969. "Repressive Tolerance." In *A Critique of Pure Tolerance,* ed. Robert Paul Wolff, Benjamin Moor, Jr., and Herbert Marcuse. Boston: Beacon Press.

———. 1972. *Counter-Revolution and Revolt.* Boston: Beacon Press.

———. 1978. "On Science and Phenomenology." In *The Essential Frankfurt School Reader,* ed. Andrew Arato and Eike Gebhardt. New York: Urizen Books.

Nietzche, F. 1966. "Aus dem Nachlass der Achtzigerjahre." In *Werke,* vol. 3, ed. Karle Schleckta. Munich: Hanser.

Wellmer, A. 1974. *Critical Theory of Society,* trans. John Cumming. New York: Seabury Press.

From *Pedagogy of the Oppressed*

PAULO FREIRE

A careful analysis of the teacher-student relationship at any level, inside or outside the school, reveals its fundamentally *narrative* character. This relationship involves a narrating Subject (the teacher) and patient, listening objects (the students). The contents, whether values or empirical dimensions of reality, tend in the process of being narrated to become lifeless and petrified. Education is suffering from narration sickness.

The teacher talks about reality as if it were motionless, static, compartmentalized, and predictable. Or else he expounds on a topic completely alien to the existential experience of the students. His task is to "fill" the students with the contents of his narration—contents which are detached from reality, disconnected from the totality that engendered them and could give them significance. Words are emptied of their concreteness and become a hollow, alienated, and alienating verbosity.

The outstanding characteristic of this narrative education, then, is the sonority of words, not their transforming power. "Four times four is sixteen; the capital of Pará is Belém." The student records, memorizes, and repeats these phrases without perceiving what four times four really means, or realizing the true significance of "capital" in the affirmation "the capital of Pará is Belém," that is, what Belém means for Pará and what Pará means for Brazil.

Narration (with the teacher as narrator) leads the students to memorize mechanically the narrated content. Worse yet, it turns them into "containers," into "receptacles" to be "filled" by the teacher. The more completely he fills the receptacles, the better a teacher he is. The more meekly the receptacles permit themselves to be filled, the better students they are.

Education thus becomes an act of depositing, in which the students are the depositories and the teacher is the depositor. Instead of communicating, the teacher issues communiqués and makes deposits which the students patiently

57

receive, memorize, and repeat. This is the "banking" concept of education, in which the scope of action allowed to the students extends only as far as receiving, filing, and storing the deposits. They do, it is true, have the opportunity to become collectors or cataloguers of the things they store. But in the last analysis, it is men themselves who are filed away through the lack of creativity, transformation, and knowledge in this (at best) misguided system. For apart from inquiry, apart from the praxis, men cannot be truly human. Knowledge emerges only through invention and re-invention, through the restless, impatient, continuing, hopeful inquiry men pursue in the world, with the world, and with each other.

In the banking concept of education, knowledge is a gift bestowed by those who consider themselves knowledgeable upon those whom they consider to know nothing. Projecting an absolute ignorance onto others, a characteristic of the ideology of oppression, negates education and knowledge as processes of inquiry. The teacher presents himself to his students as their necessary opposite; by considering their ignorance absolute, he justifies his own existence. The students, alienated like the slave in the Hegelian dialectic, accept their ignorance as justifying the teacher's existence—but, unlike the slave, they never discover that they educate the teacher.

The raison d'être of libertarian education, on the other hand, lies in its drive towards reconciliation. Education must begin with the solution of the teacher-student contradiction, by reconciling the poles of the contradiction so that both are simultaneously teachers *and* students.

This solution is not (nor can it be) found in the banking concept. On the contrary, banking education maintains and even stimulates the contradiction through the following attitudes and practices, which mirror oppressive society as a whole:

(a) the teacher teaches and the students are taught;
(b) the teacher knows everything and the students know nothing;
(c) the teacher thinks and the students are thought about;
(d) the teacher talks and the students listen—meekly;
(e) the teacher disciplines and the students are disciplined;
(f) the teacher chooses and enforces his choice, and the students comply;
(g) the teacher acts and the students have the illusion of acting through the action of the teacher;
(h) the teacher chooses the program content, and the students (who were not consulted) adapt to it;
(i) the teacher confuses the authority of knowledge with his own professional authority, which he sets in opposition to the freedom of the students;

(j)   the teacher is the Subject of the learning process, while the pupils are mere objects.

It is not surprising that the banking concept of education regards men as adaptable, manageable beings. The more students work at storing the deposits entrusted to them, the less they develop the critical consciousness which would result from their intervention in the world as transformers of that world. The more completely they accept the passive role imposed on them, the more they tend simply to adapt to the world as it is and to the fragmented view of reality deposited in them.

The capability of banking education to minimize or annul the students' creative power and to stimulate their credulity serves the interests of the oppressors, who care neither to have the world revealed nor to see it transformed. The oppressors use their "humanitarianism" to preserve a profitable situation. Thus they react almost instinctively against any experiment in education which stimulates the critical faculties and is not content with a partial view of reality but always seeks out the ties which link one point to another and one problem to another.

Indeed, the interests of the oppressors lie in "changing the consciousness of the oppressed, not the situation which oppresses them";[1] for the more the oppressed can be led to adapt to that situation, the more easily they can be dominated. To achieve this end, the oppressors use the banking concept of education in conjunction with a paternalistic social action apparatus, within which the oppressed receive the euphemistic title of "welfare recipients." They are treated as individual cases, as marginal men who deviate from the general configuration of a "good, organized, and just" society. The oppressed are regarded as the pathology of the healthy society, which must therefore adjust these "incompetent and lazy" folk to its own patterns by changing their mentality. These marginals need to be "integrated," "incorporated" into the healthy society that they have "forsaken."

The truth is, however, that the oppressed are not "marginals," are not men living "outside" society. They have always been "inside"—inside the structure which made them "beings for others." The solution is not to "integrate" them into the structure of oppression, but to transform that structure so that they can become "beings for themselves." Such transformation, of course, would undermine the oppressors' purposes; hence their utilization of the banking concept of education to avoid the threat of student *conscientização*.

The banking approach to adult education, for example, will never propose to students that they critically consider reality. It will deal instead with such vital questions as whether Roger gave green grass to the goat, and insist upon the importance of learning that, on the contrary, *Roger gave green grass to the rabbit*. The "humanism" of the banking approach masks the effort to turn men into automatons—the very negation of their ontological vocation to be more fully human.

Those who use the banking approach, knowingly or unknowingly (for there are innumerable well-intentioned bank-clerk teachers who do not realize that they are serving only to dehumanize), fail to perceive that the deposits themselves contain contradictions about reality. But, sooner or later, these contradictions may lead formerly passive students to turn against their domestication and the attempt to domesticate reality. They may discover through existential experience that their present way of life is irreconcilable with their vocation to become fully human. They may perceive through their relations with reality that reality is really a *process*, undergoing constant transformation. If men are searchers and their ontological vocation is humanization, sooner or later they may perceive the contradiction in which banking education seeks to maintain them, and then engage themselves in the struggle for their liberation.

But the humanist, revolutionary educator cannot wait for this possibility to materialize. From the outset, his efforts must coincide with those of the students to engage in critical thinking and the quest for mutual humanization. His efforts must be imbued with a profound trust in men and their creative power. To achieve this, he must be a partner of the students in his relations with them.

The banking concept does not admit to such partnership—and necessarily so. To resolve the teacher-student contradiction, to exchange the role of depositor, prescriber, domesticator, for the role of student among students would be to undermine the power of oppression and serve the cause of liberation.

Implicit in the banking concept is the assumption of a dichotomy between man and the world: man is merely *in* the world, not *with* the world or with others; man is spectator, not re-creator. In this view, man is not a conscious being *(corpo consciente);* he is rather the possessor of a consciousness: an empty "mind" passively open to the reception of deposits of reality from the world outside. For example, my desk, my books, my coffee cup, all the objects before me—as bits of the world which surrounds me—would be "inside" me, exactly as I am inside my study right now. This view makes no distinction between being accessible to consciousness and entering consciousness. The distinction, however, is essential: the objects which surround me are simply accessible to my consciousness, not located within it. I am aware of them, but they are not inside me.

It follows logically from the banking notion of consciousness that the educator's role is to regulate the way the world "enters into" the students. His task is to organize a process which already occurs spontaneously, to "fill" the students by making deposits of information which he considers to constitute true knowledge.[2] And since men "receive" the world as passive entities, education should make them more passive still, and adapt them to the world. The educated man is the adapted man, because he is better "fit" for the world. Translated into practice, this concept is well suited to the purposes of the oppressors, whose tranquility rests on how well men fit the world the oppressors have created, and how little they question it.

The more completely the majority adapt to the purposes which the dominant minority prescribe for them (thereby depriving them of the right to their own purposes), the more easily the minority can continue to prescribe. The theory and practice of banking education serve this end quite efficiently. Verbalistic lessons, reading requirements,[3] the methods for evaluating "knowledge," the distance between the teacher and the taught, the criteria for promotion: everything in this ready-to-wear approach serves to obviate thinking.

The bank-clerk educator does not realize that there is no true security in his hypertrophied role, that one must seek to live *with* others in solidarity. One cannot impose oneself, nor even merely co-exist with one's students. Solidarity requires true communication, and the concept by which such an educator is guided fears and proscribes communication.

Yet only through communication can human life hold meaning. The teacher's thinking is authenticated only by the authenticity of the students' thinking. The teacher cannot think for his students, nor can he impose his thought on them. Authentic thinking, thinking that is concerned about *reality*, does not take place in ivory tower isolation, but only in communication. If it is true that thought has meaning only when generated by action upon the world, the subordination of students to teachers becomes impossible.

Because banking education begins with a false understanding of men as objects, it cannot promote the development of what Fromm calls "biophily," but instead produces its opposite: "necrophily."

> While life is characterized by growth in a structured, functional manner,
> the necrophilous person loves all that does not grow, all that is mechanical. The
> necrophilous person is driven by the desire to transform the organic into the
> inorganic, to approach life mechanically, as if all living persons were things. . . .
> Memory, rather than experience; having, rather than being, is what counts. The
> necrophilous person can relate to an object—a flower or a person—only if he
> possesses it; hence a threat to his possession is a threat to himself; if he loses
> possession he loses contact with the world. . . . He loves control, and in the act
> of controlling he kills life.[4]

Oppression—overwhelming control—is necrophilic; it is nourished by love of death, not life. The banking concept of education, which serves the interests of oppression, is also necrophilic. Based on a mechanistic, static, naturalistic, spatialized view of consciousness, it transforms students into receiving objects. It attempts to control thinking and action, leads men to adjust to the world, and inhibits their creative power.

When their efforts to act responsibly are frustrated, when they find themselves unable to use their faculties, men suffer. "This suffering due to impotence is rooted in the very fact that the human equilibrium has been disturbed."[5] But the inability to act which causes men's anguish also causes them to reject their impotence, by attempting

. . . to restore [their] capacity to act. But can [they], and how? One way is to submit to and identify with a person or group having power. By this symbolic participation in another person's life, [men have] the illusion of acting, when in reality [they] only submit to and become a part of those who act.[6]

Populist manifestations perhaps best exemplify this type of behavior by the oppressed, who, by identifying with charismatic leaders, come to feel that they themselves are active and effective. The rebellion they express as they emerge in the historical process is motivated by that desire to act effectively. The dominant elites consider the remedy to be more domination and repression, carried out in the name of freedom, order, and social peace (that is, the peace of the elites). Thus they can condemn—logically, from their point of view—"the violence of a strike by workers and [can] call upon the state in the same breath to use violence in putting down the strike."[7]

Education as the exercise of domination stimulates the credulity of students, with the ideological intent (often not perceived by educators) of indoctrinating them to adapt to the world of oppression. This accusation is not made in the naïve hope that the dominant elites will thereby simply abandon the practice. Its objective is to call the attention of true humanists to the fact that they cannot use banking educational methods in the pursuit of liberation, for they would only negate that very pursuit. Nor may a revolutionary society inherit these methods from an oppressor society. The revolutionary society which practices banking education is either misguided or mistrusting of men. In either event, it is threatened by the specter of reaction.

Unfortunately, those who espouse the cause of liberation are themselves surrounded and influenced by the climate which generates the banking concept, and often do not perceive its true significance or its dehumanizing power. Paradoxically, then, they utilize this same instrument of alienation in what they consider an effort to liberate. Indeed, some "revolutionaries" brand as "innocents," "dreamers," or even "reactionaries" those who would challenge this educational practice. But one does not liberate men by alienating them. Authentic liberation—the process of humanization—is not another deposit to be made in men. Liberation is a praxis: the action and reflection of men upon their world in order to transform it. Those truly committed to the cause of liberation can accept neither the mechanistic concept of consciousness as an empty vessel to be filled, nor the use of banking methods of domination (propaganda, slogans—deposits) in the name of liberation.

Those truly committed to liberation must reject the banking concept in its entirety, adopting instead a concept of men as conscious beings, and consciousness as consciousness intent upon the world. They must abandon the educational goal of deposit-making and replace it with the posing of the problems of men in their relations with the world. "Problem-posing" education, responding to the essence of consciousness—*intentionality*—rejects communiqués and embodies communication. It epitomizes the special characteristic of consciousness: being *conscious of,* not only as intent on objects but as turned in upon itself in a Jasperian "split"—consciousness as consciousness *of* consciousness.

Liberating education consists in acts of cognition, not transferrals of information. It is a learning situation in which the cognizable object (far from being the end of the cognitive act) intermediates the cognitive actors—teacher on the one hand and students on the other. Accordingly, the practice of problem-posing education entails at the outset that the teacher-student contradiction be resolved. Dialogical relations—indispensable to the capacity of cognitive actors to cooperate in perceiving the same cognizable object—are otherwise impossible.

Indeed, problem-posing education, which breaks with the vertical patterns characteristic of banking education, can fulfill its function as the practice of freedom only if it can overcome the above contradiction. Through dialogue, the teacher-of-the-students and the students-of-the-teacher cease to exist and a new term emerges: teacher-student with students-teachers. The teacher is no longer merely the-one-who-teaches, but one who is himself taught in dialogue with the students, who in turn while being taught also teach. They become jointly responsible for a process in which all grow. In this process, arguments based on "authority" are no longer valid; in order to function, authority must be *on the side of* freedom, not *against* it. Here, no one teaches another, nor is anyone self-taught. Men teach each other, mediated by the world, by the cognizable objects which in banking education are "owned" by the teacher.

The banking concept (with its tendency to dichotomize everything) distinguishes two stages in the action of the educator. During the first, he cognizes a cognizable object while he prepares his lessons in his study or his laboratory; during the second, he expounds to his students about that object. The students are not called upon to know, but to memorize the contents narrated by the teacher. Nor do the students practice any act of cognition, since the object towards which that act should be directed is the property of the teacher rather than a medium evoking the critical reflection of both teacher and students. Hence in the name of the "preservation of culture and knowledge" we have a system which achieves neither true knowledge nor true culture.

The problem-posing method does not dichotomize the activity of the teacher-student: he is not "cognitive" at one point and "narrative" at another.

He is always "cognitive," whether preparing a project or engaging in dialogue with the students. He does not regard cognizable objects as his private property, but as the object of reflection by himself and the students. In this way, the problem-posing educator constantly re-forms his reflections in the reflection of the students. The students—no longer docile listeners—are now critical co-investigators in dialogue with the teacher. The teacher presents the material to the students for their consideration, and re-considers his earlier considerations as the students express their own. The role of the problem-posing educator is to create, together with the students, the conditions under which knowledge at the level of the *doxa* is superseded by true knowledge, at the level of the *logos*.

Whereas banking education anesthetizes and inhibits creative power, problem-posing education involves a constant unveiling of reality. The former attempts to maintain the *submersion* of consciousness; the latter strives for the *emergence* of consciousness and *critical intervention* in reality.

Students, as they are increasingly posed with problems relating to themselves in the world and with the world, will feel increasingly challenged and obliged to respond to that challenge. Because they apprehend the challenge as interrelated to other problems within a total context, not as a theoretical question, the resulting comprehension tends to be increasingly critical and thus constantly less alienated. Their response to the challenge evokes new challenges, followed by new understandings; and gradually the students come to regard themselves as committed.

Education as the practice of freedom—as opposed to education as the practice of domination—denies that man is abstract, isolated, independent, and unattached to the world; it also denies that the world exists as a reality apart from men. Authentic reflection considers neither abstract man nor the world without men, but men in their relations with the world. In these relations consciousness and world are simultaneous: consciousness neither precedes the world nor follows it.

> La conscience et le monde sont dormés d'un même coup: extérieur par essence à la conscience, le monde est, par essence relatif à elle.[8]

In one of our culture circles in Chile, the group was discussing (based on a codification[9]) the anthropological concept of culture. In the midst of the discussion, a peasant who by banking standards was completely ignorant said: "Now I see that without man there is no world." When the educator responded: "Let's say, for the sake of argument, that all the men on earth were to die, but that the earth itself remained, together with trees, birds, animals, rivers, seas, the stars . . . wouldn't all this be a world?" "Oh no," the peasant replied emphatically. "There would be no one to say: 'This is a world'."

The peasant wished to express the idea that there would be lacking the consciousness of the world which necessarily implies the world of consciousness.

I cannot exist without a *not-I*. In turn, the *not-I* depends on that existence. The world which brings consciousness into existence becomes the world of that consciousness. Hence, the previously cited affirmation of Sartre: *"La conscience et le monde sont dormés d'un même coup."*

As men, simultaneously reflecting on themselves and on the world, increase the scope of their perception, they begin to direct their observations towards previously inconspicuous phenomena:

> In perception properly so-called, as an explicit awareness [*Gewahren*], I am turned towards the object, to the paper, for instance. I apprehend it as being this here and now. The apprehension is a singling out, every object having a background in experience. Around and about the paper lie books, pencils, inkwell, and so forth, and these in a certain sense are also "perceived", perceptually there, in the "field of intuition"; but whilst I was turned towards the paper there was no turning in their direction, nor any apprehending of them, not even in a secondary sense. They appeared and yet were not singled out, were not posited on their own account. Every perception of a thing has such a zone of background intuitions or background awareness, if "intuiting" already includes the state of being turned towards, and this also is a "conscious experience", or more briefly a "consciousness of" all indeed that in point of fact lies in the co-perceived objective background.[10]

That which had existed objectively but had not been perceived in its deeper implications (if indeed it was perceived at all) begins to "stand out," assuming the character of a problem and therefore of challenge. Thus, men begin to single out elements from their "background awarenesses" and to reflect upon them. These elements are now objects of men's consideration, and, as such, objects of their action and cognition.

In problem-posing education, men develop their power to perceive critically *the way they exist* in the world *with which* and *in which* they find themselves; they come to see the world not as a static reality, but as a reality in process, in transformation. Although the dialectical relations of men with the world exist independently of how these relations are perceived (or whether or not they are perceived at all), it is also true that the form of action men adopt is to a large extent a function of how they perceive themselves in the world. Hence, the teacher-student and the students-teachers reflect simultaneously on themselves and the world without dichotomizing this reflection from action, and thus establish an authentic form of thought and action.

Once again, the two educational concepts and practices under analysis come into conflict. Banking education (for obvious reasons) attempts, by mythicizing reality, to conceal certain facts which explain the way men exist in the world; problem-posing education sets itself the task of demythologizing.

Banking education resists dialogue; problem-posing education regards dialogue as indispensable to the act of cognition which unveils reality. Banking education treats students as objects of assistance; problem-posing education makes them critical thinkers. Banking education inhibits creativity and domesticates (although it cannot completely destroy) the *intentionality* of consciousness by isolating consciousness from the world, thereby denying men their ontological and historical vocation of becoming more fully human. Problem-posing education bases itself on creativity and stimulates true reflection and action upon reality, thereby responding to the vocation of men as beings who are authentic only when engaged in inquiry and creative transformation. In sum: banking theory and practice, as immobilizing and fixating forces, fail to acknowledge men as historical beings; problem-posing theory and practice take man's historicity as their starting point.

Problem-posing education affirms men as beings in the process of *becoming*— as unfinished, uncompleted beings in and with a likewise unfinished reality. Indeed, in contrast to other animals who are unfinished, but not historical, men know themselves to be unfinished; they are aware of their incompletion. In this incompletion and this awareness lie the very roots of education as an exclusively human manifestation. The unfinished character of men and the transformational character of reality necessitate that education be an ongoing activity.

Education is thus constantly remade in the praxis. In order to *be,* it must *become.* Its "duration" (in the Bergsonian meaning of the word) is found in the interplay of the opposites *permanence* and *change.* The banking method emphasizes permanence and becomes reactionary; problem-posing education— which accepts neither a "well-behaved" present nor a predetermined future— roots itself in the dynamic present and becomes revolutionary.

Problem-posing education is revolutionary futurity. Hence it is prophetic (and, as such, hopeful). Hence, it corresponds to the historical nature of man. Hence, it affirms men as beings who transcend themselves, who move forward and look ahead, for whom immobility represents a fatal threat, for whom looking at the past must only be a means of understanding more clearly what and who they are so that they can more wisely build the future. Hence, it identifies with the movement which engages men as beings aware of their incompletion—a historical movement which has its point of departure, its Subjects and its objective.

The point of departure of the movement lies in men themselves. But since men do not exist apart from the world, apart from reality, the movement must begin with the men-world relationship. Accordingly, the point of departure must always be with men in the "here and now," which constitutes the situation within which they are submerged, from which they emerge, and in which they intervene. Only by starting from this situation—which determines their perception of it—can they begin to move. To do this authentically they must perceive their state not as fated and unalterable, but merely as limiting—and therefore challenging.

Whereas the banking method directly or indirectly reinforces men's fatalistic perception of their situation, the problem-posing method presents this very situation to them as a problem. As the situation becomes the object of their cognition, the naïve or magical perception which produced their fatalism gives way to perception which is able to perceive itself even as it perceives reality, and can thus be critically objective about that reality.

A deepened consciousness of their situation leads men to apprehend that situation as an historical reality susceptible of transformation. Resignation gives way to the drive for transformation and inquiry, over which men feel themselves to be in control. If men, as historical beings necessarily engaged with other men in a movement of inquiry, did not control that movement, it would be (and is) a violation of men's humanity. Any situation in which some men prevent others from engaging in the process of inquiry is one of violence. The means used are not important; to alienate men from their own decision-making is to change them into objects.

This movement of inquiry must be directed towards humanization—man's historical vocation. The pursuit of full humanity, however, cannot be carried out in isolation or individualism, but only in fellowship and solidarity; therefore it cannot unfold in the antagonistic relations between oppressors and oppressed. No one can be authentically human while he prevents others from being so. Attempting *to be more* human, individualistically, leads to *having more,* egotistically: a form of dehumanization. Not that it is not fundamental to have in order to be human. Precisely because it is necessary, some men's *having* must not be allowed to constitute an obstacle to others' having, must not consolidate the power of the former to crush the latter.

Problem-posing education, as a humanist and liberating praxis, posits as fundamental that men subjected to domination must fight for their emancipation. To that end, it enables teachers and students to become Subjects of the educational process by overcoming authoritarianism and an alienating intellectualism; it also enables men to overcome their false perception of reality. The world—no longer something to be described with deceptive words—becomes the object of that transforming action by men which results in their humanization.

Problem-posing education does not and cannot serve the interests of the oppressor. No oppressive order could permit the oppressed to begin to question: Why? While only a revolutionary society can carry out this education in systematic terms, the revolutionary leaders need not take full power before they can employ the method. In the revolutionary process, the leaders cannot utilize the banking method as an interim measure, justified on grounds of expediency, with the intention of *later* behaving in a genuinely revolutionary fashion. They must be revolutionary—that is to say, dialogical—from the outset.

NOTES

1. Simone de Beauvoir, *La Pensée de Droite, Aujord'hui* (Paris); ST, *El Pensamiento político de la Derecha* (Buenos Aires, 1963), p. 34.
2. This concept corresponds to what Sartre calls the "digestive" or "nutritive" concept of education, in which knowledge is "fed" by the teacher to the students to "fill them out." See Jean-Paul Sartre, "Une idée fundamentale de la phénomenologie de Husserl: L'intentionalité," *Situations I* (Paris, 1947).
3. For example, some professors specify in their reading lists that a book should be read from pages 10 to 15—and do this to "help" their students!
4. Eric Fromm, *The Heart of Man* (New York, 1966), p. 41.
5. *Ibid.,* p. 31.
6. *Ibid.*
7. Reinhold Niebuhr, *Moral Man and Immoral Society* (New York, 1960), p. 130.
8. Sartre, *op. cit.,* p. 32.
9. See Chapter 3.—Translator's note.
10. Edmund Husserl, *Ideas—General Introduction to Pure Phenomenology* (London, 1969), pp. 105–106.

Critical Pedagogy: A Look at the Major Concepts

PETER McLAREN

In practice, critical pedagogy is as diverse as its many adherents, yet common themes and constructs run through many of their writings. I have talked about general characteristics in the previous part. In the part that follows, I will outline in more detail the major categories within this tradition. A category is simply a concept, question, issue, hypothesis, or idea that is central to critical theory. These categories are intended to provide a theoretical framework within which you may reread my journal entries and perhaps better understand the theories generated by critical educational research. The categories are useful for the purposes of clarification and illustration, although some critical theorists will undoubtedly argue that additional concepts should have been included, or that some concepts have not been given the emphasis they deserve.

THE IMPORTANCE OF THEORY

Before we discuss individual categories, we need to examine how those categories are explored. Critical theorists begin with the premise that *men and women are essentially unfree and inhabit a world rife with contradictions and asymmetries of power and privilege.* The critical educator endorses theories that are, first and foremost, *dialectical*; that is, theories which recognize the problems of society as more than simply isolated events of individuals of deficiencies in the social structure. Rather, these problems form part of the *interactive context* between individual and society. The individual, a social actor, both creates and is created by the social universe of which he/she is a part. Neither the individual nor society is given priority in analysis; the two are inextricably interwoven, so that reference to one must by implication mean reference to the other. Dialectical theory attempts to tease out the histories and relations of accepted meanings and appearances, tracing interactions from the context to the part, from the system inward to the event. In this way, critical theory helps us focus *simultaneously on both sides of a social contradiction.*[1]

Wilfred Carr and Stephen Kemmis describe dialectical thinking as follows:

> Dialectical thinking involves searching out . . . contradictions (like the contradiction of the inadvertant oppression of less able students by a system which aspires to help all students to attain their "full potential"), but it is not really as wooden or mechanical as the formula of thesis-antithesis-synthesis. On the contrary, it is an open and questioning form of thinking which demands reflection back and forth between elements like *part* and *whole, knowledge* and *action, process* and *product, subject* and *object, being* and *becoming, rhetoric* and *reality,* or *structure* and *function.* In the process, *contradictions* may be discovered (as, for example, in a political *structure* which aspires to give decision-making power to all, but actually *functions* to deprive some access to the information with which they could influence crucial decisions about their lives). As contradictions are revealed, new constructive thinking and new constructive action are required to transcend the contradictory state of affairs. The complementarity of the elements is dynamic: it is a kind of a tension, not a static confrontation between the two poles. In the dialectical approach, the elements are regarded as mutually constitutive, not separate and distinct. Contradiction can thus be distinguished from paradox: to speak of a contradiction is to imply that a new resolution can be achieved, while to speak of a paradox is to suggest that two incompatible ideas remain inertly opposed to one another. (italics in original)[2]

The dialectical nature of critical theory enables the educational researcher to see the school not simply as an arena of indoctrination or socialization or a site of instruction, but also as a cultural terrain that promotes student empowerment and self-transformation. My own research into parochial education for instance, showed that the school functions simultaneously as a means of empowering students around issues of social justice and as a means of sustaining, legitimizing, and reproducing dominant class interests directed at creating obedient, docile, and low-paid future workers.[3]

A dialectical understanding of schooling permits us to see schools as sites of both domination and liberation; this runs counter to the overdeterministic orthodox Marxist view of schooling, which claims that schools simply reproduce class relations and passively indoctrinate students into becoming greedy young capitalists. This dialectical understanding of schooling also brushes against the grain of mainstream educational theory, which conceives of schools as mainly providing students with the skills and attitudes necessary for becoming patriotic, industrious, and responsible citizens.

Critical educators argue that any worthwhile theory of schooling *must be partisan.* That is, it must be fundamentally tied to a struggle for a qualitatively better life for all through the construction of a society based on nonexploitative relations and social justice. The critical educator doesn't believe that there are two sides to every question, with both sides needing equal attention. For the critical educator, there are *many* sides to a problem, and often these sides are linked to certain class, race, and gender interests.

Let's turn for a moment to an example of critical theorizing as it is brought to bear on a fundamental teaching practice: writing classroom objectives. In this example, I will draw on Henry Giroux's important distinction between *micro* and *macro* objectives.[4]

The common use of behavioral objectives by teachers reflects a search for certainty and technical control of knowledge and behavior. Teachers often emphasize classroom management procedures, efficiency, and "how-to-do" techniques that ultimately ignore an important question: "Why is this knowledge being taught in the first place?" Giroux recasts classroom objectives into the categories of macro and micro.

Macro objectives are designed to enable students to make connections between the methods, content, and structure of a course and its significance within the larger social reality. This dialectical approach to classroom objectives allows students to acquire a broad frame of reference or worldview; in other words, it helps them acquire a political perspective. Students can then make the hidden curriculum explicit and develop a critical political consciousness.

Micro objectives represent the course content and are characterized by their narrowness of purpose and their content-bound path of inquiry. Giroux tells us that the importance of the relationship between macro and micro objectives arises out of *having students uncover the connections between course objectives and the norms, values, and structural relationships of the wider society.* For instance, the micro objectives of teaching about the Vietnam war might be to learn the dates of specific battles, the details of specific Congressional debates surrounding the war, and the reasons given by the White House for fighting the war. The micro objectives are concerned with the organization, classification, mastery, and manipulation of data. This is what Giroux calls *productive knowledge.* Macro objectives, on the other hand, center on the relationship between means and ends, between specific events and their wider social and political implications. A lesson on the Vietnam war or the more recent invasion of Grenada for instance, might raise the following macro questions: What is the relationship between the invasion of Grenada as a rescue mission in the interests of U.S. citizens and the larger logic of imperialism? During the Vietnam era, what was the relationship between the American economy and the arms industry? Whose interests did the war serve best? Who benefited most from the war? What were the class relationships between those who fought and those who stayed home in the university?

Developing macro objectives fosters a dialectical mode of inquiry; the process constitutes a socio-political application of knowledge, what Giroux calls *directive knowledge.* Critical theorists seek a kind of knowledge that will help students recognize the *social function of particular forms of knowledge.* The purpose of dialectical educational theory, then, is to provide students with a model that permits them to examine the underlying political, social, and economic foundations of the larger society.

CRITICAL PEDAGOGY AND THE SOCIAL CONSTRUCTION OF KNOWLEDGE

Critical educational theorists view school knowledge as historically and socially rooted and interest bound. Knowledge acquired in school—or anywhere, for that matter—is never neutral or objective but is ordered and structured in particular ways; its emphases and exclusions partake of a silent logic. Knowledge is a *social construction* deeply rooted in a nexus of power relations. When critical theorists claim that knowledge is socially constructed, they mean that it is the product of agreement or consent between individuals who live out particular social relations (e.g., of class, race, and gender) and who live in particular junctures in time. To claim that knowledge is socially constructed usually means that the world we live in is constructed symbolically by the mind through social interaction with others and is heavily dependent on culture, context, custom, and historical specificity. There is no ideal, autonomous, pristine, or aboriginal world to which our social constructions necessarily correspond; there is always a referential field in which symbols are situated. And this particular referential field (e.g., language, culture, place, time) will influence how symbols generate meaning. There is no pure subjective insight. We do not stand *before* the social world; we live *in the midst* of it. As we seek the meaning of events we seek the meaning of the social. We can now raise certain questions with respect to the social construction of knowledge, such as: why do women and minorities often view social issues differently than white males? Why are teachers more likely to value the opinions of a middle-class white male student, for instance, than those of a black female?

Critical pedagogy asks how and why knowledge gets constructed the way it does, and how and why some constructions of reality are legitimated and celebrated by the dominant culture while others clearly are not. Critical pedagogy asks how our everyday commonsense understandings—our social constructions or "subjectivities"—get produced and lived out. In other words, what are the *social functions* of knowledge? The crucial factor here is that some forms of knowledge have more power and legitimacy than others. For instance, in many schools in the United States, science and math curricula are favored over the liberal arts. This can be explained by the link between the needs of big business to compete in world markets and the imperatives of the new reform movement to bring "excellence" back to the schools. Certain types of knowledge legitimate certain gender, class, and racial interests. Whose interests does this knowledge serve? Who gets excluded as a result? Who is marginalized?

Let's put this in the form of further questions: What is the relationship between social class and knowledge taught in school? Why do we value scientific knowledge over informal knowledge? Why do we have teachers using "standard English"? Why is the public still unlikely to vote for a woman or a black for president? How does school knowledge reinforce stereotypes about women, minorities, and disadvantaged peoples? What accounts for some knowledge having high status (as in the great works of philosophers or scientists) while the practical knowledge of ordinary people or marginalized or subjugated groups is often discredited and devalued? Why do we learn about the great 'men' in history and spend less time learning about the contributions of women and minorities and the struggles of people in lower economic classes? Why don't we learn more about the American labor movement? How and why are certain types of knowledge used to reinforce dominant ideologies, which in turn serve to mask unjust power relations among certain groups in society?

FORMS OF KNOWLEDGE

Critical pedagogy follows a distinction regarding forms of knowledge posited by the German social theorist Jürgen Habermas.[5] Let's examine this concept in the context of classroom teaching. Mainstream educators who work primarily within liberal and conservative educational ideologies emphasize technical knowledge (similar to Giroux's *productive knowledge*): Knowledge is that which can be measured and quantified. Technical knowledge is based on the natural sciences, uses hypothetico-deductive or empirical analytical methods, and is evaluated by, among other things, intelligence quotients, reading scores, and SAT results, all of which are used by educators to sort, regulate, and control students.

A second type, *practical knowledge,* aims to enlighten individuals so they can shape their daily actions in the world. Practical knowledge is generally acquired through *describing and analyzing social situations historically or developmentally,* and is geared toward helping individuals understand social events that are ongoing and situational. The liberal educational researcher who undertakes fieldwork in a school in order to evaluate student behavior and interaction acquires practical knowledge, for instance. This type of knowledge is not usually generated numerically or by submitting data to some kind of statistical instrument.

The critical educator, however, is most interested in what Habermas calls *emancipatory knowledge* (similar to Giroux's *directive knowledge*), which attempts to reconcile and transcend the opposition between technical and practical knowledge. Emancipatory knowledge helps us understand how social relationships are distorted and manipulated by relations of power and privilege. It also aims at creating the conditions under which irrationality, domination, and oppression can be overcome and transformed through deliberative, collective action. In short, it creates the foundation for social justice, equality, and empowerment.

CLASS

Class refers to the *economic, social, and political relationships that govern life in a given social order.* Class relationships reflect the constraints and limitations individuals and groups experience in the areas of income level, occupation, place of residence, and other indicators of status and social rank. Relations of class are those associated with surplus labor, who produces it, and who is a recipient of it. Surplus labor is that labor undertaken by workers beyond that which is necessary. Class relations also deal with the social distribution of power and its structural allocation. Today there are greater distinctions within the working classes and it is now possible to talk about the new *underclasses* within the American social structure consisting of black, Hispanic, and Asian class fractions, together with the white aged, the unemployed and under-employed, large sections of women, the handicapped, and other marginalized economic groups.

CULTURE

The concept of *culture,* varied though it may be, is essential to any under-standing of critical pedagogy. I use the term "culture" here to signify *the particular ways in which a social group lives out and makes sense of its "given" circumstances and conditions of life.* In addition to defining culture as *a set of practices, ideologies, and values from which different groups draw to make sense of the world,* we need to recognize how cultural questions help us understand who has power and how it is reproduced and manifested in the social relations that link schooling to the wider social order. The ability of individuals to express their culture is related to the power which certain groups are able to wield in the social order. The expression of values and beliefs by individuals who share certain historical experiences is determined by their collective power in society.[6]

The link between culture and power has been extensively analyzed in critical social theory over the past ten years. It is therefore possible to offer three insights from that literature that particularly illuminate the political logic that underlies various cultural/power relations. First, culture is intimately connected with the structure of social relations within class, gender, and age formations that produce forms of oppression and dependency. Second, culture is analyzed not simply as a way of life, but as a form of production through which different groups in either their dominant or subordinate social relations define and realize their aspirations through unequal relations of power. Third, culture is viewed as a field of struggle in which the production, legitimation, and circulation of particular forms of knowledge and experience are central areas of conflict. What is important here is that each of these insights raises fundamental questions about the ways in which inequalities are maintained and challenged in the spheres of school culture and the wider society.[7]

DOMINANT CULTURE, SUBORDINATE CULTURE, AND SUBCULTURE

Three central categories related to the concept of culture—dominant culture, subordinate culture, subculture—have been much discussed in recent critical scholarship. Culture can be readily broken down into "dominant" and "subordinate" parent cultures. *Dominant culture* refers to social practices and representations that *affirm the central values, interests, and concerns of the social class in control of the material and symbolic wealth of society.* Groups who live out social relations in subordination to the dominant culture are part of the *subordinate culture.* Group *subcultures* may be described as subsets of the two parent cultures (dominant and subordinate). Individuals who form subcultures often use distinct symbols and social practices to help foster an identity outside that of the dominant culture. As an example, we need only refer to punk subculture, with its distinct musical tastes, fetishistic constumery, spiked hair, and its attempt to disconfirm the dominant rules of propriety fostered by the mainstream media, schools, religions, and culture industry. For the most part, working-class subcultures exist in a subordinate structural position in society, and many of their members engage in oppositional acts against the dominant middle-class culture. It is important to remember, however, that people don't inhabit cultures or social classes but *live out class or cultural relations,* some of which may be dominant and some of which may be subordinate.[8]

Subcultures are involved in contesting the cultural "space" or openings in the dominant culture. The dominant culture is never able to secure total control over subordinate cultural groups. Whether we choose to examine British subcultural groups (i.e., working-class youth, teddy-boys, skinheads, punks, rude boys, rastafarians) or American groups (i.e., motorcycle clubs such as Hell's Angels, ethnic street gangs, or middle-class suburban gangs), subcultures are more often *negotiated* than truly *oppositional.* As John Muncie points out, this is because they operate primarily in the arena of leisure that is exceedingly vulnerable to commercial and ideological incorporation.[9] Subcultures do offer a symbolic critique of the social order and are frequently organized around relations of class, gender, style, and race. Despite the often ferocious exploitation of the subcultural resistance of various youth subcultures by bourgeois institutions (school, workplace, justice system, consumer industries), subcultures are usually able to keep alive the struggle over how meanings are produced, defined, and legitimated; consequently, they do represent various degrees of struggle against lived subjugation. Many subcultural movements reflect a crisis within dominant society, rather than a unified mobilization against it. For instance, the hippie movement in the 1960s represented, in part, an exercise of petite-bourgeoisie socialism by middle-class radicals who were nurtured both by idealist principles and by a search for spiritual and life-style comfort. This often served to draw critical attention away from the structural inequalities of capitalist society. As Muncie argues, subcultures constitute "a crisis within dominant culture rather than a conspiracy against dominant culture."[10]

The youth counterculture of the sixties served as the ideological loam that fertilized my pedagogy in Part Two. I had learned the rudiments of a middle-class radicalism that was preoccupied with the politics of expressive life and avoided examining in a minded and a critical manner the structural inequalities within the social order.

CULTURAL FORMS

Cultural forms are those symbols and social practices that express culture, such as those found in music, dress, food, religion, dance, and education, which have developed from the efforts of groups to shape their lives out of their surrounding material and political environment. Television, video, and films are regarded as cultural forms. Schooling is also a cultural form. Baseball is a cultural form. Cultural forms don't exist apart from sets of structural underpinnings which are related to the means of economic production, the mobilization of desire, the construction of social values, asymmetries of power/knowledge, configurations of ideologies, and relations of class, race, and gender.

HEGEMONY

The dominant culture is able to exercise domination over subordinate classes or groups through a process known as *hegemony*.[11] Hegemony refers to the maintenance of domination not by the sheer exercise of force *but primarily through consensual social practices, social forms, and social structures produced in specific sites such as the church, the state, the school, the mass media, the political system, and the family.* By *social practices,* I refer to what people say and do. Of course, social practices may be accomplished through words, gestures, personally appropriated signs and rituals, or a combination of these. *Social forms* refer to the principles that provide and give legitimacy to specific social practices. For example, the state legislature is one social form that gives legitimacy to the social practice of teaching. The term *social structures* can be defined as those constraints that limit individual life and appear to be beyond the individual's control, having their sources in the power relations that govern society. We can, therefore, talk about the "class structure" or the "economic structure" of our society.

Hegemony is a struggle in which the powerful win the consent of those who are oppressed, with the oppressed unknowingly participating in their own oppression. Hegemony was at work in my own practices as an elementary school teacher. Because I did not teach my students to question the prevailing values, attitudes, and social practices of the dominant society in a sustained critical manner, my classroom preserved the hegemony of the dominant culture. Such hegemony was contested when the students began to question my authority by resisting and disrupting my lessons. The dominant class secures hegemony—the consent of the dominated—by supplying the symbols, representations, and practices of social life in such a way that the basis of social authority and the unequal relations of power and privilege remain hidden. By perpetrating the myth of individual achievement and entrepreneurship in the media, the schools, the church, and the family, for instance, dominant culture ensures that subordinated groups who fail at school or who don't make it into the world of the "rich and famous" will view such failure in terms of personal inadequacy or the "luck of the draw." The oppressed blame themselves for school failure—a failure that can certainly be additionally attributed to the structuring effects of the economy and the class-based division of labor.[12]

Hegemony is a cultural encasement of meanings, a prison-house of language and ideas, that is "freely" entered into by both dominators and dominated. As Todd Gitlin puts it,

> both rulers and ruled derive psychological and material rewards in the course of confirming and reconfirming their inequality. The hegemonic sense of the world seeps into popular "common sense" and gets reproduced there; it may even appear to be generated *by* that common sense.[13]

Hegemony refers to the moral and intellectual leadership of a dominant class over a subordinate class achieved not through coercion (i.e., threat of imprisonment or torture) or the willful construction of rules and regulations (as in a dictatorship or fascist regime), but rather through the general winning of consent of the subordinate class to the authority of the dominant class. The dominant class need not impose force for the manufacture of hegemony since the subordinate class actively subscribes to many of the values and objectives of the dominant class without being aware of the source of those values or the interests which inform them.

Hegemony is not a process of active domination as much as an active structuring of the culture and experiences of the subordinate class by the dominant class. The dominant culture is able to "frame" the ways in which subordinate groups live and respond to their own cultural system and lived experiences; in other words, the dominant culture is able to manufacture dreams and desires for both dominant and subordinate groups by supplying "terms of reference" (i.e., images, visions, stories, ideals) against which all individuals are expected to live their lives. The dominant culture tries to "fix" the meaning of signs, symbols, and representations to provide a "common" worldview, disguising relations of power and privilege through the organs of mass media, state apparatus such as schools, government institutions, and state bureaucracies. Individuals are provided with "subject positions," which condition them to react to ideas and opinions in prescribed ways. For instance, most individuals in the United States, when addressed as "Americans," are generally positioned as subjects by the dominant discourse. To be an "American" carries a certain set of ideological baggage. Americans generally think of themselves as lovers of freedom, defenders of individual rights, guardians of world peace, etc.; rarely do

Americans see themselves as contradictory social agents. They rarely view their country as lagging behind other industrial economies in the world in providing security for its citizens in such areas as health care, family allowance, and housing subsidy programs. As citizens of the wealthiest country in the world, Americans generally do not question why their government cannot afford to be more generous to its citizens. Most Americans would be aghast at hearing a description of their country as a "terrorist regime" exercising covert acts of war against Latin American countries such as Nicaragua. The prevailing image of America that the schools, the entertainment industry, and government agencies have promulgated is a benevolent one in which the interests of the dominant classes supposedly represent the interests of all groups. It is an image in which the values and beliefs of the dominant class appear so correct that to reject them would be unnatural, a violation of common sense.

Within the hegemonic process, established meanings are often laundered of contradiction, contestation, and ambiguity. Resistance does occur, however, most often in the domain of popular culture. In this case, popular culture becomes an arena of negotiation in which dominant, subordinate, and oppositional groups affirm and struggle over cultural representations and meanings. The dominant culture is rarely successful on all counts. People *do* resist. Alternative groups do manage to find different values and meanings to regulate their lives. Oppositional groups do attempt to challenge the prevailing culture's mode of structuring and codifying representations and meanings. Prevailing social practices are, in fact, resisted. Schools and other social and cultural sites are rarely in the thrall of the hegemonic process since there we will also find struggle and confrontation. This is why schools can be characterized as terrains of transactions, exchange, and struggle between subordinate groups and the dominant ideology. There is a relative autonomy within school sites that allows for forms of resistance to emerge and to break the cohesiveness of hegemony. Teachers battle over what books to use, over what disciplinary practices to use, and over the aims and objectives of particular courses and programs.

One current example of the battle for hegemony can be seen in the challenge by Christian fundamentalists to public schooling. Fundamentalist critics have instigated a debate over dominant pedagogical practices that ranges all the way from textbooks to how, in science classes, teachers may account for the origins of humankind. The important point to remember, however, is that hegemony is always in operation; certain ideas, values, and social practices generally prevail over others.

Not all prevailing values are oppressive. Critical educators, too, would like to secure hegemony for their own ideas. The challenge for teachers is to recognize and attempt to transform those undemocratic and oppressive features of hegemonic control that often structure everyday classroom existence in ways not readily apparent. These oppressive features are rarely challenged since the dominant ideology is so all inclusive that individuals are taught to view it as natural, commonsensical, and inviolable. For instance, subordinate groups who subscribe to an ideology that could be described as right wing are often the very groups hurt most by the Republican government they elect in terms of cutbacks in social services, agricultural aid, etc. Yet the Republican Party has been able to market itself as no-nonsense, get-tough, anti-Communist, and hyper-patriotic—features that appeal to subordinate groups whose cultural practices may include listening to country and western music, following the televangelist programs and crusades, or cheering the pugilistic exploits of Rambo. Those who seek to chart out the ways in which the affluent are favored over subordinate groups are dismissed as wimpish liberals who don't support the "freedom fighters" in Nicaragua. Who needs to use force when ideational hegemony works this well? As Gore Vidal has observed about the United States: "The genius of our system is that ordinary people go out and vote against their interests. The way our ruling class keeps out of sight is one of the greatest stunts in the political history of any country."[14]

IDEOLOGY

Hegemony could not do its work without the support of ideology. Ideology permeates all of social life and does not simply refer to the political ideologies of communism, socialism, anarchism, rationalism, or existentialism. Ideology refers to *the production and representation of ideas, values, and beliefs and the manner in which they are expressed and lived out by both individuals and groups.*[15] Simply put, ideology refers to the production of sense and meaning. It can be described as a way of viewing the world, a complex of ideas, various types of social practices, rituals, and representations *that we tend to accept as natural and as common sense.* It is the result of the intersection of meaning and power in the social world. Customs, rituals, beliefs, and values often produce within individuals distorted conceptions of their place in the sociocultural order and thereby serve to reconcile them to that place and to disguise the inequitable relations of power and privilege; this is sometimes referred to as "ideological hegemony."

Stuart Hall and James Donald define ideology as "the frameworks of thought which are used in society to explain, figure out, make sense of or give meaning to the social and political world . . . Without these frameworks, we could not make sense of the world at all. But with them, our perceptions are inevitably structured in a particular direction by the very concepts we are using."[16] Ideology includes both positive and negative functions at any given moment: The *positive function* of ideology is to "provide the concepts, categories, images, and ideas by means of which people make sense of their social and political world, form projects, come to a certain consciousness of their place in the world and act in it;" the *negative function* of ideology "refers to the fact that all such perspectives are inevitably selective. Thus a perspective positively organizes the "facts of the case" in *this* and makes sense because it inevitably excludes *that* way of putting things."[17]

In order to fully understand the negative function of ideology, the concept must be linked to a theory of domination. *Domination* occurs when relations of power established at the institutional level are systematically asymmetrical; that is, when they are unequal, therefore privileging some groups over others. According to John Thompson, ideology as a negative function works through four different modes: legitimation, dissimulation, fragmentation, and reification. *Legitimation* occurs when a system of domination is sustained by being represented as legitimate or as eminently just and worthy of respect. For instance, by legitimizing the school system as just and meritocratic, as giving everyone the same opportunity for success, the dominant culture hides the truth of the hidden curriculum—the fact that those whom schooling helps most are those who come from the most affluent families. *Dissimulation* results when relations of domination are concealed, denied, or obscured in various ways. For instance, the practice of institutionalized tracking in schools purports to help better meet the needs of groups of students with varying academic ability. However, describing tracking in this way helps to cloak its socially reproductive function: that of sorting students according to their social class location. *Fragmentation* occurs when relations of domination are sustained by the production of meanings in a way which fragments groups so that they are placed in opposition to one another. For instance, when conservative educational critics explain the declining standards in American education as a result of trying to accommodate low income minority students, this sometimes results in a backlash against immigrant students by other subordinate groups. This "divide and rule" tactic prevents oppressed groups from working together to secure collectively their rights. *Reification* occurs when transitory historical states of affairs are presented as permanent, natural, and commonsensical—as if they exist outside of time.[18] This has occurred to a certain extent with the current call for a national curriculum based on acquiring information about the "great books" so as to have a greater access to the dominant culture. These works are revered as high status knowledge since purportedly the force of history has heralded them as such and placed them on book lists in respected cultural institutions such as universities. Here literacy becomes a weapon that can be used against those groups who are "culturally illiterate," whose social class, race, or gender renders their own experiences and stories as too unimportant to be worthy of investigation. That is, as a pedagogical tool, a stress on the great books often deflects attention away from the personal experiences of students and the political nature of everyday life. Teaching the great books is also a way of inculcating certain values and sets of behaviors in social groups, thereby solidifying the existing social hierarchy. The most difficult task in analyzing these negative functions of ideology is to unmask those ideological properties which insinuate themselves within reality as their fundamental components. Ideological functions which barricade themselves within the realm of commonsense often manage to disguise the grounds of their operations.

At this point it should be clear that ideology represents a vocabulary of standardization and a grammar of design sanctioned and sustained by particular social practices. All ideas and systems of thought organize a rendition of reality according to their own metaphors, narratives, and rhetoric. There is no "deep structure," totalizing logic, or grand theory pristine in form and innocent in effects which is altogether uncontaminated by interest, value, or judgement—in short, by *ideology*. There is no privileged sanctuary separate from culture and politics where we can be free to distinguish truth from opinion, fact from value, or image from interpretation. There is no "objective" environment that is not stamped with social presence.

If we all can agree that as individuals, we inherit a preexisting sign community, and acknowledge that all ideas, values, and meanings have social roots and perform social functions, then understanding ideology becomes a matter of investigating *which* concepts, values, and meanings *obscure* our understanding of the social world and our place within the networks of power/knowledge relations, and which concepts, values, and meanings *clarify* such an understanding. In other words, why do certain ideological formations cause us to misrecognize our complicity in establishing or maintaining asymmetrical relations of power and privilege within the sociocultural order?

The *dominant ideology* refers to patterns of beliefs and values shared by the majority of individuals. The majority of Americans—rich and poor alike—share the belief that capitalism is a better system than democratic socialism, for instance, or that men are generally more capable of holding positions of authority than women, or that women should be more passive and housebound. Here, we must recognize that the economic system requires the ideology of consumer capitalism to naturalize it, rendering it common-sensical. The ideology of patriarchy also is necessary to keep the nature of the economy safe and secured within the prevailing hegemony. We have been "fed" these dominant ideologies for decades through the mass media, the schools, and through family socialization.

Oppositional ideologies do exist, however, which attempt to challenge the dominant ideologies and shatter existing stereotypes. On some occasions, the dominant culture is able to manipulate alternative and oppositional ideologies in such a way that hegemony can be more effectively secured. For instance, *The Cosby Show* on commercial television carries a message that a social avenue now exists in America for blacks to be successful doctors and lawyers. This positive view of blacks, however, masks the fact that most blacks in the United States exist in a subordinate position to the dominant white culture with respect to power and privilege. The dominant culture secures hegemony by transmitting and legitimating ideologies like that in *The Cosby Show*, which reflect and shape popular resistance to stereotypes, but which in reality do little to challenge the real basis of power of the ruling dominant groups.

The dominant ideology often encourages oppositional ideologies and tolerates those that challenge their own rationale, since by absorbing these contradictory values, they are more often than not able to domesticate the conflicting and contradictory values. This is because the hegemonic hold of the social system is so strong, it can generally withstand dissension and actually come to neutralize it by permitting token opposition. During my teaching days in the suburban ghetto, school dances in the gym often celebrated the values, meanings, and pleasure of life on the street—some of which could be considered oppositional—but were tolerated by the administration because they helped diffuse tension in the school. They afforded the students some symbolic space for a limited amount of time; yet they redressed nothing concrete in terms of the lived subordination of the students and their families on a day-to-day basis.

The main question for teachers attempting to become aware of the ideologies that inform their own teaching is: How have certain pedagogical practices become so habitual or natural in school settings that teachers accept them as normal, unproblematic, and expected? How often, for instance, do teachers question school practices such as tracking, ability grouping, competitive grading, teacher-centered pedagogical approaches, and the use of rewards and punishments as control devices? The point here is to understand that these practices are not carved in stone; but are, in reality, socially constructed. How, then, is the distilled wisdom of traditional educational theorizing ideologically structured? What constitutes the origins and legitimacy of the pedagogical practices within this tradition? To what extent do such pedagogical practices serve to empower the student, and to what extent do they work as forms of social control that support, stabilize, and legitimate the role of the teacher as a moral gatekeeper of the state? What are the functions and effects of the systematic imposition of ideological perspectives on classroom teaching practices?

In my classroom journal, what characterized the ideological basis of my own teaching practices? How did "being schooled" both enable and contain the subjectivities of the students? I am using the word "subjectivity" here to mean forms of knowledge that are both conscious and unconscious and which express our identity as human agents. Subjectivity relates to everyday knowledge in its socially constructed and historically produced forms. Following this, we can ask: How do the dominant ideological practices of teachers help to structure the subjectivities of students? What are the possible consequences of this, for good and for ill?

PREJUDICE

Prejudice is the negative prejudgment of individuals and groups on the basis of unrecognized, unsound, and inadequate evidence. Because these negative attitudes occur so frequently, they take on a commonsense or ideological character that is often used to justify acts of discrimination.

CRITICAL PEDAGOGY AND THE POWER/KNOWLEDGE RELATION

Critical pedagogy is fundamentally concerned with understanding the relationship between power and knowledge. The dominant curriculum separates knowledge from the issue of power and treats it in an unabashedly technical manner; knowledge is seen in overwhelmingly instrumental terms as something to be mastered. That knowledge is always an ideological construction linked to particular interests and social relations generally receives little consideration in education programs.

The work of the French philosopher Michel Foucault is crucial in understanding the socially constructed nature of truth and its inscription in knowledge/power relations. Foucault's concept of "power/knowledge" extends the notion of power beyond its conventional use by philosophers and social theorists who, like American John Dewey, have understood power as "the sum of conditions available for bringing the desirable end into existence."[19] For Foucault, power comes from everywhere, from above and from below; it is "always already there" and is inextricably implicated in the micro-relations of domination and resistance.

DISCOURSE

Power relations are inscribed in what Foucault refers to as *discourse* or a family of concepts. Discourses are made up of discursive practices that he describes as

> a body of anonymous, historical rules, always determined in the time and space that have defined a given period, and for a given social, economic, geographical, or linguistic area, the conditions of operation of the enunciative function.[20]

Discursive practices, then, *refer to the rules by which discourses are formed, rules that govern what can be said and what must remain unsaid, who can speak with authority and who must listen.* Social and political institutions, such as schools and penal institutions, are governed by discursive practices.

> Discursive practices are not purely and simply ways of producing discourse. They are embodied in technical processes, in institutions, in patterns for general behavior, in forms of transmission and diffusion, and pedagogical forms which, at once, impose and maintain them.[21]

For education, discourse can be defined as a "regulated system of statements" that establish differences between fields and theories of teacher education; it is "not simply words but is embodied in the practice of institutions, patterns of behavior, and in forms of pedagogy."[22]

From this perspective, we can consider *dominant* discourses (those produced by the dominant culture) as "regimes of truth," as general economies of power/knowledge, or as multiple forms of constraint. In a classroom setting, dominant educational discourses determine what books we may use, what classroom approaches we should employ (mastery learning, Socratic method, etc.), and what values and beliefs we should transmit to our students.

For instance, neo-conservative discourses on language in the classroom would view working-class speech as undersocialized or deprived. Liberal discourse would view such speech as merely different. Similarly, to be culturally literate within a conservative discourse is to acquire basic information on American culture (dates of battles, passages of the Constitution, etc.). Conservative discourse focuses mostly on the works of "great men." A liberal discourse on cultural literacy includes knowledge generated from the perspective of women and minorities. A *critical* discourse focuses on the interests and assumptions that inform the generation of knowledge itself. A critical discourse is also self-critical and deconstructs dominant discourses the moment they are ready to achieve hegemony. A critical discourse can, for instance, explain how high status knowledge (the great works of the Western world) can be used to teach concepts that reinforce the status quo. Discourses and discursive practices influence how we live our lives as conscious thinking subjects. They shape our subjectivities (our ways of understanding in relation to the world) because it is only in language and through discourse that social reality can be given meaning. Not all discourses are given the same weight, as some will account for and justify the appropriateness of the status quo and others will provide a context for resisting social and institutional practices.[23]

This follows our earlier discussion that knowledge (truth) is socially constructed, culturally mediated, and historically situated. Cleo Cherryholmes suggests that "dominant discourses determine what counts as true, important, relevant, and what gets spoken. Discourses are generated and governed by rules and power."[24] Truth cannot be spoken in the absence of power relations, and each relation necessarily speaks its own truth. Foucault removes truth from the realm of the absolute; truth is understood only as changes in the determination of what can count as true.

> Truth is a thing of this world: it is produced only by virtue of multiple forms of constraint. And it induces regular effects of power. Each society has its regime of truth, its 'general politics' of truth: that is, the types of discourse which it accepts and makes function as true; the mechanisms and instances which enable one to distinguish true and false statements, the means by which each is sanctioned; the techniques and procedures accorded value in the acquisition of truth; the status of those who are charged with saying what counts as true.[25]

In Foucault's view, truth (educational truth, scientific truth, religious truth, legal truth, or whatever) must not be understood as a set of "discovered laws" that exist outside power/knowledge relations and which somehow correspond with the "real." We cannot "know" truth except through its "effects."

Truth is not *relative* (in the sense of "truths" proclaimed by various individuals and societies are all equal in their effects) but is *relational* (statements considered "true" are dependent upon history, cultural context, and relations of power operative in a given society, discipline, institution, etc.). The crucial question here is that if truth is *relational* and not *absolute,* what criteria can we use to guide our actions in the world? Critical educators argue that *praxis* (informed actions) must be guided by *phronesis* (the disposition to act truly and rightly). This means, in critical terms, that actions and knowledge must be directed at eliminating pain, oppression, and inequality, and at promoting justice and freedom.

Lawrence Grossberg speaks to the critical perspective on truth and theory when he argues

> the truth of a theory can only be defined by its ability to intervene into, to give us a different and perhaps better ability to come to grips with, the relations that constitute its context. If neither history nor texts speak its own truth, truth has to be won; and it is, consequently, inseparable from relations of power.[26]

An understanding of the power/knowledge relationship raises important issues regarding what kinds of theories educators should work with and what knowledge they can provide in order to empower students. *Empowerment* means not only helping students to understand and engage the world around them, but also enabling them to exercise the kind of courage needed to change the social order where necessary. Teachers need to recognize that *power relations correspond to forms of school knowledge that distort understanding and produce what is commonly accepted as "truth."* Critical educators argue that knowledge should be analyzed on the basis of whether it is oppresive and exploitative, and not on the basis of whether it is "true." For example, what kind of knowledge do we construct about women and minority groups in school texts? Do the texts we use in class promote stereotypical views that reinforce racist, sexist, and patriarchal attitudes? How do we treat the knowledge that working-class students bring to class discussions and schoolwork? Do we unwittingly devalue such knowledge and thereby disconfirm the voices of these students?

Knowledge should be examined not only for the ways in which it might misrepresent or mediate social reality, but also for the ways in which it actually reflects the daily struggle of people's lives. We must understand that knowledge not only distorts reality, but also provides grounds for understanding the actual conditions that inform everyday life. Teachers, then, should examine knowledge both for the way it misrepresents or marginalizes particular views of the world and for the way it provides a deeper understanding of how the student's world is actually constructed. Knowledge acquired in classrooms should help students participate in vital issues that affect their experience on a daily level rather than simply enshrine the values of business pragmatism. School knowledge should have a more emancipatory goal than churning out workers (human capital) and helping schools become the citadel of corporate ideology.[27] School knowledge should help create the conditions productive for student self-determination in the larger society.

CRITICAL PEDAGOGY AND THE CURRICULUM

From the perspective of critical educational theorists, the curriculum represents much more than a program of study, a classroom text, or a course syllabus. Rather, it represents the *introduction to a particular form of life; it serves in part to prepare students for dominant or subordinate positions in the existing society.*[28] The curriculum favors certain forms of knowledge over others and affirms the dreams, desires, and values of select groups of students over other groups, often discriminatorily on the basis of race, class, and gender. In general, critical educational theorists are concerned with how descriptions, discussions, and representations in textbooks, curriculum materials, course content, and social relations embodied in classroom practices benefit dominant groups and exclude subordinate ones. In this regard, they often refer to the *hidden curriculum.*

THE HIDDEN CURRICULUM

The *hidden curriculum* refers to *the unintended outcomes of the schooling process.* Critical educators recognize that schools shape students both through standardized learning situations, and through other agendas including rules of conduct, classroom organization, and the informal pedagogical procedures used by teachers with specific groups of students.[29] The hidden curriculum also includes teaching and learning styles that are emphasized in the classroom, the messages that get transmitted to the student by the total physical and instructional environment, governance structures, teacher expectations, and grading procedures.

The hidden curriculum deals with the tacit ways in which knowledge and behavior get constructed, outside the usual course materials and formally scheduled lessons. It is a part of the bureaucratic and managerial "press" of the school—the combined forces by which students are induced to comply with dominant ideologies and social practices related to authority, behavior, and morality. Does the principal expel school offenders or just verbally upbraid them? Is the ethos of the office inviting or hostile? Do the administration and teachers show respect for each other and for the students on a regular basis? Answers to these questions help define the hidden curriculum, which refers then, to the *non-subject-related* sets of behaviors produced in students.

Often, the hidden curriculum displaces the professed educational ideals and goals of the classroom teacher or school. We know, for example, that teachers unconsciously give more intellectual attention, praise, and academic help to boys than to girls. A study reported in *Psychology Today* suggests that stereotypes of garrulous and gossipy women are so strong that when groups of administrators and teachers are shown films of classroom discussion and asked who is talking more, the teachers overwhelmingly chose the girls. In reality, however, the boys in the film "out talk" the girls at a ratio of three to one. The same study also suggests that teachers behave differently depending on whether boys or girls respond during classroom discussions. When boys call out comments without raising their hands, for instance, teachers generally accept their answers; girls, however, are reprimanded for the same behavior. The hidden message is "Boys should be academically aggressive while girls should remain composed and passive." In addition, teachers are twice as likely to give male students detailed instructions on how to do things for themselves; with female students, however, teachers are more likely to do the task for them instead. Not surprisingly, the boys are being taught independence and the girls dependency.[30]

Classroom sexism as a function of the hidden curriculum results in the unwitting and unintended granting of power and privilege to men over women and accounts for many of the following outcomes:

- Although girls start school ahead of boys in reading and basic computation, by the time they graduate from high school, boys have higher SAT scores in both areas.
- By high school, some girls are less committed to careers, although their grades and achievement-test scores may be as good as boys. Many girls' interests turn to marriage or stereotypically female jobs. Some women may feel that men disapprove of women using their intelligence.
- Girls are less likely to take math and science courses and to participate in special or gifted programs in these subjects, even if they have a talent for them. They are also more likely to believe that they are incapable of pursuing math and science in college and to avoid the subjects.
- Girls are more likely to attribute failure to internal factors, such as ability, rather than to external factors, such as luck.

The sexist communication game is played at work, as well as at school. As reported in numerous studies it goes like this:

- Men speak more often and frequently interrupt women.
- Listeners recall more from male speakers than from female speakers, even when both use a similar speaking style and cover identical content.

- Women participate less actively in conversation. They do more smiling and gazing; they're more often the passive bystanders in professional and social conversations among peers.
- Women often transform declarative statements into tentative comments. This is accomplished by using qualifiers ("kind of" or "I guess") and by adding tag questions ("This is a good movie, isn't it?"). These tentative patterns weaken impact and signal a lack of power and influence.[31]

Of course, most teachers try hard not to be sexist. The hidden curriculum continues to operate, however, despite what the overt curriculum prescribes. The hidden curriculum can be effectively compared to what Australian educator Doug White calls the *multinational curriculum*. For White,

> [T]he multinational curriculum is the curriculum of disembodied universals, of the mind as an information-processing machine, of concepts and skills without moral and social judgment but with enormous manipulative power. That curriculum proposed the elevation of abstract skills over particular content, of universal cognitive principles over the actual conditions of life.[32]

White reminds us that no curriculum, policy, or program is ideologically or politically innocent, and that the concept of the curriculum is inextricably related to issues of social class, culture, gender, and power. This is, of course, not the way curriculum is traditionally understood and discussed in teacher education. The hidden curriculum, then, refers to learning outcomes not openly acknowledged to learners. But we must remember that not all values, attitudes, or patterns of behavior that are by-products of the hidden curriculum in educational settings are necessarily bad. The point is to identify the structural and political assumptions upon which the hidden curriculum rests and to attempt to change the institutional arrangements of the classroom so as to offset the most undemocratic and oppressive outcomes.

CURRICULUM AS A FORM OF CULTURAL POLITICS

Critical educational theorists view curriculum as a form of *cultural politics,* that is, as a part of the sociocultural dimension of the schooling process. The term cultural politics permits the educational theorist to highlight the political consequences of interaction between teachers and students who come from dominant and subordinate cultures. To view the curriculum as a form of cultural politics *assumes that the social, cultural, political and economic dimensions are the primary categories for understanding contemporary schooling.*[33]

School life is understood not as a unitary, monolithic, and ironclad system of rules and regulations, but as a cultural terrain characterized by varying degrees of accommodation, contestation, and resistance. Furthermore, school life is understood as a plurality of conflicting languages and struggles, a place where classroom and street-corner cultures collide and where teachers, students, and school administrators often differ as to how school experiences and practices are to be defined and understood.

This curriculum perspective creates conditions for the student's self-empowerment as an active political and moral subject. I am using the term *empowerment* to refer to the process through which students learn to critically appropriate knowledge existing outside their immediate experience in order to broaden their understanding of themselves, the world, and the possibilities for transforming the taken-for-granted assumptions about the way we live. Stanley Aronowitz has described one aspect of empowerment as "the process of appreciating and loving oneself;"[34] empowerment is gained from knowledge and social relations that dignify one's own history, language, and cultural traditions. But empowerment means more than self-confirmation. It also refers to the process by which students learn to question and selectively appropriate those aspects of the dominant culture that will provide them with the basis for defining and transforming, rather than merely serving, the wider social order.

Basing a curriculum on cultural politics consists of linking critical social theory to a set of stipulated practices through which teachers can dismantle and critically examine dominant educational and cultural traditions. Many of these traditions have fallen prey to an *instrumental rationality* (a way of looking at the world in which "ends" are subordinated to questions of "means" and in which "facts" are separated from questions of "value") that either limits or ignores democratic ideals and principles. Critical theorists want particularly to develop a language of critique and demystification that can be used to analyze those latent interests and ideologies that work to socialize students in a manner compatible with the dominant culture. Of equal concern, however, is the creation of alternative teaching practices capable of empowering students both inside and outside of schools.

CRITICAL PEDAGOGY AND SOCIAL REPRODUCTION

Over the decades, critical educational theorists have tried to fathom how schools are implicated in the process of *social reproduction.* In other words, they have attempted to explore how schools *perpetuate or reproduce the social relationships and attitudes needed to sustain the existing dominant economic and class relations of the larger society.*[35] Social reproduction refers to the intergenerational reproduction of social class (i.e., working-class students become working-class adults; middle-class students become middle-class adults). Schools reproduce the structures of social life through the colonization (socialization) of student subjectivities and by establishing social practices characteristic of the wider society.

Critical educators ask: How do schools help transmit the status and class positions of the wider society? The answers, of course, vary enormously.

Some of the major mechanisms of social reproduction include the allocation of students into private versus public schools, the socioeconomic composition of school communities, and the placement of students into curriculum tracks within schools.[36] A group of social reproduction theorists, known as *correspondence theorists,* have attempted to show how schools reflect wider social inequalities.[37] In a famous study by Bowles and Gintis (1976), the authors argue in deterministic terms that there is a *relatively simple correspondence between schooling, class, family, and social inequalities.* Bowles and Gintis maintain that children of parents with upper socioeconomic standing most often achieve upper socioeconomic status while children of lower socioeconomic parents acquire a correspondingly low socioeconomic standing. However, schooling structures are not always successful in ensuring privilege for the students' advantaged class positions. The correspondence theorists *could not explain why some children cross over from the status of their parents.* Social reproduction, as it turns out, is more than simply a case of economic and class position; it also involves social, cultural, and linguistic factors.

This brings into the debate the *conflict or resistance theorists,* such as Henry Giroux and Paul Willis, who pay significantly more attention to the *partial autonomy* of the school culture and to the role of conflict and contradiction within the reproductive process itself.[38] *Theories of resistance* generally draw upon an understanding of the complexities of culture to define the relationship between schools and the dominant society. Resistance theorists challenge the school's ostensible role as a democratic institution that functions to improve the social position of all students—including, if not especially, those groups that are subordinated to the system. Resistance theorists question the processes by which the school system reflects and sustains the logic of capital as well as dominant social practices and structures that are found in a class, race, and gender divided society.

One of the major contributions to resistance theory has been the discovery by British researcher Paul Willis that working-class students who engage in classroom episodes of resistance often implicate themselves even further in their own domination.[39] Willis's group of working-class schoolboys, known as "the lads," resisted the class-based oppression of the school by rejecting mental labor in favor of more "masculine" manual labor (which reflected the shop-floor culture of their family members). In so doing, they ironically displaced the school's potential to help them escape the shop floor once they graduated. Willis's work presents a considerable advance in understanding social and cultural reproduction in the context of student resistance. Social reproduction certainly exceeds mobility for each class, and we know that a substantial amount of class mobility is unlikely in most school settings. The work of the resistance theorists has helped us understand how domination works, even though students continually reject the ideology that is helping to oppress them. Sometimes this resistance only helps secure to an even greater degree the eventual fate of these students.

How, then, can we characterize student resistance? Students resist instruction for many reasons. As Giroux reminds us, not all acts of student misbehavior are acts of resistance. In fact, such "resistance" may simply be repressive moments (sexist, racist) inscribed by the dominant culture.[40] I have argued that the major drama of resistance in schools is an effort on the part of students to bring their street-corner culture into the classroom. Students reject the culture of classroom learning because, for the most part, it is delibidinalized (eros-denying) and is infused with a cultural capital to which subordinate groups have little legitimate access. Resistance to school instruction represents a resolve on the part of students not to be dissimulated in the face of oppression; it is a fight against the erasure of their street-corner identities. To resist means to fight against the monitoring of passion and desire. It is, furthermore, a struggle against the capitalist symbolization of the flesh. By this I mean that students resist turning themselves into worker commodities in which their potential is evaluated only as future members of the labor force. At the same time, however, the images of success manufactured by the dominant culture seem out of reach for most of them.

Students resist the "dead time" of school, where interpersonal relationships are reduced to the imperatives of market ideology. Resistance, in other words, is a rejection of their reformulation as docile objects where spontaneity is replaced by efficiency and productivity, in compliance with the needs of the corporate marketplace. Accordingly, students' very bodies become sites of struggle, and resistance a way of gaining power, celebrating pleasure, and fighting oppression in the lived historicity of the moment.

What, then, are the "regimes of truth" that organize school time, subject matter, pedagogical practice, school values, and personal truth? How does the culture of the school organize the body and monitor passion through its elaborate system of surveillance? How are forms of social control inscripted into the flesh? How are students' subjectivities and social identities produced discursively by institutionalized power, and how is this institutional power at the same time produced by the legitimization of discourses that treat students as if they were merely repositories of lust and passion (the degenerative animal instincts)? How is reason privileged over passion so that it can be used to quell the "crude mob mentality" of students? What is the range of identities available within a system of education designed to produce, regulate, and distribute character, govern gesture, dictate values, and police desire? To what extent does an adherence to the norms of the school mean that students will have to give up the dignity and status maintained through psychosocial adaptations to life on the street? To what extent does compliance with the rituals and norms of school mean that students have to forfeit their identity as members of an ethnic group? These are all questions that theorists within the critical tradition have attempted to answer. And the answers are as various as they are important.

Some versions of student resistance are undoubtedly romantic: The teachers are villains, and the students are anti-heroes. I am not interested in teacher-bashing, nor in resurrecting the resistant student as the new James Dean or Marlon Brando. I much prefer the image of Giroux's resisting intellectual, someone who questions prevailing norms and established regimes of truth in the manner of a Rosa Luxemburg or a Jean-Paul Sartre.[41]

I would like to stress an important point. Our culture in general (and that includes schools, the media, and our social institutions) has helped educate students to acquire a veritable passion for ignorance. The French psycho-analyst Jacques Lacan suggests that ignorance is not a passive state but rather an active excluding from consciousness. The passion for ignorance that has infected our culture demands a complex explanation, but part of it can be attributed, as Lacan suggests, to *a refusal to acknowledge that our subjectivities have been constructed out of the information and social practices that surround us.*[42] Ignorance, as part of the very structure of knowledge, can teach us something. But we lack the critical constructs with which to recover that knowledge *which we choose not to know.* Unable to find meaningful knowledge "out there" in the world of prepackaged commodities, students resort to random violence or an intellectual purple haze where anything more challenging than the late night news is met with retreat, or despair; and of course, it is the dominant culture that benefits most from this epidemic of conceptual anesthesia. The fewer critical intellectuals around to challenge its ideals, the better.

What do all these theories of resistance mean for the classroom teacher? Do we disregard resistance? Do we try to ignore it? Do we always take the student's side?

The answers to these questions are not easy. But let me sketch out the bare bones of a possible answer. First of all, schooling should be a process of understanding how subjectivities are produced. It should be a process of examining how we have been constructed out of the prevailing ideas, values, and world-views of the dominant culture. The point to remember is that if we have been made, then we can be "unmade" and "made over." What are some alternative models with which we can begin to repattern ourselves and our social order? Teachers need to encourage students to be self-reflexive about these questions and to provide students with a conceptual framework to begin to answer them. Teaching and learning should be a process of *inquiry,* of critique; it should also be a process of *constructing,* of building a social imagination that works within a language of hope. If teaching is cast in the form of what Henry Giroux refers to as a "language of possibility," then a greater potential exists for making learning relevant, critical, and transformative. Knowledge is relevant only when it begins with the experiences students bring with them from the surrounding culture; it is critical only when these experiences are shown to sometimes be problematic (i.e., racist, sexist); and it is transformative only when students begin to use the knowledge to help empower others, including individuals in the surrounding community. Knowledge then becomes linked to social reform. An understanding of the language of the self can help us better negotiate with the world. It can also help us begin to forge the basis of *social transformation:* the building of a better world, the altering of the very ground upon which we live and work.

Teachers can do no better than to create agendas of possibility in their classrooms. Not every student will want to take part, but many will. Teachers may have personal problems—and so may students—that will limit the range of classroom discourses. Some teachers may simply be unwilling to function as critical educators. Critical pedagogy does not guarantee that resistance will not take place. But it does provide teachers with the foundations for understanding resistance, so that whatever pedagogy is developed can be sensitive to sociocultural conditions that construct resistance, lessening the chance that students will be blamed as the sole, originating source of resistance. No emancipatory pedagogy will ever be built out of theories of behavior which view students as lazy, defiant, lacking in ambition, or genetically inferior. A much more penetrating solution is to try to understand the structures of mediation in the sociocultural world that form student resistance. In other words, what is the larger picture? We must remove the concept of student resistance from the preserve of the behaviorist or the depth psychologist and insert it instead into the terrain of social theory.

CULTURAL CAPITAL

Resistance theorists such as Henry Giroux focus on *cultural reproduction* as a function of class based differences in *cultural capital.* The concept of *cultural capital,* made popular by French sociologist Pierre Bourdieu, refers to the general cultural background, knowledge, disposition, and skills that are passed on from one generation to another. Cultural capital represents *ways of talking, acting, modes of style, moving, socializing, forms of knowledge, language practices, and values.* Cultural capital can exist in the embodied state, as long-lasting dispositions of the mind and body; in the objectified state, as cultural artifacts such as pictures, books, diplomas, and other material objects; and in the institutionalized state, which confers original properties on the cultural capital which it guarantees. For instance, to many teachers, the cultural traits exhibited by students—e.g., tardiness, sincerity, honesty, thrift, industriousness, politeness, a certain way of dressing, speaking, and gesturing—appear as natural qualities emerging from an individual's "inner essence." However, such traits are to a great extent culturally inscribed and are often linked to the social class standing of individuals who exhibit them. Social capital refers to the collectively owned economic and cultural capital of a group.[43] Taking linguistic competency as just one example of cultural capital, theorists such as Basil Bernstein contend that class membership and family socialization generate distinctive speech patterns. Working-class students learn "restricted" linguistic codes while middle-class children use "elaborated" codes. This means that the speech of working-class and middle-class children is generated by underlying regulative principles that govern their choice and combination of words and sentence structures. These, according to Bernstein, have been learned primarily in the course of family socialization.[44] Critical theorists argue that schools generally affirm and reward students who exhibit the elaborately coded "middle-class" speech while disconfirming and devaluing students who use restricted "working-class" coded speech.

Students from the dominant culture inherit substantially different cultural capital than do economically disadvantaged students, and schools generally value and reward those who exhibit that dominant cultural capital (which is also usually exhibited by the teacher). Schools systematically *devalue* the cultural capital of students who occupy subordinate class positions. Cultural capital is reflective of material capital and replaces it as a form of symbolic currency that enters into the exchange system of the school. Cultural capital is therefore symbolic of the social structure's economic force and becomes in itself a productive force in the reproduction of social relations under capitalism. Academic performance represents, therefore, not individual competence or the lack of ability on the part of disadvantaged students but *the school's depreciation of their cultural capital.* The end result is that the school's academic credentials remain indissolubly linked to an unjust system of trading in cultural capital which is eventually transformed into *economic* capital, as working-class students become less likely to get high-paying jobs.

When I worked with students in my suburban ghetto classroom, those whose cultural capital most closely resembled my own were the students with whom I initially felt most comfortable, spent the most instructional time, and most often encouraged to work in an independent manner. I could relate more readily and positively—at least at the beginning—to those students whose manners, values, and competencies resembled my own. Teachers—including myself—easily spotted Buddy, T. J., and Duke as members of the economically disadvantaged underclass, and this often worked against them, especially with teachers who registered such students as intellectually or socially deficient. Intellectual and social deficiencies had little, if anything, to do with their behavior. Class-specific character traits and social practices did.

NOTES

1. The sources for this section are as follows: Bertell Ollman, "The Meaning of Dialectics," *Monthly Review* (1986, November): 42–55; Wilfrid Carr and Stephen Kemmis, *Becoming Critical: Knowing Through Action Research* (Victoria: Deakin University, 1983); Stephen Kemmis and Lindsay Fitzclarence, *Curriculum Theorizing: Beyond Reproduction Theory* (Victoria: Deakin University, 1986); Henry A. Giroux, *Ideology, Culture and the Process of Schooling.* (Philadelphia: Temple University Press and London: Falmer Press, Ltd., 1981); Ernst Bloch, "The Dialectical Method," *Man and World* 16 (1983): 281–313.

2. Kemmis and Fitzclarence, *Curriculum Theorizing,* 36–37.

3. McLaren, *Schooling as a Ritual Performance.* London: Routledge, 1986.

4. This discussion of micro and macro objectives is taken from Henry A. Giroux, "Overcoming Behavioral and Humanistic Objectives," *The Education Forum* (1979, May): 409–419. Also, Henry A. Giroux, *Teachers as Intellectuals: Towards a Critical Pedagogy of Practical Learning* (South Hadley, MA: Bergin and Garvey Publishers, in press).

5. See Jurgen Habermas, *Knowledge and Human Interests,* trans. J. J. Shapiro (London: Heinemann, 1972); see also Jurgen Habermas, *Theory and Practice,* trans. J. Viertel, (London: Heinemann, 1974). As cited in Kemmis and Fitzclarence, *Curriculum Theorizing,* 70–72.

6. For a fuller discussion of culture, see Enid Lee, *Letters to Marcia: A Teacher's Guide to Anti-Racist Teaching.* (Toronto: Cross Cultural Communication Centre, 1985).

7. Henry A. Giroux and Peter McLaren, "Teacher Education and the Politics of Engagement: The Case for Democratic Schooling," *Harvard Educational Review* 56, (1986): 3, 232–233. Developed from Giroux's previous work.

8. For this discussion of culture, I am indebted to Raymond A. Calluori, "The Kids are Alright: New Wave Subcultural Theory," *Social Text* 4, 3 (1985): 43–53; Mike Brake, *The Sociology of Youth Culture and Youth Subculture* (London: Routledge and Kegan Paul, 1980); Graham Murdock, "Mass Communication and the Construction of Meaning," in N. Armstead (Ed.) *Reconstructing Social Psychology* (Harmondsworth: Penguin, 1974); Dick Hebidge, *Subculture: The Meaning of Style* (London and New York: Methuen, 1979); Ian Connell, D. J. Ashenden, S. Kessler and G. W. Dowsett, *Making the Difference: Schooling, Families and Social Division* (Sydney, Australia: George Allen and Unwin, 1982). Also: Stuart Hall and Tony Jefferson, *Resistance Through Rituals: Youth Subcultures in Post War Britain* (London: Hutchinson and the Centre for Contemporary Cultural Studies, University of Birmingham, 1980).

9. John Muncie, "Pop Culture, Pop Music and Post-War Youth Subcultures," *Popular Culture.* Block 5 Units 18 and 19/20, The Open University Press (1981): 31–62.

10. Muncie, "Pop Culture," 76.

11. The section on hegemony draws on the following sources: Giroux, *Ideology, Culture and the Process of Schooling,* 22–26; *Popular Culture* (1981), a second level course at The Open University, Milton Keynes, England, published by The Open University Press and distributed in the United States by Taylor and Francis (Philadelphia, PA). Several booklets in this series were instrumental in developing the sections on ideology and hegemony: Geoffrey Bourne, "Meaning, Image and Ideology," *Form and Meaning 1,* Open University Press, Block 4, Units 13, 15, and 15, 37–65; see also Tony Bennett, "Popular Culture: Defining Our Terms," *Popular Culture: Themes and Issues I,* Block I, Units 1 and 2, 77–87; Tony Bennett, "Popular Culture: History and Theory," *Popular Culture: Themes and Issues II,* Block 1, Unit 3, 29–32. Another important source is a booklet for a third level course at The Open University: *The Politics of Cultural Production,* The Open University Press, 1981. Relevant sections include: Geoff Whitty, "Ideology, Politics and Curriculum," 7–52; David Davies, "Popular Culture, Class and Schooling," 53–108. See also P. J. Hills, *A Dictionary of Education* (London: Routledge and Kegan Paul, 1982), 166–167; and Raymond Williams, *Keywords: A Vocabulary of Culture and Society* (London: Fontana, 1983), 144–146.

12. William Ryan, *Blaming the Victim* (New York: Vintage Books, 1976).

13. Todd Gitlin, *The Whole World is Watching: Mass Media in the Making and Unmaking of the New Left* (Berkeley and London: University of California Press, 1980), 253–254.

14. Gore Vidal, *Monthly Review* 19 (1986, October), as cited in Allen Fenichel "Alternative Economic Policies," *The Ecumenist* 25, 4 (1987, May–June): 49.

15. For this section on ideology, I am indebted to Henry A. Giroux, *Theory and Resistance in Education: Pedagogy for the Opposition* (South Hadley, MA: Bergin and Garvey, 1983), 143. See also Stanley Aronowitz and Herny A. Giroux, *Education Under Siege* (South Hadley, MA: Bergin and Garvey, 1985); Douglas Kellner, "Ideology, Marxism, and Advanced Capitalism," *Socialist Review* 8, 6 (1978): 38; Gibson Winter, *Liberating Creation: Foundations of Religious Social Ethics* (New York: Crossroad, 1981), 97. See also: Geoff Whitty, "Ideology, Politics and Curriculum," 7–52 and David Davies, "Popular Culture, Class and Schooling," 53–108; Williams, *Keywords,* 153–157; Tony Bennett, "Popular Culture: Defining our Terms," 77–87; and Geoffrey Bourne, "Meaning, Image and Ideology," 37–53.

16. James Donald and Stuart Hall, "Introduction," in S. Donald and S. Hall (Eds.), *Politics and Ideology* (Milton Keynes: Philadelphia, Open University Press, 1986), ix–x.

17. Donald and Hall, *Politics and Ideology,* x.
18. John Thompson, "Language and Ideology," *The Sociological Review* 35, 3 (1987, Aug.): 516–536.
19. John Dewey, in J. Ratner (Ed.), *Intelligence in the Modern World: John Dewey's Philosophy* (New York: The Modern Library, 1939), 784. See also Michael Foucault *Power/Knowledge,* in C. Gordon (Ed.), (L. Marshall, J. Mepham, and K. Spoer, Trans.), *Selected Interviews and Other Writings 1972–77* (New York: Pantheon, 1980), 187.
20. Michael Foucault, *The Archaeology of Knowledge* (New York: Harper Colophon Books, 1972), 117.
21. Foucault, *Power/Knowledge,* 200.
22. Richard Smith and Anna Zantiotis, "Teacher Education, Cultural Politics, and the Avant-Garde," in H. Giroux and P. McLaren (Eds.), *Schooling and the Politics of Culture* (Albany, NY: SUNY Press, in press), 123.
23. See Chris Weedon, *Feminist Practice and Post-Structuralist Theory* (Oxford: Basil-Blackwell, 1987).
24. Cleo Cherryholmes, "The Social Project of Curriculum: A Poststructural Analysis," *American Journal of Education* (in press): 21.
25. Foucault, *Power/Knowledge,* 131.
26. Lawrence Grossberg, "History, Politics and Postmodernism: Stuart Hall and Cultural Studies," *Journal of Communication Inquiry* 10, 2 (1987): 73.
27. For more about the relationship of power and knowledge, see Kathy Borman and Joel Spring, *Schools in Central Cities* (New York: Longman, 1984); Henry Giroux, "Public Education and the Discourse of Possibility: Rethinking the New Conservative and Left Educational Theory," *News for Teachers of Political Science* 44 (1985, Winter): 13–15.
28. See Doug White, "After the Divided Curriculum," *The Victorian Teacher* 7 (1983, March); Giroux and McLaren, "Teacher Education and the Politics of Engagement," 228.
29. See the wide range of articles in H. Giroux and D. Purple (Eds.), *The Hidden Curriculum and Moral Education: Deception or Discovery?* (Berkeley, CA: McCutchen Publishing Corp., 1983).
30. Myra Sadkev and David Sadkev, "Sexism in the Schoolroom of the '80's," *Psychology Today* (1985, March): 55–57.
31. Sadkev and Sadkev, "Sexism in the Schoolroom," 56–57. Also, the 1980 *Nova* television program, *The Pinks and the Blues* (WGBH, Boston), summarized by Anthony Wilden. "In the Penal Colony: The Body as the Discourse of the Other," *Semiotica,* 54, 1/2(1985): 73–76.
32. White, "After the Divided Curriculum," 6–9.
33. Giroux and McLaren, "Teacher Education and the Politics of Engagement," 228–229.
34. Stanley Aronowitz, "Schooling, Popular Culture, and Post-Industrial Society: Peter McLaren Interviews Stanley Aronowitz," *Orbit* (1986): 17, 18.
35. See Kemmis and Fitzclarence, *Curriculum Theorizing,* 88–89. Also, H. A. Giroux, *Ideology, Culture, and the Process of Schooling.*
36. Glenna Colclough and E. M. Beck, "The American Educational Structure and the Reproduction of Social Class," *Social Inquiry* 56, 4 (1986, Fall): 456–476.
37. Samuel Bowles and Herbert Gintis, *Schooling in Capitalist America* (New York: Basic Books, 1976); see also Kemmis and Fitzclarence, *Curriculum Theorizing,* 90; and Colclough and Beck, "The American Educational Structure," 456–476.
38. See, for instance, Peter McLaren, "The Ritual Dimensions of Resistance: Clowning and Symbolic Inversion," *Boston University Journal of Education* 167, 2 (1985): 84–97, and Giroux, *Theory and Resistance.*
39. Paul Willis, *Learning to Labour: How Working Class Kids Get Working Class Jobs* (Westmead, England: Gower, 1977).
40. Giroux, *Theory and Resistance,* 103.
41. Aronowitz and Giroux, *Education under Siege.*
42. Jacques Lacan, "Seminar XX," *Encore* (Paris: Editions du Seuil, 1975): 100. As cited in Constance Penley, "Teaching in Your Sleep: Feminism and Psychoanalysis," in C. Nelson (Ed.), *Theory in the Classroom* (Chicago: University of Chicago Press), 135.
43. Pierre Bourdieu, "Forms of Capital," in John G. Richardson (Ed.), *Handbook of Theory and Research for the Sociology of Education* (New York: Greenwood Press, 1986), 241–258. See also Henry A. Giroux, "Rethinking the Language of Schooling," *Language Arts* 61, 1 (1984, January): 36; and Henry A. Giroux, *Ideology, Culture and the Process of Schooling,* 77.
44. Paul Atkinson, *Language, Structure and Reproduction: An Introduction to the Sociology of Basil Bernstein* (London: Methuen, 1986).

In Search of a Critical Pedagogy

MAXINE GREENE

In what Jean Baudrillard describes as "the shadow of silent majorities"[1] in an administered and media-mystified world, we try to reconceive what a critical pedagogy relevant to this time and place ought to mean. This is a moment when great numbers of Americans find their expectations and hopes for their children being fed by talk of "educational reform." Yet the reform reports speak of those very children as "human resources" for the expansion of productivity, as means to the end of maintaining our nation's economic competitiveness and military primacy in the world. Of course we want to empower the young for meaningful work, we want to nurture the achievement of diverse literacies. But the world we inhabit is palpably deficient: there are unwarranted inequities, shattered communities, unfulfilled lives. We cannot help but hunger for traces of utopian visions, of critical or dialectical engagements with social and economic realities. And yet, when we reach out, we experience a kind of blankness: We sense people living under a weight, a nameless inertial mass. How are we to justify our concern for their awakening? Where are the sources of questioning, of restlessness? How are we to move the young to break with the given, the taken-for-granted—to move towards what might be, what is not yet?

Confronting all of this, I am moved to make some poets' voices audible at the start. Poets are exceptional, of course; they are not considered educators in the ordinary sense. But they remind us of absence, ambiguity, embodiments of existential possibility. More often than not they do so with passion; and passion has been called the power of possibility. This is because it is the source of our interests and our purposes. Passion signifies mood, emotion, desire: modes of grasping the appearances of things. It is one of the important ways of recognizing possibility, "the presence of the future as *that which is lacking* and that which, by its very absence, reveals reality."[2] Poets move us to give play to our imaginations, to enlarge the scope of lived experience and reach beyond from our own grounds. Poets do not give us answers; they do not solve the problems of critical pedagogy. They can, however, if we will them to do so, awaken us to reflectiveness, to a recovery of lost landscapes and lost spontaneities. Against such a background, educators might now and then be moved to go in search of a critical pedagogy of significance for themselves.

Let us hear Walt Whitman, for one:

> I am the poet of the Body and I am the poet of the Soul,
> The pleasures of heaven are with me and the pains of
> hell are with me.
> The first I graft and increase upon myself, the latter I
> translate into a new tongue.
> I am the poet of the woman the same as the man,
> And I say it is as great to be a woman as to be a man,
>
> ....
>
> I chant the chant of dilation or pride.
> We have had ducking and deprecating about enough,
> I show that size is only development.
> Have you outstript the rest? are you the President?,
> It is a trifle, they will more than arrive there every one,
> and still pass on.[3]

Whitman calls himself the poet of the "barbaric yawp"; he is also the poet of the child going forth, of the grass, of comradeship and communion and the "en masse." And of noticing, naming, caring, feeling. In a systematized, technicized moment, a moment of violations and of shrinking "minimal" selves, we ought to be able to drink from the fountain of his work.

There is Wallace Stevens, explorer of multiple perspectives and imagination, challenger of objectified, quantified realities—what he calls the "ABC of being . . . the vital, arrogant, fatal, dominant X," questioner as well of the conventional "lights and definitions" presented as "the plain sense of things." We ought to think of states of things, he says, phases of movements, polarities.

> But in the centre of our lives, this time, this day,
> It is a state, this spring among the politicians
> Playing cards. In a village of the indigenes,
> One would still have to discover. Among the dogs
> and dung,
> One would continue to contend with one's ideas.[4]

One's ideas, yes, and blue guitars as well, and—always and always—"the never-resting mind," the "flawed words and stubborn sounds."

And there is Marianne Moore, reminding us that every poem represents what Robert Frost described as "the triumph of the spirit over the materialism by which we are being smothered," enunciating four precepts:

> Feed imagination food that invigorates.
> Whatever it is, do with all your might.
> Never do to another what you would not wish done to yourself.
> Say to yourself, "I will be responsible."

Put these principles to the test, and you will be inconvenienced by being overtrusted, overbefriended, overconsulted, half adopted, and have no leisure. Face that when you come to it.[5]

Another woman's voice arises: Muriel Rukeyser's, in the poem "Käthe Kollwitz."

> What would happen if one woman told the truth about her life?
> The world would split open[6]

The idea of an officially defined "world" splitting open when a repressed truth is revealed holds all sorts of implications for those who see reality as opaque, bland and burnished, resistant both to protest and to change.

Last, and in a different mood, let us listen to these lines by Adrienne Rich:

> A clear night in which two planets
> seem to clasp each other in which the earthly grasses
> shift like silk in starlight
> If the mind were clear
> and if the mind were simple you could take this mind
> this particular state and say
> *This is how I would live if I could choose:*
> *this is what is possible*[7]

The poem is called "What Is Possible," but the speaker knows well that no mind can be "simple," or "abstract and pure." She realizes that the mind has "a different mission in the universe," that there are sounds and configurations still needing to be deciphered; she knows that the mind must be "wrapped in battle" in what can only be a resistant world. She voices her sense of the contrast between the mind as contemplative and the mind in a dialectical relation with what surrounds.

They create spaces, these poets, between themselves and what envelops and surrounds. Where there are spaces like that, desire arises, along with hope and expectation. We may sense that something is lacking that must be surpassed or repaired. Often, therefore, poems address our freedom; they call on us to move beyond where we are, to break with submergence, to transform. To transform what—and how? To move beyond ourselves—and where? Reading such works within the contexts of schools and education, those of us still preoccupied with human freedom and human growth may well find our questions more perplexing. We may become more passionate about the possibility of a critical pedagogy in these uncritical times. How can we (decently, morally, intelligently) address ourselves both to desire and to purpose and obligation? How can we awaken others to possibility and the need for action in the name of possibility? How can we communicate the importance of opening spaces in the imagination where persons can reach beyond where they are?

Poets, of course, are not alone in the effort to make us see and to defamiliarize our commonsense worlds. The critical impulse is an ancient one in the Western tradition: we have only to recall the prisoners released from the cave in *The Republic,* Socrates trying to arouse the "sleeping ox" that was the Athenian public, Francis Bacon goading his readers to break with the "idols" that obscured their vision and distorted their rational capacities, David Hume calling for the exposure of the "sophistries and illusions" by which so many have habitually lived. In philosophy, in the arts, in the sciences, men and women repeatedly have come forward to urge their audiences to break with what William Blake called "mind-forg'd manacles." Not only did such manacles shackle consciousness; their effectiveness assured the continuing existence of systems of domination—monarchies, churches, land-holding arrangements, and armed forces of whatever kind.

The American tradition originated in such an insight and in the critical atmosphere specific to the European Enlightenment. It was an atmosphere created in large measure by rational, autonomous voices engaging in dialogue for the sake of bringing into being a public sphere. These were, most often, the voices of an emerging middle class concerned for their own independence from anachronistic and unjust restraints. Their "rights" were being trampled, they asserted, rights sanctioned by natural and moral laws. Among these rights were "life, liberty, and the pursuit of happiness," which (especially when joined to justice or equity) remain normative for this nation: they are goods *to be* secured. Liberty, at the time of the founding of our nation, meant liberation from interference by the state, church, or army in the lives of individuals. For some, sharing such beliefs as those articulated by the British philosopher John Stuart Mill, liberty also meant each person's right to think for himself or herself, "to follow his intellect to whatever conclusions it may lead" in an atmosphere that forbade "mental slavery."[8]

The founders were calling, through a distinctive critical challenge, for opportunities to give their energies free play. That meant the unhindered exercise of their particular talents: inventing, exploring, building, pursuing material and social success. To be able to do so, they had to secure power, which they confirmed through the establishment of a constitutional republic. For Hannah Arendt, this sort of power is kept in existence through an ongoing process of "binding and promising, combining and covenanting." As she saw it, power springs up between human beings when they act to constitute "a worldly structure to house, as it were, their combined power of action."[9] When we consider the numbers of people excluded from this process over the generations, we have to regard this view of power as normative as well. It is usual to affirm that power belongs to "the people" at large; but, knowing that this has not been the case, we are obligated to expand the "wordly structure" until it contains the "combined power" of increasing numbers of articulate persons. A critical pedagogy for Americans, it would seem, must take this into account.

For the school reformers of the early nineteenth century, the apparent mass power accompanying the expansion of manhood suffrage created a need for "self-control" and a "voluntary compliance" with the laws of righteousness.[10] Without a common school to promote such control and compliance, the social order might be threatened. Moreover, the other obligation of the school—to prepare the young to "create wealth"—could not be adequately met. Even while recognizing the importance of providing public education for the masses of children, we have to acknowledge that great numbers of them were being socialized into factory life and wage labor in an expanding capitalist society. Like working classes everywhere, they could not but find themselves alienated from their own productive energies. The persisting dream of opportunity, however, kept most of them from confronting their literal powerlessness. The consciousness of objectively real "open" spaces (whether on the frontier, "downtown," or out at sea) prevented them from thinking seriously about changing the order of things; theoretically, there was always an alternative, a "territory ahead."[11] It followed that few were likely to conceive of themselves in a dialectical relation with what surrounded them, no matter how exploitative or cruel. As the laggard and uneven development of trade unions indicates, few were given to viewing themselves as members of a "class" with a project to pull them forward, a role to play in history.

The appearance of utopian communities and socialist societies throughout the early nineteenth century did call repeatedly into question some of the assumptions of the American ideology, especially those having to do with individualism. The founders of the experimental colonies (Robert Owen, Frances Wright, Albert Brisbane, and others) spoke of communalism, mental freedom, the integration of physical and intellectual work, and the discovery of a common good. Socialists called for a more humane and rational social arrangement and for critical insight into what Orestes Brownson described as the "crisis as to the relation of wealth and labor." He said, "It is useless to shut our eyes to the fact and, like the ostrich, fancy ourselves secure because we have so concealed our heads that we see not the danger."[12] Important as their insights were, such people were addressing themselves to educated humanitarians whose good offices might be enlisted in improving and perfecting mankind. Critical though they were of exploitation, greed, and the division of labor, they did not speak of engaging the exploited ones in their own quests for emancipation. No particular pedagogy seemed required, and none was proposed, except within the specific contexts of utopian communities. Once a decent community or society was created, it was believed, the members would be educated in accord with its ideals.

There were, it is true, efforts to invent liberating ways of teaching for children in the larger society, although most were undertaken outside the confines of the common schools. Elizabeth Peabody and Bronson Alcott, among others, through "conversations" with actual persons in classrooms, toiled to inspire self-knowledge, creativity, and communion. Like Ralph Waldo Emerson, they were all hostile to the "joint-stock company" that society seemed to have become, a company "in which the members agree, for the better securing of his bread to each shareholder, to surrender the liberty and culture of the eater."[13] Like Emerson as well, they were all hostile to blind conformity, to the ethos of "Trade" that created false relations among human beings, to the chilling routines of institutional life. It is the case that they were largely apolitical; but their restiveness in the face of an imperfect society led them to find various modes of defiance. Those at Brook Farm tried to find a communal way of challenging the social order: Fuller found feminism; Emerson, ways of speaking intended to rouse his listeners to create their own meanings, to think for themselves.

The most potent exemplar of all this was Henry David Thoreau, deliberately addressing readers "in the first person," provoking them to use their intellects to "burrow" through the taken-for-granted, the conventional, the genteel. He wanted them to reject their own self-exploitation, to refuse what we would now call false consciousness and artificial needs. He connected the "wide-awakeness" to actual work in the world, to projects. He knew that people needed to be released from internal and external constraints if they were to shape and make and articulate, to leave their own thumbprints on the world. He understood about economic tyranny on the railroads and in the factories, and he knew that it could make political freedom meaningless. His writing and his abolitionism constituted his protests; both *Walden* and *On Civil Disobedience* function as pedagogies in the sense that they seemed aimed at raising the consciousness of those willing to pay heed. His concern, unquestionably, was with his "private state" rather than with a public space; but he helped create the alternative tradition in the United States at a moment of expansion and materialism. And there are strands of his thinking, even today, that can be woven into a critical pedagogy. Whether building his house, hoeing his beans, hunting woodchucks, or finding patterns in the ice melting on the wall, he was intent on *naming* his lived world.

There were more overtly rebellious figures among escaped slaves, abolitionists, and campaigners for women's rights; but the language of people like Frederick Douglass, Harriet Tubman, Sarah Grimke, Susan B. Anthony, and Elizabeth Cady Stanton was very much the language of those who carried on the original demand for independence. The power they sought, however, was not the power to expand and control. For them—slaves, oppressed women, freedmen and freedwomen—the idea of freedom as endowment solved little; they had to take action to *achieve* their freedom, which they saw as the power to act and to choose. Thomas Jefferson, years before, had provided the metaphor of *polis* for Americans, signifying a space where persons could come together to bring into being the "worldly structure" spoken of above. Great romantics like Emerson and Thoreau gave voice to the passion for autonomy and authenticity. Black leaders, including Douglass, W. E. B. Du Bois, the Reverend Martin Luther King, and Malcolm X, not only engaged dialectically with the resistant environment in their pursuit of freedom; they invented languages and pedagogies to enable people to overcome internalized oppression. Struggling for their rights in widening public spheres, they struggled also against what the Reverend King called "nobodiness" as they marched and engaged in a civil disobedience grounded in experiences of the past. Du Bois was in many ways exemplary when he spoke of the "vocation" of twentieth-century youth. Attacking the industrial system "which creates poverty and the children of poverty . . . ignorance and disease and crime," he called for "young women and young men of devotion to lift again the banner of humanity and to walk toward a civilization which will be free and intelligent, which will be healthy and unafraid."[14] The words hold intimations of what Paulo Freire was to say years later when he, too, spoke of the "vocation" of oppressed people, one he identified with "humanization."[15] And the very notion of walking "toward a civilization" suggests the sense of future possibility without which a pedagogy must fail.

Public school teachers, subordinated as they were in the solidifying educational bureaucracies, seldom spoke the language of resistance or transcendence. It is well to remember, however, the courageous ones who dared to go south after the Civil War in the freedmen's schools. Not only did they suffer persecution in their efforts to invent their own "pedagogy of the oppressed"—or of the newly liberated; they often fought for their own human rights against male missionary administrators and even against the missionary concept itself.[16] It is well to remember, too, the transformation of the missionary impulse into settlement house and social work by women like Jane Addams and Lillian Wald. Committing themselves to support systems and adult education for newcomers to the country and for the neighborhood poor, they supported union organization with an explicitly political awareness of what they were about in a class-ridden society. They were able, more often than not, to avoid what Freire calls "malefic generosity" and develop the critical empathy needed for enabling the "other" to find his or her own way.

For all the preoccupations with control, for all the schooling "to order," as David Nasaw puts it,[17] there were always people hostile to regimentation and manipulation, critical of constraints of consciousness. Viewed from a contemporary perspective, for example, Colonel Francis Parker's work with teachers at the Cook County Normal School at the end of the nineteenth century placed a dramatic emphasis on freeing children from competitive environments and compulsions. He encouraged the arts and spontaneous activities; he encouraged shared work. He believed that, if democratized, the school could become "the one central means by which the great problem of human liberty is to be worked out."[18] Trying to help teachers understand the natural learning processes of the young, he was specifically concerned with resisting the corruptions and distortions of an increasingly corporate America. In the Emersonian tradition, he envisioned a sound community life emerging from the liberation and regeneration of individuals. And indeed, there were many libertarians and romantic progressives following him in the presumption that a society of truly free individuals would be a humane and sustaining one.

This confidence may account for the contradictions in the American critical heritage, especially as it informed education within and outside the schools. Structural changes, if mentioned at all, were expected to follow the emancipation of persons (or the appropriate molding of persons); and the schools, apparently depoliticized, were relied upon to effect the required reform and bring about a better world. If individual children were properly equipped for the work they had to do, it was believed, and trained to resist the excesses of competition, there would be no necessity for political action to transform economic relations. The street children, the tenement children, those afflicted and crippled by poverty and social neglect, were often thrust into invisibility because their very existence denied that claim.

John Dewey was aware of such young people, certainly in Chicago, where he saw them against his own memories of face-to-face community life in Burlington, Vermont. Convinced of the necessity for cooperation and community support if individual powers were to be released, he tried in some sense to recreate the Burlington of his youth in the "miniature community" he hoped to see in each classroom.[19] In those classrooms as well, there would be continuing and open communication, the kind of learning that would feed into practice, and inquiries arising out of questioning in the midst of life. Critical thinking modeled on the scientific method, active and probing intelligence: these, for Dewey, were the stuff of a pedagogy that would equip the young to resist fixities and stock responses, repressive and deceiving authorities. Unlike the libertarians and romantics, he directed attention to the "social medium" in which the individual growth occurred and to the mutuality of significant concerns.

Even as we question the small-town paradigm in Dewey's treatment of community, even as we wonder about his use of the scientific model for social inquiry, we still ought to be aware of Dewey's sensitivity to what would later be called the "hegemony," or the ideological control, implicit in the dominant point of view of a given society. He understood, for instance, the "religious aureole" protecting institutions like the Supreme Court, the Constitution, and private property. He was aware that the principles and assumptions that gave rise even to public school curricula were so taken for granted that they were considered wholly natural, fundamentally unquestionable. In *The Public and*

Its Problems, he called what we think of as ideological control a "social pathology," which "works powerfully against effective inquiry into social institutions and conditions." He went on, "It manifests itself in a thousand ways: in querulousness, in impotent drifting, in uneasy snatching at distractions, in idealization of the long established, in a facile optimism assumed as a cloak, in riotous glorification of things 'as they are,' in intimidation of all dissenters—ways which depress and dissipate thought all the more effectually because they operate with subtle and unconscious pervasiveness."[20] A method of social inquiry had to be developed, he said, to reduce the "pathology" that led to denial and to acquiescence in the status quo. For all his commitment to scientific method, however, he stressed the "human function" of the physical sciences and the importance of seeing them in human terms. Inquiry, communication, "contemporary and quotidian" knowledge of consequence for shared social life: these fed into his conceptions of pedagogy.

His core concern for individual fulfillment was rooted in a recognition that fullfillment could only be attained in the midst of "associated" or intersubjective life. Troubled as we must be fifty years later by the "eclipse of the public," he saw as one of the prime pedagogical tasks the education of an "articulate public." For him, the public sphere came into being when the consequences of certain private transactions created a common interest among people, one that demanded deliberate and cooperative action. Using somewhat different language, we might say that a public emerges when people come freely together in speech and action to take *care* of something that needs caring for, to repair some evident deficiency in their common world. We might think of homelessness as a consequence of the private dealings of landlords, an arms build-up as a consequence of corporate decisions, racial exclusion as a consequence of a private property-holder's choice. And then we might think of what it would mean to educate to the end of caring for something and taking action to repair. That would be *public* education informed by a critical pedagogy; and it would weave together a number of American themes.

Certain of these themes found a new articulation in the 1930s, during the publication of *The Social Frontier* at Teachers College. An educational journal, it was addressed "to the task of considering the broad role of education in advancing the welfare and interests of the great masses of the people who do the work of society—those who labor on farms and ships and in the mines, shops, and factories of the world."[21] Dewey was among the contributors; and, although it had little impact on New Deal policy or even on specific educational practices, the magazine did open out to a future when more and more "liberals" would take a critical view of monopoly capitalism and industrial culture with all their implications for a supposedly "common" school.

In some respect, this represented a resurgence of the Enlightenment faith. Rational insight and dialogue, linked to scientific intelligence, were expected to reduce inequities and exploitation. A reconceived educational effort would advance the welfare and interests of the masses. Ironically, it was mainly in the private schools that educational progressivism had an influence. Critical discussions took place there; attention was paid to the posing of worthwhile problems arising out of the tensions and uncertainties of everyday life; social intelligence was nurtured; social commitments affirmed. In the larger domains of public education, where school people were struggling to meet the challenges of mass education, the emphasis tended to be on "life-adjustment," preparation for future life and work, and "physical, mental, and emotional health."

There is irony in the fact that the progressive social vision, with its integrating of moral with epistemic concerns, its hopes for a social order transformed by the schools, was shattered by the Second World War. The terrible revelations at Auschwitz and Hiroshima demonstrated what could happen when the old dream of knowledge as power was finally fulfilled. Science was viewed as losing its innocence in its wedding to advanced technology. Bureaucracy, with all its impersonality and literal irresponsibility, brought with it almost unrecognizable political and social realities. It took time, as is well known, for anything resembling a progressive vision to reconstitute itself; there was almost no recognition of the role now being played by "instrumental rationality,"[22] or what it would come to signify. On the educational side, after the war, there were efforts to remake curriculum in the light of new inquiries into knowledge structures in the disciplinary fields. On the side of the general public, there were tax revolts and rejections of the critical and the controversial, even as the McCarthyite subversion was occurring in the larger world. Only a few years after the Sputnik panic, with the talent searches it occasioned, and the frantic encouragement of scientific training, the long-invisible poor of America suddenly took center stage. The Civil Rights Movement, taking form since the Supreme Court decision on integration in 1954, relit flames of critical pedagogy, as it set people marching to achieve their freedom and their human rights.

Viewed from the perspective of a critical tradition in this country, the 1960s appear to have brought all the latent tendencies to the surface. The Civil Rights Movement, alive with its particular traditions of liberation, provided the spark; the war in Vietnam gave a lurid illumination to the system's deficiencies: its incipient violence; its injustices; its racism; its indifference to public opinion and demand. The short-lived effort to reform education and provide compensation for damages done by poverty and discrimination could not halt the radical critique of America's schools. And that many-faceted critique—libertarian, Marxist, romantic, democratic—variously realized the critical potentialities of American pedagogies. Without an Emerson or a Thoreau or a Parker, there would not have been a Free School movement or a "deschooling" movement. Without a Du Bois, there would not have been liberation or storefront schools. Without a social reformist tradition, there would have been no Marxist voices asking (as, for instance, Samuel Bowles and Herbert Gintis did) for a "mass-based organization of working people powerfully articulating a clear alternative to corporate capitalism as the basis for a progressive educational system."[23] Without a Dewey, there would have been little concern for "participatory democracy," for "consensus," for the reconstitution of a public sphere.

Yes, the silence fell at the end of the following decade; privatization increased, along with consumerism and cynicism and the attrition of the public space. We became aware of living in what Europeans called an "administered society";[24] we became conscious of technicism and positivism and of the one-dimensionality Herbert Marcuse described.[25] Popular culture, most particularly as embodied in the media, was recognized (with the help of the critical theorist Theodor Adorno) as a major source of mystification.[26] The schools were recognized as agents of "cultural reproduction," oriented to a differential distribution of knowledge.[27] Numerous restive educational thinkers, seeking new modes of articulating the impacts of ideological control and manipulation, turned towards European neo-Marxist scholarship for clues to a critical pedagogy. In an American tradition, they were concerned for the individual, for the subject, which late Marxism appeared to have ignored; and the humanist dimension of Frankfurt School philosophies held an unexpected appeal. Moreover, what with its concern for critical consciousness and communicative competence, Frankfurt School thinking held echoes of the Enlightenment faith; and, in some profound way, it was recognized.

There is, of course, an important sense in which the Frankfurt School has reappropriated philosophical traditions (Kantian, Hegelian, phenomenological, psychological, psychoanalytical) which are ours as well or which, at least, have fed our intellectual past. But it also seems necessary to hold in mind the fact that European memories are not our memories. The sources of European critical theory are to be found in responses to the destruction of the Workers' Councils after the First World War, the decline of the Weimar Republic, the rise of Stalinism, the spread of fascism, the Holocaust, the corruptions of social democracy. As climactic as any contemporary insight was the realization that reason (viewed as universal in an Enlightenment sense) could be used to justify the application of technical expertise in torture and extermination. Europeans saw a connection between this and the rationalization of society by means of bureaucracy, and in the separating off of moral considerations long viewed as intrinsic to civilized life. The intimations of all this could be seen in European literature for many years: in Dostoevsky's and Kafka's renderings of human beings as insects; in Musil's anticipations of the collapse of European orders; in Camus's pestilence, in Sartre's nausea, in the Dionysian and bestial shapes haunting the structures of the arts. We have had a tragic literature, a critical literature, in the United States. We need only recall Twain, Melville, Crane, Wharton, Hemingway, Fitzgerald. But it has been a literature rendered tragic by a consciousness of a dream betrayed, of a New World corrupted by exploitation and materialism and greed. In background memory, there are images of Jeffersonian agrarianism, of public spheres, of democratic and free-swinging communities. We do not find these in European literature, *nor* in the writings of the critical theorists.

One of the few explicit attempts to articulate aspects of the Western tradition for educators has been the courageous work of Freire, who stands astride both hemispheres. He has been the pioneer of a pedagogy informed by both Marxist and existential-phenomenological thought; his conception of critical reflectiveness has reawakened the themes of a tradition dating back to Plato and forward to the theologies of liberation that have taken hold in oppressed areas of the Western world. His background awareness, however, and that of the largely Catholic peasants with whom he has worked, are not that of most North Americans. It must be granted that his own culture and education transcend his Brazilian origins and make him something of a world citizen when it comes to the life of ideas. Like his European colleagues, however, he reaches back to predecessors other than Jefferson and Emerson and Thoreau and William James and Dewey; his social vision is not that of our particular democracy. This is not intended as criticism, but as a reminder that a critical pedagogy relevant to the United States today must go beyond—calling on different memories, repossessing another history.

We live, after all, in dark times, times with little historical memory of any kind. There are vast dislocations in industrial towns, erosions of trade unions; there is little sign of class consciousness today. Our great cities are burnished on the surfaces, building high technologies, displaying astonishing consumer goods. And on the side streets, in the crevices, in the burnt-out neighborhoods, there are the rootless, the dependent, the sick, the permanently unemployed. There is little sense of agency, even among the brightly successful; there is little capacity to look at things as if they could be otherwise.

Where education is concerned, the discourse widens, and the promises multiply. The official reform reports, ranging from *A Nation at Risk* to the Carnegie Forum's *A Nation Prepared,* call for a restructuring of schools and of teacher education to the end of raising the levels of literacy in accord with the requirements of an economy based on high technology.[28] The mass of students in the schools, including the one third who will be "minorities," are to be enabled to develop "higher order skills" in preparation for "the unexpected, the nonroutine world they will face in the future."[29] The implicit promise is that, if the quality of teachers is improved (and "excellent" teachers rewarded and recognized), the majority of young people will be equipped for meaningful participation in an advanced knowledge-based economy wholly different from the mass-production economy familiar in the past.

On the other hand, there are predictions that we will never enjoy full employment in this country, that few people stand any real chance of securing meaningful work. If the military juggernaut keeps rolling on, draining funds and support from social utilities, daycare centers, arts institutions, schools and universities, we will find ourselves devoid of all those things that might make life healthier, gentler, more inviting and more challenging. At once we are reminded (although not by the authors of the educational reports) of the dread of nuclear destruction (or of Chernobyls, or of Bhopal) that lies below the surface of apparent hope for the future. This dread, whether repressed or confronted, leads numbers of people to a sense of fatalism and futility with respect to interventions in the social world. For others, it leads to a sad and often narcissistic focus on the "now." For still others, it evokes denial and accompanying extravagances: consumerism increases; a desire for heightened sensation, for vicarious violence, grows. And for many millions, it makes peculiarly appealing the talk of salvation broadcast by evangelists and television preachers; it makes seductive the promise of Armageddon.

As young people find it increasingly difficult to project a long-range future, intergenerational continuity becomes problematic. So does the confidence in education as a way of keeping the culture alive, or of initiating newcomers into learning communities, or of providing the means for pursuing a satisfying life. Uncertain whether we can share or constitute a common world, except in its most fabricated and trivialized form, we wonder what the great conversation can now include and whether it is worth keeping alive. Michael Oakeshott spoke eloquently of that conversation, "begun in the primeval forests and extended and made more articulate in the course of centuries." He said it involves passages of argument and inquiry, going on in public and in private, that it is an "unrehearsed intellectual adventure . . ." Education, for him, "is an initiation into the skill and partnership of this conversation," which gives character in the end "to every human activity and utterance."[30] We know now how many thousands of voices have been excluded from that conversation over the years. We know how, with its oppositions and hierarchies, it demeaned. As we listen to the prescriptions raining down for "common learnings" (which may or may not include the traditions of people of color, feminist criticism and literature, Eastern philosophies) and "cultural literacy," we cannot but wonder how those of us in education can renew and expand the conversation, reconstitute what we can call a common world.

Yes, there are insights into humane teaching in the latest reports; but, taking the wide view, we find mystification increasing, along with the speechlessness. We have learned about the diverse ways we Americans interpret our traditions: about those who identify with the old individualism, those who yearn for old communities, those who seek new modes of justice, those who want to lose themselves in a cause.[31] We know something about the persistence of a commitment to freedom, variously defined, and to the idea of equity. At once, we are bound to confront such extremes as a moral majority usurping talk of intimacy and family values, while neoliberals seek out technocratic, depersonalized solutions to quantified problems and speak a cost-benefit language beyond the reach of those still striving for public dialogue.

People have never, despite all that, had such vast amounts of information transmitted to them—not merely about murders and accidents and scandals, but about crucial matters on which public decisions may some day have to be made: nuclear energy, space vehicles, racism, homelessness, life-support systems, chemotherapies, joblessness, terrorism, abused children, fanatics, saints. There are whole domains of information that arouse frustration or pointless outrage. All we need to do is think of the persecution of the sanctuary-movement leaders, of children living in shelters, of the *contras* in Honduras, of adolescent suicides, of overcrowded jails. At the same time, no population has ever been so deliberately entertained, amused, and soothed into avoidance, denial, and neglect. We hear the cacophonous voices of special interest groups; we hear of discrete acts of sacrifice and martyrdom; we seldom hear of intentionally organized collaborative action to repair what is felt to be missing, or known to be wrong.

Complacency and malaise; upward mobility and despair. Sometimes we detect feelings of shame and helplessness perceived as personal failure. To be dependent, to be on welfare, is to be certified as in some manner deviant or irresponsible since good Americans are expected to fend for themselves. Even as oppressed peasants internalize their oppressors' images of them as helpless creatures, so unsuccessful Americans (young or old) internalize the system's description of them as ineffectual. They are unable to live up to the culture's mandate to control their own lives and contribute to the productivity of the whole. Our institutional responses are ordinarily technical (and we are drawn to technical solutions out of benevolence, as well as out of helplessnesss). Yet we know that to think mainly in terms of techniques or cures or remedies is often to render others and the earth itself as objects to be acted upon, treated, controlled, or used. It is to distance what we believe has to be done (efficiently, effectively) from our own existential projects, from our own becoming among other incomplete and questing human beings. It is to repress or deny the pre-reflective, tacit understandings that bind us together in a culture and connect us to our history.

Having said all this, I must ask again what a critical pedagogy might mean for those of us who teach the young at this peculiar and menacing time. Perhaps we might begin by releasing our imaginations and summoning up the traditions of freedom in which most of us were reared. We might try to make audible again the recurrent calls for justice and equality. We might reactivate the resistance to materialism and conformity. We might even try to inform with meaning the desire to educate "all the children" in a legitimately "common" school. Considering the technicism and the illusions of the time, we need to recognize that what we single out as most deficient and oppressive is in part a function of perspectives created by our past. It is a past in which our subjectivities are embedded, whether we are conscious of it or not. We have reached a point when that past must be reinterpreted and reincarnated in the light of what we have learned.

We understand that a mere removal of constraints or a mere relaxation of controls will not ensure the emergence of free and creative human beings. We understand that the freedom we cherish is not an endowment, that it must be achieved through dialectical engagements with the social and economic obstacles we find standing in our way, those we have to learn to name. We understand that a plurality of American voices must be attended to, that a plurality of life-stories must be heeded if a meaningful power is to spring up through a new "binding and promising, combining and covenanting." We understand that the Enlightenment heritage must be repossessed and reinterpreted, so that we can overcome the positivism that awaits on one side, the empty universalism on the other. But we cannot and ought not escape our own history and memories, not if we are to keep alive the awarenesses that ground our identities and connect us to the persons turning for fulfillment to our schools.

We cannot negate the fact of power. But we can undertake a resistance, a reaching out towards becoming *persons* among other persons, for all the talk of human resources, for all the orienting of education to the economy. To engage with our students as persons is to affirm our own incompleteness, our consciousness of spaces still to be explored, desires still to be tapped, possibilities still to be opened and pursued. At once, it is to rediscover the value of care, to reach back to experiences of caring and being cared for (as Nel Noddings writes) as sources of an ethical ideal. It is, Noddings says, an ideal to be nurtured through "dialogue, practice, and confirmation,"[32] processes much akin to those involved in opening a public sphere. We have to find out how to open such spheres, such spaces, where a better state of things can be imagined; because it is only through the projection of a better social order that we can perceive the gaps in what exists and try to transform and repair. I would like to think that this can happen in classrooms, in corridors, in schoolyards, in the streets around.

I would like to think of teachers moving the young into their own interpretations of their lives and their lived worlds, opening wider and wider perspectives as they do so. I would like to see teachers ardent in their efforts to make the range of symbol systems available to the young for the ordering of experience, even as they maintain regard for their vernaculars. I would like to see teachers tapping the spectrum of intelligences, encouraging multiple readings of written texts and readings of the world.

In "the shadow of silent majorities," then, as teachers learning along with those we try to provoke to learn, we may be able to inspire hitherto unheard voices. We may be able to empower people to rediscover their own memories and articulate them in the presence of others, whose space they can share. Such a project demands the capacity to unveil and disclose. It demands the exercise of imagination, enlivened by works of art, by situations of speaking and making. Perhaps we can at last devise reflective communities in the interstices of colleges and schools. Perhaps we can invent ways of freeing people to feel and express indignation, to break through the opaqueness, to refuse the silences. We need to teach in such a way as to arouse passion now and then; we need a new camaraderie, a new en masse. These are dark and shadowed times, and we need to live them, standing before one another, open to the world.

NOTES

1. Baudrillard, *In the Shadow of Silent Majorities* (New York: Semiotexte, 1983).
2. Jean-Paul Sartre, *Search for a Method* (New York: Knopf, 1968), p. 94.
3. Whitman, *Leaves of Grass* (New York: Aventine Press, 1931), pp. 49–50.
4. Stevens, *Collected Poems* (New York: Knopf, 1963), p. 198.
5. Moore, *Tell Me, Tell Me* (New York: Viking Press, 1966), p. 24.
6. Rukeyser, "Käthe Kollwitz," in *By a Woman Writt,* ed. Joan Goulianos (New York: Bobbs Merrill, 1973), p. 374.
7. Rich, *A Wild Patience Has Taken Me This Far* (New York: Norton, 1981), p. 23.
8. Mill, "On Liberty," in *The Six Great Humanistic Essays* (New York: Washington Square Press, 1963), p. 158.
9. Arendt, *On Revolution* (New York: Viking Press, 1963), pp. 174–175.
10. Horace Mann, "Ninth Annual Report," in *The Republic and the School: Horace Mann on the Education of Free Men,* ed. Lawrence A. Cremin (New York: Teachers College Press, 1957), p. 57.
11. Mark Twain, *The Adventures of Huckleberry Finn* (New York: New American Library, 1959), p. 283.
12. Brownson, "The Laboring Classes," in *Ideology and Power in the Age of Jackson,* ed. Edwin C. Rozwenc (Garden City, N.Y.: Anchor Books, 1964), p. 321.
13. Emerson, "Self-Reliance," in *Emerson on Education,* ed. Howard Mumford Jones (New York: Teachers College Press, 1966), p. 105.
14. Du Bois, *W. E. B. Du Bois: A Reader,* ed. Meyer Weinberg (New York: Harper Torchbooks, 1970), pp. 153–154.
15. Freire, *Pedagogy of the Oppressed* (New York: Continuum, 1970), pp. 27 ff.
16. Jacqueline Jones, "Women Who Were More Than Men: Sex and Status in Freedmen's Teaching," *History of Education Quarterly, 19* (1979), 47–59.
17. Nasaw, *Schooled to Order* (New York: Oxford University Press, 1981).
18. Parker, *Talks on Pedagogics* (New York: Harper, 1894).
19. Dewey, "The School and Society," in *Dewey on Education,* ed. Martin Dworkin (New York: Teachers College Press, 1959), p. 41.
20. Dewey, *The Public and Its Problems* (Athens, Oh.: Swallow Press, 1954).
21. Lawrence A. Cremin, *The Transformation of the School* (New York: Knopf, 1961), pp. 231–232.
22. Jürgen Habermas, *Knowledge and Human Interests* (Boston: Beacon Press, 1972).
23. Bowles and Gintis, *Schooling in Capitalist America* (New York: Basic Books, 1976), p. 266.
24. Marcuse, "Some Social Implications of Modern Technology," in *The Essential Frankfurt School Reader,* ed. Andrew Arato and Eike Gebhardt (New York: Urizen Books, 1978), pp. 138–162.
25. Marcuse, *One-Dimensional Man* (Boston: Beacon Press, 1966).
26. Adorno, "Cultural Criticism and Society," in *Prisms* (London: Neville Spearman, 1961), pp. 31–32 ff.
27. See Pierre Boudieu and Jean-Claude Passeron, *Reproduction* (Beverly Hills, Calif.: Sage, 1977).
28. The National Commission on Excellence in Education, *A Nation at Risk: The Imperative for Educational Reform* (Washington: U.S. Department of Education, 1983); and Carnegie Forum on Education and the Economy, *A Nation Prepared: Teachers for the 21st Century* (New York: Carnegie Forum, 1986).
29. Carnegie Forum, *A Nation Prepared,* p. 25.
30. Oakeshott, *Rationalism in Politics and Other Essays* (London: Methuen, 1962), pp. 198–199.
31. Robert N. Bellah, Richard Madsen, William M. Sullivan, Ann Swidler, and Steve M. Tipton, *Habits of the Heart: Individualism and Commitment in American Life* (Berkeley: University of California Press, 1985).
32. Noddings, *Caring: A Feminine Approach to Ethics and Moral Education* (Berkeley: University of California Press, 1984).

Suggested Readings for Future Study

CRITICAL THEORY AND RELATED THEMES

Adorno, T. (1987). *Negative dialectic.* New York: Continuum.

Ashcroft, B., Griffiths, G., and Tiffin, H. (1995). *Postcolonial studies reader.* New York: Routledge.

Ball, S., ed. (1990). *Foucault and education: Disciplines and knowledge.* New York: Routledge.

Babcock, R. (1986). *Hegemony.* New York: Tavistock.

Best, S., and Kellner, D. (1991). *Postmodern theory: Critical interrogations.* New York: Guilford, 1991.

Bhabha, H. (1994). *The location of culture.* New York: Routledge.

Bourdieu, P., and Passeron, J. (1992). *Reproduction in education, society and culture.* London: Sage.

Buck-Morss, S. (1977). *The origin of negative dialectics: Theodor W. Adorno, Walter Benjamin, and the Frankfurt School.* New York: Free Press.

Cherryholmes, C. (1988). *Power and criticism: Poststructuralist investigations in education.* New York: Teachers College.

Dubiel, H. (1985). *Theory and politics: Studies in the development of critical theory.* Cambridge, Mass.: MIT.

Eagleton, T. (1991). *Ideology: An introduction.* New York: Verso.

Fay, B. (1997). *Critical social science.* New York: Cornell University Press.

Foucault, M. (1980). *Power/knowledge: Selected interviews and other writings.* New York: Pantheon.

Fromm, E. (1941). *Escape from freedom.* New York: Avon.

Held, D. (1980). *Introduction to critical theory: Horkheimer to Habermas.* Berkeley and Los Angeles: University of California Press.

Gray, A., and McGuigan, J. (1993). *Studying culture: An introductory reader.* London: Edward Arnold.

Greene, M. (1988). *The dialectics of freedom.* New York: Teachers College.

Hoare, Q., and Smith, G., eds. (1971). *Selections from the prison notebooks of Antonio Gramsci.* New York: International.

Horkheimer, M. (1972). *Critical theory: Selected essays.* New York: Herder.

Jay, M. (1973). *The dialectical imagination: A history of the Frankfurt School and the Institute of Social Research, 1923–1959.* Boston: Little, Brown.

Jay, M. (1984). *Adorno.* Cambridge: Harvard University Press.

Karabel, J., and Halsey, A. H., eds. (1977). *Power and ideology in education.* New York: Oxford University Press.

Marcuse, H. (1966). *Eros and civilization: A philosophical inquiry into Freud.* Boston: Beacon.

Marcuse, H. (1966). *One dimensional man.* Boston: Beacon.

Marx, K. (1969). *Early writings.* New York: McGraw-Hill.

Rasmussen, D., ed. (1996). *The handbook of critical theory.* Oxford: Blackwell.

Rosado, R. (1993). *Culture and truth: The remaking of social analysis.* Boston: Beacon.

Warren, S. (1984). *The emergence of dialectical theory.* Chicago: University of Chicago Press.

CRITICAL PEDAGOGY AND DEMOCRATIC SCHOOLING

Apple, M. (1993). *Official knowledge: Democratic education in a conservative age.* New York: Routledge.

Araujo Freire, A., and Macedo, D., eds. (1998). *The Paulo Freire reader.* New York: Continuum.

Aronowitz, S., and Giroux, H. (1985). *Education under seige.* South Hadley, Mass.: Bergin & Garvey.

Barbules, N. (1992). *Dialogue in teaching: Theory and practice.* New York: Teachers College.

Darder, A. (1991). *Culture and power in the classroom.* Westport, Conn: Bergin & Garvey.

Darder, A. (2002). *Reinventing Paulo Freire: A pedagogy of love.* Boulder, Colo.: Westview.

Dewey, J. (1916). *Democracy and education.* New York: Free Press.

Forester, J. (1993). *Critical theory, public policy and planning practice: Toward a critical pragmatism.* New York: SUNY Press, 1993.

Freire, P. (1987). *The politics of education: Culture, power and liberation.* South Hadley, Mass.: Bergin & Garvey.

Freire, P. (1993). *Pedagogy of the city.* New York: Continuum.

Freire, P. (1994). *Pedagogy of the oppressed* (anniversary edition). New York: Continuum.

Freire, P. (1997). *Pedagogy of the heart.* New York: Continuum.

Freire, P., and Faundez, A. (1989). *Learning to question: A pedagogy of liberation.* New York: Continuum.

Gadotti, M. (1994). *Reading Paulo Freire: His life and work.* New York: SUNY Press.

Giroux, H. (1981). *Ideology, culture and the process of schooling.* Philadelphia: Temple University Press.

Giroux, H. (1983). *Theory and resistance in education.* South Hadley, Mass.: Bergin & Garvey.

Leistyna, P., Woodrum, A., and Sherblom, S., eds. (1996). *Breaking free. The transformative power of critical pedagogy.* Cambridge, Mass.: Harvard Educational Review.

Livingstone, D., ed. (1987). *Critical pedagogy and cultural power.* South Hadley, Mass.: Bergin & Garvey.

McLaren, P. (1986). *Schooling as ritual performance.* London: Routledge.

McLaren, P. (1989). *Life in schools: An introduction to critical pedagogy and the foundations of education.* New York: Longman.

McLaren, P. (1995). *Critical pedagogy and predatory culture: Oppositional politics in a postmodern era.* New York: Routledge.

McLaren, P., and Giarelli, J. (1995). *Critical theory and educational research.* New York: SUNY Press.

Simon, R. (1992). *Teaching against the grain: A pedagogy of possibility.* New York: Bergin & Garvey.

Shor, I., and Freire, P. (1987). *A pedagogy for liberation.* South Hadley, Mass.: Bergin & Garvey.

Sullivan, E. (1990). *Critical psychology and pedagogy: Interpretation of the personal world.* New York: Bergin & Garvey.

Part 2

SCHOOLING, CLASS, AND THE ECONOMY

INTRODUCTION

This section examines the problematic role of the market on educational policies and analyzes the ways in which the economy shapes life in schools. One of the goals of this section is to encourage students of critical pedagogy to reclaim social class as a central category of analysis in order to better understand the intricacies of the global economy and its role in the perpetuation of social inequalities.

In the first article, "Education Incorporated?" Henry Giroux speaks to the commercialization of public schools and the unrelenting imperative to form the new "democratic" citizen. As defined by a young student quoted in this article, democracy has become "the freedom to buy and consume whatever [one] wish[es] without government restrictions." This distorted notion of democracy has been shaped by the constant intrusions of corporations into the arena of schooling. Giroux eloquently describes how schools, in their effort to raise additional money to support their deprived infrastructures or simply to implement new programs, are forced to participate in the marketplace by renting their public spaces, buses, and cafeterias to big corporations. He clearly exposes how students are systematically trained to become consumers through the selling of candy and other goods to help support their schools and the constant exposure to prepackaged curricula designed by food corporations. Taking into account the marketization of schools, Giroux warns that educators must remain watchful of their democratic ideals, particularly when the school curriculum primarily speaks to the values of the marketplace. Moreover, Giroux encourages teachers to keep Dewey's vision of public education alive by defending one of the last public spaces remaining in the United States today.

Alex Molnar further contributes to this analysis with "What the Market Can't Provide." In this article, he exposes the manner in which effective educational policies—like class-size reduction in Tennessee—have been turned down and ignored because they conflict with the interests of the market. Molnar expresses real concern for the unwillingness of the public to invest in public education programs that can meet the needs of students, if they do not prove profitable to the business sector. Meanwhile, other educational policies such as school vouchers are furiously defended by supporters of big corporations, simply because they believe such programs will minimize expenditures, social costs, economic risks, and increase profit. Molnar's analysis attempts to help the reader understand how our economy has arrived at a place where profit is the priority at all cost, even when achieving it violates the basic economic and social rights of workers.

Moving the analysis of class to the arena of higher education, bell hooks essay, "Confronting Class in the Classroom," examines the different ways in which intellectuals participate in the silencing of working-class voices within the university classroom. Through their conscious or unconscious refusal to address social class in the context of their teaching, professors inadvertently fail to acknowledge the existence of a ruthless economy that is unabashedly legitimized in the daily practices of higher education.

Peter McLaren closes this section with "Revolutionary Pedagogy in Post-Revolutionary Times," a seminal critique of critical pedagogy and its retreat from class during the last decade. McLaren provides a clear discussion regarding the state of critical pedagogy under the new global economic order and expresses his concern for a radical theory of schooling that is unable to provide a systematic explanation of the uncontested impact of a relentless market economy on schools, our identities, and our rights as citizens. McLaren urges critical educators to move beyond postmodern interpretations of subjugation and a limiting politics of identity based solely on race-based explanations, and instead, deal forthrightly with the root of all domination—the lasting and continuous effects of unbridled capitalism.

QUESTIONS FOR REFLECTION AND DIALOGUE

1. In what ways are the interests of the marketplace apparent in schools today? Explain how market interests are manifested through the hidden curricula and why they represent instances of hegemony at work?
2. How does the commercialization of public education impact the development of an equitable social order?
3. Explain how the school reform movement in this country links the realignment of school programs to the interest of the global economy?
4. What is the impact of current trends to privatize social services, including public education? Would you support an initiative to privatize the Pentagon or the National Security Council? Why or why not?

5. How is the issue of class and the marketplace reflected in the course content, research objectives, student population, faculty, and administrative policies of colleges and universities?
6. How would you address and confront issues of social class in higher education?
7. What are the specific suggestions that McLaren offers those working within critical pedagogy to become more responsive to issues related to the political economy and its impact on education?

Education Incorporated?

HENRY A. GIROUX

*School is . . . the ideal time to influence attitudes, build long-term loyalties, intro-
duce new products, test markets, promote sampling and trial usage and—above
all—to generate immediate sales.*

> —Lifetime Learning System (Molnar, 1996a)

One of the most important legacies of public education has been to provide students with the critical capacities, the knowledge, and the values to become active citizens striving to realize a vibrant democratic society.
Within this tradition, Americans have defined schooling as a public good and
a fundamental right (Dewey, 1916; Giroux, 1988). Such a definition rightfully
asserts the primacy of democratic values over corporate culture and commercial
values.

Schools are an important indicator of the well-being of a democratic society. They remind us of the civic values that must be passed on to young people in order for them to think critically; to participate in policy decisions that
affect their lives; and to transform the racial, social, and economic inequities
that close down democratic social relations. Yet as crucial as the role of public
schooling has been in U.S. history, this role is facing an unprecedented attack
from proponents of market ideology who strongly advocate the unparalleled
expansion of corporate culture (Molnar, 1996a; Pecora, 1998: Consumer
Union Education Services, 1998).

PREPARING CITIZENS OR CONSUMERS?

Growing up corporate has become a way of life for youth in the United States.
This is evident as corporate mergers consolidate control of assets and markets,
particularly as such corporations extend their influence over the media and its

management of public opinion. But it is also apparent in the accelerated commercialism in everyday life, including the "commercialization of public schools, the renaming of public streets for commercial sponsors, . . . [and even] restroom advertising" (Wright, 1997, p. 181). Although many observers recognize that market culture exercises a powerful role in shaping identities, it still comes as a shock when an increasing number of young people, when asked to provide a definition for democracy, answer by referring to "the freedom to buy and consume whatever they wish, without government restriction" (Wright, 1997, p. 182).

Growing up corporate suggests that as commercial culture replaces public culture, the language of the market becomes a substitute for the language of democracy. At the same time, commercial culture erodes civil society as the function of schooling shifts from creating a "democracy of citizens [to] a democracy of consumers" (Grace, 1997, p. 315). One consequence is that consumerism appears to be the only kind of citizenship being of offered to children and adults.

Our youth are absorbing the most dangerous aspects of the commercialization of everyday life. Within corporate models of schooling, young people are now subject to the same processes of "corporatization" that have excluded all but the most profitable and most efficient from the economic life of the nation. No longer representing a cornerstone of democracy, schools within an ever-aggressive corporate culture are reduced to new investment opportunities, just as students represent a captive market and new opportunities for profits. And the stakes are high. Education becomes less a force for social improvement than a force for commercial investment. Such education promises a high yield and substantive returns for those young people privileged enough to have the resources and the power to make their choices matter— and it becomes a grave loss for those who lack the resources to participate in this latest growth industry.

CORPORATE MODELS OF SCHOOLING

According to the *Education Industry Directory*, the for-profit education market represents potential revenue of $600 billion for corporate interests (Applebome, 1996). Not only is the corporate takeover of schools rationalized in the name of profits and market efficiency alone, but it is also legitimated through the call for vouchers, privatized choice plans, and excellence. Although this discourse cloaks itself in the democratic principles of freedom, individualism, and consumer rights, it fails to provide the broader historical, social, and political contexts necessary to make such principles meaningful and applicable, particularly with respect to the problems facing public schools. For instance, advocates of privatization and choice have little to say about the relationship between choice and economic power, nor do they provide any context to explain public school failure in recent decades. They ignore factors such as joblessness, poverty, racism, crumbling school structures, and unequal school funding.

Refusing to address the financial inequities that haunt public schools, advocates of the corporate model of schooling maintain ideas and images that reek with the rhetoric of insincerity and the politics of social indifference. Most disturbing about the market approach to schooling is not only that it is bereft of a vocabulary of ethics and values but also that it has the power to override competing value systems. Such systems are not commercial in nature but critical to a just society. Once-cherished educational imperatives that enabled the capacity for democratic participation, social justice, and democratic relations—especially as counter-measures to the limits and excesses of the market—are ignored.

COMMERCIALIZATION IN SCHOOLS

Corporate culture does not reside only in the placement of public schools in the control of corporate contractors. It is also visible in the growing commercialization of school space and curriculums. Strapped for money, many public schools have had to lease out space in their hallways, buses, restrooms, and school cafeterias, transforming such spaces into glittering bill-boards for the highest corporate bidder (Consumer Union Education Services, 1998). School notices, classroom displays, and student artwork have been replaced by advertisements for Coca Cola, Pepsi, Nike, Hollywood films, and a litany of other products. Invaded by candy manufacturers, breakfast cereal makers, sneaker companies, and fast food chains, schools increasingly offer the not-so-subtle message to students that everything is for sale—including student identities, desires, and values.

Seduced by the lure of free equipment and money, schools all too readily make the transition from allowing advertising to offering commercial merchandise in the form of curricular materials designed to build brand loyalty among members of a captive public school audience. Although schools may reap small financial benefits from such transactions, the real profits go to the corporations who spend millions on advertising to reach a youth market of an estimated 43 million schoolchildren "with spending power of over $108 billion per year and the power to influence parental spending" (Sides, 1996, p. 36).

Eager to attract young customers, companies such as General Mills and Campbell Soup provide free classroom materials that blatantly hawk their products. For instance, "General Mills has sent 8,000 teachers a science curriculum about volcanoes entitled 'Gushers: Wonders of the Earth,' which uses the company's fruit Gushers candy" (Shenk, 1995, p. 52). Similarly, the *Washington Post* reported recently that McDonald's gives elementary schools curriculum packages in which students learn how a McDonald's restaurant is run and, in case they miss the point about future jobs, how to apply for employment (Sanchez, 1998).

THE GROWING DISREGARD FOR PUBLIC LIFE

As market culture permeates the social order, it threatens to diminish the tension between market values and democratic values, such as justice; freedom; equality; respect for children; and the rights of citizens as equal, free human beings. Without such values, students are relegated to the role of economic calculating machines, and the growing disregard for public life is left unchecked.

History has been clear about the dangers of unbridled corporate power. Four hundred years of slavery, ongoing through unofficial segregation; the exploitation of child labor; the sanctioning of cruel working conditions in coal mines and sweatshops; and the destruction of the environment have all been fueled by the law of maximizing profits and minimizing costs. This is not to suggest that corporations are the enemy of democracy, but to highlight the centrality of a strong democratic civil society that limits the reach of corporate culture. John Dewey (1916) rightfully argued that democracy requires work, but that work is not synonymous with democracy.

Alex Molnar (1996b) is also right to warn educators that the market does not provide "guidance on matters of justice and fairness that are at the heart of a democratic civil society" (p. 17). The power of corporate culture, when left to its own devices, respects few boundaries and even fewer basic social needs, such as the need for uncontaminated food, decent health care, and safe forms of transportation. This was made clear, for example, in recent revelations about the failure of tobacco companies to reveal evidence about the addictive nature of nicotine. In direct violation of broader health considerations, these corporations effectively promoted the addiction of young smokers to increase sales and profits. Moreover, as multi-national companies increase their control over the circulation of information in the media, little countervailing discourse remains about how these corporations undermine the principles of justice and freedom that should be at the center of our most vital civic institutions. This is particularly true for the public schools, whose function, in part, is to teach the importance of critical dialogue, debate, and decision making in a participatory democracy (Barber, 1995).

EDUCATION FOR DEMOCRATIC LIFE

Educators, families, and community members need to reinvigorate the language, social relations, and politics of schooling. We must analyze how power shapes knowledge, how teaching broader social values provides safeguards against turning citizenship skills into workplace-training skills, and how schooling can help students reconcile the seemingly opposing needs of freedom and solidarity. As educators, we need to examine alternative models of education that challenge the corporatization of public schools. For example, pioneering educators such as Deborah Meier, Ted Sizer, James Comer, the Rethinking Schools Collective, and other groups are working hard to link educational policies and classroom practices to expand the scope of freedom, justice, and democracy.

Education as a moral and political practice always presupposes a preparation for particular forms of social life, a particular vision of community, and a particular version of the future. Americans must address the problems of public schooling in the realms of values and politics, while holding firm to the possibilities of public education in strengthening the practice of active citizenship (Boyte, 1992). Schooling should enable students to involve themselves in the deepest problems of society, to acquire the knowledge, the skills, and the ethical vocabulary necessary for what the philosopher and Czech president Vaclav Havel (1998) calls "the richest possible participation in public life" (p. 45). Havel's comments suggest that educators must defend schools as essential to the life of the nation because schools are one of the few public spaces left where students can learn about and engage in the experience of democracy.

In the face of corporate takeovers, ongoing commercialization of the curriculum, and growing interest in students as consumers rather than as citizens, educators must reassert the crucial importance of public education. At issue is providing students with the opportunity to recognize the dream of a substantive democracy, particularly the idea that as citizens they are "entitled to public services, decent housing, safety, security, support during hard times, and most importantly, some power over decision making" (Kelley, 1997, p. 146). Carol Ascher, Norm Fruchter, and Robert Berne capture the gravity of such a project in their claim that

> the urgency to solve the inequities in schooling is perhaps the most important reason for continuing the struggle to reform public education. For we will not survive as a republic nor move toward a genuine democracy unless we can narrow the gap between the rich and the poor, reduce our racial and ethnic divides, and create a deeper sense of community. (1996, p. 112)

EDUCATORS AS PUBLIC INTELLECTUALS

The corporatization of U.S. education reflects a crisis of vision regarding the meaning of democracy at a time when

> market cultures, market moralities, market mentalities [are] shattering community, eroding civic society, [and] undermining the nurturing system for children. (West, 1994, p. 42)

Yet such a crisis also represents a unique opportunity for educators to connect the purpose of education to the expansion of democratic practices in order to promote economic justice and cultural diversity as a matter of politics, power, and pedagogy. As educators, it is important to confront the march of corporate power by resurrecting a noble tradition, extending from Horace Mann to Martin Luther King Jr., in which education is affirmed as a political process that encourages people to identify themselves as more than consumers, and democracy as more than a spectacle of market culture.

But more is needed than defending public education as central to nourishing the proper balance between democratic public spheres and commercial power. Given the current assault on educators at all levels of schooling, educators must also struggle against the ongoing trend to reduce teachers to the role of technicians who simply implement prepackaged curriculums and standardized tests as part of the efficiency-based relations of market democracy and consumer pedagogy.

Democratic citizenship needs teachers who have the power and autonomy to function as intellectuals working under conditions that give them the time to produce curriculums, engage in dialogues with students, use the resources of surrounding communities, and participate in the organizational decisions that affect their work. One precondition for a vibrant democracy is fostering schools that are responsive to the teachers, students, and communities that they serve. In short, I want to argue that teachers should be defended as public intellectuals who provide an indispensable service to the nation.

Such an appeal cannot be made merely in the name of professionalism, but in terms of the civic duty that educators provide. Educators who work in our nation's schools represent the conscience of a society because they shape the conditions under which future generations learn about themselves and about their relations to others and to the world. The practice of teaching is also by its very nature moral and political, rather than simply technical. At best, such teaching engages students in the ethical and political dilemmas that animate our social landscape.

RENEWING THE DEMOCRATIC MISSION OF EDUCATION

In the face of the growing corporatization of schools, educators should also organize to challenge commodified forms of learning in the public schools. This suggests producing and distributing resources that educate teachers and students to the dangers of a corporate ethos that treats schools as extensions of the marketplace and students as potential consumers. In addition to raising critical questions about advertising, educators might also consider addressing the long-standing tension between corporate culture and noncommercial values in order to contest the growing tendency to subordinate democratic values to market values. At the level of policy, public schools should ban advertising, merchandising, and commercial interests. And educators should establish a bill of rights identifying and outlining the range of noncommercial relations that can be used to mediate between the public schools and the business world.

If the forces of corporate culture are to be challenged, educators must enlist the help of diverse communities; local, state, and federal governments; and other political forces to ensure that public schools are adequately funded so that they will not have to rely on "corporate sponsorship and advertising revenues" (Consumer Union Education Services, 1998, p. 41).

How public schools educate youth for the future will determine the meaning and substance of democracy itself. Such a responsibility necessitates prioritizing democratic community, citizen rights, and the public good over market relations, narrow consumer demands, and corporate interests. Although such a challenge will be difficult in the coming era, educators must reclaim public schools as a public rather than a private good and view such a task as part of the struggle for democracy itself.

REFERENCES

Applebome, P. (1996, January 31). "Lure of the education market remains strong for business." *The New York Times,* pp. A1, A15.

Ascher, C., Fruchter, N., and Berne, R. (1996). *Hard lessons: Public schools and privatization.* New York: The Twentieth Century Fund Press.

Barber, B. (1995). "The making of McWorld." *New Perspectives Quarterly 12*(4), 13–17.

Boyte, H. (1992, Fall). "Citizenship education and the public world." *The Civic Arts Review,* 4–9.

Consumer Union Education Services. (1998). *Captive kids: A report on commercial pressures on kids at school.* Yonkers, N.Y.: Author.

Dewey, J. (1916). *Democracy and education.* New York: Free Press.

Giroux, H. (1988). *Schooling and the struggle for public life.* Minneapolis, Minn.: University of Minnesota Press.

Grace, G. (1997). "Politics, markets, and democratic schools: On the transformation of school leadership." In A. H. Halsey, H. Lauder, P. Brown, and A. S. Wells (eds.), *Education: Culture, economy, society* (pp. 311–318). New York: Oxford University Press.

Havel, V. (1998, June 2). "The state of the republic." *The New York Review of Books,* 42–46.

Kelley, R. (1997). *Yo'mama's disfunktional: Fighting the culture wars in urban America.* Boston: Beacon Press.

Molnar, A. (1996a). *Giving kids the business: The commercialization of America's schools.* Boulder, Colo.: Westview.

Molnar, A. (1996b). "School reform: Will markets or democracy prevail?" In Rethinking Schools (ed.), *Selling out our schools: Vouchers, markets, and the future of public education* (p. 17). Milwaukee, Wis.: Author.

Pecora, N. (1998). *The business of children's entertainment.* New York: Guilford.

Sanchez, R. (1998, March 2). "The billboarding of America's schools." *Washington Post National Weekly Edition,* p. 29.

Shenk, D. (1995, September). "The pedagogy of pasta source." *Harper's Magazine,* 55–53.

Sides, P. (1996). "Teaching students to be consumers." In Rethinking Schools (ed.), *Selling out our schools: Vouchers, markets, and the future of public education* (p. 36). Milwaukee, Wis.: Author.

West, C. (1994). "America's three-fold crisis." *Tikkun 9*(2), 41–44.

Wright, R. G. (1997). *Selling words: Free speech in a commercial culture.* New York: New York University Press.

What the Market Can't Provide

ALEX MOLNAR

Lamar Alexander might be called many things. But no one would ever fault his political instincts or accuse him of a lack of ambition. Alexander served two terms as governor of Tennessee, put in a stint as president of the University of Tennessee, became President George Bush's secretary of education, and then spent much of the mid-1990s in a failed effort to win the 1996 Republican presidential nomination.

Education reform is an important part of Alexander's political persona. His views on education and social policy reflect an emerging consensus between neoconservative Republicans and so-called New Democrats. He is a tireless campaigner for the "systemic" restructuring of American public education. As secretary of education, he pushed the administration's "break-the-mold" school reform initiative to create a model innovative school in each congressional district. He also talked up the New American Schools Development Corporation set up at the urging of the Bush administration to channel corporate money to school reform projects. Alexander loves private school vouchers, charter schools, and for-profit management of public schools. And as an early investor in Whittle Communications, he made a lot of money from the selling of children to advertisers.

Despite Alexander's interest in school reform, there is a successful educational initiative from his past that he does not talk about these days, a reform that holds a greater potential for improving public school performance than virtually all the ideas he now supports. How surprising it is that he has been unwilling to trumpet his accomplishment.

When Alexander entered his second term as governor of Tennessee, education was at the top of his agenda. At the same time, influential leaders in state education were intrigued by what appeared to be positive results from a statewide effort in Indiana to reduce class size. Tennessee legislators were aware, however, that years of research on class size had produced inconclusive and sometimes contradictory results. As a result, they did not want to mandate reducing class size unless they had proof that smaller classes would mean greater student achievement.

A REFORM THAT WORKS

The legislature hit upon the idea of commissioning a statewide study focusing on a specific question: What is the effect of smaller classes on student achievement and development in the early primary grades (K–3)? After some high-powered political wheeling and dealing, legislation funding the Tennessee Student Teacher Achievement Ratio (STAR) study was signed into law by Alexander in 1985.

From 1985 to 1989, researchers followed a group of more than 7,000 children attending 79 schools in 42 school districts throughout Tennessee, from kindergarten through third grade. The schools participating were in rural, urban, suburban, and innercity locations. In each school, children and teachers in the study were randomly assigned to either a small class (15 students), a regular class (24 students), or a regular class (24 students) with a teacher and a teacher's aide.

All three types of classes were used in every participating school, and all schools followed their normal practices in every other way. Results were measured on both standardized and criterion-referenced tests. A member of the research team was present during the administration of all tests to ensure that the testing situations were standard.

The study produced some remarkably clear-cut results. The researchers found, for each of the four years of the study, that students in the small classes scored significantly higher than students in the regular classes in the subjects tested—math and reading. In educational terms, the students in smaller classes were about two to six months ahead of their peers in larger classes.[1] Of particular significance for urban schools, children living in poverty and African American children (especially males) made the greatest academic gains as a result of being in smaller classes.[2] Smaller classes also seemed to prevent a gap in the achievement levels of minority and white children.[3]

The children who participated in the STAR study are still being followed by researchers in Tennessee under a follow-up project called the Lasting Benefits Study. Students involved in the original STAR study are now in high school. The latest available analysis of their educational performance (as of eighth grade) showed that the achievement advantage enjoyed by students who attended smaller K–3 classes narrowed somewhat in grades 4 and 5. However, in grade 6, students who had been in small classes once again began to widen the gap between their achievement and that of other students.[4] Besides performing better academically, students who were enrolled in smaller classes were more likely to participate in extracurricular activities and were more involved in their own education (i.e., they were taking a more active role in the class-room) than students who were in larger classes.[5]

In 1995, the American Academy of Arts and Sciences called the Tennessee STAR study "one of the great experiments in education in United States history" because of its scope, the rigor of its research design, and the significance of its findings.[6] Although the study was not initiated by Alexander, he was directly involved and had signed the related legislation. On the surface, it would seem odd that he has not sought to capitalize on its proven success. Instead, he has busied himself plugging market-oriented reforms such as private school vouchers and charter schools that have weak, if any, research support. He has even enthusiastically trumpeted for-profit failures like Education Alternatives, Inc., as successes.

There has to be an explanation for why a politician who has hitched his star to education reform would avoid taking credit for what has been widely hailed as one of the greatest achievements in the field. The most logical explanation is that reducing class size would demand a substantial investment in the public schools. It is a reform that reflects confidence that schools can be improved instead of dismantled. As Alexander no doubt knows, standing behind his initiative for smaller classes just because it works at a time when increasing the investment in education has been declared politically incorrect would make him a pariah among his market-oriented compatriots.

Reducing class size costs money—for more teachers and more space. The prevailing wisdom is that education reform can be accomplished with no additional funds. Reducing class size would represent an educational commitment to providing every child the right to learn in the best possible setting—in other words, establishing an entitlement or right to be taught in a small class.

The claim among many of those who call themselves education reformers these days is that no one knows what the most effective learning environment for children may be, so they propose to "let a thousand flowers bloom." That's why they advocate the unregulated flow of public money into all sorts of market-based experiments and innovations. If the secret ever got out that plain old public schools with smaller classes might be the best investment of all, the visionaries-for-hire and high-tech innovators would be out of work.

So, mum was the word during Alexander's campaign for the Republican presidential nomination; no mention was made of the fact that he'd actually played a leading role in commissioning "one of the great experiments in education in United States history." Political expedience and alliances required that he instead promote much less substantive but more market-oriented school reforms.

THE HIDDEN AGENDA

Despite the educational rhetoric, a major motive behind private school voucher plans, for-profit management of public schools, and, to some extent, charter schools is to fend off the traditional role of the public schools in help-ing to redistribute power and economic opportunity. Some citizens are already beginning to understand just how little these reforms have to do with edu-cation. It's true that some polls show disaffection with the performance of the public schools and support for choice. But when people are asked about specifics, it is clear they do not support turning the schools over to some unreg-ulated market. They want schools to have certified teachers, to publish test scores, to meet state academic, fiscal, and safety requirements—and they don't want voucher schools taking money out of the public school system.[7]

The prominence of market-oriented school reforms doesn't reflect the pop-ular will so much as the ascendance of economic efficiency as the *ne plus ultra* of political and social decision making. These reforms mark a radical attempt to destroy the social values built into public institutions such as schools, not an effort to improve the system. The destructive logic that drives them would put American society and culture in the service of the market rather than the other way around. Communities that have already felt the impact of the "cre-ative destruction" of the market on jobs and families are now being invited to let the market work its wonders on their schools. The characteristics of the state of grace to be achieved when that process has drawn to its logical conclusion are left eerily undescribed.

Although there are mighty attempts to obscure it, the argument that no more money can be spent on schools is, at its root, really an argument that no more money can be spent on some groups of children. It is an attempt to replace the idea that all children have an equal claim on the educational resources of the community with the idea that some children are entitled to a better education because their parents can afford to pay for it. Some voucher advocates already are arguing that parents should be free to "supplement" the amount of money provided by tax dollars as proof of their commitment to their child's school.[8]

Market-oriented school reforms are similar to the current crop of so-called welfare reforms. The fight is not fundamentally about the absolute amount of money spent. Rather, it is a struggle over the relative division of wealth in our society. Neoconservatives who favor market-oriented education reforms reject the idea that the wealth of the United States will have to be apportioned much more equitably if poor and working-class children are to attend schools that are not falling down around them, as well as to have decent homes, adequate clothing, proper nutrition, and health care.

The evidence, unlike the power, is not on the neoconservative side. After fifteen years of market-oriented government policymaking, the United States can claim the dubious distinction of having the widest disparity in incomes in the industrial world.[9] No other industrial country spends its K–12 education resources so unequally. Poor children in the United States have the least amount of money spent on them; affluent children have the most.[10] Market enthusiasts have only one solution to that gap: more competition—which the rich have been winning and working-class Americans losing.

Market-oriented school reform proposals are part of a general unwillingness to directly confront the profound economic inequality in the United States and its social implications. The need to redistribute wealth is obscured by glib arguments: If bureaucracies were leaner and teachers' unions weaker, a golden age of student learning would emerge. If money were spent more wisely, there would be more than enough to provide a good education for every child. If parents could choose schools for their children, then good schools would flourish and bad ones would fail, resulting in the continuous creation of ever higher academic standards. If corporations could make a profit by either running the schools or running commercials in them, there would be no need for increased public tax dollars. Any suggestion that all too many public schools are starved for cash instead of awash in tax dollars sends neoconservative education reformers and their allies in the pundit class screaming onto op-ed pages and into radio microphones.

The market-loving reformers that populate organizations like the conservative American Legislative Exchange Council (ALEC) realize that increasing social spending on education would redistribute wealth downward. That's why ALEC issues report after report claiming to show that increased spending on education wouldn't do any good. Echoing the cataclysmic language of the Social Security "reform" debate, ALEC published a piece entitled "Projections for Education Spending Paint a Grim Picture of the Future."[11] The grim picture is that providing public education will require spending more money as more children continue to enter the K–12 system over the next decade.

ALEC attempts to steer the reform debate away from the forest (equal educational resources for all children) to focus on the trees (individual "failed" or "successful" schools). However, there is no reason why it shouldn't be possible to consider both issues simultaneously. What do we know about successful educational practices, and how do we ensure that they are used as widely as possible? How do we go about making sure that *all* children have equal resources devoted to providing them with the highest quality education? Unfortunately, the current vogue is to pretend theoretical platitudes about the market will lead to successful practices that will make an equitable division of resources unnecessary.

THE EXPERIENCE WITH PRIVATIZATION

Market-oriented thinking has produced an international privatization boom. By the end of the 1980s, sales of state enterprises had exceeded $185 billion.[12] As of 1992, about 6,800 state-owned industries had been privatized in more than 80 countries—many of them in the old Eastern European Communist bloc and in the developing world.[13] The economic and social costs of privatization can be enormous. The saga of the Consolidated Rail Corporation (Conrail) in the United States illustrates how expensive the simplistic "public bad–private good" logic of free-market zealots can be. In the mid-1970s, the privately owned freight rail lines serving most of the eastern seaboard were on the verge of financial collapse. For years, Penn Central and the five other private freight lines that provided the bulk of the East Coast's hauling capacity had invested their profits in everything except keeping their equipment modernized and their roadbeds in good repair. In 1979, the federal government, unwilling to allow the freight rail system to collapse because of the widespread economic consequences that would have resulted, bought the operation. Over the next six years, the government invested $7 billion taxpayer dollars in Conrail.[14]

As a result of the government "throwing money" at the problem, Conrail was turning a profit by 1981. A practical person would have cheered and smiled as the government began to recoup its taxpayer-financed investment. The free-market policymakers in the Reagan administration, however, took the newly won profitability of Conrail as the signal to sell it back to private investors so that they, rather than taxpayers, could reap the benefits of the public's investment. In 1987, Conrail was privatized and sold off on the stock market for $1.65 billion[15]—a taxpayer subsidy of the "free" market of $5.4 billion.

In Great Britain, the Thatcher government sold off the state-owned power industry in 1988. The new privately owned regional distribution companies engaged in a costly race to build their own generating capacity and to convert from coal to gas power.[16] As a result, the British coal-mining industry, which had supplied the national power company, collapsed, throwing thousands of miners out of work and turning coal-mining towns into economic disaster areas. The costs—to individuals, society, and the national economy—have been enormous. The British government now has to provide for the social welfare of families that once were capable of providing for themselves. Meanwhile, in Argentina, where the economy is booming, the unemployment rate has risen sharply. That is, at least in part, the result of the widespread privatization program undertaken by the Argentinean government.[17]

In the United States, the divergence between the performance of the economy and the well-being of most workers is becoming increasingly difficult to conceal as the global market dictates the fate of America's workers. Over a decade of market-oriented social policy has created a bumper crop of billionaires at one end of the economic spectrum and wage stagnation, unemployment, and economic insecurity at the other end. Only people earning more than $80,000 a year have seen their incomes keep ahead of inflation.[18] By 1995, corporate CEOs were being paid 100 times more than the average worker, creating what one analyst called "an incredibly privileged class of people."[19]

THE HIGH COST OF THE FREE MARKET

Edward Luttwak, a senior fellow at the Center for Strategic and International Studies, argues that Americans are paying dearly for ignoring the social perspective in their political and economic decision making. He has noted the difference in how Japan and the United States measure costs. In Japan, gasoline is very expensive by American standards. The government fixes fuel prices and prohibits self-service pumps, so Japanese gas stations compete for customers by providing high levels of service. In the United States, free-market economists brag that our self-service gas stations offer consumers much "cheaper" gas than in Japan.

In Luttwak's view, however, America's "cheap" gas carries a very high price tag. Although we don't pay dearly at the gas pump, we pay a price because of all the men and women who cannot find jobs servicing cars at gas stations. We get cheap gas and high-octane social problems. Our insurance rates are higher because of vandalism and thefts, and our taxes are higher because of court and prison costs. (California spends more money on its prison system than on its universities.[20]) Of course, that's just the dollars and cents of it. The social costs also are much higher in terms of the disruptions to family and community life caused by widespread unemployment and fear of crime. In Luttwak's view, the market that cuts prices by eliminating service and jobs does not provide such a bargain after all.[21]

Most Americans don't see what the "free" market costs them because they are encouraged to consider, for example, only the nominal cost of gasoline at the pump. However, they experience the consequences of such shortsighted market logic in their community when a neighbor becomes the latest victim of corporate downsizing or their local business district disappears because a Wal-Mart has opened just outside town.

Market-oriented education reforms such as private school vouchers, for-profit schools, and charter schools bring the same costly logic to the job of educating our young. They threaten to deliver the educational equivalent of "cheap" gas by creating a structural framework to separate the interests of the educational haves from those of the educational have-nots.

THE NEW SEPARATISM

The separation is similar to that of the approximately 900 "business improvement districts" established throughout the United States. Such districts are quasi-governmental entities that tax property owners within district boundaries for the provision of special services. Run by governing boards that are frequently weighted in favor of big property owners, these districts hark back to the eighteenth century when rights were attached to the ownership of property. Improvement districts effectively allow wealthy neighborhoods to provide for themselves while reducing their interest in addressing the needs of the broader community.[22] To be sure, poor neighborhoods have the formal right to form "improvement districts," but with little property value to tax, such districts can offer little hope of true improvement.

The separation of the destinies of the haves from that of the have-nots is becoming more obvious as market-driven educational reform continues to spread. In Wisconsin, local communities faced with a chronic shortage of tax revenue are now forming their own education foundations to raise and distribute private money to their schools.[23] Obviously, as in the case of "business improvement districts," the wealthiest communities have the most resources to draw upon for such supplemental benefits.

In Michigan, the State Board of Education adopted a secessionist reform in August 1995, labeled "autonomous" districts. These new districts could be created out of existing school districts by a vote of the local school board, the electors of the district, or the electors of a school's attendance area.[24] Michigan governor John Engler announced his support for the idea.

Autonomous district legislation would almost certainly provide a legal mechanism for wealthy neighborhoods to secede from less affluent neighborhoods in the same school district. It would also facilitate the establishment of racially homogeneous districts within racially diverse communities and, as a result, create the educational equivalent of private gated communities—except the schools would be paid for by tax dollars.

If one or more wealthy attendance areas of a large school system formed autonomous districts, any remaining affluent neighborhoods would be under increasing financial pressure to do the same. As the number of affluent neighborhoods in a school district decreased, the financial burden on those remaining would necessarily intensify. The financial incentive for wealthy attendance areas to withdraw would make it harder and harder for them to remain part of the larger district even if they wished to do so.

Of course, poor neighborhoods could form autonomous districts just as they can form business improvement districts. However, the nominal right to do so would provide cold comfort. Autonomous districts in poor neighborhoods would consist of impoverished schools cut off from access to the resources of more affluent neighborhoods. They would be in worse financial shape than they were before. Although the Michigan autonomous district plan did not muster enough legislative support to pass in 1995, however, the proposal is expected to resurface.

Perversely, reforms such as the Michigan autonomous district proposal are often promoted as ways of "empowering" local communities. They do indeed empower wealthy communities to cut themselves off from any responsibility for poorer ones. Poor communities are merely empowered to struggle with their poverty alone. If there is a continued proliferation of plans that allow the winners in the global market to legally dissolve their social and political connections with the losers, the civic cost will be very high.

Paul Starr, a Princeton University sociology professor, argues that one of the main drawbacks of private school voucher plans is that they "could well drain much of the energy and life from local government" because for many people, their first taste of civic participation involves the education of their children. "Remove education to the marketplace," Starr says, "and the tendencies toward political uninvolvement, evident from declining voter participation, are only likely to be intensified."[25]

Proposals such as autonomous districts threaten to carry public education back to the dark days following *Brown* v. *The Board of Education* when "freedom of choice" plans sprang up all over the South in an attempt to avoid integration. Equally important, they are another way in which the inequality and self-interest of market relationships are spreading to civic culture and public policy. Instead of the government structuring the marketplace to ensure the general welfare, the market is allowed to reshape governmental institutions to serve special interests.

A NATURAL SELF-INTEREST

AT&T ushered in 1996 with the announcement that it was putting 40,000 more workers on the street. The move is consistent with its corporate strategy to remain competitive in global markets. The stock market loved it, and stockholders may reap considerable financial benefits. However, the social costs in communities across the United States will be enormous.[26]

Corporate leaders, no matter how enlightened, are not in a position to address such social costs. Their interests are, by definition, much narrower. It is literally not in their job description to clean up the mess their decisions leave behind for the rest of society. Only governmental action can structure the boundaries for business activities to make sure corporations play by rules that don't tear civil society apart. If the market model is adopted in public education and other institutions of civil governance, there will be few practical ways left to promote the general welfare. Individuals will be, as they increasingly are already, left to the tender mercies of the global market.

When Governor William Weld of Massachusetts asked President Clinton to declare his state's fishing industry a natural disaster in March 1995,[27] he also was announcing the inability of an unregulated market to promote the common good. The Massachusetts fishing industry was failing not because of any "natural" disaster but because of chronic overfishing. In a self-destructive pursuit of profits, fishing boat operators were taking ever smaller fish in ever bigger catches to survive economically. Members of the fishing fleet, each pursuing his or her own economic survival, were incapable of halting the devastating race to the economic bottom. Recent scientific data show that the Georges Bank off Cape Cod, once one of the most productive fishing grounds in the world, may have to be closed to commercial fishing entirely for several years in order to replenish stocks of fish depleted primarily by overfishing.[28] It is a situation that even the most competent fishing operation can now do nothing to overcome.

The market left to itself inflicted a wound that scarred not just the Massachusetts economy but also the fabric of the state's social and cultural life. As one expert on New England fishing said: "If you no longer have a reason to go to sea, you are losing more than your economy, you are losing your character, you are losing your soul."[29]

The process that destroyed the Massachusetts fishing fleet has some of the characteristics of what economists Robert Frank of Cornell and Philip Cook of Duke call a "winner-take-all" market, that is, a market in which competition is both economically wasteful and socially destructive. Frank and Cook argue that it is much wiser to limit the rewards in "winner-take-all" markets and redistribute the surplus to others who lack either the skill or talent to enter the competition. In their view, this is not only more efficient, it is also more just.[30] In addition, it is more likely to promote social stability and long-term well-being.

Edward Luttwak sees another harmful consequence of allowing the market to structure civic life. He believes that "turbo-charged" capitalism is largely responsible for the growing climate of intolerance in contemporary American life. In his judgment, the global market has made the majority of Americans economically insecure. However, this majority "does not realize that the economy too can be subject to the will of the majority (it believes in Invisible Hands, in the unchallengeable sovereignty of the market, and in the primacy of economic efficiency), so it vents its anger and resentment by punishing, restricting, and prohibiting everything it can."[31]

Not surprisingly, this majority is particularly susceptible to the kind of hectoring, punishing approach to school reform that is suggested by the Center for Education Reform's Jeanne Allen: "The 'Nation-at-risk' report was a wake-up call that change within the system would not work unless you start holding kids accountable, holding schools accountable, holding educators accountable and putting consequences there for people who don't succeed."[32]

Allen doesn't say exactly what students, teachers, and schools should be accountable for or how they should be punished if they fail to meet her demands. And she does not reveal any understanding that, to be fair, the performance standards on which people are judged need to be clear and uniform— what the private sector calls competing on a level playing field.

On the contrary, critics like Allen deny that the educational terrain has any significance at all. References to inequality in the lives of children or in the resources of the schools they attend are brushed aside as excuses for a status quo that is not performing up to par. Allen and others like her seem intent on punishing people for failing without regard for the actual circumstances in which these people may find themselves. The rhetoric of punishment in the debate over school reform, as Luttwak's analysis suggests, finds a large audience among people who are themselves on shaky economic ground and who see few positive options for improving their own situations.

THE DETERIORATING PHYSICAL AND ECONOMIC INFRASTRUCTURE

In 1991, Jonathan Kozol documented the physical degradation of the schools poor children in America attend in *Savage Inequalities*.[33] In February 1995, the

New York Times decried a New York City school system in which a second-grade class was taught in a stairwell, science classes were held in hallways, and one out of eleven children was without a desk.[34] The problems are not limited to New York. In December 1995, the General Accounting Office estimated that the nation's schools needed $112 billion to repair or rebuild them. The report detailed crumbling buildings and outdated technology at schools throughout the country.[35]

These circumstances cannot help but affect the ability of teachers to teach and children to learn effectively. They are not the result of student, teacher, or school failures. Threatening students and teachers with "consequences" will not alter these conditions. Unfortunately, rather than respond to the obvious need, school critics look for scapegoats and promote the nebulous magic of market forces while denying the need for anything so practical as money.

At a time when more and more people are in need of help to strengthen and stabilize their families, their schools, and their neighborhoods, the very idea of the government providing a framework of assistance is under attack. Instead, a bad case of nostalgia for the "good old days" of Victorian England and its alleged virtues seems to have broken out among conservative politicians, policymakers, and intellectuals.[36] Few seem willing to acknowledge that corporate decisions made in the name of economic efficiency and competitiveness are making it harder and harder for families to even survive, let alone solve the problems of their communities through grit and determination. Instead, conservative columnists such as Cal Thomas glibly mouth platitudes about "values." According to Thomas: "In the main, poverty is not caused by a lack of money. Poverty is caused by a lack of values."[37]

Actually, U.S. poverty is largely caused by economic and monetary policy. The policy of the Federal Reserve Board is to make sure that a certain percentage of Americans remain out of work to keep the economy from "overheating" and creating unacceptably high levels of inflation. Any sign that unemployment has dipped "too low" gives the financial markets the jitters, and the Federal Reserve Board notches up interest rates to cool things down (i.e., throw people out of work). As *New York Times* columnist Russell Baker has observed, paupers and welfare are essential to contemporary American capitalism.[38]

If, indeed, values cause poverty, then surely they are the values held by the occupants of corporate boardrooms, congressional offices, the White House, and Wall Street financial institutions. Laying off workers has become one of the major strategies used by profitable corporations to boost the bottom line. When Chemical Bank and Chase Manhattan Bank merged, news that their combined workforce would be reduced by 12,000 people (16 percent) sent their stock value up 11 percent. In other words, each fired worker increased the stock value of the two banks by about $216,000. One tongue-in-check commentator noted that if the banks had fired all their employees, they could have increased their share value another 53 percent.[39] Just as the best poem may be a blank page, perhaps the most profitable business of the future will have no employees at all.

The policies of the Federal Reserve and the U.S. government are no more "natural" than the "natural" disaster that overtook the Massachusetts fishing industry. They are the created disasters of government policies that serve the market instead of people. Americans are now being urged to place the education of their children—their entire futures, really—into the uncaring hands of the market.

Because market values so often define the boundaries of acceptable debate over public issues, alternatives that corporate America doesn't want to talk about are frequently ignored. For example, even when there is a sound economic reason to worry about inflationary economic "overheating," slowing the economy by raising interest rates is not the only possible response. As economist Robert Heilbroner has suggested, another way to accomplish the same result is to raise taxes. People will still lose their jobs when the economy slows, but the government will have the resources to soften the impact by spending the money on those who need help. An "anti-inflation" tax is, in Heilbroner's view, more consistent with democratic values than raising interest rates because the tax spreads the burden of fighting inflation broadly throughout the population rather than allowing a few to profit while many suffer.[40]

Heilbroner sees the market within the framework of a value-laden "political economy" that does not operate according to the dictates of objective "natural" laws. Since he doesn't see God's hand but rather human decisions at work in the market, Heilbroner is able to imagine ways of promoting the general welfare by making explicit political decisions to control the economy. That position is roundly rejected by the free-market zealots currently working their will in Washington and statehouses across the country.

As long as the market is allowed to shape American public life, schools will be asked to educate children living in poverty with fewer and fewer resources. Data released in 1995 in the Luxembourg Income Study, the most comprehensive evaluation available of the distribution of the wealth in eighteen industrial nations, found that U.S. children suffered higher levels of poverty than children in any of the other countries except Israel and Ireland. And in no other country was the gap between the most affluent households with children and the poorest households with children as wide as in the United States.[41]

Despite all the talk in the United States about welfare payments perpetuating poverty, somehow the governments of Western European countries are able to reduce the level of childhood poverty dramatically through social welfare programs. In 1991 in Great Britain, the childhood poverty rate was reduced from 27.9 percent to 8.4 percent after tax and transfer (social welfare) adjustments. In France, it was reduced from 21.2 percent to 4.6 percent; in West Germany, from 8.4 percent to 2.8 percent; and in Canada, from

15.7 percent to 9.3 percent. In the United States, on the other hand, the childhood poverty rate started at 22.3 percent and, after taking taxes and all welfare government programs into account, was reduced only slightly to 20.4 percent.[42]

THE REAL BOTTOM LINE

Any number of education reforms would help not only the children behind the statistics on poverty but also children as a whole: universal child care available on demand, comprehensive early childhood education programs for every child, small classes taught in small schools close to home for elementary-age children, learning opportunities in a variety of settings for older children, and year-round education and free access to training and education throughout life, just for starters.

Many of these reforms, plus the diverse array of innovative ideas about school structure and educational content, are already being tried in individual school districts around the country. Some will, no doubt, improve student achievement. However, no isolated success will change the grim statistics on childhood poverty. And no single success will reverse the trend toward increasing economic inequality in American society. Market-oriented school reforms provide a simple unifying idea; however, they will never improve the distribution of educational resources. Markets, left to themselves, concentrate wealth; they don't apportion it in the most socially desirable way.

Equitable school reform can succeed only as part of a more general set of economic and social reforms that equalize opportunity and distribute the wealth in American society more broadly. Market values reside entirely in the buying and selling of *things*. Corporate school reformers may be faulted for making false claims for private school vouchers or charter schools as a result of blind faith, shallow analysis, or deliberate attempts to mislead. Certainly, someone should blow the whistle on the high-tech Music Men who promise River City High a computer in every pot and gleaming Tomorrowland space needles of learning as far as the eye can see—and then waltz out of town after diverting time, attention, and resources away from the task of improving the quality of education for all children.

The basic skills and the common body of knowledge we believe every child should have cannot be allowed to succumb to a cacophony of commercials and blatant corporate and political propaganda. Unfortunately, when the market perverts educational values, it is only doing what markets are supposed to do—providing opportunities for self-interested individuals to profit.

The market can offer no guidance on matters of justice and fairness that are at the heart of democratic civil society and that *should* be at the heart of its schools and other institutions. Left to its own devices, the market is as utterly incapable of making high-quality schools available to every child, regardless of economic circumstances, as it is of providing a job for every American who needs one.

Since the market is concerned with buying and selling, it cannot represent the interests of children. Turning children over to the market assures that they will be treated as an expense to be reduced or a resource to be harvested. In the process, some children and their families will necessarily be considered more valuable than others. For the market to produce winners, there always have to be losers.

Over time, market values have eroded and debased the humane values of democratic civil society. Listen closely to the language that already fills discussions about school reform. It is the language of commerce applied to human relationships. Children are defined as "future customers," "future workers," and "future taxpayers." There is little talk of the value of children in their own right—right now. There is lots of talk about "tough love" but little mention of any other kind of love. Costs are put in terms of "the bottom line," not what justice demands. When the logic of the market is allowed to dominate society, relationships are inevitably turned into commodities to be bought and sold. And every person can be assigned a material value, either great or small. The antithesis is the democratic ideal that all people are created equal.

The hallmark of America's advanced market economy is not universal well-being. It is universal advertising. The illusion of everything from happiness to fighting hunger to health care to political leadership is substituted for the real thing. The market leads toward a virtual world in which "P.R. armies have forged a new world of pseudo-events, video press releases, informercials, letter writing campaigns, manufactured celebrities . . . all of which has made us disoriented and suspicious."[43]

In the United States, every available surface, from shopping carts to buses to computer Web pages to public schools, is now blanketed with commercials. Children are sold to advertisers from the time they are born, taught that possessions define their value, and blessed with lives filled with pseudo-events, pseudo-emotions, and pseudo-knowledge provided by marketers. Yet we expect these children to grow up capable of making independent judgments and effectively participating in democratic civic life.

The debate over public education reform cannot be understood by thinking only about schools. It is part of a much broader struggle: whether America will move in the direction of its democratic ideals or be further ensnared in the logic of the market. The outcome is by no means assured. As author Leslie Savan has written, in the United States there is now "no human emotion or concern—love, lust, war, childhood, innocence, social rebellion, spiritual enlightenment, even disgust with advertising—that cannot be turned into a sales pitch."[44]

The challenge facing American society and its children is not how to find ever more ingenious ways to speed the market on its way. The real challenge of the next century is to take control of our lives back from the market.

NOTES

1. Elizabeth R. Word, John Johnston, Helen Pate Bain, B. DeWayne Fulton, Jayne Boyd Zaharias, Charles M. Achilles, Mattha Nanette Lintz, John Folger, and Carolyn Breda, *The State of Tennessee's Student/Teacher Achievement Ratio (STAR) Project Technical Report 1985–1990* (Nashville: Tennessee Department of Education, 1990).
2. Jeremy D. Finn and Charles M. Achilles, "Answers and Questions About Class Size: A Statewide Experiment," *American Education Research Journal* 27, no. 3 (Fall 1990): 557–577.
3. C. Steven Bingham, *White-Minority Achievement Gap Reduction and Small Class Size: A Research and Literature Review,* publication #TSU-95-0025-(B)-3-531308 (Nashville: Tennessee State University Center of Excellence for Research and Policy on Basic Skills, 1995).
4. Barbara A. Nye, Jayne Boyd-Zaharias, B. DeWayne Fulton, C. M. Achilles, Van A. Cain, and Dana A. Tollett, *The Lasting Benefits Study 8th Grade Technical Report* (Nashville: Tennessee State University Center of Excellence for Research and Policy on Basic Skills, 1995); Barbara A. Nye, Jayne Boyd-Zaharias, B. DeWayne Fulton, C. M. Achilles, and Van A. Cain, *The Lasting Benefits Study 6th Grade Technical Report* (Nashville: Tennessee State University Center of Excellence for Research and Policy on Basic Skills, 1993).
5. Jeremy D. Finn and Deborah Cox, "Participation and Withdrawal Among Fourth-Grade Pupils," *American Educational Research Journal* 29, no. 1 (Spring 1992): 141–162.
6. Frederick Mosteller, "The Tennessee Study of Class Size in the Early School Grades," *The Future of Children: Critical Issues for Children and Youths* 5, no. 2 (Summer-Fall 1995): 113–127.
7. *Does the U.S. Still Want a Public Education System?* Education Writers Association backgrounder (Washington, D.C.: Education Writers Association, 1994).
8. Paul R. Peterson, "Vouching for a Religious Education," *Wall Street Journal,* December 28, 1995.
9. Keith Bradsher, "Widest Gap in Incomes? Research Points to U.S.," *New York Times,* October 27, 1995.
10. Gerald W. Bracey, "The Third Bracey Report on the Condition of Education," *Phi Delta Kappan* 75, no. 2 (October 1993): 104–117.
11. American Legislative Exchange Council (910 17th Street NW, Washington, D.C., 20006) news release, "Report Card on American Education 1994," September 20, 1994.
12. John B. Goodman and Gary W. Loveman, "Does Privatization Serve the Public Interest?" *Harvard Business Review* 69, no. 6 (November–December 1991): 26.
13. Dani Sandbery, "The Pirate Privateers," *New Internationalist,* no. 259, September 1994, p. 14.
14. "Conrail for Sale," *Time,* June 13, 1983, p. 51.
15. Richard I. Worsnop, "Privatization," *CQ Researcher* 2, no. 42 (November 13, 1992): 987.
16. William E. Schmidt, "Britain Now Seeks Marker for Coal," *New York Times,* October 22, 1992.
17. Calvin Sims, "Argentina Booming, Bypassing Jobless," *New York Times,* February 5, 1995.
18. Louis Uchitelle, "Wage Stagnation Is Seen As a Major Issue in the 1996 Election Campaign," *New York Times,* August 13, 1995.
19. Louis Uchitelle, "1995 Was Good for Companies, and Better for Alot of C.E.O.'s," *New York Times,* March 29, 1996.
20. Fox Butterfield, "Prison-Building Binge in California Casts Shadow on Higher Education," *New York Times,* April 2, 1995.
21. Edward N. Luttwak, "If the Economy Is So Good, Why Do We Feel So Bad?" *Milwaukee Journal,* December 18, 1994.
22. Doug Lasdon and Sue Halpern, "When Neighborhoods Are Privatized," *New York Times,* November 30, 1995.
23. Karen Herzog, "Network of Fund-Raising Groups Eyed to Boost Public Schools," *Milwaukee Sentinel,* January 17, 1995.
24. *Michigan Public School Governance* (Lansing: Michigan State Board of Education, 1995).
25. Richard I. Worsnop, "Privatization," *CQ Research* 2, no. 42 (November 13, 1992): 988.
26. Robert B. Reich, "How to Avoid These Layoffs?" *New York Times,* January 4, 1996.
27. "Massachusetts Seeks to Designate Fishing Industry Natural Disaster," *New York Times,* March 22, 1995.
28. Ibid.
29. Ibid.
30. Peter Passell, "Lonely, and Rich, at the Top," *New York Times,* August 27, 1995.
31. Edward Luttwak, "The Middle-Class Backlash," *Harper's,* January 1996, pp. 15–16.

32. Peter Applebome, "Have Schools Failed? Revisionists Use Army of Statistics to Argue No." *New York Times,* December 13, 1995.
33. Jonathan Kozol, *Savage Inequalities* (New York: Crown, 1991).
34. Editorial, "Students Without Desks," *New York Times,* February 5, 1995.
35. Peter Applebome, "Record Cost Cited to Fix or Rebuild Nation's Schools," *New York Times,* December 26, 1995.
36. See, for example, Gertrude Himmelfarb, "The Victorians Get a Bad Rap," *New York Times,* January 9, 1995, and Katherine Q. Seelye, "Gingrich Looks to Victorian Age to Cure Today's Social Failings," *New York Times,* March 14, 1995.
37. Cal Thomas, "The Surest Route out of Poverty Lies in Regaining Sense of Values," *Milwaukee Journal,* December 18, 1994.
38. Russell Baker, "Those Vital Paupers," *New York Times,* January 17, 1995.
39. Floyd Norris, "You're Fired! (But Your Stock Is Way Up)," *New York Times,* September 3, 1995.
40. Robert Heilbroner, "Weighing the Human Interest Rate," *Harper's,* March 1995, pp. 18–22.
41. Keith Bradsher, "Low Ranking for Poor American Children," *New York Times,* August 14, 1995.
42. Gerald Bracey, *Transforming America's Schools: An Rx for Getting Past the Blame* (Arlington, Va.: American Association of School Administrators, 1994).
43. Neal Gabler, "The Fathers of P.R.," *New York Times Magazine,* December 31, 1995, p. 29.
44. Leslie Savan, "The Bribed Soul," *Advice,* no. 18 (Summer 1995): 1.

Confronting Class in the Classroom

BELL HOOKS

Class is rarely talked about in the United States; nowhere is there a more intense silence about the reality of class differences than in educational settings. Significantly, class differences are particularly ignored in classrooms. From grade school on, we are all encouraged to cross the threshold of the classroom believing we are entering a democratic space—a free zone where the desire to study and learn makes us all equal. And even if we enter accepting the reality of class differences, most of us still believe knowledge will be meted out in fair and equal proportions. In those rare cases where it is acknowledged that students and professors do not share the same class backgrounds, the underlying assumption is still that we are all equally committed to getting ahead, to moving up the ladder of success to the top. And even though many of us will not make it to the top, the unspoken understanding is that we will land somewhere in the middle, between top and bottom.

Coming from a nonmaterially privileged background, from the working poor, I entered college acutely aware of class. When I received notice of my acceptance at Stanford University, the first question that was raised in my household was how I would pay for it. My parents understood that I had been awarded scholarships, and allowed to take out loans, but they wanted to know where the money would come from for transportation, clothes, books. Given these concerns, I went to Stanford thinking that class was mainly about materiality. It only took me a short while to understand that class was more than just a question of money, that it shaped values, attitudes, social relations, and the biases that informed the way knowledge would be given and received. These same realizations about class in the academy are expressed again and again by academics from working-class backgrounds in the collection of essays *Strangers in Paradise* edited by Jake Ryan and Charles Sackrey.

During my college years it was tacitly assumed that we all agreed that class should not be talked about, that there would be no critique of the bourgeois class biases shaping and informing pedagogical process (as well as social etiquette) in the classroom. Although no one ever directly stated the rules that would govern our conduct, it was taught by example and reinforced by a system of rewards. As silence and obedience to authority were most rewarded, students learned that this was the appropriate demeanor in the classroom. Loudness, anger, emotional outbursts, and even something as seemingly innocent as unrestrained laughter were deemed unacceptable, vulgar disruptions of classroom social order. These traits were also associated with being a member of the lower classes. If one was not from a privileged class group, adopting a demeanor similar to that of the group could help one to advance. It is still necessary for students to assimilate bourgeois values in order to be deemed acceptable.

Bourgeois values in the classroom create a barrier, blocking the possibility of confrontation and conflict, warding off dissent. Students are often silenced by means of their acceptance of class values that teach them to maintain order at all costs. When the obsession with maintaining order is coupled with the fear of "losing face," of not being thought well of by one's professor and peers, all possibility of constructive dialogue is undermined. Even though students enter the "democratic" classroom believing they have the right to "free speech," most students are not comfortable exercising this right to "free speech." Most students are not comfortable exercising this right—especially if it means they must give voice to thoughts, ideas, feelings that go against the grain, that are unpopular. This censoring process is only one way bourgeois values overdetermine social behavior in the classroom and undermine the democratic exchange of ideas. Writing about his experience in the section of *Strangers in Paradise* entitled "Outsiders," Karl Anderson confessed:

> Power and hierarchy, and not teaching and learning, dominated the graduate school I found myself in. "Knowledge" was one-upmanship, and no one disguised the fact. . . . The one thing I learned absolutely was the inseparability of free speech and free thought. I, as well as some of my peers, were refused the opportunity to speak and sometimes to ask questions deemed "irrelevant" when the instructors didn't wish to discuss or respond to them.

Students who enter the academy unwilling to accept without question the assumptions and values held by privileged classes tend to be silenced, deemed troublemakers.

Conservative discussions of censorship in contemporary university settings often suggest that the absence of constructive dialogue, enforced silencing, takes place as a by-product of progressive efforts to question canonical knowledge, critique relations of domination, or subvert bourgeois class biases. There is little or no discussion of the way in which the attitudes and values of those

from materially privileged classes are imposed upon everyone via biased pedagogical strategies. Reflected in choice of subject matter and the manner in
which ideas are shared, these biases need never be overtly stated. In his essay
Karl Anderson states that silencing is "the most oppressive aspect of middle-
class life." He maintains:

> It thrives upon people keeping their mouths shut, unless they are actually
> endorsing whatever powers exist. The free marketplace of "ideas" that is so
> beloved of liberals is as much a fantasy as a free marketplace in oil or auto-
> mobiles; a more harmful fantasy, because it breeds even more hypocrisy and
> cynicism. Just as teachers can control what is said in their classrooms, most also
> have ultra-sensitive antennae as to what will be rewarded or punished that is
> said outside them. And these antennae control them.

Silencing enforced by bourgeois values is sanctioned in the classroom by
everyone.

Even those professors who embrace the tenets of critical pedagogy (many
of whom are white and male) still conduct their classrooms in a manner that
only reinforces bourgeois models of decorum. At the same time, the subject
matter taught in such classes might reflect professorial awareness of intellectual
perspectives that critique domination, that emphasize an understanding of the
politics of difference, of race, class, gender, even though classroom dynamics
remain conventional, business as usual. When contemporary feminist movement made its initial presence felt in the academy there was both an ongoing
critique of conventional classroom dynamics and an attempt to create alternative pedagogical strategies. However, as feminist scholars endeavored to make
Women's Studies a discipline administrators and peers would respect, there
was a shift in perspective.

Significantly, feminist classrooms were the first spaces in the university
where I encountered any attempt to acknowledge class difference. The focus
was usually on the way class differences are structured in the larger society, not
on our class position. Yet the focus on gender privilege in patriarchal society
often meant that there was a recognition of the ways women were economically disenfranchised and therefore more likely to be poor or working class.
Often, the feminist classroom was the only place where students (mostly
female) from materially disadvantaged circumstances would speak from that
class positionality, acknowledging both the impact of class on our social status
as well as critiquing the class biases of feminist thought.

When I first entered university settings I felt estranged from this new environment. Like most of my peers and professors, I initially believed those feelings were there because of differences in racial and cultural background.
However, as time passed it was more evident that this estrangement was in part
a reflection of class difference. At Stanford, I was often asked by peers and professors if I was there on a scholarship. Underlying this question was the impli-

cation that receiving financial aid "diminished" one in some way. It was not just this experience that intensified my awareness of class difference, it was the constant evocation of materially privileged class experience (usually that of the middle class) as a universal norm that not only set those of us from working-class backgrounds apart but effectively excluded those who were not privileged from discussions, from social activities. To avoid feelings of estrangement, students from working-class backgrounds could assimilate into the mainstream, change speech patterns, points of reference, drop any habit that might reveal them to be from a nonmaterially privileged background.

Of course I entered college hoping that a university degree would enhance my class mobility. Yet I thought of this solely in economic terms. Early on I did not realize that class was much more than one's economic standing, that it determined values, standpoint, and interests. It was assumed that any student coming from a poor or working-class background would willingly surrender all values and habits of being associated with this background. Those of us from diverse ethnic/racial backgrounds learned that no aspect of our vernacular culture could be voiced in elite settings. This was especially the case with vernacular language or a first language that was not English. To insist on speaking in any manner that did not conform to privileged class ideals and mannerisms placed one always in the position of interloper.

Demands that individuals from class backgrounds deemed undesirable surrender all vestiges of their past create psychic turmoil. We were encouraged, as many students are today, to betray our class origins. Rewarded if we chose to assimilate, estranged if we chose to maintain those aspects of who we were, some were all too often seen as outsiders. Some of us rebelled by clinging to exaggerated manners and behavior clearly marked as outside the accepted bourgeois norm. During my student years, and now as a professor, I see many students from "undesirable" class backgrounds become unable to complete their studies because the contradictions between the behavior necessary to "make it" in the academy and those that allowed them to be comfortable at home, with their families and friends, are just too great.

Often, African Americans are among those students I teach from poor and working-class backgrounds who are most vocal about issues of class. They express frustration, anger, and sadness about the tensions and stress they experience trying to conform to acceptable white, middle-class behaviors in university settings while retaining the ability to "deal" at home. Sharing strategies for coping from my own experience, I encourage students to reject the notion that they must choose between experiences. They must believe they can inhabit comfortably two different worlds, but they must make each space one of comfort. They must creatively invent ways to cross borders. They must believe in their capacity to alter the bourgeois settings they enter. All too often, students from nonmaterially privileged backgrounds assume a position of passivity—they behave as victims, as though they can only be acted upon against their will. Ultimately, they end up feeling they can only reject or accept the norms imposed upon them. This either/or often sets them up for disappointment and failure.

Those of us in the academy from working-class backgrounds are empowered when we recognize our own agency, our capacity to be active participants in the pedagogical process. This process is not simple or easy: it takes courage to embrace a vision of wholeness of being that does not reinforce the capitalist version that suggests that one must always give something up to gain another. In the introduction to the section of their book titled "Class Mobility and Internalized Conflict," Ryan and Sackrey remind readers that "the academic work process is essentially antagonistic to the working class, and academics for the most part live in a different world of culture, different ways that make it, too, antagonistic to working class life." Yet those of us from working-class backgrounds cannot allow class antagonism to prevent us from gaining knowledge, degrees, and enjoying the aspects of higher education that are fulfilling. Class antagonism can be constructively used, not made to reinforce the notion that students and professors from working-class backgrounds are "outsiders" and "interlopers," but to subvert and challenge the existing structure.

When I entered my first Women's Studies classes at Stanford, white professors talked about "women" when they were making the experience of materially privileged white women a norm. It was both a matter of personal and intellectual integrity for me to challenge this biased assumption. By challenging, I refused to be complicit in the erasure of black and/or working-class women of all ethnicities. Personally, that meant I was not able just to sit in class, grooving on the good feminist vibes—that was a loss. The gain was that I was honoring the experience of poor and working-class women in my own family, in that very community that had encouraged and supported me in my efforts to be better educated. Even though my intervention was not wholeheartedly welcomed, it created a context for critical thinking, for dialectical exchange.

Any attempt on the part of individual students to critique the bourgeois biases that shape pedagogical process, particularly as they relate to epistemological perspectives (the points from which information is shared) will, in most cases, no doubt, be viewed as negative and disruptive. Given the presumed radical or liberal nature of early feminist classrooms, it was shocking to me to find those settings were also often closed to different ways of thinking. While it was acceptable to critique patriarchy in that context, it was not acceptable to confront issues of class, especially in ways that were not simply about the evocation of guilt. In general, despite their participation in different disciplines and the diversity of class backgrounds, African American scholars and other non-white professors have been no more willing to confront issues of class. Even when it became more acceptable to give at least lip service to the recognition of race, gender, and class, most professors and students just did not feel they were able to address class in anything more than a simplistic way. Certainly, the primary area where there was the possibility of meaningful critique and change was in relation to biased scholarship, work that used the experiences and thoughts of materially privileged people as normative.

In recent years, growing awareness of class differences in progressive academic circles has meant that students and professors committed to critical and feminist pedagogy have the opportunity to make spaces in the academy where class can receive attention. Yet there can be no intervention that challenges the status quo if we are not willing to interrogate the way our presentation of self as well as our pedagogical process is often shaped by middle-class norms. My awareness of class has been continually reinforced by my efforts to remain close to loved ones who remain in materially underprivileged class positions. This has helped me to employ pedagogical strategies that create ruptures in the established order, that promote modes of learning which challenge bourgeois hegemony.

One such strategy has been the emphasis on creating in classrooms learning communities where everyone's voice can be heard, their presence recognized and valued. In the section of *Strangers in Paradise* entitled "Balancing Class Locations," Jane Ellen Wilson shares the way an emphasis on personal voice strengthened her.

> Only by coming to terms with my own past, my own background, and seeing that in the context of the world at large, have I begun to find my true voice and to understand that, since it is my own voice, that no pre-cut niche exists for it; that part of the work to be done is making a place, with others, where my and our voices, can stand clear of the background noise and voice our concerns as part of a larger song.

When those of us in the academy who are working class or from working-class backgrounds share our perspectives, we subvert the tendency to focus only on the thoughts, attitudes, and experiences of those who are materially privileged. Feminist and critical pedagogy are two alternative paradigms for teaching which have really emphasized the issue of coming to voice. That focus emerged as central, precisely because it was so evident that race, sex, and class privilege empower some students more than others, granting "authority" to some voices more than others.

A distinction must be made between a shallow emphasis on coming to voice, which wrongly suggests there can be some democratization of voice wherein everyone's words will be given equal time and be seen as equally valuable (often the model applied in feminist classrooms), and the more complex recognition of the uniqueness of each voice and a willingness to create spaces in the classroom where all voices can be heard because all students are free to speak, knowing their presence will be recognized and valued. This does not mean that anything can be said, no matter how irrelevant to classroom subject matter, and receive attention—or that something meaningful takes place if everyone has equal time to voice an opinion. In the classes I teach, I have students write short paragraphs that they read aloud so that we all have a chance to hear unique perspectives and we are all given an opportunity to pause and listen to one another. Just the physical experience of hearing, of listening intently, to each particular voice strengthens our capacity to learn together. Even though a student may not speak again after this moment, that student's presence has been acknowledged.

Hearing each other's voices, individual thoughts, and sometimes associating theses voices with personal experience makes us more acutely aware of each other. That moment of collective participation and dialogue means that students and professor respect—and here I invoke the root meaning of the word, "to look at"—each other, engage in acts of recognition with one another, and do not just talk to the professor. Sharing experiences and confessional narratives in the classroom helps establish communal commitment to learning. These narrative moments usually are the space where the assumption that we share a common class background and perspective is disrupted. While students may be open to the idea that they do not all come from a common class background, they may still expect that the values of materially privileged groups will be the class's norm.

Some students may feel threatened if awareness of class difference leads to changes in the classroom. Today's students all dress alike, wearing clothes from stores such as the Gap and Benetton; this acts to erase the markers of class difference that older generations of students experienced. Young students are more eager to deny the impact of class and class differences in our society. I have found that students from upper- and middle-class backgrounds are disturbed if heated exchange takes place in the classroom. Many of them equate loud talk or interruptions with rude and threatening behavior. Yet those of us from working-class backgrounds may feel that discussion is deeper and richer if it arouses intense responses. In class, students are often disturbed if anyone is interrupted while speaking, even though outside class most of them are not threatened. Few of us are taught to facilitate heated discussions that may include useful interruptions and digressions, but it is often the professor who is most invested in maintaining order in the classroom. Professors cannot empower students to embrace diversities of experience, standpoint, behavior, or style if our training has disempowered us, socialized us to cope effectively only with a single mode of interaction based on middle-class values.

Most progressive professors are more comfortable striving to challenge class biases through the material studied than they are with interrogating how class biases shape conduct in the classroom and transforming their pedagogical process. When I entered my first classroom as a college professor and a feminist, I was deeply afraid of using authority in a way that would perpetuate class elitism and other forms of domination. Fearful that I might abuse power, I falsely pretended that no power difference existed between students and myself. That was a mistake. Yet it was only as I began to interrogate my fear of "power"—the way that fear was related to my own class background where I had so often seen those with class power coerce, abuse, and dominate those without—that I began to understand that power was not itself negative. It depended what one did with it. It was up to me to create ways within my professional power constructively, precisely because I was teaching in institutional structures that affirm it is fine to use power to reinforce and maintain coercive hierarchies.

Fear of losing control in the classroom often leads individual professors to fall into a conventional teaching pattern wherein power is used destructively. It is this fear that leads to collective professorial investment in bourgeois decorum as a means of maintaining a fixed notion of order, of ensuring that the teacher will have absolute authority. Unfortunately, this fear of losing control shapes and informs the professorial pedagogical process to the extent that it acts a barrier preventing any constructive grappling with issues of class.

Sometimes students who want professors to grapple with class differences often simply desire that individuals from less materially privileged backgrounds be given center stage so that an inversion of hierarchical structures takes place, not a disruption. One semester, a number of black female students from working-class backgrounds attended a course I taught on African American women writers. They arrived hoping I would use my professorial power to decenter the voices of privileged white students in nonconstructive ways so that those students would experience what it is like to be an outsider. Some of these black students rigidly resisted attempts to involve the others in an engaged pedagogy where space is created for everyone. Many of the black students feared that learning new terminology or new perspectives would alienate them from familiar social relations. Since these fears are rarely addressed as part of progressive pedagogical process, students caught in the grip of such anxiety often sit in classes feeling hostile, estranged, refusing to participate. I often face students who think that in my classes they will "naturally" not feel estranged and that part of this feeling of comfort, or being "at home," is that they will not have to work as hard as they do in other classes.

These students are not expecting to find alternative pedagogy in my classes but merely "rest" from the negative tensions they may feel in the majority of other courses. It is my job to address these tensions.

If we can trust the demographics, we must assume that the academy will be full of students from diverse classes, and that more of our students than ever before will be from poor and working-class backgrounds. This change will not be reflected in the class background of professors. In my own experience, I encounter fewer and fewer academics from working-class backgrounds. Our absence is no doubt related to the way class politics and class struggle shapes who will receive graduate degrees in our society. However, constructively confronting issues of class is not simply a task for those of us who came from working-class and poor backgrounds; it is a challenge for all professors. Critiquing the way academic settings are structured to reproduce class hierarchy, Jake Ryan and Charles Sackrey emphasize "that no matter what the politics or ideological stripe of the individual professor, of what the content of his or her teaching, Marxist, anarchist, or nihilist, he or she nonetheless participates in the reproduction of the cultural and class relations of capitalism." Despite this bleak assertion they are willing to acknowledge that "nonconformist intellectuals can, through research and publication, chip away with some success at the conventional orthodoxies, nurture students with comparable ideas and intentions, or find ways to bring some fraction of the resources of the university to the service of the . . . class interests of the workers and others below." Any professor who commits to engaged pedagogy recognizes the importance of constructively confronting issues of class. That means welcoming the opportunity to alter our classroom practices creatively so that the democratic ideal of education for everyone can be realized.

Revolutionary Pedagogy in Post-Revolutionary Times: Rethinking the Political Economy of Critical Education

PETER McLAREN

Over the last decade, the exultant pronouncements and echolalic commentaries on the demise of socialism advanced by liberal and conservative propagandists of capitalism (including the growing ranks of post-Marxists) have helped to set in train the imperatives of a revitalized global order built around the logic of the free market. As Rightist ideologues hoist the banner of unrestrained, frictionless, speculator capitalism while at the same time sounding the requiem for Marxism in the catacombs of *realpolitik,* the United States Left stands in disarray, currents of anxiety cascading through its ranks. The pivotal historical mechanisms leading to the so-called "end of ideology" have resulted in the absence of a radical Left able and ready to contest the social, cultural, and economic imperatives of the neoliberal capitalist class. The educational Left has not remained immune to the disorganization in the ranks of the Left in general, and the Marxist Left in particular. While the educational Left has made interesting advances with respect to the critique of postmodern culture, its performance has been prima facie discouraging in challenging the consolidation of global capitalist relations over the last several decades. The Marxist educational Left has, for the most part, carefully ensconced itself within the educational establishment in an uneasy alliance that has disabled its ability to do much more than engage in radical posturing, while reaping the benefits of scholarly rewards. This essay will discuss the dangerous triumph of global capitalism, will advocate for a revitalized Leftist critique of capital, and will sketch provisionally a number of directions for critical education.

The globalization of labor and capital, accompanied by technological innovation, has brought about material shifts in cultural practices and the proliferation of new contradictions between capitalism and labor that progressive educators who work in schools of education have been hard-pressed to respond to, as opposed to react to, successfully.[1]

The current phenomenon of globalization has been described as the cannibalization of the social and political by the economy[2] and the "grand finale of the explosion of Western modernity."[3] Kleptocratic capitalism is afoot today, stealing from the poor to give to the rich. The dictatorship of the free market ensures that corporate risk is socialized (through public subsidization for private wealth) while benefits are privatized (through the accumulation of personal assets). Welfare for the oppressed has been replaced by subventions to capital. The political ideology of the time legitimizes a traumatic suppression of labor income. One of the central contradictions of the new global economy is "that capitalism no longer seems able to sustain maximum profitability by means of commensurate economic growth and seems now to be relying more and more on simply *redistributing* wealth in favor of the rich, and on increasing inequalities, within and between national economies, with the help of the neoliberal state."[4] The dehumanized plight of the poor living in our midst, sleeping in cardboard boxes and eating from garbage dumpsters, is as much a part of the global economy as Los Angeles's new Mount Olympus, the shining new Getty Center atop the hill overlooking the luxury neighborhood of Bel Air.

It is undeniably the case today that capitalism has entered a global crisis of accumulation and profitability. Self-destructing as a result of intensified competition leading to overcapacity and overproduction and a fall in manufacturing profitability, the new era of flexible accumulation requires a number of ominous conditions: the total dismantling of the Fordist-Keynesian relationship between capital and labor; a shift toward the extraction of absolute surplus value; the suppression of labor incomes; a weakening of trade unions; longer working hours; more temporary jobs; and the creation of a permanent underclass. Western democracies are witnessing increasing numbers of individuals excluded from the productive and distributive spheres. Unemployment is spreading misery and misfortune throughout all sectors of United States society; where employment opportunities are available, they are too often in the "second sector" of the economy, where health insurance and pensions do not exist and where few government regulations exist to protect workers. On a more global scale, we are witnessing the progressive division of "capitalist" and "proletarian" nations.

William Greider has noted in a recent issue of *The Nation* that, "In different ways, labor incomes are suppressed on both ends of the global system—usually by labor-market forces (including mass unemployment or temp jobs) in the advanced economies, often by government edict and brutal force in developing ones. Meanwhile, companies must keep building more production or locating factories to keep up in the cost-price chase"[5] According to Greider, we are returning to a form of pre-welfare competitive capitalism that is driven by the motor of conservative political ideology—one that is capable of suturing together the discourses of freedom, family values, civic authority, nationalism, and patriotism. Of course, the term 'freedom' is used in a decidedly and perniciously manipulative fashion. Only the market remains "free" and people must submit to the dictates of the "self-correcting" market. This is most painfully evident in cases where the International Monetary Fund and the U.S. Treasury impose forced-austerity terms on poor countries (such as cutting wages and public spending and raising interest rates) so that endangered banks can fix their balance sheets.[6] Thus Jorge Larrain is compelled to write that

> unemployment is treated as laziness and pricing yourself out of a good job, workers' strikes are transformed into a problem of public order. Criminality and new forms of violence are treated as the result of lack of authority in the family, not enough law and order, lack of Victorian values, and so on. Terrorism is successful because of the free press and the excessive leniency of the law. Divisions and forms of discrimination are partly blamed on immigration and partly conjured away by patriotism and jingoism.[7]

The global restructuring of industries and work organization has had devastating consequences for developing countries. The IMF wants poor countries to improve their balance-of-payments position by liberalizing their economies, devaluing currencies, and increasing imports in proportion to exports. This has wrought nothing but havoc for the poor. And international trade conventions such as GATT have made the pursuit of ecologically sustainable food security increasingly more difficult.[8]

Today in the United States we are witnessing the emergence of a new dominant class constituted by a technological aristocracy and a cadre of business executives who work in the interests of corporate share price.[9] Within this context, capital and the state are reconfiguring race and gender; a white male comprador labor aristocracy is giving way to more decentralized, local, and flexible means of using race and gender as "divide and rule" tactics. This follows from the way in which global capitalism is relying more and more on Third World labor and on Third World labor pools in First World spaces.[10]

With the advent of the Internet, inexpensive satellite communications, multibillion dollar global software corporations, online companies, and developments in biotechnology, nanotechnology, and alternative energy technology, the new world order is unfolding by evolutionary corporate design. The new operating matrix of the biotech-based technological revolution that is following in the wake of the mergers, consolidations, and acquisitions of the life-science industry by global commercial enterprises is creating the conditions for what Jeremy Rifkin describes as a "wholesale reseeding of the Earth's biosphere with a laboratory-conceived Second Genesis, an artificially produced bio-industrial nature designed to replace nature's own evolutionary scheme."[11] The logic of unfettered capitalism is being heralded as an amplification of nature's own principles, thus justifying the emerging corporate eugenics science as a second-tier evolutionary trend, one in which genes become the "green gold" that will drive the future of the world economy. The push for patent protection of gene pools—linked to projects such as a Human Genome Diversity Project—has witnessed clandestine attempts by the U.S. government to "privatize the human body"[12] by obtaining patents on the cell-lines of Panama's Guaymi Indians and populations in the Solomon Islands, Papua New Guinea, and India so that U.S. corporations can profit from global control over the genetic blueprints of human life.

The "free market revolution," driven by continuous capitalist accumulation of a winner-take-all variety, has left the social infrastructure of the United States in tatters (not to mention other parts of the globe). Through policies of increasing its military-industrial-financial interests, it continues to purse its quivering bourgeois lips, bare its imperialist fangs, and suck the lifeblood from the open veins of South America and other regions of the globe. The sudden collapse of the Soviet Union in the 1990s and the shift to capitalism in Eastern Europe have brought nearly five billion people into the world market. The globalization of capitalism and its political bedfellow; neoliberalism, work together to democratize suffering, obliterate hope, and assassinate justice. The logic of privatization and free trade—where social labor is the means and measure of value and surplus social labor lies at the heart of profit—now shapes archetypes of citizenship, manages our perceptions of what should constitute the "good society," and creates ideological formations that produce necessary functions for capital in relation to labor.[13] As schools become increasingly financed by corporations that function as service industries for transnational capitalism, and as bourgeois think-tank profiteerism and educational professionalism continue to guide educational policy and practice, the U.S. population faces a challenging educational reality. Liberals are calling for the need for capital controls, controls in foreign exchange, the stimulation of growth and wages, labor rights enforcement for nations borrowing from the United States, and the removal of financial aid from banking and capital until they concede to the centrality of the wage problem and insist on labor rights.[14] However, very few are calling for the abolition of capital itself.

The commercialization of higher education, the bureaucratic cultivation of intellectual capital and its tethering to the machinery of capital, the rise of industrial business partnerships, the movement of research into the commercial arena of profit and service to trade organizations and academic-corporate consortia, all have garnered institutions of higher learning profound suspicion by those who view education as a vehicle for democracy. As David Noble points out, these new proprietary arrangements have turned universities into patent holding companies and marketing agencies.[15] We are witnessing the proliferation of computer-based instruction (which might offer reductions in direct labor but is more cost-intensive when you consider equipment, upgrades, maintenance, and technical and administrative support staff), and online education that reduces the number of teachers while undermining the autonomy and independence of faculty. In the hands of the technozealots, teachers are being reproletarianized and labor is being disciplined, displaced, and deskilled. Teacher autonomy, independence, and control over work is being severely reduced, while workplace knowledge and control are given over more and more to the hands of the administration.[16]

The educational Left is finding itself without a revolutionary agenda for challenging inside and outside the classrooms of the nation the effects and consequences of the new capitalism. Consequently, we are witnessing the progressive and unchecked merging of pedagogy to the productive processes within advanced capitalism. Education has been reduced to a subsector of the economy, designed to create cybercitizens within a teledemocracy of fast-moving images, representations, and lifestyle choices. Capitalism has been naturalized as commonsense reality—even as a part of nature itself—while the term "social class" has been replaced by the less antagonistic term, "socioeconomic status." As Berndt Ostendorf remarks, "With the disappearance of Socialism as a political inspiration or as a combative alternative, the laws of Capitalism have become part of nature again."[17] It is impossible to examine educational reform in the United States without taking into account the continuing forces of globalization and the progressive diversion of capital into financial and speculative channels—what some have called "tycoon capitalism" or "casino capitalism on a world scale."

Marxists have long recognized the dangers of capital and the exponentiality of its expansion into all spheres of the lifeworld. Today capital is in command of the world order as never before, as new commodity circuits and the increased speed of capital circulation works to extend and secure capital's global reign of terror. Advice given by Marx in the *Grundrisse* underscores the importance of "finding the proper level of abstraction in order to grasp the concrete nature of things."[18] The site where the concrete determinations of industrialization, corporations, markets, greed, patriarchy, and technology all come together—the center where exploitation and dominated is fundamentally articulated—"is occupied by that elusive entity known as *capital*."[19] Joel Kovel argues that "Capital is elusive because it cannot be singled out in isolation from anything else. It is a social relation grounded in the commodification of labor-power, in which labor is subject to the law of value—a relation expressed through wage labor, surplus value extraction, and the transformation of all means of production into capital."[20] The insinuation of the coherence and logic of capital into everyday life—and the elevation of the market to sacerdotal status, as the paragon of all social relationships—is an accomplished fact. The economic restructuring that we are witnessing today offers both new fears concerning capital's inevitability and some new possibilities for organizing against it. Critical pedagogy is, I maintain, a necessary (but not sufficient) element in this resistance.

Particularly during the Reagan years, hegemonic practices and regulatory forces that had undergirded postwar capitalism were dramatically destabilized, and this dynamic has continued. The halcyon days before the arrival of the New Leviathan of globalization—when liberal Keynesian policymaking established at least a provisional social safety net—have been replaced by pan-national structures of production and distribution and communication technologies that enable a "warp speed capitalism" of instant worldwide financial transactions. According to Paul Street, "the alternately fatalistic and celebratory chant of globalization has become a great capitalist smoke screen [that] disarms any resistance to capital and diverts us from seeing the real not-so novel nature of U.S. capitalists' all-too-domestic assault on U.S. workers."[21]

An international division of labor characterized by vast inequalities has become so pronounced today that it excludes entire national and continental economies from the new world order.[22] Propelled by a fragmentation of the mass market, which is split into smaller submarkets and into customized niches where competition is focused on consumer "identity," the new "fast" capitalism makes competition fiercer, creating a small number of big winners (based on large short-run profits) and a large number of losers. There is no place in America that is not a stone's throw away from the dark certainty of unemployment.

We are faced with what Pierre Bourdieu refers to as the "gospel" of neoliberalism. This gospel is one that "leads to a combat *by every means,* including the destruction of the environment and human sacrifice, against any obstacle to the maximization of profit."[23] Bourdieu describes neoliberalism as

> a powerful economic theory *whose strictly symbolic strength, combined with the effect of theory, redoubles the force of the economic realities it is supposed to express.* It ratifies the spontaneous philosophy of the people who run large multinationals and of the agents of high finance—in particular pension-fund managers. Relayed throughout the world by national and international politicians, civil servants, and most of all the universe of senior journalists—all more or less equally ignorant of the underlying mathematical theology—it is becoming a sort of universal belief, a new ecumenical gospel. This gospel, or rather the soft vulgate which is put forward everywhere under the name of liberalism, is concocted out of a collection of ill-defined words—"globalization," "flexibility," "deregulation" and so on—which, through their liberal or even libertarian connotations, may help to give the appearance of a message of freedom and liberation to a conservative ideology which thinks itself opposed to all ideology.[24]

According to Scott Davies and Neil Guppy, one of the central tenets of the neoliberal argument is that schools must bring their policies and practices in line with the importance of knowledge as a form of production.[25] According to the neoliberal educationalists, schools are largely to blame for economic decline and educational reform must therefore be responsive to the postindustrial labor market and restructured global economy. Davies and Guppy note the reasoning behind this:

As low-skill jobs vanish (because of automation or job exporting), almost all employment will require minimal skills that schools must furnish. Further, globalization is ushering in a new era of required knowledge. Curricula concentrated on consumer relations, problem solving, entrepreneurialism, and cross-cultural "multiskilling" are central to this economic transformation. Employers will recruit people with broad educations and complement this with intensive on-the-job training.[26]

Davies and Guppy also argue that globalization has led schools to stress closer links between school and the workplace in order to develop skills training and "lifelong learning." In a knowledge-intensive economy, schools can no longer provide the skills for a lifetime career. This means that schools are called upon by the market-oriented educational thinkers to focus more on adult learners through enterprise-based training.

It is growing more common to hear the refrain, "education is too important to be left to the educators," as governments make strong efforts at intervention to ensure that schools play their part in rectifying economic stagnation and ensuring global competitiveness. Standardized tests are touted as the means to ensure the educational system is aligned well with the global economy. There is now a movement to develop international standardized tests, creating pressures toward educational convergence and standardization among nations. Such an effort, note Davies and Guppy, provides a form of surveillance that allows nation-states to justify their extended influence and also serves to homogenize education across regions and nations.[27] School choice initiatives have emerged in an increasing number of nations in North America and Europe, sapping the strength of the public school system and helping to spearhead educational privatization.

Business has been given a green light to restructure schooling for its own purposes, as the image of *homo economicus* drives educational policy and practice, and as corporations and transnational business conglomerates and their political bedfellows become the leading rationalizing forces of educational reform. Because the ideologies of both democracy and socialism have lost their validity over the last several decades, and because of growing diasporic movements of immigrants in search of employment across national boundaries, there has been a renewed resurgence in the celebration of ethnicity and the development of alliance-building on the basis of race. The sociopolitical dialogue surrounding race and ethnicity has put pressure on schools to accommodate discussions and practices of diversity. And while multiculturalism in the schools has become a key factor of institutional globalization and nation-building, "with the aim of cultivating cosmopolitan world citizens,"[28] corporate multiculturalism has been able to co-opt more liberal versions of multiculturalism, with its stress on "unity in diversity," in order to link the discourse of diversity with the rationale of the business community and the new global economy.[29]

Because capital has itself invaded almost every sphere of life in the United States, the focus of the educational Left has been distracted for the most part from the great class struggles that have punctuated this century. The Leftist agenda now rests almost entirely on an understanding of asymmetrical gender and ethnic relations. While this focus surely is important, class struggle is now viewed as an outdated issue. When social class is discussed, it is usually viewed as relational, not as oppositional. In the context of discussions of "social status" rather than "class struggle," technoelite curriculum innovation has secured a privileged position that is functionally advantageous to the socially reproductive logic of entrepreneurial capitalism, private ownership, and the personal appropriation of social production. The seduction of capital is overwhelming, affecting even the most well-intentioned groups of progressive educators. Davies and Guppy remind us that "globalization is transforming education by *squeezing power from the middle.* As power is being wrestled from education professionals, teachers unions, and education officials, it is being redistributed upward to more senior state officials and downward to local groups."[30]

On the other hand, educational criticalists who stress the social character of knowledge stipulate that people can, through cooperation, increase their understanding of the social consequences of their actions, even though they will never fully know their consequences. Stressing the socially constituted way in which knowledge is produced (a fundamental axiom among Freireans, for instance) provides a basis for questioning the values and mechanisms of the dominant capitalist order. In their new book, *The New Work Order: Behind the Language of the New Capitalism,* James Paul Gee, Glynda Hull, and Colin Lankshear analyze the ways in which cognitive science has progressively shifted its concept of expertise from an association with disciplinary expertise in the academic sense, to the worldview of the new capitalism with its focus on change, speed, flexibility, and innovation.[31] They also note the way in which the academic curricula in schools have been modified to link education more securely to the job requirements of "the new work order." In this sense it is possible to view contemporary testing measures, institutional tracking, and efforts to link schools to the Internet not as strategies to prepare more creative and informed citizens, but as ways to assist in human resource planning for the global economy as we move into the new millennium.

It is undeniably the case that the capitalist class is more odious and powerful today than in the days when anticapitalist guerrillas such as Che Guevara were struggling to cut capitalism at its joints with the machete of armed guerrilla resistance. One explanation for the strength of the capitalist class in the current era of global economic restructuring is that its predatory power is more tenaciously fastened to the global commercial media system than at any other time in history. Capitalist discourses are coordinated by a small number of transnational media corporations that are mostly based in the United States.[32] This is a system, according to Robert W. McChesney, that works to advance the cause of the global market and promote commercial values, while denigrating journalism and culture not conducive to the immediate bottom line or long-run corporate interests. It is a disaster for anything but the most superficial notion of democracy—a democracy where, to paraphrase John Jay's maxim, those who own the world ought to govern it.[33]

William Robinson is worth quoting at length on this issue:

> Global capitalism is predatory and parasitic. In today's global economy, capitalism is less benign, less responsive, to the interests of broad majorities around the world, and less accountable to society than ever before. Some 400 transnational corporations own two-thirds of the planet's fixed assets and control 70 per cent of world trade. With the world's resources controlled by a few hundred global corporations, the life blood and the very fate of humanity is in the hands of transnational capital, which holds the power to make life and death decisions for millions of human beings. Such tremendous concentrations of economic power lead to tremendous concentrations of political power globally. Any discussion of "democracy" under such conditions becomes meaningless. . . . The paradox of the demise of dictatorships, "democratic transitions" and the spread of "democracy" around the world is explained by new forms of social control, and the misuse of the concept of democracy, the original meaning of which, the power *(cratos)* of the people *(demos),* has been disconfigured beyond recognition. What the transnational elite calls democracy is more accurately termed *polyarchy,* to borrow a concept from academia. Polyarchy is neither dictatorship nor democracy. It refers to a system in which a small group actually rules, on behalf of capital, and participation in decision-making by the majority is confined to choosing among competing elites in tightly controlled electoral processes. This "low-intensity democracy" is a form of consensual domination. Social control and domination is hegemonic, in the sense meant by Antonio Gramsci, rather than coercive. It is based less on outright repression than on diverse forms of ideological co-optation and political disempowerment made possible by the structural domination and "veto power" of global capital.[34]

In fact, what we are witnessing in countries such as the United States is the development of capitalist culture underwritten by privileging hierarchies that resemble those of many so-called Third World countries.[35]

What should today's global educators make of the structural power embodied within new forms of transnational capital, especially in terms of the shift in the relation between nation-states and formerly nation-based classes, the scope of economic restructuring and its ability to erode the power of organized labor, and the extent to which global mass migrations pit groups in fierce competition over very scarce resources? Robinson notes that the transnational elite has now been able to put democracy in the place of dictatorship (what can be called the neoliberal state) in order to perform at the level of the nation-state the following functions: adopting fiscal and monetary policies that guarantee macroeconomic stability; providing the necessary infra-structure for global capitalist circuitry and flows; and securing financial control for the transnational comprador elite as the nation-state moves more solidly in the camp of neoliberalism, while maintaining the illusion of "national interests" and concerns with "foreign competition." In fact, the concept of "national interests" and the term "democracy" itself function as an ideological ruse to enable authoritarian regimes to move with a relative lack of contestation toward a transformation into elite polyarchies. So many of the literacy practices in today's schools are functionally linked to this new global economy—such as "cooperative learning" and developing "communities of learners"—and promote a convenient alliance between the new fast capitalism and conventional cognitive science. While these new classroom measures are helping to design and analyze symbols, they are also being co-opted by and facilitating the new capitalism.[36]

Given current structural and conjunctural conditions such as the privatization of subjectivity, free market fundamentalism, and the moral collapse of social democracy after the defeat of communism, we need to rethink the nature and purpose of education according to the kind of "knowledge worker" proposed *by* the new capitalist order *for* the new capitalist order. This hidden curriculum or "pedagogical unsaid" is nothing new although the ideological state apparatuses have made it a more sophisticated enterprise. Its function is largely the same as it was during earlier phases of industrial capitalism: the attempt to de-form knowledge into a discreet and decontexualized set of technical skills packaged to serve big business interests, cheap labor, and ideological conformity. In fact, at a time in which real wages are being steadily ratcheted downwards, students are being prepared to become custodians of the capitalist state—a state destabilized by the constant deterritorialization and reterritorialization of capital and whose power is increasingly facilitated by the quick movement of information that permits instant turnover times within financial markets.

CRITICAL PEDAGOGY: A FRAGMENTATION OF VISION

About twenty years after the Cuban revolution, when "Che Guevara became the *prototype of a new revolutionary generation,*"[37] U.S. educational scholars on the Left began fighting the destructive logic of capital through the development of what has been variously called radical pedagogy, feminist pedagogy, and critical pedagogy. Critical pedagogy is a way of thinking about, negotiating, and transforming the relationship among classroom teaching, the production of knowledge, the institutional structures of the school, and the social and material relations of the wider community, society, and nation-state.[38] Developed by progressive teachers, literacy workers, and radical scholars attempting to eliminate inequalities on the basis of social class, it has sparked a wide array of anti-sexist, anti-racist, and anti-homophobic classroom-based curricular and policy initiatives. This follows a strong recognition that racism, sexism, and homophobia are exacerbated by capitalist exploitation.

Critical pedagogy has grown out of a number of theoretical developments such as Latin American philosophies of liberation; the pedagogy of Brazilian educator Paulo Freire;[39] the anti-imperialist struggle of Che Guevara and other revolutionary movements; the sociology of knowledge; the Frankfurt school of critical theory; feminist theory, and neo-Marxist cultural criticism. In more recent years it has been taken up by educators influenced by postmodern social theory, Derridean deconstruction, and its somewhat more politically contestatory academic partner, poststructuralism.[40] Yet at the level of classroom life, critical pedagogy is often seen as synonymous with whole language instruction, adult literacy programs, and new "constructivist" approaches to teaching and learning based on a depoliticized interpretation of Lev Vygotsky's work, and a tie-dyed optimism of "I'm okay, you're okay." While critics often decry this educational approach for its idealist multiculturalism and harmonious political vision, its supporters, including the late Paulo Freire, have complained that critical pedagogy has been frequently domesticated in practice and reduced to student-directed learning approaches devoid of social critique and a revolutionary agenda. Of course, this is due partly to the educational Left's retreat from historical materialism and metatheory as dated systems of intelligibility that have historically run their course, and to the dislocation of power, knowledge, and desire brought on by the New Left's infatuation with more conservative forms of avant-garde apostasy found in certain incarnations of French postmodernist theoretical advances.[41]

Because many postmodern theorists and their poststructuralist companions operate from a theoretical terrain built upon a number of questionable assumptions—that is, they view symbolic exchange as taking place outside the domain of value; privilege structures of deference over structures of exploitation, and relations of exchange over relations of production; emphasize local narratives over grand narratives; encourage the coming to voice of the symbolically dispossessed over the transformation of existing social relations; reduce models of reality to historical fictions; abandon the assessment of the truth value of competing narratives; replace the idea that power is class-specific and historically bound with the idea that power is everywhere and nowhere—they end up advancing a philosophical commission that propagates hegemonic class rule and reestablishing the rule of the capitalist class.[42] What this has done is precisely to continue the work of reproducing class antagonisms and creating a new balance of hegemonic relations favoring dominant class interests.[43] According to Glen Rikowksi,

> the insertion of postmodernism within educational discourses lets in some of
> the most unwelcome of guests—nihilism, relativism, educational marketisation,
> to name but a few—which makes thinking about human emancipation futile.
> Left postmodernism, in denying the possibility of human emancipation, merely

succeeds in providing complacement cocktail-bar academic gloss for the New Right project of marketising education and deepening the rule of capital within the realm of education and training.[44]

Here I am not attempting to adopt a conservative Marxist dismissal of postmodernism,[45] since, as Terry Eagleton reminds us (and as I myself have noted on numerous occasions), postmodernism, while limited as a critique of capitalism, has made considerable and important advances in explaining the construction of identity.[46] It has also contributed greatly to the construction of what has been called "radical democracy."

However, as Marxist and neo-Marxist educationalists (as well as other critical social theorists) continue to develop trenchant critiques of postmodernism, they are reinvigorating the debates over revolutionary class struggle within the current crisis of globalization in important and urgent ways.[47] Nancy Fraser, herself a neo-Weberian, has put forward a convincing case that radical democracy, which uses postmodernist and poststructuralist analyses, "remains largely confined to the cultural-political plane" and continues to "bracket political economy" and work against the development of a social politics of resource distribution.[48] Because *both capitalism and postmodern education* find virtue in diversity, in the crossing of borders, in the disavowal of hierarchical control, in the *droit à la différence* (right to difference), in the emphasis on inclusion of everyone from workers to chief executives in meaningful work decisions of the business, and in the blurring of the boundaries between life inside and outside the workplace, the language of the new capitalism can often co-opt the language of the postmodern critique of capitalism.[49] It is relatively easy for the new capitalists to align themselves with postmodernist critics of capitalism and Western hegemony. For instance, British educationalist Andy Green reports that "the postmoderns argue that greater pluralism and 'choice' in education is good because it empowers individuals and subordinated cultures. They also suggest that it is somehow inevitable in the modern world because society and culture itself has become so fragmented."[50] In actual fact, notes Green, a radically relativist postmodern approach to cultural politics may appear on the surface to valorize the marginalized and the excluded but such an approach is unable to build solidarity or genuinely pluralist forms of curricula as an alternative to an exclusionary, monocultural, national curriculum. He concludes that "[w]hat we are left with in the end is a 'free market' in classroom cultural politics where the powerful dominant discourses will continue to subordinate other voices and where equality in education will become an ever-more chimerical prospect."[51] The applied barbarism of conservative postmodernism reduces identity to a psychogram, to an instance of discourse delinked from the social totality of capitalist relations of exploitation.

In the face of the current lack of Utopia and the postmodern assault on the unified subject of the Enlightenment tradition, the "old guard" revolutionaries such as José Marti, Camilo Torres, Augusto Sandino, Leon Trotsky, Maria Lorena Barros, Emiliano Zapata, Rosa Luxemburg, and Che Guevara would have a difficult time winning the sympathy of the postmodern Left.[52] The universal proletarianism that undergirds the vision of many of these revolutionaries invites us to consider a socialist alternative to the insurgent avant-gardism of today's postmodern Left. Afflicted by a despair brought about by a Nietzschean perspectivism and the political paralysis and semiotic inertia of a cultural politics divorced from a sustained critique of capitalist social relations, it appears as if too much ground has been lost in order to rescue the revolutionary socialist project for education. Nevertheless, the "totalizing" vision of this project remains compelling and instructive, and indeed remains as urgent today as it was thirty years ago. Perhaps even more so. Not only have postmodern theorists cravenly insinuated that Marxist theory is inhospitable to issues of race, ethnicity, and gender, they have ignored the immeasurable richness of Marxist social theory that has been developed over the last several decades. Aijaz Ahmad takes issue with postmodernism's anti-Marxist assessment:

> Marxism is today often accused of neglecting all kinds of "difference", of gender, race, ethnicity, nationality, culture, and so on But it is not Marxism that recognizes no gender differences. These differences are at once abolished by capitalism, by turning women as much as men into instruments of production. These differences are also maintained through cross-class sexual exploitation, not to speak of the differential wage rate, in which women are paid less than men for the same work, or the direct appropriation of women's labor in the domestic economy.[53]

Let me make myself clear on this point. I believe that race, ethnicity, gender, and sexual orientation constitute an interconnected ensemble of social practices and to a certain extent constitute different logics. My position is not a riposte to the relative autonomy thesis (in its various incarnations throughout the years) or to non-class processes but rather a criticism of postmodernism's petit-bourgeois movement away from a "represented exterior" of signifying practices that renders an anticapitalist project not only unlikely but firmly inadmissable. Not with standing the slippage between Marxist categories and poststructuralist categories, I believe that postmodernist theories, in straddling uneasily the abyss between identity politics and class analysis, have relegated the category of class to an epiphenomena of race, ethnicity, and gender. My position is similar to that of Sherry Ortner, who remarks that "class exists in America but cannot be talked about, that it is 'hidden,' that there is no language for it, but that it is 'displaced' or 'spoken through' other languages of social difference—race, ethnicity, and gender."[54] I agree with Ortner that while to a certain extent class, race, and ethnicity are separate but interacting dimensions of U.S. social geography and while they operate at least in part on different logics, "*at the level of discourse,* class, race, and ethnicity are so deeply mutually implicated in American culture that it makes little sense to pull them apart."[55] And while "there is no class in America that is not always already racialized and ethnicized," and while racial and ethnic categories are always already class categories, the salience of race and ethnicity in the United States is such that when they are introduced into the discussion, they tend to "swamp" social class.[56] Ortner goes so far as to maintain that the persistent hiddenness of class "means that the discourse is muted and often unavailable, subordinated to virtually every other kind of claim about social success and social failure."[57] And when you mix this reality with the frenetic advance of contemporary global capitalist social relations, you have a recipe for the uncontested reproduction of global relations of exploitation.

Does this mean that I believe that the configuration of non-class processes such as race, gender, and sexuality are unimportant? Far from it. Class relations deal with the process of producing, appropriating, and distributing surplus value. This view of class is not meant to downplay or deny the importance of power and property in the structure of contemporary society. In fact, allocations of power and property *follow from* the relationships that individuals have to the production and appropriation of surplus labor.[58] I certainly acknowledge that non-class processes can compromise the conditions of existence of the fundamental class processes within capitalism. In other words, non-class processes involving race and gender relations can provide the conditions for a transformation of the class processes of Western capitalist societies. Take gender as one example. Richard Wolff and Stephen Resnick remark that

> specific changes in social processes concerned with gender relationships would provide conditions for a change in the class processes of Western capitalist societies today. A change in popular consciousness about what "male" and "female" means (i.e., a change in certain cultural processes) alongside a change in the authority distribution process within families (a change in political or power processes) might combine with a change as women sell more of their labor power as a commodity (a change in the economic process of exchange) to jeopardize capitalist class processes. With other changes in still other social processes—which our class analysis seeks to identify—such altered gender relationships might provide the conditions of existence for a revolutionary change to a new social system including a different class structure.[59]

Class and non-class processes fundamentally shape one another. My argument is not that class should subsume all other social and cultural processes, or that an analysis of class should outweigh an analysis of gender or race or sexuality, but that it should be given closer scrutiny in educational reform efforts in the sense of taking into consideration the profound effects of globalized capitalist social relations.

I am no less in favor of the development of a critical cultural consciousness, or cultural criticism in general, in relation to questions of racial or ethnic or sexual identity than I have been over recent years. As someone who for over fifteen years has contributed to analyzing those very questions, such a shift in my position would be ludicrous. I am, however, more interested today in finding a *common ground* between cultural criticism and the movement for a transformation of productive relations. The process of globalization has put too much at stake in the struggle for a pedagogy of liberation for me to be otherwise.

My position is that cultural criticism—accounting for the specific logics of non-economic factors—for the most part has not adequately addressed the liberation of humankind from economic alienation linked to capitalist economic logics that serve as the motor force for transnational oligopolies and the reproduction of established social relations. I follow Samir Amin in articulating a noneconomic-determinist interpretation of Marxism in which the capitalist mode of production is *not* reduced to the status of an economic structure.[60] In other words, the law of value governs both the economic reproduction of capitalism and all the aspects of social life under capitalism. Rather than embrace Althusserian structuralism with its famously articulated concept of "overdetermination" (that is, each aspect of society is constituted as the effect of all the others), I take the position adopted by Amin in his articulation of "underdetermination." According to Amin, the determinations of economics, politics, and culture each possess their specific logic and autonomy. There is no complementarity among these logics within the system of underdetermination; there exist only conflicts among the determining factors, conflicts which allow choice among different possible alternatives. Conflicts among logics find solutions by subordinating some logics to others. The accumulation of capital is the dominant trait of the logic of capitalism and provides the channels through which economic logic is imposed onto political, ideological, and cultural logics. Precisely because underdetermination rather than overdetermination typifies the conflictual way in which the logics governing the various factors of social causation are interlaced, all social revolutions must necessarily be cultural revolutions. The law of value, therefore, governs not only the capitalist mode of production but also all the other social determinants. In order to move beyond—to overstep—contemporary capitalism that is defined by its three basic contradictions of economic alienation, global polarization, and destruction of the natural environment, Amin charts out a project of social transformation that would initiate through its political economy, its politics, and its cultural logics a social evolution bent on reducing these contradictions rather than aggravating them. Amin also argues convincingly that postmodern criticism for the most part capitulates to the demands of the current phase of capitalist political economy in the hope of making the system more humane—a happy capitalism. My position, as well as Amin's, stresses the importance of contesting the unconstrained domination of capital that masquerades as freedom, a domination that, with the help of its political managers who pocket most of the cash, falsely sets itself up as the guarantor of human emancipation.

In retrospect, were the 1960s the last opportunity for popular revolutionary insurgency on a grand scale to be successful? Did the political disarray of prodigious dimensions that followed in the wake of the rebuff of the post-1968 Leftist intelligentsia by the European proletariat condemn the revolutionary project and the "productionist" metanarrative of Marx to the dustbin of history? Have the postmodernist emendations of Marxist categories and the rejection—for the most part—of the Marxist project by the European and North American intelligentsia signaled the abandonment of hope in revolutionary social change? What does the historical materialist approach often associated with revolutionary movements and anti-capitalist struggle have to offer educators who work in critical education? Can the schools of today build a new social order?

I raise these questions at a time in which it is painfully evident that critical pedagogy and its political partner, multicultural education, no longer serve as an adequate social or pedagogical platform from which to mount a vigorous challenge to the current social division of labor and its effects on the socially reproductive function of schooling in late capitalist society.[61] In fact, critical pedagogy no longer enjoys its status as a herald for democracy, as a clarion call for revolutionary praxis, as a language of critique and possibility in the service of a radical democratic imaginary, which was its promise in the late 1970s and early 1980s.

A nagging question has sprung to the surface of the debate over schooling and the new capitalist order: Can a renewed and revivified critical pedagogy grounded in an historical materialist approach to educational reform serve as a point of departure for a politics of resistance and counterhegemonic struggle in the twenty-first century? And if we attempt to uncoil this question and take seriously its full implications, what can we learn from the legacy and struggle of revolutionary social movements? On the surface, there are certain reasons to be optimistic. Critical pedagogy has, after all, joined antiracist and feminist struggles in articulating a democratic social order built around the imperatives of diversity, tolerance, and equal access to material resources. But surely such a role, while commendable as far as it goes, has seen critical pedagogy severely compromise an earlier, more radical commitment to anti-imperialist struggle that we often associate with the anti-war movement of the 1960s and earlier revolutionary movements in Latin America.

CRITICAL PEDAGOGY: WHAT IS TO BE DONE?

Once considered by the faint-hearted guardians of the American dream as a term of opprobrium, critical pedagogy has become so completely psychologized, so liberally humanized, so technologized, and so conceptually postmodernized, that its current relationship to broader liberation struggles seems severely attenuated if not fatally terminated. The conceptual net known as critical pedagogy has been cast so wide and at times so cavalierly that it has come to be associated with anything dragged up out of the troubled and infested waters of educational practice, from classroom furniture organized in a "dialogue friendly" circle to "feel-good" curricula designed to increase students' self-image. Its multicultural education equivalent can be linked to a politics of diversity that includes "respecting difference" through the celebration of "ethnic" holidays and themes such as "Black history month" and "Cinco de Mayo." If the term "critical pedagogy" is refracted onto the stage of current educational debates, we have to judge it as having been largely domesticated in a manner that many of its early exponents, such as Brazil's Paulo Freire, so strongly feared.

Most educationalists who are committed to critical pedagogy and multicultural education propagate versions of these that do not escape the contingency of their race, class, and gender location. One does not have to question the sincerity or commitment of these educators or dismiss their work as superficial or unimportant—for the most part it is not—to conclude that their articulations of critical pedagogy and multicultural education have been accommodated to the requirements of capital and the objectives of neoliberalism. While early exponents of critical pedagogy were denounced for their polemical excesses and radical political trajectories, a new generation of critical educators have since that time emerged who have largely adopted what could be described as a pluralist approach to social antagonisms. Their work celebrates the "end of history," and the critique of global capitalism is rarely, if ever, brought into the debate.

The reasons for the domestication of critical pedagogy have been mentioned above but I would like to elaborate here on what I consider to be some of the most important reasons. There has clearly been a strong movement among many critical educators infatuated by postmodern and poststructuralist perspectives to neglect or ignore profound changes in the structural nature and dynamics of late capitalism in the United States. Why should political economy be a concern to educators in this era of post-Marxist sympathies and multiple social antagonisms? Precisely because we are living at a particular historical juncture of doctrinaire unregulated capitalism with an overwhelming income reconcentration at the top. There currently exist 70 transnational corporations with assets greater than Cuba's—70 privately owned economic nations. Millions are unemployed in First World economic communities and millions more in Third World communities; three quarters of the new jobs in the capitalist world are temporary, low-paid, low-skill, and carry few, if any, benefits. Latin American economies are in the thrall of a decade-long crisis. In the United States in 1989 the top one percent earned more collectively than the bottom 40 percent. As Charles Handy surmised with respect to England, although the government recently stated that 82 percent of all workers are in "permanent" employment, in fact 24 percent of the labor force are part-time, 13 percent are self-employed, 6 percent are temporary, and 8 percent are unemployed, making a total of 51 percent who are not in a full-time job. Furthermore, the length of a full-time job is approximately 5.8 years. So capitalism is really about employability, not employment.[62] Overconsumption—the political subsidization of a subbourgeois, mass sector of managers, entrepreneurs, and professionals—has occurred during a time in which we are witnessing a vast redistribution of wealth from the poor to the rich as corporations are benefiting from massive tax cuts and a reorientation of consumption toward the new middle class. These trends are also accompanied by a general retreat of the labor movement.[63] The globalization of capital has unleashed new practices of social control and forms of internationalized class domination. This is not to suggest, however, that certain cultural formations and institutions do not mediate the economic or that there exist relative decommodified zones.

There has been a shifting of positions among many North American critical educators from earlier Marxist perspectives to liberal, social-democratic, neoliberal and even right-wing perspectives. Those of us on the theoretical front have lamented the conscription of some Marxist writers, such as Antonio Gramsci, into the service of a neoliberal political agenda. In all, we have witnessed the evisceration of a Marxist politics in current education debates and the accommodation of some of its positions into the capitalist state apparatus. Discussions of political and ideological relations and formations are being engaged by many North American Leftist educators as if these arenas of social power exist in antiseptic isolation from anti-imperialist struggle. It is clear that a renewed agenda for critical pedagogy must include strategies of addressing and redressing economic distribution, which will take it well beyond its current postmodernist goal of troubling fixed notions of identity and difference, or of unsettling the notion of a bounded, pre-given, or essential "self." Focusing mainly on "identity politics" is one way that the capitalist class can keep workers and subaltern groups divided against each other and less likely to form alliances challenging current efforts at national and global economic restructuring.

CRITICAL EDUCATION FOR THE NEW MILLENNIUM

Both critical pedagogy and multicultural education need to address themselves to the adaptive persistence of capitalism and to issues of capitalist imperialism and its specific manifestations of accumulative capacities through conquest (to which we have assigned the more benign term "colonialism"). In other words, critical pedagogy needs to establish a project of emancipation that moves beyond simply wringing concessions from existing capitalist structures and institutions. Rather, it must be centered around the transformation of property relations and the creation of a just system of appropriation and distribution of social wealth. It is not enough to adjust the foundational level of school funding to account for levels of student poverty, to propose supplemental funding for poverty and limited English proficiency, to raise local taxes to benefit schools, to demand that state governments partly subsidize low-property-value communities, or to fight for the equalization of funding generated by low-property-value districts (although these efforts surely would be a welcome step in the right direction). I am arguing for a fundamentally broader vision based on a transformation of global economic relations—on a different economic logic if you will—that transcends a mere reformism within existing social relations of production and the international division of labor.[64]

Marxist and neo-Marxist accounts have clearly identified imperialistic practices in recent movements toward global capital accumulation based on corporate monopoly capital and the international division of labor. The West has seen a progressive shift in its development that some liberals would champion as the rise of individuality, the rule of law, and the autonomy of civil society. Yet from a Marxist and neo-Marxist perspective these putative developments toward democracy can be seen, in effect, as

> new forms of exploitation and domination, (the constitutive "power from below" is, after all, the power of lordship), new relations of personal dependence and bondage, the privatization of surplus extraction and the transfer of ancient oppressions from the state to "society"—that is, a transfer of power relations and domination from the state to private property.[65]

Since the triumph of European capitalism in the seventeenth century, the bourgeoisie have acquired the legal, political, and military power to destroy most of society in its quest for accumulation.[66] Capitalism in advanced Western countries must be transformed if extra-economic inequalities—such as racism and sexism—are to be challenged successfully. While it is true that people have identities other than class identities that shape their experiences in crucial and important ways, anticapitalist struggle is the best means to rearticulate identities within the construction of a radical socialist project. As Ellen Meiksins Wood notes, capitalism is more than just a system of class oppression; it constitutes a ruthless totalizing process that shapes our lives in every conceivable aspect, subjecting all social life to the abstract requirements of the market.[67]

We need not accommodate ourselves to the capitalist law of value, as István Mészáros reminds us.[68] The challenge ahead is to work toward the expropriation of the capitalists but also to ensure that the socialist project remains steadfast and self-critical. The struggle for a socialist democracy, it should be noted, is intractably linked to the struggle against racism. Critical educators need to consider how racism in its present incarnations developed out of the dominant mode of global production during the seventeenth and eighteenth centuries, particularly out of colonial plantations in the new World with slave labor imported from Africa to produce consumer goods such as tobacco, sugar, and cotton.[69] How the immigrant working class has been divided historically along racial lines is a process that needs to be better understood and more forcefully addressed by multicultural educators. How, for instance, does racism give white workers a particular identity that unites them with white capitalists?[70]

Critical pedagogy as a partner with multicultural education needs to deepen its reach of cultural theory and political economy, and expand its participation in social-empirical analyses in order to address more critically the formation of intellectuals and institutions within the current forms of motion of history. Critical pedagogy and multicultural education need more than good intentions to achieve their goal. They requires a revolutionary movement of educators informed by a principled ethics of compassion and social justice, a socialist ethos based on solidarity and social interdependence, and a language of critique capable of grasping the consequences of history's narratives.[71] This is an especially difficult task, because educational imperatives linked to corporate initiatives often use the language of public democracy to mask a model of privatized democracy.[72] Given current U.S. educational policy, with its goal of serving the interests of the corporate world economy—one that effectively serves a *de facto* world government made up of the IMF, World Bank, G-7, GATT, and other structures—it is imperative that critical and multicultural educators renew their commitment to the struggle against exploitation on all fronts.[73] In emphasizing one such front—that of class struggle—I want to emphasize that the renewed Marxist approach to critical pedagogy that I envision does not conceptualize race and gender antagonisms as static, structural outcomes of capitalist social relations of advantage and disadvantage but rather locates such antagonisms within a theory of agency that acknowledges the importance of cultural politics and social difference. Far from deactivating the sphere of culture by viewing it only or mainly in the service of capital accumulation, critical pedagogy and multicultural education need to acknowledge the specificity of local struggles around the micropolitics of race, class, gender, and sexual formation. But in doing so it must not lose sight of the global division of labor brought about by the forces of capitalist accumulation. A critical pedagogy based on class struggle that does not confront racism, sexism, and homophobia will not be able to eliminate the destructive proliferation of capital.

The critical pedagogy to which I am referring needs to be made less informative and more per-formative, less a pedagogy directed toward the interrogation of written texts than a corporeal pedagogy grounded in the lived experiences of students. Critical pedagogy, as I am re-visioning it from a Marxist perspective, is a pedagogy that brushes against the grain of textual foundationalism, ocular fetishism, and the monumentalist abstraction of theory that characterizes most critical practice within teacher education classrooms. I am calling for a pedagogy in which a revolutionary multicultural ethics is performed—is lived in the streets—rather than simply reduced to the practice of reading texts (although the reading of texts with other texts, against other texts, and upon other texts is decidedly an important exercise). Teachers need to build upon the textual politics that dominates most multicultural classrooms by engaging in a politics of bodily and affective investment, which means "walking the talk" and working in those very communities one purports to serve. A critical pedagogy for multicultural education should quicken the affective sensibilities of students as well as provide them with a language of social analysis, cultural critique, and social activism in the service of cutting the power and practice of capital at its joints. Opportunities must be made for students to work in communities where they can spend time with economically and ethnically diverse populations, as well as with gay and lesbian populations, in the context of community activism and participation in progressive social movements.

Students need to move beyond simply knowing about critical multiculturalist practice. They must also move toward an embodied and corporeal understanding of such practice and an affective investment in such practice at the level of everyday life such that it is able to deflect and transform the invasive power of capital.

CRITICAL PEDAGOGY IN THE AGE OF GLOBALIZATION

As the public sphere continues to be devalued and depoliticized, transformed more and more into the culture of the shopping mall, the ongoing withdrawal of commitment to the public sphere is eroding the conditions for public schools to survive, let alone build a new social order. Defense of personal "enclaves" rather than public and collective spaces is the trend today and such enclave localism scarcely enables a macropolitics linked to the modern project of radical transformation. Given the conditions of global capitalism described throughout this essay, which is more utopian, socialism or democratic capitalism? To me it would appear to be the latter, and by far. Yet while it is unlikely that schools by themselves can serve as anything more than necessary but not sufficient public spaces of potential political, cultural, and economic transformation, there are some initiatives that are, nevertheless, worth struggling to achieve. Consequently, I wish to specify in more detail the challenge—and the possibilities—that the philosophy of revolutionary struggle poses for critical educators.

First, critical pedagogy must reflect upon the historical specificity of its own categories so that it does not come to portray its own economy of desire as representing the nature and needs of all humankind. This is crucial if critical pedagogy is going to be able to challenge the patriarchal and Eurocentric assumptions within its own ranks. As critical pedagogy has learned from feminist pedagogies, and pedagogies associated with Latin American theologies of liberation, the African diaspora, and North American pedagogies of resistance, it must disclaim any false allegations of universality that speak only or mainly to white, male, Western, working-class heterosexuals. Where critical pedagogy claims to articulate a universal position on liberation and human rights, its premises must not remain vulnerable to a masculinist, Eurocentric perspective. It is important to keep in mind that the new agent of democratic socialism is not a being predetermined by social relations but one that is never complete, one that is formed dialectically through social relations and the development of a politics underwritten by revolutionary praxis.

Second, critical pedagogy must speak to local issues and context-specific antagonisms, but at the same time it must be careful not to limit itself only to local accounts.[74] As ludic postmodern educational analysis continues to communicate better and better about itself, it appears to have less and less to say about the world and how to change it. Enlisting itself as the propaganda arm of capital, while at the same time denouncing Marxism as fixated on class struggle in a demonic, world-capitalist system abducted from its more democratic local aspects, ludic postmodern educationalists have established the importance of provisional knowledge and multiple sites of power and resistance. Yet, in doing so, they are severing the relationship between critique and action. What needs to be incorporated more fully into critical pedagogy is the trenchant work being done in critical poststructuralism, materialist feminist analysis, and the "red" feminism and pedagogy advanced by scholars such as Teresa Ebert and Rosemary Hennessy.[75] This work not only complements the Marxist pedagogy that I am advocating, but also troubles the counter-political ludic postmodernism found in so much contemporary social critique.

Critical pedagogy needs to move into the direction of challenging new carceral systems of social control through the development of a critical pedagogy of space. Following the lead of critical urban geographers such as Edward Soja, critical pedagogy should be encouraged to explore the spatiality of human life and couple this with its historicality-sociality, especially the genderizing and racializing of rural and urban cityspaces through the trialectics of space, knowledge, and power.[76]

Third, critical pedagogy must continue to speak to basic human needs, but it must do so without falling prey to a biological foundationalism or the falsely generalizing and ethnocentric tendencies of modern, Western grand theories that teleologically privilege certain historical or philosophical endpoints to the human condition such as "the end of history" or "the end of ideology," or that sound the death knell of political agency such as "the death of the subject." Such grand theories imply the redundancy of any discourse projected into the future that attempts to hold humanity accountable for its present condition. And while we should abandon the epistemological closure stipulated by "grand theories," I do not wish to suggest by any means that we should no longer see history as a series of determinative effects or view the social order in its "totality." A relentless randomness to history is affirmed in many postmodern articulations of critique, with little possibility held out for the success of struggles against patriarchy or racism or class exploitation.

Fourth, critical pedagogy must continue to challenge normative associations of intelligence and the ways in which "reason" has been differentially distributed so that it always advantages the capitalist class. Knowledge, as we have come to know, is regularly serviced in systems of representation that fix its meaning in preordained ways in order to serve special interest groups. Criticalists must never cease emphasizing that there exist determinate relations between the systems of intelligibility produced within public school institutions and those who occupy the dominant culture that houses such institutions. One of the political effects of knowledge production is to legitimate the voices of certain groups and to accord them credibility over voices of less privileged groups. In other words, a critical pedagogy must not concede any ground with respect to the position that asymmetrical relationships of power and privilege in any society have determinate effects on who will succeed and who will not. Who gets into universities, for instance, is not controlled by merit; if that were the case, then one would have to make the absurd argument that the members of the capitalist class are cognitively more gifted. However, we could easily concede that the capitalist class is considerably gifted insofar as it is able to control the definition of what counts as legitimate knowledge (for example, through test measures, official knowledge in textbooks, and the lack of challenges to "official" versions of history) and to make sure that such knowledge serves the interests of the global economy. As criticalists have pointed out, official knowledge, the ruling hierarchy of discursive authority, sovereign epistemes, and the official social transcripts of the capitalist class all oppose in one manner or another the pursuit of freedom and social justice.

The official transcript of U.S. citizenship implicitly assumes that only the white Euro-American elite are capable of achieving a universal point of view and speaking on behalf of all groups. Yet we know from Paulo Freire and other critical educationalists that the conditions of knowledge production in the "act of knowing" always involve political relationships of subordination and domination.[77] Criticalists need to excavate the coded meanings that constitute knowledge, and bring to light the rhetorical and formal strategies that go into its interpretation. Further, criticalists need to acknowledge the complex acts of investiture, fantasy, and desire that contribute to the social construction of knowledge. Dominant knowledge forms must be challenged and so must claims which try to divorce knowledge formations from their ideological and epistemic assumptions. Human capital ideas presently underwriting neoliberal educational policy fetishize education and reduce the pursuit of knowledge to the logic of commodification tied to future employment opportunities, to schooling's power of economic return, and to investment in human labor. To ensure favorable returns, education slavishly prostrates itself before the dictates of the labor marketplace and the Brain Lords of the corporate elite. These "dictates" can, in the clammy hands of neoliberal bureaucrats, raise university tuition to reduce the number of college graduates or establish quotas for certain subjects if those subjects are perceived to further the economic growth of the nation as a whole. In order to motivate "lifelong learning" among workers, corporations can cut benefits and job security so that workers are forced to keep up with the changing demands of the labor market.[78] This neoliberal ideology only ensures the eternal return of injustices and patchwork remedies, exploitation, and compensatory programs. Gee, Hull, and Lankshear argue against the vision and practices of the "new capitalist school reformers" by disavowing their consumer determinism, by making social criticism "necessary to real learning and thus as part and parcel of critical thinking and the empowerment of workers," and by reinvigorating local politics "as against the '*faux*' local of the new capitalism" so that a global community can be established "in which the interests and well-being of all become the concern of all."[79] The authors urge a critical understanding of the complex forces of the new work order that can "unmask greed and manipulation hiding behind systems and their assorted rationalizations."[80]

Fifth, criticalists must rethink the issues of "modes of production" so that educators can take into account the shift from industrialized public life to post-industrialized, post-Fordist, contexts of flexible specialization within global capitalism. Yet they must do so in a manner that revises and does not diminish the importance of the category of social class and that does not suggest—as many conservative postmodernists do—that exploitation is somehow more subjective or less concrete or severe than it was during more industrialized regimes.[81] The reproduction of economic and discursive advantage is not co-incidentally functional in school sites for the success of the capitalist project of maximizing resources and controlling the wealth in the interests of the white majority population. The exploited, the immiserated, and the wretched of the earth—*les damnés de la terre*—did not suddenly appear as a group of zombified volunteers enlisting in the ranks of the disenfranchised and destitute millions. Whether educators follow Marx's labor-value theory of exploitation or other economic explanations, it cannot be disputed that positive profits within capitalism require corresponding rates of exploitation and that this uneven distribution of wealth is unjust. As one (albeit modest) measure of resistance, teachers can incorporate into their curriculum lessons dealing with the global sweatshop.[82] Bill Bigelow reports that students from Monroe High School in Los Angeles organized to get a resolution passed by the school board committing the district not to buy soccer balls from countries that allow child labor. He also teaches against the myth that it is permissible to pay workers in undeveloped countries low wages because living expenses in those countries are much lower. He notes that milk in Haiti is 75 cents; in New York, 65 cents; eggs in Haiti are $1.50; in New York, $1.39; cereal in Haiti is $1.90; in New York, $1.60; gas in Haiti is $2.20; in New York, $1.26.[83]

Such resistance is a daunting task in the face of the recent invasion into our schools by the Barons of Capital who devise pro-capitalist strategies such as Virtual Trade Mission, now in use in growing numbers of U.S. classrooms. Backed by the Clinton administration and sponsored by the likes of MCI, Boeing, Hughes, and UPS (as well as by developing nations such as Indonesia and Singapore), the Virtual Trade Mission curriculum makes available "educational" videos and workbook exercises to approximately 50,000 students across 10 states. The videos show business executives extolling the virtues of free trade and the advantages of selling military and other industrial and commercial wares to developing countries. The V.T.M. program also includes guest lectures by corporate officials and diplomats and provides a study plan called Export Challenge. For instance, students role-play marketing executives who wish to expand their business overseas or to developing countries. To cite one example, students at the Chattanooga Arts and Sciences School helped to craft a strategy to increase Boeing's share of the Chinese commercial aircraft market.[84] With the exception of one workbook exercise produced by the International Brotherhood of Electrical Workers that provides a small amount of contrast by discussing the social dimensions of trade, the V.T.M. program presents for students an overwhelmingly glowing picture of the world of free trade. There is no mention of sweatshops, exploitation of female workers, environmental devastation, or the creation of a world of asymmetrical relations of power and privilege based on race, class, gender, and sexual orientation.

Critical pedagogy must be critical of capital as a social relation, which includes being critical of labor as the subject of capital. The struggle against capital is, after all, the main game. We as educators are also capital; capital is not just something "out there" but partially constitutes our subjectivity.[85] We are divided against ourselves, and within ourselves—as labor within (but also against) capital. Teacher unions must not shift their political center of gravity in order to appease free market privateers but rather promote social policies and social movements that address the perils of global capitalism. They can accomplish this through political coalitions with parents, students, and community groups.

Sixth, critical pedagogy must be antiracist, antisexist, and antihomophobic. Currently whiteness, heterosexuality, and maleness stand together as a leitmotif of major significations within capitalist democracy, while blackness and brownness function together as a sovereign indicator of racialization. This must be challenged, and done so as forcibly as possible.

Seventh, critical pedagogy must center around meeting the basic needs of human beings for survival and well-being in the struggle for a socialist democracy. There are material needs that must be satisfied consequent upon the common constitution of human beings as requiring food, adequate clothing, protection from the elements, and achieving self-worth and dignity. While it is surely true that needs are historical and are altered somewhat from context to context, critical pedagogy must admit to a standard of minimum material needs and human rights as integral to its socialist vision; such needs can serve as a transhistorical standard generally applied throughout the world. Self-realization and emancipation (while admittedly contingent, conjunctural, and never finished) are not possible without agreeing upon a basic standard to human capacities and surely there has to be some type of limit-concept of what we name to be relations of domination, oppression, or exploitation.

I am not appealing here for a transcendental theory of justice. I wish instead to underscore urgently the fact that as neoliberal democracy's oxygen, capitalism is predicated upon relations of uneven and unequal exchange. In order to stipulate a moral basis for a pedagogy of liberation, one must, in a strategically universalist sense at least, rely on a transhistorical claim with respect to the distribution of social wealth insofar as we are compelled to acknowledge that people suffer cruelly and die needlessly as a result of capitalist exploitation. By stressing the economic here, I am not arguing that the world of signs, symbols, and other representations are always already subsumed under capital or that the theater of discourse does not matter when the temper of the times calls for social struggle. After all, it is through discourse that we "live" social relations and make sense of them. When discourses are rendered meaningful and deconstructed for the way in which their meanings "live" through human activity, and when signs and symbols become intensified, they not only arch toward the development of critical understanding but can become hammer blows on the real. However, when discourses and interpretations become leeched of their social critique by capital-friendly policymakers, they become easily transformed into political advertisements for the neoliberal agenda.

Eighth, critical pedagogy must involve a politics of economic and resource distribution as well as a politics of recognition, affirmation, and difference. In other words, it must be a politics that speaks both to a transformative politics and to a critical and feminist multiculturalism.[86] To be colorless is to be white, and whites—in particular, white males—currently function as the colorless, normative standpoints of humanity. The social benefits in our pseudodemocracy—our emergent global polyarchy—are always the greatest the less black or brown you happen to be. The fact remains that the teaching profession is mostly white while the student population in many of our major cities is populated increasingly by students of color. Questions that must be answered in this scenario include: How are racial formations essentially social constructions? Yet, more importantly, how are these social constructions taken up, lived, and played out with devastating consequences for people of color? How are individuals and groups positioned inexorably by pseudoscientific classifications related to questions of biology or of culture both in terms of gender and ethnicity? How are these systems of classification defended by the imperatives of capitalism to exploit human labor and locate groups within the global division of labor?

Ninth, critical pedagogy needs to pursue the ideal of communicative democracy within a larger vision of socialist democracy. In the age of global capitalism, when so-called democratic schooling has become a laughable appellation, Iris Marion Young's concept of communicative democracy can prove instructive. Democracy, in Young's view, is not simply about registering one's preferences in a vote, but about becoming critically reflexive about one's preferences. This entails a move from motivated self-interest to collective interest, through examining the social knowledge available in a context free of coercion.[87] Criticalists such as Young also acknowledge that white people have the advantage in lobbying and organizing for their constituencies. And even when this constitutes majoritarian democracy, one has to acknowledge that communication is often restricted in this case. We know, for instance, that white males are now more vulnerable than ever in the global economy and that this is one of the major reasons why affirmative action is being rolled back in states such as California. Governor Pete Wilson wants to protect the considerable advantage that whites already hold. What makes this even more shameful is that he claims the moral high ground in his threat to cut back on prenatal services to undocumented women and in his stance against affirmative action. Yet criticalists understand that to abolish "preferences" for people of color is, given the present sociopolitical state of affairs in the United States, to argue for affirmative action for white people. Some of the problems currently facing us can be ameliorated by group representation and by giving voice to formerly silenced and devalued needs and experiences of oppressed groups.

Tenth, critical pedagogy must articulate its politics with a profound respect for the lived experiences and standpoint epistemology of the oppressed. Yet at the same time, criticalists must reject the all-too-familiar stance that experiences speak for themselves. This is consistent with an emphasis on gaining theoretical grounding through self-education as a means of understanding and transforming one's experiences. Experiences of the oppressed must not be silenced, they must be given voice. And a critical pedagogy must also ensure that they are heard. While a standpoint epistemology "from below" is vitally important for the perspectives that it offers, it still must be defensible and interpreted with explanatory power. This is not to say that some events are not self-evident at certain basic levels; it is, however, to argue that frameworks for interpreting experiences and building theories from those experiences is a pressing and important task. We must strive for interpretive frameworks that permit the most persuasive explanations and justifications from both ethical and epistemological pivot points. Sometimes this calls for complex theory and sometimes it does not. However, progressive educators and activists frequently resist complex theory as elitist. For some, this is partially due to a false conception of experience as transparent and, I would argue, due to a reluctance to engage in the arduous and labor-intensive task of critical theorizing. Indeed, if all experiences and relationships were politically, psychologically, and ethically self-evident, then social analysis would not be necessary. Interpretations of experience are undeniably colonized by particular definitions of what is normal from the perspective that most serves the interests of the ruling elites. Theories of liberation challenge these commonsense definitions, systems of classification, and social and material relations as being socially and historically motivated to serve the interests of the capitalist class. What is important about these theories is not their complexity, but rather their explanatory and argumentative power as well as their rhetorical persuasiveness. Critical pedagogy negates the language of commonsense description by providing a language of analysis that seeks to explain those structures of representation that give commonsense reality its "natural" appearance. This is not political advocacy in the realm of the cultural imaginary alone. If necessary, we must follow the enslaved and the toilers of the world as they take to the streets.

In a world where the latest commodity fashion and the promise of the perpetually new and different have become democracy's aphrodisiac, a call for a self-conscious return to an earlier and restorative vision of social change may seem provincial, like a player who continues to play a game already abandoned by those considered to be the trend-setters. To call for a return to a theory grounded by a reflexive relation to practical application may seem a quaint (if not politically naive) maneuver in the new Nietzschean playground of the grammatologists. However, in contrast to the conservative postmodernists' game of infinite postponement of meaning, of infinite deferral of the real, of ever-recurring promises of a future that is unattainable, the revolutionary praxis undergirding the politics of critical pedagogy speaks to an *eschaton* of peace and labor, of final victory for the oppressed. Billionaire corporate barons, jawing with their cronies in Davos, the Bohemian Grove, the Bildberg, or the Trilateral can chuckle over the fact that the combined assets of 358 of their billionaire friends are greater than that of 2.5 billion people in the world's poorest countries. Postmodern culture has provided them with a sense of irony; after all, they can even joke about themselves. The revolution that will remove the smirks from their faces and the profits from their *maquiladora* factories will not be a revolution of style, but of revolutionary struggle, by whatever means necessary.

What I would like to underscore is that the struggle over education is fundamentally linked to struggles in the larger theater of social and political life. The struggle that occupies and exercises us as school activists and critical educators should entertain global and local perspectives in terms of the way in which capitalist social relations and the international division of labor are produced and reproduced. While I am largely sympathetic to attempts to reform school practices at the level of policy, curriculum, and classroom pedagogy, such attempts need to be realized and acted upon from the overall perspectives of the struggle against capitalist social relations.

Schools must become sites for the production of both critical knowledge and sociopolitical action. Any institution worthy of the appellation "school" must educate students to become active agents for social transformation and critical citizenship. More than at any other time in world history, school practices need to address the objective, material conditions of the workplace and labor relations within global capitalism. This is an urgent task because the important challenge ahead is to educate a citizenry capable of overcoming the systemic exploitation of so many of the world's populations. Schools should provide students with a language of criticism and a language of hope. These languages should be used in order to prepare students to conceptualize systematically the relationship among their private dreams and desires and the collective dreams of the larger social order. New generations of students must be capable of analyzing the social and material conditions in which dreams are given birth, and are realized, diminished, or destroyed. More importantly, students need to be able to recognize which dreams and which dreamers are dangerous to the larger society, and why this is the case.

Schools need to foster collective dreaming, a dreaming that speaks to the creation of social justice for all groups, and the eventual elimination of classism, racism, sexism, and homophobia. This can occur only if schools are able and committed to help students analyze the ways in which their subjectivities have been ideologically formed within the exploitative forces and relations of globalized, transnational capitalism.

It is clear that if educators are to follow the example of a Marxist-inspired critical pedagogy, there must be a concerted effort to construct a social order that is not premised upon capital. As Kovel warns,

> capital must go if we are to survive as a civilization and, indeed, a species; and all partial measures and reforms should be taken in the spirit of bringing about capital's downfall. Nothing could seem more daunting than this, indeed, in the current balance of forces, it seems inconceivable. Therefore the first job must be to conceive it as a possibility, and not to succumb passively to the given situation. Capital expresses no law of nature; it has been the result of choice, and there is no essential reason to assume it cannot be unchosen. Conceiving things this way is scarcely sufficient. But it is necessary, in both a moral and a practical sense.[88]

In this essay I have tried to argue that the object of Marx's dread has not disappeared but has dramatically intensified: the exploitation of the many by the few on a worldwide scale and the increasing impoverishment of the working class. Postmodernist intellectuals who proclaim history is dead are merely attempting to deny their complicity with the unity of terror haunting humanity. The complex pedigree of thought that brings us postmodernism's *post-histoire* speculation and negative gaze would like to whisk Marxism away like a speck of dust on the stage of history. Provoked by what they perceive as the bankruptcy of the modern "we," postmodernists have provided the Left with a genre of endgame politics that not only gleefully pronounces the death of Marx, but that transmogrifies revolutionary praxis into its antithesis: a dreamscape where avant-garde theorists can effect the smirk of irony, luxuriate in the ambiguity of discursive readings of the social, besmirch the efforts of those who see an urgent need for revolutionary change, substitute "culture" for the "state," and extract excitement from the emptiness of undecidability.

The state has not diminished in importance with respect to the fashioning and management of political power, as some global analysts assert. In fact, critics such as Ellen Meiksins Wood believe that capital needs the state more today than ever before.[89] If this is indeed the case—and I believe that it is—then the working class may now be in an excellent position to challenge capital across nation-states on a global basis. Now is a precipitious time for educators to help develop the kind of critical citizenry capable of such a challenge. In the final analysis, educators need to renew their commitment to the oppressed—not in historical-teleological terms, most certainly, but in ethico-political terms that can guide political action and create the conditions for dreams to take root and liberatory praxis to be carried forward by an undaunted faith in the oppressed.

NOTES

1. Peter McLaren, "Critical Pedagogy in the Age of Global Capitalism: Some Challenges for the Educational Left," *Australian Journal of Education* 39, no. 1 (1995): 5–21. See also Peter McLaren and Ramin Farahmandpur, "Introduction," in *Charting New Terrains in Chicana(o)/Latina(o) Education,* ed. Carlos Tejeda, Zeus Leonardo, and Corinne Martinez (Creskill, N.J.: Hampton Press, forthcoming) and Peter McLaren, "The Pedagogy of Che Guevara," *Cultural Circles* (in press).
2. Jacques Adda, *La Mondalisation de l'Economie* (Paris: Decouverte, 1996), 62.
3. Philippe Engelhard, *Principes d'une Critique de l' Économie Politique* (Paris: Arléa, 1993): 543. Cited in Alain de Benoist, "Confronting Globalization," *Telos* 108 (1996): 117–37. Benoist is a radical conservative commentator.
4. Ellen Meiksins Wood, "Class Compacts, The Welfare State, and Epochal Shifts: A Reply to Frances Fox Piven and Richard A. Cloward," *Monthly Review* 49, no. 8 (1998): 25–46. The regional and liberalization pacts that emerged in the past decade—the World Trade Organization, the North American Free Trade Agreement, the European Union, Latin America's Mercosur, and the recent negotiations of the Organization for Economic Cooperation and Development surrounding the Multilateral Agreement on Investment—are shaping the New World Order in accordance with the most ideal investment conditions for transnational corporations. Anything hindering foreign investment—such as rules and regulations that protect workers and jobs, public welfare, environment, culture, and domestic businesses—will be removed. The World Trade Organization (which was created on 1 January 1995, following the signing of the GATT global free trade agreement in 1994) and the International Monetary Fund both work to obtain trade concessions from those countries whose economies are in distress and to gain access to unprotected sectors of Third World economies. The WTO, the IMF, the OECD, The International Chamber of Commerce, the European Round Table of Industrialists, the Union of Industrial and Employers Confederation of Europe, the United States Council for International Business, the International Organization of Employers, the Business Council on National Issues, the World Business Council for Sustainable Development, the United Nations Commission on Trade and Development, the Business and Industry Advisory Committee, all work to ensure market control and assist transnational corporations in becoming some of the largest economies in the world. In the United States, research centers in Silicon Valley, Route 128 in Boston, the Research Triangle in North Carolina (Raleigh-Durham) and Fairfax County, Virginia, and other locations throughout the country, are not only facilitating possibilities for electronic commerce, but are creating technological contexts for corporate mergers and take-overs.
5. William Greider, "Saving the Global Economy," *The Nation* 265, no. 20 (1997): 12.
6. Ibid., 11–16.
7. Jorge Larrain, "Stuart Hall and the Marxist Concept of Ideology," in *Stuart Hall: Critical Dialogues in Cultural Studies,* ed. David Morely and Kuan-Hsing Chen (London: Routledge, 1996), 68.
8. Ibid.
9. David Ashley, *History without a Subject* (Boulder, Colo.: Westview Press, 1997).
10. Ibid.
11. Jeremy Rifkin, "The Biotech Century: Human Life as Intellectual Property," *The Nation,* 13 April 1998, 12.

12. Ibid.
13. See Peter-McLaren, *Revolutionary Multiculturalism: Pedagogies of Dissent for the New Millennium* (Boulder, Colo.: Westview Press, 1997).
14. Greider, "Saving the Global Economy," 11–16.
15. David F. Noble, "Digital Diploma Mills: The Automation of Higher Education," *Monthly Review* 49, no. 9 (February 1998): 38–52.
16. Ibid.
17. Berndt Ostendorf, "On Globalization and Fragmentation," *2be: A Journal of Ideas* 4, nos. 9–10 (1996): 41.
18. Joel Kovel, "The Enemy of Nature," *Monthly Review* 49, no. 6 (1997): 6–14.
19. Ibid., 7.
20. Ibid.
21. Paul Street, "The Judas Economy and the Limits of Acceptable Debate: A Critique of Wolman and Colamosca." *Monthly Review* 49, no. 9 (1998): 56.
22. Manuel Castells, *The Rise of the Network Society* (Cambridge: Blackwell, 1996). See also Peter McLaren, "Introduction: Traumatizing Capital: Pedagogy, Politics, and Praxis in the Global Marketplace," in *New Perspectives in Education,* ed. Manuel Castells, Ramon Flecha, Paulo Friere, Henry Giroux, Donaldo Macedo, and Paul Willis (Boulder, Colo.: Rowman and Littlefield, in press).
23. The birth of this gospel can be traced to both turn-of-the-century Austria and the University of Chicago in the 1970s. The story begins with Austrian economist Fredrich Von Hayek, who made his debut in the bourgeois salons of "Red Vienna" in the early 1900s, enjoying Virginier cigars and Moyet cognac. Hayek rejected unfettered, laissez-faire capitalism and instead urged active government involvement to protect the smooth functioning of a free market. Later, as a University of Chicago professor, Hayek conceived of a monetarist economics of free-market constitutional liberalism, based on the idea that there is no connection between human intention and social outcome, that the results of human activity are fundamentally haphazard, and that spontaneity must be protected by the strong arm of tradition. Hayek expressed faith (almost to the point of religious zealotry) in the unregulated price mechanism as the means of economic co-ordination and argued that the role of the state must be to blunt human agency and protect the spontaneous social order from the persistently messy efforts of human design. As a philosophical naturalist, Hayek reveled in whatever transpired outside of the conscious attempt at social control; he abhorred what he believed to be the human engineering aspects of market intervention. Market ruthlessness was seen as the aggregate effort of consumer choices and in Hayek's view it was more important to protect the spontaneity of the market, despite its often deleterious consequences for the poor, than to protect individuals or groups from the shameful effects of market justice. Hayek believed that business monopolies were always more benign than the monopolies of labor and the state. Competition is what ensures the spontaneity of the market and this in turn is what creates necessary entrepreneurial opportunities that comprise the natural evolution of the market system, a natural evolution that must be safeguarded at all costs.

The educational epistemology that follows from these neoliberal perspectives flows directly from the idea that knowledge is "constitutionally and irredeemably individual." In both the United States and the United Kingdom, Hayek's ideals provided the underpinnings for discussions of school choice, national standards and curricula, eliminating the welfare state, and life-long learning. Hayekian economics, interpreted through the writings of Milton Friedman, underwrote both Thatcherism and the so-called Reagan revolution and eventually influenced global economic planning. While classical liberals reject state intervention in economics and education, neoliberals in both economic and educational arenas advocate state intervention in order to ensure the operation of a free market and the unrestricted advance of capital. Neo-liberal education policy is thus a conservative force, often blending Christianity, nationalism, authoritarian populism, and free market economics and calling for such creations as a national history curriculum that celebrates the virtues of Christian values, minimal government regulation (except to ensure a "free market") and individual freedom. See Hilary Wainwright, *Arguments for a New Left: Answering the Free Market Right* (London: Blackwell, 1994); Joel Spring, *Education and the Rise of the Global Economy* (New Jersey: Lawrence Erlbaum, 1998); see also Hayek's most influential book, *The Road to Serfdom* (Chicago: The University of

Chicago Press, 1994) and Milton Friedman, *Capitalism and Freedom* (Chicago: University of Chicago Press, 1962).

24. Pierre Bourdieu, "A Reasoned Utopia and Economic Fatalism," trans. John Howe, *New Left Review* 227 (January/February 1998): 126. Italics in original.

25. Scott Davies and Neil Guppy, "Globalization and Educational Reforms in Anglo-American Democracies," *Comparative Education Review* 41, no. 4 (November 1997): 435–59.

26. Ibid., 439.

27. Ibid.

28. Davis and Guppy, "Globalization and Educational Reforms," 444.

29. McLaren, Revolutionary Multiculturalism.

30. Davies and Guppy, 459. Italics in original.

31. James Paul Gee, Glynda Hull, and Colin Lankshear, *The New Work Order* (St. Leonard's, Australia: Allen and Unwin, 1996).

32. Douglas Kellner, *Media Culture* (New York: Routledge, 1995).

33. Robert W. McChesney, "The Global Media Giants," *Extra!* 10, no. 6 (1997): 11.

34. William Robinson, "Globalisation: Nine Theses on our Epoch," *Race and Class* 38, no. 2 (1996): 20–21.

35. Alan Toneleson, "Globalization: The Great American Non-Debate," *Current History: A Journal of Contemporary World Affairs* (November 1997): 359.

36. Gee, Hull, and Lankshear, *The New Work Order.*

37. James Petras, "Latin America: Thirty Years After Che," *Monthly Review* 49, no. 5 (October 1997): 8–21.

38. See McLaren, *Critical Pedagogy* and *Predatory Culture;* McLaren, *Revolutionary Multiculturalism;* Peter McLaren, *Life in Schools: An Introduction to Critical Pedagogy in the Foundations of Education* (New York: Longman, 1997); and Henry Giroux and Peter McLaren, *Between Borders: Pedagogy and the Politics of Cultural Studies* (New York: Routledge, 1994).

39. Peter McLaren and Peter Leonard, *Paulo Freire: A Critical Encounter* (London: Routledge, 1993); Peter McLaren and Colin Lankshear, *Politics of Liberation: Paths from Freire* (London: Routledge; 1994); and Henry A. Giroux and Peter McLaren, "Paulo Freire, Postmodernism, and the Utopian Imagination: A Blochian Reading," in *Not Yet: Reconsidering Ernst Bloch,* ed. Jamie Owen Daniel and Tom Moylan (London: Verso, 1997): 138–62.

40. See Stanley Aronowitz and Henry Giroux, *Postmodern Education* (Minneapolis: University of Minnesota Press, 1991); Patti Lather, *Getting Smart: Feminist Research and Pedagogy with/in the Postmodern* (London: Routledge, 1991); William Doll, Jr., *A Post-Modern Perspective on Curriculum* (New York: Teachers College Press, 1993); Joe Kincheloe, *Towards a Critical Politics of Teacher Thinking: Mapping the Postmodern* (Westport, Conn.: Bergin and Garvey, 1993); Robin Parker Usher and Richard Edwards, *Postmodernism and Education* (London: Routledge, 1994); Andy Hargreaves, *Changing Teachers, Changing Times* (New York: Teachers College Press, 1994); Giroux and McLaren, *Between Borders;* and Richard Smith and Philip Wexler, eds., *After Post Modernism* (London: Falmer Press, 1995).

41. See the discussion in Steven Best and Douglas Kellner, *The Postmodern Turn* (New York: Guilford Press, 1997). See also Steven Best and Douglas Kellner, *Postmodern Theory: Critical Interrogations* (New York: Guilford Press, 1991).

42. Morton Wenger, "Decoding Postmodernism: The Despair of the Intellectuals and the Twilight of the Future," *Social Science Journal* 28, no. 3 (1991): 391–407. See also Morton Wenger, "Idealism Redux: The Class-Historical Truth of Postmodernism," *Critical Sociology* 20, no. 1 (1993/94): 53–78.

43. See E. San Juan, Jr., *Beyond Postcolonial Theory* (New York: St. Martin's Press, 1998).

44. Glenn Rikowski, "Left Alone: End Time for Marxist Educational Theory?" *British Journal of Sociology of Education* 17, no. 4 (1996):442.

45. Judith Butler, "Merely Cultural," *New Left Review* 227 (January/February 1998): 33–44.

46. Terry Eagleton, *The Illusions of Postmodernism* (Cambridge: Blackwell, 1996). See my analysis of the distinction made by Teresa Ebert between "ludic postmodernism" (that celebrates the free-floating articulation of signifiers in the construction of lifestyle discourses that are viewed for the most part as detached from external determinations) and "resistance postmodernism" (which draws upon poststructuralist advances in understanding signification but views language as the product of history and links signification to class struggle through the Formalist linguistics of

Mikhail Bakhtin, V. N. Volosinov, and a sociological analysis of language associated with Lev Vygotsky and G. Plekhanov). See McLaren, *Critical Pedagogy.* See also Vered Amit-Talai and Caroline Knowles, eds., *Re-Situating Identities* (Peterborough, Canada: Broadview Press, 1996); Etienne Balibar and Immanuel Wallerstein, *Race, Nation, Class,* trans. Chris Turner (London: Verso, 1991); Judith Butler, *The Psychic Life of Power* (Stanford: Stanford University Press, 1997); Ian Chambers, *Migrancy, Culture, Identity* (London: Routledge, 1994); James D. Faubion, ed., *Rethinking the Subject* (Boulder: Westview Press, 1995); Stuart Hall, David Held, and Tony McGrew, *Modernity and its Futures* (Cambridge: The Open University, Polity Press, 1992); Stuart Hall and Paul du Gay, eds., *Questions of Cultural Identity* (London: Sage, 1996); Michael Keith and Steve Pile, eds., *Place and the Politics of Identity* (London: Routledge, 1993); John Rajchman, ed., *The Identity in Question* (London: Routledge, 1995); and Jonathan Rutherford, ed., *Identity: Community, Culture, Difference* (London: Lawrence and Wishart, 1990).

47. See Dave Hill and Mike Cole, "Marxist State Theory and State Autonomy Theory: The Case of 'Race' Education in Initial Teacher Education," *Journal of Educational Policy* 10, no. 2 (1995): 221–32; Rikowski, "Left Alone"; Mike Cole, Dave Hill, and Glenn Rikowski, "Between Postmodernism and Nowhere: The Predicament of the Postmodernist," *British Journal of Educational Studies* 45, no. 2 (June 1997): 187–200; and Andy Green, "Postmodernism and State Education," *Journal of Educational Policy* 9 (1994): 67–83.

48. Nancy Fraser, *Justice Interruptus* (New York: Routledge, 1997): 181. For a different assessment, see Iris Marion Young, "Unruly Categories: A Critique of Nancy Fraser's Dual Systems Theory," *New Left Review* 222 (March/April 1997): 147–60. Also see Mas'ud Zavarzadeh and Donald Morton, *Theory as Resistance* (New York: Guilford Press, 1994) and Teresa L. Ebert, *Ludic Feminism and After* (Ann Arbor: University of Michigan Press, 1996). See also Peter McLaren,"Beyond Phallogocentrism: Critical Pedagogy and its Capital Sins: A Response to Donna LeCourt," *Strategies* (in press) and Carole A. Stabile, "Postmodernism, Feminism, and Marx: Notes from the Abyss," in *In Defense of History,* ed. Ellen Meiksins Wood and John Bellamy Foster (New York: Monthly Review Press, 1997): 134–48.

49. Gee, Hull, and Lankshear, *The New Work Order.*

50. Andy Green, "Postmodernism and State Education," 80.

51. Ibid., 81.

52. See McLaren, "The Pedagogy of Che Guevara."

53. Aijaz Ahmad, "The *Communist Manifesto* and the Problem of Universality," *Monthly Review* 50, no. 2(1998): 22.

54. Sherry Ortner, "Identities: The Hidden Life of Class," *Journal of Anthropological Research* 54, no. 1 (Spring 1998): 8–9.

55. Ibid., 9.

56. Ibid., 4.

57. Ibid., 14.

58. Richard Wolff and Stephen Resnick, "Power, Property, and Class," *Socialist Review* 16, no. 2 (1986): 97–124.

59. Ibid., 120.

60. Samir Amin, *Specters of Capitalism: A Critique of Current Intellectual Fashions* (New York: Monthly Review Press, 1998). See also Samir Amin, *Capitalism in the Age of Globalization* (London: Zed Books, 1997) and Samir Amin, *Eurocentrism* (New York: Monthly Review Press, 1989).

61. For an expanded discussion of multiculturalism and globalization, see Peter McLaren, *Multiculturalism Critico* (Sao Paulo, Brazil: Cortez Editora and Instituto Paul Freire, 1997). See also McLaren, *Revolutionary Multiculturalism.*

62. Charles Handy, "What's It All For? Reinventing Capitalism for the Next Century," *RSA Journal* 144, no. 5475 (1996): 33–40.

63. Alex Callinicos, *Against Postmodernism: A Marxist Critique* (New York: St. Martin's Press, 1990).

64. Joe Kincheloe, *Toil and Trouble* (New York: Peter Lang, 1995).

65. Ellen Meiksins Wood, *Democracy Against Capitalism; Renewing Historical Materialism* (Cambridge: Cambridge University Press, 1995), 252.

66. James Petras and Morris Morely, *Latin America in the Time of Cholera: Electoral Politics, Market Economies, and Permanent Crisis* (New York: Routledge, 1992).

67. Wood, Democracy Against Capitalism, 262–63.
68. István Mészáros, *Beyond Capital: Toward a Theory of Transition* (New York: Monthly Review Press, 1995).
69. Callinicos, Against Postmodernism: A Marxist Critique.
70. Ibid.
71. E. San Juan, Jr., *Mediations: From a Filipino Perspective* (Pasig City, Philippines: Anvil, 1996).
72. See David T. Sehr, *Education for Public Democracy* (Albany: SUNY Press, 1997).
73. David Gabbard, "NAFTA, GATT, and Goals 2000: Reading the Political Culture of Post-Industrial America," *Taboo* 2 (Fall 1995): 184–99.
74. Joe Kincheloe and Shirley Steinberg, *Students as Researchers* (London: Falmer Press, 1998).
75. See Ebert, *Ludic Feminism and After* and Rosemary Hennessy, *Materialist Feminism and the Politics of Discourse* (New York: Routledge, 1993). The critique of postmodern discourses that I am employing is not an assault on feminist critique. It is a critique of those critical attempts—feminist, post-Marxist, and otherwise—that do not challenge sufficiently the ruling frameworks of patriarchal capitalism that deploy sexual difference to justify the unequal distribution of wealth and power. The Marxist-feminist critique I am employing locates patriarchal exploitation beyond the rhetoricization and troping of capitalism and within class, gender, and ethnic divisions of property relations and the struggle over profit and surplus labor.
76. Edward Soja, *Postmodern Geographies* (London: Verso, 1989). See also David Harvey, *Justice, Nature, and the Geography of Difference* (Cambridge: Blackwell Publishers, 1996).
77. McLaren and Leonard, Paulo Freire, *A Critical Encounter* and McLaren and Lankshear, *Politics of Liberation.*
78. Spring, *Education and the Rise of the Global Economy.*
79. Gee, Hull, and Lankshear, *The New Work Order,* 166, 152.
80. Ibid., 167.
81. Rikowski, "Left Alone" and Cole, Hill, and Rikowski, "Between Postmodernism and Nowhere."
82. Bill Bigelow, "The Human Lives Behind the Labels: The Global Sweatshop, Nike, and the Race to the Bottom," *Rethinking Schools* 11, no. 4 (1997): 1–16.
83. Ibid.
84. See the discussion by Luke Mines, "Globalization in the Classroom," *The Nation* 266, no. 20 (1998): 22–23.
85. See Rikowski, "Left Alone." See also Jack Amariglio and Antonio Calari, "Marxian Value Theory and the Problem of the Subject: The Role of Commodity Fetishism," in *Fetishism as Cultural Discourse,* ed. Emily Apter and William Pietz (Ithaca, N.Y.: Cornell University Press, 1993), 186–216; William Pietz, "Fetishism and Materialism: The Limits of Theory in Marx," in Apter and Pietz, *Fetishism as Cultural Discourse,* 119–51; and Jean Baudrillard, "The End of the Millennium or The Countdown," *Theory, Culture and Society* 15, no. 1 (February 1998): 1–9.
86. See McLaren, *Critical Pedagogy and Predatory Culture,* and McLaren, *Revolutionary Multiculturalism.*
87. Iris Marion Young, *Justice and the Politics of Difference* (Princeton, N.J.: Princeton University Press, 1990).
88. Kovel, "The Enemy of Nature," 14. See also Peter McLaren, "Introduction: Traumatizing Capital," and McLaren, "Critical Pedagogy in the Age of Global Capitalism."
89. Wood, *Democracy Against Capitalism.*

Suggested Readings
for Future Study

ON SCHOOLING, CLASS, AND THE ECONOMY

Anyon, J. (1997). *Ghetto schooling: A political economy of urban educational reform.* New York: Teachers College.

Apple, M. (1986). *Teachers and texts: A political economy of class and gender relations in education.* New York: Routledge.

Aronowitz, S. (2000). *The knowledge factory: Dismantling the corporate university and creating true higher learning:* Boston: Beacon.

Aronowitz, A. (2001). *The last good job in America: Work and education in the new global technoculture.* New York: Rowman & Littlefield.

Aronowitz, S., and Cutler, J. (1998). *Post-work: The wages of cybernation.* New York: Routledge.

Bowles, S., and Gintis, H. (1976). *Schooling in capitalist America.* New York: Basic Books.

Brosio, R. (1994). *A radical democratic critique of capitalist education.* New York: Peter Lang.

Carnoy, M. (1994). *Faded dreams: The politics and economics of race in America.* Cambridge: Cambridge University Press.

Collins, C., Leondar-Wright, B., and Sklar, H. (1999). *Shifting fortunes: The perils of the growing American wealth gap.* Boston: United for a Fair Economy.

Evans, A., Evans, R., and Kennedy, W. (1990). *Pedagogies of the non-poor.* New York: Orbis.

Gee, J. P., Hull, G., and Lankshear, C. (1996). *The new work order: Behind the language of the new capitalism.* Boulder, Colo.: Westview.

Greider, W. (1997). *One world ready or not: The manic logic of global capitalism.* New York: Simon & Schuster.

Halsey, A. H., ed. (1997). *Education: Culture, economy, and society.* New York: Oxford University Press.

Herman, E., and Chomsky, N. (1988). *Manufacturing consent: The political economy of the mass media.* New York: Pantheon.

Kozol, J. (1991). *Savage inequalities: Children in America's Schools.* New York: Harper.

Kumar, A. (1997). *Class issues: Pedagogy, cultural studies, and the public sphere.* New York: New York University Press.

Lauder, H., and Hughes, D. (1999). *Trading in futures: Why markets in education don't work.* Philadelphia: Open University Press.

McChesney, R., Wood, E. M., and Foster, J. B., eds. (1998). *Capitalism and the information age: The political economy of the global communication revolution.* New York: Monthly Review.

Milner, A. (1999). *Class.* London: Sage.

Molnar, A. (1996). *Giving kids the business: The commercialization of America's Schools.* Boulder, Colo.: Westview.

Sassen, S. (1998). *Globalization and its discontent: Essays on the new mobility of people and money.* New York: The New York Press.

Spring, J. (2001). *Globalization and educational rights.* New York: Lawrence Erlbaum.

Willis, P. (1981). *Learning to labor: How working class kids get working class jobs.* New York: Columbia University Press.

Wood, E. M. (1995). *Democracy against capitalism.* New York: Monthly Review.

Wood, E. M. (1999). *The origin of capitalism.* New York: Monthly Review.

Part 3

RACE, RACISM, AND EDUCATION

INTRODUCTION

Unlike conventional approaches often found in writings on race and education, this section addresses the process of racialization from a very distinctive perspective—it attempts to move discussions of race and racism away from the pervasiveness of an essentialist politics of identity. C. Alejandra Elenes initiates the discussion in "Reclaiming the Borderlands: Chicana/o Identity, Difference, and Critical Pedagogy" by reconceptualizing the meaning of a politics of identity and difference within the critical pedagogy movement. She readily acknowledges the contributions of critical pedagogy to the development of a "borderland" theory—one that symbolizes not the geographical boundaries but the development of an identity paradigm—but argues, that in spite of its contributions, critical pedagogy is too constraining to explain the experience of biculturalism and the borderland in an era of globalization and postcolonial concerns. Elenes clearly distinguishes the essentialist notion of Chicano/a identity developed during the 1960s from the current theoretical construct that has allowed her to conceptualize difference in a more comprehensive manner.

In "Toward a Pedagogy of Place for Black Urban Struggle," Stephen Nathan Haymes further develops the concept of racism within what he terms a "pedagogy of place" for urban movements. Inspired by the work of critical education theorists, he elaborates on racism as a lived construct within the realities of the black experience, particularly in terms of physical spaces, physical bodies, and social and economic struggles. His work here clearly attempts to move the reader beyond a postmodern reification of blackness. Further, Haymes argues that blacks in the United States have historically preserved their identity through the creation and protection of places where they could live and keep their blackness alive. Moreover, he speaks to how black public spaces within urban cities—commonly associated with the dangers of madness and the temptations of pleasure—are being appropriated by assimilationist and Afrocentric notions of development. Through his elaboration of a pedagogy of space, Haymes calls for the protection of the urban metropolis as a place to reclaim blackness, to fight against racism, and to struggle against the reification of difference by late capitalism

In her essay "Reflections on Race and Sex," the renowned feminist bell hooks speaks to the historical overlapping nature of discourses related to race and sex, beginning with slavery. Challenging the collusion of black men with patriarchal forms of domination, hooks lances a formidable critique against recurring practices of "misogynist sexism" justified as "natural" responses to racial domination. She calls for a critical feminist theory that clearly stresses an understanding of the ways racism and sexism exist as interlocking systems of domination. Hooks considers this reformulation an imperative to constructing a revolutionary vision of black liberation that can inspire new transformative models of identity for black men and women in this country.

Antonia Darder and Rodolfo Torres complete this section with their essay "Shattering the 'Race' Lens: Toward a Critical Theory of Racism" that boldly critiques the pervasive essentialism inherent in the majority of writings related to the construct of "race." Their work calls for the development of a critical theory of racism, as opposed to critical race theory, upon which to construct a new language of analysis that can dialectically engage with the relationship that exists between racism and class inequality. As such, the authors challenge critical educators who continue to privilege "race" as the primary force of oppression in their efforts to theorize social inequality. Instead, Darder and Torres call for a historical materialist analysis to help teachers more clearly understand how the hideous process of racialization has been an ongoing function and imperative for the expansion of economic domination and exploitation.

QUESTIONS FOR REFLECTION AND DIALOGUE

1. Define what is meant by a "politics of identity and difference."
2. What is meant by borderland theory? In what ways does this theory differ from other theories of identity?
3. What are the major contributions of borderland theory to the study of racism and to a critical pedagogy?
4. What are the major concepts developed by Haymes in his formulation of a pedagogy of place?
5. Define what is meant by a traditional multicultural approach to the inner cities.
6. How does Haymes define the historical and current development of black identity under the current global economy?

7. How does the discourse of economic development of inner cities relate to the perpetuation of racism?
8. What does hooks describe as the overlapping nature of race and sex in United States?
9. How does hooks explain the patriarchal bonds of men across class, race, and nationalities?
10. In what ways are the media implicated in the perpetuation of both racism and sexism?
11. According to Darder and Torres, how does a critical theory of racism differ from an the essentialist view of "race"?
12. Explain the major criticisms made by Darder and Torres of "race relations" approaches in education.
13. In what critical ways can a critical theory of racism deepen our understanding of social inequalities?

Reclaiming the Borderlands: Chicana/o Identity, Difference, and Critical Pedagogy

C. ALEJANDRA ELENES

You who understand the dehumanization of forced removal-relocation-reeducation-redefinition, the humiliation of having to falsify your own reality, your voice—you know. And often cannot say it. You try to unsay it, for if you don't, they will not fail to fill in the blanks on your behalf, and you will be said.[1]

The production and re-production of the discourse of the *Borderlands* speaks a language of fluidity, migration, postcolonialism, displacement . . . of subaltern identities. The *Borderlands* is the discourse of people who live between different worlds. It speaks against dualism, oversimplification, and essentialism. It is, a discourse, a language, that explains the social conditions of subjects with hybrid identities. Hence, it has been a discourse favored by some Chicana and Chicano scholars in the 1980s and 1990s, people in-between U.S. and Mexican culture(s), with identities that are in constant flux.[2] The border identity of Chicana/o discourse is not the essentialist nationalist identity of the Chicano movement; nor is it the identity that U.S. dominant culture has constructed. It moves beyond binary constructions. It is a discourse and identity of difference and displacement.

Identity formation is never a project that any subject constructs by herself. Identities are co-constructed by the subject and society at large; whether the subject is marked as "inferior," "deviant," "passive," or unmarked (the "norm"). Chicanas/os have been constructed as an inferior "Other" since the U.S. expanded its territory and occupied Mexico's northern territories. Much of the Chicana/o struggle has been a struggle to re-claim what was lost after 1848: land, language, culture, identity. While the Chicana/o communities have historically resisted this process of deterritorialization (physically and symbolically) in many different arenas (economic, political, cultural), education has been considered central to the struggle for a rightful place in U.S. society. It is not surprising, then, that much of the Chicana/o and Mexican-American activism has focused on access to and reform of educational institutions.

In this essay, I am analyzing the influence of *Borderlands* theories on critical pedagogy. I argue that *Borderlands* has served, and continues to do so, as a theoretical framework to advance educational theory by taking into account multiple subjectivity and difference. I will first provide a historical background of the development of Chicana/o Studies and its contribution to *Borderlands* theories and identities. Then, I analyze how critical pedagogy has adapted the concept of the *Borderlands* and the need to re-theorize difference. Finally, I elaborate on how the *Borderlands* can be incorporated into educational discourses and pedagogical practices.

THE STRUGGLE FOR ACADEMIC SPACE: CHICANA/O STUDIES

Dominant educational practices in the U.S. promote the assimilation of Chicanas/os (and other minorities) to the dominant culture, especially to its myths of equality, democracy, freedom, and individualism. According to Laura Pérez, "One of the racist, dominant culture's most effective ideological strategies has been to educate us *all*—minorities and non-minorities— to the national myths of equality, democracy, and freedom for all. We are taught that these principles are attainable realities in the U.S. and furthermore, as minorities we wish that this were true."[3] The ideology of assimilation buttresses racist notions that Chicanas/os, other minority groups, and some European ethnics, are in effect socially and culturally inferior. Thus, in order to function in schools and society they must assimilate to the dominant cultural norms. Cultural deprivation theories and the programs based on these theories were inspired by such assumptions. In its more recent incarnation, this argument claims that the U.S. is an integral part of Western civilization and the only way to avoid Balkanization is to unite in one culture and language.[4] No matter how subtle or direct, these theories and ideologies are detrimental to the educational advancement of Chicanas/os and other minorities.

The educational struggle of the civil rights movement and, even more so, that of the Chicano nationalist movement were constructed against such practices and assimilationists ideologies. The activists of the Chicana/o movement recognized that in order to achieve their political and socio-economic goals it was necessary to gain access to and reform educational institutions. The Chicano movement of the 1960s and 1970s was not the first to struggle over educational institutions. However, this was the first time that the community articulated the need to change educational institutions significantly. The educational history of Chicanas/os in the twentieth century is one of legal battles to end school segregation and to implement bilingual and multicultural education. What differentiates the Chicano movement from other educational struggles are philosophical differences.[5] For the Chicano movement, access to education meant not only the literal access of bodies into the classroom, but also to a curriculum where Chicana/o history, culture, politics, and identity were central.

One of the efforts to open Chicana/o educational spaces was the student movement's struggles to develop Chicano Studies programs and departments.[6] The point of departure for Chicano Studies was an anti-assimilationist ideology.[7] *El Plan de Santa Barbara,* the document charting the ideology of Chicano Studies, reads in part:

> Rather than accommodate Chicanos to these institutions, support programs should facilitate the development of educational processes to meet the unique interests of Chicanos . . . [and to] develop alternative goals to those prescribed by society. . . . It cannot be overemphasized that the focus of Chicano efforts on campus must provide "new" meaning and value to higher learning. Chicano programs must not employ existing goals and structures of higher education as a frame of reference. To succumb to traditional structures and approaches is to legitimize their role in indoctrinating Chicanos to become a part of gabacho . . . society.[8]

In its inception Chicano Studies was created for Chicano students. The idea was to design a curriculum that would enable Chicano youth to construct an alternative identity that promoted Chicanismo. Moreover, this curriculum would be organized to attend to the needs of the community. The connection between academia and the barrio were essential for the existence of Chicano Studies programs.

Unfortunately, the constitution of Chicana/o Studies programs was based on Chicano nationalism. The subject of Chicano nationalism was constructed as male, heterosexual, working class, and politically active. This created an obvious problem for Chicana feminists, gays, lesbians, and to a lesser extent an emerging middle class. Even though Chicano nationalism is/was a liberatory discourse, it also served as an oppressive discourse for the members of the community who were/are "othered" by Chicano nationalist discourses. Chicana feminist theorists and activists struggled to create safe spaces within Chicana/o Studies.[9]

Nevertheless, the Chicana/o Studies curriculum and scholarship has advanced in directions that were not envisioned by the Chicana/o Studies pioneers. Feminist and Queer theory, for example, have transformed the discipline from its narrow male focus. Additionally, many Chicana/o scholars are contributing to new theoretical frameworks such as poststructuralism and postmodernism.[10] Chicana/o Studies programs as well as ethnic studies programs have moved beyond the antiassimilationist ideology; the scholarship produced and the curriculum are contributing to the decentralization of Eurocentric thought. Here it is worth while to quote Kris Gutiérrez:

> One of the central aims of ethnic studies, for example, has been to make visible the essential philosophies, cultures, and histories of ethnic peoples and, thus, to produce a complete scholarship that necessarily challenges prevailing Eurocentric thought and methods. From this perspective, then, ethnic studies is not the inclusion or integration of new themes or experiences into the existing curriculum; that would simply require studying new subjects through the same Eurocentric lens, rather than a process by which students, teachers, and researchers develop new forms of agency. Instead, ethnic studies seeks to locate itself in a much broader sociocultural terrain in which groups of color and women of color are integral to the understanding of everyday life in an American context.[11]

Chicana/o Studies was based on a notion of cultural and identity difference. It was created precisely because Chicanas/os have been constituted as different who either were not "assimilable" or should be "assimilated." The antiassimilationist focus of Chicana/o Studies, and the subsequent advancement of the field, continues to depend upon the theorization of difference. While at the beginning the notion of difference was/is essentialist, more recent theorization understands difference as constituted. Chicana feminist, postmodernist, gay and lesbian, and borderlands theoretical constructions historicize and politicize the ways in which Chicanas/os are constituted as different and constitute themselves as different. As stated in the above quotation by Gutiérrez, this understanding of difference is necessary to decenter the Eurocentric curriculum.

BORDERLANDS AND THE CHICANA/O INTELLECTUAL TRADITION

The efforts and struggles of the Chicano movement to increase the presence of Chicana/o students in higher education, and to create "new" academic spaces to study systematically the experience and contributions of Chicanas/os to U.S. society, has produced significant scholarship that contributes to the reconceptualization of "American" intellectual traditions and canons. One of the contributions of Chicana/o scholars has been the theoretical notion of Borderlands.[12] Although the concept of the border is not new, it gained popularity outside of Chicana/o intellectual circles in the 1980s and 1990s, and has been adopted across many fields of study, but especially by critical pedagogy (and particularly by Henry Giroux and Peter McLaren).

Border studies have produced significant literature on the socio-economic and cultural conditions of the U.S./Mexico border.[13] The conceptualization of *Borderlands* forms part of an oppositional discourse for Chicanas/os (and Mexicans in the U.S.), constructed from the condition of living in the margins of U.S. society and culture. Publications such as Gloria Anzaldúa's *Borderlands/*

La Frontera, the anthology of Chicana/o literary criticism *Criticism in the Borderlands*, Renato Rosaldo's *Culture and Truth*, Ramón Saldívar's *Chicano Narrative*, Carl Gutiérrez-Jones's *Rethinking the Borderlands*, and Alfred Arteaga's edited volume *An Other Tongue* construct Chicana/o social and cultural critique by locating their narratives in the borderlands.[14] According to Saldívar-Hull, the borders of Chicana/o discourse are not only geopolitical, having to do with the U.S./Mexico border, but symbolic as well.[15] The borderlands are the boundaries that Chicanas/os live in that form a state of "belonging" and "not-belonging." These boundaries are the interstices between the so-called First and Third Worlds, Anglo-America and the symbolic spaces that confine people of color in the metropolis, and the formal and informal economy (the legal and the illegal). As Héctor Calderón and José David Saldívar write in the introduction to *Criticism in the Borderlands*, "Our work in the eighties and nineties, along with that of other postcolonial intellectuals' moves, travels as they say, between first and third worlds, between cores and peripheries, centers and margins. The theorists in this book see their text always 'written for' and in our local and global borderlands."[16]

Why have the borderlands gained so much currency in the 1990s? While it is not possible to find one particular answer to this complex question, I propose that the borderlands has gained popularity due to theoretical advances in ethnic studies, feminist studies, postcolonialism, and postmodernism. These advances have been critical for education scholarship. Given the limitations of neo-Marxist theories of social reproduction, especially the limitation of race, class, gender, and sexuality analyses, postmodernism offered new avenues to interpret social conditions. While many scholars in "traditional" fields "discovered" the limitation of existing paradigms, Chicana/o scholars had already provided critiques of such scholarly research.[17] It is precisely when Chicana/o scholars demonstrated the limitations of a single issue approach that the borderlands came to existence.[18] For example, Rosa Linda Fregoso historicizes the borderlands in her analysis of Chicana/o film when she writes that the concept of the border "represent[s] an alternative way of conceptualizing cultural process in the late twentieth century—a time when people, media images, and information journey across the world at the spaces 'within and between' what were once sanctified as 'homogenous' communities."[19] Fregoso argues that the borderlands gained currency because of the globalization of the economy and postcolonialism. The borderlands can explain the situation of peoples all over the globe, not only in the Southwest. Calderón and Saldívar in the introduction to their volume *Criticism in the Borderlands* argue that the discourse of the borderlands "must have emerged in the borderlands in mid-nineteenth century when Mexican-Americans, Chicanos, or mestizos began to project for themselves a positive, yet also critical, rendering of their bilingual and bicultural experience as a resistive measure against Anglo-American economic domination and ideological hegemony."[20]

Borderlands, like other discourses theorizing marginality, not only addresses philosophical/methodological questions, but also the question of subjectivity, or identity formation—two areas that, for the most part, have being interrelated in Chicana/o studies. Thus the following analysis of *Borderlands* focuses on these two areas: the notion of Border/mestiza/o identity, and the reconceptualization of social sciences methodologies, or what Renato Rosaldo calls the re-making of social analysis (*CT,* pp. 38–45).

BORDER IDENTITIES

Because Chicanas/os are marginalized people in the U.S., because they have been the objects of assimilationist policies, and because their culture, language, and customs have been considered inferior, they need to construct their own notion of identity and subjectivity. *Borderlands* as a discourse, especially that developed by Anzaldúa, constructs a Border identity of the Chicana/o subject. Anzaldúa's project leads toward an understanding of Chicana identity and subjectivity that recognizes class, race, national, and sexual discontinuities within the Chicana/o communities. Anzaldúa's project is, precisely, the construction of a mestiza identity that recognizes the relations between past and present oppression. The mestiza identity is located in the interstices of Mexican/Chicano culture, patriarchy, homophobia, and Anglo-American domination: "Alienated from her mother culture, 'alien' in the dominant culture, the woman of color does not feel safe within the inner life of her Self. Petrified, she can't respond, her face caught between *los intersticios,* the spaces between the different worlds she inhabits."[21] Anzaldúa names this identity a dual identity similar to that described by W. E. B. Du Bois,

> A kind of dual identity—we don't identify with the Anglo-American cultural values and we don't totally identify with the Mexican cultural values. We are a synergy of two cultures with various degrees of Mexicanness or Angloness. I have so internalized the borderland conflict that sometimes I feel like one cancels out the other and we are zero, nothing, no one. *A veces no soy nada ni nadie, Pero hasta cuando no lo soy, lo soy.*[22]

According to Saldívar-Hull, "Anzaldúa's text is itself a *mestizaje:* a postmodern mixture of autobiography, historical document, and poetry collection. Like the people whose lives it chronicles, *Borderlands* resists genre boundaries as well as geopolitical borders."[23] Anzaldúa chronicles the multiple forms of oppression Chicanas suffer, thus, she never lets us forget the material conditions and subordinate position of Chicanas/os, Mexicans, and Central American immigrants in the U.S.

The significance of Anzaldúa's text is in how she is able to incorporate the notion of the border as a basis for the construction of a *mestiza* consciousness. Anzaldúa combines traditional ideas of nationalism such as looking back and reclaiming an Aztec ancestry (a form of essentialism) with the destabilization of a unified subject. What this combination is able to do is incorporate the need for a Chicana identity based on an Indigenous past (a necessary political move) with a postmodernist notion of split/multiple subjectivity. Although Anzaldúa romanticizes past Chicano and Mexican cultures, she denounces their sexism, racism, and homophobia. Even though she strongly indicts Mexican and Chicano cultures, she does not disown them. The slippage in Anzaldúa's text is actually a paradox. Identity is necessary, but must be constantly deferred. In the last section I will return to this paradox.

Borderlands, according to Papusa Molina, is a "fragmented discourse . . . that is propio, or appropriate, for people like me; people in the Borderlands. I am not a one-dimensional person; I do not need to have one tongue, one language, one discourse."[24] Life in the borderlands entails living under the fear that "*la migra*" will raid your place of work and deport you, whether you are "legal" or "illegal," because in the anti-immigrant discourse all Chicanas/os and Mexicans are alien. Alfred Arteaga makes this point when he writes about his own subjectification in relation to how he conceives himself:

> I define myself as a Chicano. I was born in California and am a citizen of the United States, but my relation to that nation is problematic. U.S. Anglo-American nationalists define their nation to the exclusion of my people. Today in California, for example, the male Republican governor and the two female Democratic senators, collude in generating anti-immigrant (i.e., Mexican in the United States) hysteria: that I am rendered alien by U.S. jingoism remains a quotidian fact. My nation is not Mexico, yet I am ethnically Mexican and racially mestizo. But my people exist in the borderlands that traverse the national frontiers of the United States and Mexico.[25]

BORDERLANDS AND SOCIAL ANALYSIS

Renato Rosaldo's book *Culture and Truth* presents an anthropological approach to the reconceptualization of social analysis from a Chicano perspective. In this study, Rosaldo provides the theoretical framework for the social analysis of culture as fluid. By using the notion of *border zones* Rosaldo argues that "the fiction of the uniformly shared culture increasingly seems more tenuous than useful" (*CT,* p. 207). For Rosaldo "social borders frequently become salient around such lines as sexual orientation, gender, class, race, ethnicity, nationality, age, politics, dress, food or taste" (*CT,* pp. 207–208). The social analysis that Rosaldo proposes is the result of the demands of marginalized groups such as the counterculture, environmentalism, feminism, gay and lesbian movements, the Native American movement, and the struggles of blacks, Chicanos, and Puerto Ricans (*CT,* p. 35). The consequences for social analysis are the following:

> The salience of new topics for study created by the remaking of social analysis requires a concept of culture capacious enough to encompass both work guided

by classic norms and projects previously excluded or rendered marginal. Such previously excluded topics prominently include studies that seek out hetero-geneity, rapid change, and intercultural borrowing and lending. (*CT,* p. 208)

Rosaldo argues, following Clifford Geertz, that his remaking of social analysis blurs the boundaries between social sciences and humanities (*CT,* p. 37). The type of social analysis proposed by *Borderlands* theories uses multiple and innovative methodologies such as life histories, testimonials, and interviews, along with other forms of cultural productions such as narratives, corridos, and visual arts. In this sense, *Borderlands* constructs knowledge "from below." This knowledge is always positional and partial. Saldívar places corridos and Chicana/o narratives as social symbolic acts of resistance:

> In Chicano narrative the history of [Mexican Americans and Chicanos] is the subtext which must be recovered from the oblivion to which American social and literary history have consigned it. Our literary texts will show how aesthetic and cultural productions often turn out to be the ideological rewriting of that banished history.[26]

Carl Gutiérrez-Jones writes that Chicana and Chicano narratives have been consistently theoretical "if by *theoretical* we understand a form of discourse which comments on its own and other forms of discourse."[27] Following Fregoso and Saldívar, Gutiérrez-Jones argues that Chicana narratives in particular are counter-hegemonic. Further, he adds that the excitement of Chicano theoretical activity "lies exactly in its movement beyond encyclopedic categorization and into an analysis of the various processes by which Chicano art has engaged in dialogue with and commented on the artistic and nonartistic languages circulating around it."[28]

This analysis of the *Borderlands* can offer a way to advance educational theory. The understanding of culture as fluid is a necessary move, since much of the education scholarship under the guise of multicultural education continues to represent culture and identity as static. At the same time, the *Borderlands,* like many other theoretical formations, moves beyond the limitation of an overreliance on scientific method. I believe that in cultural productions we can find a wealth of information that can be incorporated into school practices and educational theory. One approximation of this approval has been advanced by critical pedagogy.

CRITICAL PEDAGOGY: CROSSING BORDERS

Borderlands theories have influenced the construction of knowledge in some progressive educational discourses such as critical pedagogy that contribute to the deconstruction of conservative and neoconservative views of multicultural education. A cursory examination of recent titles shows the contributions of *Borderlands* theory to educational theory and pedagogy.[29] Giroux's and

McLaren's respective work contributes to the conceptualization of the *Border-lands* applied to educational and pedagogical theory. There is an interrelationship between critical pedagogy's construction of border pedagogy and Chicana/o *Borderlands*. Both apply the concept as a metaphor and both rely on each other to advance their respective theories. However, this interrelation also raises the problematic of appropriation and erasure of difference. In this section I will elaborate on how Giroux and McLaren, respectively, develop their notion of border pedagogy, and then will critique the slippage in how they apply the notion of difference.

Giroux argues that "Border pedagogy is attentive to developing a democratic public philosophy that respects the notion of difference as part of a common struggle to extend the quality of public life" (*BC*, p. 28). For Giroux, radical educational theory and practice can be refined by border pedagogy by taking into consideration three theoretical constructs: (1) the recognition of epistemological, political, cultural, and social margins that structure the language of history, power, and difference; (2) the need to create pedagogical conditions for students to become border crossers "in order to understand otherness in its own terms"; and (3) making visible the historically and socially constructed strengths and limitations of places and borders that frame our discourses and social relations (*BC*, p. 28). Moreover, Giroux's border pedagogy is a political project particularly set as antiracist:

> What is being called for here is a notion of border pedagogy that provides educators with the opportunity to rethink the relations between the centers and the margins of power. That is, such a pedagogy must address the issue of racism as one that calls into question not only forms of subordination that create inequities among different groups as they live out their lives, but as I have mentioned previously, also challenges those institutional and ideological boundaries that have historically masked their own relations of power behind complex forms of distinction and privilege. (*BC*, p. 135)

For Giroux, then, this antiracist border pedagogy "presupposes not merely an acknowledgement of the shifting borders that both undermine and reterritorialize dominant configurations of power and knowledge" (*BC*, p. 134), but also, following Chantal Mouffe, links pedagogy with democratic practices.[30] Moreover, Giroux recognizes that the borders he is talking about are not only physical borders "but cultural borders historically constructed and socially organized within maps of rules and regulations that serve to either limit or enable particular identities, individual capacities, and social forms" (*BC*, p. 136). Giroux argues that his border pedagogy "decenters as it remaps" (*BC*, p. 136); by doing so, educators can redefine the teacher-student relation by enabling students to draw from their own experience.

Giroux and McLaren do not jettison the macrostructural in their pedagogical theorizing. McLaren, particularly, bases much of his analysis and theorization on what he calls "predatory culture." Advanced capitalism, the globalization of the economy, economic terrorism, the widening gap between the wealthy and the poor create a problem of subjectivity and agency in an era of multinational consumerism. For McLaren the conditions of the late twentieth century "are reflective of the narratives we live by. They mirror stories we tell ourselves about ourselves, stories that shape both the ecstasy and the terror of our world, disease our values, misplace our absolutes, and yet strangely give us hope, inspiration, and a framework for insights. We can't escape narratives but I believe we can resist and transform them" (*CP*, p. 89).

McLaren goes on to explain that it is through narratives that we can make sense of "our social universe" (*CP*, p. 89), since narratives form a cultural contact between individuals, groups, and our social universe. Thus, if these narratives give our lives meaning, we need to understand what those narratives are and how come they exert such an influence on us, including teachers and students. All narratives are already reading us, and "all cultural identities presuppose a certain narrative intentionality and are informed by particular stories" (*CP*, p. 89). Based on his poststructuralist analysis of narratives, McLaren proposes a pedagogy grounded in *critical narratology*. By critical narratology he means "reading personal narratives (our own and those of our students) against society's treasured stock of imperial or magisterial narratives, since not all narratives share a similar status and there are those which exist, highly devalued, within society's rifts and margins" (*CP*, p. 91). McLaren concentrates on the development of "postcolonial" narratives that unfix, unsettle, and subvert totalizing narratives (*CP*, p. 90).

McLaren's construction of border pedagogy focuses on what he calls "border identities." These are hybrid identities that can liberate "us" from "the dead weight of dominant corporate consumer narratives" (*CP*, p. 104). For McLaren, border identities are a form of autopraxis: "Border identities are anchored in and are the outcome of those social practices that configure experience and shape affective investment in such experience *in relation to narratives of liberation* which challenge the market identities produced by the New Right's narratives of consumer citizenship" (*CP*, p. 106, italics in original). Here McLaren's notion of border identities is quite different from the Chicana/o notion of border identities that I already elaborated on. Yet, McLaren argues that in the subaltern narratives of Anzaldúa, Gillermo Gómez-Peña, Trinh T. Minh-ha, and bell hooks, among others, we can find ruptures of the unified coherent subject of the Enlightenment. McLaren asserts that these subaltern narratives are necessary for critical pedagogical practices:

> Teachers and students need access to insurgent narratives that challenge phallocentic self-stories that leave out that which is contingent, irrational, or ambiguous. They need a language of narrative refusal that contests the conventional rules of self-fashioning within autobiographical identities encouraged and legitimated within patriarchy. (*CP*, pp. 114–15)

This invocation to incorporate critical narratives as educational practices, which McLaren based, among others, on the theorization of Ramón Saldívar, better coincides with Chicana/o *Borderlands* theories.

BORDER PEDAGOGIES AND DIFFERENCE

Even though there are overlaps and similarities between Chicana/o *Borderlands* and critical pedagogy, including the importance of progressive political projects, there are also crucial differences that I will elaborate here. My efforts are to open a dialogue with critical pedagogy, and to add to the continuous debates about *difference* and *erasure*. While my positions might seem contradictory (and perhaps they are) I believe that even with some of the problems I am addressing critical pedagogy has potential for Chicana/o education. This is an effort, following Trinh T. Minh-ha, to "say ourselves." Living in the borders and breaking away from specific boundaries are conditions we all live by; however, critical pedagogy does not specify how differences are incorporated into their projects. Even though Giroux and McLaren argue for the need to theorize a nonessentialist notion of difference to develop radical educational practices, in their own writings difference among students is subsumed under the universal categorization "student." For example, Giroux proposes that border pedagogy should create conditions for students to become border crossers; however, he does not specify how the different ways in which students who already are border crossers (and in some cases transgressors) can be worked out in these pedagogical contexts. In this particular sense critical pedagogy runs the risk of universalizing border identities, thus reproducing exactly what they wish to avoid. Giroux provides one of the best explanations of the problematic of modernist conceptions of a unified coherent subject. However, even though he articulates the possibilities that postmodernism can offer for radical educational practices, and thus recognizes and develops the need to take into account locality and specificity in pedagogical practices, specific instances and contingencies are missing from his theoretical discussions.

In order for border pedagogy to avoid the reproduction of universalizing tendencies, it is necessary to theorize difference further. This, of course, is problematic since much of the discussion over difference has relied on essentialist arguments. Indeed Giroux himself, in his essay "Resisting Difference: Cultural Studies and the Discourse of Critical Pedagogy," discusses the various ways in which difference has been theorized. For Giroux there are two ways of theorizing difference. One recognizes relations of inequality and how these can be expressed in multiple and contradictory ways. This form of theorizing difference has been usually advanced by women of color. The second form of theorization is based on the work of feminists (mostly white) who understand differences (usually between men and women) as inherent.[31] Linda Gordon has made a similar argument and critique of difference in feminist theorizing. One notion of difference, that between men and women, maintains the dualism and continues to promote the articulation of those areas in which men and women are different, but in which the differences of women has been subordinated, such as motherhood. The second notion of difference has also been theorized by women of color in speaking of the race, class, and sexual orientation differences among women.[32]

Both Giroux and Gordon provide necessary arguments against essentialist views of difference. If difference is innate (always biological), then there is no possibility for social change. There is, however, a part of the discussion that is left out. Differences are not inherent, rather certain groups (minorities, women, gays, and lesbians) have been constituted as different; where difference is equated with deviance. The ways in which such differences are constituted are in reference to the mythical norm: white/male/heterosexual/middle class, and so forth. The ways in which such differences are constituted are exercises of power. Then, any fruitful discussion of difference, even to understand why radical feminist and nationalist discourses have endorsed and celebrated essentialist notions of difference that claim a sense of superiority, needs to be theorized in terms of power.[33] That is, women and people of color did not at first constitute themselves as different. They were constituted as such by patriarchy and colonialism; a result of such constitution has been the struggle to construct alternative identities.

An adequate theorization of difference and its application to educational theory needs to deconstruct the essentialist notion of difference that constitutes women and people of color as different, and the ways in which people of color and women have themselves essentialized difference. It is also necessary for a theory of difference to deconstruct and decentralize white patriarchal norms from which difference is constituted as deviance. The reason why Chicanas/os and other minorities continue to discuss notions of difference—and why these are so central to the Chicana/o Studies curriculum, for example—is that difference grows out of the unequal power relations in this society. In more simple and direct ways, difference is a consequence of racism, sexism, and homophobia.[34] The "reality" is that even though these differences are socially and politically constituted, they are meaningful.

Differences are, although constituted, inevitable. Much of the problematic of this discussion over differences it that until recently only those who were marked as different were considered in the theorization of difference. If differences are going to be constituted in nonessentialist ways, it is necessary to mark, deconstruct, and decenter whiteness and privilege. Both Giroux and McLaren argue that white is an identity that must be marked and considered in conceptualizations of difference. Giroux marks himself by naming his social position:

> My own politics of location as a white, academic male positions me to speak to issues of racism and gender by self-consciously recognizing my own interests in

taking up these practices as part of a broader political project to expand the scope and meaning of democratic struggle and a politics of solidarity. Border crossing in this instance is part of an attempt to further rupture a politics of historical silence and theoretical erasure that serves to repress and marginalize the voices of the Other. (*BC,* p. 125)

Giroux indeed stands in solidarity with people of color and women, a solidarity that is welcome in these conservative times. However, as people of color are working to deconstruct essentialist constructions of subaltern identities, it is necessary to disempower white male identities. That is, progressive educators who are in solidarity with people of color must recognize their own positions of privilege and mark them as such. Giroux names his privileged position, but does not deconstruct it. Similarly, McLaren's construction of border identities does not elaborate on his own position as a border identity. Yet his notion of border identities as hybrids is based on constructions of identity that are always in flux. Thus, from a progressive or radical standpoint, the work of critical pedagogy does advance and support radical moves to transform educational practices that will enhance the educational advancement of the Chicana/o communities. In an era of constant attacks on minority communities the positions of critical pedagogy are welcome. However, in order to continue advancing a "truly" democratic notion of education it is necessary to decenter the subject positions of those who hold or symbolize power in this society. In this sense, Giroux and McLaren's appropriation of the discourse of the *Borderlands* runs the risk of not taking into account that there still is an asymmetrical position between whiteness and Chicanas/os (as well as other minorities).

TOWARD A CHICANA/O BORDER PEDAGOGY

In this final section, I want to attempt to advance critical/feminist border pedagogy by incorporating Chicana/o notions of the *Borderlands*. This first initial effort poses complicated theoretical and political questions. Who is the subject of this border pedagogy? How do we account for notions of difference? Identity and difference are necessarily for each other—how do we avoid the marginalization of the Other? The most important question is, How do we construct a Chicana/o border pedagogy without reifying the Chicana/o subject? What is at stake in this theorization is to go beyond the modernist notion of essentializing the minority subject as unified or inferior, so common in educational texts. As I have already demonstrated, the struggle for education includes a struggle to construct an alternative identity and subjectivity. As Rafael Pérez-Torres writes, "[i]n the margin, subjectivity is a condition still staunchly to be sought."[35] The issue to grapple with is how to construct a Chicana/o border pedagogy without resorting to essentialist and static definitions of identity.

A Chicana/o border pedagogy would then need to construct theoretical and political movements divorced from the limitations of dialectical analysis to an analysis that recognizes the multiple constructions within Chicana/o communities, dominant ideologies, and modes of resistance. The move that I am arguing for is a rupture (explosion) of the neat dualistic axis of a visible enemy (white America, men, or capitalism, for example) to situations where the so-called enemy is not visible, but more ideological and discursive. This movement would need to take into consideration the many contradictions and discontinuities within the Chicana/o subjects.

National (or cultural) identity is not a natural phenomenon; rather it is an identity that is constructed and that can be (re)claimed. Norma Alarcón reminds us that "the name Chicana, is not a name that women (or men) are born to or with, as is often the case with 'Mexican,' but rather it is consciously and critically assumed."[36] Thus, as a constructed identity, like all identities, it is constructed as *different from*. That is, in order for an identity to exist it has to be differentiated from an Other. As William Connolly establishes, "Identity and difference are bound together. It may be impossible to reconstitute the relation to the second without confounding the experience of the first."[37]

The understanding of identity and subjectivity as nonessentialist and at the same time subversive creates an unresolvable paradox. The Chicana/o movement constructed an "antagonistic" antiassimilationist politics; the idea was to construct a new identity that was not an "American" identity. The type of identity constructed by Anzaldúa, the Chicana/o identity, is a political identity with its own sets of values, culture, and history outside of the narrative of U.S. imperialism and assimilationist policies. But, in order for this Chicana/o identity to exist, it needs to be differentiated from Anglo-American and Mexican identities.[38] By claiming a rightful place in U.S. society, even in its own terms, Chicana/o politics must, paradoxically, reinscribe Anglo-American politics. In its most radical aspects, let us say, separatist politics, it ends up reinscribing segregation. Chicana/o politics, then, in order to exist, must inscribe itself in the impossibility of its existence. This is what Derrida calls an aporia. In his discussion of aporias, Derrida proposes that the enigma of the appearance of what *at once marks and erases* three types of limits—anthrocultural borders, delimitations of the problem of closure, and conceptual demarcations—is to trace them as still possible even while introducing the principle of their impossibility.[39] That is, identity, for example, exists precisely because of the impossibility of its existence. However, there is a way out, although the paradox is not resolvable. In his discussion of this problematic, Ernesto Laclau claims that

> The unresolved tension between universalism and particularism allows a movement away from Western Eurocentrism, through what we could call a system-

atic decentering of the West. . . . Eurocentrism was the result of a discourse that did not differentiate between the universal values that the West was advocating and the concrete historical actors that were incarnating them. Now, however, we can separate these two aspects. If the social struggles of new social actors show that the concrete practices of our society restrict the universalism of our political ideals to limited sectors of the population, it becomes possible to retain the universal dimension while widening the spheres of its application—which, in turn, will redefine the concrete contents of such a universality. Through this process, universalism as a horizon is expanded at the same time as its necessary attachment to any particular content is broken. The opposite policy—that of rejecting universalism to toto as the particular content of the West—can only lead to a political blind alley.[40]

For Laclau the unresolvability of this paradox is a precondition of democracy. "If democracy is possible, it is because the universal does not have any necessary body, any necessary content. Instead, different groups compete to give their particular aims a temporary function of universal representation."[41]

Instead of continuing to promote an essentialist and chauvinistic U.S. nationalism, and essentialist versions of Chicano nationalism, we need to develop educational theories and practices that take into account the Chicana/o Studies conceptualization of the *Borderlands*. Chicana/o border pedagogies can draw from Chicana/o aesthetic experiences that deconstruct the notion of a unified subject and essentialist notions of culture. Angie Chabram-Dernersesian asserts that Chicana aesthetics suggest that Chicana identity is not fixed; rather "they propose that its axis, terms of discourse, and points of contention change in accordance with the ways in which Chicana subjects are positioned and, in turn, position themselves within the discourses of history, culture, and society."[42] In her analysis of how Chicana artists and poets construct Chicana feminist subjectivity, Chabram-Dernersesian concludes that the "Chicana cultural producers of the 1970s and early 1980s crossed the seemingly impenetrable border of Chicano subjectivity. They transformed the language of self-representation, visualized new ethnic configurations and subject positions, and paved the way for contemporary Chicanas to explore other dimensions of the Chicana experience."[43] It is through these explorations that Chicana/o identities can be incorporated into educational discourses that are neither assimilationist nor culturally essentialist.

Cultural practices are social constructions that change over time. Moreover, they are polysemic. By applying the notion of *Borderlands* to (albeit not exclusively) historical narratives, students and teachers can analyze how these narratives are documentations of conflictual and contradictory positions societies take on the events that form that society. One strategy for this would be an analysis of the formation of mythical figures (whether historical or not). The construction of myths can be traced in the way in which historical documents (newspaper articles, diaries, chronicles, and so forth) construct the events that led to the mystification of a person or event. For example, in Mexican and Chicana/o cultures a female figure, Malintzin, has been constructed as a traitor.[44] But Malintzin did not became a traitor until Mexico's independence. The historical documentation of the conquest speaks of Malintzin's services in a positive light; the negative aspect of her role in the conquest is consolidated in the twentieth century when Mexican nationalism was forged. From a pedagogical standpoint, tracing the different constructions of Malintzin serves as a strategy to understand how flexible knowledge is. This move is an application of Rosaldo's remaking of social analysis, since it is a combination of social sciences and humanities, a blurring of disciplinary boundaries.

Critical and feminist pedagogy understand pedagogy as the construction of knowledge, not only its transmission. *Borderlands* theories can be applied to border pedagogies in order to decenter Eurocentric thought. By understanding that all knowledge in constructed it is possible to avoid the problematic of reification and essentialism. Yet, by historicizing and de-naturalizing knowledge, and focusing on hierarchical power relations and differences, it is possible to recognize how various groups construct discontinuous and dynamic forms of knowledge that neither reproduce the status quo, not unproblematically celebrate resistance.

CONCLUSION

This essay presents a theoretical perspective of how the contributions of Chicana/o scholarship, especially the *Borderlands,* can advance the construction of progressive educational discourses by deconstructing the problematic of essentialist notions of identity, culture, and difference. Thus, this is an abstract work. I present here theoretical possibilities that advance educational theory. A way to continue the construction of Chicana/o educational discourses is to analyze Chicana/o cultural productions, myths, politics, and struggles based on the theoretical construction proposed in this paper. I believe that it is possible to develop multicultural educational practices and pedagogies that take into account multiple subjectivities by incorporating as school practice and curriculum Chicana/o cultural productions.

It is through such cultural productions that Chicana/os are "saying themselves," filling in the blanks before someone else does it. For subordinated peoples, then, the power to name/construct their world is crucial to reconstruct their histories and cultures. These reconstructions and rearticulations are vehicles against cultural dominance. Given historical and contemporary racial politics in the U.S., *Borderlands* and border identities represent avenues for liberation. As marginalized communities whose histories, stories, myths, gender politics, and language are defined as "inferior," the question of and quest for cultural identity is a necessary political move.

As the quotation from Trinh Minh-ha at the beginning of this essay states, Chicanas/os must fill in the blanks before someone else does it. Filling in these blanks, trying to make sense of it all, complicates theoretical and political questions. On the one hand, the process of reclaiming "a lost identity" is a political strategy. On the other hand, it raises theoretical concerns of which the problematic of cultural reification is one. Gayatri Chakravorty Spivak had already warned us, "The subaltern cannot speak. There is no virtue in global laundry lists with 'woman' as a pious item. Representation has not withered away. The female intellectual as intellectual has a circumscribed task which she must not disown with a flourish."[45] Anzaldúa's project is a beginning and an important effort for the construction of a nonunitary identity. It is possible to construct a Chicana identity that is always in process. Chicana and Chicano Studies are contributing to a new conceptualization of knowledge beyond the confines of the marginal (yet radical) spaces of Chicano Studies. *Borderlands* theoretical constructions are not only advancing Chicana educational theory, but have also dramatically influenced critical pedagogy and theory.

NOTES

1. Trinh T. Minh-ha, *Woman, Native, Other* (Bloomington: Indiana University Press, 1989), 80.
2. In this essay I will be using the term "Chicana/o," which literally means a person of Mexican descent living in the United States. But "Chicana /o" is also a political term that gained recognition during the Chicano liberation movement of the 1960s and 1970s. For the most part, when I use "Chicana/o" I am using it in its political sense. However, there are times when it is used interchangeably with "Mexican-American." The labels used to designate persons of Latin American origin in the U.S. are complex and highly political. In the 1980s the U.S. government imposed the label "Hispanic" for all persons of Spanish descent. Liberal and progressive members of these communities have objected to "Hispanic" because it denies the Indian and African heritage. One response has been to use the term "Latina/o;" which is more palatable because it shows solidarity with Latin American struggles for liberation. However, it is also a Eurocentric term with many of the same problems as the term "Hispanic."
3. Laura Pérez, "Opposition and the Education of Chicana/os," *Race Identity and Representation in Education,* ed. Cameron McCarthy and Warren Chrichlow (New York: Routledge, 1993), 276.
4. For example, see Allan Bloom, *The Closing of the American Mind* (New York: Touchstone, 1987) and Arthur Schlesinger, Jr., *The Disuniting of America: Reflections on a Multicultural Society* (New York: Norton, 1992).
5. For a historical account of the struggle for educational equality in Texas see Guadalupe San Miguel, Jr., *"Let All of them Take Heed" Mexican Americans and the Campaign for Educational Equality in Texas, 1910–1981* (Austin: University of Texas Press, 1987).
6. In April 1969 Chicano activists in California organized a statewide conference to chart the development of Chicano Studies programs. The conference was held at the University of California, Santa Barbara. See Carlos Muñoz, Jr., "The Development of Chicano Studies, 1968–1981," in *Chicano Studies: a Multidisciplinary Approach,* ed. Eugene E. García, Francisco A. Lomelí, and Isidro D. Ortiz (New York: Teachers College Press, 1984); Carlos Muñoz, Jr., *Youth, Identity, Power: The Chicano Movement* (London: Verso, 1989); and Mario Barrera, *Beyond Aztlán: Ethnic Autonomy in Comparative Perspective* (New York: Praeger, 1988). One of the results of the conference was the drafting of *El Plan de Santa Barbara* which is the document charting the ideological map for Chicana/o Studies.
7. Carlos Muñoz, Jr., "Youth, Identity, and Power: The Chicano Generation." Unpublished manuscript, 1981.

8. Ibid., quoted in Mario Barrera, *Beyond Aztlán: Ethnic Autonomy in Comparative Perspective* (New York: Praeger, 1988), 43. Barrera defines "gabacho" as a pejorative term for Anglos.

9. See Teresa Córdova, ed., *Chicana Voices: Intersections of Class, Race, and Gender* (National Association for Chicano Studies, 1990).

10. For some the focus on abstract theorizing divides the discipline from its focus on the material conditions of the community. For critiques of the new direction in Chicano Studies see, for example, Ignacio M. García, "Juncture in the Road: Chicano Studies since 'El Plan de Santa Barbara,' " in *Chicanas/Chicanos at the Crossroads,* 181–203. García is particularly concerned with feminist, postmodernist, and lesbian "challenges" to the field and to the National Association for Chicana and Chicano Studies.

11. Kris Gutiérrez, "Pedagogies of Dissent and Transformation: a Dialogue with Kris Gutiérrez," dialogue with Peter McLaren, in *Critical Pedagogy and Predatory Culture: Oppositional Politics in a Postmodern Era* (New York: Routledge, 1995), 161–62.

12. In this essay I am concentrating on *Borderlands* theories developed by Chicana/o scholars and in the subsequent adoption by critical pedagogy. There are other border discourses that merit attention, most notably Jacques Derrida's. Derrida's writings on borders are not analyzed in this essay because, although they precede some of the Chicana/o writings, he did not influence the Chicana/o and critical pedagogy texts I am analyzing here. For Derrida's theorizing of borders see, Jacques Derrida, "Living On: Border lines," in *De-Construction and Criticism,* ed. Harold Bloom, Paul de Man, Jacques Derrida, Geoffrey H. Hartman, and J. Hillis Miller (New York: Continuum, 1979), 75–176 and Jacques Derrida, *Aporias,* trans. Thomas Dutoit (Stanford, Calif.: Stanford University Press, 1993).

13. For example, see M. Patricia Fernández-Kelly, *For We are Sold, I and My People: Women and Industry in Mexico's Frontier* (Albany: State University of New York Press, 1983); Oscar J. Martínez, *Border People: Life and Society in the U.S.-Mexico Borderlands* (Tucson: University of Arizona Press, 1994); Stanley R. Ross, ed., *Views Across the Border: The United States and Mexico* (Albuquerque: University of New Mexico Press, 1978); and Vicki Ruiz and Susan Tiano, eds., *Women on the U.S.-Mexico Border: Responses to Change* (Boulder: Westview Press, 1991). There is a difference between Border studies and *Borderlands.* Border studies literally refers to the study of the U.S./Mexico border while *Borderlands* is a metaphor of the condition of living between spaces, cultures, and languages.

14. Gloria Anzaldúa, *Borderlands/La Frontera: The New Mestiza* (San Francisco: Aunt Lute, 1987); Alfred Arteaga, ed., *An Other Tongue: Nation and Ethnicity in the Linguistic Borderlands* (London: Duke University Press, 1994); Hector Calderón and José David Saldívar, eds., *Criticism in the Borderlands* (Durham, N.C.: Duke University Press, 1991); Carl Gutiérrez-Jones, *Rethinking the Borderlands: Between Chicano Culture and Legal Discourse* (Berkeley: University of California Press, 1995); Renato Rosaldo, *Culture and Truth* (Boston: Beacon Press, 1989); and Ramón Saldívar, *Chicano Narrative* (Madison: University of Wisconsin Press, 1990). *Culture and Truth* will be referred to as *CT* with page numbers in the text for all subsequent citations.

15. Sonia Saldívar-Hull, "Feminism on the Border: From Gender Politics to Geopolitics," in *Criticism in the Borderlands,* 203–20.

16. Calderón and Saldívar, *Criticism in the Borderlands,* 7.

17. For example, Mario Barrera, *Race and Class in the Southwest* (Notre Dame, Ind.: University of Notre Dame Press, 1979); Alfredo Mirandé, *The Chicano Experience: An Alternative Perspective* (Notre Dame, Ind.: University of Notre Dame Press, 1985); Cherríe Moraga, *Loving in the War Years: lo que nunca pasó por sus labios* (Boston: South End Press, 1983); Cherríe Moraga and Gloria Anzaldúa, eds., *This Bridge Called My Back: Writings by Radical Women of Color* (New York: Kitchen Table Women of Color Press, 1981). Further, Chicana scholars and activists criticized the sexism in Chicano male-centric scholarship, and the racism and exclusion in Euro-American feminist scholarship; see Saldívar-Hull, "Feminism on the Border" and Angie Chabram-Dernersesian, "I Throw Punches for My Race, but I Don't Want to Be a Man: Writing Us— Chicanos (Girl, Us)/Chicanas—into the Movement Script," in *Cultural Studies,* ed. Lawrence Grossberg et al. (New York: Routledge, 1992).

18. This movement parallels feminist theory and poststructuralism, for example. That is, I am not arguing that Chicana/o Studies developed this critique and theoretical advancement by itself.

19. Rosa Linda Fregoso, *The Bronze Screen: Chicana and Chicano Film Culture* (Minneapolis: University of Minnesota Press, 1993), 65.

20. Calderón and Saldívar, *Criticism in the Borderlands,* 4.

21. Anzaldúa, *Borderlands/La Frontera,* 20. Italics in original.

22. Ibid., 63. Anzaldúa's project has been adopted in many women's studies classrooms and many cultural critics have praised her work. Saldívar-Hull, "Feminism on the Border"; Inderpal Grewal, "Autobiographic Subjects and Diasporic Locations: *Meatless Days* and *Borderlands,*" in *Scattered Hegemonies: Postmodernity and Transnational Feminist Practices,* ed. Inderpal Grewal and Caren Kaplan (Minneapolis: University of Minnesota Press, 1994), 231–54; and Yvonne Yarbro-Bejarano, "Gloria Anzaldúa's *Borderlands/La Frontera:* Cultural Studies, 'Difference,' and the Non-Unitary Subject," *Cultural Critique* 28 (Fall 1994): 5–28. She has also been problematized (mostly in informal conversations) for her reappropriation of Aztlán, her emphasis on Aztec (Mexican) origins, and the slippage in her theoretical and historical constructions. In spite of these contradictions and essentialist moves, Anzaldúa's project is a starting point toward the construction of *Borderlands* theories. Anzaldúa brings together the many contradictions and discontinuities within the Chicano community, so that her text has advanced Chicana feminist and *Borderlands* theory. For another example of critiques of Anzaldúa see the discussion section of Marcos Sánchez-Tranquilino and John Tagg, "The Pachuco's Flayed Hide: Mobility, Identity, and *Buenas Garras,*" in *Cultural Studies* (New York: Routledge, 1992), 556–70. In this discussion Donna Haraway raises Rosaura Sánchez's critique of Anzaldúa's reappropriation of Aztlán and remythtification of *la mestiza.*

23. Saldívar-Hull, "Feminism on the Border," 211.

24. Papusa Molina, "Fragmentation: Meditations on Separatism," *Signs: Journal of Women in Culture and Society* 19 (Winter1994): 455.

25. Arteaga, *An Other Tongue,* 3–4.

26. Saldívar, *Chicano Narrative,* 19.

27. Gutiérrez-Jones, *Rethinking the Borderlands,* 29.

28. Ibid.

29. Some of these texts include: Henry A. Giroux, *Border Crossings: Cultural Workers and the Politics of Education* (New York: Routledge, 1992), referred to as *BC* with page numbers in the text for all subsequent citations; Henry A. Giroux and Peter McLaren, eds., *Between Borders: Pedagogy and the Politics of Cultural Studies* (New York: Routledge, 1994); and Peter McLaren, "Border disputes: multicultural narrative, Rasquachismo, and critical pedagogy in postmodern America," in Peter McLaren, *Critical Pedagogy and Predatory Culture: Oppositional Politics in a Postmodern Era* (New York: Routledge, 1995), referred to as *CP* with page numbers in the text for all subsequent citations. Other titles outside the field of education include D. Emily Hicks, *Border Writing: The Multi-dimensional Text* (Minneapolis: University of Minnesota Press, 1991) and Robert C. Holub, *Crossing Borders* (Madison: University of Wisconsin Press, 1992).

30. See also, Chantal Mouffe, "Radical Democracy or Liberal Democracy?" *Socialist Review* 20, no. 2 (1990): 57–66 and Ernesto Laclau and Chantal Mouffe, *Hegemony and Socialist Strategy: Towards a Radical Democratic Politics* (London: Verso, 1985).

31. Henry A. Giroux, "Resisting Difference: Cultural Studies and the Discourse of Critical Pedagogy," in *Cultural Studies,* 205.

32. Linda Gordon, "On 'Difference,' " *Genders* 10 (Spring 1991): 91–111.

33. Gordon does recognize that difference has been constructed through power. However, in her discussion she does not theorize in-depth the workings of power.

34. For example, when Chicanas/os of any class are singled out and stopped by security guards in airports and are required to demonstrate that they are doing legitimate business, these individuals are constituted as different because of racist ideologies. They are not constituting themselves as different, rather, they are reminded of their difference and subordinate position in U.S. society.

35. Rafael Pérez-Torres, "Nomads and Migrants: Negotiating a Multicultural Postmodernism," *Cultural Critique* 26 (Winter 1993–94): 161–89.

36. See Norma Alarcón, "Chicana Feminism: In the Tracks of 'The' Native Woman," *Cultural Studies* 3 (4 August 1990): 248–56.

37. William E. Connolly, *Identity/Difference* (London: Cornell University Press, 1991), 44.

38. For a theory of oppositional consciousness see Chela Sandoval, "U.S. Third World Feminism: The Theory and Method of Oppositional Consciousness in the Postmodern World," *Genders* 10 (Spring 1991): 1–24.

39. Derrida, *Aporias,* 73.

40. Ernesto Laclau, "Universalism, Particularism, and the Question of Identity," *October* no. 61 (Summer 1992) 90.

41. Ibid.

42. Angie Chabram-Dernersesian, "And, Yes . . . The Earth Did Part: On the Splitting of Chicana/o Subjectivity," in *Building with Our Hands,* ed. A. De la Torre and Beatríz Pesquera (Berkeley: University of California Press, 1993), 34–56.

43. Ibid., 52.

44. Malintzin was a Nahuatl-speaking woman who served as Hernán Cortés' (the Spanish conqueror of Mexico) translator and lover. She is blamed for the conquest, since her services as a translator were essential for the conquest.

45. Gayatri Chakravorty Spivak, "Can the Subaltern Speak?" in *Marxism and the Interpretation of Culture,* ed. Cary Nelson and Lawrence Grossberg (Urbana: University of Illinois Press, 1988), 308.

Toward a Pedagogy of Place for Black Urban Struggle

STEPHEN NATHAN HAYMES

INTRODUCTION

What possibilities does critical pedagogy have for constructing "a pedagogy of place" for black urban struggle? An answer to this question must begin by addressing the relationship between urban struggles and the production of urban meanings. Urban conflicts can be seen as antagonism over the construction and interpretation of the city as a myth, which in turn have implications for who and how the material landscape of the city is designed (Castells, 1983; Davis, 1992). That is to say, urban conflicts are about the representation of the city, but more important, who represents the city, who produces its myths (Dennis, 1990). Mike Davis in *City of Quartz* is interested in the mythography of Los Angeles, particularly "the history of culture produced about Los Angeles—especially where that has become a material force in the city's actual evolution" (1990:20). He points out that since the 1930s cultural intellectuals such as architects, designers, artists, filmmakers, writers, and cultural theorists, at the invitation and sponsorship of the largest land developers and bankers, have played a major role in constructing the image of Los Angeles (1990:20). It is important to recognize that these images "are powerful ideological instruments of real politics because they are turned from 'vision statements' into 'general plans' for the expansion of capital in the urban" (Keith, 1993:112). Keith states: "The lofty [images] serve as a shield behind which the destruction of neighborhoods, gentrification and displacement occurs" (1993:112).

It is this context that necessitates the development of a pedagogy of place for black urban struggle that incorporates the contributions of critical pedagogy. In what follows, I argued that a sense of meaninglessness and hopelessness is becoming pervasive in contemporary black life (West, 1991b; hooks and West, 1991). For the most part, the exotic interests of the white

211

middle class consumer culture in popular black culture have been responsible for breaking down the structure of meaning in black urban communities, because mainstream white consumer culture has commodified and reified black popular culture, thereby detaching black culture from its historical and social references.

This detachment speaks to how "race" as defined in relation to blackness and black people has become in the white superemacist culture of the city a metaphor for the urban, that is, a metaphor that signifies simultaneously the pleasures and dangers of blackness in the city. Elizabeth Wilson attributes this to the postmodern culture of the post-industrial corporate city, which she argues "perceives all experience in aesthetic terms" (1991:136). However, what is important to Wilson about this is that in the postmodern city the "unpleasurable" is aestheticized to obtain a perverse pleasure. She states: "Horror, fear and ugliness are aestheticized, and thus become easier to live with, at least for the new urban aesthete, the voyeur. Postmoderism thus expresses an urban sensibility, although a perverse one" (1991:136). Cross and Keith also call attention to how in the postmodern city "ethnicity is celebrated in the collage of the exotic cultural pick-and-mix, while race remains taboo, and is anything but playful" (1993:8). In doing so, mainstream white consumer culture reappropriates the categories "race" and "urban" to signify the pleasures and dangers of blackness, controlling and regulating black cultural identity and how blacks define and use urban space. This has implications for black urban struggle in that image makers in the postmodern city tend to aestheticize experiences instead of responding morally or emotionally. They act to mask mainstream white privilege and corporate power in the city (Wilson, 1991:150).

A way to begin to think about these issues in relation to a pedagogy of place for black urban struggle is to situate black popular culture within the context of black city life. The twentieth-century city has been one of the main sources of meaning for contemporary black popular culture. And at the same time that the city has contributed to its production, black popular culture has shaped the production of urban meanings. The city for blacks has been an important site for place making, for producing black culture and black identity. The concept of place making is used here to denote that places are significant because we assign values to them in relation to our cultural projects: "Place is the fusion of space and experience, a space filled with meaning, a source of identity" (Friedland, 1992:14).

In *City and the Grassroots,* Manuel Castells asserts that "cultural identity [is] associated with and organized around a specific territory" (1983:14). Elaborating on this point, Brett Williams observes that dense living in the city has made black American culture seem vibrant: "Through the work of the street [blacks] build a vivid detailed repertoire of biographical, historical, and everyday knowledge about community life" (1988:4). In addition, the meanings and uses that blacks assign to their specific territory are defined around a popular memory of black rural southern culture: "Through the shared lore of alley gardens, through the exchange of medicines and delicacies, through fishing and feasting among metropolitan kin, and in visits, exchanges, and the construction of an alternative economy with relatives that bring Carolina harvest to the city" (Williams, 1988:3).

By producing urban meanings that recall popular memories of black rural southern culture, blacks have been able to construct alternative identities and relationships based on ties of friendship, family, history, and place. Blacks therefore define and use urban space to renegotiate an oppositional identity which knits together neighbors and draws families together across the city" (Williams, 1988:3). Renegotiating their identities as blacks is linked to place making. It involves the production of public spheres, which bell hooks refers to as "homeplace," "site[s] where one could confront the issue of humanization, where one could resist" (hooks, 1990:42). As spaces of care and nurturance, homeplaces, according to hooks, are where "all black people could be subjects, not objects, where we could be affirmed in our minds and hearts despite poverty, hardship, and deprivation, where we could restore to ourselves dignity denied us on the outside in the public world" (1990:42). The black public sphere is therefore the basis for building a community of resistance. Refering to the public sphere of marginalized or subaltern communities Nancy Fraser comes to the same conclusion:

> Subaltern counterpublics have a dual character. On the one hand, they function as spaces of withdrawal and regroupment; on the other hand, they also function as bases and training grounds for agitational activities directed toward wider publics. It is precisely in the dialectic between these two functions that their emancipatory potential resides. (1991:69)

It is this dual character of counterpublics that provides the necessary conditions for developing oppositional identities. The public sphere is not only an arena for the formation of discursive opinion; it is an arena for the formation and enactment of social identities; it is the arena that allows one to speak in one's own voice (Fraser, 1991:69). Public spheres are therefore culturally specific institutions, which, according to Fraser, include various social geographies of urban space (1991:69).

The social geography of urban space is characterized by public spaces in the city that are positioned unequally in relation to one another with respect to power. The concept of power is key to interpreting this positionality, to understanding how public spaces relate to one another in the context of the city. In particular, if power is linked to the production of urban meaning, then those public spaces located at the center of city life dominate its meaning, and in so doing define the cultural and political terrain in which marginalized public spaces, in this case black public spaces, resist, form alternative identities, and make culture in the city. In this way, the physical space of the black ghetto is a public sphere, a culturally specific institution. Because inner-city blacks live on the margins of white supremacist domination and privilege, they have no other alternative than to struggle for the transformation of their places on the margin into spaces of cultural resistance. Michael Keith and Steve Pile observe that "for those who have no place that can be safely called home, there must be a struggle for a place to be" (1993:5). This is why bell hooks argues that historically, "African American people believed that the construction of a homeplace, however fragile and tenuous (the slave hut, the wooden shack) had a radical political dimension" (1990:42). What this indicates is that the struggle by blacks for place is bound up with their identity politics. The problem with this is that if black identity is viewed as fixed, perceived in biologistic terms and not as a social construction, then the meanings attached to place are perceived as being fixed. In a white supremacist culture that equates race with being black, the meanings and uses that blacks attach to a place are believed to be derived from their biology, from their nature. As a particular kind of place, the category "urban" has been inscribed with racial meaning; it has operated as a racial metaphor for black. What this means is that black cultural politics in relation to place making should avoid essentialist constructions of blackness and black identity when defining and using their public spaces in the city. If they do not, they risk reinforcing white supremacist stereotypes that rationalize redevelopment practices that displace blacks from their public spaces.

It is imperative, then, that a pedagogy of place maintain or establish the necessary conditions for the development of black public spheres within the "ghetto territory." To do this, it should draw on the tradition of critical pedagogy. Henry Giroux argues that in relation to producing counterpublic spheres, critical pedagogy must be seen "as having an important role in the struggle of oppressed groups to reclaim the ideological and material conditions for organizing their own experiences" (1983:237). Critical pedagogy in the context of black city life has a crucial role to play in the production of counterpublics, in constructing political and cultural practices that organize human experiences enabling individuals to interpret social reality in liberating ways. However, for a "pedagogy of place" this must be understood in terms of establishing pedagogical conditions that enable blacks in the city to critically interpret how dominant definitions and uses of urban space regulate and control how they organize their identity around territory, and the consequences of this for black urban resistance.

Preceding the "Great Black Migration" to northern and midwestern cities, urban areas were mainly white. After the formation of large black urban settlements resulting from the migration, the urban was described metaphorically as a jungle, as being dominated by bestial, predatory values. With the mass migration of southern blacks to cities in the north, the "city as a jungle" began to operate as a racist metaphor to describe inner-city blacks (Gilroy, 1991: 228). "It has contributed," observes Paul Gilroy, "to contemporary definitions of 'race,' particularly those which highlight the supposed primitivism and violence of black residents in inner-city areas" (1991:229). The metaphorical construction of the urban around "race" is of particular significance given that in a white supremacist culture that identifies race with being black and not being white the urban becomes another way to signify the "evils" of blackness and black people. This can be seen in relation to current discussions about poor black urban families and the rise in black inner-city homicides, particularly in relation to black males.

Before directly commenting on this, I want to first make the argument that the ideological construction of the "city as a jungle" is related to the idea that the culture of the city is based on so-called black street culture. For example, the motif that is most prevalent in Levi blue jeans ads is "street cool," which suggests a romantic view of ghetto life. Implied in such a view "is a conception about acting in public spaces and how blacks accomplish this" (Goldman and Papson, 1992:83). The subtext of Levi ads is that "black males move without inhibition to the rhythm of the street because [t]hey signify soul, movement, expressiveness, the body unencumbered by tight, stiff middle-classness" (Goldman and Papson, 1992:83). Accompanying this is Levi's exotic use of black urban music to signify the body, hence sexuality; it is appropriated to express the physical sensuality and movement associated with jeans among youth. Thus, by stylizing and softening the black ghetto, Levi commercials detach black culture from the pain and anguish of black city life:

> In relation to the street itself, Levi's images are incomplete—they have been purged of poverty and its ill effects, streetpeople, violence, petty crime . . .
> Levi's romanticizes poverty—gives it authenticity by cleaning it up. In fact, this ad is only real in relation to what has previously been seen on television and in the mass media. Relative to the street, Levi's account is not hyperreal, but stylized. (Goldman and Papson, 1992:83)

By separating black popular urban culture from the harsh realities of black city life mainstream white consumer culture silences and marginalizes black narratives and stories of racial exclusion and racial humiliation, of daily pain and suffering experienced due to white supremacist practices in the city. It is in this context that black popular urban culture is in part an expression of the day-to-day life of inner-city blacks.

One way to begin to understand the day-to-day life of urban blacks is by looking at how the place-making practices of mainstream white institutions in the city dismantle the living spaces, and therefore public spaces or homeplaces, of inner-city blacks. This means that to address in pedagogical terms black life in the city, critical educators must have an understanding of how mainstream whites in the city—through developers, landlords, politicians, banks, and corporations—textually and visually represent space in their image of redevelopment. In an effort to attract middle-class whites and corporations to the city, urban planners, designers, and architects are employed by cities to construct a visual image of the city representing social stability. Through the restoration of neoclassical architectural forms the city is represented as harmonious. Planners believe that the aesthetics of neoclassical architecture signify orderliness, cleanliness, and whiteness, which are all articulated with civic ideals, such as national unity and national pride.

By evoking these civic ideals, neoclassical architecture is used as a way to "restore tradition" in the city. In this sense, architectural redevelopment or gentrification is tied to a nostalgia for the past. Here, however, the use of nostalgia defines and represents "tradition" as "heritage." This nostalgia for "tradition" is used to delineate "us" from "them," reinforcing old hierarchies of race (Levitas, 1990). From this point of view, the urban "place-making" practices of blacks are seen as a threat to "tradition" because of the different uses and values assigned to place as discussed above. The argument is that in "making place," the social uses and cultural values assigned by blacks to their living spaces are thought to perpetuate all those qualities associated with "blackness" in the white racist imagination, such as disorderliness, filthiness, ugliness, and irrationality. This is in contrast to those qualities associated with "whiteness" that are believed to be embodied in neoclassical architecture, such as order, purity, beauty, and rationality. It is in this context that neoclassical architecture is thought to contain essential and universal meanings (Boyer, 1986:66). The implied assumption is that the beauty and utility of neoclassical architecture is inherently functional to the creation of public spaces.

It is important to remember that black public spaces in the city have historically been centered around daily survival; it is these "spaces of survival" that serve as public spaces where black people develop self-definitions or identities that are linked to a consciousness of solidarity and to a politics of resistance. Sivanandan implies this when stating, "Regulated to a concrete ghetto and deprived of basic amenities and services, jobless for the most part . . . the inhabitants came together to create a life for themselves." Continuing this same point later, Sivanandan observes, "They set up a nursery, provide meals and a meeting place, establish a recreation centre for youth and build up in the process, a political culture." He concludes by saying that these spaces of survival "were prefigured in the black struggles of the 1960s and 1970s" (1990:52). For the Black Power movement of the 1960s and 1970s, the city was perceived as the place in which blacks could form what Sivanandan calls "organic communities of resistance." James Jenning argues that in the city black political activism equates empowerment with control of land in the black urban communities, and that this notion of empowerment surpasses affirmative action, job discrimination, or school integration (1990:120). Cynthia Hamilton argues that the significance of land for the development of oppositional political communities can constitute a threat to the dominant social order and result in the "manipulation of space" to remove certain populations from the spaces they inhabit.

> In South Africa, "forced removals" are responsible for the relocation of millions to the remote homelands. In Guatemala, the government is building model villages which grew out of army efforts in the 1980s to control rural communities by displacing the population and forcing resettlements . . . In the U.S., we have our own version of forced removal and resettlement, our own overt manipulation of behavior through spatial transformations. The form that this relocation and restructuring has taken is urban renewal and community development. The relocation and removal has had a very important consequence in the curtailing of political organization. (Hamilton, 1991:28)

How do mainstream white urban institutions legitimate or rationalize the removal of black populations living in the city? My argument is that the category space is culturally produced and ordered. According to David Goldberg, "Spatial distinctions like 'West' and 'East' are racialized in their conception and application" (1993:183). This for Goldberg means that "racial categories have been variously spatialized more or less since their inception into continental divides, national localities, and geographical regions" (1993:183). What is suggested is that through the racializing of populations, the spaces they inhabit are also racialized; therefore, in a white supremacist society like the United States, the spaces of racialized populations, black, Latino, and Asian, are differentiated from the spaces of the non-racialized population, in this case mainstream white. It is by discursively constructing populations and their spaces as racialized that mainstream white institutions in the city legitimate the removal and colonizing of the inner city. In many ways, the equating of the urban with "race" has allowed white mainstream institutions to define "urban problems"—single-parent households, violence, poverty, joblessness, drugs—as the problem of race, and therefore the problem of blacks. In doing this, black spaces in the city are represented as "spaces of pathology," as "spaces of disorder," without any consideration of how the colonizing of space by mainstream white institutions in the city removed and destroyed the communal living spaces, the "home-places" of urban blacks.

The urban renewal programs in the United States described the removal and destruction of black public spaces as "slum clearance." Goldberg argues that by definition the "slum" means filthy, foul smelling, wretched, rancorous, uncultivated, and lacking care" (1993:191). But in terms of the racial slum, he says it "is doubly determined, for the metaphorical stigma of a black blotch on the cityscape bears the added connotations of moral degeneracy, natural inferiority, and repulsiveness" (Goldberg, 1993:192). In the late 1950s and 1960s the U.S. urban renewal programs focused on the removal and destruction of black public spaces in the name of slum clearance. This process occurred simultaneously with the expansion of black northern urban settlements, during the second "Great Black Migration." The conceptualization and application of "slum clearance" originated with the removal of Africans from their land by colonial administrations to make way for European cities in Africa. Fearful that Africans would pollute the living spaces of European settlers colonial administrators segregated them.

> Uncivilized Africans, it was claimed, suffered urbanization as a pathology of disorder and degeneration of their traditional tribal life. To prevent their pollution contaminating European city dwellers and services, the idea of sanitation and public health was invoked first as the legal path to remove blacks to separate locations at the city limits and then as a principle for sustaining permanent segregation. (Goldberg, 1994:190)

In postwar Euro-American cities urban planning too produced a racialized divided cityscape. Urban renewal programs in the United States were designed around a twofold strategy, according to Goldberg. The primary motivation behind both strategies was white fear of black encroachment into white neighborhoods. One part of the strategy was to clear the slums and to rehouse the black population into towering public housing projects. The idea was to "reproduce the inner-city slum on a smaller scale." Goldberg describes this process as "warehousing the racially marginalized" (1993:191). The second part of the urban renewal strategy was to clear the slum and on a massive scale "remove the cities' racial poor with no plans to rehouse them" (Goldberg, 1993:191). The idea here was to force a "large proportion of the racialized poor to settle for slum conditions marginalized at the city limits" (Goldberg, 1993:191). This was described as "Negro Removal." Another term used by federal urban renewal programs, particularly in the 1960s and 1970s was "spatial deconcentration." As mentioned in Chapter 3, geographer Harold Rose points out in "The Future of the Black Ghetto" (1982) that in the future "ghetto centers will essentially be confined to a selected set of suburban ring communities. [There] appears to be little concern regarding the social and economic implications associated with the present spatial reorganization upon the future of urban blacks, . . . or for that matter upon the future of the city" (cited from Smith, Neil, 1992:92–93).

In the context of a white supremacist society, the culture of race and racism has much significance in terms of the spatial organization of cities in the United States. For mainstream white urban institutions the spatial "regeneration" of the city is linked to the discursive representation and control of racial differences. Goldberg points out that "regeneration" is constructed from a notion of "degeneration." From the viewpoint of white supremacist culture, the racialized urban poor are represented as "degenerate" and subsequently regressive. That is to say, the "slums" emerge because the racialized urban poor are perceived as naturally incapable of living in the modern city. "Races accordingly have their proper or natural places, geographically and biologically. Displaced from their proper or normal class, national, or ethnic positions in the social and ultimately urban setting, a 'Native' or 'Negro' would generate pathologies." Stratified by race and class, the modern city becomes a testing ground of survival, of racialized power and control (Goldberg, 1993:200). The Enlightment ideal of the modern city as a place of individualism, economic opportunity, and material progress implies that the racialized urban poor live in slums because they do not have the innate qualities needed to survive in the modern world, in the bourgeois city. Regeneration therefore is linked to the "spiritual and physical renewal" of the city for those naturally fit to live in it. Goldberg goes on to say that "gentrification is the form of regeneration that most readily defines the postmodern city" (1993:201).

In *Unheavenly City,* Banfield argues that "black slums" are not the result of "racial prejudice" because "discrimination was not the main obstacle in the way of Irish, the Italians, the Jews and others that have made it. Nor is it the main one of the Negro" (Banfield, 1968:78). Banfield then goes on to say, "If [the Negro] lives in a neighborhood that is all-black, the reason is not white prejudice. This physical separation may arise from [the Negro] having cultural characteristics that make him an undesirable neighbor" (1968:79). He also writes, "Impulse governs his behavior, either because he cannot discipline himself to sacrifice a present for a future satisfaction or because he has no sense of the future. He is therefore radically improvident: whatever he cannot use immediately he considers valueless. His bodily needs (especially sex) and his taste for 'action' take precedence over everything else" (1974:61). Banfield further suggests that "to a greater extent [the slum] is an expression of his tastes and style of life" [1974:71], implying that "the slum has its own subculture" (1974:71). Hence, for Banfield, "[t]he subcultural norms and values of the slum are reflected in poor sanitation and health practices, deviant behavior and often a real lack of interests in formal education" (1974:71). In addition, by claiming that the "subculture of the slum" rested on the premise that the Negro's bodily needs (especially sex) and his taste for "action" took precedence over everything else, Banfield moves to describe the urban riots as "outbreaks of animal spirits" (1968:297). This view of the urban uprisings was implicit in his essay "Rioting for Fun and for Profit."

Others have used this to call for the physical displacement of blacks from the city. Charles Murray, the ideologue of the New Right's antiwelfare policies and author of *Losing Ground* which was dubbed by Ronald Reagan as the "bible" of welfare reform, wants to restore the right of landlords and employers to discriminate—"without having to justify their arbitrariness" (Davis, 1992:178) "Only by letting, 'like-minded people . . . control and shape their small worlds,' and letting landlords pursue their natural instincts 'to let good tenants be and to evict bad ones,' can the larger part of urban America find its golden age of harmonious, self-regulating communities" (cited in Davis,

1992:178). Murray concludes by saying, "If the result of implementing those policies is to concentrate the bad apples into a few hyperviolent, antisocial neighborhoods, so be it" (cited in Davis, 1992:178). It is, in fact, this particular attitude that has lead to the actual dispersing of black urban settlements from downtown. David Reed argues for instance that HUD's "spatial deconcentration" program was established in the wake of the black rebellions of the 1960s as a means of dispersing blacks to remote suburban neighborhoods where geographic isolation would prevent them from organizing (1981:ii).

In addition to being spatially excluded from downtown, the dispersion of the black population to near suburbs has also been increasingly complemented with police repression and surveillance. Mike Davis, in "Fortress L.A.: The Militarization of Urban Space," discusses how efforts to criminalize inner-city communities, such as the "war" on drugs and gangs have served as a pretext for police departments to experiment with community blockades. For example, in Los Angeles, "narcotic enforcement zones" provided the LAPD with an excuse to conduct massive illegal searches and arrests under its Operation Hammer program. Comparing this to the West Bank strategy Davis writes:

> As the HAMMER mercilessly pounded away at southcentral's mean streets, it became increasingly apparent that its principle catch consisted of drunks, delinquent motorists and teenage curfew violators (offenders only by virtue of the selective application of curfews to non-Anglo neighborhoods). By 1990 the combined forces of the LAPD and the Sheriffs (implementing their own street saturation strategy) had picked up as many as 50,000 suspects. Even allowing for a percentage of Latino detainees, this remains an astonishing figure considering there are only 100,000 Black youths in Los Angeles. In some highly touted sweeps, moreover, as many as 90 percent of detained suspects have been released without charges. (1990:277)

In U.S. cities the criminalization of black youth has acted to racialize and therefore demonize the public spaces of blacks in the city. The criminalization accomplished is by using racist stereotypes that suggest that most or all black youth are members of gangs. The Urban Strategies Group in Los Angeles commented on how L.A. District Attorney Ira Reiner in a report concluded that "some of the most troubling data to emerge from this study concern the extraordinary percentage of young Black males who show up in gang data bases. The police has identified almost half of all Black men in Los Angeles County between the ages of 21 and 24 as gang members" (1992:7). The Urban Strategies Group points out that in fact, "the police simply equated being in a 'database' that they created with being in a gang."

By the assumed association with gangs, black youth are believed to be heavily involved in drug trafficking, and it is also assumed that most of the violence results from that involvement. The findings of a study conducted by Malcolm Klein, Cherly Maxson, and Lea Cunningham of the University of Southern California directly contradict the gang-drug-violence connection. They found that "gang violence is primarily related to gang issues, such as rivalries, not to drugs. . . . We find no evidence of spiralling effects of drug involvement in homicides between the mid and later years of the 1980s. Again we conclude that concern for specific gang/drug/violence connections has been overstated, at least in [south central] Los Angeles" (Urban Strategies Group, 1992:7). The Strategies Group argues that linking black youth with gangs, drugs, and violence has "create[d] a mandate for police brutality and abuse. The outcome of all this is that criminalization acts a process of racialization" (Keith, 1993).

This racialization of crime explains the increasing repression and surveillance of the black community found by the Sentencing Project (1991), which concluded that one out of every two black men will be arrested in his lifetime and that the incarceration rate for black people in the United States is four times as high as that of black people in South Africa. Interestingly, while remaining more or less constant from 1925 until 1971, U.S. incarceration rates since 1972 have tripled. This upward spiral coincides with the urban rebellions, which were an expression of black resistance to the dismantling of black settlements due to the aggressive urban renewal initiatives being sponsored by local governments.

In *City and the Grassroots,* Manuel Castells argues that although the 1968 Kerner Commission was correct that poverty has been an underlying condition of the African American community, the Commission was mistaken to assume that it was the immediate cause of the urban rebellion (1983:52). Instead, he argues that the cause of the urban rebellions was associated more with "the size of the black population; and the location of this population in the Northern regions of America" (1983:52). In addition to this, he believes that the severity of the riots had much to do with the housing crisis and with aggressive urban renewal policies, particularly within a context of police harassment and undemocratic local government (1983:52). However, the urban riots were not simply a response to the "physical" dismantling of black settlements. They were just as much or more a reaction to the consequent disruption of black civil society.

Since cultural identity is associated with and organized around territory, dismantling disrupts black identity formation by destroying the material basis of the black public sphere. By withdrawing the public sphere's physical space, urban blacks are less able to sustain the networks of family and friends necessary for organizing their experiences into a collective identity. Referring to the public sphere, Alexander Kluge in a similar vein states, "The loss of land also means a loss of community because if there is no land on which [dominated groups] may assemble, it is no longer possible to develop community" (1991: 82). The "redevelopment of space" by dominant interests in the city threatens the very material basis of black public life; that is, private use of public space is literally deterritorializing the black community. Or in the words of Rosalyn Deutsche, "The territorial conditions for situating a public sphere—at once a concrete spatial form and a social arena of radically democratic political debate—are seriously [being] undermined" (1990:175). It is in the context of deterritorialization that the "black public sphere" is being destroyed and black civil society shattered.

Nevertheless, the withdrawal of physical space is not the only threat to the formation of a collective black identity. Equally threatening is how "the architecture of redevelopment or gentrification constructs the built environment as a medium that monopolizes popular memory by controlling the representation of its own history [in urban space]" (Deutsche, 1991d:176). Put another way, mainstream white culture's image of redevelopment and its celebration of neoclassical architecture silences and marginalizes the popular stories, narratives, and memories of black place making, of black life in the city. This is significant in that these popular stories and narratives provide black urban culture with a popular vernacular. The implication is that when black urban culture is detached from its popular vernacular, from its stories and narratives of place making, blacks have less opportunity to associate their pain and anguish—unemployment, police harassment, homelessness, and hunger—with redevelopment.

It is in this context that I argue for the necessity of developing a pedagogy of place. Such a pedagogy should focus on how the loss of place-making memories by blacks is connected to how mainstream meanings and uses of urban space are naturalized by the deployment of an ideology of function, which mistakenly assumes that mainstream white definitions and uses are inherently functional to the creation of public spaces in cities. Architectural redevelopment or gentrification is believed to be functional, because it purports to "humanize" or "beautify" the environment, supposedly enhancing public use and viewer perception of the city. Also of concern is how the ideology of function obscures the role of conflict, domination, and resistance in defining what constitutes the public, and subsequently how public spaces in the city should be used and assigned meaning. A pedagogy of place must therefore facilitate blacks critically coming to voice about their own popular memories and histories of place making in the city. What this means is that black popular urban culture must be recontextualized in terms of black struggles around territory and place (Castells, 1983). This is crucial because mainstream white consumer culture detaches black popular urban culture by exoticizing black city life. Neil Smith elaborates on how artists' romanticizing the ghetto has lead to the trivializing of urban conflict:

> Especially in the context of intense media emphasis on crime and drugs in the area, the artistic invocation of danger is usually too oblique to highlight the

sharp conflicts over gentrification. . . . The world's cooptation of violent urban imagery generally trivializes real struggles and projects a sense of danger that is difficult to take seriously. Social conflict is recast as artistic spectacle danger as ambience. With the rapidity of openings and closings, moving and renamings, gentrification and decay, a landscape of happy violence becomes the stage for a dynamic and breathless new form of geographical performance art. (1992:77)

Another closely related concern of a pedagogy of place is with the impact of mainstream white consumer culture on black cultural identity. One major concern is that blacks through packaged and commodified stimulation have become addicted to the seductive images of mainstream white consumer culture—comfort, convenience, machismo, femininity, violence, and sexual stimulation (West, 1991b:224). According to West, a "market morality" is being created "where one understands oneself as living to consume" (1991:10). He says that this "mortality is creating a 'market culture' where one's communal and political identity is shaped by the adoration and cultivation of images, celebrityhood, and visibility" (1992:95). Bell hooks believes that the pervasiveness of the culture of consumption in black life "undermines our capacity to experience community" (1992:10). This is of major concern given that cultural identity is associated with territory. This is also of significance given that racist imagination of mainstream white consumer culture has re-appropriated black culture to construct "commodified" pleasure. In this way, black culture has become increasingly focused inward and individualistic. Black culture's commodification has made it less concerned with joy, that is, with "those nonmarket values—love, care, kindness, service, solidarity, the struggle for justice—values that provide the possibility of bringing people together" (Dent, 1992:1).

This being the case, blacks have become complicitous in wanting to convert the public spaces of the ghetto into private spaces of consumption. The building of public housing, community libraries, community-owned and managed cooperatives, cultural centers, and schools are subordinated to shopping malls and private homeownership. This is done under the pretext that this will bring social stability to black inner-city neighborhoods. John Logan and Harvey Molotch show how this point of view dominates black community-based organizations:

The temptation to partake in the social "upgrading" of a neighborhood is in the context of the tough problems of crime, poverty, and funding crisis, the sincere yearning of the "decent" residents is seductive; and it is easy to exclude the winos, homeless, and hoodlums as a constituency. The most efficient way to solve the neighborhood problems is perhaps through a triage system in which the best-off receive attention, the poorest are abandoned, and the middle receive the most. Raising the neighborhood's social class, even if only by a little, enables a community organization to show progress in cleaning up the neighborhood. (Logan and Molotch, 1987:145)

Underlying this is the belief that the middle-class built environment—shopping malls, single-family homes, luxury apartments and condominiums, boutiques, specialty food stores, restaurants, historic centers—forms the basis of a "stable" community. What is meant by "a stable community" is that the public spaces of the city are organized around upscale consumer-oriented entertainment and leisure. In fact, this suggests that this particular built environment corresponds with the lifestyle of the middle class, a lifestyle that Thorstein Veblen argued is defined by conspicuous consumption and conspicuous leisure. The point is that private consumption is being viewed by blacks as the way to use and define public space in the ghetto territory. In support of this view, blacks become complicitous in silencing and marginalizing their own stories and narratives about place making. The result is that blacks are rendered less able to develop oppositional public spheres.

TOWARDS A PEDAGOGY OF PLACE FOR BLACK URBAN RESISTANCE

In the context of the inner city, a pedagogy of place must be linked to black urban struggle. It must be involved in the building of oppositional public spaces, to forming spaces of care and nurturance or, as bell hooks would say, "homeplaces." However, for black urban communities to build oppositional public spaces or homeplaces a pedagogy of place must first work with them in redefining the nature of black urban struggle. One of the major contradictions of black urban struggle is its demand for redevelopment or gentrification *without* displacement. Even when blacks have control over the redevelopment process many blacks are still displaced. Black urban struggles overlook how the very notion of redevelopment or gentrification itself is premised on the racialization of certain urban populations, mainly nonwhite populations—in this case, blacks—to legitimate their forced removal or warehousing in the city. I discussed above how Goldberg points out that notions like "degeneration" and "regeneration" are informed by a racial subtext. He shows how "degeneration" is connoted with "blacks" and "slums"; "regeneration" with progress and renewal; and whites with the process of "gentrification."

> If degeneration is the dark, regressive side of progress, then regeneration is the reformation—the spiritual and physical renewal—but only of those by nature fit for it. And gentrification is the form of regeneration which most readily defines the postmodern city. Gentrification is a structural phenomenon tied to changing forms of capital accumulation and the means of maximizing ground rent. It involves tax-assisted displacement of longtime inner-city resident poor (usually the racially marginalized), renovation of the vacated residential space, upscaling the neighborhood, and resettling the area with inhabitants of higher socioeconomic status. (1993:201)

Underlying notions like redevelopment and gentrification is the discourse of development. Although much of the critical work on the discourse of development has focused on the "Third World," it is useful in terms of developing a pedagogy of place, particularly in the context of the urban, in that it would reaffirm the need of a pedagogy of place to reveal how the redevelopment of space in the city is dependent upon constructing a racial Other. According to Arturo Escobar, development is not only an instrument of economic control over the physical and social reality of much of Asia, Africa, and Latin America, it is also an "invention and strategy produced by the 'First World' about the underdevelopment of the 'Third World'" (1992:22). Escobar goes on to point out, "Development has been the primary mechanism through which these parts of the world have been produced and have produced themselves, thus marginalizing or precluding other ways of seeing and doing" (1992:22). This is of particular significance given that the discourse of development is connoted with growth, evolution, and maturation. Or as Escobar states, "The problem is complicated by the fact that the post-World War II discourse of development is firmly entrenched in Western modernity and economy" (1992:22).

What Escobar's critique of the discourse of development suggests for a pedagogy of place is that it must work with inner-city blacks in terms of how they see redevelopment. A pedagogy of place must link struggles over the definition of blackness and black identity with struggles over the image of redevelopment, with how those images construct racialized spaces and racialized Others. Though he does not talk about a pedagogy of place, Mel King recognizes the importance of why black urban struggles must deal with how black people think about themselves and what that means for the control of land by black urban communities. He writes,

> I would like to challenge people to think differently about strategies of shaping the future of cities. We are faced with a struggle for land and a struggle for the mind. This is the core of urban community organizing today, and I think it is crucial. It is my contention that, if we win the struggle for the mind, then we will win the struggle for the land. So, we have to think about where the struggle for the mind exists. Obviously, we have to deal with the issue of race. (1991:1)

King's comments indicate that it is important for a pedagogy of place to link black self-definition to how blacks define and use public space in the city. This means that the starting point for a pedagogy of place is with the "voices" of inner-city blacks. According to Henry Giroux, "The concept of voice represents forms of self and social representation that mediate and produce wider structures of meaning, experience, and history" (1991: 100). Through the concept of voice, a pedagogy of place can help blacks become more self-reflective about the construction of their racial identities, particularly when pertaining to their living spaces in the city. The concern then is with how white supremacist definitions of black public spaces shape not only black identities but also how blacks relate to the redevelopment of their spaces in the city. As Michele Wallace notes, black struggles over self-image are overwhelmingly directed towards trying to "salvage the denigrated image of blacks in the white imagination" (1990:2). Related to this, the binary logic of white supremacy sets limits on black struggles for identity and dignity, in that these struggles are defined in relation to "positive" versus "negative" images. One problem with this is that "positive images" are the bipolar opposites of negative, degrading stereotypes put forward by white supremacist ideologies. Struggles by blacks to represent themselves in a "positive" image make them complicitous in the maintenance of white supremacy, since white norms and standards define positive images. In agreement Wallace writes that

> since racism or the widespread conviction that blacks are morally and/or intellectually inferior, defines the "commonsense" perception of blacks, a positive/negative image cultural formula means that the goal of cultural production becomes simply to reverse these already existing assumptions. Not only does reversal, or the notion that blacks are more likeable, more compassionate, smarter, or even "superior," not substantially alter racist preconceptions, it also ties Afro-American cultural production to racist ideology in a way that makes the failure to alter it inevitable. (1991:2)

Wallace's critique of positive/negative images must also be extended to the cultural production of place. What her critique suggests for a pedagogy of place is that it must pay close attention to how the manufacturing of place by blacks is configured around blacks' desire for not only a "positive" image of themselves, but of their neighborhoods. A pedagogy of place must therefore help blacks understand how their struggle for a "positive image of place" is compromised by white racist stereotypes that construct and fuel black self-contempt. In addition to this, a pedagogy of place must address how black self-contempt, when expressed in terms of wanting a "positive image of place," can even be complicitous with police repression and redevelopment strategies that deterritorialize and evict some blacks from the city. Again, Logan and Molotch argue, "From the standpoint of the community organization, and this is indeed a paradox, it becomes necessary to destroy at least part of the neighborhood in order to save it" (1987:145). They are suggesting that the displacement of "undesirables" from black neighborhoods is believed by many black community organizers to be necessary to begin constructing a "positive image of place," which in turn will raise property values and bring more businesses, jobs, and the middle-class to the area. The belief of organizers, say Logan and Molotch, is that "the community can only be saved by treating it as a commodity" (1987:145).

Finally, assimilationist and Afrocentric notions of black identity have generally informed "positive images of place" in black urban communities. In addition, both notions are informed by the binary logic of white supremacy. Assimilationist notions of place are informed by the ideology of Liberal individualism, more specifically by the civil rights movement's "color-blind" consciousness. The color-blind consciousness stance of the civil rights movement represented a Eurocentric-oriented assimilationist racial consciousness. This position Cornel West argues "set out to show that black people were really like white people—thereby eliding differences (in history, culture) between blacks and whites. Black specificity and particularity were thus banished in order to gain white acceptance and approval" (1993:17). The argument of the assimilationist is that when blacks, particularly poor working-class inner-city blacks, are geographically concentrated in the same territory due to residential and employment racial segregation, they perpetuate crime, violence, single-parent households, and a cycle of poverty. From this perspective then one can understand why mainstream black scholars and leaders have shown concern over the exodus of the black middle class. They argue that this exodus has not only meant a loss in economic terms, but also in social terms. Their assumption is that the black middle class historically has been responsible for extending mainstream values to poor working-class urban blacks like family patterns and work ethics (Wilson, 1987). Assimilationist notions of place have generally supported redevelopment efforts with the hopes that this would spatially deconcentrate and integrate the "desirable" urban poor into middle-class neighborhoods, whether black or white.

Afrocentric or essentialist notions of black identity are informed racial unity. As important is the concept of self-determination, that blacks must lead and run their own organizations—that blacks can do things themselves. Related to this is the idea that "black people [should] consolidate behind their own, so that they can bargain from a position of strength" (Dyson, 1993:47). Although the concept of black self-determination it is not specific to Afrocentrism, its particular formulation by Afrocentrism is informed by a "homogeneous" notion of racial unity. It argues that a precondition for black unity is that blacks become aware that they have a history that predates slavery, one that begins on the continent of Africa. Another way of putting this is that black unity is dependent upon blacks tracing their "roots" to Africa. Michael Dyson points out that this search for racial unity has to do with "the desperate effort to replace a cultural uprooting that should have never occurred with a racial unanimity that never existed" (1993:xv). Dyson later goes on to state that while clan, community, and nation were central to African societies, only a cultural catastrophe the magnitude of chattel slavery could impose upon blacks an artificial and single racial identity (1993:xv). Motivating the quest for racial unity is the desire to preserve community life before the colonizers intervened, thus the assumption is that the future is in the past (Pieterse, 1992:12).

The Afrocentric world view therefore is to search for fixed, transcendental notions of black culture and blackness. It also believes that if black people are aware of their African roots, they would have much better self-esteem, subsequently giving them confidence to compete with their white counterparts for the American Dream—to be entrepreneurs. In addition to this, Afrocentrism has opportunistically supported the corporate redevelopment of city space as a strategy to promote black capitalism within the public spaces of the black community. This strategy has been accompanied by desire to commodify black culture, making black cultural products the basis for black capitalism, in the form of exotic black American or African restaurants, upscale jazz and blues clubs, African boutiques and art galleries, and music stores. The primary concern is to make the physical space of the black community attractive for private investment, consequently marginalizing or displacing poor working-class urban blacks (Allen, 1970). What was once an inner-city black community becomes an upscale middle-class white and black neighborhood. The implication is that the private use of black public spaces represents an attempt by black entrepreneurs, armed with the ideology of black unity, to control the political dialogue about how the "ghetto" territory should be used and defined. In a sense, the essentialist discourse of Afrocentrism is linked to an exclusionary definition and use of black urban space, to a positive image of place that is occupied by black capitalism.

For a pedagogy of place to move beyond the assimilationist versus Afrocentric dualism, it must be linked with a politics of decolonization, to the creation of new meanings of blackness and black identity. Decolonization implies a "process of cultural and historical liberation; an act of confrontation with a dominant system of thought" (hooks, 1992:1). This contestation of white supremacist systems of thought and values goes beyond addressing black self-hatred to linking political resistance, in this case, black urban resistance, to loving blackness (hooks, 1992b). According to bell hooks, "loving blackness" is a "political stance" because as a sign, blackness "primarily evokes in the public imagination of whites hatred and fear" (1992b:100). She states that "to love blackness is dangerous in a white supremacist culture—so threatening, so serious a breach in the fabric of the social order, that death is the punishment" (1992b).

A pedagogy of place must also link the process of decolonization—the loving of blackness—to the complex and contradictory positioning of the black subject. More specifically, it has to challenge the colonizing logic of white supremacist culture by first acknowledging the multiple identifications and experiences of the black subject; it must understand that locations in gender, class, race, ethnicity and sexuality complicate one another and not merely additively (Smith and Watson, 1992:xiv). Thus, the colonizing logic of white supremacy "implies a relation of structural domination and a suppression—often violent—of the heterogeneity of the [black] subject" (Mohanty and Mohanty, 1990:19). Restated, the colonizing project of white supremacist culture is related to the containment of difference by creating an essentialist and unified notion of racial identity (Smith and Watson, 1993). Decolonization implies various colonialisms or systems of racial dominations. As Cornel West notes, "racist treatment vastly differs owing to class, gender, sexual orientation, nation, region, hue and age" (1991a:28). This particular underlying assumption of decolonization has led some black feminists to challenge homogenized notions of blackness. They argue that homogenized notions of blackness are about black men gaining access to patriarchy through material privilege:

> And even though the more radical 1960s black power movement repudiated imitation of whites, emphasizing Pan-Africanist connections, their vision of liberation was not particularly distinctive or revolutionary . . . liberatory efforts centered around gaining access to material privilege, the kind of nation-building which would place black men in position of authority and power. (hooks, 1990:16)

In contrast to homogeneous constructions of black identity, bell hooks recognizes "the primacy of identity politics as an important stage in the liberation process," and proposes the notion of "radical black subjectivity" (1990:18). She uses this term to denote radical efforts to subvert static notions of black identity as a way to make visible "the complexity and variety to constructions of black subjectivity." Her equating radical black subjectivity with heterogeneity and not static notions of black identity moves black resistance from one of opposition to one of self-actualization:

> How do we create an oppositional world-view, a consciousness, an identity, a standpoint that exists not only as the struggle which also opposes dehumanization but as that movement which enables creative, expansive self-actualization. Opposition is not enough. In that vacant space after one has resisted there is still the necessity to become—to make oneself anew. That process emerges as one comes to understand how structures of domination work in one's own life, as one develops critical thinking and critical consciousness, as one invents new, alternative habits of being, and resist from that marginal space of difference inwardly defined. (1990:15)

hooks' reconceptualizing black identity around a "radical black subjectivity" is therefore opposed to static and one-dimensional notions of identity that construct black resistance in relation to binary oppositions. In this instance, black resistance involves replacing "negative" interpretations of stereotypical characterizations of blacks with "positive" ones. Nevertheless, the stereotype remains intact. In conjunction with this process is also an inversion whereby "black culture" is seen as superior to "white culture," as in the case of Afrocentricism. Within this mode of black resistance, both cultures are viewed as separate, distinct, and incompatible suggesting a notion of racial authenticity.

This search for authentic or essentialist constructions of blackness and black culture is in contradiction to a notion of resistance linked to emancipation. What is important about this linkage is that resistance is not simply reduced to a politics of oppositionality but to one of self-actualizations. This is because emancipation is "not simply about saying no, reacting, refusing, but also and primarily about social creativity, introducing new values and aims, new forms of co-operation and action" (Pieterse, 1992:13). In this way, black resistance becomes tied to a politics of identity that is transformative, a politics that moves beyond defining blackness within the white supremacist framework of binary oppositions. Although the concept of emancipation is an important corrective in redefining black resistance, there is also an aspect of it that is problematic, that is, its roots in the totalizing narratives of Western modernity. This is because in the Eurocentric, Western humanist tradition what dominates is the idea of the universality of fundamental human experiences, that experiences are identical, regardless of their wide cultural and historical differences, that underneath there is one human nature and therefore one common human essence. The assimilationist discourse is compatible with this idea of emancipation.

What is important about the concepts of decolonization, emancipation, and hooks' notion of "radical black subjectivity" is that they provide us with a way to talk about black public spaces in the city not simply as "spaces of opposition" but as "spaces of self-actualization." In this way, defining black public spaces as "places of self-actualization" is understanding the centrality of black popular urban culture in constructing such places. For one thing, it is through black popular culture that black people in the city resist mainstream white culture's racializing and therefore biologization of their spaces, bodies, and personalities. This is important in that the early twentieth-century construction of the city as jungle—an image that preceded the emergence of large-scale black urban settlements—is now connoted with black people's dark skin. In other words, the urban has become a metaphor for race, and in a white supremacist culture, like ours, race does not mean white, but black. So, in the city, urban problems, such as poverty, homelessness, joblessness, crime, violence, single-parent households, and drugs, are seen as racial problems, the problems of blacks, not of whites. And in a white supremacist culture, where race is biologized, racial problems are reduced to black people's bodies. In a sense, then, black urban popular culture attempts to construct new meanings of blackness, one that historicizes race and subsequently blackness and the spaces that blacks occupy in the city (Gilroy, 1991).

Black urban popular culture is the "voice" of the black urban movement (Gilroy, 1991:223). What distinguishes black urban social movements from working-class movements, the labor movement, for example, is that political action and organization take place outside of the workplace's political economy (Tourine, 1988; Melucci, 1989; Gilroy, 1991). Transforming the United

States from an industrial to a post-industrial capitalist society has turned blacks into a surplus population, into an expendable population, making them useless in terms of the economy. In the context of postindustrial capitalism, automation, cybernetics, neo-liberal austerity, state policies, and white racism within the labor movement have contributed to mass urban black unemployment and underemployment. Subsequently, then, the factory is not the site from which blacks develop black consciousness and solidarity. It is in their settlement spaces in the the city, their homeplaces, where the process of self-actualization occurs.

New social movement theorists, such as Alberto Melucci, Alain Tourine, and Paul Gilroy, point out that one of the key features of new movements is their alternative public spaces. Melucci refers to the public spaces of new social movements as "invisible networks of small groups submerged in everyday life." These submerged networks constitute the "laboratories" where new experiences are invented and movements question and challenge the dominant codes of everyday life (Melucci, 1989:6). In the preface to Melucci's book, *Nomads of the Present,* John Keane and Paul Mier write, "These laboratories are places in which the elements of everyday life are mixed, developed and tested, a site in which reality is given new names and citizens can develop alternative experiences of time, space and interpersonal relations" (Melucci, 1989:6). Using his concept of historicity, Tourine argues that new social movements "act upon themselves"; that is, through their cultural models they represent themselves and their actions, and in so doing challenge dominant cultural codes. Melucci similarly argues that new social movements are, in his words, "self-referential," they "are not just instrumental for their goals, they are a goal in themselves" (1989:60). For new social movements, then, the reference for social struggle is not the political system or state. This is not to say that social and political forms of struggle are not combined, but that new social movements link demands for inclusion and rights for the excluded group with the affirmation of difference. Gilroy elaborates this point by saying that

> new social movements are not primarily oriented towards instrumental objectives, such as the conquest of political power or state apparatuses, but rather towards control of a field of autonomy or independence vis à vis the system and the immediate satisfaction of collective desires. . . . The very refusal to accept mediation by the existing frameworks and institutions of the political system or to allow strategy to be dominated by the task of winning power within it, provides these movements with an important focus of group identity. (1987:226)

Melucci's, Tourine's, and Gilroy's comments about new social movements help us to recognize that it is inside the spaces of black urban settlements that blacks create new cultural models, new ways of experiencing and identifying with blackness. Black public spaces in the city challenge the cultural codes of white supremacy, and to quote bell hooks, "Loving blackness is a political stance"; "loving blackness is dangerous in a white supremacist culture" (1992:100). Because the black body has been the primary site for white supremacist repression and cultural denigration—constructing blacks as the dangerous Other, particularly in cities—it has also been the site from which black people have resisted. In support, Paul Gilroy argues that like the women's movement, the gay and lesbian movement, and sections of the peace movement, issues around the body as well play a fundamental, definitive role in black urban social movements:

> Blacks who live in the castle of their skin and have struggled to escape the biologization of their socially and politically constructed subordination are already sensitive to this issue. The attempt to articulate blackness as an historical rather than as a natural category confronts reality. The escape from bestial status into a recognized humanity has been a source of both ethics and politics since the slave system was first instituted. Black artists have thus identified the body as a seat of desires and as a nexus of interpersonal relationships in a special way which expresses the aspiration that skin colour will one day be no more significant than eye pigment and, in the meantime, announces that black is beautiful. (1991:226–227)

Gilroy's mention of black cultural workers seems to imply that through black popular culture, blacks resist and construct new meanings of blackness in relation to their bodies. It is black popular culture's deliberate use of the body as a canvas, particularly through its production of style and music, that has allowed blacks to attach new meanings of blackness to their bodies (Hall, 1992:27). According to Jefferies, style, music, and the body as a canvas, are three repertoires of black popular culture, and the city is a fourth. This is the place where black popular culture is born (Jefferies, 1992:27). The city is the place where the "language of black popular culture describes the emotions and circumstances black urban resistance encounters" (Jefferies, 1992:27). These circumstances include the control of black bodies through the manipulation of urban space (the redevelopment of space or gentrification), the surveillance and repression of black bodies through state sanctioned and organized policing, and the coercive control of black bodies in the work process (Gilroy, 1991).

Finally, a pedagogy of place for black urban struggle must use black urban popular culture as a way to recall black people's circumstances. This means that through black urban popular culture a pedagogy of place connects the voices of urban blacks to their narratives about the city. According to McLaren, "Narratives help us remember and also forget. They help shape our social reality as much by what they exclude as what they include" (1993a: 140). And, because the self is constituted in relation to multiple narratives, its contradictions and consistencies provide the context for understanding how the narratives we construct to explain our experiences marginalize and silence differences. In support of this view, Henry Giroux writes that a "viable critical pedagogy needs to [analyze] how ideologies are actually taken up in the voices and lived experiences of students as they give meaning to dreams, desires, and subject positions they inhabit" (1992a:169). He concludes by saying that "radical educators need to provide conditions for students to speak so that their narratives can be affirmed and engaged along with the consistencies and contradictions that characterize such experiences" (1992:169). Only by doing this can a pedagogy of place help urban blacks create what McLaren (1993a:140) calls a "critical narratology." By this McLaren "means reading personal narratives against society's treasured stock of narratives, since not all narratives share a similar status and there are those which exist devalued within society's rifts and margins" (1993a:140). The significance of this is that "critical narratology" can provide insights into how particular notions of difference—for instance, the binarism used by white supremacist culture to racialize the urban spaces of blacks—promote essentialist notions of blackness. Therefore, McLaren proposes that "the construction of narrative identities of liberation places a central emphasis on the meaning of difference" (1993:217). McLaren addresses this same issue when he calls for critical pedagogy to be linked to "critical multiculturalism," because critical multiculturalism highlights how the construction of difference around binarisms permits "whiteness to serve as an invisible norm against which to measure the worth of other cultures" (McLaren, 1992b:339). A pedagogy based upon critical multiculturalism is therefore relevant regarding how the invisible norm of whiteness is the narrative that informs "images of redevelopment."

Henry Giroux's notion of a critical "pedagogy of representation" and a "representational pedagogy" brings to surface similar issues regarding "the relationship between identity and culture, particularly as it is addressed in the discourse of racial difference" (1994:33). As Giroux has noted, "the identity politics of the right-wing in its attempt to block progressive political possibilities privileg[es] race as a sign of social disorder and civic decay" (1994:37). He argues that within the racial discourse of the right, "whiteness is not only privileged, it is also the only referent for social change, hope and action" (1994:45). Giroux argues, like McLaren, that whiteness is able to represent itself in this way by positioning itself as the invisible norm. A pedagogy of representation for Giroux must therefore focus on demystifying representations of racial difference by revealing whose identity, history, social forms and ethics, and view of knowledge and consensus within unequal relations of power is narrating the storyline. The primacy of a pedagogy of representation is that images of redevelopment become linked to questions of subjectivity, power, and politics, but even more important, they would be increasingly significant as pedagogical practices (Giroux, 1994:47). A pedagogy of representation is useful for developing a pedagogy for black urban struggle in that it suggests that blacks must analyze those myth-making institutions in the city that rewrite the histories of race and colonialism in the material landscape of the city (Giroux, 1994:47). Representational pedagogy, on the other hand, focuses less on the "structuring principles that inform the form and content of the representation of politics [and more on] how students and others learn to identify, challenge, and rewrite such representations" (Giroux, 1994:50). This means that a pedagogy of black urban struggles would focus on recovering new notions of blackness by looking at how black identities have been historically constructed in the city, particularly in relation to the spatial structure of the city. Blacks and others would look at how blacks have historically constructed transformative notions of blackness that recall memories of how blacks have used their living spaces to create communities of resistance. Representational pedagogy of black urban struggle would highlight the fact that black identity and black living spaces are not fixed and static. Such a pedagogy would counter the racialization of residential space through the imagery of racial segregation, an imagery that suggests that the problems experienced by black people are sharply bounded in space or that when blacks live in the same geographical area they produce social pathologies (Smith, Susan, 1993).

Furthermore, a pedagogy of black urban struggle must understand that narratives are not only constituted in relation to meaning but also around the body. Another way of putting this is that experience is not only about what is interpreted, but also about the pain and anguish felt in and on the bodies of the oppressed when deterritorialized by redevelopment and policed. The narratives that are expressed by black urban popular culture are also about the black body. Cornel West notes, "Black cultural practices emerge out of an acknowledgement of a reality they cannot not know—the ragged edges of the real, of necessity, . . . of not being able to eat, not having shelter, not having health care" (1989:89). It is "the ragged edges of the real" that shape the popular vernacular of blacks, therefore organizing the narratives and meanings they give to their lived experiences. In this way, the body plays an important role in the formation of black identity. McLaren reminds us that "[w]e cannot separate the body from the social formation, since the material density of all forms of subjectivity is achieved through the micropractices of power that are socially inscribed into our flesh" (1992:5).

It is in this context that a pedagogy for black urban struggle takes up questions regarding the black body/subject. McLaren's use of the term *body/subject* refers to "a terrain of the flesh in which meaning is inscribed, constructed, and reconstituted" (1991:150). That is, "the body [must be] conceived as the interface of the individual and society, as a site of embodied or enfleshed subjectivity which also reflects the ideological sedimentations of the social structure inscribed into it" (McLaren, 1991:150). How then do these "ideological sedimentations of the social structure regulate the black body subject? What is implied in this question is that the theoretical knowledges contained in ideologies "constitute externalized metaphors of the body" (McLaren, 1991:13). In a white supremacist culture, not only do "externalized metaphors" racialize the bodies and public spaces of blacks and establish a pretext for deterritorialization, but they also become the basis for black self-contempt.

This suggests that a pedagogy of black urban struggle be tied to Giroux's representational pedagogy: "Central to such an approach is understanding how knowledge and desire come together to promote particular forms of cultural production, investments, and counter-narratives that invoke communities of memory that are lived, felt and interrogated" (1994:51). A pedagogy of black urban struggle linked to a representational pedagogy would recognize that black self-contempt is the result of blacks essentializing (e.g., biologizing their bodies, using white supremacist definitions of race and blackness). For example, such a pedagogy would point out how phallocentric models of black masculinity, certain constructions of black femininity and of the black poor by middle-class blacks are informed by white supremacist notions about the black body (hooks, 1992; Ransby and Matthews, 1993). In addition to this, a pedagogy of place for black urban struggle would take seriously questions around the body and how mainstream white consumer culture's exoticizing of the black body has reinforced both black self-hatred and the market values of individualism, consumerism, and competitiveness. It is the values and assumptions that inform white supremacy and mainstream white consumer culture that a pedagogy of place for black urban struggle must critically interrogate in terms of their influences on the formation of black identity and black public spaces in the city.

REFERENCES

Allen, Robert. 1970. *Black Awakening in Capitalist America*. New York: Anchor Books.

Banfield, Edward C. 1968. *The Unheavenly City Revisited*. Boston: Little, Brown and Company.

Boyer, M. Christine. 1986. *Dreaming the Rational City*. Cambridge, MA: The MIT Press.

Castells, Manuel. 1983. *The City and the Grassroots*. Berkeley: University of California Press.

Cross, Michael, and Michael Keith. 1993. "Racism and the Postmodern City." In Michael Keith and Malcolm Cross, *Racism, the City and the State*. New York: Routledge.

Davis, Mike. 1990. *City of Quartz: Excavating the Future in Los Angeles*. London: Verso.

————. 1992. "Fortress Los Angeles: The Militarization of Urban Space." In Michael Sorkin (ed.), *Variations on a Theme Park: The New American City and the End of Public Space*. New York: The Noonday Press.

Dent, Gina. 1992. "Black Pleasure, Black Joy: An Introduction." In Gina Dent (ed.), *Black Popular Culture*. Seattle: Bay Press.

Dyson, Michael Eric. 1993. *Reflecting Black: African American Cultural Criticism*. Minneapolis: University of Minnesota Press.

Escobar, Arturo. 1992. "Imagining a Post-Development Era? Critical Thought, Development and Social Movement." In *Social Text*. No. 31/32.

Fraser, Nancy. 1991. "Rethinking the Public Sphere: A Contribution to the Critique of Actually Existing Democracy." In *Social Text*. Spring.

Friedland, Roger. 1992. "Space, Place and Modernity." In *A Journal of Reviews: Contemporary Sociology*. Volume 21, Number 1.

Gilroy, Paul. 1991. *"There Ain't No Black in the Union Jack": The Cultural Politics of Race and Nation*. Chicago: The University of Chicago Press.

Giroux, Henry A. 1983. *Theory and Resistance in Education: A Pedagogy for the Opposition*. South Hadley: Bergin and Garvey.

———. 1991. *Postmodernism, Feminism, and Cultural Politics: Redrawing the Educational Boundaries*. Albany: State University of New York Press.

———. 1992a. *Border Crossings: Cultural Workers and the Politics of Education*. New York: Routledge, Chapman, and Hall, Inc.

———. 1994. "Living Dangerously: Identity Politics and the New Cultural Racism." In Henry A. Giroux and Peter McLaren (eds.) *Between Borders: Pedagogy and the Politics of Cultural Studies*. New York: Routledge.

Goldberg, David Theo. 1993. *Racist Culture: Philosophy and the Politics of Meaning*. Cambridge, MA: Basil Blackwell Inc.

Goldman, Robert, and Steve Papson. 1991. "Levis and the Knowing Wink." In *Current Perspectives in Social Theory*. Volume II.

Hall, Stuart. 1992. "What Is This 'Black' in Black Popular Culture." In Gina Dent, *Black Popular Culture*. Seattle: Bay Press.

———. 1991. "The Loss of Community and Women's Space." In *Canadian Woman Studies/Les Cahiers De La Femme*.

Hamilton, Cynthia. 1988. "Apartheid in an American City." In *LA Weekly*. December 30.

hooks, bell. 1990. *Yearning: Race, Gender, and Cultural Politics*. Boston: South End Press.

———. 1992b. *Black Looks: Race and Representation*. Boston: South End Press.

hooks, bell, and Cornel West. 1991. *Breaking Bread: Insurgent Black Intellectual Life*. Boston: South End Press.

Jefferies, John. 1992. "Toward a Redefinition of the Urban: The Collision of Culture." In Gina Dent, *Black Popular Culture*. Seattle: Bay Press.

Jenning, James. 1990. "The Politics of Black Empowerment in Urban America: Reflections on Race, Class and Community." In Joseph M. Kling and Prudence S. Posner, *Dilemmas of Activism: Class, Community, and the Politics of Local Mobilization*. Philadelphia: Temple University Press.

Keith, Michael. 1993. "From Punishment to Discipline? Racism, Racialization and the Policing of Social Control." In Michael Keith and Malcolm Cross, *Racism, the City and the State*. New York: Routledge.

Keith, Michael, and Steve Pile. 1993. *Place and the Politics of Identity*. New York: Routledge.

King, Mel. 1991. "A Framework for Action." In Philip W. Nyden and Wim Wiewel (eds.), *Challenging Uneven Development: An Urban Agenda for the 1990s*. New Brunswick: Rutgers University Press.

Kluge, Alexander. 1991. "The Public Sphere." In Brian Wallis (ed.), *If You Lived Here: The City in Art, Theory, and Social Activism*. Seattle: Bay Press.

Levitas, Ruth. 1990. *The Concept of Utopia*. Syracuse: Syracuse University Press.

Logan, John R., and Harvey L. Molotch. 1987. *Urban Fortunes: The Political Economy of Place*. Los Angeles: University of California Press.

McClaren, Peter. 1991a. "Schooling the Postmodern Body: Critical Pedagogy and the Politics of Enfleshment." In Henry Giroux (ed.), *Postmodernism, Feminism, and Cultural Politics: Redrawing Educational Boundaries*. Albany: State University of New York Press.

———. 1992b. "Critical Multiculturalism and Democratic Schooling: An Interview with Peter McLaren and Joe Kincheloe." In Shirley P. Steinberg, *International Journal of Educational Reform*.

———. 1993a. "Border Disputes: Multicultural Narrative, Identity Formation, and Critical Pedagogy in Postmodern America." In Daniel McLaughlin and William G. Tierney (eds.), *Naming Silence Lives: Personal Narratives and the Process of Educational Change*. New York: Routledge.

Melucci, Alberto. 1989. *Nomads of the Present: Social Movements and Individual Needs in Contemporary Society*. Philadelphia: Temple University Press.

Mohanty, Chandra T., and Satya Mohanty. 1990. "Contradictions of Colonialism," Women's Review of Books. March (7):19.

Pieterse, Jan Nederveen. 1992. "Emancipations, Modern and Postmodern." In *Development and Change*. Volume 23, Number 3.

Ransby, Barbara, and Tracy Matthews. 1993. "Black Popular Culture and the Transcendence of Patriarchal Illusions." In *Race and Class*. Volume 35, Number 1.

Reed, David. 1981. *Education for Building a People's Movement*. Boston: South End Press.

Rose, Harold M. 1982. "The Future of the Black Ghettos." In Gary Gappert and Richard V. Knights (eds.), *Cities in the 21st Century*. Beverly Hills: Sage.

Sentencing Project. 1991. *Americans Behind Bars: A Comparision of International Rates of Incarceration*. Washington, D.C.

Smith, Neil. 1992. "New City, New Frontier: The Lower East Side as Wild, Wild West." In Michael Sorkin (ed.), *Variations on a Theme Park: The New American City and the End of Public Space*. New York: The Noonday Press.

Smith, Sidonie, and Julia Watson (eds.). 1992. *Decolonizing the Subject: The Politics of Gender in Women's Autobiography*. Minneapolis: University of Minnesota Press.

Smith, Susan J. 1993. "Residential Segregation and the Politics of Racialization." In Malcolm Cross and Michael Keith (eds.), *Racism, the City and the State*. New York: Routledge.

Tourine, Alain. 1988. *Return of the Actor: Social Theory in Postindustrial Society*. Minneapolis: University of Minnesota Press.

Urban Strategies Group. 1992. "Call to Reject the Federal Weed and Seed Program in Los Angeles." A Project of the Labor/Community Strategy Center.

Wallace, Michele. 1990. *Invisibility Blues: From Pop to Theory*. London: Verso.

West, Cornel. 1989. "Black Culture and Postmodernism." In Barbara Kruger and Phil Mariani (eds.), *Remaking History*. Seattle: Bay Press.

———. 1991a. "The New Cultural Politics of Difference." In Russell Ferguson, Martha Gever, Trinh T. Minh-ha, and Cornel West (eds.), *Out There: Marginalization and Contemporary Cultures*. Cambridge, MA: The MIT Press.

———. 1991b. "Nihilism in Black America." In *Dissent*. Spring.

———. 1992. "Philosophy and the Underclass." In *The Under-class Question*. Philadelphia: Temple University Press.

Williams, Brett. 1988. *Upscaling Downtown: Stalled Gentrification in Washington D.C.* Ithaca: Cornell University Press.

Wilson, Elizabeth. 1991. *The Sphinx in the City: Urban Life, The Control of Disorder, and Women*. Berkeley: University of California Press.

Wilson, William J. 1987. *The Truly Disadvantaged*. Chicago: University Press.

Reflections on Race and Sex

BELL HOOKS

Race and sex have always been overlapping discourses in the United States: That discourse began in slavery. The talk then was not about black men wanting to be free so that they would have access to the bodies of white women—that would come later. Then, black women's bodies were the discursive terrain, the playing fields where racism and sexuality converged. Rape as both right and rite of the white male dominating group was a cultural norm. Rape was also an apt metaphor for European imperialist colonization of Africa and North America.

Sexuality has always provided gendered metaphors for colonization. Free countries equated with free men, domination with castration, the loss of manhood, and rape—the terrorist act re-enacting the drama of conquest, as men of the dominating group sexually violate the bodies of women who are among the dominated. The intent of this act was to continually remind dominated men of their loss of power; rape was a gesture of symbolic castration. Dominated men are made powerless (i.e., impotent) over and over again as the women they would have had the right to possess, to control, to assert power over, to dominate, to fuck, are fucked and fucked over by the dominating victorious male group.

There is no psychosexual history of slavery that explores the meaning of white male sexual exploitation of black women or the politics of sexuality, no work that lays out all the available information. There is no discussion of sexual sado-masochism, of the master who forced his wife to sleep on the floor as he nightly raped a black woman in bed. There is no discussion of sexual voyeurism. And what were the sexual lives of white men like who were legally declared "insane" because they wanted to marry black slave women with whom they were sexually and romantically involved? Under what conditions did sexuality serve as a force subverting and disrupting power relations, unsettling the oppressor/oppressed paradigm? No one seems to know how to tell this story, where to begin. As historical narrative it was long ago supplanted by the creation of another story (pornographic sexual project, fantasy, fear, the origin has yet to be traced). That story, invented by white men, is about the overwhelming desperate longing black men have to sexually violate the bodies of white women. The central character in this story is the black male rapist. Black men are constructed, as Michael Dyson puts it, as "peripatetic phalluses with unrequited desire for their denied object—white women." As the story goes, this desire is not based on longing for sexual pleasure. It is a story of revenge, rape as the weapon by which black men, the dominated, reverse their circumstance, regain power over white men.

Oppressed black men and women have rarely challenged the use of gendered metaphors to describe the impact of racist domination and/or black liberation struggle. The discourse of black resistance has almost always equated freedom with manhood, the economic and material domination of black men with castration, emasculation. Accepting these sexual metaphors forged a bond between oppressed black men and their white male oppressors. They shared the patriarchal belief that revolutionary struggle was really about the erect phallus, the ability of men to establish political dominance that could correspond to sexual dominance. Careful critical examination of black power literature in the sixties and early seventies exposes the extent to which black women and men were using sexualized metaphors to talk about the effort to resist racist domination. Many of us have never forgotten that moment in *Soul on Ice* when Eldridge Cleaver, writing about the need to "redeem my conquered manhood," described raping black women as practice for the eventual rape of white women. Remember that readers were not shocked or horrified by this glamorization of rape as a weapon of terrorism men might use to express rage about other forms of domination, about their struggle for power with other men. Given the sexist context of the culture, it made sense. Cleaver was able to deflect attention away from the misogynist sexism of his assertions by poignantly justifying these acts as a "natural" response to racial domination. He wanted to force readers to confront the agony and suffering black men experience in a white supremacist society. Again, freedom from racial domination was expressed in terms of redeeming black masculinity. And gaining the right to assert one's manhood was always about sexuality.

During slavery, there was perhaps a white male who created his own version of *Soul on Ice,* one who confessed how good it felt to assert racial dominance over black people, and particularly black men, by raping black women with impunity, or how sexually stimulating it was to use the sexual exploitation of black women to humiliate and degrade white women, to assert phallocentric domination in one's household. Sexism has always been a political stance mediating racial domination, enabling white men and black men to share a common sensibility about sex roles and the importance of male domination. Clearly both groups have equated freedom with manhood, and manhood with the right of men to have indiscriminate access to the bodies of women. Both groups have been socialized to condone patriarchal affirmation of rape as an acceptable way to maintain male domination. It is this merging of sexuality with male domination within patriarchy that informs the construction of masculinity for men of all races and classes. Robin Morgan's book, *The Demon Lover: On The Sexuality of Terrorism,* begins with rape. She analyses the way men are bonded across class, race, and nationalities through shared notions of manhood which make masculinity synonymous with the ability to assert power-over through acts of violence and terrorism. Since terrorist acts are most often committed by men, Morgan sees the terrorist as "the logical incarnation of patriarchal politics in a technological world." She is not concerned with the overlapping discourses of race and sex, with the interconnectedness of racism and sexism. Like many radical feminists, she believes that male commitment to maintaining patriarchy and male domination diminishes or erases difference.

Much of my work within feminist theory has stressed the importance of understanding difference, of the ways race and class status determine the degree to which one can assert male domination and privilege and most importantly the ways racism and sexism are interlocking systems of domination which uphold and sustain one another. Many feminists continue to see them as completely separate issues, believing that sexism can be abolished while racism remains intact, or that women who work to resist racism are not supporting feminist movement. Since black liberation struggle is so often framed in terms that affirm and support sexism, is not surprising that white women are uncertain about whether women's rights struggle will be diminished if there is too much focus on resisting racism, or that many black women continue to fear that they will be betraying black men if they support feminist movement. Both these fears are responses to the equation of black liberation with manhood. This continues to be a central way black people frame our efforts to resist racist domination; it must be critiqued. We must reject the sexualization of black liberation in ways that support and perpetuate sexism, phallocentrism, and male domination. Even though Michele Wallace tried to expose the fallacy of equating black liberation with the assertion of oppressive manhood in *Black Macho and the Myth of the Superwoman,* few black people got the message. Continuing this critique in *Ain't I a Woman: Black Women and Feminism,* I found that more and more black women were rejecting this paradigm. It has yet to be rejected by most black men, and especially black male political figures. As long as black people hold on to the idea that the trauma of racist domination is really the loss of black manhood, then we invest in the racist narratives that perpetuate the idea that all black men are rapists, eager to use sexual terrorism to express their rage about racial domination.

Currently we are witnessing a resurgence of such narratives. They are resurfacing at a historical moment when black people are bearing the brunt of more overt and blatant racist assaults, when black men and especially young black men are increasingly disenfranchised by society. Mainstream white supremacist media make it appear that a black menace to societal safety is at large, that control, repression, and violent domination are the only effective ways to address the problem. Witness the use of the Willie Horton case to discredit Dukakis in the 1988 Presidential election. Susan Estrich in her post-campaign articles has done a useful job of showing how racist stereotypes were evoked to turn voters against Dukakis, and how Bush in no way denounced this strategy. In all her articles she recounts the experience of being raped by a black man fifteen years ago, describing the way racism determined how the police responded to the crime, and her response. Though her intent is to urge societal commitment to anti-racist struggle, every article I have read has carried captions in bold print emphasizing the rape. The subversive content of her work is undermined and the stereotype that all black men are rapists is re-inscribed and re-inforced. Most people in this society do not realize that the vast majority of rapes are not inter-racial, that all groups of men are more likely to rape women who are the same race as themselves.

Within popular culture, Madonna's video "Like a Prayer" also makes use of imagery which links black men with rape, reinforcing this representation in the minds of millions of viewers—even though she has said that her intention is to be anti-racist, and certainly the video suggests that not all black men who are accused of raping white women are guilty. Once again, however, this subversive message is undermined by the overall focus on sexually charged imagery of white female sexuality and black male lust. The most subversive message in the video has nothing to do with anti-racism; it has to do with the construction of white females as desiring subjects who can freely assert sexual agency. Of course the taboo expression of that agency is choosing to be sexual with black men. Unfortunately this is a continuation of the notion that ending racist domination is really about issues of interracial sexual access, a myth that must be critiqued so that this society can confront the actual material, economic, and moral consequences of perpetuating white supremacy and its traumatic genocidal impact on black people.

Images of black men as rapists, as dangerous menaces to society, have been sensational cultural currency for some time. The obsessive media focus on these representations is political. The role it plays in the maintenance of racist domination is to convince the public that black men are a dangerous threat who must be controlled by any means necessary, including annihilation. This is the cultural backdrop shaping media response to the Central Park rape case, and the media has played a major role in shaping public response. Many people are using this case to perpetuate racial stereotypes and racism. Ironically, the very people who claim to be shocked by the brutality of this case have no qualms about suggesting that the suspects should be castrated or killed. They see no link between this support of violence as a means of social control and the suspects' use of violence to exercise control. Public response to this case highlights the lack of understanding about the interconnectedness of racism and sexism.

Many black people, especially black men, using the sexist paradigm that suggests rape of white women by black men is a reaction to racist domination, view the Central Park case as an indictment of the racist system. They do not see sexism as informing the nature of the crime, the choice of victim. Many white women have responded to the case by focusing solely on the brutal assault as an act of gender domination, of male violence against women. A piece in the *Village Voice* written by white female Andrea Kannapell carried captions in bold print which began with the statement in all capitals for greater emphasis, "THE CRIME WAS MORE SEXIST THAN RACIST. . . ." Black women responding to the same issue all focused on the sexist nature of the crime, often giving examples of black male sexism. Given the work black women have done within feminist writing to call attention to the reality of black male sexism, work that often receives little or no attention or is accused of attacking black men, it is ironic that the brutal rape of a white woman by a group of young black males serves as the catalyst for admission that sexism is a serious problem in black communities. Lisa Kennedy's piece, "Body Double: The Anatomy of a Crime," also published in the *Village Voice,* acknowledges the convergence of racism and sexism as politics of domination that inform this assault. Kennedy writes:

> If I accept the premise of the coverage, that this rape is more heartbreaking than all the rapes that happen to women of color, then what happens to the value of my body? What happens to the quality of my blackness?

These questions remain unanswered, though she closes with "a call for a sophisticated feminist offensive." Such an offensive should begin with cultivating critical awareness of the way racism and sexism are interlocking systems of domination.

Public response to the Central Park case reveals the extent to which the culture invests in the kind of dualistic thinking that helps reinforce and maintain all forms of domination. Why must people decide whether this crime is more sexist than racist, as if these are competing oppressions? Why do white people, and especially feminist white women, feel better when black people, especially black women, disassociate themselves from the plight of black men in white supremacist capitalist patriarchy to emphasize opposition to black male sexism? Cannot black women remain seriously concerned about the brutal effect of racist domination on black men and also denounce black male sexism? And why is black male sexism evoked as though it is a special brand of this social disorder, more dangerous, more abhorrent and life-threatening than the sexism that pervades the culture as a whole, or the sexism that informs white male domination of women? These questions call attention to the either/or ways of thinking that are the philosophical underpinning of systems of domination. Progressive folks must then insist, wherever we engage in discussions of this crime or of issues of race and gender, on the complexity of our experience in a racist sexist society.

The Central Park crime involves aspects of sexism, male domination, misogyny, and the use of rape as an instrument of terror. It also involves race and racism; it is unlikely that young black males growing up in this society, attacking a white woman, would see her as "just a woman"—her race would be foremost in their consciousness as well as her sex, in the same way that masses of people hearing about this crime were concerned with identifying first her race. In a white supremacist sexist society all women's bodies are devalued, but white women's bodies are more valued than those of women of color. Given the context of white supremacy, the historical narratives about black male rapists, the racial identities of both victim and victimizers enable this tragedy to be sensationalized.

To fully understand the multiple meanings of this incident, it must be approached from an analytical standpoint that considers the impact of sexism and racism. Beginning there enables many of us to empathize with both the victim and the victimizers. If one reads *The Demon Lover* and thinks again about this crime, one can see it as part of a continuum of male violence against women, of rape and terror as weapons of male domination—yet another horrific and brutal expression of patriarchal socialization. And if one considers this case by combining a feminist analysis of race and masculinity, one sees that since male power within patriarchy is relative, men from poorer groups and men of color are not able to reap the material and social rewards for their participation in patriarchy. In fact they often suffer from blindly and passively acting out a myth of masculinity that is life-threatening. Sexist thinking blinds them to this reality. They become victims of the patriarchy. No one can truly believe that the young black males involved in the Central Park incident were not engaged in a suicidal ritual enactment of a dangerous masculinity that will ultimately threaten their lives, their well-being.

If one reads again Michael Dyson's piece "The Plight of Black Men," focusing especially on the part where he describes the reason many young black men form gangs—"the sense of absolute belonging and unsurpassed love"—it is easy to understand why young black males are despairing and nihilistic. And is rather naive to think that if they do not value their own lives, they will value the lives of others. Is it really so difficult for folks to see the connection between the constant pornographic glorification of male violence against women that is represented, enacted, and condoned daily in the culture and the Central Park crime? Does racism create and maintain this blindspot or does it allow black people and particularly black men to become the scapegoats, embodying society's evils?

If we are to live in a less violent and more just society, then we must engage in anti-sexist and anti-racist work. We desperately need to explore and understand the connections between racism and sexism. And we need to teach everyone about those connections so that they can be critically aware and socially active. Much education for critical consciousness can take place in everyday conversations. Black women and men must participate in the construction of feminist thinking, creating models for feminist struggle that address the particular circumstances of black people. Still, the most visionary task of all remains that of re-conceptualizing masculinity so that alternative, transformative models are there in the culture, in our daily lives, to help boys and men who are working to construct a self, to build new identities. Black liberation struggle must be re-visioned so that it is no longer equated with maleness. We need a revolutionary vision of black liberation, one that emerges from a feminist standpoint and addresses the collective plight of black people.

Any individual committed to resisting politics of domination, to eradicating sexism and racism, understands the importance of not promoting an either/or competition between the oppressive systems. We can empathize with the victim and the victimizers in the Central Park case, allowing that feeling to serve as a catalyst for renewed commitment to anti-sexist and anti-racist work. Yesterday I heard this story. A black woman friend called to say that she had been attacked on the street by a black man. He took her purse, her house keys, her car keys. She lives in one of the poorest cities in the United States. We talked about poverty, sexism, and racial domination to place what had happened in a perspective that will enable both individual healing and political understanding of this crime. Today I heard this story. A white woman friend called to say that she had been attacked in her doorway by a black man. She screamed and he ran away. Neighbors coming to her aid invoked racism. She refused to engage in this discussion even though she was shocked by the intensity and degree of racism expressed. Even in the midst of her own fear and pain, she remained politically aware, so as not to be complicit in perpetuating the white supremacy that is the root of so much suffering. Both of these women feel rage at their victimizers; they do not absolve them even as they seek to understand and to respond in ways that will enrich the struggle to end domination—so that sexism, sexist violence, racism, and racist violence will cease to be an everyday happening.

Shattering the "Race" Lens: Toward a Critical Theory of Racism

ANTONIA DARDER AND RODOLFO D. TORRES

Race has become the lens through which is refracted all of society's problems.
—Kenan Malik (1996)[1]

The truth is that there are no races. . . . The evil that is done by the concept and by easy—yet impossible—assumptions as to its application. What we miss through our obsession. . . . is, simply, reality.

—Kwame Anthony Appiah (1995)[2]

In recent years, "race"[3] has been the focus of theoretical, political, and policy debates. Dramatic national and international changes, both economic and political, have created conditions in which, on the one hand, racialized structures, processes and representations are more intricate and elusive; yet, on the other hand, the historically entrenched inequalities persist. The changing socioeconomic conditions in the United States present immense challenges and opportunities for anti-racist activists and social science scholars to rethink the nature of contemporary racialized inequality. With President Bill Clinton's recent "race initiative" commencement address at University of California, San Diego, and the acrimonious debates on affirmative action, language policy, and immigration, it is more evident now than ever before that there is a need for a critical theory of racism that can assist us to better understand the complex issues associated with the increasing racialization of American society.

"Race," though a key concept in sociological discourse and public debate, remains problematic. Policy pundits, journalists, and conservative and liberal academics alike all work within categories of "race" and use this concept in public discourse as though there is unanimity regarding its analytical value. However, like all other component elements of what Antonio Gramsci[4] called common sense, much of the everyday usage of "race" is uncritical. Gramsci argues that human beings view the world from a perspective that contains both hegemonic forms of thinking and critical insight. As such, notions of common sense are "rooted in cultural folklore but at the same time are enriched with scientific ideas and philosophical opinions, which enter into ordinary daily life."[5] Racialized group conflicts are similarly advanced and framed as a "race relations" problem, and presented largely in Black/White terms. A prime example of this confusion is the analysis of the causes of the 1992 Los Angeles riots. In the aftermath of the riots, academics and journalists analyzed the riots as a matter of "race relations"—first it was a problem between Blacks and Whites, then between Blacks and Koreans, and then between Blacks and Latinos, and back to Blacks and Whites. The interpretation of the riots as a "race relations" problem failed to take into account the economic restructuring and the drastic shifts in demographic patterns that have created new dynamics of class and racialized ethnic relations in Los Angeles.[6] These new dynamics include increasing changes in the ethnic composition of the city and a dramatic shift from a manufacturing-centered economy to one based on light manufacturing, service industries, and information technologies—urban dynamics intricately linked to "the globalizing pressure of capitalism to abandon the will to social investment within the national-domestic sphere."[7]

THE QUESTION OF IDENTITY POLITICS

[W]e work with raced identities on already reified ground. In the context of domination, raced identities are imposed and internalized, then renegotiated and reproduced. From artificial to natural, we court a hard-to-perceive social logic that reproduces the very conditions we strain to overcome.

—Jon Cruz (1996)[8]

Over the last three decades, there has been an overwhelming tendency among social science scholars to focus on notions of "race." Over the last three decades, there has been an overwhelming tendency among a variety of critical scholars to focus on the concept of "race" as a central category of analysis for interpreting the social conditions of inequality and marginalization.[9] As a consequence, much of the literature on subordinate cultural populations, with its emphasis on such issues as "racial inequality," "racial segregation," "racial identity," has utilized the construct of "race" as a central category of analysis for interpreting the social conditions of inequality and marginalization. In turn, this literature has reinforced a racialized politics of identity and representation, with its problematic emphasis on "racial" identity as the overwhelming impulse for political action. This theoretical practice has led to serious analytical weaknesses and absence of depth in much of the historical and contemporary writings on racialized populations in this country. The politics of busing in the early 1970s provides an excellent example that illustrates this phenomenon.

Social scientists studying "race relations" concluded that contact among "Black" and "White" students would improve "race relations" and the educational conditions of "Black" students if they were bused to "White" (better) schools outside their neighborhoods.[10] Thirty years later, many parents and educators adamantly denounce the busing solution (a solution based on a discourse of "race") as not only fundamentally problematic to the fabric of African American and Chicano communities, but an erroneous social policy experiment that failed to substantially improve the overall academic performance of students in these communities.

Given this legacy, it is not surprising to find that the theories, practices, and policies that have informed social science analysis of racialized populations today are overwhelmingly rooted in a politics of identity, an approach that is founded on parochial notions of "race" and representation which ignore the imperatives of capitalist accumulation and the existence of class divisions within racialized subordinate populations. The folly of this position is critiqued by Ellen Meiksins Wood[11] in her article entitled "Identity Crisis," where she exposes the limitations of a politics of identity which fails to contend with the fact that capitalism is the most totalizing system of social relations the world has ever known.

Yet, in much of the work on African American, Latino, Native American, and Asian populations, an analysis of class and a critique of capitalism is conspicuously absent. And even when it is mentioned, the emphasis is primarily on an undifferentiated plurality of identity politics or an "intersection of oppressions," which, unfortunately, ignores the overwhelming tendency of capitalism to homogenize rather than to diversify human experience. Moreover, this practice is particularly disturbing since no matter where one travels around the world, there is no question that racism is integral to the process of capital accumulation. For example, the current socioeconomic conditions of Latinos and other racialized populations can be traced to the relentless emergence of the global economy and recent economic policies of expansion, such as the North American Free Trade Agreement (NAFTA). A recent United Nations report by the International Labor Organization confirms the negative impact of globalization on racialized populations. By the end of 1998, it was projected that one billion workers would be unemployed. The people of Africa, China, and Latin America have been most affected by the current restructuring of capitalist development.[12] This phenomenon of racialized capitalism is directly linked to the abusive practices and destructive impact of the "global factory"—a global financial enterprise system that includes such transnational corporations as Coca-Cola, Wal-Mart, Disney, Ford Motor Company, and General Motors. In a recent speech on "global economic apartheid," John Cavanagh, co-executive director of the Institute for Policy Studies in Washington, D.C., comments on the practices of the Ford Motor Company.

> The Ford Motor Company has its state-of-the-art assembly plant in Mexico . . . where because it can deny basic worker rights, it can pay one-tenth the wages and yet get the same quality and the same productivity in producing goods. . . . The same technologies by the way which are easing globalization are also primarily cutting more jobs than they're creating.[13]

The failure of scholars to confront this dimension in their analysis of contemporary society as a racialized phenomenon and their tendency to continue treating class as merely one of a multiplicity of (equally valid) perspectives, which may or may not "intersect" with the process of racialization, are serious shortcomings. In addressing this issue, we must recognize that identity politics, which generally gloss over class differences and/or ignore class contradictions, have often been used by radical scholars and activists within African American, Latino, and other subordinate cultural communities in an effort to build a political base. Here, fabricated constructions of "race" are objectified and mediated as truth to ignite political support, divorced from the realities of class struggle. By so doing, they have unwittingly perpetuated the vacuous and dangerous notion that the political and economic are separate spheres of society which can function independently—a view that firmly anchors and sustains prevailing class relations of power in society.

Ramon Grosfoguel and Chloe S. Georas posit that "social identities are constructed and reproduced in complex and entangled political, economic, and symbolic hierarchy."[14] Given this complex entanglement, what is needed is a more dynamic and fluid notion of how we think about different cultural identities within the context of contemporary capitalist social formations. Such a perspective of identity would support our efforts to shatter static and frozen notions that perpetuate ahistorical, apolitical, and classless views of culturally pluralistic societies. How we analytically accomplish this is no easy matter. But however this task is approached, we must keep in mind Wood's concern:

> We should not confuse respect for the plurality of human experience and social struggles with a complete dissolution of historical causality, where there is nothing but diversity, difference and contingency, no unifying structures, no logic of process, no capitalism and therefore no negation of it, no universal project of human emancipation.[15]

Hence, if we are to effectively challenge the horrendous economic impacts of globalization on racialized communities, we must recognize that a politics of identity is grossly inept and unsuited for building and sustaining collective political movements for social justice and economic democracy. Instead, what we need is to fundamentally reframe the very terrain that gives life to our political understanding of what it means to live, work, and struggle in a society with widening class differentiation and ever-increasing racialized inequality. Through such an analytical process of reframing, we can expand the terms by which identities are considered, examined, and defined, recognizing racialized relations of power are fundamentally shaped by the profound organizational and spatial transformations of the capitalist economy.

A CRITIQUE OF "RACE RELATIONS"

If "race relations" are a feature of contemporary society, it seems obvious that academics should study them. But the casual observer could equally well conclude from personal observation that it is "obvious" that the sun circulates around the earth. In order to believe otherwise, it is necessary to confront personal experiences with analytical reasoning and forms of rational measurement. In other words, "obviousness" is a condition which depends upon the location of the observer and the set of concepts employed to conceive and interpret the object.

—Robert Miles (1993)[16]

There has been a tendency in postmodern and post-structuralist views of the anti-racism project and "race relations" to neglect or ignore profound changes in the structural nature and dynamics of U.S. capitalism, in place of obvious or common-sense appraisals of racialized inequality. This same tendency is also evident in much of the recent scholarship on cultural politics and social difference. At a time when a historical materialist analysis of capitalism is most crucially needed, many social theorists and radical educators seem reticent to engage the very idea of capitalism with any analytical rigor or methodological specificity. Yet, recent structural changes in the U.S. political economy and the increasing cultural diversity of America have made the issue of racism much more complex than ever before.

Rather than occupying a central position, these historical socioeconomic changes serve merely as a backdrop to the contemporary theoretical debates on the meaning of "race" and representation in contemporary society, debates that, more often than not, are founded on deeply psychologized or abstracted interpretations of racialized differences and conflicts. This constitutes a significant point of contention, given the dramatic changes in U.S. class formation and the demographic landscape of major urban centers. These changing conditions have resulted in major shifts in perceptions of social location, prevailing attitudes, and contemporary views of racialized populations. More so than ever, these socioeconomic conditions are linked to transnational realities shared by populations of Mexico, Taiwan, the Caribbean, and other "developing" countries, despite specific regional histories which gave rise to particular sociocultural configurations, configurations that are fundamentally shaped within the context of the ever-changing global economy.

Recent works in cultural studies, multicultural education, and critical pedagogy have brought new critical perspectives to the study of racism and cultural differences within society. U.S. scholars such as Cornel West, Michael

Omi, Howard Winant, bell hooks, Henry Giroux, and others have attempted to recast the debate on the nature of "race" and racism and its implications for social change and educational reform. More specifically, these scholars discuss the concept of "race" within the larger context of changing social and economic conditions and posit "race" as both a social construct and fluid analytical category, in an effort to challenge static notions of "race" as a biologically determined human phenomenon. Although it cannot be denied that these provocative and eloquent works represent a challenge to the mainstream analysis of "race relations" and have made contributions to our understanding of the significance of racism and anti-racist struggles, they have failed to reconceptualize the traditional social science paradigm that relies on the reified category of "race." In the final analysis, the conceptual framework utilized by these scholars is entrenched in the conventional sociology of "race relations" language.

Nowhere has this theoretical shortcoming been more evident than in the contemporary multicultural education debate—a debate that has widely informed the development of postmodern educational theory today. Despite an expressed "transformative" intent, much of the multicultural education literature has only peripherally positioned public education within the larger context of class and racialized class relations. Noticeably absent from much of the writings of even critical multicultural educators is a substantial critique of the social relations and structures of capitalism and the relationship of educational practices to the rapidly changing conditions of the U.S. political economy. The absence of an analysis of the capitalist wage-labor system and class relations with its structural inequalities of income and power represents a serious limitation in our efforts to construct a theory and practice of democratic life.

A lack of imagination in multicultural education discussions is also highly evidenced by a discourse that continues to be predominantly anchored in the Black-White framework that has for over a century shaped our thinking and scholarship related to social group differences. One of the most severe and limited aspects of the Black-White framework to the future of the anti-racist project is its tendency (albeit unintentionally) to obstruct or camouflage the need to examine the particular historical and contextual dimensions that give rise to different forms of racisms around the globe. Further, the conflation of racialized relations into a Black-White paradigm, with its consequential rendering of other subordinate cultural populations to an invisible or "second-class oppression" status, has prevented scholars from engaging with the specificity of particular groups and delving more fully into the arena of comparative ethnic histories of racism and how these are ultimately linked to class forms of social inequalities.

The habitual practice of framing social relations as "race relations" in discussions of students from subordinate cultural communities obfuscates the complexity of the problem. Here educational theorists assign certain significance to "racial" characteristics rather than attributing student responses to school conditions and how these are shaped by the structure of society and the economic and political limitations which determine the material conditions under which students must achieve. The unfortunate absence of this critique veils the real reasons why African American, Latin American, and other "minority" students underachieve, perform poorly on standardized tests, are over-represented in remedial programs and under-represented in gifted programs and magnet schools, and continue to drop out of high school at alarming rates. As a consequence, educational solutions are often derived from distorted perceptions of the problem and lead to misguided policies and practices. The politics of busing in the early 1970s discussed earlier in this chapter provides an excellent example of this phenomenon of distortion.

Although some would be quick to object to our critique, we can see the above also at work in the manner in which many education scholars have focused their studies in racialized communities. Overall, studies with minority students have placed an overwhelming emphasis on cultural and linguistic questions tied to academic achievement. This is illustrated by the large body of education literature that focuses on the cultural difference of "language minority" students, while only marginally discussing the impact of racialized inequality and class position on identity and cultural formations, as if somehow the problems of African Americans, Latinos, Native Americans, and other students from subordinate cultural populations can be resolved simply through the introduction of culturally relevant curriculum or the enactment of language policy. Moreover, it is this limited view of the problem that most informs the recent political debates between supporters of bilingual education and California's Proposition 227 (also known as the Unz Initiative or English for the Children).

FROM "RACE" TO RACIALIZATION

For three hundred years black Americans insisted that "race" was no useful distinguishing factor in human relationships. During those same three centuries every academic discipline . . . insisted that "race" was the determining factor in human development.

—Toni Morrison (1989)[17]

As Morrison implies, unproblematized "common sense" acceptance and use of "race" as a legitimate way to frame social relations has been highly prevalent in the social sciences. The use of this term, for example, among Chicano scholars in the 1960s can be linked to academic acts of resistance to the term "ethnicity" and theories of assimilation which were generally applied to discuss immigration populations of European descent. In efforts to distance Chicano scholarship from this definition and link it to a theory of internal colonialism, cultural imperialism, and racism, Chicanos were discussed as a colonized "racial" group in much the same manner that many radical theorists positioned African Americans. Consequently, the term's association with power, resistance, and self-determination has veiled the problematics of "race" as a social construct. Protected by the force of cultural nationalist rhetoric, "race" as an analytical term has remained a "paper tiger"—seemingly powerful in discourse matters but ineffectual as an analytical metaphor, incapable of moving us away from the pervasive notion of "race" as an innate determinant of behavior.

In these times, we would be hard-pressed to find a progressive scholar who would subscribe to the use of "race" as a determinant of specific social phenomena associated with inherent (or genetic) characteristics of a group. Yet the use of "race" as an analytical category continues to maintain a stronghold in both academic and popular discourse. What does it mean to attribute analytical status to the idea of "race" and use it as an explanatory concept in theoretical discussions? The use of "race" as an analytical category means to position it as a central organizing theoretical principal in deconstructing social relations of difference, as these pertain to subordinate cultural populations.

Notwithstanding provocative arguments by left theorists such as Adolph Reed Jr., who unequivocally asserts that "Race is purely a social construction; it has no core reality outside a specific social and historical context . . . its material force derives from state power, not some ahistorical 'nature' or any sort of primordial group affinities,"[18] there is an unwillingness to abandon its use. Yet, it is this persistent use of "race" in the literature and research on African Americans, Latinos, and other culturally subordinated populations that perpetuates its definition as a causal factor. As such, the notion of "race" as a social construction "only leads us back into the now familiar move of substituting a sociohistorical conception of race for the biological one . . . that is simply to bury the biological conception below the surface, not to transcend it."[19] Hence, significance and meaning are still attributed to phenotypical features, rather than to the historically reproduced complex processes of racialization. This ultimately serves to conceal the particular set of social conditions experienced by racialized groups that are determined by an interplay of complex social processes, one of which is premised on the articulation of racism to effect legitimate exclusion.[20]

This process of racialization is at work in the disturbing "scientific" assertion that "race" determines academic performance made by Richard J. Herrnstein and Charles Murray in their book *The Bell Curve*.[21] Their work illustrates the theoretical minefield of perpetuating such an analytical category in the social sciences and the potential negative consequences on racialized groups. The use of the term "race" serves to conceal the truth that it is not "race" that determines academic performance; but rather, that academic performance is determined by an interplay of complex social processes, one of which is premised on the articulation of racism (and its subsequent practices of racialization) to affect exclusion in the classroom and beyond.

It is within the historical and contemporary contexts of such scholarship that differences in skin color have been and are signified as a mark which suggests the existence of different "races." As a consequence, a primary response among many progressive activists and scholars when we call for the elimination of "race" as an analytical category is to reel off accusations of a "color-blind" discourse. This is not what we are arguing. What we do argue is that the fixation on skin color is not inherent in its existence but is a product of signification. This is to say, human beings identify skin color to mark or symbolize other phenomena in a variety of social contexts in which other significations occur. As a consequence, when human practices include and exclude people in light of the signification of skin color, collective identities are produced and social inequalities are structured.[22]

Moreover, it is this employment of the idea of "race" in the structuring of social relations that is termed racialization. More specifically, Miles in his book *Racism* defines this process of racialization as

> those instances where social relations between people have been structured by the signification of human biological characteristics in such a way as to define and construct differentiated social collectivities . . . the concept therefore refers to a process of categorization, a representational process of defining an Other (usually, but not exclusively) somatically.[23]

Hence, to interpret accurately the conditions faced by subordinate cultural populations requires us to move from the idea of "race" to an understanding of racialization and its impact on class formations. This summons a bold analytical transition from the language of "race" to recognizing the centrality of racism and the process of racialization in our understanding of exclusionary practices that give rise to structural inequalities.

BREAKING THE "RACE" FIXATION

The first task of social science is to deconstruct common sense categories and to set up rigorous analytic concepts in their place. Here, it appears to us that an excessively vague use of the vocabulary of race should be rejected, and that one should resist the extensions which banalise the evil, or remove its specificity.

—Michel Wieviorka (1997)[24]

Yet, despite the dangerous forms of distortion which arise from the use of "race" as a central analytical category, most scholars seem unable to break with the hegemonic tradition of its use in the social sciences. Efforts to problematize the reified nature of the term "race" and consider its elimination as a metaphor in our work swiftly meet with major resistance, even among progressive intellectuals of all communities—a resistance that is expressed through anxiety, trepidation, fear, and even anger. It is significant to note that even the act of questioning the existence of "races" often meets with greater suspicion that the liberal notions that perpetuate a deficit view of "race." For example, Oliver C. Cox,[25] in his 1948 treatise on "race relations," posits that "it would probably be as revealing of [negative] interracial attitudes to deliberate upon the variations in the skeletal remains of some people as it would be to question an ongoing society's definition of a race because, anthropometrically speaking, the assumed race is not a real race."[26] Similarly, in a more recent work, *The Racial Contract,* Charles W. Mills argues that:

> [T]he only people who can find it psychologically possible to deny the central-ity of race are those who are racially privileged, for whom race is invisible pre-cisely because the world is structured around them, whiteness as the grounds against which the figures of other races—those who, unlike us, are raced—appear.[27]

Inherent in these commentaries is the inability to conceive how the denial of "races" does not imply the denial of the racialization of populations and the racist ideologies that have been central to capitalist exploitation and domina-tion around the globe. Yet, it is precisely the failure to grasp this significant analytical concept that ultimately stifles the development of a critical theory of racism, a theory with the analytical depth to free us from a paradigm that explains social subordination (or domination) within the alleged nature of par-ticular populations.

It cannot be left unsaid that often uncritical responses to eliminating the concept of "race" are associated with a fear of delegitimizing the historical movements for liberation that have been principally defined in terms of "race" struggles or progressive institutional interventions that have focused on "race" numbers to evaluate success. Although understandable, such responses never-theless demonstrate the tenacious and adhesive quality of socially constructed ideas and how through their historical usage these ideas become common sense notions that resist deconstruction. The dilemma that ensues for scholars and activists in the field is well-articulated by Angela Davis:

> "Race" has always been difficult to talk about in terms not tainted by ideologies of racism, with which the notion of "race" shares a common historical evolu-tion. The assumption that a taxonomy of human populations can be con-structed based on phenotypic characteristics has been discredited. Yet, we continue to use the term "race," even though many of us are very careful to set it off in quotation marks to indicate that while we do not take seriously the notion of "race" as biologically grounded, neither are we able to think about racist power structures and marginalization processes without invoking the socially constructed concept of "race."[28]

As a consequence, "race" is retained as "an analytical category not because it corresponds to any biological or epistemological absolutes, but because of the power that collective identities acquire by means of their roots in tradition."[29] This is a tradition that oftentimes has functioned to obstruct the development of political alliances necessary to the establishment of social movements for human rights, social justice, and economic democracy.

THE OPPOSITIONAL LIMITS OF "WHITE SUPREMACY"

No one was white before he/she came to America.

—James Baldwin[30]

In efforts to sort out the complexities of "race" problems in America, many prominent intellectuals have placed an overwhelming emphasis on the notion of White supremacy. The writings of bell hooks well illustrate this particular predilection and insistence on using White supremacy as the term of choice when addressing the racialized inequalities suffered by African Americans. In *Talking Back,* she specifically notes this shift in her use of language.

> I try to remember when the word racism ceased to be the term which best expressed for me the exploitation of black people and people of color in this society and when I began to understand that the most useful term was white supremacy . . . the ideology that most determines how white people in this society perceive and relate to black people and other people of color.[31]

What seems apparent in hooks's explanation is both her belief in the existence of a White ideology that has Black people as its primary object (albeit her mention of "people of color") and the reification of skin color as the most active determinant of social relations between Black and White populations. Consequently, the persistence of such notions of racialized exploitation and domination mistakenly privileges one particular form of racism, while it ignores the historical and contemporary oppression of populations who have been treated as distinct and inferior "races" without the necessary reference to skin color.

Moreover, "White supremacy" arguments analytically essentialize Black/White relations by inferring that the inevitability of skin color ensures the reproduction of racism in the postcolonial world, where White people predominantly associate Black people with inferiority. Inherent in this perspective is the failure to recognize the precolonial origins of racism which were structured within the interior of Europe by the development of nation-states and capitalist relations of production. "The dichotomous categories of Blacks as victims, and Whites as perpetrators of racism, tend to homogenize the objects of racism, without paying attention to the different experience of men and women, of different social classes and ethnicities."[32] As such there is little room to link, with equal legitimacy, the continuing struggles against racism of Jews, Gypsies, the Irish, immigrant workers, refugees, and other racialized populations of the world (including Africans racialized by Africans) to the struggle of African Americans in the United States.

Hence, theories of racism that are founded upon the racialized idea of White supremacy adhere rigidly to a "race relations paradigm." As such, these theories anchor racialized inequality to the alleged "nature" of White people and the psychological influence of White ideology on both Whites and Blacks, rather than to the complex nature of historically constituted social relations of power and their material consequences. In light of this, hooks's preference for White supremacy represents a perspective that, despite its oppositional intent and popularity among many activists and scholars in the field, still fails to critically advance our understanding of the debilitating structures of capitalism and the nature of class formations within a racialized world. More specifically, what we argue here is that the struggle against racism and class inequality cannot be founded on either academic or popularized notions of "race" or White supremacy, notions that ultimately reify and "project a 'phantom objectivity,' an autonomy that seems so strictly rational and all-embracing as to conceal every trace of its fundamental nature."[33] Rather than working to invert racist notions of racialized inferiority, anti-racist scholars and activists should seek to develop a critical theory of racism to confront the fundamental nature and consequences of structural inequalities as reproduced by the historical processes of racialization in U.S. society and around the globe.

TOWARD A PLURALITY OF RACISMS

[T]he presumption of a single monolithic racism is being replaced by a mapping of the multifarious historical formulations of racisms.

—David Theo Goldberg[34]

In order to address these structural inequalities, an analytical shift is required, from "race" to a plural conceptualization of "racisms" and their historical articulations with other ideologies. This plural notion of "racisms" more accurately captures the historically specific nature of racism and the variety of meanings attributed to evaluations of difference and assessments of superiority and inferiority of people. Conversely, to continue our engagement of racism as a singular ideological phenomenon fails to draw on the multiplicity of historical and social processes inherent in the heterogeneity of racialized relations. This is to say, for example, that the notion of "White supremacy" can only have any real meaning within populations whose exploitation and domination is essentialized based on skin color. As such, this view severs the experience of African Americans, for instance, from meaningful comparative analysis with those racialized populations whose subordination is predicated on other social characteristics.

Consequently, "White supremacy" arguments cannot be employed to analyze, for example, the racialization of Jews in Germany during the 1930s, or Gypsy populations in Eastern Europe, or the Tutsi population in the

Congo. More close to home, the concept of "White supremacy" sheds little light on what is happening in Watts and South Central Los Angeles between the Korean petite-bourgeoisie and the African American and Latino under-class or reserve army (to use a more traditional concept!). Instead, what we are arguing for is a plural concept of racism that can free us from the "Black/White" dichotomy and, in its place, assert the historically shifting and polit-ically complex nature of racialization. More specifically, it is a pluralized concept of racism that has relevance and analytical utility in comprehending the political economy of racialized relations in South Central Los Angeles, as well as the larger sociocultural landscape that can, beyond this analysis, link the economic structures of oppression in this local context to the global context of racialized capitalism. Most importantly, we argue that the prob-lems in racialized communities are not about "race" but rather about the intricate interplay between a variety of racisms and class. It is for this reason that we do not believe that scholars should not be trying to advance a "crit-ical theory of race."[35] A persistence in attributing the idea of "race" with ana-lytical status can only lead us further down a theoretical and political dead end. Instead, the task at hand is to deconstruct "race" and detach it from the concept of racism. This is to say, what is essential for activists and social sci-ence scholars is to understand that the construction of the idea of "race" is embodied in racist ideology that supports the practice of racism. It is racism as an ideology that produces the notion of "race," not the existence of "races" that produces racism.[36]

Hence, what is needed is a clear understanding of the plurality of racisms and the exclusionary social processes that function to perpetuate the racializa-tion of members from culturally and economically marginalized communities. Robert Miles convincingly argues that these processes can be analyzed within the framework of Marxist theory without retaining the idea of race as an ana-lytical concept.

> Using the concept of racialization, racism, and exclusionary practices to identify specific means of effecting the reproduction of the capitalist mode of produc-tion, one is able to stress consistently and rigorously the role of human agency, albeit always constrained by particular historical and material circumstances, in these processes, as well as to recognize the specificity of particular forms of oppression.[37]

Miles's work also supports the notion that efforts to construct a new lan-guage for examining the nature of differing racisms requires an under stand-ing of how complex relationships of exploitation and resistance, grounded in differences of class, ethnicity, and gender, give rise to a multiplicity of ideo-logical constructions of the racialized Other. This knowledge again challenges the traditional notion of racism as predominantly a Black/White phenomenon and directs us toward a more accurately constructed and, hence, more politically and analytically useful way to identify a multiplicity of historically specific racisms.

We recognize that there are anti-racist scholars who cannot comprehend a world where the notion of "race" does not exist. Without question, mere efforts to undo and eliminate the idea of "race" as an analytical category in the social sciences is insufficient to remove its use from the popular or academic imagination and discourse of everyday life. Moreover, in a country like the United States, filled with historical examples of exploitation, violence, and murderous acts rationalized by popular "race" opinions and scientific "race" ideas, it is next to impossible to convince people that "race" does not exist as a "natural" category. So, in Colette Guillaumin's words, "let us be clear about this. The idea of race is a technical means, a machine, for committing murder. And its effectiveness is not in doubt."[38] But "races" do not exist. What does exist is the unrelenting idea of "race" that fuels racisms throughout the world.

THE NEED FOR A CRITICAL THEORY OF RACISM

> *Moreover, language presents us with resources for the construction of meanings which reach out towards the future, which point to possibilities that transcend our experience of the present. . . . And those fighting for liberation from oppression and exploitation will invariably find within language words, meanings and themes for expressing, clarifying, and coordinating their struggle for a better world.*
>
> —David McNally (1997)[39]

In considering a shift from the study of "race" to the critical study of racism, what is clear is that we need a language by which to construct culturally democratic notions of sociopolitical theory and practice. This entails the recasting and reinterpretation of social issues in a language with greater specificity, which explicitly reflects an international anti-racist notion of society. Such a language must unquestionably be linked to global histories of social movements against economic inequalities and social injustice. Although we fully recognize that theoretical language alone will not necessarily alter the power relations in any given society, it can assist us to analytically reason more accurately and, thus, to confront more effectively how power is both praticed and maintained through the systematic racialization of subordinate populations. As such, a critical language of racism can provide the foundation for developing effective public policies that are directly linked to liberatory principles of cultural and economic democracy.

In summary, we deny any place for the use of "race" as an analytical concept and support efforts to eliminate all conceptions of "race" as a legitimate entity or human phenomenon. We believe that the future struggle against racism and capitalism must at long last contend with the reality that

> There are no "races" and therefore no "race relations." There is only a belief
> that there are such things, a belief which is used by some social groups to con-

struct an Other (and therefore the Self) in thought as a prelude to exclusion and domination, and by other social groups to define Self (and so to construct an Other) as a means of resisting that exclusion. Hence, if it is used at all . . . "race" should be used only to refer descriptively to such uses.[40]

In light of this, we posit a critical conceptualization of racism with which to analyze both historical and contemporary social experiences and institutional realities. Insofar as such a concept, whether employed in social investigation or political struggle, reveals patterns of discrimination and resulting inequalities, it raises the question: What actions must be taken to dismantle these inequalities? This in turn requires nothing less than to confront racism in all its dimensions head-on. At the risk of being redundant, we must emphasize once again that rejecting "race" as having a real referent in the social world does not mean denying the existence of racism, or the denial of historical and cultural experiences predicated on a specific population's particular struggle against racism. Rather, a critical theory of racism represents a bold and forthright move to challenge common-sense notions of "race" that often lead not only to profound forms of essentialism and ahistorical perceptions of oppression, but also make it nearly impossible to dismantle the external material structures of domination that sustain racialized inequalities in schools and the larger society.

Further, we recognize the empirical reality that people believe in the existence of biologically distinct races. This can be captured analytically by stating that people employ the idea of "race" in the construction and interpretation of their social worlds. Similarly, we acknowledge that it is a common practice among the oppressed to invert the experience of exploitation. This is to say that negative notions of "race" linked to racist ideology are turned on their head and employed to fuel political movements among racialized populations. Social activists and scholars are not obliged to accept the common-sense ideas employed in the social world and use them as analytical concepts. The whole tradition of critical/Marxist analysis highlights the importance of developing an analytical framework that penetrates the surface and reified realities of social relations. (See, for example, Marx's discussion of the distinction between phenomenal forms and essential relations, his discussion of reification, and his discussion of method in the *Introduction to the Grundrisse der Kritik der Politischen Okonomie*[41] [1939].) In keeping with this tradition, we focus on racism as an analytical concept—a concept that has a real object in the social world, namely an ideology with a set of specific characteristics informed by economic imperatives—and we only refer to the idea of "race" when people use the notion in their everyday genres, utilizing it to make social distinctions based on the significance that is attached to differences between populations.

Finally, unlike scholars who argue resolutely for a critical theory of "race," we seek a critical language and conceptual apparatus that makes racism the central category of analysis in our understanding of racialized inequality, while simultaneously encompassing the multiple social expressions of racism. Undoubtedly, this entails the development of a critical language from which activists and scholars can reconstruct theories and practices of contemporary society that more accurately reflect and address capitalist forms of social and material inequities that shape the lives of racialized populations. Most importantly, we are calling for a critical theory of racism that can grapple with a radical remaking of democracy in the age of a globalized post-industrial economy. There are many who have proclaimed the death of the socialist project, but we argue that its renaissance is close at hand and will be articulated through a language that is fueled by the courage and passion to break with those hegemonic traditions on the left that fail to support a democratic vision of life for all people.

NOTES

1. Kenan Malik, *The Meaning of Race: Race History and Culture in Western Society* (New York: New York University Press, 1996), 34.
2. Kwame Anthony Appiah, "The Uncompleted Argument: Du Bois and the Illusion of Race," in *Overcoming Racism and Sexism,* Linda Bell and David Blumenfeld, eds. (Lanham, MD: Roman & Littlefield, 1995), 75.
3. Quotation marks are used around the word "race" not only to distinguish it as a social construct but to question the legitimacy of its descriptive and analytical utility. Following the example of British sociologist Robert Miles we agree that the use of "race" as an analytical concept disguises the social construction of difference, presenting it as inherent in the empirical reality of observable or imagined biological differences. For more on this issue, see *Racism* (London: Routledge, 1989) and *Racism after 'Race Relations'* (London: Routledge, 1993) both by Miles. For an insightful note on the use of quotation marks and the "racial" logic of the practice itself, see *Whiteness of a Different Color: European Immigrants and the Alchemy of Race* (Cambridge: Harvard University Press, 1998) by Mathew Frye Jacobson; ix, x.
4. Antonio Gramsci, *Selections from Prison Notebooks* (New York: International Publications, 1971).
5. Antonia Darder, *Culture and Power in the Classroom* (Westport, Conn.: Bergin & Garvey, 1991), 42.
6. Victor Valle and Rudolfo D. Torres, "The Idea of Mestizaje and the 'Race' Problematic: Racialized Media Discourse in a Post-Fordist Landscape," in *Culture and Difference.* Antonia Darder, ed. (Westport, Conn.: Bergin & Garvey, 1995), 139–153.
7. Jon Cruz, "From Farce to Tragedy: Reflections in the Reification of Race at Century's End," in *Mapping Multiculturalism,* Avery F. Gordon and Christopher Newfield, eds. (Minneapolis: University of Minnesota Press, 1996), 29.
8. Cruz, "From Farce to Tragedy," *Mapping Multiculturalism,* 35.
9. Some contemporary examples of this scholarship can be found in *Race Matters* by Cornel West (Boston: Beacon Press, 1993); *Killing Rage: Ending Racism* by bell hooks (1995); *Racial Formation in the United States: From the 1960s to the 1980s* by Michael Omi and Howard Winant (New York: Routledge, 1993); and *Loose Canons: Notes on the Culture Wars* by Henry Louis Gates Jr. (New York: Oxford University Press, 1992).
10. Gordon Allport's *The Nature of Prejudice* (Reading, Mass.: Addison-Wesley, 1954); and Kenneth Clark's *Prejudice and Your Child* (Boston: Beacon Press, 1955) strongly influenced the intellectual rationale and public policy decisions that instituted the busing solution in the United States.
11. Ellen Meiksins Wood, "Identity Crisis," *In These Times* (June 1994): 28–9.
12. Associated Press, Geneva, report released by the United Nations' International Labor Organization, entitled *Unemployment Will Reach 1 Billion Worldwide by Year's End* on Sunday, September 28, 1998.
13. John Cavanagh, "Global Economic Apartheid" (transcript from a speech delivered in Takoma Park, Maryland, September 19, 1996, p. 2); available through Alternative Radio, Boulder, Colorado. Dr. Cavanagh is a specialist in international trade, economics, and development and is

coauthor with Richard J. Barnet of *Global Dreams: Imperial Corporations in the New World Order* (New York: Simon & Schuster, 1994).

14. Ramon Grosfoguel and Chloe S. Georas, "The Racialization of Latino Caribbean Migrants in the New York Metropolitan Area," *Centro: Focus En Foco,* 1–2, No. 8, 1996: 193.

15. Ellen Meiksins Wood, *Democracy against Capitalism: Renewing Historical Materialism* (New York: Cambridge University Press, 1995), 263.

16. Robert Miles, *Racism after 'Race Relations'* (London: Routledge, 1993), 1.

17. Toni Morrison, "Unspeakable Things Unspoken: The Afro-American Presence in American Literature," *Michigan Quarterly Review* 28 (Winter 1989), 3.

18. Adolph Reed Jr., "Skin Deep," *Village Voice* 24 (September 1998), 22.

19. Appiah, "The Uncompleted Argument," *Overcoming Racism,* 74.

20. Robert Miles and Rodolfo D. Torres, "Does 'Race' Matter? Transatlantic Perspectives on Racism after 'Race Relations,' " in *Resituating Identities: The Politics of Race, Ethnicity and Culture,* Vered Amit-Talai and Caroline Knowles, eds. (Peterborough, Ontario: Broadview Press, 1996), 32.

21. Richard J. Herrnstein and Charles Murray, *The Bell Curve: Intelligence and Class Structure in American Life* (New York: Free Press, 1994).

22. Robert Miles and Rodolfo D. Torres, "Does 'Race' Matter?" *Resituating Identities,* 40.

23. Miles, *Racism* (London: Routledge, 1989), 75.

24. Michel Wieviorka, "Is It Difficult to Be an Anti-Racist?" *Debating Cultural Hybridity: Multicultural Identities and the Politics of Anti-Racism,* Pnina Werbner and Tariq Modood, eds. (London: ZED Books, 1997), 40.

25. Fifty years after the publication of *Caste, Class and Race* (New York: Doubleday, 1948) many continue to attribute Marxist analytical status to the work of Oliver C. Cox. Yet, we argue that this is misleading in that Cox, who retained race as the central category of analysis in his work, remained staunchly anchored in a "race relations" paradigm.

26. Oliver C. Cox, *Caste, Class and Race* (1948: reprint New York: Monthly Review Press, 1970), 319.

27. Charles W. Mills, *The Racial Contract* (Ithaca, NY: Cornell University Press, 1997), 76.

28. Angela Davis, "Gender, Class, and Multiculturalism: Rethinking Race Politics" in *Mapping Multiculturalism,* Avery F. Gordon and Christopher Newfield, eds. (Minneapolis: University of Minnesota Press, 1996), 43.

29. Paul Gilroy, *There Ain't No Black in the Union Jack* (Chicago: University of Chicago Press, 1991), 9.

30. James Baldwin, "On Being White . . . and Other Lies," in *Black on White,* David Roediger, ed. (New York: Shocken, 1998), 178.

31. bell hooks, *Talking Back* (Boston: South End Press, 1989), 112–13.

32. Floya Anthias and Nira Yuval-Davis, *Racialized Boundaries: Race, Nation, Gender, and Color and the Anti-racist Struggle* (New York: Routledge, 1992), 15.

33. Margaret Radin, cited in Cheryl Harris, "Whiteness as Property," in *Black on White: Black Writers on What It Means to Be White,* David Roediger (New York: Shocken Books, 1998), 107.

34. David Theo Goldberg, *Anatomy of Racism* (Minneapolis: University of Minnesota Press, 1990), xiii.

35. For recent scholarly works that focus on "critical theories of race," see *Critical Race Theory: The Cutting Edge,* Richard Delgado, ed. (Philadelphia: Temple University Press, 1995); *Critical Race Theory: The Key Writings that Formed the Movement,* Kimberlee Crenshaw, Neil Gotanda, Gary Peller, and Kendall Thomas, eds. (New York: New Press, 1995); and *Critical Race Feminism: A Reader,* Adrien King Wing (New York: New York University Press, 1997); as well as writings by Michael Omi and Howard Winant, including *Racial Condition* (Minneapolis: University of Minnesota Press, 1994).

36. Colette Guillaumin, *Racism, Sexism, Power and Ideology* (London: Routledge, 1995).

37. Robert Miles, *Racism after 'Race Relations'* (London: Routledge, 1993), 52.

38. Guillaumin, *Racism, Sexism,* 107.

39. David McNally, "Language, History and Class Struggle," in *In Defense of History: Marxism and the Postmodern Agenda,* Ellen Meiksins Wood and John Bellamy Foster, eds. (New York: Monthly Review Press, 1997), 40–41.

40. Miles, *Racism after 'Race Relations,'* 42.

41. Karl Marx, *Grundrisse der Kritik der Politischen Okonomie* (Moscow: Verlag fur Fremdsprachig Literatur, 1939).

Suggested Readings
for Future Study

RACE, RACISM, AND EDUCATION

Anzaldúa, G. (1987). *Borderlands/La frontera: The new mestiza*. San Francisco: Spinster/Aunt Lute.

Bell, D. (1992). *Faces at the bottom of the well: The permanence of racism*. New York: Basic Books.

Clark, S., ed. (1992). *Malcolm X: The final speeches, February 1965*. New York: Pathfinder.

Cox, O. (1948). *Caste, class and race*. New York: Modern Reader.

Darder, A. (1995). *Culture and difference*. Westport, Conn.: Bergin & Garvey.

Darder, A., and Torres, R., eds. (1996). The *Latino studies reader: Culture, economy and politics*. Boston: Blackwell.

Dent, G. (1992). *Black popular culture*. Seattle: Bay Press.

Dubois, W. E. B. (1903). *The souls of Black folk*. New York: Gramercy.

Dyer, R. (1993). *The matter of images: Essays on representations*. New York: Routledge.

Ferguson, R., Gever, M., Minh-ha, T., and West, C. (1990). *Out there: Marginalization and contemporary cultures*. Cambridge, Mass.: MIT Press.

Fanon, F. (1967). *Black skin, white masks*. New York: Grove Press.

Gates, H. L., Jr. (1992). *Loose Canons: Notes on the Culture Wars*. New York: Oxford University Press.

Gilroy, P. (1993). *Black Atlantic: Modernity and double consciousness*. Cambridge, Mass.: Harvard University Press.

Giroux, H. (1992). *Border crossings*. New York: Routledge.

Giroux, H. (1993). *Living dangerously: Multiculturalism and the politics of difference*. New York: Peter Lang.

Giroux, H., and McLaren, P., eds. (1994). *Between borders: Pedagogy and the politics of cultural study*. New York: Routledge.

Goldberg, D. T. (1994). *Multiculturalism: A critical reader*. Oxford: Blackwell.

Gordon, A., and Newfield, C. (1996). *Mapping multiculturalism*. Minneapolis: University of Minnesota Press.

Hauptman, L. (1995). *Tribes and tribulations: Misconceptions about American Indians and their histories*. Albuquerque: University of New Mexico Press.

hooks, b. (1994). *Outlaw culture: Resisting representations*. New York: Routledge.

hooks, b., and West, C. (1991). *Breaking bread: Insurgent Black intellectual life*. Boston: South End.

Johansen, B. (1998). *Debating democracy: Native American legacy of freedom*. Santa Fe, N.Mex.: Clear Light.

Kelley, R. (1997). *Yo' Mama's DisFUNKtional! Fighting the culture wars in urban America*. Boston: Beacon.

Leistyna, P. (1999). *Presence of mind. Education and the politics of deception*. Boulder, Colo.: Westview.

McLaren, P. (1995). *Critical pedagogy and predatory culture: Oppositional politics in a postmodern era*. New York: Bergin & Garvey.

McLaren, P. (1997). *Revolutionary multiculturalism: Pedagogies of dissent for the new millennium.* Boulder, Colo.: Westview.

Memmi, A. (1991). *The colonizer and the colonized.* Boston: Beacon.

Morrison, T. (1992) *Playing in the dark: Whiteness and the literary imagination.* Cambridge, Mass.: Harvard University Press.

McCarthy, C., and Crichlow, W., eds. (1993). *Race, identity and representation in education.* New York: Routledge.

Miles, R. (1993). *Racism after 'race relations.'* London: Routledge.

Monk, R. (1994). *Taking sides: Clashing views on controversial issues in race and ethnicity.* Guilford, Conn.: The Dushkin Publishing Group.

Omi, M., and Winant, H. (1994). *Racial formation in the United States.* New York: Routledge.

Olsen, L. (1997). *Made in America: Immigrant students in our public schools.* New York: The New Press.

Said, E. (1993). *Culture and imperialism.* New York: Knopf.

Sleeter, C., and McLaren, P. (1995). *Multicultural education, critical pedagogy and the politics of difference.* New York: SUNY Press.

Stanton-Salazar, R. (2001). *Manufacturing hope and despair: The school and kin support networks of U.S.-Mexican youth.* New York: Teachers College.

Tai, R., and Kenyatta, M., eds. (1999). *Critical ethnicity: Countering the waves of identity politics.* Lanham, Md.: Rowman and Littlefield.

Takaki, R. (1990). *Iron cages: Race and culture in 19th-century America.* New York: Oxford University Press.

Takezawa, Y. (1995). *Breaking the silence: Redress and Japanese American ethnicity.* New York: Cornell University Press.

Torres, R., and Hamamoto, D., eds. (1997). *New American destinies: A reader in contemporary Asian and Latino immigration.* New York: Routledge.

Torres, R., Miron, L., and Inda, J. X. (1999). *Race, identity and citizenship: A reader.* Boston. Blackwell.

Valenzuela, A. (1999). *Substractive schooling. U.S.-Mexican youth and the politics of caring.* New York: SUNY Press.

Wa Thiong'o, N. (1986). *Decolonizing the mind: The politics of language in African Literature.* London: James Curry.

West, C. (1993). *Race matters.* Boston: Beacon.

Winant, H. (1994). *Racial conditions.* Minneapolis: University of Minnesota Press.

Young, I. (1990). *Justice and the politics of difference.* Princeton, N.J.: Princeton University Press.

Part 4

GENDER, SEXUALITY, AND SCHOOLING

INTRODUCTION

Kathleen Weiler's essay, "Feminist Analyses of Gender and Schooling," introduces the reader to notions of gender, schooling, and sexuality with a review of the major feminist approaches to education. Her work reveals some of the problematic assumptions of traditional and liberal perspectives of gender oppression. Weiler looks at feminist research of the 1970s and 1980s conducted in response to the all-male-oriented research of the leaders of the correspondence movement. Weiler, following the tradition of other exponents of critical pedagogy, exposes the weaknesses of correspondence theories in an effort to address in a comprehensive manner issues of gender and race at work in the classroom. In particular, she engages the concept of counterhegemony, as conceptualized by Gramsci, and its utility to an emancipatory feminist approach to teaching. Weiler argues that through providing an analysis of resistance, gender, race, and social class critical pedagogy can provide a theoretical framework for the transcendence of the limitations found in earlier feminist discourses.

Michelle Fine's essay, "Sexuality, Schooling and Adolescent Females: The Missing Discourse of Desire," provides an important analysis that seeks to integrate critical pedagogy and feminist concerns. Her groundbreaking ethnography on sex education in New York city public schools exposes the hypocrisy at work in the politics of sex education—a politics that functions to suppress an ever-present (but hidden) discourse of desire among female adolescents. By so doing, she shows how this phenomenon actually works to prevent the construction of healthy sexual identities, as it perpetuates a cycle of victimization and poverty among teenage girls.

In his article on gay adolescents, "Thinking About the Gay Teen," Gerald Unks highlights the insidious conditions that exist for gay, lesbian, and bisexual students in the United States. In particular, he examines the realities of gay, lesbian, and bisexual high-school students who must survive in a society where there is license to "torment and harm people because of their sexuality." He argues that the situation of adolescents, whose sexuality exists outside the heterosexist norm of the mainstream, is far more dangerous, since they are denied many of the alternatives available to their adult counterparts for the expression of their sexuality. Unks asserts that the degree of powerlessness experienced by these students is particularly pervasive during their high school life, given the highly homophobic nature of educational institutions. As a consequence, gays, lesbian and bisexual students often live in constant fear of expressing their true sexual identity.

In her article, "What We Can Do for You! What Can "We" Do for "You"? Struggling over Empowerment in Critical and Feminist Pedagogy," Jennifer Gore launches one of the most incisive critiques of one of the most important ideological tenets of critical pedagogy and some radical feminist discourses—namely, empowerment. Grounded in a Foucauldian vision of power, Gore makes suspect the use of this concept by the leading theorists of critical pedagogy, in what she argues is a view of power as property, which can be shared, exchanged, and given. Gore problematizes the notion of responsibility attributed to teachers as agents of empowerment by critical pedagogy, for she claims it does not take into account the limitations of teachers' work and the constraint of their workplace. By so doing, Gore calls to task the traditional intellectual arrogance of theorists who keep pushing teachers to become empowering subjects, while they simultaneously protect themselves in the abstract world of academia. This article constituted a seminal piece and a significant historical critique in the development of critical pedagogy.

QUESTIONS FOR REFLECTION AND DIALOGUE

1. Describe the historical development of feminist approaches to schooling and education.
2. What are the major distinctions between liberal, radical, and socialist feminisms?
3. What are the shortcomings of reproduction theory in explaining gender oppression and human agency?
4. What are the four major approaches to sex education in public schools in the United States? How distinct are these from the experiences of other industrialized countries?
5. How efficient are these four approaches to remediating problems of teenage pregnancy, sexual violence, and school dropouts?
6. In what ways can the public's recognition of the role of "desire" in the lives of adolescents contribute to both the development of emancipated subjectivities among female students and the establishment of critical educational practices within schools?

7. In what ways are the situations of gay, lesbian, and bisexual teen-agers different from those of heterosexual teenagers?

8. How are gay, lesbian, and bisexual students affected emotionally and socially by the ostracism experienced within the high school class-room? How do you believe this might impact their academic development?

9. What are concrete steps educators can implement to address the sexuality of their students? How can they help to prevent the harass-ment of gay, lesbian, and bisexual students by their classmates?

10. How do different strands of critical pedagogy and feminist discourse conceptualize power? What are some of the problems associated with these assumptions about power?

11. What is Foucault's view of power? Positive, negative?

12. Explain how you can identify a "true" liberatory practice. What are some of the risks associated with claims to being liberatory?

Feminist Analyses
of Gender and Schooling

KATHLEEN WEILER

There are a variety of feminist approaches to the study of the relationship of gender and schooling approaches emerging from more general liberal feminist, radical feminist, and socialist feminist work.[1] This study has been most influenced by socialist feminism, and I think it is important at the outset to distinguish this form of analysis from liberal feminist theory, which underlies much of the work on sex-role stereotyping in schools. Much of the work that has been done to date on the relationship of women and schooling has emerged from liberal feminist analyses of schools. Such work has focused on sex stereotyping and bias. Theorists working from this perspective have outlined and exposed the sexual bias in curricular materials and school practices. Their focus has been on the reform of both texts and practices and on state policies toward education. Both classroom ethnographies and analyses of textbooks have emerged from this tradition.[2]

This liberal feminist work has been extremely important in documenting the biases and distortions of texts and the sexism that underlies such practices as course and career counseling for girls and boys. But it also has significant shortcomings in its narrow focus on texts and institutional structures. It has tended to ignore the depth of sexism in power relationships and the relationship of gender and class. Because this approach fails to place schools and schooling in the context of a wider social and economic analysis, it does not analyze the constraints under which the process of schooling actually takes place. Moreover, the liberal approach omits any class analysis and thus ignores not only differences between middle-class and working-class girls and women, but ignores the oppression and exploitation of working-class boys as well. As Arnot comments:

> This literature does not search too deeply into the class basis or the inequality of
> opportunity which boys suffer. . . . The implication then appears to be that girls

should match the class differentials of educational achievement and access to occupations which boys experience. Equality of opportunity in this context therefore appears to mean similar class-based inequalities of opportunity for both men and women. Or, one could say, equal oppression. (1982, p. 68)

While the strength of the liberal perspective lies in its documentation of gender discrimination and the analysis of specific sexist texts and practices, its lack of social or economic analysis limits its ability to explain the origins of these practices or the ways in which other structures of power and control affect what goes on within schools. Its lack of class analysis leads to a blurring of what actually happens in schools as individuals are described only in terms of their gender and are not viewed in terms of their class or race location as well.

In the liberal feminist studies of sex-role stereotyping, there has been an implicit assumption that changes of texts and practices will lead to changes in social relationships and that girls and boys will then be equal within capitalist society. Implicit in this view is the concept that sexism exists within the realm of ideas, and that if those ideas are changed, then social relationships will also change. Such a view ignores the constraints of the material world and the various forms of power and privilege that work together in a complex and mutually reinforced process to make up social reality as we know it. It also ignores the complexity of consciousness and the existence of ideology and culture. Thus while liberal feminist critiques of sex-role stereotyping in school texts and descriptions of classroom practices have been very useful, they are of limited analytic value in investigating the complexity of the social construction of gender in the intersection of school, family, and work.

I examine here the work of feminists influenced by socialist feminism and by critical educational theory who have investigated the relationship of schooling and gender. This critical feminist educational theory begins with certain assumptions that distinguish it from liberal feminist studies. The first assumption is that schooling is deeply connected to the class structure and economic system of capitalism; thus one focus of this work is on the relationship of women's schooling and women's work. The second assumption, again derived from more general socialist feminist theory, is that capitalism and patriarchy are related and mutually reinforcing of one another. In other words, both men and women exist in interconnected and overlapping relationships of gender and class—and, as feminists of color have increasingly emphasized, of race as well.

These theorists share the difficulties of other socialist-feminist theorists who attempt to fuse Marxism and feminism. They are deeply influenced by traditional Marxist theory, and want to apply that theory to the situation of women. But Marx and Engels were primarily concerned with the mode of production and relationships of production in class and not in gender terms. For Marx and Engels as well as for later Marxist theorists, women's oppression was subsumed within their class position and was analyzed through examining the demands of capital. Socialist-feminist theorists have argued that this traditional Marxist analysis is inadequate to reveal the nature of women's experience and oppression (Jagger, 1983; Hartsock, 1983; Eisenstein, 1979). As Kuhn and Wolpe comment, "much marxist analysis, in subsuming women to the general categories of that problematic—class relations, labour process, the state, and so on, fails to confront the specificity of women's oppression" (Kuhn and Wolpe, 1978, p. 8). This theoretical debate, what Hartmann has called "the unhappy marriage of socialism and feminism," is complex and still being worked out. The immediate task for socialist feminists is to create a synthesis of these two lines of analysis, to create a theory that can relate what Rubin has called "the sex/gender system" and the economic system through an analysis of the sexual division of labor and an understanding of the intersection of these two forms of power (Barrett, 1980; Eisenstein, 1979; Rubin, 1975). As Hartmann puts it:

> Both marxist analysis, particularly its historical and materialist method, and feminist analysis, especially the identification of patriarchy as a social and historical structure, must be drawn upon if we are to understand the development of western capitalist societies and the predicament of women within them. (1981, p. 191)

These arguments are complex and as yet incomplete. The historical development of socialist feminism itself has recently come under scrutiny and the question of its future development is hardly clear (Barrett, 1980; Ehrenreich, 1984; Rowbotham, Segal and Wainright, 1981; Tax, 1984). But while the relationship between socialism and feminism, capitalism and patriarchy is filled with tension, as Ehrenreich writes, a socialist and feminist perspective is still needed:

> Socialist—or perhaps here I should say Marxist—because a Marxist way of thinking, at its best, helps us understand the cutting edge of change, the blind driving force of capital, the dislocations, innovations, and global reshufflings. Feminist because feminism offers our best insight into that which is most ancient and intractable about our common situation: the gulf that divides the species by gender and, tragically, divides us all from nature and that which is most human in our nature. (1984, p. 57)

This study of feminist teachers is grounded in this complex and developing tradition of socialist feminist theory. But I have also been influenced by a variety of feminist theorists who have concerned themselves with the relationship of gender and schooling and who have approached these questions from less clearly defined theoretical perspectives.

In discussing ongoing feminist work on the relationship of gender and schooling, I have identified the same two perspectives that I used in discussing critical educational theory in general: theories of social and cultural reproduction and theories of cultural production and resistance. But I want to make clear at the outset of this discussion that this division is in certain ways artificial and should not be taken as connoting a rigid separation of these theorists into competing schools of thought. What I have identified in their work are tendencies, a concern with certain problems, a way of defining what is significant or causal in looking at the relationship of gender and schooling. What I think we can see here is what Althusser calls the "problematique" of theory—that is, the underlying questions that define what is significant and therefore what is to be investigated. I feel this distinction between those concerned with social and cultural reproduction and those concerned with cultural production and resistance is a valid one. But in a field of inquiry as new and fluid as this one, in which feminist scholars are in the process of generating theory, there will be a blurring and shifting of perspectives as the theorists themselves develop and refine their own concerns.[3]

The earliest of these investigations into gender and school from a critical feminist perspective can be found in what I have called feminist reproduction theory. Feminist reproduction theory is concerned with the ways in which schools function to reproduce gender divisions and oppression. In response to this emphasis on reproduction, a smaller but growing body of work has emerged which employs the concepts of resistance and cultural production to look at the lived experience of girls in schools. Most recently, the concept of counter-hegemony has been raised as a way of approaching the politically conscious work of teachers. These theoretical traditions focus on different moments in the experience of girls and women in schools, and as I have emphasized, it should be kept in mind that these categories are a kind of heuristic device, and that the individual theorists themselves may be engaged in their own process of growth and reconceptualization. But trying to clarify and identify their underlying theoretical assumptions can be of help to all of us as we attempt to generate theory and focus our own research.

FEMINIST REPRODUCTION THEORY

Although socialist feminist theory has developed rapidly in the last decade, work that explicitly addresses the role of schools in reproducing gender oppression has been somewhat limited. The most significant work has emerged in England, and has been influenced by the work of both new sociologists of education and Marxist theorists who have focused on the role of schools as ideological state apparatuses. While these feminist reproduction theorists take somewhat different approaches, they all share a common belief in the power of material historical analysis and a focus on the relationship of class and gender. Basic to their approach is the view that women's oppression in the paid workforce and in domestic work is reproduced through what happens in the schools. Thus statistical analyses of women's inferior position in the economy are tied to sexist texts and discriminatory practices in schools. Official state educational policies are examined for their overt and hidden assumptions about women and their "proper" role in the economy. The major focus of this approach is on the connection between sexist practices in the schools and women's oppression in society as a whole.

Feminist reproduction theorists are deeply influenced by traditional Marxist analysis and have been primarily concerned with social reproduction—that is, the reproduction of relationships to and control over economic production and work.[4] These theorists are concerned with the nature of women's work, both within the public sphere and within the domestic or private sphere. Thus the focus of their analysis is on the class-based nature of women's experiences in schools and the ways in which the experience of schooling reproduces gender oppression. But they also emphasize the differences between middle-class and working-class experience of gender. For them, what are being reproduced are not simply "men" and "women," but working-class or bourgeois men and women who have particular relationships to one another and to production which are the result of their class as well as their gender. As Arnot comments, this approach reveals "the diversity of class experience and the nature of class hegemony in education" (Arnot, 1982, p. 69).

The debate about the relationship of gender and class underlies the work of all of these feminist reproduction theorists who concern themselves with schooling. While they recognize the "specificity" of women's oppression and often speak of patriarchal as opposed to class oppression, they remain committed to the primacy of production. Because of the centrality of this sphere of material life and production in their thought, feminist reproduction theorists see the relationship between gender as an ideology and women's role in production as fundamental to any analysis of women and schooling. Thus for them, work, both paid and unpaid, becomes the central focus of analysis. Since they are concerned with the role of schooling in the reproduction of existing society, they focus on the way schools work ideologically to prepare girls to accept their role as low paid or unpaid workers in capitalism.

Several socialist feminist analyses of reproduction and schooling are also deeply influenced by the work of Althusser. This is particularly true of the work of Michelle Barrett. An Althusserian perspective in this case implies an emphasis on the "relative autonomy" of schools as sites of ideological reproduction. The most obvious difficulty of using an Althusserian approach for an analysis of gender is that Althusser is concerned with the category of class, not gender, and there is some question whether it is fruitful or even possible to substitute "gender" for "class" in this analysis. However, Althusser's insistence that ideological apparatuses are "relatively autonomous" from the economic sphere appears to provide the means to raise questions of gender and patriarchal practices apart from, although not unrelated to, questions of class and capitalist practices. Barrett recognizes the complexity of this issue and argues that the method of analysis must include an analysis of gender *within* specific class structures (1980). While feminist theorists of schooling influenced by Althusser provide a more complex view of the role of schools in relation to women's oppression in capitalism, they remain focused on the question of how this oppression is reproduced and, like Althusser, argue at a very abstract level of analysis that leaves little room for human agency or resistance. While a view of schools as ideological state apparatuses "relatively autonomous" from the economic base provides room for the contradictions and disjunctions evident in schools, it still remains within a paradigm of reproduction. The strengths and weaknesses of feminist reproduction theory may be clarified if we look at the work of several representative theorists.

AnnMarie Wolpe was one of the earliest socialist feminists to address the role of gender in schooling. Her work includes both a critique of official government statements on education and a critique of earlier work on sexism in schools for its lack of economic or social analysis. One of the strongest parts of Wolpe's argument is her attack on what she calls "stratification" theories, which look at women's position as the result of innate psychological differences such as lack of aggression, excessive anxiety, or orientation toward "intrinsic" rewards such as nurturing relationships (1978, p. 306). Wolpe argues that such interpretations fail to recognize the powerful forces of the capitalist economy with its need for unpaid domestic work and a reserve army of labor.

Wolpe reveals in detail the ideological assumptions about the role of women in society which underlie the official British Norwood (1943), Crowther (1959), and Newsom (1963) reports and the later unofficial Conservative Green and Black papers (1977). Wolpe shows clearly the acceptance of the role of women as wives and mothers doing unpaid work in the home and the failure to recognize either that women *do* work in paid jobs or that the paid work that they do is in low-paying and dead-end jobs. Thus by failing to recognize the reality of women's actual work as paid workers and by encouraging girls to see their own work (both paid and unpaid) as insignificant, Wolpe argues that these reports perpetuated and helped to reproduce existing inequality. She argues that in influencing school policies, these reports have played a vital ideological role in reproducing the oppression and subordination of women in the economy.

This kind of analysis is valuable since it points to the connection between hegemonic ideological views (in the consciousness of the groups—primarily men—who wrote these reports) and actual educational policy and practices as they are carried out in the schools. But what Wolpe does not address is precisely *how* these assumptions and views are put into practice in the schools or how students and teachers have accepted, incorporated, or resisted them. This is not to discredit or discount Wolpe's analysis, but to point to the limitations inherent in a view of ideology as the uncontested imposition of a view of reality or set of values. Wolpe's tendency to depict the imposition of ideology as a relatively smooth and almost mechanical process is the result of her focus on reproduction at a very abstract level of economic and structural analysis. It is Wolpe's reliance on reproduction and her failure to address the question of human agency that ultimately limits her work. While she criticizes stratification theories of education for their failure to provide any economic analysis of the role of schooling, she accepts without much criticism social reproduction theories of education. As she says:

> I want to consider the educational system first, as a mechanism of *reproduction* of "agents" in the sense that it operates, more or less successfully, to qualify them both "technically" and ideologically; and second, as a mediating agency in the *allocation* of agents into the division of labour. (Wolpe, 1978, p. 313)

Since Wolpe is concerned with women and women's oppression, the use of this reproduction paradigm ultimately leads her to depict schools as the means of reproducing women who will accept their role as workers in both paid and unpaid work. The ideology of the school is seen as important in justifying this role both for those who control the educational system and for the girls and women in the schools.

Wolpe's approach shares the limitations and shortcomings of all social reproduction theory, as we saw earlier in a discussion of the work of Bowles and Gintis and Althusser, in that it fails to address individual consciousness or the possibilities of resistance, but it also fails to address forms of women's oppression other than those of work. Wolpe later qualifies her early, rather functionalist, view by referring to the "relative autonomy" of schools. Following Althusser, she sees schools as mediating between students and the demands of capital. This "relative autonomy" recognizes the contradictions involved in the relationship between the economic base and the schools. Nonetheless, Wolpe's central concern remains the reproduction of women in relation to work. Thus, Wolpe's analysis has no place for sexuality, human needs, the historical and class-based forms of resistance of women, or the contradictory role of schooling for girls in a system of patriarchy. Ultimately Wolpe's work is valuable in pointing out the need to locate women's oppression and women's experience in schooling within a larger social structure and in making central the role of work in women's lives, but at the same time her work is frustrating in its tendency toward a mechanical form of reproduction theory.

Another early influential feminist analysis of schooling was Rosemary Deem's *Women and Schooling* (1978). In this general overview, Deem combines quantitative information about the percentage of girls in various courses, the numbers of girls taking and passing exams, and the percentage of women in various teaching and administrative jobs. She also writes from the general perspective of social reproduction, arguing that the schools are central to the process of maintaining and reproducing the existing sexual division of labor. This underlying paradigm of social reproduction leads Deem to emphasize the significance of work and the role of schooling in preparing women for certain kinds of work. Thus she emphasizes the domestic nature of working-class girls' curriculum, with its assumption that women's primary work will be unpaid labor in the home. She also points to the small number of girls in mathematics and science, and shows how that in turn excludes women from certain university courses and later technological and professional jobs. Deem points out that the schools do not create this division, but that they reinforce the present arrangement of society through their acceptance of the status quo in both class and gender terms:

> Education does not create the sexual division of labour, nor the kinds of work available in the labour market, nor the class relationships of society, but it rarely does anything to undermine them. (1978, p. 20)

Deem emphasizes that schools, in their expectations of boys and girls and in their authority structures (so heavily dominated by men in positions of power and authority), transmit different cultures to boys and to girls, and that the "choices" made by students in school reproduce the existing sexual division of labor.

One of the strengths of Deem's analysis is her emphasis on the continuity of women's work as mothers in the family and as teachers in the primary schools. As she makes clear, the role of women in doing the unpaid labor of nurturing, feeding, and caring for the material needs of children is not the reflection of some innate "women's nature," but is part of the existing social division of labor in capitalism. This arrangement may not be inevitable in capitalist societies, but in the present organization of capitalism, it is central to the reproduction of the work force. Thus Deem argues that there is a continuum between the rearing and socialization of children within the family, where the primary work is done by mothers, and the socialization that takes place in the early years of schooling, with the work done by women teachers.[5] Deem's grounding in social reproduction theory leads her to reject views of women's nurturing role as either "natural" or the "fault" of women. As she emphasizes, it is the structural organization of capitalist societies that leads to this division of labor and the resulting personal and psychological traits assumed to be natural to men and women. She criticizes the view that women teachers are inadequate because of their feminine qualities or their roles within their own families:

> Furthermore, there is the implicit assumption (in criticizing women teachers) that all these factors are the fault of women and are not attributable to their relationship with men in the sexual division of labour, or to the manner in which capitalist societies organize and reward productive and non-productive work. (1978, p. 116)

This emphasis on the existing division of capitalist societies in gender as well as class terms is one of the strongest elements in Deem's work, since it leads her to see the experiences and struggles of women teachers in the context of larger social dynamics.

Although Deem's book provides a valuable overview of the relationship of women and schooling, its strength—a recognition of the role of schools in reproducing an unequal gender and class system—is at the same time a limitation. Like Wolpe, Deem fails to deal adequately with ideology and the way in which women teachers and students exist within a structure of socially influenced needs and desires—an ideological world of male hegemony, in Arnot's phrase. Moreover, she ignores the struggles and resistance of both teachers and students to this hegemony. While her work is useful in providing specific evidence of discriminatory patterns, the picture it gives of this process is one sided. Again, what is needed here is an examination of the way in which these meanings and forms of power are negotiated and worked out in the actual lived reality of teachers and students in schools.

An interesting analysis of women's schooling from a similar perspective but in the United States context is provided by the recent work of Kelly and Nihlen (1982). Like many other socialist feminists, Kelly and Nihlen argue that an emphasis on paid work as the only meaningful form of work ignores the significance of domestic unpaid labor—a domain that has been defined as "women's sphere" in advanced capitalist societies like the United States. They argue that the ideological assumption that this work is the responsibility (and natural province) of women profoundly shapes women's working lives, making certain jobs "unnatural" for women because of the difficulties involved in doing both paid and unpaid work. Moreover, the assumption that certain characteristics are natural to women—such as nurturance, caring, sensitivity, etc.—leads women into certain jobs and not others. Kelly and Nihlen consider the evidence that links schools to this division of labor, but unlike some of the earlier writers who focus on reproduction, they also raise the question of the extent to which students "do in fact become what the messages of the schools would have them become" (Kelly and Nihlen, 1982, p. 174). Thus, while they work from the perspective of reproduction theory, seeking to delineate the reproductive role of schools in the creation of the sexual division of labor, they also begin to question the adequacy of that perspective in addressing the realities of women's experience in schools.

In looking at the relationship of schooling and women's work, Kelly and Nihlen focus on several areas of schooling. They look first at authority patterns and staffing. Using available statistics and data, they show clearly the unequal representation of women in positions of authority and status and note the *decline* of women in higher paying and higher status jobs since the 1950s. They also examine the formal curriculum, and, citing the numerous studies of curriculum and texts that exist, particularly in the 1970s, show again the sex-stereotyping prevalent in curricular material at both the primary and secondary levels. They then examine the ways in which knowledge is distributed in the classroom itself and in the social relationships of schooling. As they point out, this area is least researched; we know the least about the ways in which girls and boys are treated by male and female teachers. But the studies that do exist point to discrimination and stereotyped expectations based not only on gender, but on race and class as well. Thus working-class girls of color receive the least attention and have the lowest expectations from teachers. On the other hand, there is evidence that teachers tend to prefer white middle-class girls to black working-class boys, for example.

The most interesting part of Kelly and Nihlen's discussion is the final section on the possible resistance of girls. As they make clear, girls do continue to higher education (although disproportionally to two-year colleges as opposed to more elite public and private four-year colleges) despite the ideological message of the school curriculum that their place is at home doing domestic work. As Kelly and Nihlen point out, women do not accept the ideological message of the school unproblematically. Instead, they obviously "negotiate" that knowledge in light of their own emotional, intellectual and material needs:

> While the above suggests that women may not necessarily incorporate all "school knowledge" it should not be taken by any means to deny what school knowledge in fact is or its attempted transmission in the classroom. Rather, it is to point out that within the classroom sets of knowledge renegotiation and/or active filtering occurs that may counter what the schools consider legitimate. How this renegotiation occurs we do not know, yet there is ample evidence to suggest its existence. (1982, p. 175)

Kelly and Nihlen's work is valuable in pointing to the weaknesses of the reproduction paradigm and in calling for an examination of the ways in which girls appropriate or reject school knowledge about the roles of women in paid and domestic work. They point to evidence that girls do not unproblematically accept the vision of sexual identity transmitted to them through the social relationships, authority patterns, and curriculum of the schools. However, despite their valuable work in recognizing the need to take into account resistance in looking at girls in schools, Kelly and Nihlen's work has certain limitations. First, I think, is their failure to apply or develop the concept of resistance to account for contradictory relationships to schooling on the part of both students and teachers. And second, they are still tied to a theory of work and work value that does not address the sexuality and power in the relationships of men and women which are extremely important in school settings, as in all socially contructed gender relationships.

Certainly the most sophisticated and fully developed theoretical work in the socialist feminist sociology of education can be found in the work of Madeleine Arnot. A sociologist of education versed in the theories of Bernstein and Bourdieu, Arnot has developed a critique of their work and an analysis of traditional reproduction theory from a feminist perspective. Her work combines a thorough knowledge of both reproduction and resistance theory. Her use of these difficult and sometimes contradictory traditions provides a complex analysis of the relationship of gender, class, and schooling. As Arnot defines her own position: "I do not believe that one can disassociate the ideological forms of masculinity and femininity, in their historical specificity, from either the material basis of patriarchy or from the class structure" (1980, p. 60). Underlying all of her work is the central understanding that social relationships are always in process and are constructed by individual human beings within a web of power and material constraints.

While Arnot has been influenced by reproduction theory and is sympathetic to a materialist analysis, she is critical of feminist reproduction theory for its failure to deal with the question of resistance and the contested nature of the construction of both class and gender identities. Arnot argues that socialist feminist social reproduction theorists, like social reproduction theorists in general, project too total a vision of domination and oppression. In some of these accounts, girls are turned into women through the effects of schooling in a mechanical process in which their humanity and consciousness is simply ignored. Thus Arnot suggests replacing the concept of reproduction with Gramsci's concept of hegemony. As she says:

> By putting the concept of hegemony, rather than "reproduction" at the fore of an analysis of class and gender, it is less easy in research to forget the *active* nature of the learning process, the existence of dialectical relations, power struggles, and points of conflict, the range of alternative practices which may exist inside, or exist outside and be brought into the school. (1982, p. 66)

In seeking a way to address questions of cultural production, Arnot looks back to the work of Bernstein and Bourdieu. While Arnot criticizes their work for their failure to address gender, she is also deeply influenced by this work, particularly that of Bernstein and his theories of the framing and transmission of knowledge. She uses his concept of a code to suggest that "one can develop a theory of gender codes which is class based and which can expose the structural and interactional features of gender reproduction and conflict in families, in schools and in work places" (1982, p. 80). What this focus on gender codes would allow us, Arnot argues, is to remain conscious of the different moments and crossing structures of power which are negotiated by individuals in social settings. Thus she emphasizes that girls negotiate and construct their own gendered identities through different definitions of what it means to be a woman from their families, their peers, the school, the media, etc., and that this involves both contradictions and conflict. Arnot argues that feminist educational theorists, by emphasizing hegemony, the existence of competing codes of meaning and the continual *process* of social relationships, will be able to unravel the complexities of the effects of both capitalism and patriarchy on individual lives without falling into the mechanical functionalism of repro-duction theory or the atheoretical stance of liberal theory.

The work of Arnot and Kelly and Nihlen draws attention to the need to take into account agency and the production of meaning on the part of girls and women in schools. It also reiterates the basic argument of Barrett and other socialist feminists that we must try to understand the construction of gender within specific historical and social sites. While this project is only beginning, the basis for this investigation can be found in the work of feminists who have turned to the lived experience of girls and women in school. The most devel-oped of this work has come from feminists using the concept of resistance to investigate the lived reality of working-class girls in and out of schools. But other work is in process and emerging that considers the lives and work of women teachers as well as students. This new work builds upon the earlier reproduction studies, but its basic focus is quite different. It is to this work that I now want to turn.

FEMINIST RESISTANCE AND CULTURAL PRODUCTION THEORY

As we have seen, feminist reproduction theory has emphasized the ways in which schooling *reproduces* existing gender inequalities. This work has focused on the ideological function of texts and classroom practices in reinforcing patriarchal hegemony. And because much of this work is grounded in tradi-tional Marxist class analysis, it has also focused on the connection between schooling and women's work in the paid work force. I have argued that the limitation of this approach lies in its failure to consider human beings as agents who are able to contest and redefine the ideological messages they receive in schools. It is a much too mechanistic and all-encompassing view of social real-ity. In response to these limitations, some feminists have begun to examine girls' and women's experiences in schools from the perspective of resistance and cultural production theories.

While traditionally the concept of resistance has been used to describe pub-lic counter-school or antisocial actions, there is an emerging view that this def-inition is inadequate to explain or understand the lives of girls or women. Some feminist theorists argue that resistance has different meanings for boys and for girls and that girls' resistance can only be understood in relation to both gen-der and class position (Connell, 1982; Davies, 1983; Kessler et al., 1985). These theorists insist that women as well as men can resist domination and oppression and they as well as men negotiate social forces and possibilities in an attempt to meet their own needs. This is the same dialectic between human needs and human will that we see in other critical studies. Women, as well as men, are enmeshed in social relationships and ideological, as well as material, webs of meaning and power. But because they are oppressed by sexism as well as class, the form of their resistance will be different from that of men. More-over, schooling may have a different meaning for them than it has for boys of their same class or race. As Gaskell comments:

. . . schools, operating in their traditional function, do not simply reproduce sex-stereotypes or confirm girls in subordinate positions. Certainly they do that much of the time. But they have also long been a vehicle for women who wish to construct their own intellectual lives and careers. (1985, p. 35)

Girls and women with different race and class subjectivities will have different experiences in schools. Both their resistance and their "reading" of the ideological messages of schools will differ in specific school settings. And of course girls of different class and race subjectivities will be met with varying expectations on the part of white and black, male and female teachers, depending on these teachers' own views of what is gender appropriate. By adding the categories of race and class to that of gender, we can begin to reveal the diversity and complexity of girls' and women's experiences in schools.

Among the most important work addressing the experiences of working-class girls in schools has come from feminist sociologists of education who have studied groups of antisocial or antischool girls. The work of these theorists has emerged from a wider sociological investigation of youth subcultures as the site of working-class resistance to the hegemonic ideology of capitalism. Much of this research has come from the Centre for Contemporary Cultural Studies at the University of Birmingham in England and the feminist research group there has engaged on a number of valuable projects and critiques (Women's Study Group, 1978). While these feminist sociologists have worked closely with the male sociologists using this perspective, they have also generated sharp criticisms of this male-focused work. In particular, feminist sociologists interested in the question of working-class girls' resistance have been both influenced by and critical of the work of Willis. As we saw in the first chapter, Wills's study of working-class boys, *Learning to Labour,* made an immediate impact on critical educational theory, and particularly on critical ethnographic studies of schools. However, despite its originality and richness, it shared the weakness of earlier studies in its exclusive examination of the public subcultures of young men. This exclusive interest in men and a subsequent (sometimes subtle, and sometimes not) definition of male counterculture as working-class culture evoked a feminist response, both in the form of critiques of Willis and also in the sociological investigation of working-class girls' experiences and subcultures on the part of feminist sociologists (McRobbie, 1980; Acker, 1981).

The feminist critique of Willis centers around two general points. First is the fundamental question of the reliability of descriptions of working-class culture by male sociologists. The question raised here is whether Willis has given weight to certain aspects of that culture because of his own ideological valuing of male actions. That is, does Willis, in common with other male sociologists, "see" male activities and spheres as significant, but remain "blind" to the significance of female spheres. This criticism follows the line of argument of feminist anthropologists who have critiqued male anthropologists for their own form of male ethnocentrism (Reiter, 1975).

The second feminist criticism of Willis's work highlights his failure to address the sexist oppression inherent in male working-class culture. As McRobbie puts it:

> Shopfloor culture may have develped a toughness and resilience to deal with the brutality of capitalist productive relations, but these same "values" can be used internally. . . . They can also be used, and often are, against women and girls in the form of both wife and girlfriend battering. A fully *sexed* notion of working class culture would have to consider such features more centrally. (1980, p. 41)

Thus a failure to recognize the oppressive sexism of male subcultures and an acceptance of the absence of girls in these subcultures are clearly inter-related. In fact, of course, the boys' own sexism reproduces the role of girls in working-class culture as oppressed and subordinate.

While these relationships may in some sense reflect a logic of capitalism, it is not the ideology or state policies of capitalism that directly pressures these working-class girls, but rather the immediate and oppressive sexism of working-class boys. As we will see, feminists argue that the moral failure to condemn or even to see the sexism of male subcultures leads in turn to a fail-ure to understand the full dynamics of working-class culture and life.

In response to this feminist critique of Willis and other male work on boys' public subcultures, feminists have turned to an examination of girls' antisocial and counter-school groups. While studies of girls' subcultures are still relatively few in comparison to studies of boys', McRobbie, Fuller and others in Eng-land, and Thomas in Australia have contributed ethnographic studies that raise new questions about the intersection of gender, race, and class in the lives of working-class girls.

Studies of white working-class girls have been undertaken by McRobbie and her associates at the Centre for Contemporary Cultural Studies in Eng-land and by Thomas in Australia. These studies have been deeply influenced by the cultural production theories of Willis and others at the CCCS and pro-vide an alternative approach to similar problems. McRobbie worked with a group of 14–16 year-old-girls at a Birmingham youth club for six months, while Thomas studied two groups of antischool or antiacademic girls—one group in a middle-class and one in a working-class school—for an academic year. In both cases, there was a clear and stated recognition that the experiences and actions of girls could not be explained solely through an analysis of class, but that, as McRobbie put it, "their culture would be linked to and partly determined by, although not mechanically so, the material position occupied by the girls in society" (1978, p. 97). Thus unlike comparable studies of male subcultures, McRobbie and Thomas begin with an awareness of the dual oppression of working-class girls through both capitalism and patriarchy. And in looking at the gender-specific nature of their oppression and their resistance, they focus on the private, domestic world of sexuality and the family as well as the public world of the street and paid work.

Both McRobbie and Thomas studied girls who rejected the values of school and official state institutions. In both cases, these girls rejected school values of propriety and behavior. They challenged dominant views of what a "proper girl" should be like by asserting the values of their own sexuality in sites where that sexuality was deemed inappropriate. Both McRobbie and Thomas emphasize the ways in which these girls use sexuality as opposition to the authority of the school or to middle-class definitions of femininity. As McRobbie comments:

> One way in which girls combat the class-based and oppressive features of the school is to assert their "femaleness," to introduce into the classroom their physical maturity in such a way as to force the teachers to take notice. A class instinct then finds expression at the level of jettisoning the official ideology for girls in the school (neatness, diligence, appliance, femininity, passivity, etc.) and replacing it with a more feminine, even sexual one. (1978, p. 104)

Thomas found that counterculture girls in opposition to school authority vacillated between aggressive defiance and an assertive and sometimes coy sexuality, particularly toward younger men teachers (Thomas, 1980, p. 148). What these girls appear to be doing, then, is using their sexuality as an act of resistance to accepted norms of female behavior. They take what society tells them is their most significant characteristic and exaggerate it as an assertion of their own individuality. Thus their aggressive use of sexuality becomes a form of power. This use of sexuality, however, is particularly true of working-class girls, and only in the context of situations defined by school or state authorities. Thomas found that antischool middle-class girls were much more likely to be immersed in the ideology of romance, and to view marriage as a way out of the boring and irrelevant world of school and the dead-end world of work (Thomas, 1980, p. 152). And working-class girls, although they would flaunt their sexuality in such sites as schools, were in fact very cautious in entering into sexual relationships, since they were very much aware of the dangers of becoming labeled "loose" in the context of their own working-class culture.

This attitude toward sexuality among working-class girls is supported by Wilson's study of "delinquent" or "semi-delinquent" girls in a northern England working-class community (Wilson, 1978). She found that girls categorized themselves into three groups based on sexual activity—virgins, one-man girls, and lays. Most of the girls categorized themselves as one-man girls, which meant they engaged in sex, but with an ideology of romance and the intention of marriage. For them, marriage seemed the only possible future. Thomas points out that in the groups of antischool girls she studied, working-class girls, although committed to marriage and in particular to motherhood, had far fewer illusions about what married life would be like. Middle-class girls, on the other hand, were immersed in an ideology of heterosexual romance (Thomas, 1980, p. 152). In fact, for working-class girls with no education and no skills, marriage is virtually an economic necessity. Thus what the girls have to oppose to the dominant-class culture and ideology of the school and the state is the assertion of their own exploited and submissive role in working-class culture. Just as Willis's lads emphasize their masculinity as manual workers and thus end up in dead-end and exploited unskilled jobs, so these girls emphasize their femininity in a traditional sense and end up exploited both in their unpaid labor in the home as well as in the marginal and low-paying jobs they can get as waged workers. As Thomas comments:

> In this way, counter-school youth subcultures serve to reproduce working-class culture in the new generation; by providing a vehicle for the expression of opposition to the school's central academic purpose, they help to ensure the perpetuation of a voluntary labouring class under capitalism. (1980, p. 131)

In the case of girls, this reproduction is achieved not only through the conflict of class cultures, but within the context of patriarchal definitions of sexuality and exploitative sexual relationships that *appear* to provide girls with their only source of personal power.

Feminists have argued that a definition of working-class culture that only considers the public world of paid labor and public sites such as the pub or the street corner in fact ignores the domestic world of unpaid labor, sexuality, and childcare that is found in the private world of the family. They call for studies of girls and women that can reveal the ways in which their lives reflect the forces of production and reproduction and the ways in which they experience the social world and negotiate within it. Such studies should reveal the ways in which women's lives also reflect and are shaped by the forces of production and reproduction in different configurations but just as powerfully as men. In this way, a more complete picture of working-class culture and of the process that Willis calls cultural production would be illuminated. Such studies would approach both public and private sites, definitions of work that include both waged and nonwaged work, and an analysis of sexuality and deep human needs as they are mediated in all aspects of class culture, for both men and women.

In order to understand the totality of working-class life both for men and women it is necessary to realize that culture is produced in *both* public and private sites and that social relationships, the production of culture, and the values given to both work and individual experience are profoundly influenced by both capitalism and patriarchy in both sites. This is not to argue that the public and private are unrelated. Quite the contrary. They are deeply related and intertwined as they make up a whole cultural world. But because boys and girls, men and women, are associated in sometimes very rigid ways with one sphere or the other, they work out individual and collective cultural responses that are quite different, though at the same time complementary. The central argument here is that to ignore the cultural world of women is to distort any understanding of the *totality* of working-class culture or resistance. A focus solely on the public male world of waged work and public oppositional culture is inadequate to come to grips with the ways in which the logics of both capitalism and patriarchy structure the individual experiences of working-class men and women and their common class culture as well as their separate men's and women's cultures.

The emphasis on the production of meaning and culture in public and private sites is, I think, instructive when we turn back to the question of schooling and the nature of the resistance of girls to the school. As both McRobbie and Thomas make clear, while the official ideology of schooling for girls sometimes reinforces the messages of working-class culture, at other times it is in opposition to that culture. But the working-class girls studied by McRobbie and Thomas fall back on an exaggerated form of the definitions of gender from wider working-class culture (as well as the ideological messages of the dominant culture as expressed in advertisements and the media). Their resistance thus simply embeds them more deeply in the culture of domination and submission, of double work, both waged and nonwaged.

The concept of resistance is used by McRobbie and Thomas to address the complexity of class and gender experience of working-class girls. But that concept is also useful in examining the nature of race and its relation to gender and class. The work of Fuller is particularly interesting in raising questions about the nature and implications of girls' resistance. Fuller studied groups of Afro-Caribbean, Indo-Pakistani, and white British girls in a London comprehensive school (Fuller, 1980; 1983). By making the category of race central to her work, she brings the realities of racism and the need to consider racial identity as well as gender and class position into her work in a fundamental way.[6]

Thus the question of cultural production and resistance takes on a more complex meaning, since these girls have to negotiate structures of what Amos and Parmar have called "triple oppression" (Amos and Parmar, 1981). Fuller explores the strategies these girls of color employ to try to gain some control over their lives. She points to three areas of control that emerged from her observation and interviews with these girls: "Firstly, their being controlled by others in and out of school; secondly, their wish for control for themselves at some time in the future; and lastly (and perhaps paradoxically) their need to exercise forms of self-control and resentment now in order to achieve self-determination later" (1983, p. 127). While Fuller has been influenced by the work of Willis and male sociological theorists of resistance, her work is more concerned with the ways in which girls, both individually and collectively, make sense of and try to negotiate oppressive social relationships and structures in order to gain more control over their own lives.

Fuller's work calls into question certain qualities of the concept of resistance that are relatively unquestioned in work that has focused on counter-school girls' subcultures. Basic to Fuller's analysis is the idea that critical understanding (what Willis would call "penetration") and the formation of an oppositional subcultural view of society is not necessarily tied to public antiauthority and counter-school groups. Instead, she argues in the case of black British girls in particular that they can combine a critical view of schools with an ability to manipulate and succeed within the school system of examinations and certification. She sees these girls' ability to combine two apparently contradictory perspectives as the result of their own social identities as black girls in a racist and sexist society. In their negotiation of these double or triple forms of oppression, the girls create complex responses. As Fuller points out:

> Indeed in regard to many aspects of their current and likely future lives some of the fifth-year girls were markedly *more* critical and politically sophisticated than most of the boys. Yet in terms of overt "symptoms" within the school the girls' opposition to what was actually and what in the future they thought was likely to be happening to them, did not come across as obviously oppositional or troublesome in the terms that others describe "troublesome" male pupils. (1983, p. 125)

Thus while the black girls were conscious of the racism and sexism they faced, they did not express that criticism as opposition to the school and the system of certification that the school represented. Instead, they overtly conformed to school mores (although in a way that was often on the edge of overt rejection of the rules) and more specifically saw the school as the means to resist the sexism of black British culture and the racism of white British culture. As Fuller puts it:

> I would suggest that in concentrating on pupils rather than on opposition we can get away from seeing pupils' cultural criticism as residing solely or even mainly in overt resistance to schooling. It may be that girls are too busy resisting other aspects of their life for resistance to schooling to have a high priority for them. (1983, p. 140)

Fuller argues that black girls saw the obtaining of academic qualifications as an assertion of their own sense of competence and intelligence that was denied them in black culture as girls. In her interviews, Fuller cites the girls' consciousness of and rejection of the sexist and sometimes sexually violent attitudes of black boys. In the face of this they asserted their own toughness and, in particular, their ability to work for wages and thus have a basis for their own identity and autonomy. They were also conscious of the double standard within their own families in which they were expected to do unpaid domestic work while their brothers were allowed and even expected to be out of the house. The success of black girls in state schools caused resentment among black boys, who saw this as a challenge to accepted women's roles. Here is Marcia, a black fifteen-year-old girl:

> I've always got my head in a book. I don't think they like it because they [black boys] are always commenting on it and they say, "You won't get anywhere," and sometimes I think they don't want me to learn or something like that, you know, but I spoke to my mum about it, and she said I shouldn't listen and I should keep working hard. (Fuller, 1983, p. 131)

This is not to argue that the sexism these black girls face is unique to black culture, or that they are not equally or more affected by racism. Fuller argues that it is in in fact the conjunction of these two forms of oppression along with their assertion of their value as girls and as blacks that gives them the anger and power to resist dominant definitions of themselves and to assert their own control over their futures by taking control of the educational system of certification and examinations:

> The conjunction of all these—their positive identity as black but knowledge of racial discrimination in Britain, their positive identity as female but belief that both in Britain and in the Caribbean women were often accorded less than their due status—meant that the girls were angry at the foreclosing of options available to them as blacks and as women. (Fuller, 1980, p. 57)

Fuller's work raises important issues not only for the study of resistance and cultural production, but also about the nature of subcultures in general. First of all, the combination of critical consciousness and an apparent acceptance of the official ideology of school success needs to be examined. Fuller argues that these girls have achieved a certain "penetration" of the ideology of certification, in that they consciously intend to use school examinations to gain some control over their lives. However, this might also be viewed as a form of individual accommodation to existing social conditions rather than a collective cultural pattern that can be called resistance. I think the question that is not addressed in Fuller's work concerns the nature of class in capitalist societies. By positing only race and gender as relationships of oppression, Fuller's black girls fail to critique the nature of work in class society and thus in one sense oppose one relationship of oppression to another in just the way Willis's lads do. That is, just as the lads use racial and sexual domination to assert themselves and thus obscure their own class oppression and the nature of the work that they will do, so these black girls use "success" in school and an acceptance of the dominant definitions of work in capitalism to oppose the racism and sexism they experience in both black and white culture. The individual manipulation of school and certification may allow them to oppose oppressive aspects of their own lives, but without a more political and public expression, it may be more individual accommodation than collective resistance.

The other question raised by Fuller's work is about the nature of subcultures in general. Because as we have seen girls are usually excluded from the public arena of the street, the subcultural groups they form are private and exist in the domestic sphere of the home or in friendship groups among girls. While the black boys in the school in which Fuller worked joined a wider Rastafarian culture and adopted the style and clothes of that subculture, the girls were excluded. Thus what Fuller calls a subculture in fact was based on a kind of common understanding and attitude toward both whites and boys and an assertion of a common pride in being black and female. While this common understanding was very significant as the girls struggled to assert their own autonomy and to gain some measure of control over their lives, it did not have the weight of more public male subcultures. What Fuller does not address is the need for a more public and politically conscious assertion of black women's identity and strength that could be the basis for more organized resistance. As Amos and Parmar state:

> Existing political organizations cannot always incorporate all these struggles and although we feel that as black women we should organize with other black people against the racism in this society, and as part of the working class we should organize around the issues of work and non-work, and as women we should organize with other women, as black women we also need to organize separately around the issues that are particular to our experience as black women, experiences which come out of the triple oppression we face. (1981, p. 146)

Resistance is an important concept in looking at the lives of girls and women in schools, because it highlights their ability as human agents to make meaning and to act in social situations as well as to be acted upon. However, resistance must be used with some caution and careful definition if it is to help us understand social processes. We can see some of the difficulties involved in the use of the term resistance in Anyon's work on girls in fifth-grade classrooms. Anyon's research rests on a more general and shallow study of the cultural life of younger girls. She studied one hundred students in five different schools and depended on one seemingly quite structured interview with each child. Anyon's data is rather weak in comparison with the work of Fuller, McRobbie, and Thomas, but she does raise similar issues in her theoretical discussion. Like the cultural production theorists, Anyon questions the view of ideology as complete and uncontested. Instead, she argues that girls and women do not passively accept the dominant ideology of sexism, but rather negotiate ideology and needs. She argues that "gender development involves not so much passive imprinting as active response to social contradictions" (Anyon, 1983, p. 26).

Like Fuller, Anyon questions the depiction of resistance as solely found in public antisocial or counter-school actions. Instead, and following Genovese in his work on black slavery, she argues that women employ a "simultaneous process of accommodation and resistance" in their negotiation of social relationships. However, the line between accommodation and resistance is somewhat blurred in Anyon's discussion and it is not always clear when exaggerated feminine behavior or acquiescence to school authority can be viewed as accommodation or resistance. What is lacking in this work is a more rigorous discussion of what resistance might mean in complex and overlapping relationships of domination and oppression. Because Anyon does not locate the girls she interviews in a more complete social world, she is left with a description of attitudes or actions in school and must interpret them outside of a social totality. In this use, terms like resistance and accommodation become convenient categories into which observed behavior or beliefs can be slotted. Anyon's work is frustrating in this regard. Consider, for example her analysis of this incident in one of the working-class fifth-grade classrooms she observed:

> She told me that she wanted to be a veterinarian, and that she did not want to work in a factory like her mother did. I watched her persist at her desk to do her school work as the teacher screamed at the other children and gave confusing directions, and as belligerent boys roamed the classroom. Thus, I interpret her hard work not only as an accommodation to expectations that she do what is demanded in school, but also that through this accommodation she can resist both present and future social discomfort. (Anyon, 1983, p. 41)

There is something in this picture of a hostile school world ("screaming" teacher, "belligerent" boys) and the obedient, hardworking girl that smooths over the complexity of the competing forms of social power that this girl (not to mention the teacher and boys) negotiates in order to make sense of the world and to try to assert herself. I think the problem here rests ultimately in the lack of depth in our understanding of this girl, the school, the class and gender ideology that is embodied in the texts and social relationships of the school and among school children and in the dynamics of the girl's own family. In this case, the terms accommodation and resistance feel like empty generalities that can, in fact, be applied to any social action.

Anyon does make some valuable points about the need to make "resistance" cultural and public if it is to serve as the basis for social change. Like McRobbie, McCabe, and Garber, Anyon points out that individual resistance to sexism and the negotiation of existing concepts of femininity lead to an acceptance of the status quo: "While accommodation and resistance as modes of daily activity provide most females with ways of negotiating individually felt social conflict or oppression, this individual activity of everyday life remains just that: individual, fragmented, and isolated from group effort" (Anyon, 1984, p. 45). It has been argued that the failure of girls and women to participate in public antisocial groups and activities is the result of a certain psychological tendency to turn opposition and anger inward in private, self-destructive activities. (Cloward and Piven, 1979) However, it may be that girls and women resist dominant and oppressive patriarchal values and relationships, though in different ways from men. But the question for women is how the human ability to create meaning and resist an imposed ideology can be turned to praxis and social transformation.

The recent work of Gaskell (1985) and Kessler, Ashenden, Connell, and Dowsett (1985) develops the question of women's relationships to schooling by examining the activities and choices of girls and women in particular school settings. Both of these studies argue that schools are contradictory sites for girls and women and, despite the existence of sexist texts and practices, provide the possibility of resistance to male hegemony on the part of both students and teachers. Kessler et al. argue:

> Yet the central fact, perhaps the most important point our interviews have demonstrated, is that the complex of gender inequality and patriarchal ideology is not a smoothly functioning machine. It is a mass of tensions, contradictions, and complexities that always have the potential for change. (1985, p. 47)

By looking at girls and women teachers in both a working-class public school and an elite private school, Kessler et al. show the need to analyze power relations and the intersection of family and school in each particular site. They argue that we need to understand the intersection of the family, the workplace, and the state in terms of sexual ideology and structural constraints on girls and women. Thus the struggles of elite girls will be quite different from those of working-class women teachers. To ignore class and racial difference in studying gender is to distort both the realities of their experience and the possibilities for resistance in each site.

Gaskell argues along similar lines. In studying working-class girls' course choices, Gaskell argues that girls were not simply "reproduced" by male hegemony, but that they made choices according to what their own understanding of the world was like:

> They knew, for their own good reasons, what the world was like, and their experience acted as a filter through which any new message was tested, confirmed, rejected, challenged, and reinterpreted. Changing their minds would have meant changing the world they experienced, not simply convincing them of a new set of ideals around equality of opportunity and the desirability of a different world. (1985, p. 58)

Gaskell emphasizes the need to hear the girls' own stories. She argues that reproduction theories that view women as simply the creation of male hegemony or sexist institutions obscure and fail to see the realities of women's strengths and agency.

> There is . . . a tradition in feminist scholarship that has emphasized that women's consciousness is not simply an internalization of male forms but con-

tains its own alternative interpretations, commitments and connections. . . .
The relation between women's consciousness and man's world is complex and
involves accommodation, resistance, and self-imposed and externally imposed
silences. Correspondence does not account for their relationship. (1985, p. 58)

These studies point out and analyze oppressive practices and ideology, but
at the same time insist that the schooling of girls is a complex process that contains contradictions and points of resistance which must be analyzed in each
particular historical instance.

Throughout the feminist studies of resistance and cultural production certain themes are illuminated. First is the assertion that all people have the capacity to make meaning of their lives and to resist oppression. This is expressed in
Giroux's remark that "inherent in a radical notion of resistance is an expressed
hope, an element of transcendence" (1983, p. 108). Second, that that capacity to resist and to understand is limited and influenced by class, race, and gender position. People will use the means at hand, the power that they can
employ to meet their needs and assert their humanity. This is clear in the work
of Fuller, Gaskell, and Kessler, and Ashenden, Connell, and Dowsett. Third,
as is clear from the work of Willis, McRobbie, and Thomas in particular, the
various "solutions" sought by people embedded in sexist, racist, and classist
society can lead in fact to deeper forms of domination and the oppression of
others. Willis's lads "partially penetrate" the logic of capitalism, but that
rejection leads them to a rejection of mental work and to the celebration of a
masculinity defined by sexism and racism. McRobbie's and Thomas's girls'
rejection of school ideology leads them to a definition of their own sexuality
that leads back to the oppressive sexism of working-class culture. And Fuller's
girls, in succeeding in school and gaining certification, assert their abilities and
value as black women, but accept the logic of work in capitalism. For women,
who are so often excluded from the public sphere, the question of whether
resistance can lead to change if it is only expressed in individual critique or private opposition is a very real one. And this leads back to the schools. Can
schools become a possible "public sphere" for the encouragement of resistance
and the building of a critical counter-hegemony for girls?

FEMINIST TEACHING AS COUNTER-HEGEMONY

I have argued that the concept of resistance has been used as a heuristic device
to explore the possibilities of human agency. But various theorists have argued
that we need to expand our view of agency to include not only resistance in the
form of various kinds of opposition to oppressive beliefs and practices, but also
to include more critical and politicized work in the form of organized and conscious collective oppositional actions. This kind of opposition has been called
counter-hegemony. By this is meant the creation of a self-conscious analysis of
a situation and the development of collective practices and organization that
can oppose the hegemony of the existing order and begin to build the base

for a new understanding and transformation of society. Feminist counter-hegemonic teaching has been developed and refined at the university level in a variety of women's studies programs (Bunch and Pollack, 1983; Spanier, Bloom and Borovak, 1984). In these programs both feminist theory and methods have been developed to provide a counter-hegemonic vision and critique. (Bunch, 1983; Schniedewind, 1983). Teaching in public schools, although more profoundly bounded by institutional constraints, also contains the possibility of transformative work. This does not imply that this work will be achieved without enormous and sometimes overpowering opposition. As Freire says, critical teaching in dominant institutions means that teachers are constantly living a contradiction. But possibilities for critical work exist within that very contradiction. It is vital that teachers recognize not only the structural constraints under which they work, but also the potential inherent in teaching for transformative and political work. As Connell comments:

> The doctrine that tells teachers the schools are captive to capitalism and exhorts them to get on with the revolution outside, could not be more mistaken; it is teachers' work as teachers that is central to the remaking of the social patterns investing education. (1985, p. 4)

If the work of critical teachers can be viewed as counter-hegemonic work, the latent and unarticulated resistance of students can in turn become the focus of critical teaching. As Giroux points out, "the concept of resistance highlights the need for classroom teachers to decipher how modes of cultural production displayed by subordinate groups can be analyzed to reveal both their limits and their possibilities for enabling critical thinking, analytic discourse, and new modes of intellectual appropriation" (1983, p. 111). Thus the ability of students to resist the forms of subcultural resistance become the focus of critical teaching, which can be part of the creation of a counter-hegemony.

As several feminist educational theorists have argued, the schools can provide the site for feminist teachers to raise issues of sexism and gender oppression. Kelly and Nihlen, for example, mention the potential significance of the women's movement in legitimating an alternative vision of gender. As they comment, "It well may be—and more research is needed—that the presence of a woman's movement provides a means of making resistance 'count' and sets the tenor for the renegotiation of knowledge within the classroom" (1982, p. 176). McRobbie and Garber have argued along the same lines that the school can be a progressive force if it can serve as a site for feminist teachers to introduce the ideas of the women's movement to girls and to open up a discussion of the structural limitations and oppression they face (McRobbie, 1978, p. 102). Kessler et al. argue the need to "democratize the curriculum by reorganizing knowledge to advantage the disadvantaged; and to mobilize support for democratization of the schools in relation to gender, as much as other structures of power" (1985, p. 46).

This view of teaching as critical work leads us to see the resistance of students as an important basis for the building of a counter-hegemony, as teachers and students together struggle to understand the forces acting upon their lives. Many feminists have argued that feminist teaching can contribute to the building of this alternative vision of social reality and morality (Hartsock, 1979; Lather, 1984). The outline of this kind of argument can be found in the work of Lather (1984). Lather's work has focused on the impact of feminism and women's studies courses on the education of teachers. She has argued that while male critical educational theorists speak of the need for critical teaching, they have overlooked the power of feminism to challenge the status quo through the creation of women's studies courses and critiques of sexist texts and practices. Looking back to Gramsci for a theoretical perspective to understand the work of feminist teachers, she argues that his call for a progressive social group who can create what he calls a new historical bloc can be found in the women's movement.

> Adopting gender as a basic analytic tool will enable critical theory to see what is right under its nose: the possibilities for fundamental social changes that open up when we put women at the center of our transformation. (Lather, 1984, p. 52)

In Gramsci's view, revolutionary theory had to be grounded in the struggles of everyday life. Lather argues that feminist theory and the women's movement are grounded in precisely these struggles to make the personal political. A critical, materialist feminism could illuminate these relationships of personal and public and begin to create a new politics that would be truly revolutionary. Lather applies the Gramscian concept of counter-hegemony to this feminist work. She emphasizes the difference between counter-hegemony and the more commonly used term of *resistance*. *Resistance* is "usually informal, disorganized, and apolitical," but *counter-hegemony* implies a more critical theoretical understanding and is expressed in organized and active political opposition. As Lather defines it:

> The task of counter-hegemonic groups is the development of counter-institutions, ideologies, and cultures that provide an ethical alternative to the dominant hegemony, a lived experience of how the world can be different. (1984, p. 55)

While the starting point of counter-hegemonic work is the world of students, both their oppression and their opposition, it must move beyond that point to provide more democratic relationships, an alternative value system and a critique of existing society.[7]

While feminist teaching has focused on gender oppression, we need to remember that feminists in teaching and outside of it tend to be middle class and white. Thus although they share with working-class girls the common oppression of being female in a patriarchal and sexist society, they are divided from them by class and, in the case of girls of color, by race as well. Nonetheless, the work of conscious feminists *is* important in building counter-hegemony; schools can be sites for critical teaching and work in specific sites and under certain conditions. What we need to do is to be very clear about the specific meanings of class, race, and gender for people in differing relationships of control and power in a society dominated by capitalism, racism, and patriarchy. We need to locate ourselves in these complex webs of relationships and then attempt to act at whatever sites we find ourselves, in ways that will encourage both resistance to oppression and the building of a counter-hegemony through critical understanding.

REFERENCES

Acker, Sandra. No-woman's land: British sociology of education 1960–1979. *The Sociological Review* (1981) 29, 1.

Amos, Valerie and Parmar, Pratibha. Resistances and responses: The experiences of black girls in Britain. In Angela McRobbie and Trisha McCabe, eds., *Feminism for girls.* London and Boston: Routledge and Kegan Paul, 1981.

Anyon, Jean. Intersections of gender and class: Accommodation and resistance by working class and affluent females to contradictory sex-role ideologies. *Journal of Education* (1984) 166, 1, 25–48.

Arnot, Madeleine. Male hegemony, social class and women's education. *Journal of Education* (1982) 164, 1, 64–89.

Barrett, Michele. *Women's oppression today.* London: Virago Press, 1980.

Bunch, Charlotte. Not by degrees: Feminist theory and education. In Charlotte Bunch and Sandra Pollack, eds. *Learning our way.* Trumansburg, N.Y.: Crossing Press, 1983.

Bunch, Charlotte and Pollack, Sandra, eds. *Learning our way.* Trumansburg, N.Y.: Crossing Press. 1983.

Cloward, Richard and Piven, Frances Fox. Hidden protest: The channeling of female innovation and resistance. *Signs* (1979) 4, 4, 651–669.

Connell, R. W. *Teachers' work.* London: George Allen and Unwin, 1985.

Connell, R. W., Dowsett, G. W., Kessler, S., and Aschenden, D. J. *Making the difference.* Boston: Allen and Unwin, 1982.

Davies, Lynn. Gender, resistance and power. In Stephen Walker and Len Barton, eds. *Gender class and education.* Lewes, Sussex: The Falmer Press, 1983.

Deem, Rosemary. *Women and schooling.* London and Boston: Routledge and Kegan Paul, 1978.

Ehrenreich, Barbara. Life without father: Reconsidering socialist-feminist theory. *Socialist Review* (Jan.–Feb., 1984) 73, 48–58.

Eisenstein, Zillah. ed. *Capitalist patriarchy and the case for socialist feminism.* New York and London: Monthly Review Press, 1979.

———. Qualified criticism, critical qualifications. In Jane Purvis and Margaret Hales. *Achievement and inequality in education.* London: Routledge and Kegan Paul, 1983.

Fuller, Mary. Black girls in a London comprehensive school. In Rosemary Deem, ed. Schooling for women's work. London and Boston: Routledge and Kegan Paul, 1980.

———. Qualified criticism, critical qualifications. In Jane Purvis and Margaret Hales. *Achievement and inequality in education.* London: Routledge and Kegan Paul, 1983.

Gaskell, Jane. Course enrollment in the high school: The perspective of working class females. *Sociology of Education* (1985) 58, 1, 48–59.

Giroux, Henry. *Theory, resistance, and education.* South Hadley, Mass.: Bergin and Garvey, 1983.

Hartsock, Nancy. Feminist theory and the development of revolutionary strategy. In Zillah Eisenstein, ed. *Capitalist patriarchy and the case for socialist feminism.* London and New York: Monthly Review Press, 1979.

Hartmann, Heidi. The unhappy marriage of socialism and feminism. In Lydia Sargent, ed. *Women and Revolution.* Boston: South End Press, 1981.

Jagger, Alison. *Feminist theory and human nature.* Sussex: Harvester Press, 1983.

Kelly, Gayle and Nihlen, Ann. Schooling and the reproduction of patriarchy: Unequal workloads, unequal rewards. In Michael Apple, ed. *Cultural and economic reproduction in education.* London and Boston: Routledge and Kegan Paul, 1982.

Kessler, S., Ashenden, R., Connell, R., and Dowsett, G. Gender relations in secondary schooling. *Sociology of Education* (1985) 58, 1, 34–48.

Kuhn, Annette and Wolpe, AnnMarie, eds. *Feminism and materialism.* London and Boston: Routledge and Kegan Paul, 1978.

Lather, Patti. Critical theory, curricular transformation and feminist mainstreaming. *Journal of Education* (1984) 166, 1, 49–62.

McRobbie, Angela. Working class girls and the culture of femininity. In Centre for Contemporary Cultural Studies Women's Group. *Women take issue.* London: Hutchison, 1978.

———. Settling accounts with subcultures. *Screen Education* (1980) 34, 37–51.

Reiter, Rayna, ed. *Toward an anthropology of women.* New York and London: Monthly Review Press, 1975.

Rowbotham, Sheila, Segal, Lynne, and Wainwright, Hilary. *Beyond the fragments: Feminism and the making of socialism.* Boston: Alyson Publications, 1981.

Rubin, Gayle. The traffic in women: Notes on the political economy of sex. In Rayna Reiter, ed. *Toward an anthropology of women.* New York and London: Monthly Review Press, 1975.

Schniedewind, Nancy. Feminist values: Guidelines for teaching methodology in women's studies. In Charlotte Bunch and Sandra Pollack, eds. Learning our way: Essays in feminist education. Trumansburg, N.Y.: Crossing Press, 1983.

Spanier, Bonnie, Bloom, Alex, and Boroviak, Darlene. *Toward a balanced curriculum.* Cambridge, Mass.: Schenkman Publishing Company, 1984.

Tax, Meredith. Learning how to bake. *Socialist Review* (Jan.–Feb. 1984) 73, 36–41.

Thomas, Claire. Girls and counter-school culture. *Melbourne Working Papers.* Melbourne, 1980.

Wilson, Deirdre. Sexual codes and conduct: A study of teenage girls. In Carol Smart and Barry Smart, eds. *Women, sexuality and social control.* London and Boston: Routledge and Kegan Paul, 1978.

Wolpe, AnnMarie. Education and the sexual division of labour. In Annette Kuhn and AnnMarie Wolpe, eds. *Feminism and materialism.* Boston and London: Routledge and Kegan Paul, 1978.

Women's Study Group. *Women take issue.* London: CCCS/Hutchison, 1978.

NOTES

1. See Jagger (1983) for the clearest and most accessible discussion of the differences among radical feminism, liberal feminism, and socialist feminism in terms of feminist theory in general.
2. Significant examples of this approach are Frazier and Sadker (1973); Levy (1974); Chetwynd and Harnett (1978); Byrne (1978); and Delamont (1980). See Acker (1982) for an overview of various feminist approaches to the question of the relationship of gender and schooling from the perspective of the early 1980s, particularly with reference to British studies.
3. Feminist inquiry into the relation of gender and schooling has continued in recent British works which have addressed the existence of sex bias in schools and have begun to focus on potential strategies to redress those practices from a variety of theoretical perspectives. *Girl-friendly schooling* (1985), a selection of papers from the 1984 conference on girl-friendly schooling, provides both studies of sexist practices and discussions of feminist intervention and policy suggestions. Weiner's *Just a bunch of girls* (1985) contributes a valuable perspective on race that has been missing from most accounts. Mahony's *Schools for the boys* (1985) presents a powerful indictment of co-education from a radical feminist perspective. Like Walkerdine (1981) Mahony raises significant questions about the nature of male sexual power and privilege that have not been adequately addressed in either liberal or socialist feminist studies.
4. Representative theorists in this tradition are Barrett (1980); David (1980); Deem (1978; 1980); Kelly and Nihlen (1982); and Wolpe (1978; 1981).
5. As Mannicom has shown, this shared nurturing role of mothers and primary teachers does not necessarily lead to mutual understanding and cooperation between mothers and primary teachers, even though sexist assumptions about the "natural" nurturing qualities of women are at work in both instances. (Mannicom, 1984)
6. See also the recent articles by Brak and Mihas (1985), Foster (1985) and Riley (1985).
7. Examples of curriculum and teaching can be found that begin to bring together feminist and critical thinking. For example, a group of radical teachers at the Group School in Cambridge, Mass., created various curricula with working-class girls. This work has been published as *Changing learning, changing lives.* (Gates, Klaw, and Steinberg, 1979) These teachers used the life experiences of working-class girls to draw out themes of race, class, and gender for critical analysis. Schneidewind and Davidson have provided a feminist curriculum for public schools in *Open minds to equality* (1983). McRobbie and her associate Trisha McCabe have published *Feminism for girls,* directed at both students and teachers and youth workers. McRobbie and McCabe raise questions of the transmission of images and values through the media and texts, both in school and outside of school. Articles in this collection critique such areas as the depiction of girls in the literature curriculum, the nature of secretarial work, and the overt and hidden meanings of *Jackie,* the British equivalent of *Seventeen.* In providing analyses and critiques of sites and texts that make up the cultural world of teenage girls, McRobbie and McCabe hope to provide these girls with the kind of critical vision that will lead them to see their experiences critically as socially created and thus open to resistance and change.

Sexuality, Schooling, and Adolescent Females: The Missing Discourse of Desire

MICHELLE FINE

Since late 1986, popular magazines and newspapers have printed steamy stories about education and sexuality. Whether the controversy surrounds sex education or school-based health clinics (SBHCs), public discourses of adolescent sexuality are represented forcefully by government officials, New Right spokespersons, educators, "the public," feminists, and health-care professionals. These stories offer the authority of "facts," insights into the political controversies, and access to unacknowledged fears about sexuality (Foucault, 1980). Although the facts usually involve the adolescent female body, little has been heard from young women themselves.

This article examines these diverse perspectives on adolescent sexuality and, in addition, presents the views of a group of adolescent females. The article is informed by a study of numerous current sex education curricula, a year of negotiating for inclusion of lesbian and gay sexuality in a citywide sex education curriculum, and interviews and observations gathered in New York City sex education classrooms.[1] The analysis examines the desires, fears, and fantasies which give structure and shape to silences and voices concerning sex education and school-based health clinics in the 1980s.

Despite the attention devoted to teen sexuality, pregnancy, and parenting in this country, and despite the evidence of effective interventions and the widespread public support expressed for these interventions (Harris, 1985), the systematic implementation of sex education and SBHCs continues to be obstructed by the controversies surrounding them (Kantrowitz et al., 1987; Leo, 1986). Those who resist sex education or SBHCs often present their views as based on rationality and a concern for protecting the young. For such opponents, sex education raises questions of promoting promiscuity and immorality, and of undermining family values. Yet the language of the challenges suggests an affect substantially more profound and primitive. Gary Bauer,

Undersecretary of Education in the U.S. Department of Education, for example, constructs an image of immorality littered by adolescent sexuality and drug abuse:

> There is ample impressionistic evidence to indicate that drug abuse and promiscuity are not independent behaviors. When inhibitions fall, they collapse across the board. When people of any age lose a sense of right and wrong, the loss is not selective. . . . [T]hey are all expressions of the same ethical vacuum among many teens. . . . (1986)

Even Surgeon General C. Everett Koop, a strong supporter of sex education, recently explained: "[W]e have to be as explicit as necessary. . . . You can't talk of the dangers of snake poisoning and not mention snakes" (quoted in Leo, 1986, p. 54). Such commonly used and often repeated metaphors associate adolescent sexuality with victimization and danger.

Yet public schools have rejected the task of sexual dialogue and critique, or what has been called "sexuality education." Within today's standard sex education curricula and many public school classrooms, we find: (1) the authorized suppression of a discourse of female sexual desire; (2) the promotion of a discourse of female sexual victimization; and (3) the explicit privileging of married heterosexuality over other practices of sexuality. One finds an unacknowledged social ambivalence about female sexuality which ideologically separates the female sexual agent, or subject, from her counterpart, the female sexual victim. The adolescent woman of the 1980s is constructed as the latter. Educated primarily as the potential victim of male sexuality, she represents no subject in her own right. Young women continue to be taught to fear and defend in isolation from exploring desire, and in this context there is little possibility of their developing a critique of gender or sexual arrangements.

PREVAILING DISCOURSES OF FEMALE SEXUALITY INSIDE PUBLIC SCHOOLS

> If the body is seen as endangered by uncontrollable forces, then presumably this is a society or social group which fears change—change which it perceived simultaneously as powerful and beyond its control. (Smith-Rosenberg, 1978, p. 229)

Public schools have historically been the site for identifying, civilizing, and containing that which is considered uncontrollable. While evidence of sexuality is everywhere within public high schools—in the halls, classrooms, bathrooms, lunchrooms, and the library—official sexuality education occurs sparsely: in social studies, biology, sex education, or inside the nurse's office. To understand how sexuality is managed inside schools, I examined the major discourses of sexuality which characterize the national debates over sex education and SBHCs. These discourses are then tracked as they weave through the curricula, classrooms, and halls of public high schools.

The first discourse, *sexuality as violence,* is clearly the most conservative, and equates adolescent heterosexuality with violence. At the 1986 American Dreams Symposium on education, Phyllis Schlafly commented: "Those courses on sex, abuse, incest, AIDS, they are all designed to terrorize our children. We should fight their existence, and stop putting terror in the hearts and minds of our youngsters." One aspect of this position, shared by women as politically distinct as Schlafly and the radical feminist lawyer Catherine MacKinnon (1983), views heterosexuality as essentially violent and coercive. In its full conservative form, proponents call for the elimination of sex education and clinics and urge complete reliance on the family to dictate appropriate values, mores, and behaviors.

Sexuality as violence presumes that there is a causal relationship between official silence about sexuality and a decrease in sexual activity—therefore, by not teaching about sexuality, adolescent sexual behavior will not occur. The irony, of course, lies in the empirical evidence. Fisher, Byrne, and White (1983) have documented sex-negative attitudes and contraceptive use to be negatively correlated. In their study, sex-negative attitudes do not discourage sexual activity, but they do discourage responsible use of contraception. Teens who believe sexual involvement is wrong deny responsibility for contraception. To accept responsibility would legitimate "bad" behavior. By contrast, Fisher et al. (1983) found that adolescents with sex-positive attitudes tend to be both more consistent and more positive about contraceptive use. By not teaching about sexuality, or by teaching sex-negative attitudes, schools apparently will not forestall sexual activity, but may well discourage responsible contraception.

The second discourse, *sexuality as victimization,* gathers a much greater following. Female adolescent sexuality is represented as a moment of victimization in which the dangers of heterosexuality for adolescent women (and, more recently, of homosexuality for adolescent men) are prominent. While sex may not be depicted as inherently violent, young women (and today, men) learn of their vulnerability to potential male predators.

To avoid being victimized, females learn to defend themselves against disease, pregnancy, and "being used." The discourse of victimization supports sex education, including AIDS education, with parental consent. Suggested classroom activities emphasize "saying no," practicing abstinence, enumerating the social and emotional risks of sexual intimacy, and listing the possible diseases associated with sexual intimacy. The language, as well as the questions asked and not asked, represents females as the actual and potential victims of male desire. In exercises, role plays, and class discussions, girls practice resistance to trite lines, unwanted hands, opened buttons, and the surrender of other "bases" they are not prepared to yield. The discourses of violence and victimization both portray males as potential predators and females as victims. Three problematic assumptions underlie these two views:

—First, female subjectivity, including the desire to engage in sexual
activity, is placed outside the prevailing conversation (Vance, 1984).

—Second, both arguments present female victimization as contingent
upon unmarried heterosexual involvement—rather than inherent in
existing gender, class, and racial arrangements (Rubin, 1984). While
feminists have long fought for the legal and social acknowledgment of
sexual violence against women, most have resisted the claim that
female victimization hinges primarily upon sexual involvement with
men. The full range of victimization of women—at work, at home, on
the streets—has instead been uncovered. The language and emotion
invested in these two discourses divert attention away from structures,
arrangements, and relationships which oppress women in general, and
low-income women and women of color in particular (Lorde, 1980).

—Third, the messages, while narrowly anti-sexual, nevertheless buttress
traditional heterosexual arrangements. These views assume that as long
as females avoid premarital sexual relations with men, victimization
can be avoided. Ironically, however, protection from male victimization is available primarily through marriage—by coupling with a man.
The paradoxical message teaches females to fear the very men who will
ultimately protect them.

The third discourse, *sexuality as individual morality,* introduces explicit
notions of sexual subjectivity for women. Although quite judgmental and
moralistic, this discourse values women's sexual decisionmaking as long as
the decisions made are for premarital abstinence. For example, Secretary of
Education William Bennett urges schools to teach "morality literacy" and to
educate towards "modesty," "chastity," and "abstinence" until marriage. The
language of self-control and self-respect reminds students that sexual immorality breeds not only personal problems but also community tax burdens.

The debate over morality in sex education curricula marks a clear contradiction among educational conservatives over whether and how the state may
intervene in the "privacy of families." Non-interventionists, including Schlafly
and Onalee McGraw, argue that educators should not teach about sexuality at
all. To do so is to take a particular moral position which subverts the family.
Interventionists, including Koop, Bennett, and Bauer, argue that schools
should teach about sexuality by focusing on "good values," but disagree about
how. Koop proposes open discussion of sexuality and the use of condoms,
while Bennett advocates "sexual restraint" ("Koop's AIDS Stand Assailed,"
1987). Sexuality in this discourse is posed as a test of self-control; individual
restraint triumphs over social temptation. Pleasure and desire for women as
sexual subjects remain largely in the shadows, obscured from adolescent eyes.

The fourth discourse, a *discourse of desire,* remains a whisper inside the official work of U.S. public schools. If introduced at all, it is as an interruption of

the ongoing conversation (Snitow, Stansell, & Thompson, 1983). The naming of desire, pleasure, or sexual entitlement, particularly for females, barely exists in the formal agenda of public schooling on sexuality. When spoken, it is tagged with reminders of "consequences"—emotional, physical, moral, reproductive, and/or financial (Freudenberg, 1987). A genuine discourse of desire would invite adolescents to explore what feels good and bad, desirable and undesirable, grounded in experiences, needs, and limits. Such a discourse would release females from a position of receptivity, enable an analysis of the dialectics of victimization and pleasure, and would pose female adolescents as subjects of sexuality, initiators as well as negotiators (Golden, 1984; Petchesky, 1984; Thompson, 1983).

In Sweden, where sex education has been offered in schools since the turn of the century, the State Commission on Sex Education recommends teaching students to "acquire a knowledge . . . [which] will equip them to experience sexual life as a source of happiness and joy in fellowship with other [people]" (Brown, 1983, p. 88). The teachers' handbook goes on, "The many young people who wish to wait [before initiating sexual activity] and those who have had early sexual relations should experience, in class, [the feeling] that they are understood and accepted" (p. 93). Compare this to an exercise suggested in a major U.S. metropolitan sex education curriculum: "Discuss and evaluate: things which may cause teenagers to engage in sexual relations before they are ready to assume the responsibility of marriage" (see Philadelphia School District, 1986; and New York City Board of Education, 1984).

A discourse of desire, though seldom explored in U.S. classrooms, does occur in less structured school situations. The following excerpts, taken from group and individual student interviews, demonstrate female adolescents' subjective experiences of body and desire as they begin to articulate notions of sexuality.

In some cases young women pose a critique of marriage:

> I'm still in love with Simon, but I'm seeing Jose. He's OK but he said, "Will you be my girl?" I hate that. It feels like they own you. Like I say to a girlfriend, "What's wrong? You look terrible!" and she says, "I'm married!" (Millie, a 16-year-old student from the Dominican Republic)

In other cases they offer stories of their own victimization:

> It's not like last year. Then I came to school regular. Now my old boyfriend, he waits for me in front of my building every morning and he fights with me. Threatens me, gettin' all bad. . . . I want to move out of my house and live 'cause he ain't gonna stop no way. (Sylvia, age 17, about to drop out of twelfth grade)

Some even speak of desire:

> I'm sorry I couldn't call you last night about the interview, but my boyfriend came back from [the] Navy and I wanted to spend the night with him, we

don't get to see each other much. (Shandra, age 17, after a no-show for an interview)

In a context in which desire is not silenced, but acknowledged and discussed, conversations with adolescent women can, as seen here, educate through a dialectic of victimization and pleasure. Despite formal silencing, it would be misleading to suggest that talk of desire never emerges within public schools. Notwithstanding a political climate organized around the suppression of this conversation, some teachers and community advocates continue to struggle for an empowering sex education curriculum both in and out of the high school classroom.

Family life curricula and/or plans for a school-based health clinic have been carefully generated in many communities. Yet they continue to face loud and sometimes violent resistance by religious and community groups, often from outside the district lines (Boffey, 1987; "Chicago School Clinic," 1986; Dowd, 1986; Perlez, 1986a, 1986b; Rohter, 1985). In other communities, when curricula or clinics have been approved with little overt confrontation, monies for training are withheld. For example, in New York City in 1987, $1.7 million was initially requested to implement training on the Family Life education curriculum. As sex educators confronted community and religious groups, the inclusion of some topics as well as the language of others were continually negotiated. Ultimately, the Chancellor requested only $600,000 for training, a sum substantially inadequate to the task.[2]

In this political context many public school educators nevertheless continue to take personal and professional risks to create materials and foster classroom environments which speak fully to the sexual subjectivities of young women and men. Some operate within the privacy of their classrooms, subverting the official curriculum and engaging students in critical discussion. Others advocate publicly for enriched curricula and training. A few have even requested that community-based advocates *not* agitate for official curricular change, so "we [teachers] can continue to do what we do in the classroom, with nobody looking over our shoulders. You make a big public deal of this, and it will blow open."[3] Within public school classrooms, it seems that female desire may indeed be addressed when educators act subversively. But in the typical sex education classroom, silence, and therefore distortion, surrounds female desire.

The blanketing of female sexual subjectivity in public school classrooms, in public discourse, and in bed will sound familiar to those who have read Luce Irigaray (1980) and Hélène Cixous (1981). These French feminists have argued that expressions of female voice, body, and sexuality are essentially inaudible when the dominant language and ways of viewing are male. Inside the hegemony of what they call The Law of the Father, female desire and pleasure can gain expression only in the terrain already charted by men (see also Burke, 1980). In the public school arena, this constriction of what is called sexuality allows girls one primary decision—to say yes or no—to a question not necessarily their own. A discourse of desire in which young women have a voice would be informed and generated out of their own socially constructed sexual meanings. It is to these expressions that we now turn.

THE BODIES OF FEMALE ADOLESCENTS: VOICES AND STRUCTURED SILENCES

If four discourses can be distinguished among the many positions articulated by various "authorities," the sexual meanings voiced by female adolescents defy such classification. A discourse of desire, though absent in the "official" curriculum, is by no means missing from the lived experiences or commentaries of young women. This section introduces their sexual thoughts, concerns, and meanings, as represented by a group of Black and Latina female adolescents—students and dropouts from a public high school in New York City serving predominantly low-income youths. In my year at this comprehensive high school I had frequent opportunity to speak with adolescents and listen to them talk about sex. The comments reported derive from conversations between the young women and their teachers, among themselves, and with me, as researcher. During conversations, the young women talked freely about fears and, in the same breath, asked about passions. Their struggle to untangle issues of gender, power, and sexuality underscores the fact that, for them, notions of sexual negotiation cannot be separated from sacrifice and nurturance.

The adolescent female rarely reflects simply on sexuality. Her sense of sexuality is informed by peers, culture, religion, violence, history, passion, authority, rebellion, body, past and future, and gender and racial relations of power (Espin, 1984; Omolade, 1983). The adolescent woman herself assumes a dual consciousness—at once taken with the excitement of actual/anticipated sexuality and consumed with anxiety and worry. While too few safe spaces exist for adolescent women's exploration of sexual subjectivities, there are all too many dangerous spots for their exploitation.

Whether in a classroom, on the street, at work, or at home, the adolescent female's sexuality is negotiated by, for, and despite the young woman herself. Patricia, a young Puerto Rican woman who worried about her younger sister, relates: "You see, I'm the love child and she's the one born because my mother was raped in Puerto Rico. Her father's in jail now, and she feels so bad about the whole thing so she acts bad." For Patricia, as for the many young women who have experienced and/or witnessed sexual violence, discussions of sexuality merge representations of passion with violence. Often the initiator of conversation among peers about virginity, orgasm, "getting off," and pleasure, Patricia mixed sexual talk freely with references to force and violence. She is a poignant narrator who illustrates, from the female adolescent's perspective, that sexual victimization and desire coexist (Benjamin, 1983).

Sharlene and Betty echo this braiding of danger and desire. Sharlene explained: "Boys always be trying to get into my panties," and Betty added: "I don't be needin' a man who won't give me no pleasure but take my money and expect me to take care of him." This powerful commentary on gender relations, voiced by Black adolescent females, was inseparable from their views of sexuality. To be a woman was to be strong, independent, and reliable—but not too independent for fear of scaring off a man.

Deidre continued this conversation, explicitly pitting male fragility against female strength: "Boys in my neighborhood ain't wrapped so tight. Got to be careful how you treat them. . . ." She reluctantly admitted that perhaps it is more important for Black males than females to attend college, "Girls and women, we're stronger, we take care of ourselves. But boys and men, if they don't get away from the neighborhood, they end up in jail, on drugs or dead . . . or wack [crazy]."

These young women spoke often of anger at males, while concurrently expressing a strong desire for male attention: "I dropped out 'cause I fell in love, and couldn't stop thinking of him." An equally compelling desire was to protect young males—particularly Black males—from a system which "makes them wack." Ever aware of the ways that institutional racism and the economy have affected Black males, these young women seek pleasure but also offer comfort. They often view self-protection as taking something away from young men. Lavanda offered a telling example: "If I ask him to use a condom, he won't feel like a man."

In order to understand the sexual subjectivities of young women more completely, educators need to reconstruct schooling as an empowering context in which we listen to and work with the meanings and experiences of gender and sexuality revealed by the adolescents themselves. When we refuse that responsibility, we prohibit an education which adolescents wholly need and deserve. My classroom observations suggest that such education is rare.

Ms. Rosen, a teacher of a sex education class, opened one session with a request: "You should talk to your mother or father about sex before you get involved." Nilda initiated what became an informal protest by a number of Latino students: "Not our parents! We tell them one little thing and they get crazy. My cousin got sent to Puerto Rico to live with her religious aunt, and my sister got beat 'cause my father thought she was with a boy." For these adolescents, a safe space for discussion, critique, and construction of sexualities was not something they found in their homes. Instead, they relied on school, the spot they chose for the safe exploration of sexualities.

The absence of safe spaces for exploring sexuality affects all adolescents. It was paradoxical to realize that perhaps the only students who had an in-school opportunity for critical sexual discussion in the comfort of peers were the few students who had organized the Gay and Lesbian Association (GALA) at the high school. While most lesbian, gay, or bisexual students were undoubtedly closeted, those few who were "out" claimed this public space for their display and for their sanctuary. Exchanging support when families and peers would offer little, GALA members worried that so few students were willing to come out, and that so many suffered the assaults of homophobia individually. The gay and lesbian rights movement had powerfully affected these youngsters, who were comfortable enough to support each other in a place not considered very safe—a public high school in which echoes of "faggot!" fill the halls.

In the absence of an education which explores and unearths danger and desire, sexuality education classes typically provide little opportunity for discussions beyond those constructed around superficial notions of male heterosexuality (see Kelly, 1986, for a counterexample). Male pleasure is taught, albeit as biology. Teens learn about "wet dreams" (as the onset of puberty for males), "erection" (as the preface to intercourse), and "ejaculation" (as the act of inseminating). Female pleasures and questions are far less often the topic of discussion. Few voices of female sexual agency can be heard. The language of victimization and its underlying concerns—"Say No," put a brake on his sexuality, don't encourage—ultimately deny young women the right to control their own sexuality by providing no access to a legitimate position of sexual subjectivity. Often conflicted about self-representation, adolescent females spend enormous amounts of time trying to "save it," "lose it," convince others that they have lost or saved it, or trying to be "discreet" instead of focusing their energies in ways that are sexually autonomous, responsible, and pleasurable. In classroom observations, girls who were heterosexually active rarely spoke, for fear of being ostracized (Fine, 1986). Those who were heterosexual virgins had the same worry. And most students who were gay, bisexual, or lesbian remained closeted, aware of the very real dangers of homophobia.

Occasionally, the difficult and pleasurable aspects of sexuality were discussed together, coming either as an interruption, or because an educational context was constructed. During a social studies class, for example, Catherine, the proud mother of two-year-old Tiffany, challenged an assumption underlying the class discussion—that teen motherhood devastates mother and child; "If I didn't get pregnant I would have continued on a downward path, going nowhere. They say teenage pregnancy is bad for you, but it was good for me. I know I can't mess around now, I got to worry about what's good for Tiffany and for me."

Another interruption came from Opal, a young Black student. Excerpts from her hygiene class follow.

Teacher: Let's talk about teenage pregnancy.
Opal: How come girls in the locker room say, "You a virgin?" and if you say "Yeah" they laugh and say "Ohh, you're a virgin. . . ." And some Black teenagers, I don't mean to be racial, when they get ready to tell their mothers they had sex, some break on them and some look funny. My friend told her mother and she broke all the dishes. She told her mother so she could get protection so she don't get pregnant.

Teacher: When my 13-year-old (relative) asked for birth control
I was shocked and angry.
Portia: Mothers should help so she can get protection and not get
pregnant or diseases. So you was wrong.
Teacher: Why not say "I'm thinking about having sex?"
Portia: You tell them after, not before, having sex but before pregnancy.
Teacher (now angry): Then it's a fait accompli and you expect my
compassion? You have to take more responsibility.
Portia: I am! If you get pregnant after you told your mother and you
got all the stuff and still get pregnant, you the fool. Take up hygiene
and learn. Then it's my responsibility if I end up pregnant. . . .

Field Note, October 23, Hygiene Class

Two days later, the discussion continued.

Teacher: What topics should we talk about in sex education?
Portia: Organs, how they work.
Opal: What's an orgasm?
[laughter]
Teacher: Sexual response, sensation all over the body. What's
analogous to the male penis on the female?
Theo: Clitoris.
Teacher: Right, go home and look in the mirror.
Portia: She is too much!
Teacher: Why look in the mirror?
Elaine: It's yours.
Teacher: Why is it important to know what your body looks like?
Opal: You should like your body.
Teacher: You should know what it looks like when it's healthy, so
you can recognize problems like vaginal warts.

Field Note, October 25, Hygiene Class

The discourse of desire, initiated by Opal but evident only as an interruption, faded rapidly into the discourse of disease—warning about the dangers of sexuality.

It was in the spring of that year that Opal showed up pregnant. Her hygiene teacher, who was extremely concerned and involved with her students, was also quite angry with Opal: "Who is going to take care of that baby, you or your mother? You know what it costs to buy diapers and milk and afford child care?"

Opal, in conversation with me, related, "I got to leave [school] 'cause even if they don't say it, them teachers got hate in their eyes when they look at my belly." In the absence of a way to talk about passion, pleasure, danger, and responsibility, this teacher fetishized the latter two, holding the former two hostage. Because adolescent females combine these experiences in their daily lives, the separation is false, judgmental, and ultimately not very educational.

Over the year in this high school, and in other public schools since, I have observed a systematic refusal to name issues, particularly issues that caused adults discomfort. Educators often projected their discomfort onto students in the guise of "protecting" them (Fine, 1987). An example of such silencing can be seen in a (now altered) policy of the school district of Philadelphia. In 1985 a student informed me, "We're not allowed to talk about abortion in our school." Assuming this was an overstatement, I asked an administrator at the District about this practice. She explained, "That's not quite right. If a student asks a question about abortion, the teacher can define abortion, she just can't discuss it." How can definition occur without discussion, exchange, conversation, or critique unless a subtext of silencing prevails (Greene, 1986; Noddings, 1986)?

Explicit silencing of abortion has since been lifted in Philadelphia. The revised curriculum now reads:

Options for unintended pregnancy:

(a) adoption
(b) foster care
(c) single parenthood
(d) teen marriage
(e) abortion

A footnote is supposed to be added, however, to elaborate the negative consequences of abortion. In the social politics which surround public schools, such compromises are apparent across cities.

The New York City Family Life Education curriculum reads similarly (New York City Board of Education, 1984, p. 172):

List: The possible options for an unintended pregnancy. What considerations should be given in the decision on the alternatives?

—adoption
—foster care
—mother keeps baby
—elective abortion

Discuss:

—religious viewpoints on abortion
—present laws concerning abortion
—current developments in prenatal diagnosis and their implication for abortion issues
—why abortion should not be considered a contraceptive device

List: The people or community services that could provide assistance in the event of an unintended pregnancy.

Invite: A speaker to discuss alternatives to abortion; for example, a social worker from the Department of Social Services to discuss foster care.

One must be suspicious when diverse views are sought only for abortion, and not for adoption, teen motherhood, or foster care. The call to silence is easily identified in current political and educational contexts (Fine, 1987; Foucault, 1980). The silence surrounding contraception and abortion options and diversity in sexual orientations denies adolescents information and sends the message that such conversations are taboo—at home, at church, and even at school.

In contrast to these "official curricula," which allow discussion and admission of desire only as an interruption, let us examine other situations in which young women were invited to analyze sexuality across categories of the body, the mind, the heart, and of course, gender politics.

Teen Choice, a voluntary counseling program held on-site by non–Board of Education social workers, offered an instance in which the complexities of pleasure and danger were invited, analyzed, and braided into discussions of sexuality. In a small group discussion, the counselor asked of the seven ninth graders, "What are the two functions of a penis?" One student responded, "To pee!" Another student offered the second function: "To eat!" which was followed by laughter and serious discussion. The conversation proceeded as the teacher asked, "Do all penises look alike?" The students explained, "No, they are all different colors!"

The freedom to express, beyond simple right and wrong answers, enabled these young women to offer what they knew with humor and delight. This discussion ended as one student insisted that if you "jump up and down a lot, the stuff will fall out of you and you won't get pregnant," to which the social worker answered with slight exasperation that millions of sperm would have to be released for such "expulsion" to work, and that of course, it wouldn't work. In this conversation one could hear what seemed like too much experience, too little information, and too few questions asked by the students. But the discussion, which was sex-segregated and guided by the experiences and questions of the students themselves (and the skills of the social worker), enabled easy movement between pleasure and danger, safety and desire, naiveté and knowledge, and victimization and entitlement.

What is evident, then, is that even in the absence of a discourse of desire, young women express their notions of sexuality and relate their experiences. Yet, "official" discourses of sexuality leave little room for such exploration. The authorized sexual discourses define what is safe, what is taboo, and what will be silenced. This discourse of sexuality miseducates adolescent women. What results is a discourse of sexuality based on the male in search of desire and the female in search of protection. The open, coed sexuality discussions so many fought for in the 1970s have been appropriated as a forum for the primacy of male heterosexuality and the preservation of female victimization.

THE POLITICS OF FEMALE SEXUAL SUBJECTIVITIES

In 1912, an education committee explicitly argued that "scientific" sex education "should . . . keep sex consciousness and sex emotions at the minimum" (Leo, 1986). In the same era G. Stanley Hall proposed diversionary pursuits for adolescents, including hunting, music, and sports, "to reduce sex stress and tension . . . to short-circuit, transmute it and turn it on to develop the higher powers of the men [sic]" (Hall, 1914, pp. 29, 30). In 1915 Orison Marden, author of *The Crime of Silence,* chastised educators, reformers, and public health specialists for their unwillingness to speak publicly about sexuality and for relying inappropriately on parents and peers, who were deemed too ignorant to provide sex instruction (Imber, 1984; Strong, 1972). And in 1921 radical sex educator Maurice Bigelow wrote:

> Now, most scientifically-trained women seem to agree that there are no corresponding phenomena in the early pubertal life of the normal young woman who has good health (corresponding to male masturbation). A limited number of mature women, some of them physicians, report having experienced in the pubertal years localized turnescence and other disturbances which made them definitely conscious of sexual instincts. However, it should be noted that most of these are known to have had a personal history including one or more such abnormalities such as dysmenorrhea, uterine displacement, pathological ovaries, leucorrhea, tuberculosis, masturbation, neurasthenia, nymphomania, or other disturbances which are sufficient to account for local sexual stimulation. In short such women are not normal. . . . (p. 179)

In the 1950s public school health classes separated girls from boys. Girls "learned about sex" by watching films of the accelerated development of breasts and hips, the flow of menstrual blood, and then the progression of venereal disease as a result of participation in out-of-wedlock heterosexual activity.

Thirty years and a much-debated sexual revolution later (Ehrenreich, Hess, & Jacobs, 1986), much has changed. Feminism, the Civil Rights Movement, the disability and gay rights movements, birth control, legal abortion with federal funding (won and then lost), and reproductive technologies are part of these changes (Weeks, 1985). Due both to the consequences of, and the backlashes against, these movements, students today do learn about sexuality—if typically through the representations of female sexuality as inadequacy or victimization, male homosexuality as a story of predator and prey, and male heterosexuality as desire.

Young women today know that female sexual subjectivity is at least not an inherent contradiction. Perhaps they even feel it is an entitlement. Yet when public schools resist acknowledging the fullness of female sexual subjectivities, they reproduce a profound social ambivalence which dichotomizes female heterosexuality (Espin, 1984; Golden, 1984; Omolade, 1983). This ambivalence surrounds a fragile cultural distinction between two forms of female sexuality: *consensual* sexuality, representing consent or choice in sexuality, and *coercive* sexuality, which represents force, victimization, and/or crime (Weeks, 1985).

During the 1980s, however, this distinction began to be challenged. It was acknowledged that gender-based power inequities shape, define, and construct experiences of sexuality. Notions of sexual consent and force, except in extreme circumstances, became complicated, no longer in simple opposition. The first problem concerned how to conceptualize power asymmetries and consensual sexuality. Could *consensual* female heterosexuality be said to exist within a context replete with structures, relationships, acts, and threats of female victimization (sexual, social, and economic) (MacKinnon, 1983)? How could we speak of "sexual preference" when sexual involvement outside of heterosexuality may seriously jeopardize one's social and/or economic well-being (Petchesky, 1984)? Diverse female sexual subjectivities emerge through, despite, and because of gender-based power asymmetries. To imagine a female sexual self, free of and uncontaminated by power, was rendered naive (Foucault, 1980; Irigaray, 1980; Rubin, 1984).

The second problem involved the internal incoherence of the categories. Once assumed fully independent, the two began to blur as the varied practices of sexuality went public. At the intersection of these presumably parallel forms—coercive and consensual sexualities—lay "sexual" acts of violence and "violent" acts of sex. "Sexual" acts of violence, including marital rape, acquaintance rape, and sexual harassment, were historically considered consensual. A woman involved in a marriage, on a date, or working outside her home "naturally" risked receiving sexual attention; her consent was inferred from her presence. But today, in many states, this woman can sue her husband for such sexual acts of violence; in all states, she can prosecute a boss. What was once part of "domestic life" or "work" may, today, be criminal. On the other hand, "violent" acts of sex, including consensual sadomasochism and the use of violence-portraying pornography, were once considered inherently coercive for women (Benjamin, 1983; Rubin, 1984; Weeks, 1985). Female involvement in such sexual practices historically had been dismissed as nonconsensual. Today such romanticizing of a naive and moral "feminine sexuality" has been challenged as essentialist, and the assumption that such a feminine sexuality is "natural" to women has been shown to be false (Rubin, 1984).

Over the past decade, understandings of female sexual choice, consent, and coercion have grown richer and more complex. While questions about female subjectivities have become more interesting, the answers (for some) remain deceptively simple. Inside public schools, for example, female adolescents continue to be educated as though they were the potential *victims* of sexual (male) desire. By contrast, the ideological opposition represents only adult married women as fully consensual partners. The distinction of coercion and consent has been organized simply and respectively around age and marital status—which effectively resolves any complexity and/or ambivalence.

The ambivalence surrounding female heterosexuality places the victim and subject in opposition and derogates all women who represent female sexual subjectivities outside of marriage—prostitutes, lesbians, single mothers, women involved with multiple partners, and particularly, Black single mothers (Weitz, 1984). "Protected" from this derogation, the typical adolescent woman, as represented in sex education curricula, is without any sexual subjectivity. The discourse of victimization not only obscures the derogation, it also transforms socially distributed anxieties about female sexuality into acceptable, and even protective, talk.

The fact that schools implicitly organize sex education around a concern for female victimization is suspect, however, for two reasons. First, if female victims of male violence were truly a social concern, wouldn't the victims of rape, incest, and sexual harassment encounter social compassion, and not suspicion and blame? And second, if sex education were designed primarily to prevent victimization but not to prevent exploration of desire, wouldn't there be more discussions of both the pleasures and relatively fewer risks of disease or pregnancy associated with lesbian relationships and protected sexual intercourse, or of the risk-free pleasures of masturbation and fantasy? Public education's concern for the female victim is revealed as deceptively thin when real victims are discredited, and when nonvictimizing pleasures are silenced.

This unacknowledged social ambivalence about heterosexuality polarizes the debates over sex education and school-based health clinics. The anxiety effectively treats the female sexual victim as though she were a completely separate species from the female sexual subject. Yet the adolescent women quoted earlier in this text remind us that the female victim and subject coexist in every woman's body.

TOWARD A DISCOURSE OF SEXUAL DESIRE AND SOCIAL ENTITLEMENT: IN THE STUDENT BODIES OF PUBLIC SCHOOLS

I have argued that silencing a discourse of desire buttresses the icon of woman-as-victim. In so doing, public schooling may actually disable young women in their negotiations as sexual subjects. Trained through and into positions of passivity and victimization, young women are currently educated away from positions of sexual self-interest.

If we re-situate the adolescent woman in a rich and empowering educational context, she develops a sense of self which is sexual as well as intellectual, social, and economic. In this section I invite readers to imagine such a context. The dialectic of desire and victimization—across spheres of labor, social relations, and sexuality—would then frame schooling. While many of the curricula and interventions discussed in this paper are imperfect, data on the effectiveness of what *is* available are nevertheless compelling. Studies of sex education curricula, SBHCs, classroom discussions, and ethnographies of life inside public high schools demonstrate that a sense of sexual and social entitlement for young women *can* be fostered within public schools.

SEX EDUCATION AS INTELLECTUAL EMPOWERMENT

Harris and Yankelovich polls confirm that over 80 percent of American adults believe that students should be educated about sexuality within their public schools. Seventy-five percent believe that homosexuality and abortion should be included in the curriculum, with 40 percent of those surveyed by Yankelovich et al. (N = 1015) agreeing that 12-years-olds should be taught about oral and anal sex (see Leo, 1986; Harris, 1985).

While the public continues to debate the precise content of sex education, most parents approve and support sex education for their children. An Illinois program monitored parental requests to "opt out" and found that only 6 or 7 of 850 children were actually excused from sex education courses (Leo, 1986). In a California assessment, fewer than 2 percent of parents disallowed their children's participation. And in a longitudinal 5-year program in Connecticut, 7 of 2,500 students requested exemption from these classes (Scales, 1981). Resistance to sex education, while loud at the level of public rhetoric and conservative organizing, is both less vocal and less active within schools and parents' groups (Hottois & Milner, 1975; Scales, 1981).

Sex education courses are offered broadly, if not comprehensively, across the United States. In 1981, only 7 of 50 states actually had laws against such instruction, and only one state enforced a prohibition (Kirby & Scales, 1981). Surveying 179 urban school districts, Sonnenstein and Pittman (1984) found that 75 percent offered some sex education within senior and junior high schools, while 66 percent of the elementary schools offered sex education units. Most instruction was, however, limited to 10 hours or less, with content focused on anatomy. In his extensive review of sex education programs, Kirby (1985) concludes that less than 10 percent of all public school students are exposed to what might be considered comprehensive sex education courses.

The progress on AIDS education is more encouraging, and more complex (see Freudenberg, 1987), but cannot be adequately reviewed in this article. It is important to note, however, that a December 1986 report released by the U.S. Conference of Mayors documents that 54 percent of the 73 largest school districts and 25 state school agencies offer some form of AIDS education (Benedetto, 1987). Today, debates among federal officials—including Secretary of Education Bennett and Surgeon General Koop—and among educators question *when* and *what* to offer in AIDS education. The question is no longer *whether* such education should be promoted.

Not only has sex education been accepted as a function of public schooling, but it has survived empirical tests of effectiveness. Evaluation data demonstrate that sex education can increase contraceptive knowledge and use (Kirby, 1985; Public/Private Ventures, 1987). In terms of sexual activity (measured narrowly in terms of the onset or frequency of heterosexual intercourse), the evidence suggests that sex education does not instigate an earlier onset or increase of such sexual activity (Zelnick & Kim, 1982) and may, in fact, postpone the onset of heterosexual intercourse (Zabin, Hirsch, Smith, Streett, & Hardy, 1986). The data for pregnancy rates appear to demonstrate no effect for exposure to sex education alone (see Dawson, 1986; Marsiglio & Mott, 1986; Kirby, 1985).

Sex education as constituted in these studies is not sufficient to diminish teen pregnancy rates. In all likelihood it would be naive to expect that sex education (especially if only ten hours in duration) would carry such a "long arm" of effectiveness. While the widespread problem of teen pregnancy must be attributed broadly to economic and social inequities (Jones et al., 1985), sex education remains necessary and sufficient to educate, demystify, and improve contraceptive knowledge and use. In conjunction with material opportunities for enhanced life options, it is believed that sex education and access to contraceptives and abortion can help to reduce the rate of unintended pregnancy among teens (Dryfoos, 1985a, 1985b; National Research Council, 1987).

SCHOOL-BASED HEALTH CLINICS: SEXUAL EMPOWERMENT

The public opinion and effectiveness data for school-based health clinics are even more compelling than those for sex education. Thirty SBHCs provide on-site health care services to senior, and sometimes junior, high school students in more than 18 U.S. communities, with an additional 25 communities developing similar programs (Kirby, 1985). These clinics offer, at a minimum, health counseling, referrals, and follow-up examinations. Over 70 percent conduct pelvic examinations (Kirby, 1985), approximately 52 percent prescribe contraceptives, and 28 percent dispense contraceptives (Leo, 1986). None performs abortions, and few refer for abortions.

All SBHCs require some form of general parental notification and/or consent, and some charge a nominal fee for generic health services. Relative to private physicians, school-based health clinics and other family planning agencies are substantially more willing to provide contraceptive services to unmarried minors without specific parental consent (consent in this case referring explicitly to contraception). Only one percent of national Planned Parenthood affiliates require consent or notification, compared to 10 percent of public health department programs and 19 percent of hospitals (Tores & Forrest, 1985).

The consequences of consent provisions for abortion are substantial. Data from two states, Massachusetts and Minnesota, demonstrate that parental consent laws result in increased teenage pregnancies or increased numbers of out-of-state abortions. The Reproductive Freedom Project of the American Civil Liberties Union, in a report which examines the consequences of such consent provisions, details the impact of these statutes on teens, on their familial relationships, and ultimately, on their unwanted children (Reproductive Freedom Project, 1986). In an analysis of the impact of Minnesota's mandatory parental notification law from 1981 to 1985, this report documents over 7,000 pregnancies in teens aged 13–17, 3,500 of whom "went to state court to seek the right to confidential abortions, all at considerable personal cost." The report also notes that many of the pregnant teens did not petition the court, "although their entitlement and need for confidential abortions was as strong or more so than the teenagers who made it to court. . . . Only those minors who are old enough and wealthy enough or resourceful enough are actually able to use the court bypass option" (Reproductive Freedom Project, p. 4).

These consent provisions, with allowance for court bypass, not only increase the number of unwanted teenage pregnancies carried to term, but also extend the length of time required to secure an abortion, potentially endangering the life of the teenage woman, and increasing the costs of the abortion. The provisions may also jeopardize the physical and emotional well-being of some young women and their mothers, particularly when paternal consent is required and the pregnant teenager resides with a single mother. Finally, the consent provisions create a class-based health care system. Adolescents able to afford travel to a nearby state, or able to pay a private physician for a confidential abortion, have access to an abortion. Those unable to afford the travel, or those who are unable to contact a private physician, are likely to become teenage mothers (Reproductive Freedom Project, 1986).

In Minneapolis, during the time from 1980 to 1984 when the law was implemented, the birth rate for 15- to 17-year-olds increased 38.4 percent, while the birth rate for 18- and 19-year-olds—not affected by the law—rose only 3 percent (Reproductive Freedom Project, 1986). The state of Massachusetts passed a parental consent law which took effect in 1981. An analysis of the impact of that law concludes that ". . . the major impact of the Massachusetts parental consent law has been to send a monthly average of between 90 and 95 of the state's minors across state lines in search of an abortion. This number represents about one in every three minor abortion patients living in Massachusetts" (Cartoof & Klerman, 1986). These researchers, among others, write that parental consent laws could have more devastating effects in larger states, from which access to neighboring states would be more difficult.

The inequalities inherent in consent provisions and the dramatic consequences which result for young women are well recognized. For example, twenty-nine states and the District of Columbia now explicitly authorize minors to grant their own consent for receipt of contraceptive information and/or services, independent of parental knowledge or consent (see Melton & Russo, 1987, for full discussion; National Research Council, 1987; for a full analysis of the legal, emotional, and physical health problems attendant upon parental consent laws for abortion, see the Reproductive Freedom Project report). More recently, consent laws for abortion in Pennsylvania and California have been challenged as unconstitutional.

Public approval of SBHCs has been slow but consistent. In the 1986 Yankelovich survey, 84 percent of surveyed adults agree that these clinics should provide birth control information; 36 percent endorse dispensing of contraceptives to students (Leo, 1986). In 1985, Harris found that 67 percent of all respondents, including 76 percent of Blacks and 76 percent of Hispanics, agree that public schools should establish formal ties with family planning clinics for teens to learn about and obtain contraception (Harris, 1985). Mirroring the views of the general public, a national sample of school administrators polled by the Education Research Group indicated that more than 50 percent believe birth control should be offered in school-based clinics; 30 percent agree that parental permission should be sought, and 27 percent agree that contraceptives should be dispensed, even if parental consent is not forthcoming. The discouraging news is that 96 percent of these respondents indicate that their districts do not presently offer such services (Benedetto, 1987; Werner, 1987).

Research on the effectiveness of SBHCs is consistently persuasive. The three-year Johns Hopkins study of school-based health clinics (Zabin et al., 1986) found that schools in which SBHCs made referrals and dispensed contraceptives noted an increase in the percentage of "virgin" females visiting the program as well as an increase in contraceptive use. They also found a significant reduction in pregnancy rates: There was a 13 percent increase at experimental schools after 10 months, versus a 50 percent increase at control schools; after 28 months, pregnancy rates decreased 30 percent at experimental schools versus a 53 percent increase at control schools. Furthermore, by the second year, a substantial percentage of males visited the clinic (48 percent of males in experimental schools indicated that they "have ever been to a birth control clinic or to a physician about birth control," compared to 12 percent of males in control schools). Contrary to common belief, the schools in which clinics dispensed contraceptives showed a substantial postponement of first experience of heterosexual intercourse among high school students and an increase in the proportion of young women visiting the clinic prior to "first coitus."

Paralleling the Hopkins findings, the St. Paul Maternity and Infant Care Project (1985) found that pregnancy rates dropped substantially in schools with clinics, from 79 births/1,000 (1973) to 26 births/1,000 (1984). Teens who delivered and kept their infants had an 80 percent graduation rate, relative to approximately 50 percent of young mothers nationally. Those who stayed in school reported a 1.3 percent repeat birth rate, compared to 17 percent nationally. Over three years, pregnancy rates dropped by 40 percent. Twenty-five percent of young women in the school received some form of family planning and 87 percent of clients were continuing to use contraception at a 3-year follow-up. There were fewer obstetric complications; fewer babies were born at low birth weights; and prenatal visits to physicians increased relative to students in the control schools.

Predictions that school-based health clinics would advance the onset of sexual intimacy, heighten the degree of "promiscuity" and incidence of pregnancy, and hold females primarily responsible for sexuality were countered by the evidence. The onset of sexual intimacy was postponed, while contraception was used more reliably. Pregnancy rates substantially diminished and, over time, a large group of males began to view contraception as a shared responsibility.

It is worth restating here that females who received family planning counseling and/or contraception actually postponed the onset of heterosexual intercourse. I would argue that the availability of such services may enable females to feel they are sexual agents, entitled and therefore responsible, rather than at the constant and terrifying mercy of a young man's pressure to "give in" or of a parent's demands to "save yourself." With a sense of sexual agency and not necessarily urgency, teen girls may be less likely to use or be used by pregnancy (Petchesky, 1984).

NONTRADITIONAL VOCATIONAL TRAINING: SOCIAL AND ECONOMIC ENTITLEMENT

The literature reviewed suggests that sex education, access to contraception, and opportunities for enhanced life options, in combination (Dryfoos, 1985a, 1985b; Kirby, 1985; Select Committee on Children, Youth and Families, 1985), can significantly diminish the likelihood that a teenager will become pregnant, carry to term, and/or have a repeat pregnancy, and can increase the likelihood that she will stay in high school through graduation (National Research Council, 1987). Education toward entitlement—including a sense of sexual, economic, and social entitlement—may be sufficient to affect adolescent girls' views on sexuality, contraception, and abortion. By framing female subjectivity within the context of social entitlement, sex education would be organized around dialogue and critique, SBHCs would offer health services, options counseling, contraception, and abortion referrals, and the provision of real "life options" would include nontraditional vocational training programs and employment opportunities for adolescent females (Dryfoos, 1985a, 1985b).

In a nontraditional vocational training program in New York City designed for young women, many of whom are mothers, participants' attitudes toward contraception and abortion shifted once they acquired a set of vocational skills, a sense of social entitlement, and a sense of personal competence (Weinbaum, personal communication, 1986). The young women often began the program without strong academic skills or a sense of competence. At the start, they were more likely to express more negative sentiments about contraception and abortion than when they completed the program. One young woman, who initially held strong anti-abortion attitudes, learned that she was pregnant midway through her carpentry apprenticeship. She decided to abort, reasoning that now that she has a future, she can't risk losing it for another baby (Weinbaum, paraphrase of personal communication, 1986). A developing sense of social entitlement may have transformed this young woman's view of reproduction, sexuality, and self.

The Manpower Development Research Corporation (MDRC), in its evaluation of Project Redirection (Polit, Kahn, & Stevens, 1985) offers similar conclusions about a comprehensive vocational training and community-based mentor project for teen mothers and mothers-to-be. Low-income teens were enrolled in Project Redirection, a network of services designed to instill self-sufficiency, in which community women served as mentors. The program included training for what is called "employability," Individual Participation Plans, and peer group sessions. Data on education, employment, and pregnancy outcomes were collected at 12 and 24 months after enrollment. Two years after the program began, many newspapers headlined the program as a failure. The data actually indicated that at 12 months, the end of program involvement, Project Redirection women were significantly *less likely* to experience a repeat pregnancy than comparison women; *more likely* to be using contraception; *more likely* to be in school, to have completed school, or to be in the labor force; and twice as likely (20 percent versus 11 percent, respectively) to have earned a Graduate Equivalency Diploma. At 24 months, however, approximately one year out of the program, Project and comparison women were virtually indistinguishable. MDRC reported equivalent rates of repeat pregnancies, dropout, and unemployment.

The Project Redirection data demonstrate that sustained outcomes cannot be expected once programs have been withdrawn and participants confront the realities of a dismal economy and inadequate child care and social services. The data confirm, however, the effectiveness of comprehensive programs to reduce teen pregnancy rates and encourage study or work as long as the young women are actively engaged. Supply-side interventions—changing people but not structures or opportunities—which leave unchallenged an inhospitable and discriminating economy and a thoroughly impoverished child care/social welfare system are inherently doomed to long-term failure. When such programs fail, the social reading is that "these young women can't be helped." Blaming the victim obscures the fact that the current economy and social welfare arrangements need overhauling if the sustained educational, social, and psychological gains accrued by the Project Redirection participants are to be maintained.

In the absence of enhanced life options, low-income young women are likely to default to early and repeat motherhood as a source of perceived competence, significance, and pleasure. When life options are available, however, a sense of competence and "entitlement to better" may help to prevent second pregnancies, may help to encourage education, and, when available, the pursuit of meaningful work (Burt, Kimmich, Goldmuntz, & Sonnenstein, 1984).

FEMININITY MAY BE HAZARDOUS TO HER HEALTH: THE ABSENCE OF ENTITLEMENT

Growing evidence suggests that women who lack a sense of social or sexual entitlement, who hold traditional notions of what it means to be female—self-sacrificing and relatively passive—and who undervalue themselves, are disproportionately likely to find themselves with an unwanted pregnancy and to maintain it through to motherhood. While many young women who drop out, pregnant or not, are not at all traditional in these ways, but are quite feisty and are fueled with a sense of entitlement (Fine, 1986; Weinbaum, personal communication, 1987), it may also be the case that young women who do internalize such notions of "femininity" are disproportionately at risk for pregnancy and dropping out.

The Hispanic Policy Development Project reports that low-income female sophomores who, in 1980, expected to be married and/or to have a child by age 19 were disproportionately represented among nongraduates in 1984. Expectations of early marriage and childbearing correspond to dramatic increases (200 to 400 percent) in nongraduation rates for low-income adolescent women across racial and ethnic groups (Hispanic Policy Development Project, 1987). These indicators of traditional notions of womanhood bode poorly for female academic achievement.

The Children's Defense Fund (1986) recently published additional data which demonstrate that young women with poor basic skills are three times more likely to become teen parents than women with average or above-average basic skills. Those with poor or fair basic skills are four times more likely to have more than one child while a teen; 29 percent of women in the bottom skills quintile became mothers by age 18 versus 5 percent of young women in the top quintile. While academic skill problems must be placed in the context of alienating and problematic schools, and not viewed as inherent in these young women, those who fall in the bottom quintile may nevertheless be the least likely to feel entitled or in control of their lives. They may feel more vulnerable to male pressure or more willing to have a child as a means of feeling competent.

My own observations, derived from a year-long ethnographic study of a comprehensive public high school in New York City, further confirm some of these conclusions. Six months into the ethnography, new pregnancies began showing. I noticed that many of the girls who got pregnant and carried to term were not those whose bodies, dress, and manner evoked sensuality and experience. Rather, a number of the pregnant women were those who were quite passive and relatively quiet in their classes. One young woman, who granted me an interview anytime, washed the blackboard for her teacher, rarely spoke in class, and never disobeyed her mother, was pregnant by the spring of the school year (Fine, 1986).

Simple stereotypes, of course, betray the complexity of circumstances under which young women become pregnant and maintain their pregnancies.

While U.S. rates of teenage sexual activity and age of "sexual initiation" approximate those of comparable developed countries, the teenage pregnancy, abortion, and childbearing rates in the United States are substantially higher. In the United States, teenagers under age fifteen are at least five times more likely to give birth than similarly aged teens in other industrialized nations (Jones et al., 1985; National Research Council, 1987). The national factors which correlate with low teenage birthrates include adolescent access to sex education and contraception, and relative equality in the distribution of wealth. Economic and structural conditions which support a class-stratified society, and which limit adolescent access to sexual information and contraception, contribute to inflated teenage pregnancy rates and birthrates.

This broad national context acknowledged, it might still be argued that within our country, traditional notions of what it means to be a woman—to remain subordinate, dependent, self-sacrificing, compliant, and ready to marry and/or bear children early—do little to empower women or enhance a sense of entitlement. This is not to say that teenage dropouts or mothers tend to be of any one type. Yet it may well be that the traditions and practices of "femininity" as commonly understood may be hazardous to the economic, social, educational, and sexual development of young women.

In summary, the historic silencing within public schools of conversations about sexuality, contraception, and abortion, as well as the absence of a discourse of desire—in the form of comprehensive sex education, school-based health clinics, and viable life options via vocational training and placement—all combine to exacerbate the vulnerability of young women whom schools, and the critics of sex education and SBHCs, claim to protect.

CONCLUSION

Adolescents are entitled to a discussion of desire instead of the anti-sex rhetoric which controls the controversies around sex education, SBHCs, and AIDS education. The absence of a discourse of desire, combined with the lack of analysis of the language of victimization, may actually retard the development of sexual subjectivity and responsibility in students. Those most "at risk" of victimization through pregnancy, disease, violence, or harassment—all female students, low-income females in particular, and non-heterosexual males—are those most likely to be victimized by the absence of critical conversation in public schools. Public schools can no longer afford to maintain silence around a discourse of desire. This is not to say that the silencing of a discourse of desire is the primary root of sexual victimization, teen motherhood, and the concomitant poverty experienced by young and low-income females. Nor could it be responsibly argued that interventions initiated by public schools could ever be successful if separate from economic and social development. But it is important to understand that by providing education, counseling, contraception, and abortion referrals, as well as meaningful educational and vocational opportunities, public schools could play an essential role in the construction of the female subject—social and sexual.

And by not providing such an educational context, public schools contribute to the rendering of substantially different outcomes for male and female students, and for male and female dropouts (Fine, 1986). The absence of a thorough sex education curriculum, of school-based health clinics, of access to free and confidential contraceptive and abortion services, of exposure to information about the varieties of sexual pleasures and partners, and of involvement in sustained employment training programs may so jeopardize the educational and economic outcomes for female adolescents as to constitute sex discrimination. How can we ethically continue to withhold educational treatments we know to be effective for adolescent women?

Public schools constitute a sphere in which young women could be offered access to a language and experience of empowerment. In such contexts, "well-educated" young women could breathe life into positions of social critique and experience entitlement rather than victimization, autonomy rather than terror.

NOTES

1. The research reported in this article represents one component of a year-long ethnographic investigation of students and dropouts at a comprehensive public high school in New York City. Funded by the W. T. Grant Foundation, the research was designed to investigate how public urban high schools produce dropout rates in excess of 50 percent. The methods employed over the year included: in-school observations four days/week during the fall, and one to two days/week during the spring; regular (daily) attendance in a hygiene course for twelfth graders; an archival analysis of more than 1200 students who compose the 1978–79 cohort of incoming ninth graders; interviews with approximately 55 recent and long-term dropouts; analysis of fictional and autobiographical writings by students; a survey distributed to a subsample of the cohort population; and visits to proprietary schools, programs for Graduate Equivalency Diplomas, naval recruitment sites, and a public high school for pregnant and parenting teens. The methods and preliminary results of the ethnography are detailed in Fine (1986).
2. This information is derived from personal communications with former and present employees of major urban school districts who have chosen to remain anonymous.
3. Personal communication.

REFERENCES

Bauer, G. (1986). *The family: Preserving America's future.* Washington, DC: U.S. Department of Education.
Benedetto, R. (1987, January 23). AIDS studies become part of curricula. *USA Today,* p. D1.
Benjamin, J. (1983). "Master and slave: The fantasy of erotic domination." In A. Snitow, C. Stansell, and S. Thompson (eds.), *Powers of desire* (pp. 280–299). New York: Monthly Review Press.
Bennett, W. (1987, July 3). "Why Johnny can't abstain." *National Review,* pp. 36–38, 56.
Bigelow, M. (1921). *Sex-Education.* New York: Macmillan.
Boffey, P. (1987, February 27). "Reagan to back AIDS plan urging youths to avoid sex." *New York Times,* p. A14.
Brown, P. (1983). "The Swedish approach to sex education and adolescent pregnancy: Some impressions." *Family Planning Perspectives,* 15(2), 92–95.
Burke, C. (1980). "Introduction to Luce Irigaray's 'When our lips speak together.' " *Signs,* 6, 66–68.
Burt, M., Kimmich, M., Goldmuntz, J., and Sonnenstein, F. (1984). *Helping pregnant adolescents: Outcomes and costs of service delivery.* Final Report on the Evaluation of Adolescent Pregnancy Programs. Washington, DC: Urban Institute.

Cartoof, V., & Klerman, L. (1986). "Parental consent for abortion: Impact of the Massachusetts law." *American Journal of Public Health, 76,* 397–400.

"Chicago school clinic is sued over birth control materials." (1986, October 16). *New York Times,* p. A24.

Children's Defense Fund. (1986). *Preventing adolescent pregnancy: What schools can do.* Washington, DC: Children's Defense Fund.

Children's Defense Fund. (1987). *Adolescent pregnancy: An anatomy of a social problem in search of comprehensive solutions.* Washington, DC: Children's Defense Fund.

Cixous, H. (1981). "Castration or decapitation?" *Signs, 7,* 41–55.

Dawson, D. (1986). "The effects of sex education on adolescent behavior." *Family Planning Perspectives, 18,* 162–170.

Dowd, M. (1986, April 16). "Bid to update sex education confronts resistance in city." *New York Times,* p. A1.

Dryfoos, J. (1985a). "A time for new thinking about teenage pregnancy." *American Journal of Public Health, 75,* 13–14.

Dryfoos, J. (1985b). "School-based health clinics: A new approach to preventing adolescent pregnancy?" *Family Planning Perspectives, 17*(2), 70–75.

Ehrenreich, B., Hess, E., and Jacobs, G. (1986). *Re-making love.* Garden City, NY: Anchor Press.

Espin, O. (1984). "Cultural and historical influences on sexuality in Hispanic/Latina women: Implications for psychotherapy." In C. Vance (ed.), *Pleasure and danger* (pp. 149–164). Boston: Routledge & Kegan Paul.

Fine, M. (1986). "Why urban adolescents drop into and out of high school." *Teachers College Record, 87,* 393–409.

Fine, M. (1987). "Silencing in public school." *Language Arts, 64,* 157–174.

Fisher, W., Byrne, D., and White, L. (1983). "Emotional barriers to contraception." In D. Byrne & W. Fisher (eds.), *Adolescents; sex, and contraception* (pp. 207–239). Hillsdale, NJ: Lawrence Erlbaum.

Foucault, M. (1980). *The history of sexuality* (vol.1). New York: Vintage Books.

Freudenberg, N. (1987). "The politics of sex education." *Health PAC Bulletin.* New York: HealthPAC.

Golden, C. (1984, March). *Diversity and variability in lesbian identities.* Paper presented at Lesbian Psychologies Conference of the Association of Women in Psychology.

Greene, M. (1986). "In search of a critical pedagogy." *Harvard Educational Review, 56,* 427–441.

Hall, G. S. (1914). "Education and the social hygiene movement." *Social Hygiene,* 1 (1 December), 29–35.

Harris, L., and associates. (1985). *Public attitudes about sex education, family planning and abortion in the United States.* New York: Louis Harris and Associates, Inc.

Hispanic Policy Development Project. (1987, Fall). *1980 high school sophomores from poverty backgrounds: Whites, Blacks, Hispanics look at school and adult responsibilities,* vol. 1, no. 2. New York: Author.

Hottois, J., and Milner, N. (1975). *The sex education controversy.* Lexington, MA: Lexington Books.

Imber, M. (1984). "Towards a theory of educational origins: The genesis of sex education." *Educational Theory, 34,* 275–286.

Irigaray, L. (1980). "When our lips speak together." *Signs, 6,* 69.

Jones, E., Forrest, J., Goldman, N., Henshaw, S., Lincoln, R., Rosoff, J., Westoff, C., and Wulf, D. (1985). "Teenage pregnancy in developed countries." *Family Planning Perspectives, 17*(1), 55–63.

Kantrowitz, B., Hager, M., Wingert, S., Carroll, G., Raine, G., Witherspoon, D., Huck, J., and Doherty, S. (1987, February 16). "Kids and contraceptives." *Newsweek,* pp. 54–65.

Kelly, G. (1986). *Learning about sex.* Woodbury, NY: Barron's Educational Series.

Kirby, D. (1985). *School-based health clinics: An emerging approach to improving adolescent health and addressing teenage pregnancy.* Washington, DC: Center for Population Options.

Kirby, D., and Scales, P. (1981, April). "An analysis of state guidelines for sex education instruction in public schools." *Family Relations,* pp. 229–237.

Koop, C. E. (1986). *Surgeon General's report on acquired immure deficiency syndrome.* Washington, DC: Office of the Surgeon General.

"Koop's AIDS stand assailed." (1987, March 15). *New York Times,* p. A25.

Leo, J. (1986, November 24). "Sex and schools." *Time,* pp. 54–63.

Lorde, A. (1980, August). *Uses of the erotic: The erotic as power.* Paper presented at the Fourth Berkshire Conference on the History of Women, Mt. Holyoke College.

MacKinnon, C. (1983). "Complicity: An introduction to Andrea Dworkin's 'Abortion,' Chapter 3, 'Right-Wing Women.' " *Law and Inequality,* 1, 89–94.

Marsiglio, W., and Mott, F. (1986). "The impact of sex education on sexual activity, contraceptive use and premarital pregnancy among American teenagers." *Family Planning Perspectives,* 18(4), 151–162.

Melton, S., and Russon, N. (1987). "Adolescent abortion." *American Psychologist,* 42, 69–83.

National Research Council. (1987). *Risking the future: Adolescent sexuality, pregnancy and childbearing* (vol. 1). Washington, DC: National Academy Press.

New York City Board of Education. (1984). *Family living curriculum including sex education. Grades K through 12.* New York City Board of Education, Division of Curriculum and Instruction.

Noddings, N. (1986). "Fidelity in teaching, teacher education, and research for teaching." *Harvard Educational Review,* 56, 496–510.

Omolade, B. (1983). "Hearts of darkness." In A. Snitow, C. Stansell, and S. Thompson (eds.), *Powers of desire* (pp. 350–367). New York: Monthly Review Press.

Perlez, J. (1986a, June 24). "On teaching about sex." *New York Times,* p. C1.

Perlez, J. (1986b, September 24). "School chief to ask mandatory sex education." *New York Times,* p. A36.

Petchesky, R. (1984). *Abortion and woman's choice.* New York: Longman.

Philadelphia School District. (1986). *Sex education curriculum.* Draft.

Polit, D., Kahn, J., and Stevens, D. (1985). *Final impacts from Project Redirection.* New York: Manpower Development Research Center.

Public/Private Ventures. (1987, April). *Summer training and education program.* Philadelphia: Author.

Reproductive Freedom Project. (1986). *Parental consent laws on abortion: Their catastrophic impact on teenagers.* New York: American Civil Liberties Union.

Rohter, L. (1985, October 29). "School workers shown AIDS film." *New York Times,* p. B3.

Rubin, G. (1984). "Thinking sex: Notes for a radical theory of the politics of sex." In C. Vance (ed.), *Pleasure and danger* (pp. 267–319). Boston: Routledge & Kegan Paul.

St. Paul Maternity and Infant Care Project. (1985). *Health services project description.* St. Paul, MN: Author.

Scales, P. (1981). "Sex education and the prevention of teenage pregnancy: An overview of policies and programs in the United States." In T. Ooms (ed.), *Teenage pregnancy in a family context: Implications for policy* (pp. 213–253). Philadelphia: Temple University Press.

Schlafly, P. (1986). *Presentation on women's issues.* American Dreams Symposium, Indiana University of Pennsylvania.

"Selected group to see original AIDS tape." (1987, January 29). *New York Times,* p. B4.

Smith-Rosenberg, C. (1978). "Sex as symbol in Victorian purity: An ethnohistorical analysis of Jacksonian America." *American Journal of Sociology,* 84, 212–247.

Snitow, A., Stansell, C., and Thompson, S. (eds.). (1983). *Powers of desire.* New York: Monthly Review Press.

Sonnenstein, F., and Pittman, K. (1984). "The availability of sex education in large city school districts." *Family Planning Perspectives,* 16(1), 19–25.

Strong, B. (1972). "Ideas of the early sex education movement in America, 1890–1920." *History of Education Quarterly,* 12, 129–161.

Thompson, S. (1983). "Search for tomorrow: On feminism and the reconstruction of teen romance." In A. Snitow, C. Stansell, and S. Thompson (eds.), *Powers of desire* (pp. 367–384). New York: Monthly Review Press.

Torres, A., and Forest, J. (1985). "Family planning clinic services in the United States, 1983." *Family Planning Perspectives,* 17(1), 30–35.

Vance, C. (1984). *Pleasure and danger.* Boston: Routledge & Kegan Paul.

Weeks, J. (1985). *Sexuality and its discontents.* London: Routledge & Kegan Paul.

Weitz, R. (1984). "What price independence? Social reactions to lesbians, spinsters, widows and nuns." In J. Freeman (ed.), *Women: A feminist perspective* (3rd ed.). Palo Alto, CA: Mayfield.

Werner, L. (1987, November 14). "U.S. report asserts administration halted liberal 'anti-family agenda.' " *New York Times,* p. A12.

Zabin, L., Hirsch, M., Smith, E., Streett, R., and Hardy, J. (1986). "Evaluation of a pregnancy prevention program for urban teenagers." *Family Planning Perspectives,* 18(3), 119–126.

Zelnick, M., and Kim, Y. (1982). "Sex education and its association with teenage sexual activity, pregnancy and contraceptive use." *Family Planning Perspectives,* 14(3), 117–126.

Thinking About the Gay Teen

GERALD UNKS

Homosexuals are arguably the most hated group of people in the United States. While other minorities have gained a modicum of protection and acceptance, homosexuals remain essentially outside the pale. In their public lives, few Americans any longer use words such as "nigger," "kike," "gook," or "wop." Yet, "faggot," "fairy," "homo," and "queer" are used by many without hesitation. Picking on persons because of their ethnicity, class, religion, gender, or race is essentially taboo behavior, but adults and children alike are given license to torment and harm people because of their sexuality. The civil liberties of most minorities are fairly secure; those of homosexuals are tenuous at best, and nonexistent at worst. In spite of mighty gains by other minorities, homosexuals stand alone, outside, despised, and ripe for discrimination.

Unlike most minorities, the majority of homosexuals have the option of hiding their identities from a hostile society. Although the damage to their mental health may be considerable, they can conceal their most-despised status, and act publicly as if they were not homosexuals. Most choose this charade as a way of life, for to self-identify as a homosexual is to invite persecution by society and rejection by family, peers, organized religion, and community. In the past two decades, homosexuality has received increasing governmental, medical, and media attention, and several notable people have identified themselves as homosexuals. The topic, homosexuality, has become the acceptable stuff of public discourse, but there is little to suggest that *the subjects* of the topic—homosexuals themselves—are much better off than they were a generation ago. No longer plagued by the "I'm the only one in the world" syndrome, most homosexuals must still continue to choose to lead a lie as a lifestyle. Secretly all around us, fearing to reveal a part of their being, they are nonetheless there. They are our celebrities, our politicians, our manual laborers, our

322

professionals, our acquaintances, our tradespeople, our religious leaders, our friends, our coworkers, our bosses—and our adolescents.

There is little evidence to suggest that adolescent homosexuals experience any less prejudice and discrimination than is visited on their adult counterparts. Indeed, there is compelling data suggesting that they may suffer *more*. First, as is typical of all youth, their political, economic, and social expression is restricted because of their age. However, unlike their counterparts, they do not enjoy the sort of social allegiances, educational resources, or cultural support that are routinely established by the adult society for other youth subcultures. Second, they are children in a minority that society has chosen to regard as solely adult. The most apparent parts of gay and lesbian culture—particularly bars and social clubs—are highly adult-centered, and there are legal, social, financial, and political barriers that prevent any legitimate adolescent participation in them. The youthful homosexual receives messages, implied and explicit, that suggest that homosexuality is an exclusively adult characteristic or privilege, sort of like voting or getting married. The cry of gay teens, "I have no place to go, nowhere to meet people like me, no one to look up to and learn from, no place to turn," echoes their essentially powerless position.

A cursory search for support systems typically available to adolescent homosexuals reveals that there are essentially none. Further, adolescent homosexuals cannot find comfort in family, church, or peer groups, nor are there role models with whom they can identify. In virtually every way, lesbian, gay, and bisexual adolescents are *worse off* than their adult counterparts. While forces in the larger adult society might hint at political correctness, acceptance, and accommodation, the high school—the center of most adolescent life and culture—stands staunchly aloof and rigidly resistant to even a suggestion that any of its faculty or student body might be homosexual or that homosexuals deserve anything but derision and scorn within its walls. High schools may be the most homophobic institutions in American society, and woe be to anyone who would challenge the heterosexist premises on which they operate.

Heterosexism, an ideology "[t]hat denies, denigrates, and stigmatizes any nonheterosexual form of behavior, identity, relationship, or community" (Herek, 1992, p.89), permeates the typical high school. Consistently, the very existence of homosexuality is denied—on the faculty, in the student body, and even in the curriculum. There is an extraordinarily narrow definition of what is acceptable male and female dress and conduct (much more restrictive than one would find in the college or the adult community), and those who transgress are likely to be taunted. The array of social conventions, mores, folkways, and institutional norms that support the belief that heterosexuality is the best and only lifestyle is overwhelming. It affects what is taught, who takes which subjects, and who is "in" and "out" in the cultural life of the school.

Within the typical secondary school curriculum, homosexuals do not
exist. They are "nonpersons" in the finest Stalinist sense. They have fought
no battles, held no offices, explored nowhere, written no literature, built
nothing, invented nothing, and solved no equations. Ironically, they were neither Greeks nor Romans, and they did not write poetry, compose music,
paint, or sculpt. The lesson to the heterosexual student is abundantly clear:
homosexuals do nothing of consequence. To the homosexual student, the
message has even greater power: no one who has ever felt as you do has done
anything worth mentioning. This omission almost certainly contributes to
homophobia, "the fear and hatred that heterosexuals experience when around
homosexuals and the discomfort *and self-hatred* (our italics) homosexuals have
about their own homosexuality" (Weinberg, 1972). The absence from the
curriculum of valid information about homosexuality cuts both ways; heterosexual students are given no reasons not to hate homosexuals, while homosexual students are given no reason not to hate themselves. Both groups suffer
a loss, for they are denied important information about a significant group of
human beings.

Over time, subjects in the high school have acquired dubious gender
association; some are "masculine," others are "feminine." In reality, math,
auto shop, and science are not male domains; nor are literature, home economics, and music the province of females. Yet in the *unreality* of the school
environment, this has become the case. The impact of this gender association on female scores in math has been widely documented. However, coupled with a strong strain of heterosexism, it takes its toll on all students. Only
a few females take auto shop, just as only a few males take home economics.
Fearing homophobic labels, most students stick to their own gender-defined
subjects. Does the male who takes his musical ability seriously fear being
called a "fairy?" Does the female who excels in sports invite taunts of "dyke?"
Some students consider history to be "male," and they do not like female history teachers, just as some believe that literature is somehow "female." In the
context of the high school, anything that might even remotely be considered
"queer" is avoided, and this includes the study of subjects which could
help all students. The entire student body—heterosexual and homosexual—
suffers by being denied access to *all* of the subjects in the school curriculum simply because the school allows heterosexism to go unanswered (see
Klein, 1992).

Anyone who studies the culture of the typical high school realizes that the
curriculum is only half—perhaps less than half—of the "life of the school."
Apart from courses and schedules, there is the rich brew of growth, pride, anxiety, hope, wonder, fear, experimentation, anger, and challenge that is the
essence of being a high school student. *Sexuality* is also part of that mix, for it
is usually during high school that most adolescents have their first serious sexual encounters. Indeed, the high school culture expects and promotes these

liaisons with dances, newspaper gossip columns, yearbook signings, class ring exchanges, locker sharings, and—perhaps above all—the prom. It is, however, *heterosexuality* that is being championed; there is no room for homosexuality in the high school culture, for it challenges the blatant heterosexism that infuses the institution's mores and folkways. Any same-sex affection is closely and carefully proscribed—even in athletics. Should students feel any same-sex attraction, and should they act upon those feelings, they will be vigorously punished with ostracism at best, and physical abuse at worst. There is evidence that adolescents, more than any other age group, are likely to commit violence against homosexuals (Masters, Johnson, and Kolodny, 1992, p. 394; Greer, 1986). Again, all students suffer from a heterocentric high school culture. Certainly, the homosexual student is most abused, but heterosexual students are also losers, for they must conform to rigid standards of behavior that admit no individual differences. These unilateral, unbending expectations may be particularly troublesome for a heterosexual male who is small, quiet, serious, or sensitive, and for the heterosexual female who finds it awkward or difficult to display stereotypic feminine traits.

Another factor contributing to the marginalization of homosexual adolescents is their lack of viable support groups. While virtually all students of any other identifiable group have advocates and support in the high school, homosexual students typically have none. They have no equivalent of the African-American student's protection against hate words, slurs, and discrimination. They receive no special programs or assistance. The guidance office is not the place where they can tell it all. There are seldom role models on the faculty, and even the most understanding faculty member may not be an appropriate person with whom to confide "their most secret secret." Indeed, heterosexual faculty members who are empathetic to homosexuals are placed in a particular bind; if they champion gay rights, they may themselves be accused of being gay. And should there be "out" gay teachers on the faculty, and should they work for gay student rights, they might well be accused of "recruiting." Lacking any significant support system, it is not surprising that the homosexual adolescent may achieve poorly, drop out of school, engage in substance abuse, run away from home, or attempt suicide.

The occurrence of suicide among adolescent homosexuals is possibly the most widely publicized data about them. That this is the case is perhaps the cruelest irony in the chronicle of the woes of gay teens. How unfortunate it is that they must make the *ultimate* statement about their condition in order to get a significant cohort of the public to pay attention to them. The reports about a disproportionately large number of suicides among young homosexuals have been beneficial in that they have prompted a positive public response in some areas of the country to the problems of gay teens. These reports, however, have not been without their critics (see Shaffer, 1993), and the issue of how many homosexual adolescents commit suicide has become politicized (see Bull, 1994). Kielwasser and Wolf (1994) have evaluated these arguments:

> While suicidal ideation among lesbian and gay youth is not uncommon, the statistical profiles used to document a high rate of suicidality are problematic. Random samples of homosexual youth are impossible to generate, and many studies of lesbian and gay youth suicide are based on convenience samples of adolescents already involved in various counseling, suicide prevention, and delinquency abatement programs. Additionally, and perhaps more importantly, this historic emphasis on the psychosocial problems faced by lesbian and gay youth has frequently obscured any systematic consideration of their particular talents. Certainly, most lesbian and gay youth do survive adolescence. They move willfully into adulthood by virtue of an extraordinarily powerful and creative resilience. At least one research psychologist (Gregory M. Herek, 1993, personal communication) has suggested that we adjust our research agenda to include homosexual youth as gifted children. (p. 59)

Herek's suggestion makes sense. Most teens who feel deficient in one area of development will compensate by being even better in others. And there are few areas of life that are as subject to compensation as is sexuality. Indeed, it would be very useful to examine the "outstanding students" in every field. Almost certainly, there would be homosexual students among them. If, however, there was *a disproportionately large number* of homosexual students among "the success class"—the football captains, the honor students, the Eagle Scouts, the cheerleaders, the school officers, and the rest—(and we suspect that there would be), then it would tend to take some of the focus of public attention away from the negative area of suicide, a condition too long associated with homosexuality. To engage in such inquiry, however, would entail gathering accurate *random* sample data, and this requires honest responses. As long as heterosexism and homophobia reign in the high school, this condition is unlikely to obtain. Finally, the point must be made: irrespective of how many young homosexuals commit suicide, numbers are not what is important. If just one young homosexual commits suicide, that is a problem deserving of public attention and community action.

There are certain themes that run through much of the literature about gay teens—oppression, anger, silence, desperation, guilt, and death. Not all of the themes, however, are depressing and negative; there is also a great deal that is positive. As Kielwasser and Wolf pointed out above, in spite of the staggering figures about misery and suicide, it is a fact that most gay teens do survive adolescence—they make it through along with most other adolescents— and they become useful and well-adjusted adults; this is the life pattern for the majority of homosexuals in America. Further, it is extremely positive to remember the closeted gay *Wunderkinder*—born of sublimation and compensation—who bubble as adolescents and star as adults. Few of them would admit to life's being tragic, and some would cite their adolescent discomfort as a wellspring for their adult accomplishments. Karen Harbeck is correct, however, when she reminds us that, in the main, homosexuals—even adolescent ones—are neither miserable wretches nor superachievers. They are mostly ordinary people who accept the challenges and solve the problems that are the essence of life for everyone. Indeed, a case can be made that gay teens will be truly well off only when these, the average homosexuals, are accepted for what *they* are—outstanding only in that they are human beings. Then homosexuals will have no stereotypes attached to them. They will all be thought of neither as the limp-wristed drag queen, the brutish dyke, nor the genius conductor of the symphony. They will be seen as just plain individuals—possessed of all the same warts and wrinkles or shining complexions as are all people.

Perhaps the most positive themes in the literature about gay teens are the descriptions of what is now being done to assist them. In a growing number of schools across the nation, parts of a gay-friendly curriculum are in place, and they are working. Certainly, these curricula and units became a reality only after a fight, but—in spite of the flack—they are still in place. Project 10, the Harvey Milk School, Spectrum, and OutRight! are models that are working. They have their critics, but these are usually more vocal than numerous. School officials who wish to ease the plight of gay adolescents in their student bodies do not have to invent the wheel; pioneering efforts are already in place to show them the way. All that they must do is to seize the initiative in their own school district, recognizing that there will be opposition, but also realizing that it may be far less intense than they expect.

Yet gay-friendly curricula and student organizations may be simply too much for some faculties and administrators to imagine in their districts. For them there is still a task: strongly oppose any "epithets of hate," and enact policies against harassment. At the very least, any school system can implement these reforms. They do not broaden the curriculum, they do not "recruit," nor do they celebrate a particular lifestyle. What they do is extend basic civil liberties to a minority of students who do not currently enjoy them. And if some faculty or administrators respond that there are none of "them" in their student body, there is still a reason to institute the reforms. There *are* several of "them" in the student body, and while fear may keep them in hiding while they are in school, the positive action of passing these reforms may give them a bit of self-confidence.

Still, suggesting that homosexuality and homosexual accomplishments should be a part of the curriculum is usually an invitation to trouble. Accusations will almost certainly be made about the person's own sexuality. There is a

heterosexist/homophobic presumption that those who have any interest in homosexuals (other than to ferret them out for persecution) must
themselves be homosexual. This absurdity is roughly equivalent to assuming
that only African-Americans are interested in matters of race, or that one
must be poor to be interested in poverty. Aspersions about their sexuality
aside, those who want to consider homosexuality in schools may be accused
of "causing trouble" by bringing up a "controversial issue." This is the
censor's historic weapon—attempting to destroy an idea by refusing to
acknowledge or discuss it. A controversial issue is by definition one on which
reasonable people can honestly disagree. However, it is *unreasonable* to
claim that homosexuals do not exist or that no homosexuals have accomplished anything of worth. To claim that homosexuals—including adolescent homosexuals—do not exist is equivalent to claiming that baseball
players do not exist. To discuss baseball players—how many there are, what
they do, what they have done, where they live, their good points and their
bad—is not at all controversial in schools. Intrinsically, neither is homosexuality; however, it becomes "a problem" when a society is forced to choose
between acknowledging the existence of homosexuality, on the one hand,
and holding on to the heterosexist notion that homosexuals do not exist, on
the other.

However, in the presence of an avalanche of media attention, it is
difficult—even for the most rabid heterosexist—to deny the very existence of
homosexuals. Robbed of this position, the heterosexist retreats to name-calling,
identifying homosexuals *only* as child molesters, men who wear women's clothing, and dirty old men who have sex in public toilets. Above all, heterosexists
cling to three ideas that are apparently crucial to their mind-set: being lesbian
or gay is in and of itself evil, homosexuals could "change" if they wanted to, and
no lesbian or gay person has ever done anything worthwhile. Most curriculum
proposals that suggest the importance of studying homosexuality directly challenge these three ideas, and affront the heterosexist mentality because these
plans suggest that the curriculum should acknowledge the legitimate existence
of a homosexual community and that it should recognize the contemporary and
historical contributions of this community to the larger society. This is not a
controversial idea at all—unless one wishes to claim that there is no homosexual community and that its scientists, writers, composers, athletes, public officials, and all of the other contributors to the varieties of human accomplishment
do not and never did exist. To make such a claim, in the presence of the scholarship on the subject, is not simply unreasonable; to the extent that it denies
reality, it is insane.

Three words—myth, reality, and dream—surround the problems of and
prospects for the gay teen in American society. Up to the present, much of society and its schools has embraced an elaborate, unchallenged collection of myths
about homosexuality and the gay teen. It derives a sort of perverse security

from not talking about it, denying it, and persecuting it—as if a strange combination of uncomfortable silence and selective rage would make it go away. Myths unexamined do not, however, become truths; and those who order their lives on myth are doomed. Still, a great number of Americans seek out and cherish myths. They lament the good old days, and call for a return to values and patterns that had the appearance of utility in the past. They refuse to look at reality; they embrace the soothing balm of the political and religious soothsayer who reinforces their parochial beliefs. Authoritarian societies have many "thou shalt nots" in their lexicon, the most dangerous of which is "thou shalt not think." That the American society and its schools have adopted the posture of not thinking about homosexuality and the gay teen is a perilous course to take. For when one rejects thinking as the foundation of an educational system, one is in reality rejecting one of the most promising ways of disciplining ideas with facts.

It is unfortunate that the literature and scholarship about gay teens does not usually address the issue of the student's right to know. Censoring homosexuality as an appropriate topic for reflective examination in a high school is a breach of a student's academic freedom. It is in the same category as all of the other topics that self-appointed thought police have historically sought to keep out of the classroom—evolution, Communism, and the rest. Powerful arguments as they are, gay teen suicide prevention and establishing the civil liberties of gay teens may be second-order reasons for talking about homosexuality in schools. In a truly democratic society, the primary reason in support of studying about homosexuality in schools may be to assure freedom of thought. Societies are totalitarian to the extent that they have areas of belief and attitude that are closed to reflective examination and thought. The real importance of thinking about the gay teen, and homosexuality generally, is to open up one of those areas which American society has chosen to close. In that, it is a search for truth.

In school—if nowhere else—our youth should sate their desire for reliable knowledge. When society, however well-intentioned, denies its youth this sort of information, it perpetrates the most insidious form of intellectual rape upon its children. However, instructing in realities entails an examination of the controversial and what some might consider the down-right unpleasant. But it can also involve suggesting dreams—the possibility of hope and of change. In the final analysis, it is the fusion of these realities and dreams—in a process called thinking—which makes people responsible citizens, and it is thinking about all ideas, including homosexuality, which will make the United States and its citizens—including its gay teens—truly free.

REFERENCES

Bull, C. "Suicidal Tendencies," *The Advocate,* 652 (April 5, 1994), pp. 34–42.
Greer, W. R. (1986). "Violence Against Homosexuals Rising, Groups Seeking Wider Protection Say." *New York Times,* November 23, p. 36.

Herek, G. M. (1992). "The Social Context of Hate Crimes: Notes on Cultural Heterosexism." In *Hate Crimes: Confronting Violence Against Lesbians and Gay Men.* G. Herek and K. Berril, eds. Newbury Park, CA: Sage Publications.

Kielwasser, A. P., and Wolf, M. A. (1994). "Silence, Difference, and Annihilation: Understanding the Impact of Mediated Heterosexism on High School Students." *The High School Journal,* 77 (January 2), pp. 58–79.

Klein, S. S. (1992). "Why Should We Care About Gender and Sexuality in Education?" In *Sexuality and the Curriculum: The Politics and Practices of Sexuality Education.* James Sears, ed. New York: Teachers College Press.

Masters, W., Johnson, V., and Kolodny, R. (1992). *Human Sexuality.* Fourth Edition. New York: HarperCollins Publishers.

Shaffer, D. (1993). "Political Science." *The New Yorker,* 69, no. 11 (May 3, 1993), p. 116.

Weinberg, G. (1972). *Society and the Healthy Homosexual.* New York: Anchor.

What We Can Do for You!
What *Can* "We" Do for "You"?:
Struggling over Empowerment
in Critical and Feminist Pedagogy

JENNIFER GORE

"**E**mpowerment" is a term used in a range of current educational discourses. For example, there are conservative discourses (e.g., Maeroff, 1988) which equate empowerment with professionalization and seem to employ the term for rhetorical purposes which result in little shift in relations of power; liberal humanist discourses (e.g., Yonemura, 1986) which aim at the "empowerment" of *individual* teachers, student teachers and students and the alteration of power relations *within* the classroom; and critical and feminist discourses (e.g., Culley, 1985; Giroux, 1988; McLaren, 1988; Miller, 1990; Shor & Freire, 1987; Shrewsbury, 1987; Simon, 1987) which are concerned with societal relations of power and hold more collective and avowedly political notions of empowerment. Because of their roots in specific liberatory and emancipatory political projects, we might be least likely to question the claims to empowerment of the critical and feminist discourses. Precisely for this reason, and because my own practice as a teacher educator is grounded in critical and feminist traditions, I limit this paper to an analysis of discourses within those traditions.[1]

My major aim is to point to some weaknesses or shortcomings in the construction of "empowerment" by critical and feminist educational discourses which create problems internal to those discourses. Rather than seek to legitimate or celebrate critical and feminist discourses, I want to look for their dangers, their normalizing tendencies, for how they might serve as instruments of domination despite the intentions of their creators (Sawicki, 1988). Michel Foucault says "Thought is freedom in relation to what one does, the motion by which one detaches oneself from it, establishes it as an object and reflects on it as a problem" (Rabinow, 1984, p. 388). As is consistent with many post-structural analyses (e.g., Ellsworth, 1989; Popkewitz, 1991; Sawicki, 1988), my aim is to be "thoughtful" about constructions of truth, power, knowledge, the self, and language in these discourses. Specifically, I draw on Foucault's notion of "regime of truth" to reflect on problems of power relations and knowledge internal to the critical and feminist discourses which are my focus here. To do so, I have selected examples which illustrate clearly the potential dangers of those discourses. At the same time, however, I wish to acknowledge that some work within the critical and feminist traditions at least begins to address the kinds of weaknesses I outline here (e.g., Britzman, 1991; Cherry-holmes, 1988; Ellsworth, 1989; Lather, 1991; Lewis, 1988, 1989; Marshall, 1989). Of particular relevance to my argument is the feminist poststructural-ist work of scholar/teacher Elizabeth Ellsworth (1989). Following her initia-tive, this paper cautions those of us who profess and practice empowerment within critical and feminist discourses against didactic claims of "what we can do for you." My aim is not to immobilize or paralyze us from continuing that work. Rather, I hope to strengthen my own, and others', understanding and practice within critical and feminist traditions.

My focus is on those critical and feminist educational discourses that emphasize empowerment. Interestingly, the same discourses seem to also claim for themselves the label "pedagogy"; that is, discourses of "critical pedagogy" and "feminist pedagogy." While other critical educational discourses and other feminist discourses address pedagogy and have relevance to pedagogy, they do not claim to be centrally about pedagogy. Nor, curiously, is "empowerment" central to these "non-pedagogy" discourses. This observation leads me to pon-der, as a secondary aim of the paper, the connection of empowerment and ped-agogy in discourses of critical and feminist pedagogy. I shall explicitly address this issue near the end of the paper.

The fields of critical pedagogy and feminist pedagogy are complex and fragmented. Through an analysis of contemporary academic literature that claims for itself the label "critical pedagogy" or "feminist pedagogy," I have begun to explore not only the separation of these two fields, but distinctions within each field (Gore, 1989b, 1993). Within the field of critical pedagogy two main discursive strands can be identified. The central distinction between the two strands centers on different approaches to the question of pedagogy, whereby one strand emphasizes the articulation of a broad (and shifting) social and educational vision while the other shows greater concern for instructional practices in specific contexts. In making this distinction between "systems of thought" in critical pedagogy, the prominence of its "authors," the proponents of the two strands, is striking, with Henry Giroux and Peter McLaren the key advocates and representatives of the first strand and Paulo Freire and Ira Shor the key advocates and representatives of the second. In the field of feminist pedagogy, two discursive strands can also be identified. The central distinction between these strands lies in the empha-sis of one strand on instructional aspects of pedagogy and the emphasis of the other strand on feminism(s). While "authors" can be named (e.g., Margo

Culley, Carolyn Shrewsbury, and Nancy Schniedewind as representative of the first strand; Madeleine Grumet and Frances Maher as representative of the second), these "systems of thought" are most closely linked to the institutional location of their proponents, with the first strand of feminist pedagogy emerging from Women's Studies departments and the second from schools of education. Another distinction within feminist pedagogy can be drawn around the variety of stances within feminism that are reflected but often not acknowledged in the discourses of feminist pedagogy. Simply stated, much of the feminist pedagogy literature to date has emerged out of liberal and radical feminist traditions.[2] It is not within the scope of this paper to map out these distinctions in detail. However, acknowledging the complexity of the "objects" of my analysis is important in countering any "unity" implied in the following discussion of points of coincidence in constructions of empowerment.

It is from the outlined discursive strands of critical and feminist pedagogy that I will be drawing examples as I return to my primary aim of identifying weaknesses in constructions of empowerment. It is not my purpose to criticize specific discourses as having specific weaknesses so much as I hope to illustrate, through examples, general tendencies among the critical and feminist pedagogy discourses. The normalizing tendencies, or dangers, of these discourses can be located in: (1) presuppositions inherent in the term empowerment which are taken on by the discourses and, closely related, (2) their unreflexive use of empowerment rhetoric. I elaborate each of these in turn.

PROBLEMATIC PRESUPPOSITIONS

The term "empowerment" has no particular meaning prior to its construction within specific discourses; that is, it is important to acknowledge that the meanings of words are always "up for grabs," that there are no essential meanings—only ascribed meanings (Weedon, 1987). Social definitions of terms are products of the contexts surrounding their use and the discourses in which they are embedded.

Nevertheless, while its specific meanings must be identified within discourses, the term "empowerment" often does, more generally, presuppose (1) an agent of empowerment, (2) a notion of power as property, and (3) some kind of vision or desirable end state. It is my contention that discourses of critical and feminist pedagogy construct empowerment in ways consistent with these underlying presuppositions. I elaborate these arguments by addressing each of the three presuppositions in turn: first, clarifying how the presupposition seems inherent to the term "empowerment"; next, illustrating its manifestation in some discourses of critical and feminist pedagogy; and finally, pointing to theoretical weaknesses and oversights within these discourses that are created by taking on the presupposition in the construction of empowerment.

THE AGENT OF EMPOWERMENT

To em-power denotes to give authority, to enable, to license. As such, it is a process which requires an agent—someone, or something, to em-power. Even the notion of "self-empowerment" presumes an agent—the self.

When discourses of critical and feminist pedagogy espouse "self-empowerment" the distinction made is not around the agent of empowerment but around the subject of empowerment—that is, who is (to be) empowered. Giroux (1988) and McLaren (1989), for instance, speak frequently of "self and social empowerment," distinguishing between, and connecting, the empowerment of individuals and social positions. The following statement by McLaren (1989) provides an example: "Teachers must engage unyieldingly in their attempt to empower students both as individuals and as potential agents of social change by establishing a critical pedagogy that students can use in the classroom and in the streets" (221). The agent of empowerment in this example, and generally in critical pedagogy, is the teacher while the subject of empowerment is more than the individual student.

Strong senses of human agency and optimism pervade claims about the teacher as empower-er in ways which portray the teacher's role as crucial and sometimes even as omnipotent. Culley (1985) provides an extreme example of this approach to empowerment: "The feminist teacher can be a potent agent of change who, through combinations of course content and process, has the power to replace self-hatred with self-love, incapacity with capacity, unfreedom with freedom, blindness with knowledge" (21). Likewise in critical pedagogy, we find statements which place the teacher as the agent of empowerment. For example, McLaren (1989) in addressing the "kinds of theories educators should work with" and the "knowledge they can provide in order to empower students," says "empowerment means not only helping students to understand and engage the world around them, but also enabling them to exercise the kind of courage necessary to change the social order where necessary" (182). The teacher, as the agent of empowerment, is accorded great importance in these discourses.

My major concerns are that these claims to empowerment attribute extraordinary abilities to the teacher, and hold a view of agency which risks ignoring the context(s) of teachers' work. Teachers are constrained by, for example, their location in patriarchal institutions (Grumet, 1988) and by the historical construction of pedagogy as, and within, discourses of social regulation (Gore, 1993; Hamilton, 1989; Luke, 1989). Overly optimistic views of the agent of empowerment also set up serious shortcomings in the use of empowerment rhetoric which shall be elaborated later.

POWER AS PROPERTY

Another major shortcoming of constructions of empowerment in critical and feminist pedagogy discourses is that they conceive of power as property, something the teacher has and can give to students. To *em*-power suggests that power can be given, provided, controlled, held, conferred, taken away. For example, Shrewsbury (1987) describes the vision of feminist pedagogy as including "a participatory, democratic process in which at least some power is shared" (7) and "the goal is to increase the power of all actors, not to limit the power of some" (8). While Giroux (1988) and McLaren (1989) have recently begun to refer to power as embodied in concrete practices, they still talk of "sharing power" in ways which remained locked within a view of power as property. "Giroux assumes that schools must be seen . . . as complexes of dominant and subordinate cultures, each ideologically linked to *the power they possess* to define and legitimate a particular construction of reality" (McLaren, 1989, 200) (emphasis added).

Power as property is often, but not necessarily, connected with a "zero-sum" understanding of power which suggests that there is only so much power and that if teachers "give" some of it to students, they must "give up" some of their own power. Such an understanding of power is implied in Kathryn Pauly Morgan's (1987) characterization of the paradox of democratic pedagogy:

> If the feminist teacher actively assumes any of the forms of power available to her—expert, reward, legitimate, maternal/referent—she eliminates the possibility of educational democracy in the feminist classroom; if she dispenses with these in the name of preserving democracy, she suffers personal alienation, fails to function as a role model, and abandons the politically significant role of woman authority. In short, she stops functioning as a feminist teacher. (51)

Some of the early "resistance" work in education points to the inadequacy of conceptions of power as property or zero-sum. For example, in Paul Willis's (1977) study, *Learning to Labour,* the teachers were not alone in being able to exercise power. The "lads" exercised their own power also. And the effects of the exercise of power were contradictory and partial.

While Willis's study only pointed to the operation of power as contradictory, Foucault (among others) has elaborated a view of power which reveals weaknesses of the property and zero-sum conceptions. Rather than conceiving of power as a possession or a commodity, a thing to be held or exchanged, Foucault (1980) argued instead that power is "exercised, and . . . only exists in action" (89):

> Power must be analysed as something which circulates, or rather as something which only functions in the form of a chain. It is never localised here or there, never in anybody's hands, never appropriated as a commodity or piece of wealth. Power is employed and exercised through a net-like organisation. And not only do individuals circulate between its threads; they are always in the position of simultaneously undergoing and exercising this power. They are not only its inert or consenting target. They are always also the elements of its articulation. In other words, individuals are the vehicles of power, not its points of application. (98)

Theoretically, Foucault's analysis of power raises questions about the possibility of empowering. First, it refutes the idea that one can give power to (can *em*-power) another. Thus, to accept a view of one's work as giving power (as property) to others/Others (I will return to this in my discussion of the use of empowerment) is to overly simplify the operation of power in our society. Given Foucault's conception of power as "circulating," "exercised" and existing "only in action," empowerment cannot mean the giving of power. It could, however, mean the exercise of power in an attempt (that might not be successful) to help others to exercise power. That is, Foucault's analysis of power doesn't preclude purposeful or politically motivated action; it does point out the rather strong possibility that our purposes might not be attained.

Second, conceiving of power *as exercised* points immediately to the need for empowerment to be context-specific and related to practices. As I have already indicated, discourses of critical and feminist pedagogy have tended to "decontextualize" empowerment. Their concern for context at the broad level of societal relations and institutions and ideologies (be they capitalist and/or patriarchal) leads to totalizing or universalizing tendencies which imply their concern is for "all teachers" or "all students" or "all women." Understanding power as exercised, rather than as possessed, requires more attention to the microdynamics of the operation of power as it is exercised in particular sites, that is conducting an "*ascending* analysis of power, starting . . . from its infinitesimal mechanisms" (Foucault, 1980, 99).

WHAT IS THE VISION OF EMPOWERMENT ANYWAY?

Critical and feminist pedagogy discourses frequently perpetuate a simplistic dichotomy between empowerment and oppression through a level of abstraction which mystifies the meanings ascribed to either term (empowerment or oppression). Ellsworth (1989) has illustrated this point by citing some of the ways in which critical discourses answer the question "Empowerment for what?" The vision is of empowerment

> for "human betterment", for expanding "the range of possible social identities people may become" and "making one's self present as part of a moral and political project that links production of meaning to the possibility for human agency, democratic community, and transformative social action." (307)

But what does all this mean at the level of the school or classroom? And how are teachers to turn this "macro" vision into the "micro" of their daily practices in classrooms? Such questions have historically plagued radical educational work, as it struggles with the contradictory demands of traditional radical political ideals and institutional work in the academy (Ladwig, 1992; Liston & Zeichner, 1991; Wexler, 1987).

The perpetuation of a dichotomy between empowerment and oppression also stems from a shift in conceptions of power as repression to power as productive, such that empowerment is linked with a productive conception of power and oppression is linked with a repressive conception. For example, Shrewsbury (1987) states that "by focusing on empowerment, feminist pedagogy embodies a concept of power as energy, capacity, and potential rather than as domination" (8). In this view, power is *either* productive *or* repressive. I will argue shortly that attempts to empower can (and probably will) have inconsistent effects.

What I find most troubling is the theoretical *pronouncement* of these discourses as empowering or liberatory. For example, McLaren (1989) claims that:

> We can consider *dominant* discourses (those produced by the dominant culture) as "regimes of truth", as general economies of power/knowledge, or as multiple forms of constraint. . . . A critical discourse is . . . self-critical and deconstructs dominant discourses the moment they are ready to achieve hegemony. (181)

In this statement, critical discourses are presented as liberatory because they challenge dominant discourses, not because they have been liberatory for particular people or groups. Meanwhile, the "self critical" nature claimed for critical discourses seems more rhetorical than actual. While Giroux and McLaren occasionally reframe or clarify aspects of their argument as their project continues to shift with time, the possibility that their own academic construction of critical pedagogy might not be the emancipatory discourse it is intended to be is rarely articulated by these theorists. Rather, teachers are exhorted to "take as their first concern the issue of empowerment"; empowerment which "depends on the ability of teachers in the future to struggle collectively in order to create those ideological and material conditions of work that enable them to share power, to shape policy, and to play an active role in structuring school/community relations" (Giroux, 1988, 214). In short, empowerment depends on teachers using and actualizing this discourse of critical pedagogy.

Contrary to this view, Sawicki (1988) argues that "no discourse is inherently liberating or oppressive. . . . The liberatory status of any discourse is a matter of historical inquiry, not theoretical pronouncement" (166). Does this suggest that by focussing only on "dominant" discourses McLaren has missed an opportunity afforded by the concept "regime of truth"? Bové (1988) argues that many leading humanistic intellectuals misread Foucault "to blunt the political consequences of his critique of their disciplines', their discourses', and their own positions within the knowledge/power apparatus" (xi). The political consequences of Foucault's critique include questioning of the ideological, discursive, and political positions of "oppositional" discourses. To capitalize on this interpretation of Foucault's work would require more contextualization of empowerment rhetoric. That is, in addition to the theoretical pronouncement about emancipatory potential currently found, there would need to be more historical or empirical inquiry of empowerment in particular sites and discourses.

This general problem of decontextualization is perhaps more apparent in the critical discourses than it is in the feminist pedagogy discourses where there can be found many more attempts to address specific contexts. With the 1960s radical feminist premise that "the personal is political" (Jaggar, 1983), an insight which still has currency in contemporary feminisms, the feminist pedagogy literature reveals a much greater emphasis on actual classrooms and classroom practices (e.g., consider the collections edited by Bunch & Pollack, 1983; Culley & Portuges, 1985; Schniedewind & Maher, 1987) and seems less inclined toward grand theorizing. However, many of these accounts are rather descriptive and individualistic in their presentation of context and pay little attention to the location of their practices in educational institutions. Despite any differences related to "feminist process" or "feminist pedagogy," or to a student population consisting primarily of women, teaching feminism in a Women's Studies classroom remains an act of pedagogy in an educational institution.

When much of the empowerment rhetoric pertains to practices which could or should take place within universities and schools, we must ask how much freedom can there be within the institutional and pedagogical exigencies of teaching? More attention to contexts would help shift the problem of empowerment from dualisms of power/powerlessness, and dominant/subordinate, that is, from purely oppositional stances, to a problem of multiplicity and contradiction. It may be helpful to think of social actors negotiating actions within particular contexts. I hasten to add here that I am not advocating a notion of context as simply a pseudonym/synonym for the present or the immediate. Rather, I would argue that context must be conceived as filled with social actors whose personal and group histories position them as subjects immersed in social patterns. Thus, contexts for the work of empowerment need to be defined historically and politically with acknowledgment of the unique struggles that characterize the exercise of power at the micro levels.

UNREFLEXIVE USE

My major concern about the politics of empowerment within discourses of critical and feminist pedagogy stems from conceptions of the agent of empowerment. Having established that the agent of empowerment is usually the teacher, and that the subject (or object) of empowerment is Others, a distinction is immediately set up between "us" and "them." Even if some teachers attempted to empower other teachers, the distinction remains between those who aim to empower and those who are to be empowered. As a given in any relation which aims at empowerment, the agent becomes problematic when the us/them relationship is conceived as requiring a focus only on "them." When the agent of empowerment assumes to be already empowered, and so apart from those who are to be empowered, arrogance can underlie claims of "what we can do for you." This danger is apparent both in the work of the teacher who is to empower students, and in the work of the academic whose discourse is purportedly empowering for the teachers (and others).

In the focus on Others there is a danger of forgetting to examine one's own (or one's group's) implication in the conditions one seeks to affect. Consider, for example, the following statement by Giroux (1988):

> Teachers' work has to be analyzed in terms of its social and political function within particular "regimes of truth". That is, teachers can no longer deceive themselves

into believing they are serving on behalf of truth when, in fact, they are deeply involved in battles "about the status of truth and the political role it plays." (212)

In his insistence that teachers are intellectuals who need to be conscious of the contradictory effects of their work, it seems Giroux has ignored the possibility that his own position as an intellectual is also vulnerable as a "regime of truth." Although Giroux (1991) argues that "educators need to be skeptical regarding any notion of reason [that] purports to reveal the truth by denying its own historical construction and ideological principles" (51), he does not articulate, with any specificity, his own complicity. It is possible that he has misread Foucault in a way which costs him his critical openness (Bové, 1988). His insight on teachers seems to be his oversight when it comes to his own work. In the (well-intentioned) focus on empowering others there is a danger of overlooking the reflexivity which, rhetorically,[3] is considered integral to critical practice.

Moreover, setting oneself apart as teacher/intellectual/leader can easily foster an arrogance which assumes to know what empowerment means for teachers or students. And it assumes that "we *can* do for you." Bové (1986) puts it like this:

> Leading intellectuals tend to assume responsibility for imagining alternatives and do so *within* a set of discourses and institutions burdened genealogically by multifaceted complicities with power that make them dangerous to people. As agencies of these discourses that greatly affect the lives of people one might say leading intellectuals are a tool of oppression and most so precisely when they arrogate the right and power to judge and imagine efficacious alternatives—a process that we might suspect, sustains leading intellectuals at the expense of others. (277)

Rather than making pronouncements about what we can do, we need to ask "what *can* we do for you?"

If empowerment is constructed as the exercise of power in an attempt to help others to exercise power (rather than as the giving of power), we confront the unforeseeable and contradictory effects of the exercise of power and must be more humble and reflexive in our claims. It is not at all clear we can do anything. For example, in my own practice as a teacher educator, I have encouraged student teachers to question practices of the education systems in which they will work and have exposed them to ideas of collective political action as having potential for social change. These efforts were aimed at "empowering" student teachers as they enter the salaried workforce. But my teaching will not/has not always had the effects I hoped it would (Gore, 1990; Gore & Zeichner, 1991). Some students decided that they couldn't bear to teach in such an oppressive system and never entered teaching. Some taught for only a brief time and then pursued alternative careers. Some have struggled to find peers with whom to engage in "collective political action" and, in "going it alone," have been ostracized within their schools and have risked job security. Others have accepted "the way things are."

In attempts to empower others we need to acknowledge that our agency has limits, that we might "get it wrong" in assuming we know what would be empowering for others, and that no matter what our aims or how we go about "empowering," our efforts will be partial and inconsistent.

REGIMES OF TRUTH

Each of the concerns about empowerment I have articulated above—an overly optimistic view of agency, a tendency to overlook context, an overly simplistic conception of power as property, the theoretical pronouncement of discourses as liberatory, a lack of reflexivity—can be illuminated through Foucault's notion of "regimes of truth".

In pointing to the nexus of power and knowledge, regime of truth highlights the potential dangers and normalizing tendencies of all discourses, including those which aim to liberate. Foucault (1983) said "My point is not that everything is bad, but that everything is dangerous" (231). Foucault (1980) explains "regime of truth" as follows: " 'Truth' is linked in circular relation with systems of power which produce and sustain it, and to effects of power which it induces and which extend it" (133), and

> Each society has its regime of truth, its general politics of truth: that is, the types of discourse which it accepts and makes function as true; the mechanisms and instances which enable one to distinguish true and false statements, the means by which each is sanctioned; the techniques and procedures accorded value in the acquisition of truth; the status of those who are charged with saying what counts as true. (131)

McLaren and Giroux, from whose work I have drawn many of my examples thus far, both employ the concept "regime of truth" to talk about the nexus of power and knowledge. My interpretation of the concept differs however, in my application of it to more than one "society" (the "dominant" society) with a single regime. My use allows us to posit that, for example, feminisms may have their own power-knowledge nexuses which, in particular contexts or at particular historical moments, will operate in ways which are oppressive and repressive to people within and/or outside of that "society." As evidence, consider the anger many women of color have expressed at the alienation and marginalization they felt from what developed as a primarily white, middle-class form of feminism in the academy (e.g., hooks, 1984; Lorde, 1984; Omolade, 1985; Spelman, 1988). Similarly, I argue, contemporary discourses of critical and feminist pedagogy have their own politics of truth—systems of power which produce and sustain truth and effects of power which the discourses induce and by which the discourses are extended—at the same time as they are positioned within the larger regimes of our present.

Michel Foucault (1983) and Michel Feher (1987) have articulated points of focus that can be used as a methodological guide for the study of regimes of truth.[4] The framework articulates two sets of questions or concerns central to Foucault's work; the first identifies the *political* aspects of the regime, focussing on the relations of power, what goes on between people; the second identifies the *ethical* aspects of the regime, the relation to one's self and the way that relation shifts. The political aspects of the regime can be identified through a study of the system of differentiations made, the functions and objectives of those differentiations (or relations of power), the specific techniques and practices which actualize the relations of power, the institutions which integrate these practices, and the formation of knowledge which describes the regime. The ethical component of the regime can be identified by studying the aspects of the self or body that are considered problematic or in need of disciplining in any given regime, in the name of what the self is disciplined or styled, the specific techniques that are developed to achieve a particular self-styling, toward what goal. The ethical "is at once intertwined with and autonomous to the political. . . . The two . . . work together. . . . The ethical affects the mechanisms of power as much as the political, and there is as much resistance in the political as there is in the ethical" (Feher, 1987, 165).

It is not within the scope of this paper, nor it is my aim, to attempt a detailed analysis of regimes of truth in critical and feminist pedagogy. Rather, I elaborate central features of regimes of truth in critical and feminist pedagogy which might help in understanding their constructions of empowerment rhetoric and practices. In particular, I focus on some of the differentiations made, the institutions involved, and the relations to "self" articulated within the discourses. I emphasize that these aspects of the regime are connected to each other and separated here for purposes of analysis and clarity.

In the Neo-Marxist discourses of critical pedagogy there has been a self-proclaimed shift from "a language of critique" to "a language of possibility" (e.g., Aronowitz & Giroux, 1985; Simon, 1987). This differentiation is connected with the shift from conceptions of power as repressive to power as productive, and with a shift from an emphasis on ideology and structure to an emphasis on agency. Resistance theories can be located at the transition between critique and possibility. Willis's (1977) study, for example, pointed to a productive aspect of power but concluded with an elucidation of the oppressive structures which kept "the lads" in their class position. "Empowerment" has been constructed in ways that take the productive moment of power further, and so go "beyond resistance." This movement to a language of possibility is part of a general shift in critical educational discourse toward acknowledging that education has played a role in social movement and not just in social reproduction (Wexler, 1987). There has been movement beyond encouraging teachers to recognize the structural constraints under which they work to having them also acknowledge "the potential inherent in teaching for transformative and political work" (Weiler, 1988, 52). The strong sense of agency found in empowerment rhetoric (particularly in critical pedagogy) can be connected to the language of possibility in which it is embedded. Indeed, it is with this shift to a language of possibility that we saw the emergence of "critical pedagogy" discourse and the linking of empowerment and pedagogy which I shall examine shortly.

Despite this move to power as productive, the Neo-Marxist roots of the discourse perhaps account for the retention of a notion of power as property which still pervades the rhetoric of critical pedagogy. In its "vulgar" form, the Neo-Marxist conception of power is clearly encapsulated in the following passage from Burbules' (1986) "A Theory of Power in Education":

> In order to identify power relations in schools, we have to begin with the questions Where are the conflicts of interest? Where are the zero-sum games? In principle, education need not involve power relations at all; the learning of one student does not necessarily entail the disadvantaging of another. In principle, teachers can function as legitimate authorities, not as authoritarian masters. In principle, schools can *educate* and . . . minimize power relations and promote the basis for informed, consensual, and egalitarian human relations. (109)

While Giroux and McLaren might argue with Burbules's theory, traces of power as property can still be found in their work; for example, critical pedagogy retains dualisms of the dominant and subordinate, the oppressed and the privileged, in which power is located in the hands of the dominant and the privileged.

Likewise, in feminist pedagogy conceptions of power as property remain. For example, Clare Bright (1987) says:

> Discussion of the student/teacher relationship must include a frank look at the power of the teacher. Feminists have often avoided the topic of power, preferring structures and situations where power is shared. However, the educational system is not an egalitarian one, and regardless of the extent to which a teacher tries to minimize her power, it can not be completely given away. (98)

Inasmuch as feminisms seek to change "patriarchal structures" and "existing power relations between men and women" (Weedon, 1987), notions of power as property and power as productive inhere and are carried into the discourses of feminist pedagogy. For instance, Shrewsbury (1987) claims that

> Empowering pedagogy does not dissolve the authority or power of the instructor. It does move from power as domination to power as creative energy . . . a view of power as creative community energy would suggest that strategies be developed to counteract unequal power arrangements. Such strategies recognize the potentiality for changing traditional unequal relationships. Our classrooms need not always reflect an equality of power, but they must reflect movement in that direction. (9, 8)

When we consider the specific practices that are to empower we confront what Michael Apple (1988) has discussed as a paradox in the democratic call for social change from "the ground up" and the need to offer possibilities or models from which people can act. This paradox helps account for the tendency toward abstract and decontextualized (at the micro levels) claims for empowerment. In the attempt not to impose an agenda on others, critical (and, to a lesser extent, some feminist) pedagogy discourses have opted instead for rather abstract theories of empowerment. And yet, they have imposed a requirement on teachers to do the work of empowering, to be the agents of empowerment, without providing much in the way of tangible guidance for that work. An exception is the recent feminist poststructuralist attention to pedagogy which situates itself in particular contexts but has also begun to raise questions about the possibility of empowering (e.g., Ellsworth, 1989; Gardner, Dean & McKaig, 1989; Lather, 1991; Lewis, 1989; Mahony, 1988)—questions that point to multiplicity, contradiction and partialness.

The institutional location of much critical and feminist pedagogy discourse, in an academy which rewards the development of theory over struggles to teach, can account for some of the theoretical pronouncement and inattention to context which I have been discussing. As part of *academic* discourses, the constructions of empowerment discussed in this paper often reveal a "will to knowledge," characteristic of much intellectual work, that is so strong that the need, desire or willingness to question one's own work is lost in the desire to believe that one has found "truth," that one is "right." This aspect of the regime of truth is manifested (and problematic) in critical and feminist pedagogy discourses of empowerment by a tendency to present the discourses in a fixed, final, "founded" form which "protects *them* from rethinking and change. It turns what was once 'critical' in their work into a kind of norm or law—a final truth, a final emancipation. For Foucault that is just what critical 'truth' cannot be" (Rajchman, 1985, 93).

Taubman (1986) makes this point in his review of *Gendered Subjects: The Dynamics of Feminist Teaching* claiming it is

> informed by essentialist and separatist arguments and assumptions. . . .
> Therein . . . lies the danger of a feminist pedagogy. The old dualities are preserved. The origin of truth is found in anatomy. . . . Feminist pedagogy loses its usefulness to the extent that it sees itself as synonymous with good teaching, having an exclusive claim on good teaching. . . . It loses its force to the extent that it locates the origin and horizon of pedagogy in and on the bodies of women. (93)

These essentializing tendencies might be accounted for by the emergence of much feminist pedagogy from liberal and radical feminist traditions, both of which have tended to "attempt to define women's nature once and for all" (Weedon, 1987, p. 135). Similarly, the connection of critical pedagogy to Neo-Marxism might account for its totalizing tendencies, whereby dominant discourses are bad and must be overturned and oppositional discourses are liberatory.

The will to knowledge of much academic work also helps us understand the lack of reflexivity which is a danger in the use of empowerment rhetoric in some of these discourses. A more detailed attempt to map out the regimes of truth of critical and feminist pedagogy[5] (Gore, 1989b) reveals a tendency to neglect the ethical[6]—one's relation to oneself. That is, these discourses rarely address ways in which teachers, students, or the theorists themselves need to style or discipline their gestures, postures or attitudes. The rhetoric is of freedom, not of control. And yet, the discourses have the effect of disciplining teachers to practice critical and feminist pedagogies. This neglect of the ethical brings us full circle to the institutions which integrate critical and feminist discourses, primarily universities, and to the differentiations made in the academy and within the discourses themselves. The focus is generally on the broader political questions of interests and institutions with, especially in some discourses of critical pedagogy, little attention to self. How then, does the rhetoric of empowerment connect with the practice of pedagogy?

PEDAGOGY AND EMPOWERMENT

To understand the relation of pedagogy to empowerment in these discourses of critical and feminist pedagogy, I want to highlight two aspects of the preceding analysis. First, my analysis of presuppositions points to a general congruence between the two enterprises of pedagogy and empowerment. In very general terms, pedagogy seems to involve a teacher (an agent) who "gives" knowledge, responsibility, and more (as property) to students, and aims to produce a particular conception of the educated student (a vision, a desired end state); that is, pedagogy seems to hold the same presuppositions as empowerment. It is not surprising, then, that it is the critical and feminist discourses which claim a focus on pedagogy that also emphasize empowerment.

Moreover, constructions of critical and feminist pedagogies and of empowerment have both occurred within discourses that have gone beyond a conception of power as primarily repressive: empowerment suggests the productive capacity of power (while frequently posing it in opposition to power as domination and so maintaining the dichotomy); critical and feminist pedagogy come out of a history of "progressive" schooling in which instead of controlling/disciplining/constraining learners, the teacher was to use her or his authority to facilitate/to empower.

While the congruence of empowerment and critical and feminist pedagogies can be understood, it remains to be seen whether they can be actualized as conceived. That is, while the desire may be to move from a conception of power as repression to em-power-ment (in a dichotomous fashion with great optimism and human agency), the institutional location (context, again) of much pedagogical practice may militate against it. The pedagogical relation of teacher to students is, at some fundamental level, one in which the teacher is able to exercise power in ways unavailable to students. Teaching remains embedded within a history of moral and cultural regulation. Moreover, as Foucault (1977) and others (e.g., Walkerdine, 1985, 1986; Walkerdine & Lucey, 1989) have argued about disciplinary power, practices which decrease overt regulation can increase surveillance and regulation through covert and more dangerous means. These conditions suggest that attempts to "give up power" and "share power" in the name of empowerment might be misdirected. Rather, the energies of those of us who advocate critical and feminist pedagogies might be better directed at seeking ways to exercise power toward the fulfilment of our espoused aims, ways that include humility, skepticism and self-criticism.

Second, my reconstruction (following Foucault) of empowerment as the exercise of power in an attempt to help others to exercise power, suggests that empowerment must occur in sites of practice. Indeed if pedagogy is conceived as the process of knowledge production (Lusted, 1986), a meaning consistent with much critical and feminist work that tends to deny constructions of pedagogy as "instruction," then we can argue that empowerment must be pedagogical—a process of knowledge production. Of course, the work of theorizing can certainly be pedagogical to the degree that we can identify processes of knowledge production. But when we consider the rhetoric of much of this work to be for the empowerment of teachers and students as teachers and students and as "critical citizens" (critical pedagogy) or women (feminist pedagogy), while the primary site of knowledge production is the university, we can better understand why these discourses have seemed to some critics to be rather ineffectual. For example, Giroux's work has certainly been pedagogical and empowering for many of us *in the academic field.* Critiques of his work for the inaccessibility of its language (e.g., Bowers, 1991; Schrag, 1988; Miedema, 1987) point out that his work may not have been as pedagogical or empowering at the ostensibly targeted sites of school and classroom. Of course, we need to take these criticisms cautiously, given that they are other academic articulations, just as my own critique must be positioned within the academic context of its construction.

Nevertheless, the argument that empowerment must be linked to pedagogical practice reiterates and strengthens two threads of this paper: first, discourses of critical and feminist pedagogy need to pay much closer attention to the contexts in which they aim to empower; second, they need to provide better guidance for the actions of the teachers they hope to empower or they hope will empower students. This is not to suggest that detailed prescriptions for practice should, or even could, be given. But if teachers are to exercise power in an attempt to help their students exercise power both in and outside of the classroom or, as McLaren (1989) put it, "in the classroom and in the streets," then teachers need some contextualized guidance as to ways in which they might proceed. I am fully aware that this paper does not directly assist with the task of providing such contextualized guidance. My purpose here was limited to an elaboration of concerns with constructions of empowerment as a precursor to such a task for my own work in teacher education and, hopefully, for the work of others within the critical and feminist traditions.

CONCLUSION

None of this discussion of shortcomings or power or regimes of truth is to say that the impulse to empower groups who have historically been oppressed is bad or wrong, or that academics should divorce themselves from struggles that are not perceived to be immediately their own. On the contrary, I believe academics must continue the kinds of political struggles which are the concern of critical and feminist pedagogies but should do so while constantly questioning the "truth" of their/our own thought and selves. Of course, my own thoughts presented here must also be questioned. They represent a moment in my ongoing struggle to understand and practice pedagogies informed by the feminist and critical traditions.

In this paper I have tried to demonstrate ways in which (my interpretations of) Foucault's analyses of power and intellectual work are useful for this endeavor. Foucault's rejection of conceptions of power as property points to a rethinking of empowerment as the exercise of power in an attempt to help others to exercise power. And, in the emphasis on power as action, Foucault's work demands greater attention to the contexts in which empowerment is advocated and/or attempted. Furthermore, Foucault's analysis of power and knowledge as connected through regimes of truth, calls for greater reflexivity and acknowledgment of the limitations of what "we" can do for "you."

ACKNOWLEDGMENT

My thanks to James Ladwig for his insightful comments and criticisms on numerous versions of this paper. I am also grateful to Elizabeth Ellsworth, Tom Popkewitz, Michael Apple, Ken Zeichner and Alison Dewar, each of whom has had significant influences on my thinking about "empowerment."

NOTES

1. See Gore (1989a) for an elaboration of the construction of empowerment within conservative and liberal humanist discourses.
2. See Jaggar (1983) and Weedon (1987) for characterizations of the variety of stances within feminism. Also see Acker (1987) for a consideration of the educational applications of the various theoretical frameworks. The recent poststructuralist feminist attention to pedagogy differs from this earlier work in feminist pedagogy in several ways, not the least of which, given my delimitations in this paper, is its reluctance to call itself "feminist pedagogy."
3. Consider, for example, McLaren's (1989) statement cited earlier in this paper that critical discourses are "self-critical" or the statement "Nor must we ever give up becoming more theoretically vigilant on the basis that we are morally innocent. To claim immunity from our exercising domination over others on the basis that we have good intentions is to euphemistically dodge Michel Foucault's injunction that we judge truth by its effects and to deny our complicity in economies of oppression on the grounds of our theoretical ignorance" (McLaren, 1988, p. 70). There is a confessional nod of complicity here, but no explication, elaboration, or articulation of the *specific* form that complicity takes.
4. I thank Elizabeth Ellsworth for introducing me to Feher's (1987) work and for suggesting its relevance as a methodology for my work on critical and feminist pedagogies.
5. See Gore (1989b) for an attempt to map out the regimes of truth in critical and feminist pedagogy around issues of authority.
6. This sense in which Foucault uses "ethical" is not to be confused with the commonsense use of the term, which often conflates ethics with morality.

REFERENCES

Acker, S. (1987). "Feminist theory and the study of gender and education." *International Review of Education,* 33(4), 419–435.

Apple, M. W. (1988). "Curriculum, capitalism, and democracy: A response to Whitty's critics." *British Journal of Sociology of Education,* 7(3), 319–327.

Aronowitz, S., and Giroux, H. A. (1985). *Education under siege.* South Hadley, Mass.: Bergin & Garvey.

Bové, P. A. (1986). *Intellectuals in power: A genealogy of critical humanism.* New York: Columbia University Press.

Bové, P. A. (1988). "Foreword: The Foucault phenomenon: The problematics of style." In G. Deleuze *Foucault* (trans. S. Hand), (pp. vii–xl). Minneapolis: University of Minnesota Press.

Bowers, C. A. (1991). "Some questions about the anachronistic elements in the Giroux-McLaren theory of a critical pedagogy." *Curriculum Inquiry,* 21(2), 239–252.

Bunch, C., and Pollack, S. (eds). (1983). *Learning our way: Essays in feminist education.* Trumansburg, NY: The Crossing Press.

Bright, C. (1987). "Teaching feminist pedagogy: An undergraduate course." *Women's Studies Quarterly,* 15(3–4), 96–100.

Britzman, D. (1991). *Practice makes practice: A critical study of learning to teach.* Albany: State University of New York Press.

Burbules, N. C. (1986). "A theory of power in education." *Educational Theory,* 36(2), 95–114.

Cherryholmes, C. (1988). *Power and criticism: Poststructural investigations in education.* New York: Teachers College Press.

Culley, M. (1985). "Anger and authority in the introductory Women's Studies classroom." In M. Culley and C. Portuges (eds). *Gendered subjects: The dynamics of feminist teaching* (pp. 209–218). Boston & London: Routledge & Kegan Paul.

Culley M., and Portuges, C. (eds). (1985). *Gendered subjects: The dynamics of feminist teaching.* Boston & London: Routledge & Kegan Paul.

Ellsworth, E. (1989). "Why doesn't this feel empowering? Working through the repressive myths of critical pedagogy." *Harvard Educational Review,* 59(3), 297–324.

Feher, M. (1987). "On bodies and technologies." In H. Foster (ed). *Discussions in contemporary culture* (pp. 159–172). Seattle: Bay Press.

Foucault, M. (1977). *Discipline and punish: The birth of the prison.* New York: Pantheon.

Foucault, M. (1980). "Truth and power." In C. Gordon (ed). *Power/knowledge: Selected interviews and other writings 1972–1977* (pp. 109–133). New York: Pantheon Books.

Foucault, M. (1983). "The subject and power." In H. L. Dreyfus and P. Rabinow (eds). *Michel Foucault: Beyond structuralism and hermeneutics,* 2nd edition (pp. 208–228). Chicago: University of Chicago Press.

Gardner, S., Dean, C., and McKaig, D. (1989). "Responding to difference in the classroom: The politics of knowledge, class, and sexuality." *Sociology of Education,* 62 (Jan.), 64–74.

Giroux, H. A. (1988). *Schooling and the struggle for public life: Critical pedagogy in the modern age.* Minneapolis: University of Minnesota Press.

Giroux, H. A. (ed). (1991). *Postmodernism, feminism, and cultural politics: Redrawing educational boundaries.* Albany: State University of New York Press.

Gore, J. M. (1989a). "Agency, structure and the rhetoric of teacher empowerment." Paper presented at the American Educational Research Association Annual Conference, San Francisco, California, March 27–31.

Gore, J. M. (1989b). "The struggle for pedagogies: Critical and feminist discourses as 'regimes of truth.'" Paper presented at the Eleventh Conference on Curriculum Theory and Classroom Practice, Bergamo Conference Center, Dayton, Ohio, October 18–22.

Gore, J. M. (1990). "Pedagogy as text in physical education teacher education." In D. Kirk and R. Tinning (eds). *Physical education, curriculum and culture: Critical issues in the contemporary crisis* (pp. 101–138). London, New York & Philadelphia: The Falmer Press.

Gore, J. M. (1993). *The struggle for pedagogies: Critical and feminist discourses as "regimes of truth."* New York: Routledge.

Gore, J. M., and Zeichner, K. M. (1991). "Action research and reflective teaching in preservice teacher education: A case study from the United States." *Teaching and Teacher Education,* 7(2), 119–136.

Grumet, M. (1988). *Bitter milk.* Amherst: The University of Massachusetts Press.

Hamilton, D. (1989). *Towards a theory of schooling.* London, New York & Philadelphia: The Falmer Press.

hooks, b. (1984). *Feminist theory: From margin to center.* Boston: South End Press.

Jaggar, A. M. (1983). *Feminist politics and human nature.* Sussex: The Harvester Press.

Ladwig, J. G. (1992). A theory of methodology for the sociology of school knowledge. Ph.D. thesis, University of Wisconsin-Madison.

Lather, P. (1991). *Getting smart: Feminist research and pedagogy with/in the postmodern.* New York: Routledge.

Lewis, M. (1988). *Without a word: Sources and themes for a feminist pedagogy.* Ph.D. thesis, University of Toronto.

Lewis, M. (1989). "Problems of practice in radical teaching. A feminist perspective on the psycho/social/sexual dynamics in the mixed gender classroom." Paper presented at the American Educational Research Association Annual Conference, San Francisco, California, March 27–31.

Liston, D., and Zeichner, K. (1991). *Teacher education and the conditions of schooling.* New York: Routledge.

Lorde, A. (1984). *Sister outsider.* Trumansburg, NY: Crossing Press.

Luke, C. (1989). *Pedagogy, printing and protestantism: The discourse on childhood.* Albany: State University of New York Press.

Lusted, D. (1986). "Why pedagogy?" *Screen,* 27(5), 2–14.

Maeroff, G. I. (1988). *The empowerment of teachers: Overcoming the crisis of confidence.* New York & London: Teachers College Press.

Mahony, P. (1988). "Oppressive pedagogy: The importance of process in Women's Studies." *Women's Studies International Forum,* 11(2), 103–108.

Marshall, J. D. (1989). "Foucault and education." *Australian Journal of Education,* 33(2), 99–113.

McLaren, P. (1988). "Schooling the postmodern body: Critical pedagogy and the politics of enfleshment." *Journal of Education,* 170(3), 53–83.

McLaren, P. (1989). *Life in schools: An introduction to critical pedagogy in the foundations of education.* New York & London: Longman.

Miedema, S. (1987). "The theory-practice relation in critical pedagogy." *Phenomenology + Pedagogy,* 5(3), 221–229.

Miller, J. L. (1990). *Creating spaces and finding voices: Teachers collaborating for empowerment.* Albany: State University of New York Press.

Morgan, K. P. (1987). "The perils and paradoxes of feminist pedagogy." *Resources for Feminist Research,* 16(3), 49–52.

Omolade, B. (1985). "Black women and feminism." In H. Eisenstein and A. Jardine (eds). *The future of difference.* New Brunswick: Rutgers University Press.

Popkewitz, T. S. (1991). *A political sociology of educational reform: Power/knowledge in teaching, teacher education, and research.* New York: Teachers College Press.

Rabinow, P. (1984). "Polemics, politics, and problemizations: An interview with Michel Foucault." In P. Rabinow (ed). *The Foucault reader* (pp. 381–390). New York: Pantheon Books.

Rajchman, J. (1985). *Michel Foucault: The freedom of philosophy.* New York: Columbia University Press.

Sawicki, J. (1988). "Feminism and the power of Foucauldian discourse." In J. Arac (ed). *After Foucault: Humanistic knowledge, postmodern challenges* (pp. 161–178). New Brunswick and London: Rutgers University Press.

Schniedewind, N., and Maher, F. (eds). (1987). "Special feature: Feminist pedagogy." *Women's Studies Quarterly,* 15(3–4).

Schrag, F. (1988). "Response to Giroux." *Educational Theory,* 38(1), 143–144.

Shor, I., and Freire, P. (1987). *A pedagogy for liberation: Dialogues on transforming education.* South Hadley, Mass.: Bergin & Garvey.

Shrewsbury, C. M. (1987). "What is feminist pedagogy?" *Women's Studies Quarterly,* 15(3–4), 6–14.

Simon, R. I. (1987). "Empowerment as a pedagogy of possibility." *Language Arts,* 64(4), 370–382.

Spelman, E. V. (1988). *Inessential woman: Problems of exclusion in feminist thought.* Boston: Beacon Press.

Taubman, P. (1986). Review article "Gendered subjects: The dynamics of feminist teaching," Margaret Culley and Catherine Portuges (eds.) *Phenomenology + Pedagogy,* 4(2), 89–94.

Walkerdine, V. (1985). "On the regulation of speaking and silence: Subjectivity, class and gender in contemporary schooling." In C. Steedman, C. Unwin, and V. Walkerdine (eds). *Language, gender and childhood* (pp. 203–241). London, Boston & Henley: Routledge & Kegan Paul.

Walkerdine, V. (1986). "Progressive pedagogy and political struggle." *Screen,* 27(5), 54–60.

Walkerdine, V., and Lucey, H. (1989). *Democracy in the kitchen: Regulating mothers and socialising daughters.* London: Virago Press.

Weedon, C. (1987). *Feminist practice and poststructuralist theory.* Oxford: Basil Blackwell.

Weiler, K. (1988). *Women teaching for change: Gender, class and power.* South Hadley, Mass.: Bergin & Garvey.

Wexler, P. (1987). *Social analysis of education: After the new sociology.* London & New York: Routledge & Kegan Paul.

Willis, P. (1977). *Learning to labour.* Westmead: Saxon House.

Yonemura, M. (1986). "Reflections on teacher empowerment and teacher education." *Harvard Educational Review,* 56(4), 473–480.

Suggested Readings
for Future Study

GENDER, SEXUALITY, AND SCHOOLING

Abelove, H., Barale, M., and Halperin, D. (1993). *Lesbian and gay studies reader.* New York: Routledge.

Anzaldúa, G., ed. (1990). *Haciendo caras: Creative and critical perspectives by feminists of color.* San Francisco: Aunt Lute Books, 1990.

Butler, J. (1990). *Gender trouble: Feminisim and the subversion of identity.* New York: Routledge.

Butler, J. and Scott, J. (1992). *Feminists theorize the political.* New York: Routledge.

Fischman, G. (2000). *Imagining teachers: Rethinking gender dynamics in teacher education.* Lanham, Md.: Rowman and Littlefield.

Fuss, D. (1991). *Inside/outside: Lesbian theories, gay theories.* New York: Routledge.

Garcia, A., ed. (1997). *Chicana feminist thought.* New York: Routledge.

Gore, J. (1993). *The struggle for pedagogies: Critical and feminist discourses as regimes of truth.* New York: Routledge.

Giroux, H., ed. (1991). *Postmodernism, feminism, and cultural politics.* Albany: SUNY Press.

Guillaumin, C. (1995). *Racism, sexism, power and ideology.* London: Routledge.

Haymes, S. (1995). *Race, culture and the city: Pedagogy for black urban struggle.* Albany: SUNY Press

Hernandez, A. (1987). *Pedagogy, democracy and feminism: Rethinking the public sphere.* Albany: SUNY Press.

hooks, b. (1990). *Yearning: Race, gender and cultural politics.* Boston: South End Press.

hooks, b. (1999). *Talking back: Thinking feminist, thinking back.* Boston: South End Press.

Irvine, J. (1994). *Sexual cultures and the construction of adolescent identity.* Philadephia: Temple University Press.

Keohane, N., et. al. (1982). *Feminist theory: A critique of ideology.* Chicago: University of Chicago Press.

Lancaster, R., and Di Leonardo, M., eds. (1997). *The gender sexuality reader.* New York: Routledge.

Letts, W., IV, and Sears, T. (1999). *Queering elementary education: Advancing the dialogue about sexuality and schooling.* Lanham, Md: Rowman and Littlefield.

Luke, C., and Gore, J. (1992). *Feminism and critical pedagogy.* New York: Routledge.

McRobbie, A. (1991). *Feminism and youth culture: From Jackie to just seventeen.* London: Macmillan.

McRobbie, A. (1994). *Postmodernism and popular culture.* New York: Routledge.

Minh-ha, T. (1989). *Woman native other: Writing postcoloniality and feminism.* Bloomington: Indiana University Press.

Mohanty, C., Russo, A., and Torres, L. (1991). *Third world women and the politics of feminism.* Bloomington: Indiana University Press.

Sudbury, J. (1998). *Other kinds of dreams.* New York: Routledge.

Trujillo, C. (1998). *Living Chicana theory.* Berkeley, Calif.: Third Woman Press.

Unks, G., ed. (1995). *The gay teen. Educational practice and theory for lesbian, gay and bisexual adolescents.* New York: Routledge.

Wallace, M. (1990). *Invisibility blues: From pop to theory.* New York: Routledge.

Warren, K., ed. (1997). *Ecofeminism: Women, culture, nature.* Bloomington: Indiana University Press.

Weiler, K. (2001). *Feminist engagements: Reading, resisting, and revisioning male theorists in education and cultural studies.* New York: Routledge.

Weiler, K. (1998). *Women teaching for change: Gender, class and power.* South Hadley, Mass.: Bergin & Garvey.

Welton, D. (1998). *Body and flesh.* Boston: Blackwell.

Part 5

LANGUAGE, LITERACY, AND PEDAGOGY

This section on language, literacy and pedagogy begins with a dialogue between Paulo Freire and Donaldo Macedo about the meaning of emancipatory literacy. Selected from their book, *Literacy: Reading the Word and the World* (1987), "Rethinking Literacy" provides the reader with a glimpse into Freire and Macedo's vision of literacy within the context of critical pedagogy. Here, a radical literacy is understood as far more than the simple ability to decode a text. Instead, it is understood as a process of personal and social emancipation carried out through the development of both consciousness and a language of critique and possibility. As such, Freire and Macedo's contribution provided the groundwork for the growing field of critical literacy, biliteracy, and multiple literacies.

In "Teaching How to Read the World and Change It," Robert Peterson (1990) further contributes to our understanding of a the role of language and literacy in the classroom through his powerful narrative account of his own critical teaching experience. This article provides an excellent example of how critical pedagogy is lived in one classroom, even under the constraints of a very conservative school movement. Peterson's account offers many practical applications, from thematic teaching—or generative themes as Freire termed them—to experiential learning for second language students. Peterson's focus here is to provide detailed descriptions of how he works to implement a problem-posing approach, the incorporation of cultural capital, the use of dialogue and conscientization in the classroom, and the idea of empowerment and cultural politics in his practice as a middle school teacher.

Lisa Delpit's essay, "Language Diversity and Learning" from her prize-winning book *Other People's Children,* contributes to this section by examining the role of language in the construction of literate identities as defined by mainstream society. She offers important insights into the manner in which language forms, language use, language performance, language competency, cultural communication styles, and linguistic knowledge play significant roles in how teachers both perceive and teach literacy in their classroom. More important, she extends this analysis to the development of low expectations among teachers of second language learners and speakers of "nonstandard" forms of English. Delpit reveals the ways in which speakers of non-mainstream forms of English are systematically disabled from reading, as a consequence of debilitating reading intervention programs that dismiss the existing literacy skills of students from diverse linguistic backgrounds.

QUESTIONS FOR REFLECTION AND DIALOGUE

1. What are some of the major distinctions between the traditional approach to literacy and the one advocated by Freire and Macedo?
2. What are the roles of consciousness, dialectical theory, language, and experience to a theory of critical literacy?
3. What classroom suggestions does Peterson offer in order to counterbalance the debilitating impact of teacher-proof reading programs (i.e., Open Court)?
4. Explain Peterson's incorporation of dialogue, reflection, political action, and critical literacy in his middle school teaching.
5. How does the concept of linguistic reproduction (derived from social reproduction theory) apply to Delpit's analysis of language diversity?
6. In what ways do teachers legitimate and reward the communication styles of mainstream society? What are the implications of these actions to the accumulation of cultural capital and the education of working-class students?
7. What approach would you take to teach critical literacy to second language learners and speakers of "nonstandard" English. Explain why.
8. Research question: Given the critical views of literacy included in this volume, provide an analysis of traditional reading intervention programs in public schools today.

Rethinking Literacy: A Dialogue

PAULO FREIRE AND DONALDO MACEDO

Macedo: The notion of *emancipatory literacy* suggests two dimensions of literacy. *On the one hand, students have to become literate about their histories,* experiences, and the culture of their immediate environments. *On the other hand, they must also appropriate those codes and cultures of the dominant spheres so they can transcend their own environments.* There is often an enormous tension between these two dimensions of literacy. How can emancipatory literacy deal effectively with this tension so as not to suffocate either dimension?

Freire: First, *I think consciousness is generated* through the *social practice in which we participate.* But it also has an individual dimension. That is, my comprehension of the world, my dreams of the world, my judgment of the world—all of these are part of my individual practice; all speak of my presence in the world. I need all of this to begin to understand myself. But it is not sufficient to explicate my action. In the final analysis, consciousness is socially bred. In this sense, I think my subjectivity is important. But I cannot separate my subjectivity from its social objectivity.

When you ask me how to deal with the individual dimension of social consciousness, your question implies a certain relationship of tension. I believe that a critical education, an education along the lines of what Henry Giroux calls radical pedagogy, has to consider this tension and has to understand how this tension between the individual and the social practice takes place. One has to learn to deal with this relationship. In formulating a theory of education one should neither deny the social, the objective, the concrete, the material, nor emphasize only the development of the individual consciousness. In understanding the role of objectivity one must stimulate the development of the individual dimension as well.

Macedo: The fundamental question is how to deal with the individual consciousness as emphasized in an emancipatory literacy when this consciousness may be at odds with the collective social consciousness.

Freire: If you study the various ways of living and being validated in a society as complex as that of the United States, you find, for example, an undeniable taste for individualism. But the taste each person shows for individualism is that person's particular expression of a social consciousness.

Macedo: This is part of the point I wanted to address: how can one develop critical consciousness without looking at the concept of the reality of social consciousness? That is, is it possible to avoid the permanent shock that exists between individual consciousness and collective consciousness?

Freire: If we take the individualist's treatment of the social dimension, a pedagogy becomes critical when an educator like Henry Giroux or Stanley Aronowitz has a dialogue with students and methodically challenges them to discover that a critical posture necessarily implies the recognition of the relationship between objectivity and subjectivity. I would call this critical because in many cases individuals have not yet perceived themselves as conditioned; on the contrary, they passionately speak of their freedom.

When challenged by a critical educator, students begin to understand that the *more profound dimension of their freedom lies exactly in the recognition of constraints that can be overcome.* Then they discover for themselves in the process of becoming more and more critical that *it is impossible to deny the constitutive power of their consciousness in the social practice in which they participate.* On the other hand, they perceive that *through their consciousness,* even when they are not makers of their social reality, *they transcend the constituting reality and question* it. This behavioral difference leads one to become more and more critical; that is, students assume a critical posture to the extent that they comprehend how and what constitutes the consciousness of the world.

Macedo: Does the assumption of this critical posture put an end to the tension we discussed earlier?

Freire: Not at all. The tension continues. But for me, a delineated pedagogy can underscore the presence of this tension. *Yet the role of critical pedagogy is not to extinguish tensions.* The prime role of critical pedagogy is to lead students to recognize various tensions and enable them to deal effectively with them. Trying to deny these tensions ends up negating the very role of subjectivity. The negation of tension amounts to the illusion of overcoming these tensions when they are really just hidden.

We cannot exist outside an interplay of tensions. Even those who live passively cannot escape some measure of tensions. Frequently there is an ongoing denial of tensions, but these tensions should be understood. I believe, in fact, that one task of radical pedagogy is to clarify the nature of tensions and how best to cope with them.

Macedo: What role can a critical literacy program play in the interrelationship between productive discourse, text, and oral discourse?

Freire: It is impossible to carry out my literacy work or to understand literacy (and here I will have to repeat myself because I have no better way to answer your question) by divorcing the reading of the word from the reading of the world. *Reading the word and learning how to write the word so one can later read it are preceded by learning how to write the world, that is, having the experience of changing the world and touching the world.*

Macedo: How do you specifically develop the consciousness of the world in the process of literacy?

Freire: The consciousness of the world is constituted in relation to the world; it is not a part of the self. The world enables me to constitute the self in relation to "you," the world. The transformation of objective reality (what I call the "writing" of reality) represents precisely the starting point where the animal that became human began to write history. It started when these animals started to use their hands differently. As this transformation was taking place, the consciousness of the "touched" world was constituting itself. It is precisely this world consciousness, touched and transformed, that bred the consciousness of the self.

For a long time these beings, who were making themselves, wrote the world much more than they spoke the world. They directly touched and affected the world before they talked about it. Sometime later, though, these beings began to speak about the transformed world. And they began to speak about this transformation. After another long period of time, these beings began to register graphically the talk about the transformation. For this reason, I always say that before learners attempt to learn how to read and write they need to read and write the world. They need to comprehend the world that involves talk about the world.

Literacy's oral dimension is important even if it takes place in a culture like that of the United States, whose memory is preponderantly written, not oral like that of Africa, for example. Considering these different moments, which took place over millennia, and also considering the modern experience, it is not viable to separate the literacy process from general educational processes. It is not viable to separate literacy from the productive process of society. The ideal is a concomitant approach in which literacy evolves in various environments, such as the workplace. But even when literacy cannot take place in various environments, I think it is impossible to dichotomize what takes place in the economic process of the world from the process of discourse.

As to your question of whether economic discourse is an act of production relative to acts of literacy, I would say that a critical pedagogy would have to stimulate students to reflect. Since this reflection by its very nature should be critical, learners will begin to comprehend the relationship among many different discourses. In the final analysis, these discourses are interrelated. Productive discourse and discourse about or accompanying productive discourse always intersect at some level. The problem of understanding the culture in which education takes place cannot negate the presence and influence of economic production.

Macedo: Speaking of cultural production, I would like to ask you about the relationship between education, including literacy, and culture. We have to take into account various definitions of culture, however. By "culture" I do not mean that which is representative of those dominant elements of the elite class, that is, culture with a capital C. Culture is not an autonomous system, but a system characterized by social stratification and tensions. To be precise, I have in mind Richard Johnson's definition of culture, which includes the following three main premises:

1. Cultural processes are intimately connected with social relations, especially *with class relations and class formations, with sexual divisions, with the racial structuring of social relations, and with age oppressions as a form of dependency.*
2. *Culture involves power and helps to produce asymmetries* in the abilities of individual and social groups to define and realize their needs.
3. Culture is neither autonomous nor an externally determined field, but a *site of social differences and struggles.*[1]

Given the range of factors that interact in cultural production and reproduction, how can an emancipatory literacy transcend social class barriers to interface with all these other factors related to culture? Can you also speak about education generally and literacy in particular as factors of culture?

Freire: Literacy and education in general are cultural expressions. You cannot conduct literacy work outside the world of culture because education in itself is a dimension of culture. Education is an act of knowledge (knowledge here is not to be restricted to a specific object only) on the part of the very subject who knows. Education has to take the culture that explains it as the object of a curious comprehension, as if one would use education to question itself. And every time that education questions itself, in response it finds itself in the larger body of culture. Evidently, the more it continues to interrogate itself about its purpose in culture and society, the more education discovers that culture is a totality cut across by social classes.

In Brazilian society, for example, one cannot deny certain behavior patterns characteristic of different social class behavior. For example, taste, which is also cultural, is heavily conditioned by social class boundaries.

Macedo: I did not intend to focus only on social classes in cultural production and reproduction. I think we need to investigate other cultural influences on education.

Freire: When a pedagogy tries to influence other factors that could not be strictly explained by a theory of class, you still have to pass through class analysis.

Given this understanding, we still must acknowledge that social classes exist and that their presence is contradictory. That is, the existence of social classes provokes a conflict of interests. It provokes and shapes cultural ways of being and, therefore, generates contradictory expressions of culture.

In general, dominant segments of any society talk about their particular interests, their tastes, their styles of living, which they regard as concrete expressions of nationality. Thus the subordinated groups, who have their own tastes and styles of living, cannot talk about their tastes and styles as national expressions. They lack the political and economic power to do so. Only those who have power can generalize and decree their group characteristics as representative of the national culture. With this decree, the dominant group necessarily depreciates all characteristics belonging to subordinated groups, characteristics that deviate from the decreed patterns.

This is especially interesting when you understand the asymmetry generated by social institutions, and how important a role critical literacy programs play in demystifying the artificial parameters imposed on people. Critical literacy has to explicate the validity of different types of music, poetry, language, and world views.

From this viewpoint the dominant class, which has the power to define, profile, and describe the world, begins to pronounce that the speech habits of the subordinate groups are a corruption, a bastardization of dominant discourse. It is in this sense that sociolinguists are making an enormous contribution to the demystification of these notions. What they show is that, scientifically, all languages are valid, systematic, rule-governed systems, and that the inferiority/superiority distinction is a social phenomenon. A language is developed to the degree that it reaches a certain stability in a particular area and to the extent that it is used in the comprehension and expression of the world by the groups that speak it.

One cannot understand and analyze a language, then, without a class analysis. Even though we may have to go beyond class boundaries to understand certain universal properties of language, we should neither reduce the investigation of language to a mechanical comprehension, nor reduce it to only social class analysis. But we have to do the latter to gain a global view of the total system under investigation.

I think all of us ultimately speak the same language (in the abstract sense) and express ourselves in different ways.

This has to do with the question you asked concerning different discourses. If you take the Brazilian case, you have the type of language spoken by the dominant class and other types spoken by workers, peasants, and similar groups. These are part of the abstract notion we call Brazilian Portuguese. This is not language as an abstraction, but language as a concrete system spoken by different groups. It is important, then, to comprehend these different varieties of language. They involve different grammars and different syntactical and semantic representations that are conditioned and explicated by people in varying positions relative to forces of production.

Language is also culture. Language is the mediating force of knowledge; but it is also knowledge itself. I believe all of this also passes through the social classes. A critical pedagogy poses this dynamic, contradictory cultural comprehension and the dynamic, contradictory nature of education as a permanent object of curiosity on the part of the learners. We find a general simplicity concerning the appreciation of these phenomena. It is as if all had been already known and decreed by the dominant groups. It is as if all that takes place at the level of culture had nothing to do with other discourses, such as the discourse of production. *A pedagogy will be that much more critical and radical the more investigative and less certain of "certainties" it is.* The more "unquiet" a pedagogy, the more critical it will become.

A pedagogy preoccupied with the uncertainties rooted in the issues we have discussed is, by its nature, a pedagogy that requires investigation. This pedagogy is thus much more a pedagogy of question than a pedagogy of answer.

Macedo: Let's talk about literacy as the "language of possibility," enabling learners to recognize and understand their voices within a multitude of discourses in which they must deal. *How can an emancipatory literacy guarantee the legitimation of one's own discourse, which may be in a relationship of tension with other discourses?* That is, if emancipatory literacy calls for the celebration of one's discourse, you will inevitably have competing discourses, all with the same goal in mind. Is it possible to have enough space within an emancipatory literacy effort to enable learners to appropriate their own discourses and simultaneously move beyond them, so as to develop competency and ease while dealing with other discourses? What roles can black American discourse, women's discourse, and the discourse of ethnic groups play in the emancipatory literacy process?

Freire: This question transcends a mechanical and strict comprehension of the reading act, that is, the act of learning the word so one can then read and write it. This question involves a dream that goes beyond the expectation of just learning to read the word. Your question implies a profound comprehension of the act of reading. To respect different discourses and to put into practice the understanding of plurality (which necessitates both criticism and creativity in the act of saying the word and in the act of reading the word) require a political and social transformation.

Your question reminds me of my dream of a different society, one in which saying the word is a fundamental right and not merely a habit, in which *saying the word is the right to become a part of the decision to transform the world.* To read the word that one says in this perspective presupposes the reinvention of today's society. The reinvention of society, on the other hand, requires the reinvention of power. A political perspective that only dreams of a radical change of the bourgeoisie and the seizing of power is not sufficient.

The issue is the role of subjectivity in the transformation of history. *For me, historical transformation, which is part of your question, is more important than taking power.* We ought not to be concerned with the mere shifting of power from one group to another. It is necessary to understand that in seizing power one must transform it. This *re-creation and reinvention of power* by necessity passes through the reinvention of the productive act. And the reinvention of the productive act takes place to the degree that people's discourse is legitimized in terms of people's wishes, decisions, and dreams, not merely empty words.

Discourse as a transformative act begins to assume an active and decisive participation relative to what to produce and for whom. The reinvention of power that passes through the reinvention of production cannot take place without the amplification of voices that participate in the productive act. In other words, people, not merely a minority of specialists, would have to decide on what to produce based on real necessities, not invented ones that ultimately benefit only the dominant group.

The reinvention of production, without which there would be no reinvention of power, would stimulate the reinvention of culture and the reinvention of language. Why are the majority of the people silenced today? Why should they have to muffle their own discussion? When they are called upon to read, why do they read only the dominant discourse? Literacy programs generally give people access to a predetermined and preestablished discourse while silencing their own voices, which should be amplified in the reinvention of the new society I am dreaming of. The reinvention of power that passes through the reinvention of production would entail the reinvention of culture within which environments would be created to incorporate, in a participatory way, all of those discourses that are presently suffocated by the dominant discourse.

The legitimation of these different discourses would authenticate the plurality of voices in the reconstruction of a truly democratic society. Then, in this envisioned society the comprehension of the reading act and the writing act would forcibly change. Present understanding of literacy would also have to change. By definition, there would be real respect for those learners who have not yet become familiar with saying the word to read it. This respect involves the understanding and appreciation of the many contributions nonreaders make to society in general.

You, Donaldo, told me that you are often shocked to learn that some African peoples, for example, who fought brilliantly to reappropriate their culture and throw out the colonizers, are later depreciated by the new leadership because they cannot read the word. Any people who can courageously break the chains of colonialism can also easily read the word, provided the word belongs to them. Their new leadership fails to recognize that in the struggle for liberation these people were involved in an authenic literacy process by which they learned to read their history, and that they also wrote during their struggle for liberation. This is a fundamental way to write history without writing words. It is shocking that even though they were successful in the most difficult aspect of literacy, to read and write their world, they were belittled in this much easier aspect, that which involved reading and writing the word. Your question highlights the profoundly political aspect of literacy, making me see that what you refer to as "the language of possibility" has to be based on respect for existing possibilities.

Another point that arises from your question is that of the rights of multiple voices. Taking Latin America as an example, let's think about the so-called indigenous populations. These populations were in place before the white population arrived. Thus, the white population became involved with an established civilization that also had its own voice or voices. These populations have the right to the voices that were silenced by the Hispanic-Portuguese invasion. Any literacy project for these populations necessarily would have to go through the reading of the word in their native languages. This literacy cannot require that the reading of the word be done in the colonizer's language.

If we foresee a possible revolution in these societies, we have to develop space for the literacy of possibility to take place. I remember vividly a conversation I had with Fernando Cardenal and Ernesto Cardenal in Nicaragua in which they both expressed sentiments similar to those we are now discussing. They spoke extensively about the Mosquito Indians. They both felt that in any literacy campaign, Mosquito culture had to be respected totally. Also, they felt that the Mosquitos' language would have to be a fundamental element in the literacy process. A literacy program that negates the plurality of voice and discourse is authoritarian, antidemocratic.

Macedo: Could you elaborate on the ways in which subjectivities are constituted in the schools? That is, the ways in which schools influence and shape students' ideologies, personalities, and needs.

Freire: First, I would say that schools do not really create subjectivity. Subjectivity functions within schools. Schools can and do repress the development of subjectivity, as in the case of creativity, for example. A critical pedagogy must not repress students' creativity (this is true throughout the history of education). Creativity needs to be stimulated, not only at the level of students' individuality, but also at the level of their individuality in a social context. Instead of suffocating this curious impetus, educators should stimulate risk taking, without which there is no creativity. Instead of reinforcing the purely mechanical repetitions of phrases and lists, educators should stimulate students to doubt.

Schools should never impose absolute certainties on students. They should stimulate the certainty of never being too certain, a method vital to critical pedagogy. Educators should also stimulate the possibilities of expression, the possibilities of subjectivity. They should challenge students to discourse about the world. Educators should never deny the importance of technology, but they ought not to reduce learning to a technological comprehension of the world.

We can conceive of two positions that are false here. The first would be to simplify or negate the importance of technology, to associate all technological processes with a concomitant dehumanizing process. In truth, technology represents human creativity, the expression of the necessity of risk. On the other hand, one should not fall into a denial of humanism.

The world is not made up of certainties. Even if it were, we would never know if something was really certain. The world is made of the tension between the certain and uncertain. The type of critical pedagogy I am calling for is not easy to attain in a society like that of the United States, one that has historically acquired an extraordinary advancement in technology and capital production. This extraordinary advancement has given birth to a series of myths, including the myth of technology and science. Educators should assume a scientific position that is not scientist, a technological position that is not technologic.

Macedo: How can this critical pedagogy fundamentally stimulate the influence of subjectivity in terms of the development of students' creativity, curiosity, and needs? In societies that are technologically advanced it becomes that much more difficult to avoid falling victim to the myths to which you refer, myths that may discourage the possible role of students' subjectivities.

Freire: Yes, but at the same time these societies stimulate the role of individuality, that is, the individuality within an "individualistic" frame. The individualistic frame, in the end, also negates subjectivity. This is a curious phenomenon and we need to understand it dialectically. It could appear that a position that is profoundly individualistic would end up stimulating and respecting the role of the human agency. In truth, it denies all dimensions of human agency. Why does the individualistic position end up working against the real role of human agency? Because the only real subjectivity is that which confronts its contradictory relationship to objectivity.

And what does the individualistic position advocate? It dichotomizes the individual from the social. Generally, this cannot be accomplished, since it is not viable to do so. Nevertheless, the individualistic ideology ends up negating social interests or it subsumes social interests within individualistic interests.

The comprehension of the social is always determined by the comprehension of the individual. In this sense, the individualistic position works against the comprehension of the real role of human agency. *Human agency makes sense and flourishes only when subjectivity is understood in its dialectical, contradictory, dynamic relationship with objectivity, from which it derives.*

This leads to an enormous problem for critical pedagogy in technologically advanced societies. One method the critical educator can try is what you and I are doing right now, using discussion as an attempt to challenge each other so that we can understand the relationship between subjectivity and objectivity, so that we can in the final analysis understand the enormous and undeniable role of science and technology, and also so that we can understand the risk taking inherent in a humanized life. This type of discourse is one method a critical educator could use to demystify a whole network of mythology: the myth that one should not waste time, for instance. What does wasting time mean? Does one avoid wasting time only in order to make money? Or does it mean one cannot waste time making money? *What is it to waste time and what is it to make time?* In the end, the work of an educator in a critical and radical perspective is the work of unveiling the deep dimensions of reality that are hidden in these myths.

Macedo: You often mention the role of subject that should be assumed by students. Your preoccupation leads us to Giroux's treatment of what he calls "human agency." What do you think about the role of human agency in the dominant society regarding the complex relationship between literacy campaigns in particular and education in general?

Freire: This is one of the central themes of a radical pedagogy. It is a theme that has been accompanying the history of thought and dividing the various positions vis-à-vis the answers given. For me, this theme is another profound issue for the end of the century.

Your question brings to mind a statement by Marx. When he referred to the making of history he said that man makes history based on the concrete conditions that he finds. Evidently, it is not from the legitimate dream that a dominated class, for example, has to liberate itself. It is from concrete conditions, or more accurately, from the relationship between the concrete and the possible.

A generation inherits concrete conditions in a given society. It is from this concrete, historical situation that a generation finds it is possible to continue the continuity of history. However, the present generation has to elaborate and work on the transformation of the present concrete conditions, because without such effort it is impossible to make the future. If the present conditions are only fundamental, the present does not envelop the future within it.

For this reason the present is always a time of possibility (as Giroux has said so eloquently in his introduction to *The Politics of Education*). I think Giroux understands this perfectly when he asserts that outside the present it is impossible to make history. That is, the making of history has to take into consideration the present that came from a particular past, the base lines of this present which demarcate the making of history. When Giroux says that the present is a present possibility, not determinism, he is situating human agency in a key way, because in the relationship between the subjectivity of the present and the objectivity of the present, there is the undeniable role of subjectivity.

If subjectivity were always the result of historical transformations, objectivity would, ironically, then become the subject of the transforming subjectivity. To the extent that Giroux says that this present is a present of possibility, he is raising the issue of the role of human agency, and this is important in any critical, radical pedagogy.

Macedo: Following Giroux's discussion of public spheres' expansion of opportunities for cultivating democratic principles, to what extent do you think such areas as labor unions, the church, and social movements can be expected to play a role compatible with the goals of a critical pedagogy?

Freire: An educator who does not develop himself, who does not consider Giroux's reflections and exigencies, is out of touch with his times. In Brazil I have stressed Giroux's perspective, using a terminology that is apparently somewhat different. For example, I have insisted that a radical and critical education has to focus on what is taking place today inside various social movements and labor unions. Feminist movements, peace movements, and other such movements that express resistance generate in their practices a pedagogy of resistance. They show us that it is impossible to think of education as strictly reduced to the school environment. One cannot always deny the possibility of the schools, but we have to recognize that historically there are times when the school environment provides more or fewer opportunities.

I would say that in twenty years of military rule in Brazil there were times when there were severe repercussions if one rejected the dominant ideology. There were times when the schools were totally closed to any form of critical pedagogy. The period during the 1970s when most of the Latin American countries (for example, Uruguay, Chile, Argentina) experienced military dictatorships coincided with the emergence of Parisian theories of reproduction derived from the work of Pierre Bourdieu. These theories led a number of Latin American educators to refine the possibilities of using the school environment to promote an education of resistance.

In the past four years or so, with both social and political changes in Latin America—the attempt to redemocratize Brazil, for example, or the struggle for liberation in Nicaragua—there has been a certain confidence in reestablishing the use of institutional space for experimenting with the development of a critical pedagogy.

I think, though, that even today, in an era when using the schools is possible, in order to counter the introduction of dominant ideologies, it is necessary to recognize that public environments are extremely important for pedagogical production of political and social resistance. Within this landscape of spheres of resistance, educators who seek transformation now have choices. Some may choose to work in public environments outside the schools. Others may prefer to work in their specialized fields in the schools.

I do not deny either approach. The ideal would be to establish and appreciate the relationship between these two approaches: the more traditional, structured, and systematized education that takes place in the schools versus the more dynamic, free, and contradictory (though more creative) approach within social movements. A point I developed extensively in the book I did with António Faundes is that educators' comprehension of what is taking place today in these social movements and spheres of public action is most vital for critical pedagogy. Political organizations that fail to learn from the agents of these public movements will also fail to achieve historical and political resonance.

I totally agree with Giroux's view relative to the roles of public movements in the promotion of democratic principles. Giroux's critical appreciation of these movements centers on seeing them as agencies of discussion. It is within these public spheres, in fact, that antihegemonic movements have been generated. For me, the basic problem for educators and political people who dream of change lies in how to apprehend the struggle, in the sense of generating a new hegemony evolving from the manifestations and experiences within these movements.

The task of a critical educator is to approach the real world of these public spheres and social agencies, to make a contribution. An educator's major contribution would be to appreciate the theoretical elements within these movements' practices. The critical educator should make the inherent theory in these practices flourish so that people can appropriate the theories of their own practice. The role of the educator, then, is not to arrive at the level of social movements with a priori theories to explicate the practice taking place, but to discover the theoretical elements rooted in practice.

NOTE

1. Richard Johnson, "What Is Cultural Studies Anyway?" *Angistica* nos. 1, 2 (1983).

Teaching How to Read the World and Change It: Critical Pedagogy in the Intermediate Grades

ROBERT E. PETERSON

INTRODUCTION

Monday morning a child brings a stray dog into the classroom. The traditional teacher sees that it is removed immediately.

The progressive teacher builds on the students' interest; perhaps measures and weighs the animal with the children, has the children draw and write about the dog, and eventually calls the humane society.

The Freirian teacher does what the progressive teacher does but more. She asks questions, using the dog as the object of reflection. "Why are there so many stray dogs in our neighborhood?" "Why are there more here than in the rich suburbs?" "Why do people have dogs?" "Why doesn't the city allocate enough money to clean up after the dogs and care for the strays?" While accepting stray animals into a classroom isn't the bellwether mark of an elementary Freiran teacher, engaging children in reflective dialogue on topics of their interest is.

Not surprisingly, the classroom of an elementary teacher applying a Freirian method is markedly different than that of a traditional teacher. What perhaps is not as expected is that a Freirian approach also differs significantly from the methods of many progressive teachers, that is, those who organize their classes in child-centered and holistic ways.

Going to public school in the 1960s I became a proponent of progressive education as a student, but it was only when I read, Freire as a junior in high school, that I realized education could be more than just "relevant" and "student-centered." However, the political reality of being a high school student activist in the late 1960s and early 1970s made me doubt the likelihood of a Freiran method being used in the public schools.

It wasn't until a decade later, that I came back to Freire and reexamined his applicability to the public school setting. I was on the other side of the teacher's desk, now looking at things as an educator rather than a student. I had traveled to Nicaragua and observed the week-long celebration that concluded the National Literacy Campaign in August of 1980, and the experience convinced me that I should look again at Freire's work. I knew that the conditions of teaching and learning in the United States differed greatly from those encountered by Freire in the Third World, and yet I felt that the essence of Freire's approach would be appropriate for an urban school setting.

Throughout the 1980s, I worked on applying Freire's ideas in my fourth and fifth grade bilingual inner-city classrooms. My approach contrasted sharply with the numerous "educational reforms" being tried elsewhere. These mainstream proposals were often state and system mandates; their goal was to "teacher-proof" the curricula through the use of basal reader programs, direct instruction, the methods of Madeline Hunter and an expansion of standardized testing (Fairtest, 1988; Gibboney, 1988; Levine, 1988). Under the banners of "back to the basics" and "improving student achievement" these efforts further reinforced and strengthened what Freire calls the "banking" method of education, whereby the teacher puts periodic deposits of knowledge into the students' heads. Such classrooms are very teacher- and text-centered. Little discussion and reflection take place. While the relevance of a banking-type approach appears to go counter to what recent research on literacy suggests (Calkins, 1983; Goodman 1986; Goodman, Smith, & Meredith, & Goodman 1987; Graves, 1983; Smith 1985) this model continues to be the most prevalent method in public school classrooms. Goodlad (1984), for example, found that not even 1 percent of the instructional time in high schools was devoted to discussion that "required some kind of open response involving reasoning or perhaps an opinion from students." As he notes, "the extraordinary degree of student passivity stands out" (p. 229).

Freire posits a dialogic "problem posing" method of education as an alternative. Here, teachers and students both become actors in figuring out the world through a process of mutual communication. In the banking method of education the teacher and the curricular texts have the "right answers" which the students are expected to regurgitate periodically onto criterion referenced tests. However in Freire's model, questions and not answers are the core of the curriculum; open-ended questions prod students to critically analyze their social situation and encourage them to ultimately work towards changing it.

To apply Freire's approach in the elementary classroom one has to have a perspective about the learners and learning which runs counter to the dominant educational ideology. A Freirian approach relies on the experience of the students and implies a respect and use of the students' culture, language, and dialect. It values dialogue and reflection over lecture and repetition. It means constructing a classroom in which students have the maximum amount of power that is legally permitted and that they can socially handle. It means challenging the students to reflect on the social nature of knowledge and the curriculum, to get them to think about why they think and act the way they do.

Ultimately a Freirian approach means moving beyond thought and words to action. This is done on the one hand by teachers themselves modeling social responsibility and critical engagement in community and global issues. On the other hand it means constructing with the students an atmosphere in the classroom and the school where students feel secure and confident enough to interrogate their own realities, see them in a different light, and act on their developing convictions to change their own social reality. In order to do all this, the teachers themselves have to go through a transformative process, breaking the ideological chains of their own formal education, of past training, and the inertia of habit of past teaching.

TEACHING ORGANICALLY

Freire uses generative words and themes in his teaching, words that invoke passion and feeling among his students. In North American jargon this is sometimes called a "language experience" approach for it utilizes students' own language and experiences as the basis of instruction. An example from European literature and from the experience of a New Zealand teacher illustrate the significance of this approach.

In Bertolt Brecht's (1978) famous play *The Mother,* which takes place during the 1905 revolution in Czarist Russia, the mother and a metal worker go to ask a professor to teach them to read and write. The professor, begrudgingly and condescendingly, agrees and proceeds to write two words on a slate board: "Branch" and "nest." The two workers immediately become frustrated by the irrelevance of the situation and demand to know how to spell "worker," "class struggle," and "exploitation." Not clear as to why his initial words were inappropriate, the professor obligingly changes his plans. And, thus, through the power of their own words, the workers learn how to read and write rapidly.

In her work with Maori children in New Zealand, Sylvia Ashton-Warner (1965) developed an educational approach very similar to that of Freire. She understood that the failure of the Aborigine children in New Zealand schools was mainly due to their cultural clash with the Anglosized system. She drew on the interests and experience of her students, within the context of the culture they brought to school. Her use of "organic vocabulary" to teach reading, spelling, and writing was based on the belief that words significant to the learner would motivate the learner into learning. As she explained:

> Pleasant words won't do. Respectable words won't do. They must be words organically tied up, organically born from the dynamic life itself. They must be words that are already part of the child's being. (1965, p. 33)

The proof of her method was in the students themselves. While it took four months for them to learn words like "come, look, and," in four minutes they could learn words like "police, bulldog, knife, cry, yell, fight, Daddy, Mummy, ghost, kiss, and frightened."

The meaningfulness of these words stands in sharp contrast to the first words taught to many children in urban school settings in the United States. One widely used basal company chose eight words as the primary starting point for reading: "red, yellow, blue, girl, boy, the, a, has." In fact, an entire kindergarten workbook is devoted to the word "the." The Commission on Reading of the national Council of Teachers of English (1988) documents how basal reading programs control vocabulary and syntax to such an extent as to make the initial exposure to reading irrelevant and boring to most children.

Children's learning should be centered in their own experience, language, and culture. For this to happen, the classroom environment should be "language rich," allowing the children to develop their language and thinking abilities in as natural a setting as possible. This applies equally to first and second language learning (Krashen & Terrell, 1983; Goodman, 1986). A generative theme approach fosters the development of such an environment.

Practical application. A generative theme is an issue or topic that catches the interest of students in such a way that discussion, study, and project work can be built around it. Themes may come from an incident in a particular student's life, a problem in the community, or an idea that a student latched onto from the media, the news, or a classroom activity. Writing, reading, talking, acting, and reflecting are the key ways through which generative themes develop. I start the year with a unit on the child's own family and background—placing their birthdates on the class timeline. The second day we place their parents dates on the timeline, the third, their grandparents. We put pins in a world map indicating the places of birth. I ask them to talk to their parents or other family members and collect at least one story, joke, or memory from their family and either write it down or prepare to tell it orally.

The first day of school I also have the students in my class write a book. Inspired by Ashton-Warner's (1965) continual construction of books based on her children's writings and drawings, I do the same. Quality is not important on the first day. I want to show students that we can write, draw, and accomplish things they would not have dreamed of. We choose a topic or topics together, write, draw, and put the unedited papers into a plastic theme binder creating an instant book. This action of collaboratively producing a book based on the students' own experiences provides both a model of what can be accomplished the rest of the year and a benchmark upon which the teacher and the students can judge growth in their abilities. "If we can accomplish this in only one day by working together," I tell my students, "Just imagine what we can do in an entire year!"

Throughout the year I use the "writing process" approach (Graves 1983, Calkins, 1986) which focuses on production of student generated and meaningful themes. Students write for a purpose, whether it is for publication, a pen pal or display. We publish in the school newsletter, the city newspaper, children's magazines,[1] or our own books. Never have I seen students think so much about a piece of writing than when they know it is to be published.

The most ambitious writing we do is for the publication of our own books. Usually this is in the form of anthologies of students' prose, poetry, and drawings—*Kid Power, Colors Laugh, Splashing in Action* are the titles of a few that we have produced. I especially encourage writings on the students' own communities and families (Wigginton, 1989). At times children have written entire booklets—legends, adventures, autobiographies—that they may give to a parent or sibling as a gift for a birthday or holiday. These booklets validate the children's lives, give them self-confidence in their ability to do projects, help focus reflection on our common field trips and areas of study, provide an inspiration to write and a motivation to read. They are also useful for me, not only as the basis for future writing lessons, but because I learn more about my students and their communities.

Generative themes can be discovered and reflected upon not only through writing in the classroom but through a variety of other language and performance arts activities. Mime, drama, role playing, reading aloud from their own writings, chants, and oral story telling allow students to describe and reflect on their world while improving their basic first language and second language abilities.

Even when standardized curricula must be used, a teacher can utilize the life experiences of their students. For example, if by state law or local decree a teacher must use a basal reader, approaches can be taken that downplay its segmented skills orientation. A student could: Write or tell about what would happen if she were to take the main character home for dinner; write a letter to the main character comparing the student's life to that of the main characters; or write a version of the story that draws on some comparable situation in their school community. Teachers can also supplement basals by having students read quality children's literature in decent anthologies[2] or in whole books. My experience has shown that if children shelve the basal a few times a week and instead read classroom sets of entire novels, they are more likely to think longer and more deeply about a piece of literature and how it relates to their lives.

But there are some problems with this organic style of teaching. Given class oppression in our society, poor children usually have a narrower range of experiences than those from more affluent homes. This does not mean they are culturally or experientially deprived—as spending the summer in Mexico or the Mississippi delta or even playing in the back alleys of one of our big cities can be a rich experience. Their culture and experience is just different than that of many teachers; it is also in discordance with the texts of the dominant curricula. I believe though that we should stretch what is organic in the children's lives by taking them out into the world and by bringing the world into the classroom (Searle, 1977). Field trips, speakers, movies, and current events studies are obvious ways to do this.

Poetry and music can also bring the world into the classroom. For example, Langston Hughes' poems "Colored Child at the Carnival" or "The Ballad of the Landlord," speak to the experience of many African-Americans and poor people and spark critical discussions. I have had similar success with songs such as "Harriet Tubman" and "I Cried" sung by Holly Near, "Lives in the Balance" and "Lawless Avenue" by Jackson Browne, "Sambo Lando" sung by Inti Illimani, "El Pueblo Unido Jamas Sera Vencido" by Quilapayun. Whenever I use poems or songs I reproduce the words so that each student can follow along and keep a copy.

As we delve deeper into the nature of students' experiences in urban America, new problems with the application of Freire's theory confront us. Freire (1970) assumes that what will most inspire the learner is discussion and reflection on his or her own experiences, particularly his or her own oppression. In my eyes, many children in urban America are oppressed by a few key institutions: school, family, and community.

For an elementary teacher to apply Freire by focusing on such oppression raises difficult problems. The degree to which a teacher can "deviate" from the standard curriculum depends on a number of factors—the amount of peer and parental support, the political situation in the school and district, and the sophistication and maturity of the particular group of students, to name a few. But there is deviation and there is deviation. To study the Plains Indians instead of the Pilgrims is one thing. To help students become aware and critical about how they are being oppressed in society can be quite another. I have found two ways to approach this problem. First is to deal with power relationships and "oppression" within my own classroom. The second way is to bring the world into the classroom, so that children start reflecting on their own lives. I will first explain the latter.

One year I showed my students the video *The Wrath of Grapes* (United Farm Workers, 1987) about the current grape boycott and followed it up with a field trip to see Cesar Chavez speak at the local technical college. All sorts of good things came out of this activity, but the most interesting was that on the Monday after our trip my students came to school and the first thing they yelled was "Mr. Peterson, Sixth Street is on strike."

"What?" I replied?

"Sixth and National Ave. is on strike!"

Now the streets in Milwaukee have a lot of pot holes after the long winter but I had never heard of a street being on strike. What had in fact occurred was a strike by workers at a local factory. Later that week during art period I took six students armed with a tape recorder over to the company so they could interview the workers. I believe they learned more during their half-hour interview than they had in years of social studies lessons. We debriefed in the teachers' lounge. When we were reviewing the reason for the strike—a wage cut from $7.00 down to $4.00. Cecilia said rather unemotionally, "That's more money than my mom makes now." We examined where each of the children's parents worked and if they were in a union. "Grievance" became a spelling word the next week and pretty soon there seemed to be grievances about all sorts of things in the children's lives. By bringing the world into the classroom they were better able to reflect upon their own lives.

But as I enlarge the world in which my students operate through sharing of such experiences, always tying issues to and building upon the students' own realities, I habitually confront another problem. The "generative themes" of many media-saturated children often seem to have more to do with life on the cathode ray tube than life in our community. During writing workshop or group discussions I sometimes feel I am in another world of professional wrestlers, super heros, and video games. The average child watches television six hours a day and in one year sees 800 war toy commercials, 250 episodes of war cartoons; the violent commercials and episodes being the equivalent of 22 days of school (Liebert & Sprafkin, 1988).[3]

One consequence of this television addiction is physical atrophy, but the deadening of the child's imagination and the imposition of a violent, consumeristic ideology are other results that have a direct affect on a "generative theme"-based classroom. When my kids moan about the President, their solution is to kill him. A child doesn't like gangs—solve the problem by machine gunning them down or by sending them to the electric chair. There is no simple or short-term solution to this problem, and certainly a single classroom teacher is not going to solve this problem alone. I challenge these ideas through dialogue attempting to get children to think about why they think the way they do (which I explain in more detail in the section on critiquing curriculum and the media). I take what I hear and try to rework it from a different angle—codify it to use Freire's term—and bring it up again in the future in the context of other curricular areas.

In a generative theme-oriented classroom, the tendency is often to try to cover too much too fast. My most successful experiences have been when I've had the class concentrate on one thing in depth. The concept of "less is more" (Coalition of Essential Schools, 1984) applies equally well to a single classroom as it does to an entire school curricula. I have ensured this by using a variety of methods: a word for the day, a quotation of the week, a short poem, a graphic, a cartoon, story, or news article.

When I have a special word for the day it often relates to a topic the children have been discussing or studying. I or one of the students present it in both English and Spanish, explain its epistomology, teach the others how to sign it in American Sign Language, discuss its significance and use it as a "password" as we move through the day's activities. Sometimes the word comes from the conversations I hear, or from a topic of interest that we have discussed in our studies. The focus on one word, particularly in a bilingual setting, helps students become aware of language in a metacognitive sense. Through word webbing or semantic mapping I help connect this word again to the life experiences of the students.

Regardless of whether it's a word, a scripted dialogue, a story, or a discussion which serves to organize classroom dialogue, the focus of instruction and locus of control is learner- rather than teacher-centered. The essence of an organic theme-based approach thus lies in the connections it builds between the topic at hand, the students' lives and broader world around them (Ellwood, 1989).

THE EMPOWERMENT OF STUDENTS

Since students have so few rights, they rarely develop responsibility. By fifth grade I get children who are so damaged by society that they are only able to behave if they are given no rights—even going to the pencil sharpener without having to ask permission is too much for some to handle. This irresponsibility is rooted in the teacher-centered and textbook-driven curriculum which serves to disempower children. Because students are denied rights and kept from decision making throughout their school life and subjected to tedious worksheets and boring curriculum, school life prevents them from developing the responsibility and self-discipline necessary to be independent thinkers and actors in our society.[4] Freire (1970) maintains that through this subjugation students become *objects* acted upon by the authoritarian school system and society. He argues, instead, for a pedagogical process of dialogue, reflection, dramatization, and interaction, whereby students move towards being subjects capable of understanding the world and their social context, and ultimately engaging in activity based on this new understanding. Again, the realization of students as subjects is not always easily attained.

I want my students to take responsibility for their own learning, when I begin to encourage this many see it as license to goof off. Shor and Freire (1987) speak of the need to develop transitionary models and activities to train people to be more responsible. In making the transition to empower students, one must therefore be prepared for a sometimes enormous struggle.

The first step in this transition is to enhance the students' self-esteem and reduce the anxiety level. This is done through creating an overall positive atmosphere in the classroom and by planning very specific activities which stress self-awareness, respect, and cooperation. Activities like those suggested by Canfield and Wells (1976), Prutzman, Stern, Burger, and Bodenhamer (1988), and Schniedewind (1987) help students become more aware about their own attitudes about themselves and others while developing skills of listening, speaking, and cooperating.

I have children interview each other at the beginning of the year and report on it to the whole class. This shows them that they should take each other seriously and it practices public speaking and careful listening. I play circle games involving drama, storytelling, and physical activity as well as small group activities which stress brainstorming, problem solving, and creative writing and dramatics. Instead of segregating affective education activities off into an afternoon corner of the curriculum I try as much as possible to integrate group process and self-esteem-building activities into the curriculum as a whole. No matter where such activities are during the day, however, I have found that I need to model, role play, and teach many of these social skills. I model something, involve a small group of students with me doing the activity in front of the class, then have another small group do it again in front without my participation. Finally, after a short discussion with the whole class everyone becomes involved in the activity. Later, it is important for the class to discuss both the content and the process of the activity, with both strengths and shortcomings being highlighted. Modeling and discussing with students how to manage their time and to stay organized—from one's desk to one's three-ring binder—are also very powerful tools for the development of independence and high self-esteem.

Finally, I have found that I can reach even more students by linking my attempts at developing self-confidence and responsibility to history. For example, each year I make sure to focus for a while on the fact that in our nation's past females were not allowed to attend many schools, not allowed to speak at political meetings or vote. Through role play, storytelling, discussion, and project work about the past, some students are inspired to take a stronger and more self-conscious role in the classroom.

Beyond the building of self-esteem, students need to be involved with establishing and periodically reviewing the rules and curriculum of the classroom. Students' ability to do this depends on several factors including their maturity and previous schooling experience. At the beginning of the year, I carefully plan lessons which give students a taste of what it would mean to have a large say over what happens in the class. At the same time I am quick to restrict student decision making at the first signs that students are using the increased power as a license to goof off. As I restrict it, I go through a long process of explanation: discussion, role playing, and a lessening of the restrictions. After several cycles of this process, students usually become better able to take on increased responsibility and freedom. Sometimes such restrictions must be done on an individual level. For example, if the desks are arranged in clusters, those students who demonstrate they are capable of sitting close to their classmates and yet still listen to class discussions are permitted to stay in the clusters, while those who are disruptive have as a logical consequence their desk being placed in a "row."

Empowerment does not mean "giving" someone their freedom. Nor does it mean creating a type of surface "empowerment" in which one gives the students the impression that they are "equal" to the teacher. The challenge for the teacher who believes in student empowerment is to create an environment which is both stimulating and flexible in which students can exercise increasing levels of power while regularly reflecting upon and evaluating the new learner-teacher relationship.

One element of this environment is class organization. We arrange our classroom according to our needs: Rows for presentations, a circle of chairs for large group discussion, and clusters of desks for small group discussion and work.

For class meetings, for instance, desks are pushed to the walls and the chairs are placed in a big circle. Such meetings form the basis of democraticizing the classroom (Glasser, 1969, 1986; Schmuck & Schmuck, 1983) through discussions, voting, and class problem-solving. At the beginning of each school year, I chair the meetings but eventually the students take over. One person takes notes each session into a spiral notebook that we keep hung on the wall. I have a special rock which is passed from person to person so we know whose turn it is to speak. The first part of the year is often spent just improving our listening skills so that we can have an interactive dialogue instead of a series of monologues. I do this through modeling what a good listener does and playing listening games, such as having each person repeat one thing or the main idea of the person who spoke immediately before them prior to their speaking.

I start the class meetings with a circle game and then pass the rock and let people state the concern or problem they would like to discuss. I note these and then decide what will be discussed that day, usually starting off with a smaller, solvable problem and then moving into the hot and heavy ones. We use a five-step plan:

1. What is the problem?
2. Are you sure about it?
3. What can we do about it?
4. Try it.
5. How did it work?

Through this five-step process, students begin to work collectively, reflecting upon the problem and together seeking solutions. While many of the problems poor and minority children and communities face cannot be easily or immediately "solved" a "problem-posing" pedagogy can encourage a questioning of why things are the way they are and the identification of actions, no matter how small, to begin to address them. Inherent is a recognition of the complexity and time needed for solutions with individuals and communities" (Wallerstein & Bernstein, 1988).

A DIALOGICAL INSTRUCTIONAL METHOD

If "student empowerment" is going to be meaningful, students not only need to be involved in some of the problem-solving and posing practices outlined above, but teachers must fundamentally change their methods. Education should not be viewed as the transmission of knowledge by trained technicians, but rather as an interactive process through which problems are posed and answers collaboratively sought. Dewey (1916) felt similarly and spoke of a conception of instruction for knowledge as opposed to instruction for habit. Like Freire, he saw education as an interactive process based on the history, experience, and culture of the student. Dewey said a mechanic taught mechanically would not be able to solve a new problem that might arise, but one taught to understand the whole machine and machines in general would be able to adapt to the new situation. The difference between Dewey and Freire is in part defined by the kinds of activities they advocate as ways for students to gain knowledge. Dewey took a deliberate apolitical stance. The practical educational activities he advocated usually involved students transforming the natural world, that is, gardening or laboratory experiments. Freire, on the other hand, defines practical education activities as critical discussion and collective action aimed at solving political and social problems (also see Walsh's Introduction, this volume).

The centerpiece of Freire's method, and what distinguishes it so sharply from the dominant practices in classrooms of most of North America, is its emphasis on dialogue. *Dialogue,* as Freire defines it, is not just permissive talk, but *conversation with a focus and a purpose.* Dialogue shows that the object of study is not the exclusive property of the teacher; knowledge is not produced somewhere in textbook offices and then transferred to the student. By discussion and extensive use of open-ended questioning by the teacher, students begin to think about the object or topic under study. Freire (Shor & Freire, 1987) is not opposed to lectures per se and in fact suggests the use of a variety of formats in the classroom. Since factual knowledge is the foundation upon which many discussions and opinions should be based, short lectures are sometimes important even at the elementary level. However, with the recent trend towards direct instruction, teachers too often demonstrate an overreliance on lecture to convey knowledge, even though only a small amount of such information is retained.

To initiate dialogue, I may use a motivating drawing, photo, cartoon, poem, written dialogue, oral story, or piece of prose. These dialogue "triggers" are useful for full classroom or small group discussions. Wallerstein and Bernstein (1988) have used a simple acronym "SHOWED" as a way to help students systematically respond to such a trigger.

S   what do you *See?*
H   what's *Happening* to your feelings?
O   relate it to your *Own* lives
W   *Why* do we face these problems?
E
D   what can we *Do* about it?

The students are encouraged to use this format to help facilitate their dialogue. It helps to direct students away from spontaneous conversation to a progression that moves from personal reactions to social analysis to consideration of action. A few examples from my class serve to illustrate this process.

One year as my class played at recess, a student slipped and fell on to a broken bottle, putting a ghastly wound into the back of her thigh—over 50 stitches. After the police and ambulance had carried her off on a stretcher, we tearfully retreated back into the safety of our classroom and I thought, "What the heck should I do now?" I sent two kids out to retrieve the guilty piece of glass. We put the piece in an open box and passed it around. The rest of the afternoon we discussed everything from the high school students who share our playground, to the bottle manufacturing companies who have prevented the Wisconsin state legislature from passing a bottle deposit law. One of my students, Fernando Valadez, put his thoughts to poetry:

Pig Pen

Nobody likes to live
in the pigpen of broken bottles,
muddy papers and squished cans.
In our neighborhood of
lonely streets, messy parks,
dirty alleys and dangerous playgrounds
you might get hurt like a friend
of mine who got a big cut on the back
of her leg when she was running
by the swings and fell on some glass.
The ambulance came
and took her away.
Who's going to take the junk
away?

At times the triggers I use are more explicitly value-laden and often cut across the curricula integrating language arts, history, and other subject areas. Some of the best dialogue in my class has come from discussions following the reading of poems or short historical pieces. Will Fisher's poem, for instance, helped initiate discussion of history and justice. The context is ice cream cones and mud, one that a child can relate to and understand:

A COMMAND TO DRIVE HORSE RECKLESSLY

The first warm day in May, a line of common folk in front of the Dairy Queen shop. A carriage dashes by, spraying mud. Women curse and shake their fists. Two men rush after the carriage. It has been stopped by a traffic light. The men angrily threaten the coachman. Clutching his fifty-cent cone, a child catches up and, ignoring the others, flings the cone through the open window into the face of the nobleperson.

Utilizing the "SHOWED" question format with this simple poem has enabled my students to discuss a wide variety of topics ranging from racial and class discrimination, inflation, splashing each other on the playground, to the invention of traffic lights and cars.

CRITIQUE THE CURRICULUM AND SOCIETY

There is more to Freire than generative themes of the learners' lives and a dialogic style. He speaks of the need to illuminate reality to the student, as opposed to the standard curriculum which obscures reality. Freire (1985) suggests that the "question is a different relationship to knowledge and society and that the only way to truly understand the curriculum of the classroom is to go beyond its walls into the society." (Walsh expands on this relationship to knowledge and society in her Introduction.)

In most schools, facts are presented as value-free. Conceptual analysis—to the degree it exists—does not make contact with the real world. History is presented as a series of nonrelated sequential facts. Scientific "truths" are presented without historical context with little regard to the ramifications such matters have on the learners' environment or global ecology. Students are expected to learn—usually memorize and occasionally "discover"—such facts without regard to the values or interests which inform such perspectives (Shor, 1980, 1987).

As stated previously teachers should help students draw connections between their own lives, communities, and environment. But we must also *help them reflect upon why they think the way they do; to discover* that *knowledge is socially constructed, that truth is relative not only to time and place but to class, race, and gender interests as well.* Students need to know that what they have before them in their textbooks, in the newspapers, or on the television is not always true. We should thus engage our students in thinking about the validity of texts (Bigelow, 1989). In fact, this is one of the few uses I have found for them in my classroom.

The third-grade basal reader, *Golden Secrets* (Scott Foresman, 1980), for example, has a story on inventions. The anonymous author states that the traffic light was invented by an anonymous policeman. Actually it was invented by the African-American scientist Garrett A. Morgan. I give my students a short piece on Morgan that is from a black history book (Adams, 1969) and we compare and question. Some of my classes decided to write to Scott Foresman and complain.

The problem with textbooks is also what they omit (Council on Interracial Books for Children, 1977a). The Silver Burdett Social Studies Series, *The World and Its People* (Helmus, Arnsdorff, Toppin, and Pounds 1984), used in over two-thirds of the nation's school districts, has a 502-page reader on U.S. History. Only five paragraphs of this text mention unions and working-class struggle, only one labor leader, Samuel Gompers, is mentioned and most of the text is written in the passive tense. "Why?" I ask the students, as I provide interesting stories and we role-play the true history of working-class struggle in our country. I connect this to local history, like the several-day general strike for the eight-hour day in 1886 which ended with the massacre of seven people including a 13-year-old boy. I have the students survey their parents and neighbors as to knowledge of this strike and other important events in our community's history and then we reflect on why people do not know such things. We recreate such history through readers' theater, role plays, simulations, dramas, and special projects.

Similarly, a Heath science textbook (Barufaldi, Ladd, & Moses 1981) has a short biography on an African-American scientist Charles Drew, who pioneered blood transfusions and plasma research. Omitted is the fact that Dr. Drew died after a car accident in the South when a southern hospital refused to treat him and give him a blood transfusion because of his skin color.

One example that I particularly like to use in my bilingual class is the story of Sequoyah and the Cherokees. Most history books mention Sequoyah's creation of the alphabet and the Trail of Tears, but few mention that the Cherokee nation had a bilingual weekly newspaper and a bilingual school system with over 200 of their own schools including a normal school—that is, until the early 1900s when the federal government stepped in and disbanded it.[5] I tell the children this story of the Cherokees and say, "Let's see what the history books and encyclopedias say." Usually there are gross omissions and we proceed to discuss why and what impact these omissions have on how we view the world. I ask, "Why didn't the government want the Cherokees to maintain their language?" This is a crucial question in my classroom since, by fifth grade, many of the students have already developed negative attitudes toward their native Spanish language.

There are many stories from the untold history of the oppressed that expose the social nature of knowledge and nurture civic courage and a sense of social justice. I find the history of Shea's Rebellion and the Seminole Wars particularly worthwhile because not only was there a struggle for a just cause but a key ingredient was unity among nationalities, a persistent problem in our nation's history.

Another important way to deal with the socially constructed nature of knowledge is to directly deal with racist and sexist stereotypes.[6] Around Thanksgiving time I show my students the filmstrip, *Unlearning "Indian" Stereotypes* (Council on Interracial Books for Children, 1977b). It is narrated by Native American children who visit a public library and become outraged at the various stereotypes of Indians in the books.

One year after viewing the filmstrip the students seemed particularly outraged at what they had learned. They came the next day talking about how their siblings in first grade had come home with construction paper headdresses with feathers. "That's a stereotype," the students proudly proclaimed. "What did you do about it?" I responded. "I ripped it up." "I slugged him," came the chorus of responses. As we continued the discussion, I asked why their brothers and sisters had the objects and interrogated them as to how children learn about such things. Finally they decided there were more productive things they could do. They first scoured the school library for books with stereotypes but since they found few, they decided to investigate their sibling's first grade room and look for stereotypes there. They wrote a letter to the teacher asking permission and then went in armed with clipboards, paper, and pens. Results were a picture of an Indian next to the letter "I" in the alphabet strip on the wall. They came back and decided they wanted to teach the first graders about stereotypes. I was skeptical but agreed and after much rehearsal they entered the first grade classroom to give their lesson—rather unsuccessfully I am afraid. But, they reflected on it and later Paco Resendez and Faviola Alvarez wrote in our school newspaper:

> We have been studying stereotypes on Native Americans. What is a stereotype? It's when somebody says something that's not true about another group of people. For example, it is a stereotype if you think all Indians wear feathers or say "HOW!" Or if you think that all girls are delicate. Why? Because some girls are strong.

Another way to show students that knowledge is socially constructed is to get different newspaper or magazine articles about the same subject, from different points of view. Subscribe to newspapers from another country, like *La Barricada,* or use excerpts from papers such as *The Nation, In These Times, Food and Justice,* or the *Guardian* to contrast the reporting from the established press. Or videotape a children's cartoon or tape record lyrics of a popular tune and then watch or play it, analyze it as a class, and draw out its values. I watch for outrageous stories or advertisements in the paper—these can be real thought provokers—or invite in guests who will shock the students out of their complacency. I also use posters, quotations, and maps.

I place a "poster of the week" on a special moveable bulletin board on my classroom wall. By using dramatic, historical, and/or controversial posters I encourage writing, discussion, and critique.[7] I also use a quotation of the week— in English, Spanish, or both. I begin the year providing the quotations myself, but as time passes children offer ones that they have found or created. Some quotations in particular, lend themselves to comparison, analysis, and critique:

> When the missionaries first came to Africa they had bibles and we had the land. They said, "Let us pray." We closed our eyes. When we opened them we had the bibles and they had the land. (Bishop Desmond Tu Tu, Nobel Peace Prize Recipient)

Pointing out the biases in maps is also particularly thought provoking. The Mercator projection map, for example, places the equator two-thirds of the way down and depicts Europe as larger than South America although the area of the latter is approximately (6.9 million square miles) double that of Europe (3.8). The newly created Peter Projection may corrects this. Another map challenges the conception that Argentina is on the bottom and North America is on top, by reversing the North and South Poles. Such media invoke considerable dialogue and thinking, including who makes maps, why they are the way they are, and how maps shape our thinking about the world.[8]

TEACHING SOCIAL RESPONSIBILITY

As students develop the interest and ability to discuss and reflect on their lives, communities, and the broader world, questions inevitably arise as to how people change the world. This concern and interest in social change can be encouraged by consciously fostering what Giroux (1985) calls "civic courage": stimulating "their passions, imaginations, and intellects so that they will be moved to challenge the social, political and economic forces that weigh so heavily upon their lives" (p. 201). In other words, students should be encourage to act *as if* they were living in a democracy.

One way this can be done is through class meetings and positive reinforcement of socially responsible actions in the classroom. In other words, the first way to build social responsibility is to try to democratize and humanize the educational setting. In my classroom, for example, there is a small quartz rock which is given to the student who has helped someone else. At the beginning of each day, the student who had been awarded for her or his social responsibility the day before chooses the next recipient.

The central theme in my classroom is that the quest for social justice is a neverending struggle in our nation and world; that the vast majority of people have benefited by this struggle; that we must understand this struggle; and that we must make decisions about whether to be involved in it. The academic content areas can be woven around this theme. In reading poetry and literature to children, social issues can be emphasized through books that specifically empower children (Peterson, 1987). Contemporary struggles can be highlighted through curricular materials and readings on Central America, apartheid, and on racism at home.[9] And pictures of real people who have worked for social justice can help children see these struggles as human. In my classroom there is a gallery of freedom fighters, the "luchadores por la justicia" or strugglers for justice that we have studied in social studies and current events. The large portraits—some commercially purchased and others drawn by the children—serve as reminders that women and men of all races have made important contributions to society and serve as keys to unlock our past discussions and studies about people and their struggles. A few years ago one of my students reflected on Cesar Chavez in this way:

Cesar Chavez is a good man. He is very famous but he is poor. I thought that if people are famous they have to be rich. But this man is poor because he has a group of people and the money he earns he gives to them.

In most curricula, struggle is omitted and conflict forgotten. History is not of social movements or eras but rather the succession of rules from the earliest Egyptian pharaohs to the most recent presidential administration. It has been fragmented, distorted, and rewritten. With our common history of struggle denied us, the past rewritten, the rulers of our society find the present much easier to manipulate. When Nixon said, "History will absolve our roles in Vietnam," he knew what he was talking about, for corporate textbook companies continue to write and rewrite our history—at least for the immediate future.

In contrast, Freire points to the positive role of struggle in history. He calls conflict the "midwife of real consciousness" and says it should be the focus of learning (Freire, 1970). The cynic might say that with all the conflict in our schools our students must be of very high consciousness. The key point here is to reflect on and critique conflict, in our daily lives, classrooms, and communities, as well as in history.[10]

Focusing on societal conflict—both historic and contemporary—is not only highly motivating and educational but also helps children, even the very young, to analyze and evaluate different points of view and express opinions as to what they think is just. The study of conflicts can be integrated into social studies units, for example, personal conflicts like Fredrick Douglass's struggle to learn to read; historic conflicts like the wars to take the land from American Indians, slave rebellions, worker strikes, bus boycotts, civil rights marches, antiwar movements; and contemporary conflicts like the United Farm Worker grape boycott, the war in El Salvador, apartheid, the antitoxin "Not in My Back Yard Movement." In my classroom, each conflict studied and any other historical event encountered in the normal course of our school day, is recorded on a 3 × 5 file card with a word description and the date. This card is hung on the class timeline which circles three sides of the room. This process provides students with a visual representation of time, history, and sequence while fostering the understanding that everything is interrelated.

Historical conflict is best understood through engaging students in participatory activities. Often I will read or tell a story about a conflict and have children role-play parts of it either during or after the story. Occasionally such stories lead to small group or whole class drama presentations. I also use readers theater, that is, scripted plays written so that no acting needs to take place.[11] Sometimes I also encourage students to draw a conflict either together as a mural on large sheets of paper for display or separately for publication.

In addition, each student builds a people's textbook—a three-ring binder in which they put alternative materials. There are sections for geography, history, science, songs, poetry, and quotations. One year after *Rethinking Schools*

printed an article on an important Milwaukee event of 1854 when 5,000 people stormed the county jail to free a runaway slave the students used the information to write their own bilingual book about the historic incident. By
examining local history in which European Americans fought alongside
African-Americans for the abolition of slavery, my students began to understand that social responsibility in a race-divided society means working
together on issues that might not necessarily be deemed as in ones immediate
self-interest.[12]

Freire takes liberating education even one step further—to action or praxis.
He believes learners should use their newfound analysis to transform the world.
In the school setting transforming-type activities depend on the nature of the
group of students, the community, and the school system, and the courage and
seniority of the teacher. My students have gone with me to marches that
protested police brutality, demanded that King's birthday be made a national
holiday, asked that Congress not fund the Contras, and requested nuclear dis-
armament. Two of my students testified before the City Council, asking that
a Jobs with Peace referendum be placed on the ballot. In another instance, the
students went to observe the court proceedings in the case of a police killing of
an African-American man. Obviously teachers need to be involved in the community in order to know what's happening and what possibilities exist for
involvement of children.

Projects that are less overtly political can also stimulate critical thinking:
Joining Amnesty International as a class and adopting a political prisoner,
adopting a section of beach on a lake or river and keeping it clean, interviewing people involved in a local strike or community struggle, raising money for
earthquake or famine relief, writing letters to governmental representatives,
having such representatives or social activists visit the classroom, or corresponding with children in other parts of the USA, Puerto Rico, USSR, El Salvador and Mozambique.[13] Discussion, writing, and critical reflection on these
activities, however, are crucial so these are not to be just "interesting" field trips
or projects.

One year we studied the underground railroad as part of the fifth grade
U.S. history curriculum. We also studied the second underground railroad, the
sanctuary movement. I invited a speaker to my class who had lived in El Salvador for several years. He showed slides of the people. My children at first
laughed at the distended bellies of the starving Salvadoran children, but their
chuckles turned to horror and then anger as they began to understand that U.S.
bombs are being dropped on these children. The class meeting after the presentation was quite informative. The kids asked "Why?" Why was the U.S.
government doing this? "Why did Reagan do it?" We asked them "Why do
you think?" "Because Regan supports the rich," said one. "Yeah," agreed the
others. But others were still not satisfied. "Why? Why does he support the
rich?" Finally the speaker responded. "Because it is the job of the president in

this country to support the rich." Paco's hand shot up. "If that's the case," he argued, "what about Kennedy?" The bell rang before the speaker could answer. As I drove him home he said the discussion was better than many he had had on university campuses.

In a group meeting the following day the children decided to write letters to our representatives and the president on the issue. The next day one boy, Michael, came in and said, "Mr. Peterson, we have to send weapons down to Central America or else the Russians will take over and no one will believe in God anymore." I said, "Michael, you've been talking to your mom . . . Great. Keep it up. We'll talk about that later." But that day we didn't get to it and as he left I gave him some *Food First* leaflets about hunger in Central America being the real enemy and asked him to read them with his mom. The following day he did not show up for school—I was a bit concerned. The day after he was back and we talked in detail about the various perspectives on Nicaragua, El Salvador, the USSR, and the United States of America. The children decided that even if the Sandinistas received money and weapons from aliens from Saturn they had that right because all they wanted to do was run their own country.

A week later at a group meeting, Emma announced that we had to discuss the letters we wrote to the President. "They won't do any good," she lamented, "I bet he just tore them up." She then proposed we go on a field trip to Washington DC to meet the President in person and that I, the teacher, finance it. I politely declined. At that point there was what Freire (Shor & Freire 1987) would call an inductive moment—when the students are stalled and need direction—I said that sometimes people protested in Washington, DC, but often people protested right here in Milwaukee, as the Pledge of Resistance was doing regularly. The kids immediately said they wanted to go, and before I knew it I was sending home letters to the parents explaining that although it was not part of the official curriculum, if they consented, I would supervise a public bus trip after school up to the Federal Building to protest U.S. aid to the contras. I bought tag board and markers from the local bookstore careful not to use the school's supplies. Half the class—12 children—brought back signed notes. The next Monday the students stayed after school and made their signs. At first they asked me what they should say, but I responded that if they were going on a protest march they had better know what they were protesting. They could make the signs themselves. They did. Their signs included:

Let them run their land!
Support the Poor! Not the "freedom fighters." They're the Rich.
Help Central America Don't Kill Them
Give the Nicaraguans their Freedom
Let Nicaragua Live!
Give Nicaragua Some Food Instead of Weapons

We want Freedom and Peace
Stop spending money to make bombs.

When they were finished making their signs we walked two blocks to the
public bus stop and during a steady drizzle headed downtown to the Federal
Building. They were the only Hispanics at the march of 150 people and were
welcomed with open arms. We walked, marched, chanted, and finally went
home wet and exhausted.

The next day we had a panel discussion and the kids talked and listened
like they were on top of the world. Paula Martinez wrote about it later in our
magazine, *Kid Power*:

> On a rainy Tuesday in April some of the students from our class went to
> protest against the contras. The people in Central America are poor and being
> bombed on their heads. When we went protesting it was raining and it seemed
> like the contras were bombing us. A week before we had visitor, Jim Harney.
> He had been to El Salvador. He talked to our class about what was going on in
> El Salvador. He said it was terrible. A lot of people are dying. He showed us
> slides of El Salvador and told us its bad to be there. He hoped that our govern-
> ment will give them food and money and not bombs.

Michael, the boy who had come back from home concerned about the
Russians and God did not go to the march. He said he had to babysit his little
brother. Parent conferences were a week later and I was a bit apprehensive to
see his mother—a socially mobile Puerto Rican studying to become a nurse.
She walked into the room, sat down and said, "Mr Peterson, I want to thank
you. Michael has become interested in everything. He watches the news, he
talks to me about what's going on, he knows more about things than me sometime. I don't know what you did. But thanks." As our conversation progressed
it was clear her conservative political views on Central America had not
changed, but our differences were secondary, because what was central to both
of us was that her son had started to read the world.

REFERENCES

Adams, R. (1969). *Great Negroes: Past and present.* Chicago: Afro-Am Publishing Co.
All London Teachers Against Racism and Facism (ALTARF). (1984). *Challenging racism.* Nottingham,
    UK: Russell Press. Available from ALTARF, Room 216, Panther House, 38 Mount Pleasant,
    London WCIX OAP.
Ashton-Warner, S. (1965). *Teacher.* New York: Simon & Schuster.
Barufaldi, J., Ladd, G., and Moses, A. (1981). *Heath Science.* Lexington, MA: D.C. Heath.
Bigelow, W. (1985). *Strangers in their own land: A curriculum guide to South Africa.* New York: Africa
    World Press.
Bigelow, W. (1989, October/November). "Discovering Columbus: Re-reading the past." *Rethinking
    Schools,* 4(1), 1, 12–13.
Bigelow, W., and Diamond, N. (1988). *The power in our hands: A curriculum on the history of work
    and workers in the United States.* New York: Monthly Review Press.
Brecht, B. (1978). *The mother.* New York: Grove Press.

Calkins, L. (1983). *Lessons from a child.* Portsmouth, NH: Heinemann.

Calkins, L. (1986). *The art of teaching writing.* Portsmouth, NH: Heinemann.

Canfield, J., and Wells, H. (1976). *100 ways to enhance self-concept in the classroom: A handbook for teachers and parents.* Englewood Cliffs, NJ: Prentice-Hall.

Coalition of Essential Schools. (1984). *Prospectus: 1984–1994.* Providence, RI: Brown University.

Commission on Reading by the National Council of Teachers of English. (1988). *Report card on basal readers.* Katonah, NY: Richard C. Owen.

Council on Interracial Books for Children (CIBC). (1977a). *Stereotypes, distortions and omissions in U.S. history textbooks.* New York: Racism and Sexism Resource Center for Educators.

Council on Interracial Books for Children. (1977b). *Unlearning "Indian" stereotypes.* New York: Racism and Sexism Resource Center for Educators.

Council on Interracial Books for Children. (1982a). *Unlearning Chicano and Puerto Rican stereotypes.* New York: Racism and Sexism Resource Center for Educators.

Council on Interracial Books for Children. (1982b). *Unlearning Asian American stereotypes.* New York: Racism and Sexism Resource Center for Educators.

Dewey, J. (1916). *Democracy and education.* New York: Macmillan.

Dreikurs, R., Grunwald, B., and Pepper, F. (1982). *Maintaining sanity in the classroom.* New York: Harper & Row.

Ellwood, C. (1989). "Making connections: Challenges we face." *Rethinking Schools,* 3(3), 1, 12–13.

Fairtest (National Center for Fair and Open Testing). (1988). *Fallout from the testing explosion: How 100 million standardized exams undermine equity and excellence in American's public schools.* Available from P.O. Box 1272, Harvard Square Station, Cambridge, MA 02238.

Freire, P. (1970). *Pedagogy for the oppressed.* New York: Seabury.

Freire, P. (1985). *The politics of education.* South Hadley, MA: Bergin & Garvey.

Gibboney, R. A. (1988). "Madeline Hunter's teaching machine." *Rethinking Schools,* 2(3), 10–11.

Giroux, H. (1985). *Theory and resistance in education.* South Hadley, MA: Bergin and Garvey.

Glasser, W. (1969). *Schools without failure.* New York: Harper & Row.

Glasser, W. (1986). *Control theory in the classroom.* New York: Harper & Row.

Goodlad, J. (1984). *A place called school: Prospects for the future.* New York: McGraw-Hill.

Goodman, K. (1986). *What's whole in whole language?* Richmond Hill, Ontario; Canada Scholastic TAB. (Distributed in the United States by Heinemann.)

Goodman, K., Smith, E. B., Meredith, R., and Goodman, Y. (1987). *Language and thinking in school: A whole language curriculum.* New York: Richard C. Owen.

Graves, D. H. (1983). *Writing: Teachers and children at work.* Portsmouth, NH: Heinemann.

Helmus, T., Arnsdorf, V., Toppin, E., and Pounds, N. (1984). *The United States and its neighbors.* Atlanta: Silver Burdett Co.

Krashen, S., and Terrell, T. (1983). *The natural approach: Language acquisition in the classroom.* Hayward, CA: Alemany Press.

Levine, D. (1988). "Outcome based education: Grand design or blueprint for failure?" *Rethinking Schools,* 2(2), 1, 12–13.

Liebert, R., and Sprafkin, J. (1988). *The early window: Effects of television on children and youth.* New York: Pergamon Press.

Meyers, R., Banfield, B., and Colon, J. (eds.). (1983). *Embers: Stories for a changing world.* Old Westbury, NY: The Feminist Press.

New York City Board of Education. (1988). *Resolving conflict creatively: A draft teaching guide for grades Kindergarten through six.* New York: Board of Education.

Payne, C. (1984). "Multicultural education and racism in American schools." *Theory into Practice,* 33(2), 124–131.

Peterson, R. (1987). "Books to empower young people." *Rethinking Schools,* 1(3), 9–10.

Prutzman, P., Stern, L., Burger, M. L., and Bodenhamer, G. (1988). *The friendly classroom for a small planet: A handbook on creative approaches to living and problem solving for children.* Philadelphia, PA: New Society Publishers.

Racism and Sexism Resource Center. (1981). *Winning justice for all: A supplementary curriculum unit on sexism and racism, stereotyping and discrimination.* New York: Council on Interracial Books for Children.

Rubin, L. (1984). *Food First curriculum.* San Francisco: Food First.

Schniedewind, N. (1987). *Cooperative learning, cooperative lives: A sourcebook of learning activities for building a peaceful world.* Somerville, MA: Circle Press.

Schiedewind, N., and Davidson, E. (1983). *Open minds to equality: A sourcebook of learning activities to promote race, sex, class, and age equity.* Englewood Cliffs, NJ: Prentice-Hall.

Schmuck P. A., and Schmuck, R. A. (1983). *Group process in the classroom.* Dubuque, IA: Wm. C. Brown Company.

Scott, Foresman & Co. (1981). *Scott Foresman reading.* New York.

Searle, C. (1977). *The world in a classroom.* London: Writers and Readers Publishing Cooperative.

Shor, I. (1980). *Critical teaching and everyday life.* Boston: South End Press.

Shor, I. (1987). *Freire for the classroom: A sourcebook for liberatory teaching.* Portsmouth, NH: Heinemann.

Shor, I., and Freire, P. (1987). *A pedagogy for liberation: Dialogues on transforming education.* South Hadley, MA: Bergin and Garvey.

Smith, F. (1985). *Reading without nonsense.* New York: Teachers College Press.

United Farm Workers. (1987). *The wrath of grapes* (video). Keene, CA: The United Farm Workers.

Wallerstein, N., and Bernstein, E. (1988). "Empowerment education: Freire's ideas adapted to health education." *Health Education Quarterly,* 15(4), 379–394.

Weinberg, M. (1977). *A chance to learn: The history of race and education in the United States.* New York: Cambridge University Press.

Wigginton, E. (1989). "Foxfire grows up." *Harvard Educational Review,* 59(1), 24–49.

Winn, M. (1987). *Unplugging the plug-in drug.* New York: Penguin.

Wodtke, K. (1986). "Inequality at age five?" *Rethinking Schools,* 1(1), 7.

NOTES

1. Publications which accept children's writings include: *Children's Album,* PO Box 6086, Concord, CA 94524 ($10/year); *Rethinking Schools,* 1001 E. Keefe Ave., Milwaukee, WI 53212 ($10/year); *Stone Soup,* PO Box 83, Santa Cruz, CA 95063 ($17.50/year); *Reflections,* Box 368, Ducan Falls, OH 43734 ($3/year); *The McGuffey Writer,* 400A McGuffey Hall, Miami University, Oxford, OH 45056 ($3/year); *Chart Your Course,* PO Box 6448, Mobile, AL., 36660, ($20/yr); *Creative Kids,* PO Box 637, 100 Pine Ave., Holmes, PA 19043 ($10/yr.); *A Young Author's Guide to Publishing* lists submission guidelines for children's magazines; send $2.50 to Dr. Nicholas Spennato, Delaware County Reading Council, 6th and Olive St., Media, PA 19063.

2. One excellent anthology is called *Embers: Stories for a Changing World* edited by Meyers, Banfield, and Colon, J. (1983) distributed by the Council on Interracial Books for Children, 1841 Broadway, New York, NY, 10023. For a bibliography of children's books that have young people as protagonists who are working for social justice see Peterson (1987). Books to empower young people. *Rethinking Schools,* vol. 1, no. 3, pp. 9–10, available from *Rethinking Schools,* 1001 E., Keefe Ave., Milwaukee, WI 53212.

3. Marie Winn (1987) offers some innovative ideas to both parents and teachers to help children kick the television habit, including plans for classroom and school wide television turnoff campaigns.

4. This generalization ignores the class, race, and gender factors which profoundly affect school structure and student self-esteem. For example, Wodtke (1986) found discrepancies between instructional approaches received by suburban kindergarten and those in poor, working-class settings. The suburban kindergartens tended to encourage children to participate in show-and-tell and speak in front of the class, while the predominantly poor and working-class kindergartens rarely utilized such activities instead relying more heavily on worksheets and drill because of the pressures to cover standardized curriculum and the emphasis put on direct instruction. This differentiated approach tends to inculcate certain habits and outlooks in children based on class and race factors.

5. In 1838, the United States government forced the Cherokee people and other southeastern tribes to abandon their land in Georgia and move to Oklahoma. The Indians suffered such hardships along the way that the path they followed became known as the Trail of Tears. For more information on the bilingual education system established by the Cherokees see Payne (1984) and Weinberg (1977).

6. The recognition of the importance of dealing with racism among children leads some educators (ALTARF, 1984) to argue that multicultural education is limited if not accompanied by an anti-racist component.

7. High-quality, politically progressive posters can be found through a number of outlets. Particularly good sources are the Syracuse Cultural Worker, Box 6367, Syracuse, NY 13217 and Northern Sun Merchandising, 2916 E. Lake St., Minneapolis, MN 55406. A source for excellent posters of Native American leaders is the Perfection Form Company, Logan, Iowa and for women posters contact: TABS, 438 Fourth St., Brooklyn, NY 11215 (718) 788-3478.

8. The Peter Projection Map can be ordered from Friendship Press, PO Box 37844, Cincinnati, Ohio 45237. The Turnabout map is distributed by Laguna Sales, Inc., 7040 Via Valverde, San Jose, CA 95135.

9. I collect and weave into our class curricula parts of progressive curricula such as *Winning "Justice for All"* (Racism & Sexism Resource Center, 1981), *Open Minds to Equality* (Schniedewind & Davidson, 1983) *Food First Curriculum,* (Rubin, 1984), *Cooperative Learning, Cooperative Lives* (Schniedewind 1987), and a variety of curriculum on contemporary issues such as Central America (contact Network of Educators' Committees on Central America, PO Box 43509, Washington DC 20010-9509. 202-667-2618); apartheid (Bigelow, 1985); U.S. labor struggles (Bigelow & Diamond, 1988); women (contact National Women's History Project, PO Box 316 Santa Rosa Ca 95402 (707)526-5974); peace (contact the Wilmington College Peace Resource Center, Pyle Center Box 1183, Willmington, OH 45177); and racism (see the "Unlearning Stereotypes" filmstrips and guides from the CIBC, 1977a, 1982a, 1982b).

10. Simulating classroom and interpersonal conflict through trigger cartoons, scripted dialogues, and role plays helps students to develop the skills and responsibility to analyze and resolve their own interpersonal problems. In classroom conflict, such reflection helps children understand the purposes behind the "misbehavior" and allows them to develop strategies and skills to diffuse and mediate such conflict. For a theoretical and practical approach to helping children understand the reasons for misbehavior see Dreikurs, Grunwald, and Pepper (1982) and for additional ways to mediate conflict see Prutzman et al. (1988), Schniedewind (1987), and the curriculum produced by teachers and administrators in NYC Community School District 15 in collaboration with the New York Chapter of Educators for Social Responsibility (New York Board of Education, 1988).

11. Dozens of high-quality reader theaters which deal with a host of conflicts in the history of labor, women, and racial minorities are available from Stevens and Shea, Dept. S, PO Box 794, Stockton, CA 95201.

12. The pamphlet *Joshua Glover: The freeing of a runaway slave in Milwaukee—La liberación de un esclavo fugitivo en Milwaukee* is available from Communicate! Rural Route 2, Pulaski, WI 54162.

13. One such telecommunications linkup is De Orilla a Orilla (from Shore to Shore) which can be contacted by writing Dennis Sayers, De Orilla a Orilla, N.E. MRC, University of Massachusetts, 250 Stuart St., Rm 1105, Boston, MA 02116. Additional information about communication linkups can be obtained from the book, *School Links International: A New Approach to Primary School Linking Around the World,* by Rex Deddis and Cherry Mares (1988), published by the Avon County Council, Tidy Britain Group Schools Research Project.

Language Diversity and Learning

LISA DELPIT

A brand-new black teacher is delivering her first reading lesson to a group of first-grade students in inner-city Philadelphia. She has almost memorized the entire basal-provided lesson dialogue while practicing in front of a mirror the night before.

"Good morning, boys and girls. Today we're going to read a story about where we live, in the city."

A small brown hand rises.

"Yes, Marti."

Marti and this teacher are special friends, for she was a kindergartner in the classroom where her new teacher student-taught.

"Teacher, how come you talkin' like a white person? You talkin' just like my momma talk when she get on the phone!"

I was that first-year teacher many years ago, and Marti was among the first to teach me the role of language diversity in the classroom. Marti let me know that children, even young children, are often aware of the different codes we all use in our everyday lives. They may not yet have learned how to produce those codes or what social purposes they serve, but children often have a remarkable ability to discern and identify different codes in different settings. It is this sensitivity to language and its appropriate use upon which we must build to ensure the success of children from diverse backgrounds.

One aspect of language diversity in the classroom—*form* (the code of a language, its phonology, grammar, inflections, sentence structure, and written symbols)—has usually received the most attention from educators, as manifested in their concern about the "nonstandardness" of the code their students speak. While form is important, particularly in the context of social success, it is considerably less important when concern is lodged instead in the area of cognitive development. This area is related to that aspect of language diversity reflected in Marti's statement—language *use*—the socially and cognitively based linguistic determinations speakers make about style, register, vocabulary, and so forth, when they attempt to interact with or achieve particular goals within their environments. It is the purpose of this paper to address a broad conception of language diversity as it affects the learning environments of linguistically diverse students; it focuses on the development of the range of linguistic alternatives that students have at their disposal for use in varying settings.

ACQUIRING ONE LANGUAGE VARIETY AND LEARNING ANOTHER

The acquisition and development of one's native language is a wondrous process, drawing upon all of the cognitive and affective capacities that make us human. By contrast, the successful acquisition of a second form of a language is essentially a rote-learning process brought to automaticity. It is, however, a process in which success is heavily influenced by highly charged affective factors. Because of the frequency with which schools focus unsuccessfully on changing language form, a careful discussion of the topic and its attendant affective aspects is in order.

THE AFFECTIVE FILTER IN LANGUAGE LEARNING

Learning to orally produce an alternate form is not principally a function of cognitive analysis, thereby not ideally learned from protracted rule-based instruction and correction. Rather, it comes with exposure, comfort level, motivation, familiarity, and practice in real communicative contexts. Those who have enjoyed a pleasant interlude in an area where another dialect of English is spoken may have noticed a change in their own speech. Almost unconsciously, their speech has approached that of those native to the area. The evidence suggests that had these learners been corrected or drilled in the rules of the new dialect, they probably would not have acquired it as readily.

Stephen Krashen, in his work on second-language acquisition, distinguishes the processes of conscious learning (rule-based instruction leading to the monitoring of verbal output) from unconscious *acquisition* ("picking up" a language through internalizing the linguistic input-derived immersion in a new context—what happens, say, when the North American enjoys a visit to the Caribbean).[1] Krashen found unconscious acquisition to be much more effective. In further studies, however, he found that in some cases people did not easily "acquire" the new language. This finding led him to postulate the existence of what he called the "affective filter." The filter operates "when affective conditions are not optimal, when the student is not motivated, does not identify with the speakers of the second language, or is overanxious about his performance, . . . [causing] a mental block . . . [which] will prevent the input from reaching those parts of the brain responsible for language acquisition."[2] Although the process of learning a new dialect cannot be completely equated with learning a new language, some processes seem to be similar. In this case, it seems that the less stress attached to the process, the more easily it is accomplished.

The so-called affective filter is likely to be raised when the learner is exposed to constant correction. Such correction increases cognitive monitoring of speech, thereby making talking difficult. To illustrate with an experiment anyone can try, I have frequently taught a relatively simple new "dialect" in my work with preservice teachers. In this dialect, the phonetic element "iz" is added after the first consonant or consonant cluster in each syllable of a word. (*Teacher* becomes tiz-ea-chiz-er and *apple,* iz-ap-piz-le.) After a bit of drill and practice, the students are asked to tell a partner why they decided to become teachers. Most only haltingly attempt a few words before lapsing into either silence or into "Standard English," usually to complain about my circling the room to insist that all words they utter be in the new dialect. During a follow-up discussion, all students invariably speak of the impossibility of attempting to apply rules while trying to formulate and express a thought. Forcing speakers to monitor their language for rules while speaking, typically produces silence.

Correction may also affect students' attitudes toward their teachers. In a recent research project, middle-school, innercity students were interviewed about their attitudes toward their teachers and school. One young woman complained bitterly, "Mrs.——— always be interrupting to make you 'talk correct' and stuff. She be butting into your conversations when you not even talking to her! She need to mind her own business."

In another example from a Mississippi preschool, a teacher had been drilling her three- and four-year-old charges on responding to the greeting, "Good morning, how are you?" with "I'm fine, thank you." Posting herself near the door one morning, she greeted a four-year-old black boy in an interchange that went something like this:

Teacher: Good morning, Tony, how are you?
Tony: I be's fine.
Teacher: Tony, I said, How *are* you?
Tony: (with raised voice) I be's *fine.*
Teacher: No, Tony, I said *how are you?*
Tony: (angrily) I done told you *I be's fine* and I ain't telling you no more!

Tony must have questioned his teacher's intelligence, if not sanity. In any event, neither of the students discussed above would be predisposed, as Krashen says, to identify with their teachers and thereby increase the possibility of unconsciously acquiring the latter's language form.

ETHNIC IDENTITY AND LANGUAGE PERFORMANCE

Issues of group identity may also affect students' oral production of a different dialect. Nelson-Barber, in a study of phonologic aspects of Pima Indian language found that, in grades 1–3, the children's English most approximated the standard dialect of their teachers.[3] But surprisingly, by fourth grade, when one might assume growing competence in standard forms, their language moved significantly toward the local dialect. These fourth graders had the *competence* to express themselves in a more standard form, but chose, consciously or unconsciously, to use the language of those in their local environments. The researcher believes that, by ages 8–9, these children became aware of their group membership and its importance to their well-being, and this realization was reflected in their language. They may also have become increasingly aware of the school's negative attitude toward their community and found it necessary—through choice of linguistic form—to decide with which camp to identify.

A similar example of linguistic *performance* (what one does with language) belying linguistic *competence* (what one is capable of doing) comes from researcher Gerald Mohatt (personal communication), who was at the time teaching on a Sioux reservation. It was considered axiomatic among the reservation staff that the reason these students failed to become competent readers was that they spoke a nonstandard dialect. One day Mohatt happened to look, unnoticed, into a classroom where a group of boys had congregated. Much to his surprise and amusement, the youngsters were staging a perfect rendition of his own teaching, complete with stance, walk, gestures, *and* Standard English (including Midwestern accent). Clearly, the school's failure to teach these children to read was based on factors other than their inability to speak and understand Standard English. They could do both; they did not often choose to do so in a classroom setting, however, possibly because they chose to identify with their community rather than with the school.

APPRECIATING LINGUISTIC DIVERSITY IN THE CLASSROOM

What should teachers do about helping students acquire an additional oral form? First, they should recognize that the linguistic form a student brings to school is intimately connected with loved ones, community, and personal identity. To suggest that this form is "wrong" or, even worse, ignorant, is to suggest that something is wrong with the student and his or her family. On the other hand, it is equally important to understand that students who do not have access to the politically popular dialect form in this country, that is, Standard English, are less likely to succeed economically than their peers who do. How can both realities be embraced?

Teachers need to support the language that students bring to school, provide them input from an additional code, and give them the opportunity to use the new code in a nonthreatening, real communicative context. Some teachers accomplish this goal by having groups of students create bidialectal dictionaries of their own language form and Standard English. Others have had students become involved with standard forms through various kinds of role-play. For example, memorizing parts for drama productions will allow students to "get the feel" of speaking Standard English while not under the threat of correction. Young students can create puppet shows or role-play cartoon characters. (Many "superheroes" speak almost hypercorrect Standard English!) Playing a role eliminates the possibility of implying that the *child's* language is inadequate, and suggests, instead, that different language forms are appropriate in different contexts. Some other teachers in New York City have had their students produce a news show every day for the rest of the school. The students take on the persona of some famous newscaster, keeping in character as they develop and read their news reports. Discussions ensue about whether Walter Cronkite would have said it that way, again taking the focus off the child's speech.

ACTIVITIES FOR PROMOTING LINGUISTIC PLURALISM

It is possible and desirable to make the actual study of language diversity a part of the curriculum for all students. For younger children, discussions about the differences in the ways television characters from different cultural groups speak can provide a starting point. A collection of the many children's books written in the dialects of various cultural groups can also provide a wonderful basis for learning about linguistic diversity, as can audiotaped stories narrated by individuals from different cultures.[4] Mrs. Pat, a teacher chronicled by Shirley Brice Heath, had her students become language "detectives," interviewing a variety of individuals and listening to the radio and television to discover the differences and similarities in the ways people talked.[5] Children can learn that there are many ways of saying the same thing, and that certain contexts suggest particular kinds of linguistic performances.

Inevitably, each speaker will make his or her own decision about the appropriate form to use in any context. Neither teachers nor anyone else will be able to force a choice upon an individual. All we can do is provide students with the exposure to an alternate form, and allow them the opportunity to practice that form *in contexts that are nonthreatening, have a real purpose, and are intrinsically enjoyable.* If they have access to alternative forms, it will be their decision later in life to choose which to use. We can only provide them with the knowledge base and hope they will make appropriate choices.

ETHNIC IDENTITY AND STYLES OF DISCOURSE

Thus far, we have primarily discussed differences in grammar and syntax. There are other differences in oral language of which teachers should be aware in a multicultural context, particularly in discourse style and language use. Michaels and other researchers identified differences in children's narratives at "sharing time."[6] They found that there was a tendency among young white children to tell "topic-centered" narratives—stories focused on one event—and a tendency among black youngsters, especially girls, to tell "episodic" narratives—stories that include shifting scenes and are typically longer. While these differences are interesting in themselves, what is of greater significance is adults' responses to the differences. Cazden reports on a subsequent project in which a white adult was taped reading the oral narratives of black and white first graders, with all syntax dialectal markers removed.[7] Adults were asked to listen to the stories and comment about the children's likelihood of success in school. The researchers were surprised by the differential responses given by black and white adults.

In responding to the retelling of a black child's story, the white adults were uniformly negative, making such comments as "terrible story, incoherent" and "[n]ot a story at all in the sense of describing something that happened." Asked to judge this child's academic competence, all of the white adults rated her below the children who told "topic-centered" stories. Most of these adults also predicted difficulties for this child's future school career, such as, "This child might have trouble reading," that she exhibited "language problems that affect school achievement," and that "family problems" or "emotional problems" might hamper her academic progress.[8]

The black adults had very different reactions. They found this child's story "well formed, easy to understand, and interesting, with lots of detail and description." Even though all five of these adults mentioned the "shifts" and "associations" or "nonlinear" quality of the story, they did not find these features distracting. Three of the black adults selected the story as the best of the five they had heard, and all but one judged the child as exceptionally bright, highly verbal, and successful in school.[9]

When differences in narrative style produce differences in interpretation of competence, the pedagogical implications are evident. If children who produce stories based in differing discourse styles are expected to have trouble reading, and viewed as having language, family, or emotional problems, as was the case with the informants quoted by Cazden, they are unlikely to be viewed as ready for the same challenging instruction awarded students whose language patterns more closely parallel the teacher's. It is important to emphasize that those teachers in the Cazden study who were of the same cultural group as the students recognized the differences in style, but did not assign a negative valence to those differences. Thus, if teachers hope to avoid negatively stereotyping the language patterns of their students, it is important that they be encouraged to interact with, and willingly learn from, knowledgeable members of their students' cultural groups. This can perhaps best become a reality if teacher education programs include diverse parents, community members, and faculty among those who prepare future teachers, and take seriously the need to develop in those teachers the humility required for learning from the surrounding context when entering a culturally different setting.

QUESTIONING STYLES

Heath has identified another aspect of diversity in language use which affects classroom instruction and learning.[10] She found that questions were used differently in a southeastern town by young black students and their teachers. The students were unaccustomed to responding to the "known-answer" test questions of the classroom. (The classic example of such questions is the contrast between the real-life questioning routine: "What time is it?" "Two o'clock." "Thanks." and the school questioning routine: "What time is it?" "Two o'clock." "*Right!*"[11]) These students would lapse into silence or contribute very little information when teachers asked direct factual questions which called for feedback of what had just been taught. She found that when the types of questions asked of the children were more in line with the kinds of questions posed to them in their home settings—questions probing the students' own analyses and evaluations—these children responded very differently. They "talked, actively and aggressively became involved in the lesson, and offered useful information about their past experiences."[12] The author concludes not only that these kinds of questions are appropriate for all children rather than just for the "high groups" with which they have typically been used, but that awareness and use of the kinds of language used in children's communities can foster the kind of language and performance and growth sought by the school and teachers.

ORAL STYLES IN COMMUNITY LIFE

I would be remiss to end this section without remarking upon the need to draw upon the considerable language strengths of linguistically diverse populations. Smitherman and many others have made note of the value placed upon oral expression in most African-American communities.[13] The "man (person) of words," be he or she preacher, poet, philosopher, huckster, or rap song creator, receives the highest form of respect in the black community. The verbal adroitness, the cogent and quick wit, the brilliant use of metaphorical language, the facility in rhythm and rhyme, evident in the language of preacher Martin Luther King, Jr., boxer Muhammad Ali, comedienne Whoopi Goldberg, rapper L. L. Cool J., singer and songwriter Billie Holiday, and many inner-city black students, may all be drawn upon to facilitate school learning.

Other children, as well, come to school with a wealth of specialized linguistic knowledge. Native American children, for example, come from communities with very sophisticated knowledge about storytelling, and a special way of saying a great deal with a few words. Classroom learning should be structured so that not only are these children able to acquire the verbal patterns they lack, but they are also able to strengthen their proficiencies, and to share these with classmates and teachers. We will then all be enriched.

THE DEMANDS OF SCHOOL LANGUAGE—ORALITY AND LITERACY

There is little evidence that speaking another dialectal form perse, negatively affects one's ability to learn to read.[14] For commonsensical proof, one need only reflect on nonstandard-dialect-speaking slaves who not only taught themselves to read, but did so under threat of severe punishment or death. But children who speak nonmainstream varieties of English do have a more difficult time becoming proficient readers. Why?

One explanation is that, where teachers' assessments of competence are influenced by the dialect children speak, teachers may develop low expectations for certain students and subsequently teach them less.[15] A second explanation, which lends itself more readily to observation, rests in teachers' confusing the teaching of reading with the teaching of a new dialect form.

Cunningham found that teachers across the United States were more likely to correct reading miscues that were dialect related ("Here go a table" for "Here is a table") than those that were nondialect related ("Here is the dog" for "There is the dog").[16] Seventy-eight percent of the dialect miscues were corrected, compared with only 27 percent of the nondialect miscues. He concludes that the teachers were acting out of ignorance, not realizing that "here go" and "here is" represent the same meaning in some black children's language.

In my observations of many classrooms, however, I have come to conclude that even when teachers recognize the similarity of meaning, they are likely to correct dialect-related miscues. Consider a typical example:

Text: Yesterday I washed my brother's clothes.
Student's rendition: Yesterday I wash my bruvver close.

The subsequent exchange between student and teacher sounds something like this:

T: Wait, let's go back. What's that word again? [Points at *washed.*]
S: Wash.
T: No. Look at it again. What letters do you see at the end? You see "e-d." Do you remember what we say when we see those letters on the end of a word?
S: "ed"
T: OK, but in this case we say wash*ed.* Can you say that?
S: Wash*ed.*
T: Good. Now read it again.
S: Yesterday I wash*ed* my bruvver . . .
T: Wait a minute, what's that word again? [Points to *brother.*]
S: Bruvver.
T: No. Look at these letters in the middle. [Points to *th.*] Remember to read what you see. Do you remember how we say that sound? Put your tongue between your teeth and say /th/ . . .

The lesson continues in such a fashion, the teacher proceeding to correct the student's dialect-influenced pronunciations and grammar while ignoring the fact that the student had to have comprehended the sentence in order to translate it into her own dialect. Such instruction occurs daily and blocks reading development in a number of ways. First, because children become better readers by having the opportunity to read, the overcorrection exhibited in this lesson means that this child will be less likely to become a fluent reader than other children who are not interrupted so consistently. Second, a complete focus on code and pronunciation blocks children's understanding that reading is essentially a meaning-making process. This child, who understands the text, is led to believe that she is doing something wrong. She is encouraged to think of reading not as something you do to get a message, but something you pronounce. Third, constant corrections by the teacher are likely to cause this student and others like her to resist reading and to resent the teacher.

Robert Berdan reports that, after observing the kind of teaching routine described above in a number of settings, he incorporated the teacher behaviors into a reading instruction exercise that he used with students in a college class.[17] He put together sundry rules from a number of American social and regional dialects to create what he called the "language of Atlantis." Students were then called upon to read aloud in this dialect they did not know. When they made errors he interrupted them, using some of the same statements/comments he had heard elementary school teachers routinely make to their students. He concludes:

> The results were rather shocking. By the time these Ph.D. candidates in English or linguistics had read 10–20 words, I could make them sound totally illiterate. By using the routines that teachers use of dialectally different students, I could produce all of the behaviors we observe in children who do not learn to read successfully. The first thing that goes is sentence intonation: they sound like they are reading a list from the telephone book. Comment on their pronunciation a bit more, and they begin to subvocalize, rehearsing pronunciations for themselves before they dare to say them out loud. They begin to guess at pronunciations . . . They switch letters around for no reason. They stumble; they repeat. In short, when I attack them for their failure to conform to my demands for Atlantis English pronunciations, they sound very much like the worst of the second graders in any of the classrooms I have observed.
>
> They also begin to fidget. They wad up their papers, bite their fingernails, whisper, and some finally refuse to continue. They do all the things that children do while they are busily failing to learn to read. Emotional trauma can result as well. For instance, once while conducting this little experiment, in a matter of seconds I actually had one of my graduate students in tears.[18]

The moral of this story is not to confuse dialect intervention with reading instruction. To do so will only confuse the child, leading her away from those intuitive understandings about language that will promote reading development, and toward a school career of resistance and a lifetime of avoiding reading. For those who believe that the child has to "say it right in order to spell it right," let me add that English is not a phonetically regular language. There is no particular difference between telling a child, "You may *say* /bruvver/, but it's spelled b-r-o-*t-h*-e-r," and "You say /com/, but it's spelled c-o-m-*b*."

For this and other reasons, writing may be an arena in which to address standard forms. Unlike unplanned oral language or public reading, writing lends itself to editing. While conversational talk is spontaneous and must be responsive to an immediate context, writing is a mediated process which may be written and rewritten any number of times before being introduced to public scrutiny. Consequently, writing is amenable to rule application—one may first write freely to get one's thoughts down, and then edit to hone the message and apply specific spelling, syntactical, or punctuation rules. My college students who had such difficulty talking in the "iz" dialect, found writing it, with the rules displayed before them, a relatively easy task.

STYLES OF LITERACY

There are other culturally based differences in language use in writing as well. In a seminal article arguing for the existence of "contrastive rhetoric," Robert Kaplan proposes that different languages have different rhetorical norms, representing different ways of organizing ideas.[19]

Such style differences have also been identified in public school classrooms. Gail Martin, a teacher-researcher in Wyoming, wrote about her work with Arapaho students:

> One of our major concerns was that many of the stories children wrote didn't seem to "go anywhere." The stories just ambled along with no definite start or finish, no climaxes or conclusions. I decided to ask Pius Moss [the school elder] about these stories, since he is a master Arapaho storyteller himself. I learned about a distinctive difference between Arapaho stories and stories I was accustomed to hearing, reading, and telling. Pius Moss explained that Arapaho stories are not written down, they're told in what we might call serial form, continued night after night. A "good" story is one that lasts seven nights . . .
>
> When I asked Pius Moss why Arapaho stories never seem to have an "ending," he answered that there is no ending to life, and stories are about Arapaho life, so there is no need for a conclusion. My colleagues and I talked about what Pius had said, and we decided that we would encourage our students to choose whichever type of story they wished to write: we would try to listen and read in appropriate ways.[20]

Similarly, Native Alaskan teacher Martha Demientieff has discovered that her students find "book language" baffling. To help them gain access to this unfamiliar use of language, she contrasts the "wordy," academic way of saying things with the metaphoric style of Athabaskan. The students discuss how book language always uses more words, but how in Heritage language, brevity is always best. Students then work in pairs, groups, or individually to write papers in the academic way, discussing with Martha and with each other whether they believe they have said enough to "sound like a book." Next they take those papers and try to reduce the meaning to a few sentences. Finally, students further reduce the message to a "saying" brief enough to go on the front of a T-shirt, and the sayings are put on little paper tee shirts that the students cut out and hang throughout the room. Sometimes the students reduce other authors' wordy texts to their essential meanings as well. Thus, through winding back and forth through orality and literacy, the students begin to understand the stylistic differences between their own language and that of standard text.

FUNCTIONS OF PRINT

Print may serve different functions in some communities than it does in others, and some children may be unaccustomed to using print or seeing it used in the ways that schools demand. Shirley Brice Heath, for example, found that the black children in the community she called Trackton engaged with print as a group activity for specific real-life purposes, such as reading food labels when shopping, reading fix-it books to repair or modify toys, reading the names of cars to identify a wished-for model, or reading to participate in church. There was seldom a time anyone in the community would read as a solitary recreational activity; indeed, anyone who did so was thought to be a little strange.[21]

The children in Trackton, in short, read to learn things, for real purposes. When these children arrived in school they faced another reality. They were required, instead, to "learn to read," that is, they were told to focus on the *process* of reading with little apparent real purposes in mind other than to get through a basal page or complete a worksheet—and much of this they were to accomplish in isolation. Needless to say, they were not successful at the decontextualized, individualized school reading tasks.

Researchers have identified other differences in the use of language in print as well. For example, Ron Scollon and Suzanne Scollon report that, in the Athabaskan Indian approach to communicative interaction, each individual is expected to make his or her own sense of a situation and that no one can unilaterally enforce one interpretation. Consequently, they were not surprised when, in a story-retelling exercise intended to test reading comprehension, Athabaskan children tended to modify the text of the story in their retellings.[22] The school, however, would be likely to interpret these individually constructed retellings as evidence that the students had not comprehended the story.

TALK ACROSS THE CURRICULUM

A debate over the role of language diversity in mathematics and science education was fueled recently by the publication of a book by Eleanor Wilson Orr titled *Twice as Less: Black English and the Performance of Black Students in Mathematics and Science.*[23] Orr is a teacher of math and science who, as director of the elite Hawthorne School, worked out a cooperative program with the District of Columbia to allow several Washington, D.C., public high school students to attend the prestigious school. Orr and her colleagues were dismayed to find that despite their faithfully following time-tested teaching strategies, and despite the black D.C. students' high motivation and hard work, the newcomers were failing an alarming percentage of their math and science courses.

Noting the differences in the language the black students used, Orr decided to investigate the possibility that speaking Black English was preventing these students from excelling in math and science. In a detailed argument she contends that the students' nonstandard language is both the cause and the expression of the real problem—their "nonstandard *perceptions.*"[24] She cites student statements such as "So the car traveling *twice as faster* will take *twice as less* hours" to support her thesis, and suggests that it is the difference between Black English and Standard English forms in the use of prepositions, conjunctions, and relative pronouns that is the basis for the students' failures.

It is important to critique this position in order that the failures of those responsible for teaching mathematics and science to poor and black students not be attributed to the students themselves, that is, so that the victims not be blamed. There are many problems with the Orr argument. One is her assumption that black students, by virtue of speaking Black English, do not have access to certain concepts needed in mathematical problem solving. For example, she makes much of the lack of the "as-as" comparison, but I have recorded Black English—speaking six- to eleven-year-olds frequently making such statements as, "She big as you" and "I can too run fast as you."

A second problem is that Orr compares the language and performance of low-income, ill-prepared students with upper-income students who have had superior scholastic preparation. I contend that it was not their language which confused the D.C. students, but mathematics itself! Any students with a similar level of preparation and experience, no matter what their color or language variety, would probably have had the same difficulties.

The most basic problem with the Orr argument, however, is Orr's apparent belief that somehow mathematics is linked to the syntactical constructions of standard English: "[T]he *grammar* of standard English provides consistently for what is *true mathematically.*"[25] What about the grammar of Chinese or Arabic or German? Orr's linguistic naïve determinist position can only lead to the bizarre conclusion that speakers of other languages would be equally handicapped in mathematics because they, too, lacked standard English constructions!

Even though Orr asserts that the cause of the problem is the speaking of Black English, she seems unaware that her proposed solution is not linked to this conceptualization. She does not recommend teaching Standard English, but rather, teaching *math* through the use in instruction of irregular number systems which force students to carefully work out concepts and prevent their dependence on inappropriate rote memorized patterns. One can surmise that as students and teachers work through these irregular systems, they create a shared language, developing for the students what they truly lack, a knowledge of the *content* of the language of mathematics, not the form.

Interviews with black teachers who have enjoyed long-term success teaching math to black-dialect-speaking students suggest that part of the solution also lies in the kind and quality of talk in the mathematics classroom. One teacher explained that her black students were much more likely to learn a new operation successfully when they understood to what use the operation might be put in daily life. Rather than teach decontextualized operations, she would typically first pose a "real-life" problem and challenge the students to find a solution. For example, she once brought in a part of a broken wheel, saying that it came from a toy that she wished to fix for her grandson. To do so, she had to reconstruct the wheel from this tiny part. After the students tried unsuccessfully to solve the problem, she introduced a theorem related to constructing a circle given any two points on an arc, which the students quickly assimilated.

Another black math teacher spoke of putting a problem into terms relevant to the student's life. He found that the same problem that baffled students when posed in terms of distances between two unfamiliar places or in terms of numbers of milk cans needed by a farmer, were much more readily solved when familiar locales and the amount of money needed to buy a leather jacket were substituted. I discovered a similar phenomenon when my first-grade inner-city students did much better on "word problems" on standardized tests when I merely substituted the names of people in our school for the names in the problems.

All of these modifications to the language of instruction speak to Heath's findings in Trackton: some youngsters may become more engaged in school tasks when the language of those tasks is posed in real-life contexts than when they are viewed as merely decontextualized problem completion. Since our long-term goal is producing young people who are able to think critically and creatively in real problem-solving contexts, the instructional—and linguistic—implications should be evident.

CONCLUSION

One of the most difficult tasks we face as human beings is communicating meaning across our individual differences, a task confounded immeasurably when we attempt to communicate across social lines, racial lines, cultural lines, or lines of unequal power. Yet, all U.S. demographic data points to a society becoming increasingly diverse, and that diversity is nowhere more evident than in our schools. Currently, "minority" students represent a majority in all but two of our twenty-five largest cities, and by some estimates, the turn of the century will find up to 40 percent nonwhite children in American classrooms. At the same time, the teaching force is becoming more homogeneously white. African-American, Asian, Hispanic, and Native American teachers now comprise only 10 percent of the teaching force, and that percentage is shrinking rapidly.

What are we educators to do? We must first decide upon a perspective from which to view the situation. We can continue to view diversity as a problem, attempting to force all differences into standardized boxes. Or we can recognize that diversity of thought, language, and worldview in our classrooms cannot only provide an exciting educational setting, but can also prepare our children for the richness of living in an increasingly diverse national community. (Would any of us really want to trade the wonderful variety of American ethnic restaurants for a standard fare of steak houses and fast-food hamburgers?)

I am suggesting that we begin with a perspective that demands finding means to celebrate, not merely tolerate, diversity in our classrooms. Not only should teachers and students who share group membership delight in their own cultural and linguistic history, but all teachers must revel in the diversity of their students and that of the world outside the classroom community. How can we accomplish these lofty goals? Certainly, given the reality of the composition of the teaching force, very few educators can join Martha Demientieff in taking advantage of her shared background with her culturally unique students and contrasting "*our* Heritage language" or "the way we say things" with "Formal English." But teachers who do not share the language and culture of their students, or teachers whose students represent a variety of cultural backgrounds, can also celebrate diversity by making language diversity a part of the curriculum. Students can be asked to "teach" the teacher and other students aspects of their language variety. They can "translate" songs, poems, and stories into their own dialect or into "book language" and compare the differences across the cultural groups represented in the classroom.

Amanda Branscombe, a gifted white teacher who has often taught black students whom other teachers have given up on, sometimes has her middle school students listen to rap songs in order to develop a rule base for their creation. The students would teach her their newly constructed "rules for writing rap," and she would in turn use this knowledge as a base to begin a discussion of the rules Shakespeare used to construct his plays, or the rules poets used to develop their sonnets.[26]

Within our celebration of diversity, we must keep in mind that education, at its best, hones and develops the knowledge and skills each student already possesses, while at the same time adding new knowledge and skills to that base. All students deserve the right both to develop the linguistic skills they bring to the classroom and to add others to their repertoires. While linguists have long proclaimed that no language variety is intrinsically "better" than another, in a stratified society such as ours, language choices are not neutral. The language associated with the power structure—"Standard English"—is the language of economic success, and all students have the right to schooling that gives them access to that language.

While it is also true, as this chapter highlights, that no one can force another to acquire an additional language variety, there are ways to point out to students both the arbitrariness of designating one variety over another as "standard," as well as the political and economic repercussions for not gaining access to that socially designated "standard." Without appearing to preach about a future which most students find hard to envision, one teacher, for example, has high school students interview various personnel officers in actual workplaces about their attitudes toward divergent styles in oral and written language and report their findings to the entire class. Another has students read or listen to a variety of oral and written language styles and discuss the impact of those styles on the message and the likely effect on different audiences. Students then recreate the texts or talks, using different language styles appropriate for different audiences (for example, a church group, academicians, rap singers, a feminist group, politicians, and so on).

Each of us belongs to many communities. Joseph Suina, a Pueblo Indian scholar, has proposed a schematic representation of at least three levels of community membership. He sets up three concentric circles. The inner circle is labeled "home/local community," the middle circle is "national community," and the outer circle represents the "global community."[27] In today's world it is vital that we all learn to become active citizens in all three communities, and one requisite skill for doing so is an ability to acquire additional linguistic codes. We can ignore or try to obliterate language diversity in the classroom, or we can encourage in our teachers and students a "mental set for diversity." If we choose the latter, the classroom can become a laboratory for developing linguistic diversity. Those who have acquired additional codes because their local language differs significantly from the language of the national culture may actually be in a better position to gain access to the global culture than "mainstream" Americans who, as Martha says, "only know one way to talk." Rather than think of these diverse students as problems, we can view them instead as resources who can help all of us learn what it feels like to move between cultures and language varieties, and thus perhaps better learn how to become citizens of the global community.

NOTES

1. Stephen D. Drashen, *Principles and Practice in Second Language Acquisition* (New York: Pergamon, 1982).
2. Ibid., p. 22.

3. S. Nelson-Barber, "Phonologic Variations of Pima English," in R. St. Clair and W. Leap, eds., *Language Renewal among American Indian Tribes: Issues, Problems and Prospects* (Rosslyn, Va.: National Clearinghouse for Bilingual Education, 1982).

4. Some of these books include Lucille Clifton, *All Us Come 'Cross the Water* (New York: Holt, Rinehart, and Winston, 1973); Paul Green (aided by Abbe Abbott), *I Am Eskimo—Aknik My Name* (Juneau, Alaska: Alaska Northwest Publishing, 1959); Howard Jacobs and Jim Rice, *Once upon a Bayou* (New Orleans, La.: Phideaux Publications, 1983); Tim Edler, *Santa Cajun's Christmas Adventure* (Baton Rouge, La.: Little Cajun Books, 1981); and a series of biographies produced by Yukon-Koyukkuk School District of Alaska and published by Hancock House Publishers in North Vancouver, British Columbia, Canada.

5. Shirley Brice Heath, *Ways with Words* (Cambridge, Eng.: Cambridge University Press, 1983).

6. S. Michaels and C. B. Cazden, "Teacher-Child Collaboration on Oral Preparation for Literacy," in B. Schieffer, ed., *Acquisition of Literacy: Ethnographic Perspectives* (Norwood, N.J.: Ablex, 1986).

7. C. B. Cazden, *Classroom Discourse* (Portsmouth, N.H.: Heinemann, 1988).

8. Ibid., p. 18.

9. Ibid.

10. Heath, *Ways with Words.*

11. H. Mehan, "Asking Known Information," *Theory into Practice* 28 (1979), pp. 285–94.

12. Ibid., p. 124.

13. G. Smitherman, *Talkin and Testifyin* (Boston: Houghton Mifflin, 1977).

14. R. Sims, "Dialect and Reading: Toward Redefining the Issues," in J. Langer and M. T. Smith-Burke, eds., *Reader Meets Author/Bridging the Gap* (Newark, Dela.: International Reading Association, 1982).

15. Ibid.

16. P. M. Cunningham, "Teachers' Correction Responses to Black-Dialect Miscues Which Are Nonmeaning-Changing," *Reading Research Quarterly* 12 (1976–77).

17. Robert Berdan, "Knowledge into Practice: Delivering Research to Teachers," in M. F. Whiteman, ed., *Reactions to Ann Arbor: Vernacular Black English and Education* (Arlington, Va.: Center for Applied Linguistics, 1980).

18. Ibid., p. 78.

19. R. Kaplan, "Cultural Thought Patterns in Intercultural Education," *Language Learning* 16 (1966), pp. 1–2.

20. Cazden, *Classroom Discourse,* p. 12.

21. Heath, *Ways with Words.*

22. Ron Scollon and Suzanne B. K. Scollon, "Cooking It Up and Boiling It Down: Abstracts in Athabaskan Children's Story Retellings," in D. Tannen, ed., *Spoken and Written Language* (Norwood, N.J.: Ablex, 1979).

23. Eleanor Wilson Orr, *Twice as Less: Black English and the Performance of Black Students in Mathematics and Science* (New York: W.W. Norton, 1987).

24. Ibid., p. 30.

25. Ibid., 149 (emphasis added).

26. Personal communication, 1988.

27. Personal communication, 1989.

Suggested Readings
for Future Study

LANGUAGE, LITERACY, AND PEDAGOGY

Bartolome, L. (1998). *The misteaching of academic discourses: The politics of language in the classroom.* Boulder, Colo.: Westview.

Bizell, P. (1992). *Academic discourse and critical consciousness.* Pittsburgh: University of Pittsburgh Press, 1992.

Chomsky, N. (1977). *Language and responsibility.* New York: Pantheom.

Courts, P. (1991) *Literacy and empowerment: The menaning makers.* New York: Bergin & Garvey.

Crawford, J. (1992). *Hold your tongue: Bilingualism and the politics of "English only."* New York: Addison-Wesley.

Cummins, J. (1996). Negotiating identities: Education for empowerment in a diverse society. Ontario, Calif.: California Association for Bilingual Education.

Delpit, L. (1995). *Other peoples' children: Cultural conflict in the classroom.* New York: The New Press.

Diaz-Soto, L. (1997). *Language, culture and power.* Albany: SUNY Press.

Fairclough, N. (1995). *Critical discourse analysis: The critical study of language.* New York: Longman.

Freire, P., and Macedo, D. (1987*). Literacy. Reading the word and the world.* South Hadley, Mass.: Bergin & Garvey.

Fowler, R., Hodge, B., Kress, G., and Trew, T. (1979). *Language and control.* Boston: Routledge.

Frederickson, J., and Ada, A. eds. (1995). *Reclaiming our voices: Bilingual education, critical pedagogy, and praxis.* Ontario, Calif.: California Association for Bilingual Education.

Gallego, M., and Hollingsworth, S., eds. (2000). *What counter as literacy: Challenging the school standard.* New York: Teachers College.

Gee, J. (1992). *The social mind: Language, ideology and social practice.* New York: Bergin & Garvey.

Holquist, M. (1981). *The dialogic imagination: Four essays by M. M. Bakhtin.* Austin: University of Texas Press.

Illich, I., and Sanders, B. (1988). *ABC: The Alphabetization of the popular mind.* New York: Vintage.

Nettle, D., and Romaine, S. (2000). *Vanishing voices: The extinction of the world's languages.* New York: Oxford University Press.

Macedo, D. (1994). *Literacies of power: What Americans are not allowed to know.* Boulder, Colo.: Westview.

Mitchell, C., and Weiler, K. (1991). *Rewriting literacy: Culture and the discourse of the other.* New York: Bergin & Garvey.

Pruyn, M. (1999). *Discourse wars in Gotham-West: A Latino immigrant urban tale of resistance and agency.* Boulder, Colo.: Westview.

Shannon, P. (1989). *Broken premises: Reading instruction in twentieth-century America.* South Hadley, Mass.: Bergin & Garvey.

Skutnabb-Kangas, T. (2000). *Linguistic genocide in education or worldwide diversity and human rights?* Mahwah, N.J.: Lawrence Erlbaum.

Skutnabb-Kangas, T., and Phillipson, R., eds. (1995). *Linguistic human rights: Overcoming linguistic discrimination.* New York: Mouton de Gruyter.

Walsh, C. (1991). *Pedagogy and the struggle for voice: Issues of language, power, and schooling for Puerto Ricans.* Westport, Conn.: Bergin & Garvey

Part 6

CRITICAL ISSUES IN THE CLASSROOM

INTRODUCTION

This section on critical issues in the classroom, begins with Lilia Bartolomé's well-known essay, "Beyond the Methods Fetish." Bartolomé examines the common and persistent demands of classroom teachers for appropriate methods to assist them in the teaching of culturally diverse students. In response, she warns against the reification of instructional approaches designed to supposedly help teachers to deal (or cope) with the exceptionality of diverse working-class students. Bartolomé's work reveals the ways in which an obsessional focus on instructional methods can actually become an obstacle to the critical development of the very students it proposes to serve. Instead, she encourages educators to embrace a humanizing pedagogy that is inclusive of particular educational methods, but whose focus centers on students as subjects, rather than dehumanized objects upon which instruction is applied. Unlike some critical educators in the field, Bartolomé reaffirms here the significance of process writing, language experience, cooperative learning, strategic teaching, and whole language activities—but only when these are implemented within the context of a liberating educational process.

Teresa McKenna's "Borderness and Pedagogy" serves to illustrate the tensions often at work when cultural issues are critically engaged in the setting of a multicultural classroom. Her discussion will undoubtedly cause the reader to recall Elenes's view of borderlands (in Part Three), particularly when McKenna asserts that a politics of difference in this country is certainly a politics of borderland, since any notion of national identity is, like it or not, grounded firmly on a "syncretism of cultures," a view that sets the foundation for her conclusion that there is indeed the potential within the United States for constructing a more coalescing view of identity—but possible only once people begin to recognize that the binary racial oppositions currently at work have been artificially fabricated and are not in the interest of public democratic life. In the last analysis, McKenna argues that "cultural difference" is perhaps the only real commonality shared by all groups in this country, and hence, the only real basis for any potential sense of unity among us, an issue she considers significant to pedagogy, given the increasing level of diversity among the students we teach.

In an era when computer technology has become commonplace and its value rarely question within public schools, Michael Apple brings important concerns to bear in "Is the New Technology Part of the Solution or Part of the Problem in Education?" His essay examines the implications of a relentless and uncontested expansion of technology within schools today. His discussion effectively critiques this phenomenon within the realities of the global economy, and also includes historical background information that helps to illustrate how intense pressure is placed upon schools to conform to the needs of the marketplace. Apple clearly exposes how pedagogical practices that can appear benign on the surface, such as the use of computers in schools, can actually have disastrous effects on working-class populations.

QUESTIONS FOR REFLECTION AND DIALOGUE

1. What are some of the instructional approaches to cultural differences described by Bartolomé?
2. What does Bartolomé mean when she uses the phrase "teachers' political clarity"? How do you understand the importance of this concept within critical pedagogy?
3. What is meant by "cultural responsive instruction" and "strategic teaching"? What are the implications of these instructional methods on the education of culturally diverse students?
4. How does McKenna define the notion of difference?
5. What importance or usefulness do concepts like consciousness and dialogue have within culturally diverse classroom settings?
6. In what ways does the massive use of computers in schools contribute to the "proletarianization and deskilling" of both people and jobs?
7. What predictions does Apple make about the future economic climate in the United States? In what ways does the current phenomenon resemble the transition of the 1800s from an agricultural society to an industrial social order?
8. What implications do rapid changes in the economic conditions of U.S. society have for the education of poor, working-class, and racialized populations?

Beyond the Methods Fetish: Toward a Humanizing Pedagogy

LILIA I. BARTOLOMÉ

Much of the current debate regarding the improvement of minority student academic achievement occurs at a level that treats education as a primarily technical issue (Giroux, 1992).[1] For example, the historical and present-day academic underachievement of certain culturally and linguistically subordinated student populations in the United States (e.g., Mexican Americans, Native Americans, Puerto Ricans) is often explained as resulting from the lack of cognitively, culturally, and/or linguistically appropriate teaching methods and educational programs.[2] As such, the solution to the problem of academic underachievement tends to be constructed in primarily methodological and mechanistic terms dislodged from the sociocultural reality that shapes it. That is, the solution to the current underachievement of students from subordinated cultures is often reduced to finding the "right" teaching methods, strategies, or prepackaged curricula that will work with students who do not respond to so-called "regular" or "normal" instruction.

Recent research studies have begun to identify educational programs found to be successful in working with culturally and linguistically subordinated minority student populations (Carter & Chatfield, 1986; Lucas, Henze, & Donato, 1990; Tikunoff, 1985; Webb, 1987). In addition, there has been specific interest in identifying teaching strategies that more effectively teach culturally and linguistically "different" students and other "disadvantaged" and "at-risk" students (Knapp & Shields, 1990; McLeod, in press; Means & Knapp, 1991; Tinajero & Ada, 1993). Although it is important to identify useful and promising instructional programs and strategies, it is erroneous to assume that blind replication of instructional programs or teacher mastery of particular teaching methods, in and of themselves, will guarantee successful student learning, especially when we are discussing populations that historically have been mistreated and miseducated by the schools.

This focus on methods as solutions in the current literature coincides with many of my graduate students' beliefs regarding linguistic minority education improvement. As a Chicana professor who has taught anti-racist multicultural education courses at various institutions, I am consistently confronted at the beginning of each semester by students who are anxious to learn the latest teaching methods—methods that they hope will somehow magically work on minority students.[3] Although my students are well-intentioned individuals who sincerely wish to create positive learning environments for culturally and linguistically subordinated students, they arrive with the expectation that I will provide them with easy answers in the form of specific instructional methods. That is, since they (implicitly) perceive the academic underachievement of subordinated students as a technical issue, the solutions they require are also expected to be technical in nature (e.g., specific teaching methods, instructional curricula and materials). They usually assume that: 1) they, as teachers, are fine and do not need to identify, interrogate, and change their biased beliefs and fragmented views about subordinated students; 2) schools, as institutions, are basically fair and democratic sites where all students are provided with similar, if not equal, treatment and learning conditions; and 3) children who experience academic difficulties (especially those from culturally and linguistically low-status groups) require some form of "special" instruction since they obviously have not been able to succeed under "regular" or "normal" instructional conditions. Consequently, if nothing is basically wrong with teachers and schools, they often conclude, then linguistic minority academic underachievement is best dealt with by providing teachers with specific teaching methods that promise to be effective with culturally and linguistically subordinated students. To further complicate matters, many of my students seek *generic* teaching methods that will work with a variety of minority student populations, and they grow anxious and impatient when reminded that instruction for any group of students needs to be tailored or individualized to some extent. Some of my students appear to be seeking what Maria de la Luz Reyes (1992) defines as a "one size fits all" instructional recipe. Reyes explains that the term refers to the assumption that instructional methods that are deemed effective for mainstream populations will benefit *all* students, no matter what their backgrounds may be.[4] She explains that the assumption is

> similar to the "one size fits all" marketing concept that would have buyers believe that there is an average or ideal size among men and women . . . Those who market "one size fits all" products suggest that if the article of clothing is not a good fit, the fault is not with the design of the garment, but those who are too fat, too skinny, too tall, too short, or too high-waisted. (p. 435)

I have found that many of my students similarly believe that teaching approaches that work with one minority population should also fit another (see Vogt, Jordan, & Tharp, 1987, for an example of this tendency). Reyes argues that educators often make this "one size fits all" assumption when discussing instructional approaches, such as process writing. For example, as Lisa Delpit (1988) has convincingly argued, the process writing approach that has been blindly embraced by mostly White liberal teachers often produces a negative result with African American students. Delpit cites one Black student:

> I didn't feel she was teaching us anything. She wanted us to correct each other's papers and we were there to learn from her. She didn't teach anything, absolutely nothing.

> Maybe they're trying to learn what Black folks knew all the time. We understand how to improvise, how to express ourselves creatively. When I'm in a classroom, I'm not looking for that, I'm looking for structure, the more formal language.

> Now my buddy was in a Black teacher's class. And that lady was very good. She went through and explained and defined each part of the structure. This [White] teacher didn't get along with that Black teacher. She said she didn't agree with her methods. But I don't think that White teacher had any methods. (1988, p. 287)

The above quote is a glaring testimony that a "one size fits all" approach often does not work with the same level of effectiveness with all students across the board. Such assumptions reinforce a disarticulation between the embraced method and the sociocultural realities within which each method is implemented. I find that this "one size fits all" assumption is also held by many of my students about a number of teaching methods currently in vogue, such as cooperative learning and whole language instruction. The students imbue the "new" methods with almost magical properties that render them, in and of themselves, capable of improving students' academic standing.

One of my greatest challenges throughout the years has been to help students to understand that a myopic focus on methodology often serves to obfuscate the real question—which is why in our society, subordinated students do not generally succeed academically in schools. In fact, schools often reproduce the existing asymmetrical power relations among cultural groups (Anyon, 1988; Gibson & Ogbu, 1991; Giroux, 1992; Freire, 1985). I believe that by taking a sociohistorical view of present-day conditions and concerns that inform the lived experiences of socially perceived minority students, prospective teachers are better able to comprehend the quasi-colonial nature of minority education. By engaging in this critical sociohistorical analysis of subordinated students' academic performance, most of my graduate students (teachers and prospective teachers) are better situated to reinterpret and reframe current educational concerns so as to develop pedagogical structures that speak to the day-to-day reality, struggles, concerns, and dreams of these students. By understanding the historical specificities of marginalized students, these teachers and prospective teachers come to realize that an uncritical focus on methods makes invisible the historical role that schools and their personnel have played (and continue to play), not only in discriminating against many culturally different groups, but also in denying their humanity. By robbing students of their culture, language, history, and values, schools often reduce these students to the status of subhumans who need to be rescued from their "savage" selves. The end result of this cultural and linguistic eradication represents, in my view, a form of dehumanization. Therefore, any discussion having to do with the improvement of subordinated students' academic standing is incomplete if it does not address those discriminatory school practices that lead to dehumanization.

In this article, I argue that a necessary first step in reevaluating the failure or success of particular instructional methods used with subordinated students calls for a shift in perspective—a shift from a narrow and mechanistic view of instruction to one that is broader in scope and takes into consideration the sociohistorical and political dimensions of education. I discuss why effective methods are needed for these students, and why certain strategies are deemed effective or ineffective in a given sociocultural context. My discussion will include a section that addresses the significance of teachers' understanding of the political nature of education, the reproductive nature of schools, and the schools' continued (yet unspoken) deficit views of subordinated students. By conducting a critical analysis of the sociocultural realities in which subordinated students find themselves at school, the implicit and explicit antagonistic relations between students and teachers (and other school representatives) take on focal importance.

As a Chicana and a former classroom elementary and middle school teacher who encountered negative race relations that ranged from teachers' outright rejection of subordinated students to their condescending pity, fear, indifference, and apathy when confronted by the challenges of minority student education, I find it surprising that little minority education literature deals explicitly with the very real issue of antagonistic race relations between subordinated students and White school personnel (see Ogbu, 1987, and Giroux, 1992, for an in-depth discussion of this phenomenon).

For this reason, I also include in this article a section that discusses two instructional methods and approaches identified as effective in current education literature: culturally responsive education and strategic teaching. I examine the methods for pedagogical underpinnings that—under the critical use of politically clear teachers—have the potential to challenge students academically and intellectually while treating them with dignity and respect. More importantly, I examine the pedagogical foundations that serve to humanize the educational process and enable both students and teachers to work toward breaking away from their unspoken antagonism and negative beliefs about each other and get on with the business of sharing and creating knowledge. I argue that the informed way in which a teacher implements a method can serve to offset potentially unequal relations and discriminatory structures and practices in the classroom and, in doing so, improve the quality of the instructional process for both student and teacher. In other words, politically informed teacher use of methods can create conditions that enable subordinated students to move from their usual passive position to one of active and critical engagement. I am convinced that creating pedagogical spaces that enable students to move *from object to subject position* produces more far-reaching, positive effects than the implementation of a particular teaching methodology, regardless of how technically advanced and promising it may be.

The final section of this article will explore and suggest the implementation of what Donaldo Macedo (1994) designates as an

> anti-methods pedagogy that refuses to be enslaved by the rigidity of models and methodological paradigms. An anti-methods pedagogy should be informed by a critical understanding of the sociocultural context that guides our practices so as to free us from the beaten path of methodological certainties and specialisms. (p. 8)

Simply put, it is important that educators not blindly reject teaching methods across the board, but that they reject uncritical appropriation of methods, materials, curricula, etc. Educators need to reject the present methods fetish so as to create learning environments informed by both action and reflection. In freeing themselves from the blind adoption of so-called effective (and sometimes "teacher-proof") strategies, teachers can begin the reflective process, which allows them to recreate and reinvent teaching methods and materials by always taking into consideration the sociocultural realities that can either limit or expand the possibilities to humanize education. It is important that teachers keep in mind that methods are social constructions that grow out of and reflect ideologies that often prevent teachers from understanding the pedagogical implications of asymmetrical power relations among different cultural groups.

THE SIGNIFICANCE OF TEACHER POLITICAL CLARITY[5]

In his letter to North American educators, Paulo Freire (1987) argues that technical expertise and mastery of content area and methodology are insufficient to ensure effective instruction of students from subordinated cultures. Freire contends that, in addition to possessing content area knowledge, teachers must possess political clarity so as to be able to effectively create, adopt, and modify teaching strategies that simultaneously respect and challenge learners from diverse cultural groups in a variety of learning environments.

Teachers working on improving their political clarity recognize that teaching is not a politically neutral undertaking. They understand that educational institutions are socializing institutions that mirror the greater society's culture, values, and norms. Schools reflect both the positive and negative aspects of a society. Thus, the unequal power relations among various social and cultural groups at the societal level are usually reproduced at the school and classroom level, unless concerted efforts are made to prevent their reproduction. Teachers working toward political clarity understand that they can either maintain the status quo, or they can work to transform the sociocultural reality at the classroom and school level so that the culture at this micro-level does not reflect macro-level inequalities, such as asymmetrical power relations that relegate certain cultural groups to a subordinate status.

Teachers can support positive social change in the classroom in a variety of ways. One possible intervention can consist of the creation of heterogeneous learning groups for the purpose of modifying low-status roles of individuals or groups of children.[6] Elizabeth Cohen (1986) demonstrates that when teachers create learning conditions where students, especially those perceived as low status (e.g., limited English speakers in a classroom where English is the dominant language, students with academic difficulties, or those perceived by their peers for a variety of reasons as less able), can demonstrate their possession of knowledge and expertise, they are then able to see themselves, and be seen by others, as capable and competent. As a result, contexts are created in which peers can learn from each other as well.

A teacher's political clarity will not necessarily compensate for structural inequalities that students face outside the classroom; however, teachers can, to the best of their ability, help their students deal with injustices encountered inside and outside the classroom. A number of possibilities exist for preparing students to deal with the greater society's unfairness and inequality that range from engaging in explicit discussions with students about their experiences, to more indirect ways (that nevertheless require a teacher who is politically clear), such as creating democratic learning environments where students become accustomed to being treated as competent and able individuals. I believe that the students, once accustomed to the rights and responsibilities of full citizenship in the classroom, will come to expect respectful treatment and authentic estimation in other contexts. Again, it is important to point out that it is not the particular lesson or set of activities that prepares the student; rather, it is the teacher's politically clear educational philosophy that underlies the varied methods and lessons/activities she or he employs that make the difference.

Under ideal conditions, competent educators simultaneously translate theory into practice *and* consider the population being served and the sociocultural reality in which learning is expected to take place. Let me reiterate that command of a content area or specialization is necessary, but it is not sufficient for effectively working with students. Just as critical is that teachers comprehend that their role as educators is a political act that is never neutral (Freire, 1985, 1987, 1993; Freire & Macedo, 1987). In ignoring or negating the political nature of their work with these students, teachers not only reproduce the status quo and their students' low status, but they also inevitably legitimize schools' discriminatory practices. For example, teachers who uncritically follow school practices that unintentionally or intentionally serve to promote tracking and segregation within school and classroom contexts continue to reproduce the status quo. Conversely, teachers can become conscious of, and subsequently challenge, the role of educational institutions and their own roles as educators in maintaining a system that often serves to silence students from subordinated groups.

Teachers must also remember that schools, similar to other institutions in society, are influenced by perceptions of socioeconomic status (SES), race/ethnicity, language, and gender (Anyon, 1988; Bloom, 1991; Cummins, 1989; Ogbu, 1987). They must begin to question how these perceptions influence classroom dynamics. An important step in increasing teacher political clarity is recognizing that, despite current liberal rhetoric regarding the equal value of all cultures, low SES and ethnic minority students have historically (and currently) been perceived as deficient. I believe that the present methods-restricted discussion must be broadened to reveal the deeply entrenched deficit orientation toward "difference" (i.e., non-Western European race/ethnicity, non-English language use, working-class status, femaleness) that prevails in the schools in a deeply "cultural" ideology of White supremacy. As educators, we must constantly be vigilant and ask how the deficit orientation has affected our perceptions concerning students from subordinated populations and created rigid and mechanistic teacher-student relations (Cummins, 1989; Flores, Cousin, & Diaz, 1991; Giroux & McLaren, 1986). Such a model often serves to create classroom conditions in which there is very little opportunity for teachers and students to interact in meaningful ways, establish positive and trusting working relations, and share knowledge.

OUR LEGACY: A DEFICIT VIEW OF SUBORDINATED STUDENTS

As discussed earlier, teaching strategies are neither designed nor implemented in a vacuum. Design, selection, and use of particular teaching approaches and strategies arise from perceptions about learning and learners. I contend that the most pedagogically advanced strategies are sure to be ineffective in the hands of educators who implicitly or explicitly subscribe to a belief system that renders ethnic, racial, and linguistic minority students at best culturally disadvantaged and in need of fixing (if we could only identify the right recipe!), or, at worst, culturally or genetically deficient and beyond fixing[7]. Despite the fact that various models have been proposed to explain the academic failure of certain subordinated groups—academic failure described as *historical, pervasive,* and *disproportionate*—the fact remains that these views of difference are deficit-based and deeply imprinted in our individual and collective psyches (Flores, 1982, 1993; Menchaca & Valencia, 1990; Valencia, 1986, 1991).

The deficit model has the longest history of any model discussed in the education literature. Richard Valencia (1986) traces its evolution over three centuries:

Also known in the literature as the "social pathology" model or the "cultural deprivation" model, the deficit approach explains disproportionate academic problems among low status students as largely being due to pathologies or deficits in their sociocultural background (e.g., cognitive and linguistic deficiencies, low self-esteem, poor motivation) . . . To improve the educability of such students, programs such as compensatory education and parent-child intervention have been proposed. (p. 3)

Barbara Flores (1982, 1993) documents the effect this deficit model has had on the schools' past and current perceptions of Latino students. Her historical overview chronicles descriptions used to refer to Latino students over the last century. The terms range from "mentally retarded," "linguistically handicapped," "culturally and linguistically deprived," and "semilingual," to the current euphemism for Latino and other subordinated students: the "at-risk" student.

Similarly, recent research continues to lay bare our deficit orientation and its links to discriminatory school practices aimed at students from groups perceived as low status (Anyon, 1988; Bloom, 1991; Diaz, Moll, & Mehan, 1986; Oaks, 1986). Findings range from teacher preference for Anglo students, to bilingual teachers' preference for lighter skinned Latino students (Bloom, 1991), to teachers' negative perceptions of working-class parents as compared to middle-class parents (Lareau, 1990), and, finally, to unequal teaching and testing practices in schools serving working-class and ethnic minority students (Anyon, 1988; Diaz et al., 1986; Oaks, 1986; U.S. Commission on Civil Rights, 1973). Especially indicative of our inability to consciously acknowledge the deficit orientation is the fact that the teachers in these studies—teachers from all ethnic groups—were themselves unaware of the active role they played in the differential and unequal treatment of their students.

The deficit view of subordinated students has been critiqued by numerous researchers as ethnocentric and invalid (Boykin, 1983; Diaz et al., 1986; Flores, 1982; Flores et al., 1991; Sue & Padilla, 1986; Trueba, 1989; Walker, 1987). More recent research offers alternative models that shift the source of school failure away from the characteristics of the individual child, their families, and their cultures, and toward the schooling process (Au & Mason, 1983; Heath, 1983; Mehan, 1992; Philips, 1972). Unfortunately, I believe that many of these alternative models often unwittingly give rise to a kinder and more liberal, yet more concealed version of the deficit model that views subordinated students as being in need of "specialized" modes of instruction—a type of instructional "coddling" that mainstream students do not require in order to achieve in school. Despite the use of less overtly ethnocentric models to explain the academic standing of subordinated students, I believe that the deficit orientation toward difference, especially as it relates to low socioeconomic and ethnic minority groups, is very deeply ingrained in the ethos of our most prominent institutions, especially schools, and in the various educational programs in place at these sites.

It is against this sociocultural backdrop that teachers can begin to seriously question the unspoken but prevalent deficit orientation used to hide SES, racial/ethnic, linguistic, and gender inequities present in U.S. classrooms. And it is against this sociocultural backdrop that I critically examine two teaching approaches identified by the educational literature as effective with subordinated student populations.

POTENTIALLY HUMANIZING PEDAGOGY: TWO PROMISING TEACHING APPROACHES

Well-known approaches and strategies such as cooperative learning, language experience, process writing, reciprocal teaching, and whole language activities can be used to create humanizing learning environments where students cease to be treated as objects and yet receive academically rigorous instruction (Cohen, 1986; Edelsky, Altwerger, & Flores, 1991; Palinscar & Brown, 1984; Pérez & Torres-Guzmán, 1992; Zamel, 1982). However, when these approaches are implemented uncritically, they often produce negative results, as indicated by Lisa Delpit (1986, 1988). Critical teacher applications of these approaches and strategies can contribute to discarding deficit views of students from subordinated groups, so that they are treated with respect and viewed as active and capable subjects in their own learning.

Academically rigorous, student-centered teaching strategies can take many forms. One may well ask, is it not merely common sense to promote approaches and strategies that respect, recognize, utilize, and build on students' existing knowledge bases? The answer would be, of course, yes, it is. However, it is important to recognize, as part of our effort to increase our political clarity, that these practices have *not* typified classroom instruction for students from marginalized populations. The practice of learning from and valuing student language and life experiences *often* occurs in classrooms where students speak a language and possess cultural capital that more closely matches that of the mainstream (Anyon, 1988; Lareau, 1990; Winfield, 1986).[8]

Jean Anyon's (1988) classic research suggests that teachers of affluent students are more likely than teachers of working-class students to utilize and incorporate student life experiences and knowledge into the curriculum. For example, in Anyon's study, teachers of affluent students often designed creative and innovative lessons that tapped students' existing knowledge bases; one math lesson, designed to teach students to find averages, asked them to fill out a possession survey inquiring about the number of cars, television sets, refrigerators, and games owned at home so as to teach students to average. Unfortunately, this practice of tapping students' already existing knowledge and language bases is not commonly utilized with student populations traditionally perceived as deficient. Anyon reports that teachers of working-class students viewed them as lacking the necessary cultural capital, and therefore imposed content and behavioral standards with little consideration and respect for student input. Although Anyon did not generalize beyond her sample, other studies suggest the validity of her findings for ethnic minority student populations (Diaz et al., 1986; Moll, 1986; Oaks, 1986).

The creation of learning environments for low SES and ethnic minority students, similar to those for more affluent and White populations, requires that teachers discard deficit notions and genuinely value and utilize students' existing knowledge bases in their teaching. In order to do so, teachers must confront and challenge their own social biases so as to honestly begin to perceive their students as capable learners. Furthermore, they must remain open to the fact that they will also learn from their students. Learning is not a one-way undertaking.

It is important for educators to recognize that no language or set of life experiences is inherently superior, yet our social values reflect our preferences for certain language and life experiences over others. Student-centered teaching strategies such as cooperative learning, language experience, process writing, reciprocal teaching, and whole language activities (if practiced consciously and critically) can help to offset or neutralize our deficit-based failure and recognize subordinated student strengths. Our tendency to discount these strengths occurs whenever we forget that learning only occurs when prior knowledge is accessed and linked to new information.

Beau Jones, Annemarie Palinscar, Donna Ogle, and Eileen Carr (1987) explain that learning is the act of linking new information to prior knowledge. According to their framework, prior knowledge is stored in memory in the form of knowledge frameworks. New information is understood and stored by calling up the appropriate knowledge framework and then integrating the new information. Acknowledging and using existing student language and knowledge makes good pedagogical sense, and it also constitutes a humanizing experience for students traditionally dehumanized and disempowered in the schools. I believe that strategies identified as effective in the literature have the potential to offset reductive education in which "the educator as *the one who knows* transfers existing knowledge to the learner as *the one who does not know*" (Freire, 1985, p. 114, emphasis added). It is important to repeat that mere implementation of a particular strategy or approach identified as effective does not guarantee success, as the current debate in process writing attests (Delpit, 1986, 1988; Reyes, 1991, 1992).

Creating learning environments that incorporate student language and life experiences in no way negates teachers' responsibility for providing students with particular academic content knowledge and skills. It is important not to link teacher respect and use of student knowledge and language bases with a laissez-faire attitude toward teaching. It is equally necessary not to confuse academic rigor with rigidity that stifles and silences students. The teacher is the authority, with all the resulting responsibilities that entails; however, it is not necessary for the teacher to become authoritarian in order to challenge students intellectually. Education can be a process in which teacher and students mutually participate in the intellectually exciting undertaking we call learning. Students *can* become active subjects in their own learning, instead of passive objects waiting to be filled with facts and figures by the teacher.

I would like to emphasize that teachers who work with subordinated populations have the responsibility to assist them in appropriating knowledge bases and discourse styles deemed desirable by the greater society. However, this process of appropriation must be additive, that is, the new concepts and new discourse skills must be added to, not subtracted from, the students' existing background knowledge. In order to assume this additive stance, teachers must discard deficit views so they can use and build on life experiences and language styles too often viewed and labeled as "low class" and undesirable. Again, there are numerous teaching strategies and methods that can be employed in this additive manner. For the purposes of illustration, I will briefly discuss two approaches currently identified as promising for students from subordinated populations. The selected approaches are referred to in the literature as culturally responsive instructional approaches and strategic teaching.

CULTURALLY RESPONSIVE INSTRUCTION: THE POTENTIAL TO EQUALIZE POWER RELATIONS

Culturally responsive instruction grows out of cultural difference theory, which attributes the academic difficulties of students from subordinated groups to cultural incongruence or discontinuities between the learning, language use, and behavioral practices found in the home and those expected by the schools. Ana Maria Villegas (1988, 1991) defines culturally responsive instruction as attempts to create instructional situations where teachers use teaching approaches and strategies that recognize and build on culturally different ways of learning, behaving, and using language in the classroom.

A number of classic ethnographic studies document culturally incongruent communication practices in classrooms where students and teachers may speak the same language but use it in different ways. This type of incongruence is cited as a major source of academic difficulties for subordinated students and their teachers (see Au, 1980; Au & Mason, 1983; Cazden, 1988; Erickson & Mohatt, 1982; Heath, 1983; Philips, 1972). For the purposes of this analysis, one form of culturally responsive instruction, the Kamehameha Education Project reading program, will be discussed.

The Kamehameha Education Project is a reading program developed as a response to the traditionally low academic achievement of native Hawaiian students in Western schools. The reading program was a result of several years of research that examined the language practices of native Hawaiian children in home and school settings. Observations of native Hawaiian children showed them to be bright and capable learners; however, their behavior in the classroom signaled communication difficulties between them and their non-Hawaiian teachers. For example, Kathryn Hu-Pei Au (1979, 1980) reports that native Hawaiian children's language behavior in the classroom was often misinterpreted by teachers as being unruly and without educational value. She found that the children's preferred language style in the classroom was linked to a practice used by adults in their homes and community called "talk story." She discusses the talk story phenomenon and describes it as a major speech event in the Hawaiian community, where individuals speak almost simultaneously and where little attention is given to turn taking. Au explains that this practice may inhibit students from speaking out as individuals because of their familiarity with and preference for simultaneous group discussion.

Because the non-Hawaiian teachers were unfamiliar with talk story and failed to recognize its value, much class time was spent either silencing the children or prodding unwilling individuals to speak. Needless to say, very little class time was dedicated to other instruction. More important, the children were constrained and not allowed to demonstrate their abilities as speakers and possessors of knowledge. Because the students did not exhibit their skills in mainstream accepted ways (e.g., competing as individuals for the floor), they were prevented from exhibiting knowledge via their culturally preferred style. However, once the children's interaction style was incorporated into classroom lessons, time on task increased and, subsequently, students' performance on standardized reading tests improved. This study's findings conclude that educators can successfully employ the students' culturally valued language practices while introducing the student to more conventional and academically acceptable ways of using language.

It is interesting to note that many of the research studies that examine culturally congruent and incongruent teaching approaches also inadvertently illustrate the equalization of previous asymmetrical power relations between teachers and students. These studies describe classrooms where teachers initially imposed participation structures upon students from subordinated linguistic minority groups and later learned to negotiate with them rules regarding acceptable classroom behavior and language use (Au & Mason, 1983; Erickson & Mohatt, 1982; Heath, 1983; Philips, 1972). Thus these studies, in essence, capture the successful negotiation of power relations, which resulted in higher student academic achievement and increased teacher effectiveness. Yet there is little explicit discussion in these studies of the greater sociocultural reality that renders it perfectly normal for teachers to automatically disregard and disrespect subordinated students' preferences and to allow antagonistic relations to foment until presented with empirical evidence that legitimizes the students' practices. Instead, the focus of most of these studies rests entirely on the cultural congruence of the instruction and not on the humanizing effects of a more democratic pedagogy. Villegas (1988) accurately critiques the cultural congruence literature when she states:

> It is simplistic to claim that differences in languages used at home and in school are the root of the widespread academic problems of minority children. Admittedly, differences do exist, and they can create communication difficulties in the

classroom for both teachers and students. Even so, those differences in language must be viewed in the context of a broader struggle for power within a stratified society. (p. 260)

Despite the focus on the cultural versus the political dimensions of pedagogy, some effort is made to link culturally congruent teaching practices with equalization of classroom power relations. For example, Kathryn Au and Jana Mason (1983) explain that "one means of achieving cultural congruence in lessons may be to *seek a balance between the interactional rights of teachers and students,* so that the children can participate in ways comfortable to them" (p. 145, emphasis added). Their study compared two teachers and showed that the teacher who was willing to negotiate with students either the topic of discussion or the appropriate participation structure was better able to implement her lesson. Conversely, the teacher who attempted to impose both topic of discussion *and* appropriate interactional rules was frequently diverted because of conflicts with students over one or the other.

Unfortunately, as mentioned earlier, interpretations and practical applications of this body of research have focused on the *cultural* congruence of the approaches. I emphasize the term *cultural* because in these studies the term "culture" is used in a restricted sense devoid of its dynamic, ideological, and political dimensions. Instead, culture is treated as synonymous with ethnic culture, rather than as "the representation of lived experiences, material artifacts and practices *forged within the unequal and dialectical relations* that different groups establish in a given society at a particular point in historical time" (Giroux, 1985, p. xxi, emphasis added). I use this definition of culture because, without identifying the political dimensions of culture and subsequent unequal status attributed to members of different ethnic groups, the reader may conclude that teaching methods simply need to be ethnically congruent to be effective—without recognizing that not all ethnic and linguistic cultural groups are viewed and treated as equally legitimate in classrooms. Interestingly enough, there is little discussion of the various socially perceived minority groups' subordinate status vis-à-vis White teachers and peers in these studies. All differences are treated as ethnic cultural differences and not as responses of subordinated students to teachers from dominant groups, and vice versa.

Given the sociocultural realities in the above studies, the specific teaching strategies may not be what made the difference. Indeed, efforts to uncritically export the Kamehameha Education Project reading program to other student populations resulted in failure (Vogt et al., 1987). It could well be that the teacher's effort to negotiate and share power by treating students as equal participants in their own learning is what made the difference in Hawaii. Just as important is the teachers' willingness to critically interrogate their deficit views of subordinated students. By employing a variety of strategies and techniques, the Kamehameha students were allowed to interact with teachers in egalitarian and meaningful ways. More importantly, the teachers also learned to recognize, value, use, and build upon students' previously acquired knowledge and skills. In essence, these strategies succeeded in creating a comfort zone so students could exhibit their knowledge and skills and, ultimately, empower themselves to succeed in an academic setting. Teachers also benefitted from using a variety of student-centered teaching strategies that humanized their perceptions of treatment of students previously perceived as deficient. Ray McDermott's (1977) classic research reminds us that numerous teaching approaches and strategies can be effective, so long as trusting relations between teacher and students are established and power relations are mutually set and agreed upon.

STRATEGIC TEACHING: THE SIGNIFICANCE OF TEACHER-STUDENT INTERACTION AND NEGOTIATION

Strategic teaching refers to an instructional model that explicitly teaches students learning strategies that enable them consciously to monitor their own learning. This is accomplished through the development of reflective cognitive monitoring and metacognitive skills (Jones, Palinscar, Ogle, & Carr, 1987). The goal is to prepare independent and metacognitively aware students. This teaching strategy makes explicit for students the structures of various text types used in academic settings and assists students in identifying various strategies for effectively comprehending the various genres. Although text structures and strategies for dissecting the particular structures are presented by the teacher, a key component of these lessons is the elicitation of students' knowledge about text types and their own strategies for making meaning before presenting them with more conventional academic strategies.

Examples of learning strategies include teaching various text structures (i.e., stories and reports) through frames and graphic organizers. *Frames* are sets of questions that help students understand a given topic. Readers monitor their understanding of a text by asking questions, making predictions, and testing their predictions as they read. Before reading, frames serve as an advance organizer to activate prior knowledge and facilitate understanding. Frames can also be utilized during the reading process by the reader to monitor self-learning. Finally, frames can be used after a reading lesson to summarize and integrate newly acquired information.

Graphic organizers are visual maps that represent text structures and organizational patterns used in texts and in student writing. Ideally, graphic organizers reflect both the content and text structure. Graphic organizers include semantic maps, chains, and concept hierarchies, and assist the student in visualizing the rhetorical structure of the text. Beau Jones and colleagues (1987) explain that frames and graphic organizers can be "powerful tools to help the student locate, select, sequence, integrate and restructure information—both from the perspective of understanding and from the perspective of producing information in written responses" (p. 38).

Although much of the research on strategic teaching focuses on English monolingual mainstream students, recent efforts to study linguistic minority students' use of these strategies show similar success. This literature shows that strategic teaching improved the students' reading comprehension, as well as their conscious use of effective learning strategies in their native language (Avelar La Salle, 1991; Chamot, 1983; Hernandez, 1991; O'Malley & Chamot, 1990; Reyes, 1987). Furthermore, these studies show that students, despite limited English proficiency, were able to transfer or apply their knowledge of specific learning strategies and text structure to English reading texts. For example, Jose Hernandez (1991) reports that sixth-grade limited English proficient students learned, in the native language (Spanish), to generate hypotheses, summarize, and make predictions about readings. He reports:

> Students were able to demonstrate use of comprehension strategies even when they could not decode the English text aloud. When asked in Spanish about English texts the students were able to generate questions, summarize stories, and predict future events in Spanish. (p. 101)

Robin Avelar La Salle's (1991) study of third- and fourth-grade bilingual students shows that strategic teaching in the native language of three expository text structures commonly found in elementary social studies and science texts (topical net, matrix, and hierarchy) improved comprehension of these types of texts in both Spanish and English.

Such explicit and strategic teaching is most important in the upper elementary grades, where students are expected to focus on the development of more advanced English literacy skills. Beginning at about third grade, students face literacy demands distinct from those encountered in earlier grades. Jeanne Chall (1983) describes the change in literacy demands in terms of stages of readings. She explains that at a stage three of reading, students cease to "learn to read" and begin "reading to learn." Students in third and fourth grade are introduced to content area subjects such as social studies, science, and health. In addition, students are introduced to expository texts (reports). This change in texts, text structures, and in the functions of reading (reading for information) calls for teaching strategies that will prepare students to comprehend various expository texts (e.g., cause/effect, compare/contrast) used across the curriculum.

Strategic teaching holds great promise for preparing linguistic minority students to face the new literacy challenges in the upper grades. As discussed before, the primary goal of strategic instruction is to foster learner independence. This goal in and of itself is laudable. However, the characteristics of strategic instruction that I find most promising grow out of the premise that teachers and students must interact and negotiate meaning as equals in order to reach a goal.

Teachers, by permitting learners to speak from their own vantage points, create learning contexts in which students are able to empower themselves throughout the strategic learning process. Before teachers attempt to instruct students in new content or learning strategies, efforts are made by the teacher to access student prior knowledge so as to link it with new information. In allowing students to present and discuss their prior knowledge and experiences, the teacher legitimizes and treats as valuable student language and cultural experiences usually ignored in classrooms. If students are encouraged to speak on what they know best, then they are, in a sense, treated as experts—experts who are expected to refine their knowledge bases with the additional new content and strategy information presented by the teacher.

Teachers play a significant role in creating learning contexts in which students are able to empower themselves. Teachers act as cultural mentors of sorts when they introduce students not only to the culture of the classroom, but to particular subjects and discourse styles as well. In the process, teachers assist the students in appropriating the skills (in an additive fashion) for themselves so as to enable them to behave as "insiders" in the particular subject or discipline. Jim Gee (1989) reminds us that the social nature of teaching and learning must involve apprenticeship into the subject's or discipline's discourse in order for students to do well in school. This apprenticeship includes acquisition of particular content matter, ways of organizing content, and ways of using language (oral and written). Gee adds that these discourses are not mastered solely through teacher-centered and directed instruction, but also by "apprenticeship into social practices through scaffolded and supported interaction with people who have already mastered the discourse" (p. 7). The apprenticeship notion can be immensely useful with subordinated students if it facilitates the acceptance and valorization of students' prior knowledge through a mentoring process.

Models of instruction, such as strategic teaching, can promote such an apprenticeship. In the process of apprenticing linguistic minority students, teachers must interact in meaningful ways with them. This human interaction not only assists students in acquiring new knowledge and skills, but it also often familiarizes individuals from different SES and racial/ethnic groups, and creates mutual respect instead of the antagonism that so frequently occurs between teachers and their students from subordinated groups. In this learning environment, teachers and students learn from each other. The strategies serve, then, not to "fix" the student, but to equalize power relations and to humanize the teacher-student relationship. Ideally, teachers are forced to challenge implicitly or explicitly held deficit attitudes and beliefs about their students and the cultural groups to which they belong.

BEYOND TEACHING STRATEGIES: TOWARD A HUMANIZING PEDAGOGY

When I recall a special education teacher's experience related in a bilingualism and literacy course that I taught, I am reminded of the humanizing effects of teaching strategies that, similar to culturally responsive instruction and strategic teaching, allow teachers to listen, learn from, and mentor their students. This teacher, for most of her career, had been required to assess her students through a variety of closed-ended instruments, and then to remediate their diagnosed "weaknesses" with discrete skills instruction. The assessment instruments provided little information to explain why the student answered a question either correctly or incorrectly, and they often confirmed perceived student academic, linguistic, and cognitive weaknesses. This fragmented discrete skills approach to instruction restricts the teacher's access to existing student knowledge and experiences not specifically elicited by the academic tasks. Needless to say, this teacher knew very little about her students other than her deficit descriptions of them.

As part of the requirements for my course, she was asked to focus on one Spanish-speaking, limited English proficient special education student over the semester. She observed the student in a number of formal and informal contexts, and she engaged him in a number of open-ended tasks. These tasks included allowing him to write entire texts, such as stories and poems (despite diagnosed limited English proficiency), and to engage in "think-alouds" during reading.[9] Through these open-ended activities, the teacher learned about her student's English writing ability (both strengths and weaknesses), his life experiences and world views, and his meaning-making strategies for reading. Consequently, the teacher constructed an instructional plan much better suited to her student's academic needs and interests. And even more important, she underwent a humanizing process that allowed her to recognize the varied and valuable life experiences and knowledge her student brought into the classroom.

This teacher was admirably candid when she shared her initial negative and stereotypic views of the student and her radical transformation. Despite this teacher's mastery of content area, her lack of political clarity blinded her to the oppressive and dehumanizing nature of instruction offered to linguistic minority students. Initially, she had formed an erroneous notion of her student's personality, worldview, academic ability, motivation, and academic potential on the basis of his Puerto Rican ethnicity, low SES background, limited English proficiency, and moderately learning-disabled label. Because of the restricted and closed nature of earlier assessment and instruction, the teacher had never received information about her student that challenged her negative perceptions. Listening to her student and reading his poetry and stories, she discovered his loving and sunny personality, learned his personal history, and identified academic strengths and weaknesses. In the process, she discovered and challenged her deficit orientation. The following excerpt from this student's writing exemplifies the power of the student voice for humanizing teachers:

My Father

I love my father very much. I will never forget what my father has done for me and my brothers and sisters. When we first came from Puerto Rico we didn't have food to eat and we were very poor. My father had to work three jobs to put food and milk on the table. Those were hard times and my father worked so hard that we hardly saw him. But even when I didn't see him, I always knew he loved me very much. I will always be grateful to my father. We are not so poor now and so he works only one job. But I will never forget what my father did for me. I will also work to help my father have a better life when I grow up. I love my father very much.

The process of learning about her student's rich and multifaceted background enabled this teacher to move beyond the rigid methodology that had required her to distance herself from the student and to confirm the deficit model to which she unconsciously adhered. In this case, the meaningful teacher-student interaction served to equalize the teacher-student power relations and to humanize instruction by expanding the horizons through which the student demonstrated human qualities, dreams, desires, and capacities that closed-ended tests and instruction never captured.

I believe that the specific teaching methods implemented by the teacher, in and of themselves, were not the significant factors. The actual strengths of methods depend, first and foremost, on the degree to which they embrace a humanizing pedagogy that values the student's background knowledge, culture, and life experiences, and creates learning contexts where power is shared by students and teachers. Teaching methods are a means to an end—humanizing education to promote academic success for students historically underserved by the schools. A teaching strategy is a vehicle to a greater goal. A number of vehicles exist that may or may not lead to a humanizing pedagogy, depending on the sociocultural reality in which teachers and students operate.

The critical issue is the degree to which we hold the moral conviction that we must humanize the educational experience of students from subordinated populations by eliminating the hostility that often confronts these students. This process would require that we cease to be overly dependent on methods as technical instruments and adopt a pedagogy that seeks to forge a cultural democracy where all students are treated with respect and dignity. A true cultural democracy forces teachers to recognize that student's lack of familiarity with the dominant values of the curriculum "does not mean . . . that the lack of these experiences develop in these children a different 'nature' that determines their absolute incompetence" (Freire, 1993, p. 17).

Unless educational methods are situated in the student's cultural experiences, students will continue to show difficulty in mastering content area that is not only alien to their reality, but is often antagonistic toward their culture and lived experiences. Further, not only will these methods continue to fail students, particularly those from subordinated groups, but they will never lead to the creation of schools as true cultural democratic sites. For this reason, it is imperative that teachers problematize the prevalent notion of "magical" methods and incorporate what Macedo (1994) calls an anti-methods pedagogy, a process through which teachers 1) critically deconstruct the ideology that informs the methods fetish prevalent in education, 2) understand the intimate relationships between methods and the theoretical underpinnings that inform these methods, and 3) evaluate the pedagogical consequences of blindly and uncritically replicating methods without regard to students' subordinate status in terms of cultural, class, gender, and linguistic difference. In short, we need

> an anti-methods pedagogy that would reject the mechanization of intellectualism . . . [and] challenge teachers to work toward reappropriation of endangered dignity and toward reclaiming our humanity. The anti-methods pedagogy adheres to the eloquence of Antonio Machado's poem, "Caminante, no hay camino, se hace camino al andar." (Traveler, there are no roads. The road is created as we walk it [together])." (Macedo, 1994, p. 8)

REFERENCES

Anyon, J. (1988). "Social class and the hidden curriculum of work." In J. R. Gress (ed.), *Curriculum: An introduction to the field* (pp. 366–389). Berkeley, CA: McCutchan.

Au, K. H. (1979). "Using the experience text relationship method with minority children." *The Reading Teacher,* 32, 677–679.

Au, K. H. (1980). "Participant structures in a reading lesson with Hawaiian children: Analysis of a culturally appropriate instructional event." *Anthropology and Educational Quarterly,* 11, 91–115.

Au, K. H., and Mason, J. M. (1983). "Cultural congruence in classroom participation structures: Achieving a balance of rights." *Discourse Processes,* 6, 145–168.

Avelar La Salle, R. (1991). *The effect of metacognitive instruction on the transfer of expository comprehension skills: The interlingual and cross-lingual cases.* Unpublished doctoral dissertation, Stanford University.

Bloom, G. M. (1991). *The effects of speech style and skin color on bilingual teaching candidates' and bilingual teachers' attitudes toward Mexican American pupils.* Unpublished doctoral dissertation, Stanford University.

Boykin, A. W. (1983). "The academic performance of Afro-American children." In J. T. Spence (ed.), *Achievement and achievement motives: Psychological and sociological approaches* (pp. 322–369). San Francisco: W. H. Freeman.

Carter, T. P., and Chatfield, M. L. (1986). "Effective bilingual schools: Implications for policy and practice." *American Journal of Education,* 95, 200–232.

Cazden, C. (1988). *Classroom discourse: The language of teaching and learning.* Portsmouth, NH: Heinemann.

Chall, J. (1983). *Stages of reading development.* New York: McGraw-Hill.

Chamot, A. U. (1983). "How to plan to transfer curriculum from bilingual to mainstream instruction." *Focus,* 12. (A newsletter available from The George Washington University National Clearinghouse for Bilingual Education, 1118 22nd St. NW, Washington, DC 20037)

Cohen, E. G. (1986). *Designing groupwork: Strategies for the heterogeneous classroom.* New York: Teachers College Press.

Cummins, J. (1989). *Empowering minority students.* Sacramento: California Association of Bilingual Education.

Delpit, L. (1986). "Skills and other dilemmas of a progressive black educator." *Harvard Educational Review,* 56, 379–385.

Delpit, L. (1988). "The silenced dialogue: Power and pedagogy in educating other people's children." *Harvard Educational Review,* 58, 280–298.

Diaz, S., Moll, L. C., and Mehan, H. (1986). "Sociocultural resources in instruction: A context-specific approach." In *Beyond language: Social and cultural factors in schooling language minority students* (pp. 187–230). Los Angeles: California State University, Evaluation, Dissemination and Assessment Center.

Edelsky, C., Altwerger, B., and Flores, B. (1991). *Whole language: What's the difference?* Portsmouth, NH: Heinemann.

Erickson, F., and Mohatt, G. (1982). "Cultural organization of participation structures in two class-rooms of Indian students." In G. Spindler (ed.), *Doing the ethnography of schooling: Educational anthropology in action* (pp. 133–174). New York: Holt, Rinehart and Winston.

Flores, B. M. (1982). *Language interference or influence: Toward a theory for Hispanic bilingualism.* Unpublished doctoral dissertation, University of Arizona at Tucson.

Flores, B. M. (1993, April). *Interrogating the genesis of the deficit view of Latino children in the educational literature during the 20th century.* Paper presented at the American Educational Research Association Conference, Atlanta.

Flores, B., Cousin, P. T., and Diaz, E. (1991). "Critiquing and transforming the deficit myths about learning, language and culture." *Language Arts,* 68, 369–379.

Freire, P. (1985). *The politics of education: Culture, power and liberation.* South Hadley, MA: Bergin & Garvey.

Freire, P. (1987). "Letter to North-American teachers." In I. Shor (ed.), *Freire for the classroom* (pp. 211–214). Portsmouth, NJ: Boynton/Cook.

Freire, P. (1993). *A pedagogy of the city.* New York: Continuum Press.

Freire, P., and Macedo, D. (1987). *Literacy: Reading the word and the world.* South Hadley, MA: Bergin & Garvey.

Gee, J. P. (1989). "Literacy, discourse, and linguistics: Introduction." *Journal of Education,* 171, 5–17.

Gibson, M. A., and Ogbu, J. U. (1991). *Minority status and schooling: A comparative study of immigrant and involuntary minorities.* New York: Garland.

Giroux, H. (1985). "Introduction." In P. Freire, *The politics of education: Culture, power and liberation* (pp. xi–xxv). South Hadley, MA.: Bergin & Garvey.

Giroux, H. (1992). *Border crossing: Cultural workers and the politics of education.* New York: Routledge.

Giroux, H., and McLaren, P. (1986). "Teacher education and the politics of engagement: The case for democratic schooling." *Harvard Educational Review,* 56, 213–238.

Golnick, D. M., and Chinn, P. C. (1986). *Multicultural education in a pluralistic society.* Columbus, OH: Merrill.

Heath, S. B. (1983). *Ways with words.* New York: Cambridge University Press.

Hernandez, J. S. (1991). "Assisted performance in reading comprehension strategies with non-English proficient students." *Journal of Educational Issues of Language Minority Students,* 8, 91–112.

Jones, B. F., Palinscar, A. S., Ogle, D. S., and Carr, E. G. (1987). *Strategic teaching and learning: Cognitive instruction in the content areas.* Alexandria, VA: Association for Supervision and Curriculum Development.

Knapp, M. S., and Shields, P. M. (1990). *Better schooling for the children of poverty: Alternatives to conventional wisdom: Vol. 2. Commissioned papers and literature review.* Washington, DC: U.S. Department of Education.

Lamont, M., and Lareau, A. (1988). "Cultural capital-allusions, gaps and glissandos in recent theoretical developments." *Sociological Theory,* 6, 153–168.

Langer, J. A. (1986). *Children reading and writing: Structures and strategies.* Norwood, NJ: Ablex.

Lareau, J. A. (1990). *Home advantage: Social class and parental intervention in elementary education.* New York: Falmer Press.

Lucas, T., Henze, R., and Donato, R. (1990). "Promoting the success of Latino language-minority students: An exploratory study of six high schools." *Harvard Educational Review,* 60, 315–340.

Macedo, D. (1994). "Preface." In P. McLaren and C. Lankshear (eds.), *Conscientization and resistance* (pp. 1–8). New York: Routledge.

McDermott, R. P. (1977). "Social relations as contexts for learning in school." *Harvard Educational Review,* 47, 198–213.

McLeod, B. (Ed.). (in press). *Cultural diversity and second language learning.* Albany: State University of New York Press.

Means, B., and Knapp, M. S. (1991). *Teaching advanced skills to educationally disadvantaged students.* Washington, DC: U.S. Department of Education.

Mehan, H. (1992). "Understanding inequality in schools: The contribution of interpretive studies." *Sociology of Education,* 65(1), 1–20.

Menchaca, M., and Valencia, R. (1990). "Anglo-Saxon ideologies in the 1920s–1930s: Their impact on the segregation of Mexican students in California." *Anthropology and Education Quarterly,* 21, 222–245.

Moll, L. C. (1986). "Writing as communication: Creating learning environments for students." *Theory Into Practice*, 25, 102–110.

Oaks, J. (1986). "Tracking, inequality, and the rhetoric of school reform: Why schools don't change." *Journal of Education*, 168, 61–80.

Ogbu, J. (1987). "Variability in minority responses to schooling: Nonimmigrants vs. immigrants." In G. Spindler and L. Spindler (eds.), *Interpretive ethnography of education* (pp. 255–280). Hillsdale, NJ: Lawrence Erlbaum Associates.

O'Malley, J., and Chamot, A. U. (1990). *Learning strategies in second language acquisition.* New York: Cambridge University Press.

Palinscar, A. S., and Brown, A. L. (1984). "Reciprocal teaching of comprehension fostering and comprehension-monitoring activities." *Cognition and Instruction*, 1(23), 117–175.

Pérez, B., and Torres-Guzmán, M. E. (1992). *Learning in two worlds: An integrated Spanish/English biliteracy approach.* New York: Longman.

Philips, S. U. (1972). "Participant structures and communication competence: Warm Springs children in community and classroom." In C. B. Cazden, V. P. John, and D. Hymes (eds.), *Functions of language in the classroom* (pp. 370–394). New York: Teachers College Press.

Reyes, M. de la Luz. (1987). "Comprehension of content area passages: A study of Spanish/English readers in the third and fourth grade." In S. R. Goldman and H. T. Trueba (eds.), *Becoming literate in English as a second language* (pp. 107–126). Norwood, NJ: Ablex.

Reyes, M. de la Luz. (1991). "A process approach to literacy during dialogue journals and literature logs with second language learners." *Research in the Teaching of English*, 25, 291–313.

Reyes, M. de la Luz. (1992). "Challenging venerable assumptions: Literacy instruction for linguistically different students." *Harvard Educational Review*, 62, 427–446.

Sue, S., and Padilla, A. (1986). "Ethnic minority issues in the U.S.: Challenges for the educational system." In *Beyond language: Social and cultural factors in schooling language minority students* (pp. 35–72). Los Angeles: California State University, Evaluation, Dissemination and Assessment Center.

Tikunoff, W. (1985). *Applying significant bilingual instructional features in the classroom.* Rosslyn, VA: National Clearinghouse for Bilingual Education.

Tinajero, J. V., and Ada, A. F. (1993). *The power of two languages: Literacy and biliteracy for Spanish-speaking students.* New York: Macmillan/McGraw-Hill.

Trueba, H. T. (1989). "Sociocultural integration of minorities and minority school achievement." In *Raising silent voices: Educating the linguistic minorities for the 21st century* (pp. 1–27). New York: Newbury House.

U.S. Commission on Civil Rights. (1973). *Teachers and students: Report V. Mexican-American study: Differences in teacher interaction with Mexican-American and Anglo students.* Washington, DC: Government Printing Office.

Valencia, R. (1986, November 25). *Minority academic underachievement: Conceptual and theoretical considerations for understanding the achievement problems of Chicano students.* Paper presented to the Chicano Faculty Seminar, Stanford University.

Valencia, R. (1991). *Chicano school failure and success: Research and policy agendas for the 1990s.* New York: Falmer Press.

Villegas, A. M. (1988). "School failure and cultural mismatch: Another view." *Urban Review*, 20, 253–265.

Villegas, A. M. (1991). *Culturally responsive pedagogy for the 1990s and beyond.* Paper prepared for the Educational Testing Service, Princeton, NJ.

Vogt, L. A., Jordan, C., and Tharp, R. G. (1987). "Explaining school failure, producing school success: Two cases." *Anthropology & Education Quarterly*, 18, 276–286.

Walker, C. L. (1987). "Hispanic achievement: Old views and new perspectives." In H. T. Trueba (ed.), *Success or failure: Learning and the language minority student* (pp. 15–32). New York: Newbury House.

Webb, L. C. (1987). *Raising achievement among minority students.* Arlington, VA: American Associates of School Administrators.

Winfield, L. F. (1986). "Teachers beliefs toward academically at risk students in inner urban schools." *Urban Review*, 18, 253–267.

Zamel, V. (1982). "Writing: The process of discovering meaning." *TESOL Quarterly*, 16, 195–209.

NOTES

1. The term "technical" refers to the positivist tradition in education that presents teaching as a precise and scientific undertaking and teachers as technicians responsible for carrying out (preselected) instructional programs and strategies.
2. "Subordinated" refers to cultural groups that are politically, socially, and economically subordinate in the greater society. While individual members of these groups may not consider themselves subordinate in any manner to the White "mainstream," they nevertheless are members of a greater collective that historically has been perceived and treated as subordinate and inferior by the dominant society. Thus it is not entirely accurate to describe these students as "minority" students, since the term connotes numerical minority rather than the general low status (economic, political, and social) these groups have held and that I think is important to recognize when discussing their historical academic underachievement.
3. "Chicana" refers to a woman of Mexican ancestry who was born and/or reared in the United States.
4. "Mainstream" refers to the U.S. macroculture that has its roots in Western European traditions. More specifically, the major influence on the United States, particularly on its institutions, has been the culture and traditions of White, Anglo-Saxon Protestants (WASP) (Golnick & Chinn, 1986). Although the mainstream group is no longer composed solely of WASPs, members of the middle class have adopted traditionally WASP bodies of knowledge, language use, values, norms, and beliefs.
5. "Political clarity" refers to the process by which individuals achieve a deepening awareness of the sociopolitical and economic realities that shape their lives and their capacity to recreate them. In addition, it refers to the process by which individuals come to better understand possible linkages between macro-level political, economic, and social variables and subordinated groups' academic performance at the micro-level classroom. Thus, it invariably requires linkages between sociocultural structures and schooling.
6. Elizabeth Cohen (1986) explains that in the society at large there are status distinctions made on the basis of social class, ethnic group, and gender. These status distinctions are often reproduced at the classroom level, unless teachers make conscious efforts to prevent this reproduction.
7. For detailed discussions regarding various deficit views of subordinated students over time, see Flores, Cousin, and Diaz, 1991; also see Sue and Padilla, 1986.
8. "Cultural capital" refers to Pierre Bourdieu's concept that certain forms of cultural knowledge are the equivalent of symbolic wealth in that these forms of "high" culture are socially designated as worthy of being sought and possessed. These cultural (and linguistic) knowledge bases and skills are socially inherited and are believed to facilitate academic achievement. See Lamont and Lareau, 1988, for a more in-depth discussion regarding the multiple meanings of cultural capital in the literature.
9. "Think-alouds" refers to an informal assessment procedure where readers verbalize all their thoughts during reading and writing tasks. See J. A. Langer, 1986, for a more in-depth discussion of think-aloud procedures.

Borderness and Pedagogy: Exposing Culture in the Classroom

TERESA McKENNA

Acknowledgment of the cultural annihilation to which Adrienne Rich alerts us in the first epigraph to this chapter has begun to alter what we teach and how we teach it. Because of this new awareness, the classroom has become the focal point of theoretical and practical debate regarding the viability of certain culturally diverse materials for instruction and the effects of this material on the values and the future of life as they have been known in the United States. For those of us who have attempted to realize change in the institutionalized center of cultural formation and dissemination—the classroom— the debate has led to vociferous and at times discomfiting opposition.

Turning the collective gaze of the classroom to an examination of culture, which includes consideration of the effects of difference (gender, race, class, and ethnicity), is not a comfortable or a highly prized objective of most institutions of education. The rhetoric of diversity, such as celebration of our culture as the great melting pot or the freshest salad bowl, belies the ambivalence and fear of difference so pervasive in our society. This fear finds its greatest rootedness in differences of race and gender.

The issue is not just an insider/outsider problem, a simple we/they opposition, or a masculine/feminine construction. Nor is the issue just a matter of access to a dominant culture. Rather, it is a questioning of culture as determined by conscious and unconscious policies of exclusion based on inequalities perceived in some cultural differences. Many scholars, critics, artists, and political activists have complicated the debate by realigning the issues along progressive lines—that is, through consideration of the perspectives of people of color.

Color, however, is not necessarily equivalent to our inherited notions of race or ethnicity. Even now, when speaking of race, most people refer to a black/white racial binary. Yet the notion of race, as we all know, is far more problematic. The "Other" that is stigmatized by race is not confined to African Americans, Asian Americans, or Native Americans. Some ethnic "Others" are perceived as racial, particularly in certain incarnations of oppositional culture; moreover, some manifestations of gender differences are similarly stigmatized. What we have here is an intersection of race, ethnicity, and gender, which the self-designation "people of color" underscores by making the larger, stigmatized "Other" visible and a vortex of political solidarity.

The perspective of "people of color" indicates an acceptance of racialness not only as inevitable, but as a creative focal point for art, politics, and education. The performance artist Guillermo Gómez-Peña, who finds himself between nations, languages, and monetary and artistic economies, claims himself as one of the "children of the chasm that is opening between the 'first' and the 'third' worlds." He too is one of the indisputable heirs to a new *mestizaje* (the fusion of the Amerindian and European races)" (1988, p. 130). He concludes: "As a result of this process I have become a cultural topographer, border-crosser, and hunter of myths. And it doesn't matter where I find myself, in Califas or Mexico City, or Barcelona or West Berlin; I always have the sensation that I belong to the same species: the migrant tribe of fiery pupils" (p. 128).

We are all implicated in this chasm "between the 'first' and the 'third' worlds," because those "fiery pupils" find themselves in our classrooms; the literature we are attempting to integrate into the curriculum emerges from this zone. Is acknowledging this situation of "Otherness" and incorporating culturally diverse texts into the curriculum enough? Indeed it is not. We can no longer assume that a common culture exists into which these "recalcitrant cultural anomalies" can be made to fit. The dream of a common culture is gone, and we have in its place a dynamic flowering of multiplicities. The crisis of identity does not lie within the cultural "Other" but within United States society itself. Gómez-Peña (1988, p. 129) gives us an insight into this situation:

> I am a child of crisis and cultural syncretism, half hippie and half punk. My generation grew up watching movies about cowboys and science fiction, listening to *cumbias* and tunes from the Moody Blues, constructing altars and filming in Super-8, reading the *Corno Emplumado* and *Artforum,* traveling to Tepoztlán and San Francisco, creating and decreating myths. We went to Cuba in search of political illumination, to Spain to visit the crazy grandmother and to the U.S. in search of the instantaneous musico-sexual paradise. We found nothing. Our dreams wound up getting caught in the webs of the border.

Gómez-Peña and his generation are not the only ones caught within that web. This syncretism of cultures aptly describes the cultural situation of the United States itself. And borderness, a consciousness of living in the borderlands, is a useful empathetic tool for understanding the discomfort that educators who face the "web of the border" feel when we enter classrooms throughout this country.

Henry Louis Gates, in different terms, articulates a similar political understanding when he writes in his introduction to his collection of essays *Loose Canons: Notes on the Culture Wars* (1992, p. xv):

> Ours is a late-twentieth-century world profoundly fissured by nationality, ethnicity, race, class, and gender. And the only way to transcend those divisions—to forge, for once, a civic culture that respects both differences and commonalities—is through education that seeks to comprehend the diversity of human culture. Beyond the hype and the high-flown rhetoric is a pretty homely truth: There is no tolerance without respect—and no respect without knowledge.

Similarly, in an address at the University of California, Riverside (1991), Cornel West remarks that "we as human beings are part of civilizations that have always had ambiguous legacies, cultures that are always already hybrid that are built on the elements and fragments of antecedent cultures. So that the notion of pristine cultures falls by the wayside." Consequently, for West, a critical sensibility that recovers an understanding of difference as integral to cultural production is one that is rooted in a moral imperative. He explains that "it is a perspective that forces us to understand any society, any culture in terms of its complexity, how in fact we as human beings interact with one another" (unpublished oral recording).

Yet Guillermo Gómez-Peña further complicates the dimensions of this morality play. His multiracial, multigendered border culture alters the mix in the proverbial pot. As it is, the ideology of "Americanness" in terms of race has been characterized by a simple binary, whether that be "us versus them" or "black versus white" rhetoric. Gómez-Peña's incipient manifesto shatters once again the dream of a common culture that is based on the illusion of civility and civic participation. The interaction among peoples in the United States traditionally has not been characterized by equality or common sharing of power and social control. It has been marked by a need to normalize, to reduce cultural hybridity into its lowest common denominator in order, many have believed, to effect a manageable idea of cultural and national identity. But that common culture—as West, Gómez-Peña, and Gates among others have pointed out—has been based on obfuscation, cultural destruction, and repression of difference. The ideal of a common culture did not reflect the reality of the increasingly hybrid cultural profile that has been shown to be historically resilient and permanent.

Many have feared that difference only divides; it cannot bind peoples together under one national rubric. Yet if we understand difference as the common cultural reference point it becomes the basis for unity—a paradoxical concept that has proven difficult for many to grasp. At the root of this paradox is an imperative that releases us from the debilitating tension between anarchy and order that has characterized the ways in which culture, invariably conceived as icon, has driven our social order including our educational system. The "rage for order" dominates Allan Bloom and E. D. Hirsch's manifestos as well as Arthur Schlesinger's more recent concern about the "fraying of American Culture." Their ideas fundamentally reflect a fear of anarchy. Yet a critical sensibility that deals with cultural hybridity as a resource puts into play other terms of analysis that point to the enabling complexities of our cultural multiplicities and reestablishes a self-critical moment in which we regain the richness and cultural resources that have been denied through the urge to reduce, to make common. This is a moment in which we redirect our agenda as educators and as participants in civic culture.

So if—and this is a big if—the question about "What is to be done?" has been addressed, the follow-up question "How do we do it?" has not. Do we argue for a form of common culture through "exposure" to other cultures through texts? Does this agenda mask a call for a form of that consensus out of which the "Americanization" programs of the turn of the century proceeded?

In a critique of the theoretical positing of the consensus versus descent paradigm advocated by Werner Sollors, Ramón Saldívar (1991, p. 19) cautions:

> The American ideological consensus . . . takes on a very different quality when we take into account the ways that class origins and racial and gender differences affect literary and social history. At the very least, people of different classes, races, and gender will feel the effects of that consensus and its hegemony differently. And if Jameson's notion of expressive causality is to be taken seriously as a way of regarding history as the "absent cause" accessible to us only through its "narrativization in the political unconscious," then we must not easily dismiss the real power of difference to resist the reifying tendencies of studies such as Sollors' with their presumptuous claims to move "beyond ethnicity" toward the formation of an unitary American culture.

What do a theory of difference and a pedagogy of difference have in common? How does the experience of difference translate into the classroom environment? The answer necessitates sustaining a delicate balance between theory and practice. At the same time that critics have argued for an unmasking of the political suppositions undergirding the traditional canon, they have also at times consciously and unconsciously supported the goal of the classroom as the site of political transformation. Henry Louis Gates (*Loose Canons,* pp. xiii–xiv) correctly observes:

> But is the political and social significance of our work as immediate as all that? Or is the noisy spectacle of the public debate a kind of stage behind which far narrower gains are secured or relinquished? I must confess to considerable ambivalence on the matter. The "larger issues" that frame the classroom clamor

are profoundly real: but the significance of our own interventions is easily over-stated; and I do not exempt myself from this admonition.

Either the political nature of pedagogy is perceived to be tantamount to a national betrayal or the classroom is indeed a limited space of transformation. The answer lies, again, somewhere in between, in the teacher's imperative to "teach," to establish new frameworks for interacting together. In *Race Matters* (1993, p. 4), Cornel West argues for the necessity for a moral understanding of the American "Educational" project:

> To establish a new framework, we need to begin with a frank acknowledgment of the basic humanness and Americanness of each of us. And we must acknowledge that as a people—*E Pluribus Unum*—we are on a slippery slope toward economic strife, social turmoil, and cultural chaos. If we go down, we go down together. The Los Angeles upheaval forced us to see not only that we are not connected in ways we would like to be but also, in a more profound sense, that this failure to connect binds us even more tightly together. The paradox of race in America is that our common destiny is more pronounced and imperiled precisely when our divisions are deeper.

Those divisions are multiple. They are race, class, gender, sexuality, and linguistically based. And it is in the classroom that these divisions are played out most dynamically. The refractions of difference are staggeringly multiple, as Gloria Anzaldúa (1987, pp. 77–78) eloquently reminds us:

> Because I, a *mestiza,*
> continually walk out of one culture
> and into another,
> because I am in all cultures at the same time,
> *alma de dos mundos, tres, cuatro,*
> *me zumba la cabeza con lo contradictorio.*
> *Estoy norteada por todas las voces que me hablan*
> *simultáneamente.*

In a constant state of mental nepantilism, an Aztec word meaning torn between ways, *la mestiza* is a product of the transfer of the cultural and spiritual values of one group to another. Being tricultural, monolingual, bilingual, or multi-lingual, speaking in a patois, and in a state of perpetual transition, the *mestiza* faces the dilemma of the mixed breed: which collectivity does the daughter of a darkskinned mother listen to?

The dilemma of the mestiza resonates in the dilemma of the Americas, and in particular the United States. It is a dilemma that in many ways informs the pedagogical situation when we as professors and as students are called upon to educate and to be educated in the paradigmatic border space of the classroom. In Anzaldúa's theorizing about *mestizaje,* the only way to survive the borderlands is to acknowledge the multiplicity of difference and to acquire a tolerance for ambiguity. I suggest that herein lies that edge on which we might leverage both a theory and practice of difference.

With her book *Borderlands/La Frontera* Gloria Anzaldúa has emerged as a major theorist regarding borderness and border consciousness, ideas that have become useful particularly for critics of Chicano/a and Latino/a literatures. In this volume she posits a problematic of contradiction. As explained above, she asks the hard questions about the effects of cultural multiplicity: "which collectivity does the daughter of a darkskinned mother listen to?" And she claims, as we all would like to, that the "answer to the problem between the white race and the colored, between males and females, lies in healing the split that originates in the very foundation of our lives, our cultures, our languages, our thoughts" (p. 78). The consciousness of the mestiza is the key to that healing. It is a coming together based on race, ethnicity, class, and gender. It is a vortex of difference. Anzaldúa concludes that we must all empathetically project ourselves into the borderland and from there change the "symbolic contract" with which we have been defined: "To survive the Borderlands/you must live *sin fronteras*/be a crossroads (p. 195).

Being a crossroads does not imply a denial of difference; rather it promotes an articulation of difference. It means living without borders, but it also means living as an intersection of all the border spaces that define: race, class, gender, sexuality, ethnicity. Norma Alarcón has argued, along with other feminists of color, that there can be no totalizing "we" female subject. Similarly there can be no essential "we" of a "common culture." Chicana feminists are calling into question the imperative to homogenize, particularly in mainstream feminist theory. Seeking ways to uncover multiplicity in theory is an equally challenging prospect in the classroom. The complexity of this theoretical and pedagogical project clearly underscores that merely changing the course lists is not enough.

Race, gender, and sexuality among other elements inform border consciousness and contribute to the problematic nature of a pedagogical project that attempts to expose the multiplicity of cultures. As mentioned above, to be conscious of the borderlands is to tolerate ambiguity since the search for homogeneity is frustrated in the border regions. Thus to change the lists is not sufficient. If the subjectivities of teacher and student are not questioned, exposed, integrated into the process of the classroom, then the "reading" or even "rereading" of texts will not make a qualitative difference. We must ask ourselves as feminists and as educators, "What is our objective in the classroom?" Is it to "expose" students to a new angle on Western culture or is it to transform their and our relationship to culture?

Central to understanding this point is acknowledging that the classroom is a politicized space. It has always been a politicized space because the systems of thought, as well as cultural and political hierarchies, are affirmed and denied there. In the classroom, authority and, as we all know, patriarchy are replicated. Do we carry on the traditions of those systems which we learned in the classrooms of our childhoods, colleges, and graduate schools? Do we avert this by merely reading Chicana, Native American, African American, or Asian American texts? Clearly, integrating these texts into the curriculum is a necessary first step, but it must be followed by redefining the classroom itself as a process externalizing the intersections of race, class, ethnicity, and gender that underlie all texts—as well as the text of the classroom itself.

Adrienne Rich has written about the various manifestations of the "culture of passivity." We internalize and perpetuate old systems by not asking questions, by accepting a situation as if it were the natural order of things. And this applies to the "old" canon, as well as to the reconstruction of the "new" canon. If we do not account for our own subjectivity in the classroom, then we risk what Rich calls "passive collusion" in the process of accepting the world always according to someone else, whether that be Emerson, Thoreau, or Cherríe Moraga. As teachers in a classroom, either we can participate in a passive collusion with the culture of passivity or we can attempt to become agents of transformation and thus begin to forge an active culture that acknowledges the true catalytic power of difference.

The issue should not rest solely within our ability as teachers to effect this active culture. Students must also become agents in this transformation. Ernesto Cardenal, Nicaraguan poet and activist, used "exteriorization" as a core process in his poetry workshops that functioned as the building blocks of literacy in his country. The objective was not to interpret, not to embellish, but to make concrete the individual's experience; and words are the concrete vehicles for translating subjectivity to exteriorization. As N. Scott Momaday explains in *The Names* (1976), "had I known it, even then language bore all the names of my being." We need not replicate the model of the poetry workshop, but we do need to underscore the notion that the classroom, workshop if you will, can be a creative space in which students and teachers alike work through their subjectivity to achieve an externalization of the intersecting elements of race, class, ethnicity, and gender that define us all. In other words, the political nature of the classroom can be externalized in a process in which the nexus of race, class, and gender is questioned and activated. In this situation, the student is not just "informed," "taught," or "exposed"; rather, the class together *informs, teaches,* and *exposes.* The focus is on the process, not on the informational product.

This is not an easy task, as we all know. If a form of communitas (to borrow Victor Turner's term) is momentarily achieved within the communal space of the classroom, tensions also threaten to pull it apart. We have all experienced the resistance and denial that accompany the reading of all literature, especially culturally different, linguistically diverse texts. When we are attempting to divest the classroom of its authoritative structure and mode of analysis, who will mediate between clashing subjectivities? The answer is that all persons involved in the learning project will have to do so. As each participant is decentered in the class process, each in some fashion becomes an educator and a student. Each assumes an interactive role with the others. In this sense, we must work through this discomfort with texts and use that resistance to expose difference. Only in this way can we combat the silence that, unfortunately, we have all had to contend with in the traditional classrooms of our past and that falls over into the classrooms of our own making.

Richard Yarborough suggests that we use the notion of diverse "voices" that speak the multiplicity of cultures when we talk about texts. To this fruitful direction, I would add that the voices are not only those of the texts, but also those of the students, teachers, and other participants in the learning project. We cannot understand the difference in voice of a text without understanding our own voice and difference in relationship to it. By focusing on this type of conversation, the classroom can become a space in which a vibrant new discourse can qualitatively challenge the official dominant discourse of the canon. It is a conversation in which questions are asked, contradictions are exposed, and no solutions are reached. In order to teach the new canon, we must be able to live with contradiction, ambiguity, and nonclosure. Although frequently uncomfortable, the process is at the very least consciously active. By participating in this fluid space (the classroom) in which contradictions and conflict are played out, we can create an empathetic moment in which the classroom participants feel what it might be like to cross into the borderlands. Anzaldúa reminds us that the border is a transitional space in which differences are articulated and a "tolerance for ambiguity" is an operational mode. Yet this type of activity will strain everyone's tolerance for ambiguity.

I recently organized a seminar for college seniors called "Chicano Literature in a Cross-Cultural Perspective" that used Chicano literature and its formulation of the border as a paradigm for understanding other culturally diverse writing by African Americans, Asian Americans, Caribbean Islanders, and other Latinos. I began by studying three Chicano texts and analyzing their representation of the border. The final text in this initial unit was *Borderlands/ La Frontera* by Anzaldúa, a feminist, lesbian writer, and activist. The students' reactions to the first two texts, which were by male authors, were at times difficult since issues of race and cultural difference were not easy for them to address. The discussions of Chicano history, the reading of the texts, and finally the reference to contemporary issues produced uncomfortable responses, particularly from students of color. Indeed, Adrienne Rich correctly names the detrimental effects of never seeing yourself in the "mirror" of literature as a profound "disequilibrium." At the same time, internalized racial biases surfaced, and reluctant understanding of difference within racial communities was addressed more than prejudice within the dominant culture.

When Anzaldúa's text was read, however, all students (male and female, white/nonwhite) reacted swiftly and severely. Sexuality and issues of sexual orientation clearly elicit fear across the board, regardless of race or class. The discussions were painful and substantive, ranging from a critical assessment of Anzaldúa's aesthetics based on lesbianism to a reluctant review of homophobia within families and university classrooms. Issues such as "outing" and homophobic joking provoked uncomfortable, yet engaged discussion. The debate was heated. At one point, I asked the students to describe the kinds of emotions that had surfaced during the hour of critical dialogue. Once they had analyzed and chronicled their responses and engagement in the discussion, I addressed the main objective of the lesson: the discomfort they felt was analogous to experiencing the border. Their feelings of conflict, discomfort, excitement, moments of confusion and clarification, contradictions and solidarities placed them empathetically in the border zone. They were not expected to resolve either their feelings or the issues; but they had instead exposed their racial, gendered, and class selves in an active performance of difference.

One of the by-products of this class experience was a borrowing and lending across borders that occurred for a transient time. I would not characterize this process as "consciousness-raising" (a form of pedagogy of which, along with Henry Louis Gates, I have a deep suspicion). Consciousness-raising connotes a permanent transformation of consciousness. The illuminations I am seeking are at their best transient. They may appear for a brief time and then retreat. The classroom, like the border, is a transitory space. The transformation of culture is not secured; at best it can be activated. And this occurs through the reading of the texts under assignment and through the self-reflexive "reading" of the text of the class. I don't know whether a form of coalition building based on a knowledge of difference is reached at any given moment. Perhaps. I tend to think of each classroom experience as another layer drawn on the palimpsest of a student's education. With any luck, the residue of that layer will emerge at future times. Perhaps it is key to achieving what Cornel West has called "a prophetic framework of moral reasoning rather than a narrow framework of racial reasoning." Perhaps through a borrowing and lending across borders some sort of articulation of moral and civic culture will emerge that better reflects the enabling resources of our multiple differences. Yet it is not a comfortable place to be. Anzaldúa the poet puts it for us best: "This is my home/this thin edge of/ barbwire."

Like Anzaldúa's "edge of barbwire," our society and its future lie in jeopardy in the educational institutions of our nation. In order to survive, our classrooms must "be a crossroads." We must acknowledge that due to our racial, class, and gendered subjectivities we have all been caught in the implications of the "web of the border." It is a place of creative learning; it is the site of our survival. And it is clear that our ability to connect theory and pedagogy is critical to this survival.

REFERENCES

Anzaldúa, G. 1987. *Borderlands/La Frontera.* San Francisco: Aunt Lute Books.

Gates, H. L. Jr. 1992. *Loose Canons: Notes on the Culture Wars.* New York: Oxford University Press.

Gomez-Peña, G. 1988. "Documented/Undocumented." In *The Greywolf Annual Five: Multicultural Literacy.* ed. R. Simonson and S. Walker. pp. 127–134. Saint Paul: Graywolf Press.

Momaday, N. S. 1976. *The Names.* New York: Harper Colophon Books.

Saldivar, J. 1991. *The Dialectics of Our America: Geneology, Cultural Critique, and Literary History.* Durham, N.C.: Duke University Press.

Is the New Technology Part of the Solution or Part of the Problem in Education?

MICHAEL APPLE

So far, I have discussed two different kinds of texts: those produced for the many classrooms and lecture halls throughout our school system, and those produced for the consumption of parents, educators, and others as slogan systems to convince them of the need to change what education is for. These texts take a particular form. They are printed on paper and are bound as books. However, there is a different sort of text—among the most popular today—that must be considered if our analysis is to be complete. This is one that is plugged into an electrical outlet and is marketed by IBM, Apple (no, this company is not a relative of mine), and other large corporations. Technology as text and as transformer of the labor process of both students and teachers cannot be ignored, not only because so many of the national reports make recommendations directly sponsoring 'computer literacy,' but also because a considerable number of parents and educators believe that the computer will revolutionize the classroom and their children's chances of a better life. Will it?

THE POLITICS OF TECHNOLOGY

In our society, technology is seen as an autonomous process. It is set apart and viewed as if it had a life of its own, independent of social intentions, power, and privilege. We examine technology as if it were something constantly changing, and something that is constantly changing our lives in schools and elsewhere. This is partly true, of course, and is fine as far as it goes. However, by focusing on what is changing and being changed, we may neglect to ask what relationships are remaining the same. Among the most important of these are the sets of cultural and economic inequalities that dominate even societies like our own.[1]

By thinking of technology in this way, by closely examining whether the changes associated with "technological progress" are really changes in certain relationships after all, we can begin to ask political questions about their causes and especially their multitudinous effects. Whose idea of progress? Progress for what? And fundamentally, once again, who benefits?[2] These questions may seem rather weighty ones to be asking about schools and the curricular and teaching practices that now go on in them or are being proposed. Yet, we are in the midst of one of those many educational bandwagons that governments, industry, and others so like to ride. This wagon is pulled in the direction of a technological workplace, and carries a heavy load of computers as its cargo.

The growth of the new technology in schools is definitely not what one would call a slow movement. In one recent year, there was a 56 percent reported increase in the use of computers in schools in the United States, and even this may be a conservative estimate. Of the 25,642 schools surveyed, over 15,000 schools reported some computer usage.[3] In the United States alone, it is estimated that over 350,000 microcomputers have been introduced into the public schools in the past four years.[4] This is a trend that shows no sign of abating. Nor is this phenomenon only limited to the United States. France, Canada, England, Australia, and many other countries have "recognized the future." At its center seems to sit a machine with a keyboard and a screen.

I say "at its center" since both in industry and governmental agencies and in schools themselves the computer and the new technology have been seen as something of a savior economically and pedagogically. "High tech" will save declining economies and will save our students and teachers in schools. In the latter, it is truly remarkable how wide a path the computer is now cutting.

The expansion of its use, the tendency to see all areas of education as a unified terrain for growth in the use of new technologies, can be seen in a two-day workshop on integrating the microcomputer into the classroom held at my own university. Among the topics covered were computer applications in writing instruction, in music education, in secondary science and mathematics, in primary language arts, for the handicapped, for teacher record keeping and management, in business education, in health occupation training programs, in art, and in social studies. To this is added a series of sessions on the "electronic office," how technology and automation are helping industry, and how we all can "transcend the terror" of technology.[5]

Two things are evident from this list. First, vast areas of school life are now seen to be within the legitimate purview of technological restructuring. Second, there is a partly hidden but exceptionally close linkage between computers in schools and the needs of management for automated industries, electronic offices, and "skilled" personnel. Thus, recognizing both what is happening inside and outside of schools and the connections between these areas is critical to any understanding of what is likely to happen with the new technologies, especially the computer, in education.

As I have argued elsewhere, educational debates are increasingly limited to technical issues. Questions of "how to" have replaced questions of "why."[6] In this chapter, I shall want to reverse this tendency. Rather than dealing with what the best way might be to establish closer ties between the technological requirements of the larger society and our formal institutions of education, I want to step back and raise a different set of questions. I want us to consider a number of rather difficult political, economic, and ethical issues about some of the tendencies in schools and the larger society that may make us want to be very cautious about the current technological bandwagon in education. In so doing, a range of areas will need to be examined. Behind the slogans of technological progress and high-tech industry, what are some of the real effects of the new technology on the future labor market? What may happen to teaching and curriculum if we do not think carefully about the new technology's place in the classroom? Will the growing focus on technological expertise, particularly computer literacy, equalize or further exacerbate the lack of social opportunities for our most disadvantaged students?

At root, my claim will be that the debate about the role of the new technology in society and in schools is not and must not be just about the technical correctness of what computers can and cannot do. These may be the least important kinds of questions, in fact. Instead, at the very core of the debate, are the ideological and ethical issues concerning what schools should be about and whose interests they should serve.[7] The question of interests is very important at the moment since, because of the severe problems currently besetting economies like our own, a restructuring of what schools are *for* has reached a rather advanced stage.

Thus, while there has always been a relatively close connection between the two, as I demonstrated in the last chapter there is now an even closer relationship between the curriculum in our schools and corporate needs.[8] In a number of countries, educational officials and policy-makers, legislators, curriculum workers, and others have been subject to immense pressure to make the 'needs' of business and industry the primary goals of the school system. Economic and ideological pressures have become rather intense and often very overt. The language of efficiency, production, standards, cost-effectiveness, job skills, work discipline, and so on—all defined by powerful groups and always threatening to become the dominant way we think about schooling[9]—has begun to push aside concerns for a democratic curriculum, teacher autonomy, and class, gender, and race equality. Yet, we cannot fully understand the implications of the new technology in this restructuring unless we gain a more complete idea of what industry is now doing not only in the schools but in the economy as well.

TECHNOLOGICAL MYTHS AND ECONOMIC REALITIES

Let us look at the larger society first. It is claimed that the technological needs of the economy are such that unless we have a technologically literate labor force we will ultimately become outmoded economically. But what will this labor force actually look like?

A helpful way of thinking about this is once more to use the concepts of increasing *proletarianization* and *deskilling* of jobs. These concepts signify a complex historical process in which the control of labor has altered—one in which the skills workers have developed over many years are broken down and reduced to their atomistic units, automated, and redefined by management to enhance profit levels, efficiency, and control. In the process, the employee's control of timing, over defining the most appropriate way to do a task, and over criteria that establish acceptable performance, are slowly taken over as the prerogatives of management personnel who are usually divorced from the place where the actual labor is carried out. Loss of control by the worker is almost always the result. Pay is often lowered. And the job itself becomes routinized, boring, and alienating as conception is separated from execution and more and more aspects of jobs are rationalized to bring them into line with management's need for a tighter economic and ideological ship.[10] Finally, and very importantly, many of these jobs may simply disappear.

There is no doubt that the rapid developments in, say, micro-electronics, genetic engineering, and associated "biological technologies," and other high-tech areas, are in fact partly transforming work in a large number of sectors in the economy. This may lead to economic prosperity in certain sections of our population, but its other effects may be devastating. Thus, as the authors of a recent study that examined the impact of new technologies on the future labor market demonstrate:

> This transformation . . . may stimulate economic growth and competition in the world marketplace, but it will displace thousands of workers and could sustain high unemployment for many years. It may provide increased job opportunities for engineers, computer operators, and robot technicians, but it also promises to generate an even greater number of low level, service jobs such as those of janitors, cashiers, clericals, and food service workers. And while many more workers will be using computers, automated office equipment, and other sophisticated technical devices in their jobs, the increased use of technology may actually reduce the skills and discretion required to perform many jobs.[11]

This scenario requires further elaboration.

Rumberger and Levin make a distinction that is very useful to this discussion. They differentiate between high-tech industries and high-tech occupations—in essence between what is made and the kinds of jobs these goods require. High-tech industries that manufacture technical devices such as computers, electronic components, and the like currently employ less than 15 percent of the paid workforce in the United States and other industrialized nations. Just as importantly, a substantial knowledge of technology is required by *less than one-fourth* of all occupations within these industries. On the contrary, the largest share of jobs created by high-tech industries are in areas such as clerical and office work or in production and assembly. These actually pay below average wages.[12] Yet this is not all. High-tech occupations that do require considerable skill—such as computer specialists and engineers—may indeed expand. However, most of these occupations actually "employ relatively few workers compared to many traditional clerical and service fields."[13] Rumberger and Levin summarize a number of these points by stating that "although the percentage growth rate of occupational employment in such high technology fields as engineering and computer programming was higher than the overall growth rate of jobs, far more jobs would be created in low-skilled clerical and service occupations than in high technology ones."[14]

Some of these claims are supported by the following data. It is estimated that even being generous in one's projections, only 17 percent of new jobs that will be created between now and 1995 will be in high-tech industries. (Less generous and more restrictive projections argue that only 3 to 8 percent of future jobs will be in such industries.)[15] As I noted, though, such jobs will not be all equal. Clerical workers, secretaries, assemblers, warehouse personnel, etc.—these will be the largest occupations within the industry. If we take the electronic components industry as an example here, this is made much clearer. Engineering, science, and computing occupations constituted approximately 15 percent of all workers in this industry. The majority of the rest of the workers were engaged in low-wage assembly work. Thus, in the late 1970s, nearly two-thirds of all workers in the electronic components industry took home hourly wages "that placed them in the bottom third of the national distribution."[16] If we take the archetypical high-tech industry—computers and data processing—and decompose its labor market, we get similar results. In 1980, technologically oriented and skilled jobs accounted for only 26 percent of the total.[17]

These figures have considerable weight, but they are made even more significant by the fact that many of that 26 percent may themselves experience a deskilling process in the near future. That is, the reduction of jobs down into simpler and atomistic components, the separation of conception from execution, and so on—processes that have had such a major impact on the labor process of blue-, pink-, and white-collar workers in so many other areas—are now advancing into high-technology jobs as well. Computer programming provides an excellent example. New developments in software packages and machine language and design have meant that a considerable portion of the job of programming now requires little more than performing "standard, routine, machine-like tasks that require little in-depth knowledge."[18]

What does this mean for the schooling process and the seemingly widespread belief that the future world of work will require increasing technical competence on the part of all students? Consider the occupations that will contribute the most number of jobs not just in high-tech industries but throughout the society by 1995. Economic forecasts indicate that these will include building custodians, cashiers, secretaries, office clerks, nurses, waiters and waitresses, elementary school teachers, truck drivers, and other health workers such as nurses' aides and orderlies.[19] None of these are directly related to high technology. Excluding teachers and nurses, none of them require any postsecondary education. (Their earnings will be approximately 30 percent below the current average earnings of workers, as well.)[20] If we go further than this and examine an even larger segment of expected new jobs by including the forty job categories that will probably account for about half of all the jobs that will be created, it is estimated that only about 25 percent will require people with a college degree.[21]

In many ways, this is strongly related to the effects of the new technology on the job market and the labor process in general. Skill levels will be raised in some areas, but will decline in many others, as will jobs themselves decline. For instance, "a recent study of robotics in the United States suggests that robots will eliminate 100,000 to 200,000 jobs by 1990, while creating 32,000 to 64,000 jobs."[22] My point about declining skill requirements is made nicely by Rumberger and Levin. As they suggest, while it is usually assumed that workers will need computer programming and other sophisticated skills because of the greater use of technology such as computers in their jobs, the ultimate effect of such technology may be somewhat different. "A variety of evidence suggests just the opposite: as machines become more sophisticated, with expanded memories, more computational ability, and sensory capabilities, the knowledge required to use the devices declines."[23] The effect of these trends on the division of labor will be felt for decades. But it will be in the sexual division of labor that it will be even more extreme. As I argued, since historically *women's work* has been subject to these processes in very powerful ways, we shall see increased proletarianization and deskilling of women's labor and, undoubtedly, a further increase in the feminization of poverty.[24]

These points clearly have implications for our educational programs. We need to think much more rigorously about what they mean for our transition from school to work programs, especially since many of the "skills" that schools are currently teaching are transitory because the jobs themselves are being transformed (or lost) by new technological developments and new management offensives.

Take office work, for example. In offices, the bulk of the new technology has not been designed to enhance the quality of the job for the largest portion of the employees (usually women clerical workers). Rather it has usually been designed and implemented in such a way that exactly the opposite will result. Instead of accommodating stimulating and satisfying work, the technology is there to make managers' jobs "easier," to eliminate jobs and cut costs, to divide work into routine and atomized tasks, and to make administrative control more easily accomplished.[25] The vision of the future society seen in the microcosm of the office is inherently undemocratic and perhaps increasingly authoritarian. Is this what we wish to prepare our students for? Surely, our task as educators is neither to accept such a future labor market and labor process uncritically nor to have our students accept such practices uncritically either. To do so is simply to allow the values of a limited but powerful segment of the population to work through us. It may be good business but I have my doubts about whether it is ethically correct educational policy.

In summary, then, what we will witness is the creation of enhanced jobs for a relative minority and deskilled and boring work for the majority. Furthermore, even those boring and deskilled jobs will be increasingly hard to find. Take office work again, an area that is rapidly being transformed by the new technology. It is estimated that between one and five jobs will be lost for every new computer terminal that is introduced.[26] Yet this situation will not be limited to office work. Even those low-paying assembly positions noted earlier will not necessarily be found in the industrialized nations with their increasingly service-oriented economies. Given the international division of labor, and what is called "capital flight," a large portion of these jobs will be moved to countries such as Korea, the Philippines and Indonesia.[27]

This is exacerbated considerably by the fact that many governments now find "acceptable" those levels of unemployment that would have been considered a crisis a decade ago. "Full employment" in the United States is now often seen as between 7 and 8 percent *measured* unemployment. (The actual figures are much higher, of course, especially among minority groups and workers who can only get part-time jobs or who have given up looking for paid work after so many disappointments.) This is a figure that is *double* that of previous economic periods. Even higher rates are now seen as "normal" in other countries. The trend is clear. The future will see fewer jobs. Most of those that are created will not necessarily be fulfilling, nor will they pay well. Finally, the level of technical skill will continue to be lowered for a large portion of them.[28]

Because of this, we need convincing answers to some very important questions about our future society and the economy before we turn our schools into "production plants" for creating new workers. *Where* will these new jobs be? *How many* will be created? Will they *equal* the number of positions lost in offices and factories, and service jobs in retailing, banks, telecommunications, and elsewhere? Are the bulk of the jobs that will be created relatively unskilled, less than meaningful, and themselves subject to the "inexorable" logics of management so that they too will be likely to be automated out of existence?[29]

These are not inconsequential questions. Before we give the schools over to the requirements of the new technology and the corporation, we must be very certain that it will benefit all of us, not primarily those who already possess economic and cultural power. This requires continued democratic discussion, not a quick decision based on the economic and political pressure now being placed on schools.

Much more could be said about the future labor market. I urge the interested reader to pursue it in greater depth, since it will have a profound impact on our school policies and programs, especially in vocational areas, in working-class schools, and among programs for young women. The difficulties with the high-tech vision that permeates the beliefs of the proponents of a technological solution will not remain outside the school door, however. Similar disproportionate benefits and dangers await us inside our educational institutions as well, and it is to this that we now turn.

INEQUALITY AND THE TECHNOLOGICAL CLASSROOM

Once we go inside the school, a set of questions concerning "who benefits?" also arises. We shall need to ask about what may be happening to teachers and students given the emphasis now being placed on computers in schools. I shall not talk about the individual teacher or student here. Obviously, some teachers will find their jobs enriched by the new technology and some students will find hidden talents and will excel in a computer-oriented classroom. What we need to ask instead (or at least before we deal with the individual) is what may happen to classrooms, teachers, and students differentially. Once again, I shall seek to raise a set of issues that may not be easy to solve, but cannot be ignored if we are to have a truly democratic educational system not just in name only.

Though I have dealt with this in greater detail in *Ideology and Curriculum* and *Education and Power,*[30] let me briefly situate the growth of the technologized classroom into what seems to be occurring to teaching and curriculum in general. Currently, considerable pressure is building to have teaching and school curricula be totally prespecified and tightly controlled for the purposes of "efficiency," "cost effectiveness," and "accountability." In many ways, the deskilling that is affecting jobs in general is now having an impact on teachers as more and more decisions are moving out of their hands and as their jobs become even more difficult to do. This process is more advanced in some countries than others, but it is clear that the movement to rationalize and control the act of teaching and the content and evaluation of the curriculum is very real.[31] Even in those countries that have made strides away from centralized examination systems, powerful inspectorates and supervisors, and tightly controlled curricula, there is an identifiable tendency to move back toward state control. Many reforms have only a very tenuous hold at the present time. This is in part due to economic difficulties and partly due as well to the importing of American styles and techniques of educational management—styles and techniques that have their roots in industrial bureaucracies and have almost never had democratic aims.[32] Even though a number of teachers may support computer-oriented curricula, an emphasis on the new technology needs to be seen in this context of the rationalization of teaching and curricula in general.

Given these pressures, what will happen to teachers if the new technology is accepted uncritically? One of the major effects of the current (over) emphasis on computers in the classroom may again be the deskilling and depowering of a considerable number of teachers. Given the already heavy workload of planning, teaching, meetings, and paperwork for most teachers, and given the expense, it is probably wise to assume that the largest portion of teachers will not be given more than a very small amount of training in computers, their social effects, programming, and so on. This will be especially the case at the primary and elementary school level, where most teachers are already teaching a wide array of subject areas. Research indicates in fact that few teachers in any district are actually given substantial information before computer curricula are implemented. Often only one or two teachers are the "resident experts."[33] Because of this, most teachers have to rely on pre-packaged sets of material, existing software, and specially purchased material from any of the scores of software manufacturing firms that are springing up in a largely unregulated way. This will be heightened by the contradictory sense of professionalism and technical expertise many teachers already have.

The impact of this can be striking. What is happening is the exacerbation of trends we have begun to see in a number of nations. Instead of teachers having the time and the skill to do their own curriculum planning and deliberation, they become isolated executors of someone else's plans, procedures, and evaluative mechanisms. In industrial terms, this is very close to what I noted in my previous discussion of the labor process—the separation of conception from execution.[34]

The reliance on pre-packaged software can have a number of long-term effects. First, it can cause a decided loss of important skills and dispositions on the part of teachers. When the skills of local curriculum planning, individual evaluation, and so on are not used, they atrophy. The tendency to look outside of one's own or one's colleagues' historical experience about curriculum and teaching is lessened as considerably more of the curriculum, and the teaching and evaluative practices that surround it, is viewed as something one purchases. In the process—and this is very important—the school itself is transformed into a lucrative market. The industrialization of the school I talked of previously is complemented, then, by further opening up the classroom to the mass-produced commodities of industry. The technological "text" joins the existing textbook in the political economy of commodified culture. And once again, financial capital will dominate. In many ways, it will be a publisher's and salesperson's delight. Whether students' educational experiences will markedly improve is open to question.

The issue of the relationship of purchased software and hardware to the possible deskilling and depowering of teachers does not end here, though. The problem is made even more difficult by the rapidity with which software developers have constructed and marketed their products. There is no guarantee that the mass of such material has any major educational value. Exactly the opposite is often the case. One of the most knowledgeable government officials has put it this way: "High quality educational software is almost non-existent in our elementary and secondary schools."[35] While perhaps overstating his case to emphasize his points, the director of software evaluation for one of the largest school systems in the United States has concluded that of the more than 10,000 programs currently available, approximately 200 are educationally significant.[36]

To their credit, the fact that this is a serious problem is recognized by most computer enthusiasts, and reviews and journals have attempted to deal with it. However, the sheer volume of material, the massive amounts of money spent on advertising software in professional publications, at teachers' and administrators' meetings, and so on, the utter "puffery" of the claims made about much of this material, and the constant pressure by industry, government, parents, some school personnel, and others to institute computer programs in schools *immediately*—all of this makes it nearly impossible to do more than make a small dent in the problem. As one educator put it, "There's a lot of junk out there."[37] The situation is not made any easier by the fact that teachers simply do not now have the time to thoroughly evaluate the educational strengths and weaknesses of a considerable portion of the *existing* curricular material and texts before they are used. Adding one more element, and a sizable one at that, to be evaluated only increases the load. Teachers' work is increasingly becoming what students of the labor process call *intensified.* More and more needs to be done; less and less time is available to do it.[38] Thus, one has little choice but to buy readymade material, in this way continuing a trend in which all of the important curricular elements are not locally produced but purchased from commercial sources whose major aim may be profit, not necessarily educational merit.[39]

A significant consideration here, besides the loss of skill and control, is expense. This is at least a three-pronged issue. First, we must recognize that we may be dealing with something of a "zero-sum game." While dropping, the cost of computers is still comparatively high, though some manufacturers may keep purchase costs relatively low, knowing that a good deal of their profits may come from the purchase of software later on or through a home-school connection, something I shall discuss shortly. This money for the new technology *must come from somewhere.* This is an obvious point, but one that is very consequential. In a time of fiscal crisis, where funds are already spread too thinly and necessary programs are being starved in many areas, the addition of computer curricula most often means that money must be drained from one area and given to another. What will be sacrificed? If history is any indication, it may be programs that have benefited the least advantaged. Little serious attention has been paid to this, but it will become an increasingly serious dilemma.

A second issue of expense concerns staffing patterns, for it is not just the content of teachers' work and the growth of purchased materials that are at stake. Teachers' jobs themselves are on the line here. At a secondary school level in many nations, for example, layoffs of teachers have not been unusual as funding for education is cut. Declining enrollment in some regions has meant a loss of positions as well. This has caused intense competition over students within the school itself. Social studies, art, music, and other subjects must fight it out with newer, more "glamorous" subject areas. To lose the student numbers game for too long is to lose a job. The effect of the computer in this situation has been to increase competitiveness among staff, often to replace substance with both gloss and attractive packaging of courses, and to threaten many teachers with the loss of their livelihood.[40] Is it really an educationally or socially wise decision to tacitly eliminate a good deal of the choices in these other fields so that we can support the "glamor" of a computer future? These are not only financial decisions, but are ethical decisions about teachers' lives and about what our students are to be educated in. Given the future labor market, do we really want to claim that computers will be more important than further work in humanities and social sciences or, perhaps even more significantly in working-class and ethnically diverse areas, in the students' own cultural, historical, and political heritage and struggles? Such decisions must not be made by only looking at the accountant's bottom line. These too need to be arrived at by the lengthy democratic deliberation of all parties, including the teachers who will be most affected.

Third, given the expense of microcomputers and software in schools, the pressure to introduce such technology may increase the already wide social imbalances that now exist. Private schools to which the affluent send their children and publicly funded schools in more affluent areas will have more ready access to the technology itself.[41] Schools in inner-city, rural, and poor areas will be largely priced out of the market, even if the cost of "hardware" continues to decline. After all, in these poorer areas, and in many public school systems in general in a number of countries, it is already difficult to generate enough money to purchase new textbooks and to cover the costs of teachers' salaries. Thus, the computer and literacy over it will "naturally" generate further inequalities. Since, by and large, it will be the top 20 percent of the population who will have computers in their homes[42] and many of the jobs and institutions of higher education their children will be applying for will either ask for or assume "computer skills" as keys of entry or advancement, the impact can be enormous in the long run.

The role of the relatively affluent parent in this situation does not go unrecognized by computer manufacturers.

> Computer companies . . . gear much of their advertising to the educational possibilities of computers. The drive to link particular computers to schools is a frantic competition. Apple, for example, in a highly touted scheme proposed to 'donate' an Apple to every school in America. Issues of philanthropy and intent aside, the clear market strategy is to couple particular computer usages to schools where parents—especially middle class parents with the economic wherewithal and keen motivation [to insure mobility]—purchase machines compatible with those in schools. The potentially most lucrative part of such a scheme, however, is not in the purchase of hardware (although this is also substantial) but in the sale of proprietary software.[43]

This very coupling of school and home markets, then, cannot fail to further disadvantage large groups of students. Those students who already have computer backgrounds—be it because of their schools or their homes or both—will proceed more rapidly. The social stratification of life chances will increase. These students' original advantage—one *not* due to "natural ability," but to *wealth*—will be heightened.[44]

We should not be surprised by this, nor should we think it odd that many parents, especially middle-class parents, will pursue a computer future. The knowledge itself is part of the technical-administrative "cultural capital" of the new middle class. Computer skills and "literacy," however, is partly a strategy for the maintenance of middle-class mobility patterns.[45] Having such expertise, in a time of fiscal and economic crisis, is like having an insurance policy. It partly guarantees that certain doors remain open in a rapidly changing labor market. In a time of credential inflation, more credentials mean fewer closed doors.[46] (This also works within the school. Some teachers will support computerization because it offers a real sense of competence and control that may be missing in their jobs now and perhaps because it offers paths to upward mobility within the school bureaucracy as well.)

The credential factor here is of considerable moment. In the past, as gains were made by ethnically different people, working-class groups, women, and others in schooling, one of the latent effects was to raise the credentials required by entire sectors of jobs. Thus, class, race, and gender barriers were partly maintained by an ever-increasing credential inflation. Though this was more of a structural than a conscious process, the effect over time has often been to again disqualify entire segments of a population from jobs, resources and power. This too may be a latent outcome of the computerization of the school curriculum. Even though, as I have shown, the bulk of new jobs will not require "computer literacy," the establishment of computer requirements and mandated programs in schools will condemn many people to even greater economic disenfranchisement. Since the requirements are in many ways artificial— computer knowledge will not be so very necessary and the number of jobs requiring high levels of expertise will be relatively small—we will simply be affixing one more label to these students. "Functional illiteracy" will simply be broadened to include computers.[47]

Thus, rather than blaming an unequal economy and a situation in which meaningful and fulfilling work is not made available, rather than seeing how the new technology for all its benefits is "creating a growing underclass of displaced and marginal workers," the lack is personalized. It becomes the students' or workers' fault for not being computer literate. One significant social and ideological outcome of computer requirements in schools, then, is that they can serve as a means "to justify those lost lives by a process of mass disqualification, which throws the blame for disenfranchisement in education and employment back on the victims themselves."[48]

Of course, this process may not be visible to many parents of individual children. However, the point does not revolve around the question of individual mobility, but around large-scale effects. Parents may see such programs as offering important paths to advancement and some will be correct. However, in a time of severe economic problems, parents tend to overestimate what schools can do for their children.[49] As I documented earlier, there simply will not be sufficient jobs, and competition will be intense. The uncritical introduction of and investment in hardware and software will by and large hide the reality of the transformation of the labor market and will support those who are already advantaged unless thought is given to these implications now.

Let us suppose, however, that it was important that everyone become computer literate and that these large investments in time, money, and personnel were indeed so necessary for our economic and educational future. Given all this, what is currently happening in schools? Is inequality in access and outcome now being produced? While many educators are continually struggling against these effects, we are already seeing signs of this disadvantagement being created.

There is evidence of class-, race-, and gender-based differences in computer use. In middle-class schools, for example, the number of computers is considerably more than in working-class or inner-city schools populated by children of color. The ratio of computers to children is also much higher. This in itself is an unfortunate finding. However, something else must be added here. These more economically advantaged schools not only have more contact hours and more technical and teacher support, but the very manner in which the computer is used is often different from what would be generally found in schools in less advantaged areas. Programming skills, generalizability, a sense of the multitudinous things one can do with computers both within and across aca-

demic areas—these tend to be stressed more[50] (though simply drill and practice uses are still widespread even here).[51] Compare this to the rote, mechanistic, and relatively low-level uses that tend to dominate the working-class
school.[52] These differences are not unimportant, for they signify a ratification
of class divisions.

Further evidence to support these claims is now becoming more readily
available as researchers dig beneath the glowing claims of a computer future
for all children. The differential impact is made clearer in the following figures.
In the United States, while over two-thirds of the schools in affluent areas have
computers, only approximately 41 percent of the poorer public schools have
them. What one does with the machine is just as important as having one, of
course, and here the differences are again very real. One study of poorer elementary schools found that white children were four times more likely than
black children to use computers for programming. Another found that the
children of professionals employed computers for programming and for other
"creative" uses. Non-professional children were more apt to use them for drill
and practice in mathematics and reading, and for "vocational" work. In general, in fact, "programming has been seen as the purview of the gifted and tal-
ented" and of those students who are more affluent. Less affluent students seem
to find that the computer is only a tool for drill and practice sessions.[53]

Gender differences are also very visible. Two out of every three students
currently learning about computers are boys. Even here these data are deceptive, since girls "tend to be clustered in the general introductory courses," not
the advanced level ones.[54] One current analyst summarizes the situation in a
very clear manner:

> While stories abound about students who will do just about anything to
> increase their access to computers, most youngsters working with school com-
> puters are [economically advantaged], white and male. The evergrowing num-
> ber of private computer camps, after-school and weekend programs serve
> middle class white boys. Most minority [and poor] parents just can't afford to
> send their children to participate in these programs.[55]

This class, race, and gendered impact will also occur because of traditional
school practices such as tracking or streaming. Thus, vocational and business
tracks will learn operating skills for word processing and will be primarily filled
with (working-class) young women.[56] Academic tracks will stress more general
programming abilities and uses and will be disproportionately male.[57] Since
computer programs usually have their home bases in mathematics and science
in most schools, gender differences can be heightened even more given the
often differential treatment of girls in these classes and the ways in which mathematics and science curricula already fulfill "the selective function of the school
and contribute to the reproduction of gender differences."[58] While many
teachers and curriculum workers have devoted considerable time and effort to

equalizing both the opportunities and outcomes of female students in mathematics and science (and such efforts are important), the problem still remains a substantive one. It can be worsened by the computerization of these subjects.

TOWARD SOCIAL LITERACY

We have seen some of the possible negative consequences of the new technology in education, including the deskilling and depowering of teachers and the creation of inequalities through expense, credential inflation, and limitations on access. Yet it is important to realize that the issues surrounding the deskilling process are not limited to teachers. They include the very ways students themselves are taught to think about their education, their future roles in society, and the place of technology in that society. Let me explain what I mean by this.

The new technology is not just an assemblage of machines and their accompanying software. It embodies a *form of thinking* that orients a person to approach the world in a particular way. Computers involve ways of thinking that are primarily *technical*.[59] The more the new technology transforms the classroom in its own image, the more a technical logic will replace critical political and ethical understanding. The discourse of the classroom will center on technique, and less on substance. Once again "how to" will replace "why," but this time at the level of the student. This situation requires what I shall call social, not technical, literacy for all students.

Even if computers make sense technically in all curricular areas and even if all students, not mainly affluent white males, become technically proficient in their use, critical questions of politics and ethics remain to be dealt with in the curriculum. Thus, it is crucial that whenever the new technology is introduced into schools, students have a serious understanding of the issues surrounding their larger social effects, many of which I raised earlier.

Unfortunately, this is not often the case. When the social and ethical impacts of computers are dealt with, they are usually addressed in a manner that is less than powerful. One example is provided by a recent proposal for a statewide computer curriculum in one of the larger states in the United States. The objectives that dealt with social questions in the curriculum centered around one particular set of issues. The curriculum states that "the student will be aware of some of the major uses of computers in modern society . . . and the student will be aware of career opportunities related to computers."[60] In most curricula the technical components of the new technology are stressed. Brief glances are given to the history of computers (occasionally mentioning the role of women in their development, which is at least one positive sign). Yet in this history, the close relationship between military use and computer development is largely absent. "Benign" uses are pointed to, coupled with a less than realistic description of the content and possibility of computer careers and what Douglas Noble has called "a gee-whiz glance at the marvels of the future." What is almost never mentioned is job loss or social disenfranchisement. The very real destruction of the lives of unemployed autoworkers, assemblers or clerical work-ers is marginalized.[61] The political, economic, and ethical dilemmas involved when we choose between, say, "efficiency" and the quality of the work people experience, between profit and someone's job—these too are made invisible.

How would we counterbalance this? By making it clear from the outset that knowledge about the new technology that it is necessary for students to have goes well beyond what we now too easily take for granted. A considerable portion of the curriculum would be organized around questions concerned with social literacy: "Where are computers used? What are they used to do? What do people *actually* need to know in order to use them? Does the com-puter enhance anyone's life? Whose? Does it hurt anyone's life? Whose? Who decides when and where computers will be used?"[62] Unless these are *fully* inte-grated in a school program at *all* levels, I would hesitate to advocate the use of the new technology in the curriculum. To do less makes it much more diffi-cult for students to think critically and independently about the place the new technology does and should have in the lives of the majority of people in our society. Our job as educators involves skilling, not deskilling. Unless students are able to deal honestly and critically with these complex ethical and social issues, only those now with the power to control technology's uses will have the capacity to act. We cannot afford to let this happen.

CONCLUSION

I realize that a number of my points in this chapter may prove to be rather con-tentious. But stressing the negative side can serve to highlight many of the crit-ical issues that are too easy to put off given the immense amount of work that school personnel are already responsible for. Decisions often get made too quickly, only to be regretted later on when forces are set in motion that could have been avoided if the implications of one's actions had been thought through more fully.

As I noted at the outset of this discussion, there is now something of a mad scramble to employ the computer in every content area. In fact, it is nearly impossible to find a subject that is not being "computerized." Though math-ematics and science (and some parts of vocational education) remain the home base for a large portion of proposed computer curricula, other areas are not far behind. If it can be packaged to fit computerized instruction, it will be, even if this is inappropriate, less effective than the methods that teachers have devel-oped after years of hard practical work, or it will be less than sound educa-tionally or economically. Rather than the machine fitting the educational needs and visions of the teacher, students, and community, all too often these needs and visions are made to fit the technology itself.

Yet, as I have shown, the new technology does not stand alone. It is linked to transformations in real groups of people's lives, jobs, hopes, and dreams. For some of these groups, their lives will be enhanced. For others, their dreams will be shattered. Wise choices about the appropriate place of the new technology in education, then, are not only educational decisions. They are fundamentally choices about the kind of society we shall have, about the social and ethical responsiveness of our institutions to the majority of our future citizens. Here educators can be guided by the critical positions on the introduction and use of the new technology that have been taken by some of the more progressive unions in a number of countries.

My discussion here has not been aimed at making us all neo-Luddites, people who go out and smash the machines that threaten our jobs or our children. The new technology is here. It will not go away. Our task as educators is to make sure that when it enters the classroom it is there for politically, economically, and educationally wise reasons, not because powerful groups may be redefining our major educational goals in their own image. We should be very clear about whether or not the future it promises our students is real, not fictitious. We need to be certain that it is a future *all* of our students can share in, not just a select few. After all, the new technology is expensive and will take up a good deal of our time and that of our teachers, administrators, and students. It is more than a little important that we question whether the wagon we have been asked to ride on is going in the right direction. It's a long walk back.

NOTES

1. David Noble, *Forces of Production: A Social History of Industrial Automation* (New York: Alfred A. Knopf, 1984), pp. xi–xii. For a more general argument about the relationship between technology and human progress, see Nicholas Rescher, *Unpopular Essays on Technological Progress* (Pittsburgh: University of Pittsburgh Press, 1980).
2. Noble, *Forces of Production,* p. xv.
3. Paul Olson, "Who Computes? The Politics of Literacy," unpublished paper, Ontario Institute for Studies in Education, Toronto, 1985, p. 6.
4. Patricia B. Campbell, "The Computer Revolution: Guess Who's Left Out?" *Interracial Books for Children Bulletin* 15 (No. 3, 1984), 3.
5. "Instructional Strategies for Integrating the Microcomputer into the Classroom," The Vocational Studies Center, University of Wisconsin, Madison, 1985.
6. Michael W. Apple, *Ideology and Curriculum* (Boston and London: Routledge & Kegan Paul, 1979).
7. Olson, "Who Computes?" p. 5.
8. See Michael W. Apple, *Education and Power* (Boston and London: Routledge & Kegan Paul, 1982).
9. For further discussion of this, see Apple, *Ideology and Curriculum,* Apple, *Education and Power,* and Ira Shor, *Culture Wars* (Boston and London: Routledge & Kegan Paul, 1986).
10. This is treated in greater detail in Richard Edwards, *Contested Terrain* (New York: Basic Books, 1979). See also the more extensive discussion of the effect these tendencies are having in education in Apple, *Education and Power.*
11. Russell W. Rumberger and Henry M. Levin, "Forecasting the Impact of New Technologies on the Future Job Market," Project Report No. 84-A4, Institute for Research on Educational Finance and Government, School of Education, Stanford University, February, 1984, p. 1.
12. *Ibid.,* p. 2.
13. *Ibid.,* p. 3.
14. *Ibid.,* p. 4.
15. *Ibid.,* p. 18
16. *Ibid.*
17. *Ibid.,* p. 19.
18. *Ibid.,* pp. 19–20.

19. *Ibid.,* p. 31.
20. *Ibid.,* p. 21.
21. *Ibid.*
22. *Ibid.,* p. 25.
23. *Ibid.*
24. On the history of women's struggles against proletarianization, see Alice Kessler-Harris, *Out to Work* (New York: Oxford University Press, 1982).
25. Ian Reinecke, *Electronic Illusions* (New York: Penguin Books, 1984), p. 156.
26. See the further discussion of the loss of office jobs and the deskilling of many of those that remain in *ibid.,* pp. 136–58. The very same process could be a threat to middle- and low-level management positions as well. After all, if control is further automated, why does one need as many supervisory positions? The implications of this latter point need to be given much more consideration by many middle-class proponents of technology since their jobs may soon be at risk too.
27. Peter Dwyer, Bruce Wilson, and Roger Woock, *Confronting School and Work* (Boston and London: George Allen & Unwin, 1984), pp. 105–6.
28. The paradigm case is given by the fact that, as I mentioned in the previous chapter, three times as many people now work in low-paying positions for McDonald's as for U.S. Steel. See Martin Carnoy, Derek Shearer, and Russell Rumberger, *A New Social Contract* (New York: Harper & Row, 1983), p. 71. As I have argued at greater length elsewhere, however, it may not be important to our economy if all students and workers are made technically knowledgeable by schools. What is just as important is the production of economically useful knowledge (technical/administrative knowledge) that can be used by corporations to enhance profits, control labor, and increase efficiency. See Apple, *Education and Power,* especially chapter 2.
29. Reinecke, *Electronic Illusions,* p. 234. For further analysis of the economic data and the effects on education, see W. Norton Grubb, "The Bandwagon Once More: Vocational Preparation for High-Tech Occupations," *Harvard Educational Review* 54 (November 1984), 429–51.
30. Apple, *Ideology and Curriculum,* and Apple, *Education and Power.* See also Michael W. Apple and Lois Weis (eds.), *Ideology and Practice in Schooling* (Philadelphia: Temple University Press, 1983).
31. Apple, *Ideology and Curriculum*; Apple, *Education and Power*; Apple and Weis (eds.), *Ideology and Practice in Schooling.* See also Arthur Wise, *Legislated Learning: The Bureaucratization of the American Classroom* (Berkeley: University of California Press, 1979).
32. Apple, *Ideology and Curriculum,* and Apple, *Education and Power.* On the general history of the growth of management techniques, see Richard Edwards, *Contested Terrain.*
33. Douglas Noble, "The Underside of Computer Literacy," *Raritan* 3 (Spring 1984), 45.
34. See the discussion of this in Apple, *Education and Power,* especially chapter 5.
35. Douglas Noble, "Jumping Off the Computer Bandwagon," *Education Week,* October 3, 1984, 24.
36. *Ibid.*
37. *Ibid.* See also, Noble, "The Underside of Computer Literacy," 45.
38. For further general discussion of the intensification and transformation of other kinds of work, see Robert Thomas, "Citizenship and Gender in Work Organization: Some Considerations for Theories of the Labor Process," in Michael Burawoy and Theda Skocpol (eds.), *Marxist Inquiries: Studies of Labor, Class, and States* (Chicago: University of Chicago Press, 1982), pp. 86–112.
39. Apple, *Education and Power.* For further analysis of the textbook publishing industry, see Michael W. Apple, "Curriculum Conflict in the United States," in Anthony Hartnett and Michael Naish (eds.), *Education and Society Today* (Barcombe, Sussex: Falmer Press, in press).
40. I am endebted to Susan Jungck for this point. See her excellent dissertation, "Doing Computer Literacy," unpublished Ph.D. dissertation, University of Wisconsin, Madison, 1985.
41. Reinecke, *Electronic Illusions,* p. 176.
42. *Ibid.,* p. 169.
43. Olson, "Who Computes?" p. 23.
44. *Ibid.,* p. 31. Thus, students' familiarity and comfort with computers becomes a form of what has been called the "cultural capital" of advantaged groups. For further analysis of the dynamics of cultural capital, see Apple, *Education and Power,* and Pierre Bourdieu and Jean-Claude Passeron, *Reproduction in Education, Society and Culture* (Beverly Hills: Sage, 1977).
45. Olson, "Who Computes?" p. 23. See also the discussion of interclass competition over academic qualifications in Pierre Bourdieu, *Distinction: A Social Critique of the Judgement of Taste* (Cambridge, Mass.: Harvard University Press, 1984), pp. 133–68.

46. Once again, I am endebted to Susan Jungck for this argument.

47. Noble, "The Underside of Computer Literacy," 54.

48. Douglas Noble, "Computer Literacy and Ideology," *Teachers College Record* 85 (Summer 1984), 611. This process of "blaming the victim" has a long history in education. See Apple, *Ideology and Curriculum,* especially chapter 7.

49. R. W. Connell, *Teachers' Work* (Boston and London: George Allen & Unwin, 1985), p. 142.

50. Olson, "Who Computes?" p. 22.

51. For an analysis of the emphasis on and pedagogic problems with such limited uses of computers, see Michael J. Streibel, "A Critical Analysis of the Use of Computers in Education," unpublished paper, Department of Curriculum and Instruction, University of Wisconsin, Madison, 1984.

52. Olson, "Who Computes?" p. 22.

53. Campbell, "The Computer Revolution: Guess Who's Left Out?" Many computer experts, however, are highly critical of the fact that students are primarily taught to program in BASIC, a less than appropriate language for later advanced computer work. Michael Streibel, personal communication.

54. Campbell, "The Computer Revolution."

55. *Ibid.*

56. An interesting analysis of what happens to young women in such business programs and how they respond to both the curricula and their later work experiences can be found in Linda Valli, "Becoming Clerical Workers: Business Education and the Culture of Femininity," in Apple and Weis (eds.), *Ideology and Practice in Schooling,* pp. 213–34. See also her more extensive treatment in Linda Valli, *Becoming Clerical Workers* (Boston and London: Routledge & Kegan Paul, 1986).

57. Jane Gaskell in Olson, "Who Computes?" p. 33.

58. Feodora Fomin, "The Best and the Brightest: The Selective Function of Mathematics in the School Curriculum," in Lesley Johnson and Deborah Tyler (eds.), *Cultural Politics: Papers in Contemporary Australian Education, Culture and Politics* (Melbourne: University of Melbourne Sociology Research Group in Cultural and Educational Studies, 1984), p. 220.

59. Michael Streibel's work on the models of thinking usually incorporated within computers in education is helpful in this regard. See Streibel, "A Critical Analysis of the Use of Computers in Education." The more general issue of the relationship between technology and the control of culture is important here. A useful overview of this can be found in Kathleen Woodward (ed.), *The Myths of Information: Technology and Postindustrial Culture* (Madison: Coda Press, 1980).

60. Quoted in Noble, "The Underside of Computer Literacy," 56.

61. *Ibid.,* 57. An interesting but little-known fact is that the largest proportion of computer programmers actually work for the military. See Joseph Weizenbaum, "The Computer in Your Future," *New York Review of Books* 30 (October 27, 1983), 58–62.

62. Noble, "The Underside of Computer Literacy," 40. For students in vocational curricula especially, these questions would be given more power if they were developed within a larger program that would seek to provide these young men and women with extensive experience in and understanding of *all* aspects of operating an entire industry or enterprise, not simply those "skills" that reproduce workplace stratification. See Center for Law and Education, "Key Provision in New Law Reforms Vocational Education: Focus is on Broader Knowledge and Experience for Students/Workers," *Center for Law and Education, Inc. D.C. Report,* December 28, 1984, 1–6.

Suggested Readings
for Future Study

CRITICAL ISSUES IN THE CLASSROOM

Apple, M. (1979). *Ideology and curriculum.* New York: Routledge.

Boal, A. (1982). *The theater of the oppressed.* New York: Routledge.

Burbules, N. (1992). *Dialogue in teaching: Theory and practice.* New York: Teachers College.

Ellworth, E. (1997). *Teaching positions: Difference, pedagogy and the power of address.* New York: Teachers's College.

Fine, M. (1990). *Framing dropouts: Notes on the politics of an urban public high school.* Albany: SUNY Press.

Freire, P. (1998). *Teachers as cultural workers.* Boulder, Colo.: Westview.

Giroux, H. (1999). *The mouse that roared: Disney and the end of innocence.* Lanham, Md.: Rowman and Littlefield.

Giroux, H., and Purpel, D. (1983). *The hidden curriculum and moral education.* New York: McCutchan.

Greene, M. (2000). *Releasing the imagination: Essays on education, the arts and social change.* New York: Jossy-Bass.

hooks, b. (1994). *Teaching to transgress: Education as the practice of freedom.* New York: Routledge.

Kampol, B. (1997). *Issues and trends in critical pedagogy.* Cresskill, N.J.: Hampton.

Kecht, M. (1992). *Pedagogy is politics: Literary theory and critical teaching.* Chicago: University of Illinois Press.

McNeil, L. (2000). *Contradictions of school reform: Educational costs of standardized testing.* New York: Routledge.

Oakes, J., and Lipton, M. (1999). *Teaching to change the world.* New York: McGraw-Hill.

Shor, I. (1996). *When students have power: Negotiating authorities in a critical pedagogy.* Chicago: University of Chicago Press.

Shor, I., ed. (1987). *Freire for the classroom: A sourcebook for liberatory teaching.* Portsmouth, N.H.: Boynton-Cook.

Trifonas, P., ed. (2000). *Revolutionary pedagogies: Cultural politics, instituting education and the discourse of theory.* New York: Routledge.

Spina, S., ed. (2000). *Smoke and mirrors: The hidden context of violence in schools and society.* Lanham, Md.: Rowman and Littlefield.

Wheelock, A. (1992). *Crossing the tracks: How "untracking" can save America's schools.* New York: New Press.

Zinn, H. (1980). *A people's history of the United States.* New York: Harper.

Part 7

TEACHING AND SOCIAL TRANSFORMATION

INTRODUCTION

The intent of this last section is to focus squarely on the relationship between teaching and activism. As such, the articles here speak to the common obstacles that those who dare to struggle for a liberatory pedagogy face in their efforts to realize their dream. "Knowing Ourselves as Instructors," written by Lee Anne Bell, Sharon Washington, Gerald Weinstein, and Barbara Love, examines the role of the teacher within the context of social justice content and classroom life. The primary concern is to shed light on the manner in which teachers are implicated when raising questions of oppression and social inequalities. In specific and grounded ways, the authors explore the role of teachers' social identities and competency (or knowledge gaps), when responding to biased and emotionally charged comments by students, as well as when confronting their own unexamined biases and emotions in the process. Central to this discussion is a view of "teachers as texts" for their students, particularly with respect to the reconstruction of power, within a context where there exist real institutional risks when challenging traditional classroom formats and content.

In a dialogue entitled "What Are the Fears and Risks of Transformation?" Ira Shor and Paulo Freire discuss the meaning of education as social activism and its implications. In this conversation, Freire deconstructs the origin of fears and links it to the existence of dreams people have for a better world. He advocates for an acceptance of those fears as part of their commitment to work for change, but simultaneously advocates for a realistic analysis of the possibilities and consequences of political activity. Freire does not believe in "blind activism," particularly when the tactics and strategies to develop change have not been researched well. He encourages critical educators to limit their fears— but not their dreams—by constantly assessing the ideological development of their students and the ideological maps of the institutions in which they work. He strongly cautions the critical educator about becoming paralyzed by fear or suffering elimination by a burst of impulsive acts that lead to political suicide.

Antonia Darder's essay, "Teaching as an Act of Love," concludes this volume on critical pedagogy. Although her essay pays tribute to Paulo Freire's contributions to the struggle for an emancipatory vision of society, her underlying intent here is to demonstrate the political power inherent in a praxis of everyday life, where the personal and political dialectically exist in an ongoing process of reflection, action, struggle, and renewal. Such a praxis entails an unwavering commitment to humanity, a clear political vision, the courage to challenge limitations, the capacity to begin anew, the discipline "to stay the course," and the humility and grace to cultivate a loving relationship of solidarity with others in the world. As Freire well knew, these constitute the building blocks for a transformative pedagogy of activism—a pedagogy that does not end when the school day is over but rather exists as a historical force within the very consciousness of freedom that fuels our political dreams.

QUESTIONS FOR REFLECTION AND DIALOGUE

1. According to Bell and her associates, in what different ways are the social and cultural identities of teachers implicated in the context of classroom transformation?

2. What issues are at work when teachers move to "intentionally create tension to disrupt complacent and unexamined attitudes" within their classrooms?

3. What does it mean when Bell and her associates say that teachers are texts for their students?

4. What are the problems associated with a fear of transformation? How do Shor and Freire suggest teachers deal with this fear?

5. What are some of the concrete suggestions offered by Shor and Freire to activist teachers that relate directly to their work in schools?

6. Describe Freire's perspectives on capitalism, racism, and feminism? How do these views impact the work of critical educators?

7. Describe the qualities of progressive teachers. In what ways are these traits addressed (or not addressed) within in the traditional curriculum of teacher education programs?

8. What conditions do you think need to change within public schools in order to establish a more democratic environment for students, teachers, parents, and administrators? Give specific examples.

9. What do you believe prevents teachers from joining together to improve the quality of life, for themselves and their students, within public schools? How might such a process be cultivated among educators, students, parents, and community members?

Knowing Ourselves as Instructors

LEE ANNE BELL, SHARON WASHINGTON, GERALD WEINSTEIN, AND BARBARA LOVE

While much has been written about how to engage students in social justice courses, little attention has been paid to the teachers in these classrooms. Yet few teachers would claim that raising issues of oppression and social justice in the classroom is a neutral activity. Content as cognitively complex and socially and emotionally charged as social justice, is inevitably challenging at both personal and intellectual levels. In the social justice classroom, we struggle alongside our students with our own social identities, biases, fears, and prejudices. We too need to be willing to examine and deal honestly with our values, assumptions, and emotional reactions to oppression issues. The self-knowledge and self-awareness that we believe are desirable qualities in any teacher become crucial in social justice education.

For most faculty, our professional training has not prepared us to address emotionally and socially charged issues in the classroom. Social justice education is not simply new content but often a radical change in process as well. "Among educators there has to be an acknowledgement that any effort to transform institutions so that they reflect a multicultural standpoint must take into consideration the fears teachers have when asked to shift their paradigms" (hooks, 1994, 36).

Weinstein and O'Bear (1992) asked a group of twenty-five university faculty colleagues from different disciplines to respond anonymously to the question, "What makes you nervous about raising issues of racism in your classroom?" These faculty expressed several concerns that are relevant to our topic. Here, we examine these and other concerns identified in our discussions for this chapter. Sometimes we use a common voice in which "we" refers to the four authors. Other times we use a single voice, identified as Sharon, Jerry, Lee, or Barbara. These quotes come from our taped discussions or from the article by Weinstein and O'Bear.

Below, we describe each concern with examples to illustrate how we grapple with it in our own teaching. Although we treat each issue separately, they do in fact overlap and interact constantly. Further, the strategies we discuss are not intended as standardized responses applicable to any teaching situation. Raising oppression issues in the classroom can be exciting and rewarding, but never entirely comfortable or predictable, especially when group interaction is such a central part of the process.

AWARENESS OF OUR OWN SOCIAL IDENTITIES

In most traditional classrooms, our particular social and cultural identities as teachers usually remain in the background, but in the social justice classroom where social identity is central to the content, the significance of who we are often takes center stage. In the study by Weinstein and O'Bear (1992), faculty expressed heightened awareness about their social identities that required them to be more conscious of their attitudes and assumptions, and often raised feelings of guilt, shame, or embarrassment at behaviors and attitudes of members of their own social group(s). Whether we are members of the privileged or targeted group with respect to particular issues inevitably influences how we react to material under discussion as well as how our students are likely to perceive us.

> Jerry: Even though I come into the classroom as a professional teacher, I do not leave my social identities at the door. I am a blend of such identities, for example, white, male, Jewish, heterosexual, beyond middle age, working-class background, now middle class. Especially when I am conducting antisemitism courses, I am constantly reminded of my conflicts about being at the same time a member of a group that is targeted by antisemitism and a member of the dominant white, male group in this society, with all of the inequities and privileges associated with each status.

As teachers we can offer our experience with both dominant and targeted identities as a way to join with students, expand the boundaries in the room for discussing these subjects, and model being open to exploring our own relative positions of power and privilege in relation to different oppression issues.

> Barbara: African American students often express difficulty in seeing themselves in the role of dominant or agent of oppression. They are so closely identified with the role of target or victim of oppression that they fail to see how they benefit from agent aspects of their identity. I grew up with a keen awareness of myself as a black person, but with no understanding at all of the ways I benefit from my status as a Christian. I gathered lots of information about disability oppression, but gained a much deeper understanding of systematic exclusion of people with disabilities when I suffered an injury that left me temporarily disabled.

The historical and experiential complexity of social identity further complicates awareness. The various meanings of group membership for people from different geographic regions, historical periods, and family experiences, yet who are members of the same social group, are important to note. As teachers we need to be careful about the categories we use and conscious of how individual members of a social group experience oppression in diverse ways.

> Barbara: Being Black means different things to different African heritage people. A light-skinned middle- or upper-class African heritage person growing up in the Northeast in the 1990s will describe the experience of being Black very differently from a dark-skinned working-class person raised in the South in the 1950s. Neither experience is any more or less authentically Black. While different, both experiences interact with a system of racism that extends through time, geographic region, and particular individual/family locations.

Exploration of our own social identities and relationships with other members of the groups to which we belong can help us as teachers to remember these complexities. Though as individuals we experience the oppression directed toward our group, no one individual can ever embody the totality of group subjugation. This is one of the central limitations of identity politics. We are constantly balancing the broad strokes of group oppression with the finer shadings of individual experience. This balancing extends to assumptions we make about our students. If we can be conscious of our own identity explorations we may be more likely to remember that that they too may be coming from a range of different places.

> Sharon: What may be in the forefront for a student of color at a particular moment may not be race, but sexual orientation, physical ability, or age. Just because a student is in a wheelchair does not mean disability is the issue that is currently primary. At that point in life, a student may be more engaged with issues of gender, race, or sexual orientation.

As faculty, we find it helpful to reflect on the experiences that have shaped our various identities and note the particular issues with which we feel most comfortable as well as those we tend to avoid, distort, or fear. This knowledge can be helpful preparation for engaging with social justice issues in the classroom, and enable us to respond thoughtfully to students even when we ourselves feel exposed.

> Lee: As a white woman, racism is an ongoing learning process for me. I keep realizing new areas where I'm unaware, learning and hopefully growing, but it is never closed and finished content. If I acknowledge my own ongoing learning I can be more open to what students raise for me to look at. Being aware of my own struggles to be honest with myself and open to new information hopefully also helps me to be more empathetic and supportive of their struggles.

As teachers, we can also try to be thoughtful about our own different levels of awareness on particular issues and realize that our own consciousness is likely to shift and change through our ongoing learning about the various forms and manifestations of oppression in our society.

CONFRONTING OUR OWN BIASES

A second issue noted by faculty in the Weinstein and O'Bear study had to do with fear of being labeled racist, sexist, and so on, or discovering previously unrecognized prejudices within ourselves. This included having to question our own assumptions, being corrected or challenged publicly (especially by members of the targeted group), and encountering our own fears and romanticized notions about members of targeted groups.

No one who has taken on the task of teaching about oppression wants to be thought of as homophobic, racist, sexist, classist, antisemitic, or ableist. Yet we know that recognizing and rooting out deeply socialized, and often unconscious, prejudices and practices is difficult. Faculty understandably feel a sense of vulnerability that what is out of our awareness will emerge to confront us as we engage these issues in our classrooms.

> Lee: I grew up in the Midwest and didn't meet a Jewish person, or at least was not aware I had, until I went to college. I thought that meant I couldn't be antisemitic. Slowly I came to realize all the assumptions and stereotypes I breathe in just living in this culture. I still have unexpected moments of new learning when I suddenly become aware of something I have missed or overlooked that is tied to antisemitism. And I think, "Oh no, how could I not have seen this?" I can berate myself for not noticing, or try to avoid the discomfort of this awareness, or I can try to be grateful that at least now I can do something about it.

One example of an activity that went awry because of unexamined assumptions is illustrative. Lee had planned an activity to elicit a discussion of male and female gender socialization, using a fishbowl format in which men and women could listen to each other without interruption.

> I was so intent on gender issues in my planning that I didn't anticipate the discomfort a gay man might feel in the rather raucous male-bonding discussion that took place among the men in the fish bowl emphasizing sports and heterosexual dating. I had not anticipated the way a gay man might have a very different relationship to his experiences of maleness. I noticed the student's discomfort and began to guess my mistake, which he confirmed when we talked about it later.

This lesson serves as a helpful reminder in planning courses to continually ask, "Who are the students I am imagining as I do this planning?" and "Who might I be leaving out?"

Barbara notes how encountering previously unrecognized prejudice enables her to be more effective and empathetic with her students:

> An important part of my own learning has been to recognize the ways I have internalized oppression and how it permeates my consciousness without my awareness. For example, learning to confront the homophobia at the heart of my own religious tradition has been vital to being able to support students who are seeking to learn about heterosexism and homophobia while remaining loyal to their own religious beliefs.

This self-examination is a lifelong process. We all have areas of limited vision, particularly where we are members of the dominant group. If we can model openness to ongoing learning, our students will benefit and we can be less judgmental and more self-accepting when we make mistakes or uncover new areas of ignorance or lack of awareness, and not retreat from this difficult but important work.

RESPONDING TO BIASED COMMENTS IN THE CLASSROOM

Faculty anxiety about how to respond to biased comments in the classroom is understandable. Those interviewed by Weinstein and O'Bear expressed fears about dealing with biased comments from dominant members in the presence of targeted members, especially when such remarks were made by members of a dominant social group to which they themselves belonged.

Language plays such an important role in perpetuating oppression that miscommunication and misunderstanding can easily arise. Targeted group members usually have a long history of developing sensitivity to negative cues that signal oppressive attitudes. They have been subjected to, suffered from, discussed and thought about such cues throughout the course of their lives and so are highly tuned to note them. Dominant group members on the other hand are often oblivious to the effects of their language on targeted group members and in fact are often shocked to realize this effect. Thus the potential for breakdown in communication, hurt feelings, defensiveness, and recriminations is high. As educators we want to insure that our language does not inhibit discussion or contribute to any student feeling excluded. Setting ground rules and establishing a commonly agreed upon procedure for addressing offensive statements when they arise are ways to address this problem through classroom process.

As teachers, we ourselves are not immune to these triggers either and need to recognize beforehand those to which we are most vulnerable.

> Jerry: As a Jew, particularly when I am teaching about antisemitism, I am vulnerable to all the dominant signals concerning my group. Some version of all the stereotyped statements and attitudes that have pursued me my entire life are bound to be expressed. I always experience those expressions and attitudes with some degree of pain, for they restimulate past fears. When I hear those expres-

sions I may get angry and want to retaliate, but I know that acting directly on my feelings would be inappropriate and counterproductive to the goals of the session and my role as teacher and facilitator. By anticipating typical responses that I have experienced before I can prepare myself to use these triggers intentionally and constructively during the class.

Greater self-knowledge about how we typically react in situations of tension can give us more options for responding in thoughtful ways when conflicts arise. For example, we can examine our motives for avoiding conflict, or proving ourselves as unprejudiced, or wanting people to like us. When we pay attention to our internal dialogue in these situations, we can make more conscious choices in the moment:

> Sharon: I make sure that I know myself in relation to the material and the particular issues that give me the most discomfort or anxiety. If I feel like a well of emotion, I remind myself this class is for the students. Once I had someone co-teaching a particular session and this person just lost it and raged at the class. I went away thinking, "Wow, she just threw up all over the class!"

There are several ways to prepare beforehand to deal with our own triggers as they arise. Having a support system, a person or group with whom we can discuss these issues, share feelings, and get support is very important. For example, Sharon regularly meets with a friend and colleague, another African American woman, to debrief and talk about her classes. She has also at times used a journal to note her feelings and reactions as the class progresses. This process is often a helpful reminder at points in a course where resistance is particularly high or she is feeling down on herself, and allows her to recognize that these are predictable parts of the process rather than flaws in the class or her own teaching. These realizations can be very reassuring.

An appreciation for the process people go through in developing awareness about oppression can also help us acquire patience and understanding when dealing with our own feelings as teachers.

> Lee: I can feel very impatient sometimes. But when I shift my frame of reference to one of trying to understand the process by which people can be engaged in unlearning oppressive attitudes, it kind of unhooks me. Then it becomes a challenge to figure out, "Okay, how is this person thinking about these issues now and what is going to be the way to help them to try out a different perspective?"

Attention to process in the moment occurs on two levels. One level relates to our awareness about how students may be thinking about or experiencing what is going on in the classroom: "Why does that student say or think that, and what is getting triggered for him or her?" On a parallel track, we note and try to understand our own reactions to what is occuring: "Why am I so annoyed at this person; What does it trigger for me?"

It is often easy to hold romanticized notions that those who are themselves victimized by bigotry will be more sensitive and vigilant when groups other than their own are targeted. Unfortunately experiencing oppression does not automatically render one an expert or liberate one from bias toward another group. We can easily be triggered when such expectations are shattered.

> Jerry: I have been exposed to Jewish racism and sexism, African American anti-semitism and sexism, and white, Gentile women who are racist and antisemitic. I always harbor the wish that all targeted group members would be allies in interrupting bias in all of its forms. However, wishing doesn't make it so. When I am confronted with bias toward my group from other targeted people, I have to overcome my fear of alienating those whom I thought were "on my side" and challenge their beliefs in the same way I would anyone else. However, in the process I try to provide continuous evidence that I am also sensitive to their target group issues.

The challenge is to maintain an openness to both our own internal process and to what may be going on for our students, so that we can respond to biased comments clearly and directly, but also with compassion and understanding for what it means to discover and change oppressive beliefs and behaviors in ourselves.

DOUBTS AND AMBIVALENCE ABOUT ONE'S OWN COMPETENCY

Weinstein and O'Bear found that faculty often worry about having to expose their own struggles with the issues, reveal uncertainty, or make mistakes. As college faculty members we are assumed to have expertise in what we teach. To the degree that we expect ourselves to appear certain about what we know, we may find it difficult to encounter hot spots or knowledge gaps exposed by our interactions with students.

> Jerry: This is especially true when targeted group members other than my own describe perspectives to which I am not yet sensitive. Unless I can admit to students that I am still in the process of learning and that there are areas about which I still need to be educated, I may give the impression that there are simple solutions to which I have access. This places great pressure on me to have "the answer." One way of diminishing the pressure is to disclose my own uncertainties to students. It also models that unlearning prejudice is a lifelong process in which there are rarely simple answers.

The issues students raise that challenge our awareness and sensitivity can create a valuable space for opening up the learning process. As we confront misinformation or ignorance and the blindspots of privilege, we create the possibility for modeling honesty and openness to what can be learned by listening to others who are different from us, especially those who have been targets of dominant stereotypes and assumptions.

In our discussions for this chapter, Lee recalled a course in which classism was a central focus. Since most of the class were teachers or human service professionals, she had assumed a predominantly middle-class perspective and focused the class accordingly, only to discover a simmering anger at the cost of textbooks and the amount of time outside of class needed to complete the homework felt by students who were working two jobs and struggling to make ends meet. Once Lee realized her mistake, she told the class the false assumptions she had made and initiated a discussion about how the problems students were experiencing could be addressed in ways that would be supportive and promote learning. The discussion provided an opportunity for the whole class to engage in an exploration of classism and the unexamined assumptions that reinforce class privilege. The discussion also gave Lee useful new ideas about how to select texts for courses, develop a library of books to loan to students, and think about new ways to construct assignments and build a supportive classroom community.

> Sharon: You can't come into the class saying, in effect, "I know everything there is to know about this and let me tell you." When you make a mistake you have to be willing to say, "Well, that was a mistake" or "I've learned something about this now and I'll do it differently next time." I don't know how comfortable most teachers are with doing this, but there is a way to say, "It didn't occur to me" or "I didn't notice, I'm sorry."

Teaching in ways that invite challenge and model ongoing learning demonstrates a different definition of competence than the traditional one of mastery and expertise. Competence becomes instead skill in creating an atmosphere where difficult dialogues can occur (Goodman, 1995), developing processes that enable people (including the teacher) to expose and look critically at their own assumptions and biases, and building a community that encourages risk-taking and action to challenge oppressive conditions within and beyond the classroom.

NEED FOR LEARNER APPROVAL

Most faculty hope that our students will like and respect us, and leave our classes feeling positive about their experience. Those interviewed by Weinstein and O'Bear named such fears as making students frustrated, frightened, or angry, leaving them feeling shaken and confused and not being able to fix it.

> Lee: I think I'm good at creating community in the classroom and making people feel welcome and supported. Where I have to push myself is to introduce and not smooth over conflict, to challenge students, and risk their not liking me. I do it, but I realize I'm much more comfortable with the community-building part. It makes me feel good, I want students to like me. But there are times when that can get in the way of productive learning.

In the social justice classroom we intentionally create tension to disrupt complacent and unexamined attitudes about social life. These very conditions can cause students to dislike or feel hostile toward us at various points in the course. Confronting oppression invariably involves a range of feelings from anxiety, confusion, anger, and sadness, to exhilaration and joy. We need to remind ourselves that as much as we crave approval from our students, a sense of well-being and long-term learning are not necessarily synonymous. A better indication of our effectiveness might be whether students leave with more questions than they came in with, wanting to know more and questioning core assumptions in their own socialization.

> Jerry: When students left feeling frustrated, upset, and confused I used to regard it as evidence of my failure as a teacher: It was not until we ran a racism workshop for a community college in which the entire faculty and administration were involved that my concept of what constituted successful teaching began to change. On finishing the weekend-long session the participants were not smiling. On the way home my co-leader and I felt that the workshop had been a failure. Over the next three to five years, however, we kept getting reports of systematic changes in that institution that promoted greater racial equity and awareness and that were directly attributed to the workshop.

DEALING WITH EMOTIONAL INTENSITY, AND FEAR OF LOSING CONTROL

Faculty worry about not knowing how to respond to angry comments, having discussions blow up, dealing with anger directed at them, and being overwhelmed by their own strong emotions engendered by the discussion (Weinstein & O'Bear, 1992). Johnella Butler describes this process well:

> All the conflicting emotions, the sometimes painful movement from the familiar to the unfamiliar, are experienced by the teacher as well. We have been shaped by the same damaging, misinformed view of the world as our students. Often, as we try to resolve their conflicts, we are simultaneously working through our own. (1989, 160)

Many faculty have been taught that emotions have no place in academia. Traditional modes of teaching distance us from the core issues and conflicts that are central to social justice education and can often result in simply skimming the surface. Ultimately, it is questionable whether intellectual and abstract reflection alone effectively change oppressive attitudes and behaviors.

Dealing with tension, anger, and conflict in the classroom is difficult. However, avoiding the feelings that are stimulated by oppression ignores how deeply it is embedded in our psyches and reinforces norms of silence and discounting that ultimately support oppression (Aguilar & Washington, 1990). Often the most significant learning results from the disequilibrium that open confrontation with feelings and contradictory information can generate (Keil, 1984; Zaharna, 1989).

In preparing ourselves to deal with difficult emotions it can be helpful to examine how our own history with the expression of emotion may affect the way we respond to emotion in the classroom.

Barbara: I have had to examine how anger and other intense emotions were handled in my household to get a better understanding of my current response to emotions in the classroom. Quite apart from my professional training to be carefully neutral and suppress any display of emotion, I was raised in a household where feelings were denied until they erupted. My response has been to deny feelings any place in discussions, and especially to disallow loud voices. Learning to listen to loud voices and to encourage others to be receptive to them has been important for my ability to facilitate authentic discussion. Reminding learners that loud voices sometimes indicate that a person cares a lot about an issue can provide a context that allows "heated" discussion to take place.

If we learn to accept emotional expression as a valid and valuable part of the learning process, we can turn our focus to finding effective ways to enable its expression in the service of learning.

Sharon: I actually don't really try to control emotions, but I do try to manage outlets for expressing emotions through dyads or journals for example. If people are upset, I say "Be upset! Be angry, whatever, and we'll just notice it." And I just sort of acknowledge that it's part of the process.

We also acknowledge that there may be times when we feel overwhelmed and uncertain about what to do. When emotions are running high and we are uncertain about how to proceed, we have found it helpful to create time-out to reflect and decide on next steps.

Jerry: There have been a number of times during my anti-bias teaching when I have felt totally helpless in dealing with certain interactions. A participant may say something that stimulates great tension and anxiety, and a dense silence overtakes the group. I may feel upset and paralyzed as all eyes turn to me to see what I will do, expecting me to take care of the situation. I cannot think of any helpful intervention. I am too upset to think clearly. It is a fearsome moment, one I anticipate with dread.

Over the years Jerry has accumulated a few emergency procedures that help him survive these moments:

- Give participants a brief time-out.
- Ask people to record their own immediate responses in their notebooks.
- Invite each participant to share their responses with one other person.

The purpose of these strategies is to change the focus momentarily from public to private, so that participants and instructor can reflect upon and articulate to themselves what they are feeling. It then becomes more possible to return to the discussion with greater thoughtfulness and honesty.

In many cases when a supportive climate has been previously established, losing control or facing strong emotions can be a constructive event, one from which both professor and students learn. In fact, students often make fundamental shifts in their perspectives after they have experienced someone "losing" control, letting go enough to share deeper feelings, fears, and experiences.

> Barbara: I teach social justice education from a position of hope and belief that our efforts can make a difference in the elimination of oppression. I was co-teaching an antisemitism course with a Jewish colleague who said that she did not think antisemitism would ever be entirely eliminated and that other Holocausts were and are possible. Before I could catch them, tears coursed down my face as I felt the enormity of the task before me and the challenge to my own optimism. Several students later told me that this was a powerful learning moment for them.

PERSONAL DISCLOSURE AND USING OUR EXPERIENCE AS EXAMPLE

We as instructors are also in many ways texts for our students. Our social group identities, behavior in the classroom, and openness about our own process of learning can all be important and challenging aspects of course content. Who we are affects student perceptions of the issues we raise. In some respects we are both the messenger and the message.

Asking students to engage experientially with oppression material requires that we be willing to take the risks we ask of them. Self-disclosure is an important part of this process and one of the most powerful ways of teaching is through modeling the behavior we hope to encourage in others.

> Lee: If we want to create an environment where our students can be vulnerable enough to look at painful issues that challenge our faith in a fair society and ourselves as good human beings, then we have to give ourselves the same permission to be vulnerable and confused. I'm constantly struggling against this image that teachers are supposed to be perfect, in control, totally aware. Which is ridiculous! Nobody can be that. The question is how can I try to be skillful, and at the same time give myself permission to be a fallible human being? If I'm going to ask my students to disclose something, then I should be willing to do that too. I try to disclose ways in which I've made mistakes and where I felt really stupid when I realized what I was saying, to let students know there's not perfection. There's just human beings trying to be humane with each other and not perpetuate this bloody system.

Sharing our own struggles with the issues provides important permission for our students to engage in the difficult process of doing so themselves. This stance can help to avoid expectations of perfection which often block action. Better to take imperfect action and continue to engage with the issues, than to avoid responsibility for action altogether while we search for perfection.

Sharon: I want students to understand that learning about social justice is part of a life-long process. I will share with them stories of my own development, both in areas where I was a target of oppression, or stood in the shoes of an agent of oppression with the accompanying privileges.

The amount, context, and nature of personal information that we disclose is a matter of judgment, depending on the nature and size of the group and the amount of time we have together. We try to make clear the relation of our own disclosure to the topic under discussion.

For many teachers, especially those from targeted groups, the risk of self-disclosure needs to be thoughtfully taken. For example, self-disclosure by a gay or lesbian teacher can be a significant boon to learning, especially if the topic is heterosexism. The instructor, however, should be aware of the homophobia and misinformation sure to exist among her students and plan carefully about how and when she will come out.

Sharon: I know that for myself I'm always conscious about when it is that I'll come out in class, or even if I will. Because I want them to still see me as credible and I believe that as soon as I come out, that piece of knowledge looms in their eyes over everything else. Like all of a sudden their teacher is sexual, and they have to deal with the internal contradictions of respect for teacher along with societal messages that gay men and lesbians are bad, perverse, immoral, etc. So I know that I'm very conscious about when to share that information. I try to wait until after I've gotten their trust so that any trust I lose during that time period can hopefully be re-established before the end of the semester. I have had students deny my being lesbian and think I was only saying it to create a learning opportunity for them!

Our role in disclosing personal experiences differs from that of our students. Students will use their experiences to probe and understand the personal implications of a specific issue. As instructors, we often use personal experience to illustrate a point. Our role is to be inclusive. Understanding the limits of our own experience allows us to consciously develop examples that go beyond our own personal range.

NEGOTIATING AUTHORITY ISSUES

In the social justice classroom, we deliberately challenge the traditional classroom hierarchy in order to build a community of learning in which the teacher participates as a facilitator of process rather than an authority delivering knowledge (Tompkins, 1990). Issues of authority in the classroom are especially complicated for faculty who are members of targeted groups. Much has been written, for example, about the dilemmas faced by faculty of color and female and gay/lesbian faculty who often cope with both institutional and student devaluation of their professional status (Ahlquist, 1991: Arnold, 1993; hooks, 1994; Ladson-Billings, 1996; Aguilar & Washington, 1990; Maher &

Tetreault, 1994). Students sometimes perceive them as less authoritative and may discount the legitimacy of what they teach or accuse them of pushing their own agenda.

A professor of color and a white professor teaching about racism, for example, are likely to be perceived quite differently by students of color and white students. Sharon describes the various issues she often juggles and the common student perceptions she faces as an African American woman teaching about racism.

> The fact that my students are often 99 percent white means that I have to set up an environment where they can talk about their perceptions of reverse discrimination, quotas, affirmative action, etc. I also don't want to come off appearing like it's only my issue, or it's my personal thing, or that I've got a chip on my shoulder. And if I do have students of color in the class, then I'm also concerned about trying to keep them from having to be the authority on all issues of race.

Gender also casts authority issues in particular ways. We are socialized to expect females to defer to male authority, not to be authorities themselves. Women who achieve professional roles often juggle negative social messages about women in power with an internal sense of being imposters in these roles (McIntosh, 1988; Bell, 1990). When we are dealing with emotional issues and feelings in the classroom, female professors can be easily typecast. Students often expect female teachers to be nurturing or to smile; they become angry or challenge our authority when we do not fulfill their expectations (see Culley, 1985).

INSTITUTIONAL RISKS AND DANGERS

One additional concern is the fear related to the institutional risks involved in departing from traditional teaching formats and content. As we engage with social justice issues and change our classrooms accordingly, we often come into conflict with institutional norms of professed objectivity, authority, and professorial distance in ways that can undermine our confidence, lose the support of some of our colleagues, and in some cases jeopardize our positions as faculty.

When we take on the challenge of teaching social justice content and developing a democratic, participatory process in our classrooms, we run very real risks of getting in trouble with our institutions. We are challenging traditional content as well as traditional teaching processes and norms about the teacher-student relationship. We also often encounter problems with grading and evaluation that other instructors rarely deal with.

> Sharon: A student's mother wrote to the Dean and told him that I was a bad teacher and that if her daughter didn't get a B, she was going to take this to the Provost and the President of the university and have them call me on the carpet. And it was really hard holding my own ground. [Did the Dean support you?] The Dean did support me but not without questioning me.

Here, we see multiple vulnerabilities. There's the jeopardy of being an African American teacher in a white institution where she cannot necessarily count on the support that white faculty can usually rely on. Then she is introducing subject matter that may not be supported by the institution. Finally she is engaging in a process of teaching that also may not be valued institutionally.

Many of the faculty teaching social justice courses are women, often among them the few people of color on the faculty, and often untenured. Thus the most vulnerable group takes on the most difficult and institutionally risky teaching. Faculty who teach social justice courses also sometimes receive lower ratings on teaching evaluations than those who teach traditional courses, adding yet another layer of institutional danger to an already exposed position. Thus faculty who take on the challenge of teaching social justice, especially if they are members of targeted groups, are often in an extremely vulnerable position institutionally.

Team teaching, particularly with a tenured faculty member, can be a valuable way of building in support for untenured faculty. Other support systems also need to be developed and nurtured so that faculty who teach social justice education can survive and hopefully thrive in these institutions.

CONCLUSION

We hope that through naming and discussing the fears and concerns faced by faculty who teach about oppression, we can begin a dialogue of support and encouragement that will enable teachers to sustain their commitment to social justice education. More often that not, people who write about multicultural education say very little about their own struggles in the classroom. We want to contribute to a discussion where teachers can expose the problems and difficulties we all face in this work and support each other in being more effective.

We also want to recognize that we are part of a much larger process of change and affirm the importance of the small part each of us individually plays in this process. What we do counts, often in ways that will not come back to us for validation.

> Sharon: I just think it's helpful to know that I am doing the best I can do and not to be too wedded to the here and now. I know ancestors who came before fought for freedom, equality, and justice and made it possible for me to live this life. Even if I don't change the world for me, I have faith that my work can contribute to a better world for the generations yet to come. That's what keeps me doing it, keeps me grounded, being grateful and knowing that my little part counts.

We hope that nurturing this perspective in our students will make it possible for them to become engaged in social justice action and to believe in the importance of the role each of them can play in creating change.

REFERENCES

Aguilar, T., and Washington, S. (1990). Towards an inclusion of multicultural issues in leisure studies curricula. *Schole: A journal of leisure studies and recreation education*, 5, 41–52.

Ahlquist, R. (1991). Position and imposition: Power relations in a multicultural foundations class. *Journal of Negro Education, 60*, 158–169.

Arnold, M. S. (1993). *Breaking the pot: Melting student resistance to pluralism in counseling programs*. Paper presented at The Association for Counselor Education and Supervision, San Antonio, TX.

Bell, L. A. (1990). The gifted woman as imposter. *Advanced Development, 2*, 55–64.

Butler, J. E. (1989). Transforming the curriculum: Teaching about women of color. In J. A. Banks and C. A. M. Banks (Eds.), *Multicultural education: Issues and perspectives* (pp. 145–63). Boston: Allyn & Bacon.

Culley, M. (1985). Anger and authority in the introductory women's studies classroom. In M. Culley and C. Portuges (Eds.), *Gendered subjects: The dynamics of feminist teaching* (pp. 209–17). Boston: Routledge & Kegan Paul.

Goodman, D. (1995). Difficult dialogues: Enhancing discussions about diversity. *College Teaching, 43* (2), 47–52.

hooks, b. (1994). *Teaching to transgress: Education as the practice of freedom*. New York: Routledge.

Keil, F. C. (1984). Mechanisms of cognitive development and the structure of knowledge. In R. J. Sternberg (Ed.), *Mechanisms of cognitive development*. New York: W. H. Freeman.

Ladson-Billings, G. (1996). Silence as weapons: Challenges of a black professor teaching white students. *Theory into Practice, 35*, (2), 79–85.

Maher, F. A., and Tetreault, M. K. T. (1994). *The feminist classroom*. New York: Basic Books.

McIntosh, P. (1988). *White privilege and male privilege: A personal account of coming to see correspondences through work in women's studies*, Working paper #189. Wellesley, MA: Wellesley College Center for Research on Women.

Tomkins, J. (1990). Pedagogy of the distressed. *College English, 52*(6), 653–60.

Weinstein, G., and Obear, K. (1992). Bias issues in the classroom: Encounters with the teaching self. In M. Adams (Ed.), *Promoting diversity in college classrooms: Innovative responses for the curriculum, faculty, and institutions,* New Directions for Teaching and Learning, no. 52. San Francisco: Jossey-Bass.

Zaharna, R. S. (1989). Self-shock: The double-binding challenge of identity. *International Journal of Intercultural Relations, 13* (4), 501–25.

What Are the Fears and Risks of Transformation?

IRA SHOR AND PAULO FREIRE

FEAR AND RISK: THE RESULTS OF DREAMING INSIDE HISTORY

Ira   We've discussed the transformation of students and teachers but I think we need to examine the special fears teachers have about transforming themselves. I've heard teachers talk directly and indirectly about their fears. They worry about being fired if they practice emancipating education instead of the transfer-of-knowledge pedagogy. They speak about the risks to their careers if they express opposition ideology, if they engage in opposition politics in their institutions. They also fear the awkwardness of relearning their profession in front of their students. Teachers want to feel expert, so the need to recreate ourselves on the job is intimidating to many. Dialogic classes are creative and unpredictable, invented in-progress, making some teachers worry that they will make mistakes in class and lose control or respect.

Teachers who fear transformation can also be attracted to liberating pedagogy. The regular curriculum often fails them, boring them and the students. They can feel stifled by the routine syllabus or by the familiar limits of their academic discipline. They want to breathe deeply as educators instead of taking gulps of air in a closet of official knowledge.

Teacher burn-out, student resistance, and conservative cuts in school budgets have made many teachers wonder why they are in education. It's never been a place to get rich or famous. The pay and prestige of the profession have fallen in the last fifteen years, in the United States. It has some amenities like long vacations and the morale of working for human development. Many teachers came into the profession inspired by the human good they could do, even as a public service, looking for their students to experience the joy of learning. But now more than ever, teachers are getting fewer rewards and more distress. They find it harder to celebrate their love of knowledge and their devotion to human growth. This is a moment of crisis in the teaching profession which opens some teachers to liberating dreams.

Those open to transformation feel a Utopian appeal but many feel fear also. They are attracted out of a conviction that education *should* liberate. They turn away because they understand the risks of opposition politics. They fear standing out as radicals, as people who rock the boat. The 70s and 80s have been lonely conservative years in which to take a stand against the authorities. The decline of mass movements since the 60s meant you no longer joined large crowds challenging the system. Your challenge now makes you individually more visible, and thus more vulnerable. If you're in the opposition instead of safely inside the establishment consensus (the official curriculum), you risk being fired, or not getting a promotion, or not getting a pay raise, or not getting the courses you want to teach or the schedule you want or the leave you apply for, or even in some cases you become the target of ultra-conservative groups.

When I speak with teachers, fear is like a damp presence hovering in the room. I suspect that more people feel this fear than speak openly about it. It's embarrassing to admit publicly that what stands in the way is not only the difficulty of experimenting with students, but also the professional or political risks accompanying opposition. There is also, Paulo, something I referred to earlier, a fear of the students' rejection of liberating pedagogy. A conservative restoration from Nixon to Reagan in the U.S. has made students less willing to take risks. Resurgent authorities have imposed on students such things as careerism, new testing and curricular requirements, ethics of self-interest, and dismal regimes in back-to-basics. Students worry about getting jobs. They are anxious and impatient. They want to know how any course helps them gain skills and credentials for the tough job market. They face under-employment and declining entry-level wages, while shabby schools and colleges pursue them with tests, tests, and more tests! Such a repressive, business-oriented milieu makes students resist experimental pedagogy.

We should investigate this cloud of fear above the teacher's head when she or he holds class. Fear of punishment may be only the beginning of other kinds of fear that inhibit teacher transformation. Are these fears unreasonable? Are they sensible? Are people *so* socialized into fearing punishment that *we censor ourselves* in advance of becoming an effective opposition, or even before attempting opposition? How can dialogical pedagogy deal with the teacher's fear of student rejection, student resistance?

Paulo   First of all, I think that when we speak about fear, we must be absolutely clear that we are speaking about something very concrete. That is, "fear" is *not* an abstraction. Secondly, I think we must know that we are speaking about something very normal. Another point I find right now when I am trying to touch the question is that when we think of fear in these situations it leads us to reflect about the need we have to be very, very clear concerning our choices, which in turn demands some kinds of concrete procedures or practices, which in turn are the actual experiences that provoke fear. To the extent that I become more and more clear concerning my choices, my dreams, which are substantively political and adjunctively pedagogical, to the extent to which I recognize that as an educator I am a politician, I also understand better the reasons for me to be afraid; because I begin to foresee the consequences of such teaching. Putting into practice a kind of education that critically challenges the consciousness of the students necessarily works *against* some myths which *deform* us.

Those deforming myths come out of the dominant ideology in society. By challenging the myths, we also challenge the dominant power. When we begin to feel ourselves involved in concrete fears, like losing our jobs, having to walk from college to college sending out curricula vitae without receiving positive answers, or the fear of little by little losing credibility in our profession, when we see all these things, we have to add some other clarifications to the original clarification of our political dreams. We must establish some limits for our fear.

First of all, we recognize that having fear is normal. Having fear is a manifestation of being alive. I don't have to hide my fears. But, what I cannot permit is that my fear is unjustified, immobilizing me. If I am clear about my political dream, then one of the conditions for me to continue to have this dream is not to immobilize myself in walking towards its realization. And fear can be immobilizing. At this moment, I am trying to be didactic, in the interpretation of this problem. Now, I am recognizing the right to have fear. Nevertheless, I must establish the limits, to "cultivate" my fear. (Laughs) To cultivate means to accept it.

Ira Instead of denying it?

Paulo Yes. Look, of course, I don't need to make public speeches about my fear. But, I don't need to rationalize my fear and I must not deny it, to call it something else and to give the impression that I am not afraid. In the moment in which you begin to rationalize your fear, you begin to deny your dream.

Ira Fear comes from the dream you have about the society you want to make and to unmake through teaching and other politics.

Paulo Yes! Fear exists in you precisely because you have the dream. If your dream was to preserve the status quo, what should you fear then? Your fear might concern the forces in society which are fighting *against* the status quo. Do you see? Then, you don't have to deny your fear, because you would have the power of the elite behind you in protecting the status quo. If your dream is one of transformation, then you fear the reaction of the powers that are now in power.

If you rationalize your fear then you deny your dream. For me, it must be absolutely clear concerning these two points: Fear comes from your political dream and to deny the fear is to deny your dream.

Ira Making a dream of transformation concrete puts you in experiences that involve risk, but if you do not get to those experiences then you prevent your dream from entering reality. But, Paulo, let's think also about the *heroism,* even heroic posturing, that often accompanies being a radical, someone who dreams of revolutionary transformation. There's mystique of heroism, of personal sacrifice, that possesses many people who want radical change. They might feel obliged to act heroic and to show no fear. This burdens them with the need to deny what they feel and distorts the kind of work they do. They might feel that having fear makes them an inadequate person, an inadequate militant. Fear is a sign of inadequacy from this point of view, rather than a sign you are testing ways to make your political dream concrete, to make it real in society.

Your analysis is entirely different. You say that fear is a sign that you are doing your transformational work well. It means that you are making critical opposition, engaging the status quo in a contention for social change. Your dream is entering reality, contending in history, and provoking unavoidable reaction and risk.

WHAT FEAR CAN TEACH US: LIMITS AND LESSONS

Paulo   The more you recognize your fear as a consequence of your attempt to practice your dream, the more you learn how to put into practice your dream! Do you see? Look, Ira, I never had interviews with the great revolutionaries of this century about their fears! I never asked Fidel Castro, for example, about his fears. I could not ask this question to Amilcar Cabral, another fantastic revolutionary. Or to Che Guevara, for example. But, *all* of them felt fear, to the extent that all of them were very faithful to their dreams.

But there is another point which I think is very important. This understanding of fear is not something which diminishes me but which makes me recognize that I am a human being. This recognition gains my attention in order to set limits when fear tells me *not* to do this or that. Is it clear? I have to establish the limits for my fear.

Ira   First you make some concessions to it, and then you understand the concessions you make, saying I can't do this because I am afraid, but I won't allow my fear to prevent me from doing *that*.

Paulo   This is what I am trying to say. What happens as a consequence is that in some moments instead of rationalizing fear, you understand it *critically*. Then, the recognition of the fear limiting your action allows you to arrive at a very critical position in which you begin to act according to the dialectical relationships between tactics and strategy. What do I mean?

If you consider that strategy means your dream, the tactics are just the mediations, the ways, the methods, the roads, the instruments to concretize the dream, to materialize the strategy. This relationship cannot be dichotomized. Tactics cannot be allowed to contradict strategy. Because of that, you cannot have authoritarian tactics to materialize democratic dreams. Another thing: the more you bring strategy and tactics into agreement, the more you recognize the space which limits your actions.

In some moments, for example, you discover that today historically it is not possible to do a certain kind of action because the repression should come easily on you. Then, it is as if your fear is more or less domesticated by your clarity. You just know that in that moment it is impossible to walk one kilometer. So, you walk 800 meters! And you wait for tomorrow to walk more, when another 200 meters can be walked. Of course, one of the serious questions is how to learn the *position* where the limit is. You don't find that in books! With whom do you learn how to establish limits? You learn by practicing it. You learn by experiencing. You learn by being punished! (Laughs)

Ira   The same idea applies to educational politics. Teachers learn the limits for doing liberatory education by doing it. It's the same for any act of political transformation. By attempting transformation, we learn how to do it and also the limits within which we act. When we learn limits, *real* limits in our classrooms or in other arenas of society, we also gain some concrete knowledge on how much or even how little can be accomplished right now. Then this concrete feedback on our attempts protects us from wild fantasies of fear that could immobilize us, or which could drive us into ultra-militance if we fail to recognize limits or if we feel we have to deny our fear and act heroic. If we read our reality well, we don't imagine repression, don't project our future punishment for daring opposition, but rather test the actual circumstances of our politics and design our interventions within those limits. This calls on the teacher to take a very experimental attitude in her or his classes. But the experimental attitude is common to all transformational politics. You might say that politics inside or outside the classroom requires on-going research. You research your field of action to see the results and limits of your interventions, Then, you discover how far you can go or if you've gone beyond the limits. For example, these limits could mean, in the classroom, the transformational potential of the students. One way to go beyond the limits is to violate student openness to accepting the liberatory option offered by the teacher. You raise "correct" issues of racism or sexism or nuclear war or class inequality, and get no response from the students, who are hearing you speak in tongues, as far as they're concerned. If you go beyond student desire or ability, or if you work outside their language or themes, you see the results, their resistance. Your approach was not systematically rooted in the real potentials for change.

Another way to violate the real limits in a school or college is to organize a militant action which is abstractly "correct" but practically disastrous. This happened at my college in 1973 when a racist geneticist came to lecture, at the President's invitation. Our small group of activist teachers and students wanted to disrupt the event. I argued that the student majority would not support such an action and that the liberal administration would go after the militants instead of uniting with us to keep the conservative majority of the faculty at bay. I marvelously failed to convince anybody of my point of view and the group militantly disrupted the lecture. The aftermath was a break between the left and the liberal administration including the firing of some radical teachers. In addition, because the left shouted down the speaker, the issue became "free speech" on campus, instead of racism in school and society. This was one step forward and three steps back, thanks to a wrong assessment of the limits. The limits back then suggested we could engage the racist in a big public debate, win the contest, and increase awareness about the nature of racism.

There are authorities policing the teacher. If the teacher tries to squeeze through a political opening too small for the project she or he has started, the teacher will feel the pressure of official response, some form of reaction or repression, which is a sign that the limits have been stepped over at this moment, in this situation, using these kinds of methods. In the incident I cited above, I could see the administration mobilizing for this event in ways that threatened the position of the left. Repression calls upon us to do a tactical retreat and figure out a new way to work. If you are fired, you are erased as a factor in that place and have to begin somewhere else. Getting fired often makes people more cautious politicians wherever they wind up next. In many cases, it silences the teacher, especially those with families to support. We've had so many examples of radical teachers being fired at all levels of education in the U.S. The mere threat of losing your job is enough to silence many teachers. Teachers who speak up, organize, or deviate from the official curriculum are made an example of, and the example of their disappearance is not lost on the faculty who remain.

I remember also, Paulo, when I was just out of graduate school, starting as a professor, when the 60s upheavals were winding down. It was 1972 and my college was hit by political attacks against Open Admissions. The traditionalists wanted a return to the old elite curriculum and the previous decorum. The civil authorities and the private sector wanted to restrain the mass movements of the 60s, one of which was a struggle for open access to higher education. They wanted to reverse the politics of equality and also to cut the costs of education and other social services to working people. So, waves of attacks on Open Admissions and on free tuition started in New York in the spring of 1972, my first year as a professor.

I recall that we were in the large college auditorium for a crisis meeting, and I was sitting there with another professor, a friend ten years older than me. During the hot faculty debate on what to do with threatened budget cuts, I raised my hand to speak. As my hand went up, my professor friend grabbed my arm and pulled it down quickly. I looked at him in surprise and saw real concern, even a cynical wisdom in his face. He said to me, "If you want to keep your job, shut up and publish!" He was a a liberal and he had a wonderful New York sense of humor. But, the lesson he shared with me at that moment of crisis was to shut up. I felt sorry for him. I felt sorry that he feared talking.

I did feel fear also. I wanted to keep my job—I needed the money and I liked the work. It had taken me two years to find that job, even though I was the top student in my graduate department at the University of Wisconsin. No senior professor went to bat for me there because my politics offended the old boy network. I heard that one of them put a poison pen letter in my job file to discourage other colleges from hiring me. So, after nine years in college and a Ph.D. in my pocket, you can imagine how I felt racing all over the country looking for work. This was one price of dissent here in the States. I felt fear once again because my whole doctoral committee was fired for political reasons. I finished my thesis just before my major professor's contract expired. Still, sitting in my budget-college auditorium in 1972, it was my habit to put my hand up, and speak at crisis meetings. That year, in my English Department, I faced being fired by conservatives, and was observed in my class five times in five months. It was a hard time that almost gave me an ulcer, but I managed to keep my job and do politics, feeling fear. Each year was a research for me in new political conditions.

Paulo   You are right—politics is a research also.

Ira   But not a very genteel research, not safely locked away in the archives. I can understand the fear of doing this kind of research, this testing of political practice. The moment you begin opposition you reveal yourself, you expose yourself for the "dream" you want and against the "dream" held by the authorities and their supporters.

ACTING IN SPITE OF FEAR

Paulo   This is the question. But, you know the limits of the establishment to the extent you work or act in your location. That is, without acting you never can know what the limits are for you.

Ira   My professor friend in 1972 was stopping short of the limits we had to act. But, he had a family to support and he had already lost one job.

Paulo   The problem is to act without being paralyzed by your fear. In the case of teachers, for example, it's very good when we take risks in different spaces, not just in the schools. Now, I said "risks" because this is one of the concrete parts of the action. If you don't command your fear, you no longer risk. And if you don't risk, you don't create anything. Without risking, for me, there is no possibility to exist.

Let us suppose we work in a faculty of education in some university. We are afraid because we are trying to do something different. What is terrible is that what we can do in some faculties is nothing that could seriously endanger the establishment. But, the establishment is *so* demanding concerning its preservation that it does not allow anything, even something naive, which can say NO! to it. Then, facing the sensitivity of the establishment, we are afraid. But, as I said before, we are clarifying our choice. We are knowing more or less what we would like to do. I think that one of the first things to do is to begin to know the space in which we are. This means to know the different departments of the faculty, the dean of the faculty and his or her approach, his or her comprehension of the world, his or her ideological position, his or her choice. We need to know the teachers in the different departments. It is a kind of research. I call it making an "ideological map" of the institution.

By doing this, sooner or later, we begin to know who we can count on at certain moments. Acting alone is the *best* way to commit suicide. It's impossible to confront the lion romantically! You have to know who you can count on and who you have to fight. To the extent you more or less know that, you can begin to be *with* and not to be *alone.* The sensation of not being alone diminishes fear.

Let me say here, now, why I insist constantly on the politicity of education. There was a time in my life as an educator when I did not speak about politics and education. It was my most naive moment. There was another time when I began to speak about the political aspects of education. That was a *less* naive moment, when I wrote *Pedagogy of the Oppressed* (1970). In the second moment, nevertheless, I was still thinking that education was not politics but only had an *aspect* of politics. In the *third* moment, today, for me there is *not* a political aspect. For me, now I say that education is politics. Today, I say education has the quality of being politics, which shapes the learning process. Education is politics and politics has *educability.* Because education is politics, it makes sense for the liberating teacher to feel some fear when he or she is teaching.

Then, when I am convinced of this, and being convinced that education is politics does *not* abolish fear, I treat my fear not as a ghost that commands me. *I* am the subject of my fear. This command over fear did not happen soon. It took time in my life. When rumors of a coup came up in early 1964, many people in Brazil preferred not to believe them. Instead of "cultivating" their fears, they chose to say a coup was impossible. My feelings then were different. I felt the coup was possible, even though I leaned towards thinking that maybe it wouldn't happen. Before the coup I had less fear of a military move because of the optimism of the people at that time. After the coup, everyone's fears and mine in general increased. Getting control of fear is not the same thing for everyone. It depends on the intensity of the practice. It depends on the results of your practice. For example, my experience in jail was very good for me. No? (Laughs) Every time I say that I insist on adding that I am *not* a masochist! But I learned a lot in jail.

Some months after the coup in 1964 I spent 75 days in jail. I had different experiences there, concerning the kinds of cells, the kinds of human relationships with the people in prison and with the people who put us in prison, many things. My experience in exile taught me a great deal also.

Ira   Such punishments for teachers are still extreme here in the U.S. It's easy to lose your job for radical teaching or for opposing school policy or for organizing students, but it is far less likely that you would be put in jail, unless you broke some laws. It is almost impossible to be forced into exile. At this moment, those are punishments that teachers in the U.S. do not have to face for being in the opposition.

My doctoral committee in Madison was fired during the Vietnam era because they were outspoken against the war and also took militant stands against racism, sexism, and authoritarian education. But they were not put in jail. They lost their jobs, their incomes, had their careers broken, and their families' lives disrupted. You might say they were forced into a kind of internal exile, because they had to leave town, give up their homes, pack up their families and move far away. Could you say something more of your experiences in jail or in exile, concerning fear?

Paulo   I had several difficult moments of cultivating my fear after I was arrested at my home in the coup.

One afternoon, I was in my cell with five or six colleagues, intellectuals, lawyers, doctors, liberal professionals. Lunch was just given to us by the jailers, but we had all thrown away more than we had eaten of the horrible food. Some of us were silent, some talked. Then, a policeman marched into the cell and demanded, "Who is Paulo Freire?" I answered "Present!" like a student in school. He then said, "I love prisoners like you with a good sense of obedience. Take your things and come with me." I asked, "Where to?" But he only answered, "You'll find out when you get there."

He put me in a jeep which sped off. While the jeep was moving, I felt fear enveloping me. I asked myself, "Where am I going now? What is my destination? Am I going somewhere I can return from? How can I let Elza know I am being moved?" For a prisoner, being moved is something to worry about. The jeep traveled 30–40 minutes during which I was invaded by fear of the unknown. At some moment in the ride, I realized that if I did not get control of my fear, it would destroy me.

To get some control, I established a relationship between my individual experience and the larger political moment I was in. This comparison of my situation with the problems of the country gave me some detachment. Also, I perceived that my class position as an educator might protect me, at least at that moment in the coup. Those 40 minutes in the jeep were my strongest moments of wrestling with my fear, even though I had felt fear earlier, when I was first arrested.

When the jeep finally stopped, the police handed me over to a lieutenant in an army barracks. Now I had a new fear to overcome after dealing with my first fear of the unknown in the jeep. At the barracks, they put me in a box, a kind of small closet perhaps two feet by three feet, with no windows. I spent a day and a night in that box. When I first recognized the barracks and knew where I was, my fear of the unknown decreased, but I then had a second fear, whether or not I could survive biologically in such a box, and how long would they keep me in it. I was not sure I could deal with such a space. My body would have to invent surviving in a box where the walls were rippled so that I could not rest against them without pain.

After finally accepting that I was in such a box, I had to confront the size of the space to avoid its damaging effects, how to sit or stand or kneel, and so on. While I was deep in thought about this, a sergeant suddenly came to the box and spoke to me when he knew we were alone. He said through an iron grate in the door, "Professor, I know who you are and I also know you have no experience in being in such a space. Don't stand up or sit down too long. You must walk in the box. Every hour or so, call for me or someone else on duty and say you need to go to the toilet, even if you don't have to, just to get out, and don't hurry back in." This advice helped me a lot to deal with my fear in the box.

My story took place during the coup. But, in terms of dealing with fear, I can also speak of a fantastic testimony about this question a few years ago from a black worker in Brazil, when I was visiting a Christian base community, a Catholic grassroots community. There was a public meeting of about 1,000 people where I was received in the community. This was in 1980, when I had just arrived back in Brazil after my exile since 1964. This community was in a local neighborhood in Sao Paulo. The meeting was especially for us to have a conversation together after sixteen years of separation, when I was far from Brazil.

At one moment, this man, a tall, strong, beautiful man, began to talk. He said, "Some years ago, I learned how to read and to write with the proposals of this man here," and he put his hand out like this, pointing to me. He then said, "But to the extent that I began to read, to write the words, simultaneous with understanding better how Brazilian society worked, I became strongly motivated to do the same with other workers who also could not read. And then I became a teacher of literacy. I began to teach some other people, to do with them what the other teachers did with me. Of course, I began to discuss with the others the problems of Brazil, the coup d'état in Brazil, the violence against the workers. One day the police came, and arrested me. They took me to the prefect's office, the police station, to put me in jail."

He said then, "When I was going to the police office, to be put in jail, to speak with the prefect, I began to think of my seven children. And the more I thought of the seven children, the more I was afraid. When the police car stopped at the station, they took me out and I was introduced to the chief in the district office. He stared at me and said, 'Look, I have some information about you. They say you are a good man, not a bad man. Your behavior is good. But, they say you were influenced by the ideas of a *bad Brazilian,* the so-called Paulo Freire, and now you are teaching people according to the ideas of this bad Brazilian. I brought you here to tell you this is your first time, your first warning, so I will let you go back, but please stop teaching people with the ideas of this bad Brazilian.' "

The black worker from the community looked around and then said, "At the moment when the chief made his speech to me I had the temptation to feel happy because I was being released. And I almost denied using Paulo Freire. And I came home feeling happy because I was free, crying out, I am free! I am free! I embraced my kids and I kissed my wife, and I spent three days without giving class. On the fourth day, I said to myself, No, it is impossible, I must continue to teach. At the same time, I said to myself, What am I going to do with my seven kids? I can't go on teaching because of the kids. Finally, I taught the classes. The next week I was called in again to the police station, by the same man. He said, 'You did not accept my suggestion, so you will stay here now. I don't know when I will let you go.' "

I can't forget the speech of this man, his testimony! I must always think of him as one of *my* best educators, one of *my* best teachers.

And then he said, that in jail, he began to think again of his seven kids, and about his wife. Finally, some people intervened and he was released. When he got out, he insisted again on teaching the classes.

This story is beautiful because we can see in it the question of fear associated with the dream, how he learned to control fear *without* rejecting it.

He said that the third time, when he began teaching the classes, he was called again to the police station. The chief said to him, "Look, it was just told me that you know fifty percent of the slum in which you live. And fifty percent of the people know you. Why don't you leave this area? Why don't you forget Paulo Freire? Why don't you go far away and live in another slum where you don't know anyone, start a new life?"

The answer he gave to the police chief was, "Oh, Mr. Prefect, yes I know fifty percent of the people of my slum. How can I leave the slum right now when I must get to know the *other* fifty percent?"

The worker stopped his story and stared at me in the great silence of this big meeting. I am sure he heard the silence gripping the attention of the people there. Finally, he said, "And about my seven kids, what happened to them?"

He answered his own question in such a *fantastic* way! Look, I am sweating from the memory of his speech! He said, "There was a moment in my fear in which I discovered that *precisely* because of the seven kids I could not be silent!" Do you see?

Ira   His dream was their hope for the future. His fear meant that their hope was alive, their future was coming to life.

Paulo   Yes! His dream, absolutely concrete, is his future and his hope. In no sense was there a future for his kids without his hope. Then, knowing this, he overcame his fear. No paralyzing fear. This, Ira, is what is not easy to explain, or to live with. After seeing the sweetness of this fantastic man, this Brazilian worker, this story of his fear, when I left the meeting that night in Sao Paulo, I also felt more or less changed. That is, finally, that man added to me some dimension of courage.

Ira   The Brazilian worker was knitted into a community that helped him know what he was fighting for, but he also faced more severe repression than teachers face in the First World, who may lose their jobs but won't be locked up for doing liberatory education.

When I think of getting knitted into a location and acting for a dream of transformation, I'm taken back to the 'ideological profile' you spoke about earlier, as a way of preparing myself for opposition. I know I didn't understand this in the 60s, when the upheavals were immature and not well-organized. Now, I see better the value of research and preparation, to make opposition count, and also as a way of reducing fear by reducing mistakes and unnecessary risks. If you do a careful institutional profile, a map of who is on what side politically, then you can find allies, scout your enemies in advance, get a feel for what terrain offers some political opening. This preparation not only reduces the chances of miscalculating the room for opposition, but it also starts knitting you into your location. I found that I also had to learn what the history of politics had been in my college before I arrived there as a new professor. It's very easy to discredit yourself if you stand up naively and propose something that had been just fought over before you arrived.

The black worker in your story had friends who could intervene for him. He worked in concert with others in his community so the police could not simply isolate him. He wasn't a romantic hero. If teacher-militants can become 'institutional citizens' knitted into the school or college, the authorities cannot so easily uproot us or characterize us as outsiders. Doing the institutional profile helps this knitting, I think. Another political method that helps is called 'deviance credits.' I think of this as taking on some of the harmless tasks of the institution so that you get recognized as a legitimate part of the scenery. There are many things formal schools or colleges do, from buying books for the library to planning how to decorate the buildings to judging student essay contests and appeals on grades. On the whole, society and its subsystems like education are authoritarian. But, not every piece is captured by authority or closed to democratic opposition. Finding cracks in the wall helps, like locating less obnoxious parts of the school or college to take part in for deviance credits. If you take part in a variety of small tasks, you begin slowly to root yourself in the life of the institution. The recognition you get for doing this is like an account of credits that allows you more room to deviate.

Confrontations are inevitable over pedagogy and policy, so there will be some risk and fear. You are bound to make interventions that offend the status quo. It matters to pick our battles carefully, but we also can store up weapons for the fight. If you accumulate deviance credits, the right to deviate, you gain more legitimacy for radical criticisms, for liberatory experiments, for opposition programs. You are not a total outsider and you are not a total insider. You have one leg in the life of the institution and one leg outside. Gaining this kind of credibility by doing some legitimate institutional tasks strengthens your chance to make opposition. You could say that it prolongs your life in the institution because you did something for the life of the institution as you found it when you arrived. This will simply make it harder for the authorities to fire you. After all, the point of making opposition is not to get fired fast!

Paulo   Yes (laughs).

Ira   The goal of opposition is not to get fired, but to make long opposition, so you can gradually research your efforts and feel out your territory, slow enough to cope with your fears, like the black worker in the story. If you can prolong your opposition, you'll take it farther. There's no way to avoid risk, fear, or offending the status quo, but maybe you can limit the response by the authorities, by keeping them off-balance, with something like deviance credits. I think the black worker in the story had deviance credits because of his association with the Church in Brazil, which is a powerful and legitimate institution there, and here in the U.S., too. He not only had half the slum as his acquaintance but he was also inside one of the pillars of his society, which made it harder for the police to pull him out and eliminate him. The police had less running room because of his connections. Still, he, a liberatory educator, had to work through his fear and convictions, to use the possibilities of his environment.

THE FEAR OF STUDENT RESISTANCE

Ira   Paulo, I'd like to go on here to talk about a different fear teachers speak about in the U.S. They fear *student* rejection of liberating pedagogy. Teachers who are transforming themselves to liberating methods often complain that students resist the invitation. The students often have traditional expectations.

Now, in the U.S., there are discipline problems. Students are reacting to resurgent authorities full of tests and new requirements. The economic crisis is also anxiety-producing. The job-market is poor, the cost of living high, the cost of college going up. So students want to know quickly what the market value of a course is. They resent taking required liberal arts courses that "waste" their time by distracting them from their career majors in business, nursing, engineering, or computers, the new hot programs that pushed humanities into a depression in the 70s.

Students worry about their futures. How do they get a good job out of this education? Liberating educators face student cynicism on a grand scale. Teachers often find themselves possessing a dream for society that is light years distant from the universe of their students. Some student militancy is reviving now, especially around apartheid in South Africa and the arms race and the war in Central America, but the premier problem has been a decade of careerism rather than liberating possibilities. How would you speak to this question?

Paulo   This fear of student rejection is a very concrete problem. First of all, it is *not* the students' thinking about jobs and money which makes society like it is now. On the contrary, it is society becoming a certain way which creates this preoccupation among students. There are some very concrete, historical conditions which create students' expectations about pedagogy. Secondly, I think that expecting a job after traditional education is not a problem for the official curriculum, not a problem for teachers who use the transfer-of-knowledge approach. Getting a job is a very concrete and realistic expectation which easily fits into the regular way of schooling. It is normal for traditional classrooms to respond to the students' preoccupation with getting a job. They agree with the status quo, including the job market the students must enter. Thirdly, I think that *both* the traditional and the liberating or democratic educator, in my view, have to answer the expectations of the students. Let me be more concrete.

Because I, the liberating educator, have some dreams perhaps completely different from the students, I don't have the right to accomplish my tasks in an irresponsible way. I cannot teach only to their demand that this course do nothing but help them get a job. Is that clear?

Ira   It's an important point. Explain it again.

Paulo   Both the traditional and the liberating educator do not have the right to deny the students' goals for technical training or for job credentials. Neither can they deny the technical aspects of education. There is a realistic need for technical expertise which education from a traditional or a liberatory perspective must speak to. Also, the students' need for technical training in order to qualify for jobs is a realistic demand on the educator.

Nevertheless, what is the *only* difference a liberating educator has on this question? The traditional educator and the democratic educator both have to be competent in their ability to educate students around skills needed for jobs. But the traditionalist does it with an ideology concerned with the preservation of the establishment. The liberating educator will try to be efficient in training, in forming the educatees scientifically and technically, but he or she will try to *unveil* the ideology enveloped in the *very* expectations of the students.

Ira   The traditional educator offers technical training in a way that strengthens the hold of dominant ideology on student consciousness. Training does not reveal the politics of doing such work. The liberatory teacher does not mystify jobs, careers or working, but poses critical questions while teaching them?

Paulo   Yes! No mystification.

Ira   Job skills must be criticized at the same time they are learned because the current conditions of society require students to enter a predatory job market.

Paulo   Yes, it is required! How is it possible *before* transforming society to deny students the knowledge they need to survive? For me, (laughing) it is an absurdity.

Ira   Then, our task as liberating educators with the necessity of training students for jobs is to raise critical questions about the very training we are giving. The students must earn a living, and no one can deny that need or have contempt for that expectation of theirs. At the same time, the pedagogical problem is how to intervene in the training so as to raise critical consciousness about the jobs and the training, too.

Paulo   I don't deny or question the need for training. But I absorb this aspect into my criticism of the whole system, in the class. Still, what is impossible is to be an *incompetent* educator because I am a revolutionary! (Laughing) Do you see? It would be a contradiction. The more seriously you are engaged in a search for transformation the more you have to be rigorous, the more you have to seek for knowledge, the more you have to challenge the students to be scientifically and technically prepared for the real society they are still living in. If the students use the course *just* to get jobs and be happy with that, you *cannot* kill them! (Laughing) You have to challenge them at the very same moment you are helping them to be prepared.

Ira   Won't students see this as a confusion? You are endorsing and criticizing the material at the same time.

Paulo   Ah, no, it is not a confusion. It is a contradiction. They must understand what contradiction means, that human action can move in several directions at once, that something can contain itself and its opposite also. for example, at the same time that architecture or nursing students get competent training, the liberating teacher has to raise questions about how people live in slums, and what are their medical and housing needs. It is not enough to prepare students to build for the rich or to treat the rich only. Neither is it enough to feel sorry for the poor. The politics of housing and medicine have to be integrated into the program.

Ira   Right now, vocational, career, and professional programs, like nursing, accounting, computers, engineering, business, marketing, teach job skills that funnel students uncritically into an unpredictable job market. The critical side of the curriculum resides almost exclusively in some liberal arts courses, in the college program. Sociologists, philosophers, anthropologists, historians, literature teachers, in some courses, not all, ask students to think critically, and only a small part of this reflection is actually devoted to critical scrutiny of work, careers, or domination in the job market. In my book *Critical Teaching and Everyday Life* (1980), I devoted some chapters to writing courses where "work" was investigated as a theme. There is now a radical separation in the curriculum between the programs that do the most concrete training for jobs and the programs that do the most critical reflection. This separation is political, not accidental. It prevents future labor from escaping dominant ideology. It segregates critical thinking from training. Such job preparation reduces the capacity of workers to challenge the system.

The problem for liberating educators is that they often wind up in the departments which do the *least* job training, with the least career orientation, like me in an English Department teaching writing, media and literature courses, with very few English majors at my college. My courses are filled with business, tech, nursing and computer majors, who are pumped full of career anxiety by their prime programs. So, from the start, students arriving in my classes or in other humanities courses know that the education offered there will be marginal to their career goals, to their getting the training required by the job-market. Still, I like to make a virtue of necessity, so I've found that the writing course has been able to raise some critical awareness even though it is not a career program. Perhaps that's because reading, writing and thinking have been defined as basic job skills, required for all careers, even though writing itself is a limited career choice for most students. The writing teacher can insert critical literacy closer to the job world precisely because writing classes can absorb social themes as their subject matter for literacy development. The techniques of writing need concrete subjects to create compositions, so the writing class is open to critical study of the most anticritical theme of education, career training.

Paulo   Let me go on with your example of the writing course or the writing teacher. Think about two English teachers. One is a convinced reactionary who does not want anything concerning social change. He or she thinks all things that exist are good and should stay that way. He thinks that those who fail are to blame for their own failure. The other English teacher on the contrary knows that his colleague is wrong. From the point of view of the interests of the mass of the people, he or she knows the reactionary is wrong, but the liberatory educator also knows that the traditional writing teacher is absolutely right from the point of view of the dominant class, which has the greatest stake in keeping things as they are.

Then, the liberatory educator has a different approach concerning language, teaching, learning. She or he knows very well that language is an ideological problem. Language has to do with social classes, the identity and power of each class being expressed in its language. But the liberating teacher also knows that today the standard that rules language is a very elitist one. The powers that rule society at large also have a standard by which language is judged. If the liberatory teacher wants to teach competently, he or she must know well the elite criterion by which language is valued. This is a hard criterion of language for common people from lower economic backgrounds to achieve, something which the liberatory teacher accepts without blaming the students for their problems with correct usage. By understanding the elite and political aspects of standard usage, the liberatory teacher avoids blaming the students for the clash of their own language with the ruling forms. Knowing these things, the liberatory teacher works with students who must gain a good command of standard English and correct usage.

Ira   You are saying that standard English is a job skill, a social skill that students must possess? The liberating educator is obliged to teach correct usage?

Paulo   Yes, the liberatory teacher has to know this, or see the language problem in this way. The so-called standard is a deeply *ideological* concept, but it is necessary to teach correct usage while also criticizing its political implications.

Now the question is, knowing all these things, does the liberating educator have the right *not* to teach standard usage? Does he or she have the right to say "I am a revolutionary so I don't teach the 'good' English?" No. In my point of view, she or he will have to make it possible for the students to command standard English but here is the big difference between him or her and the other reactionary teacher. While the traditionalist teaches the rules of the *famous English* (laughs) he or she *increases* the students' domination by elitist ideology which is inserted into these rules. The liberatory teacher teaches standard usage in order for them to survive while discussing with them *all* the ideological ingredients of this unhappy task. Do you see? This is how I think teachers can reflect on their fear of student rejection and also on their fear of standard usage.

Ira   We study standard usage and technical skills because of political realities facing students and teachers both, the fact that society is not yet an egalitarian one where elite standards no longer dominate. What we need to invent are liberatory methods which develop student command of correct usage and of job skills while encouraging them to respect their own idioms and to criticize the very nature of the unequal job-market. This is a complicated dual task which has taken up my attention since I began teaching at my worker college, to develop language skills and criticism of domination at the same time.

Paulo   Yes. This is the position I take in Brazil when I talk to teachers. A year or two ago, I opened a Brazilian congress of teachers of Portuguese. In my speech, I talked precisely about how the standard form or correct usage can be absorbed into a democratic pedagogy. This problem is very great for teachers in Brazil because there is such a vast social class difference between the Portuguese I speak and the Portuguese the workers speak. They are two separate worlds of language. The syntax is completely different. The structure of thinking is also different. The problem of concordance between subject and verb, for example, is constantly different from one class to another in Brazil.

To my thinking, teachers in popular areas of Brazil need first to give testimony to common students that they respect the language of the people. Secondly, they would have to give testimony that the language of the people is as beautiful as ours. Thirdly, they would have to help them believe in their own speech, not to be ashamed of their own language, but to discover the beauty in their own words. Fourthly, teachers who work among ordinary people would have to demonstrate that the common form of language also has a grammar which is invisible at the moment to them. Their ordinary way of speaking also has rules and structure. Their language exists because it is spoken. If it is spoken, it has a structure. If it has a structure, then it has grammatical rules too. Behind this ordinary speech, there is an unwritten grammar and an unrecognized beauty, which of course the dominant class would not draw to the attention of the common people. To organize such knowledge and make it clear to the people would be to challenge the dominance of the elite forms and thus of the elite class itself.

Finally, teachers have to say to students, Look, in spite of being beautiful, this way you speak also includes the question of *power*. Because of the political problem of power, you need to learn how to command the dominant language, in order for you to survive in the struggle to transform society.

Someone may ask me, But, Paulo, if you teach correct usage, the poor or working-class student may just get ruling ideology through the elite usage. Yes! It is a danger. But dominant ideology is not being reproduced *exclusively* through language or through school. There are other ways of reproduction in society, and language is only one mechanism. For me, what we cannot deny to working-class students is the grasp of some principles of the grammar common to the dominant class. Not grasping the elite forms would only make it more difficult for them to survive in the struggle. The testimony that must be given to students as we teach the standard form is that they need to command it not exclusively in order to survive, but *above all* for fighting better against the dominant class.

Ira   This is political wisdom for liberatory teachers. Still, I must criticize the word "survival," because "survival" is a conservative theme that put teachers and students on the defensive after the egalitarian '60s. The word "survival" has poisoned the educational atmosphere in the States with more fear than is necessary. The student fear of survival has helped conservatives tilt the curriculum towards careerism and back-to-basics. By alarming students, teachers and parents about survival, conservatives in the recent period were helped in narrowing the experimental and democratic curricula from the '60s. From another angle, I'd say that the overblown talk about survival is also an unnecessary paternalism by teachers. Students are very resourceful in dealing with the predatory job market. They know that connections, aggressiveness, luck, moxie, and chutzpah play as big a role as paper credentials. Students need critical education, skills, degrees, and adult mentoring, but they don't benefit from an alarming picture of reality, where careerism and back-to-basics are falsely posed as the keys to a fearful kingdom. Fears of survival only strengthen conservatism by encouraging students and teachers to think of career programs as the solution, while critical learning and politics are only distractions. Job training and vocationalism have always been the curricula of choice by business forces for the mass of students. Workbased programs also have a poor historical record of connecting schoolish training with future employment.

I said these things because the theme of survival has become too angelic in my culture. I always remind myself that the great masters of survival are the cockroaches of New York! I've read that they reproduce every few generations a new breed that resists the insecticides deadly to their grandparents. Cockroaches can beam with pride at their children's survival powers. I've also read that cockroaches are likely to be the best survivors of a nuclear war. Not too long ago, the '60s was a time when masses of people thought about "thriving," not just "surviving." Cockroach "survival" has served the authorities' need to restrain the mass movements of the '60s and to limit demands for power, equality, and prosperity.

When the political pendulum swings back to social movements, fears teachers have about student rejection of liberatory education will change with the changing tides of history. These fears, I think, are the size of this conservative age. You're right, Paulo, about the need to make concessions to the limits of the moment, the need to insert critical learning into correct usage and career issues. But, conservative eras that set such limits are made and unmade in history. As conservatism ebbs and popular militancy returns, student resistance to transformative learning should decline. Will teachers then fall behind the experimental desires of the students?

Teaching as an Act of Love: Reflections on Paulo Freire and His Contributions to Our Lives and Our Work

ANTONIA DARDER

As individuals or as peoples, by fighting for the restoration of [our] humanity [we] will be attempting the restoration of true generosity. And this fight, because of the purpose given it, will actually constitute an act of love.

—Paulo Freire
Pedagogy of the Oppressed (1970)

For days, I have reflected on the writings of Paulo Freire; and with every turn of ideas, I've been brought back to the notion of love and its manifestation in our work and our lives. Here, let me say quickly that I am neither speaking of a liberal, romanticized, or merely feel-good notion of love that so often is mistakenly attributed to this term nor the long-suffering and self-effacing variety associated with traditional religious formation. Nothing could be further from the truth. If there was anything that Freire consistently sought to defend, it was the freshness, spontaneity, and presence embodied in what he called an "armed loved—the fighting love of those convinced of the right and the duty to fight, to denounce, and to announce" (Freire, 1998, p. 42). A love that could be lively, forceful, and inspiring, while at the same time, critical, challenging, and insistent. As such, Freire's brand of love stood in direct opposition to the insipid "generosity" of teachers or administrators who would blindly adhere to a system of schooling that fundamentally transgresses every principle of cultural and economic democracy.

Rather, I want to speak to the experience of love as I came to understand it through my work and friendship with Freire. I want to write about a political and radicalized form of love that is never about absolute consensus, or unconditional acceptance, or unceasing words of sweetness, or endless streams of hugs and kisses. Instead, it is a love that I experienced as unconstricted, rooted in a committed willingness to struggle persistently with purpose in our life and to intimately connect that purpose with what he called our "true vocation"—to be human.

A COMMITMENT TO OUR HUMANITY

> *A humanizing education is the path through which men and women can become conscious about their presence in the world. The way they act and think when they develop all of their capacities, taking into consideration their needs, but also the needs and aspirations of others. (Freire & Betto, 1985, p. 14–15)*

For Freire, a liberatory education could never be conceived without a profound commitment to our humanity. Once again, I must point out that his notion of humanity was not merely some simplistic or psychologized notion of "having positive self-esteem," but rather a deeply reflective interpretation of the dialectical relationship between our cultural existence as individuals and our political and economic existence as social beings. From Freire's perspective, if we were to solve the educational difficulties of students from oppressed communities, then educators had to look beyond the personal. We had to look for answers within the historical realm of economic, social, and political forms, so that we might better understand those forces that give rise to our humanity as it currently exists. In so many ways, his work pointed to how economic inequality and social injustice dehumanize us, distorting our capacity to love ourselves, each other, and the world. In the tradition of Antonio Gramsci before him, Freire exposed how even well-meaning teachers, through their lack of critical moral leadership, actually participate in disabling the heart, minds, and bodies of their students—an act that disconnects these students from the personal and social motivation required to transform their world and themselves.

There is no question that Freire's greatest contribution to the world was his capacity to be a loving human being. His regard for children, his concern for teachers, his work among the poor, his willingness to share openly his moments of grief, disappointment, frustration, and new love, all stand out in my mind as examples of his courage and unrelenting pursuit of a coherent and honest life. I recall our meeting in 1987, six months after the death of his first wife, Elza. Freire was in deep grief. During one of his presentations, he literally had to stop so that he could weep the tears that he had been trying to hold back all morning. For a moment, all of us present were enveloped by his grief and probably experienced one of the greatest pedagogical lessons of our life. I don't believe anyone left the conference hall that day as they had arrived. Through the courageous vulnerability of his humanity—with all its complexities and contradictions—Freire illuminated our understanding of not only what it means to be a critical educator, but what it means to live a critical life.

In the following year, I experienced another aspect of Freire's living praxis. To everyone's surprise, Freire remarried a few months later. Many were stunned by the news and it was interesting to listen to and observe the responses of his followers in the States. Some of the same radical educators who had embraced him in his grief now questioned his personal decision to remarry so quickly after the death of Elza. Much to my surprise, the news of his marriage and his public gestures of affection and celebration of his new wife, Nita, were met with a strange sort of suspicion and fear. Despite these reverberations, Freire spoke freely of his new love and the sensations that now stirred in him. He shared his struggle with loneliness and grief and challenged us to *live and love* in the present—as much personally as politically.

FEAR AND REVOLUTIONARY DREAMS

The more you recognize your fear as a consequence of your attempt to practice your dream, the more you learn how to put into practice your dream! I never had interviews with the great revolutionaries of this century about their fears! But all of them felt fear, to the extent that all of them were very faithful to their dreams. (Shor & Freire, 1987, p. 57)

Challenging the conditioned fears with which our dreams of freedom are controlled and the "false consciousness" that diminishes our social agency are common themes in Freire's work. In *Pedagogy of the Oppressed* (1970), he wrote of the *fear of freedom* that afflicts us, a fear predicated on prescriptive relationships between those who rule and those who are expected to follow. As critical educators, he urged us to question carefully our ideological beliefs and pedagogical intentions and to take note of our own adherence to the status quo. He wanted us to recognize that every *prescribed behavior* represents the imposition of one human being upon another—an imposition that moves our consciousness away from what we experience in the flesh to an abstracted reality and false understanding of our ourselves and our world. If we were to embrace a pedagogy of liberation, we had to prepare ourselves to replace this conditioned fear of freedom with sufficient autonomy and responsibility to struggle for an educational praxis and a way of life that could support democratic forms of economic and cultural existence.

Freire often addressed the notion of fear in his speeches and in his writings. In his eyes, fear and revolutionary dreams were unquestionably linked. The more that we were willing to struggle for an emancipatory dream, the more apt we were to know intimately the experience of fear, how to control and educate our fear, and finally, how to transform that fear into courage. Moreover, we could come to recognize our fear as a signal that we are engaged in critical opposition to the status quo and in transformative work toward the manifestation of our revolutionary dreams.

In many ways, Freire attempted to show us through his own life that facing our fears and contending with our suffering are inevitable and necessary human dimensions of our quest to make and remake history, of our quest to make a new world from our dreams. Often, he likened our movement toward greater humanity as a form of *childbirth, and a painful one*. This *labor of love* constitutes a critical process in our struggle to break the *oppressor-oppressed* contradiction and the conflicting beliefs that incarcerate our humanity. Freire's description of this duality is both forthright and sobering.

> The oppressed suffer from the duality which has established itself in their innermost being. They discover that without freedom they cannot exist authentically. Yet, although they desire authentic existence, they fear it. They are at one and the same time themselves and the oppressor whose consciousness they have internalized. The conflict lies in the choice between wholly themselves or being divided; between ejecting the oppressor within or not ejecting him; between human solidarity or alienation; between following prescriptions or having choices; between being spectators or actors, between acting or having the illusion of acting through the action of the oppressors; between speaking out or being silent, castrated in their power to create and re-create, in their power to transform the world. (1970, p. 33)

Freire firmly believed that if we were to embrace a pedagogy of freedom, we had to break out of this duality. We had to come to see how the domesticating power of the dominant ideology causes teachers to become ambiguous and indecisive, even in the face of blatant injustice. Critical educators had to struggle together against a variety of punitive and threatening methods used by many administrators to instill a fear of freedom. Because if this domesticating role were not rejected, even progressive teachers could fall prey to *fatalism*—a condition that negates passion and destroys the capacity to dream—making them each day more politically vulnerable and less able to face the challenges before them.

Fatalism is a notion that Freire, until the end, refused to accept. At every turn, he emphatically rejected the idea that nothing could be done about the educational consequences of economic inequalities and social injustice. If the economic and political power of the ruling class denied subordinate populations the space to survive, it was not because "it should be that way" (Freire, 1997, p. 41). Instead, the asymmetrical relations of power that perpetuate fatalism among those with little power had to be challenged. This required teachers to problematize the conditions of schooling with their colleagues, students, and parents, and through a critical praxis of reflection, dialogue, and action, become capable of *announcing justice*. But such an announcement required a total *denouncement of fatalism*, which would unleash our power to push against the limits, create new spaces, and begin redefining our vision of education and society.

CAPITALISM AS THE ROOT OF DOMINATION

> *Brutalizing the work force by subjecting them to routine procedures is part of the nature of the capitalist mode of production. And what is taking place in the reproduction of knowledge in the schools is in large part a reproduction of that mechanism. (Freire & Faundez, 1989, p. 42)*

The question of power is ever present in Freire's work, as is his intimacy with the struggle for democracy. At this juncture, it is vitally important that we turn to Freire's ideological beginnings—a dimension of his work that often has been negated or simply ignored by many liberals and progressives who embraced his pedagogical ideas. A quick scan of the writings cited in *Pedagogy of the Oppressed* clearly illustrates that Freire's work was unabashedly grounded in Marxist-Socialist thought. Without question, when Freire spoke of the *ruling class* or the *oppressors,* he was referring to historical class distinctions and class conflict within the structure of capitalist society—capitalism was the root of domination. As such, his theoretical analysis was fundamentally rooted in notions of class formation, particularly with respect to how the national political economy relegated the greater majority of its workers to an exploited and marginalized class. However, for Freire, the struggle against economic domination could not be waged effectively without a humanizing praxis that could both engage the complex phenomenon of class struggle and effectively foster the conditions for critical social agency among the masses.

Although heavily criticized on the left for his failure to provide a more systematic theoretical argument against capitalism, Freire's work never retreated from a critique of capitalism and a recognition of capitalist logic as the primary totalizing force in the world. This is to say that he firmly believed that the phenomenon of cultural invasion worldwide was fundamentally driven by the profit motives of capitalists. During my early years as a critical educator, I, like so many, failed to adequately comprehend and incorporate this essential dimension of Freire's work. For critical educators of color in the United States, we saw racism as the major culprit of our oppression and insisted that Freire engage this issue more substantively. Although he openly acknowledged the existence of racism, he was reticent to abandon the notion of class struggle and often warned us against losing sight of the manner in "which the class factor is hidden within both sexual and racial discrimination" (Freire, 1997, p. 86). Our dialogues with him on this issue often were lively and intense because in many ways, Freire questioned the limits of cultural nationalism and our blind faith in a politics of identity. At several different conferences, where educators of color called for separate dialogues with him, he told us that he could not understand why we insisted in dividing ourselves. With true angst, Freire explained to us: "I cannot perceive in my mind how Blacks in America can be liberated without Chicanos being liberated, or how Chicanos can be liberated without Native Americans being liberated, or Native Americans liberated without Whites being liberated" (Freire, 1987). He insisted that the struggle against oppression was a human struggle in which we had to build solidarity across our differences, if we were to change a world engulfed by capitalism. "The lack of unity among the reconcilable 'different' helps the hegemony of the antagonistic 'different'. The most important fight is against the main enemy" (Freire, 1997, p. 85). As might be expected, many of us walked away frustrated. Only recently have I come to understand the political limits of our parochial discourse.

The world economy has changed profoundly since the release of *Pedagogy of the Oppressed,* yet Freire's message remains more relevant than ever. As capital, labor, and knowledge increasingly are conceived of in global terms, the influential role of capital is expanded exponentially, and the globalization of national and local economies is changing the underlying basis of the nation-state (Carnoy, 1997), these structural changes are reflected in the theories and practices of public schooling. As a consequence, "there is now a radical separation in the curriculum between the programs that do the most concrete training for jobs and the programs that do the most critical reflection. Such job separation reduces the capacity of workers to challenge the system" (Shor & Freire, 1987, p. 47).

Moreover, as Ladislau Dowbor (1997) eloquently argues in his preface to *Pedagogy of the Heart,* we must remove the blinders and see capitalism as the generator of scarcity. We cannot afford to ignore the growing gap between the rich and the poor caused by an increasing economic polarization that belies neoliberal theories of the trickle-down effect. And despite an abundance of technological devices flooding the market place, clean rivers, clean air, clean drinking water, chemical-free food, free time, and the space for adults and children to socialize freely has diminished. "Capitalism requires that free-of-charge happiness be substituted for what can be bought and sold" (p. 26). Yet, seldom do we find with the resounding praises paid to technology a discussion of how technological revolutions have exposed the wretchedness of capitalism—millions of people dying from starvation alongside unprecedented wealth. And even more disconcerting is the deleterious impact of globalized capitalism upon the social and environmental interests of humanity—interests that seem to receive little concern next to the profit motives of transnational corporations.

CHALLENGING OUR LIMITATIONS

In order to achieve humanization, which presupposes the elimination of dehumanizing oppression, it is absolutely necessary to surmount the limit-situations in which men [and women] are reduced to things. (Freire, 1970, p. 93)

Although Freire's historical, regional, and class experiences were different from many of ours, his political purpose was clear and consistent. To achieve a liberatory practice, we had to challenge those conditions that limit our social agency and our capacity to intervene and transform our world. In light of this, Freire's frequent response to questions about issues that perpetuate educational injustice was to challenge us to consider the nature of the limits we were confronting and how we might transcend these limitations in order to discover that beyond these situations, and in contradiction to them, lie *untested feasibilities* for personal, institutional, and socioeconomic restructuring. For example, in thinking back to how many educators of color responded to Freire's insistence that we create alliances to struggle against capitalism, many of us could not break loose from our deep-rooted (and objectified) distrust of "Whites," nor could we move beyond our self-righteous justification of our sectarianism. These represented two of the limit situations that prevented us from establishing the kind of democratic solidarity or *unity within diversity* that potentially could generate profound shifts in the political and economic systems that intensify racism. Freire knew this and yet listened attentively to our concerns and frustrations within the context of our dialogues, always with respect and a deep faith in the power of our political commitment and perseverance.

Freire deeply believed that the rebuilding of solidarity among educators was a vital and necessary radical objective because solidarity moved against the grain of "capitalism's intrinsic perversity, its anti-solidarity nature" (Freire, 1998, p. 88). Throughout his writings, Freire warned us repeatedly against sectarianism. "Sectarianism in any quarter is an obstacle to the emancipation of [human] kind" (Freire, 1970, p. 22). "While fighting for my dream, I must not become passionately closed within myself" (Freire, 1998, p. 88). In many instances, he linked our ability to create solidarity with our capacity for *tolerance.*

At a critical scholars' conference in Boston during the summer of 1991, I came face to face with Freire's notion of tolerance. The meetings had been quite intense, particularly with respect to the concerns of feminist scholars within the field. Rather than exemplifying dialogue, I felt the exchanges began to take on a rather virulent tone. In my frustration, I stood up and fired away at one of the presenters. Freire seemed upset with my response. The following day during my presentation, I again proceeded to critique passionately the lack of substantive commitment to the principles of dialogue and solidarity among the group, focusing my critique on issues of cultural and class differences among many of us. Freire's response to my comments that afternoon remain with me to this day. He was particularly concerned with what he judged as my lack of tolerance and besieged me to behave with greater tolerance in the future, if I was to continue this work effectively. With great political fervor, I rejected Freire's position making the case that what we needed was to be more *intolerant*—of oppression and social injustice! For years, I licked my wounds over being *scolded* in public by Freire. But eight years later, I must confess that I recognize great wisdom in Freire's advise. Despite my undeniable political commitment, I was lacking tolerance as "revolutionary virtue—the wisdom of being able to live with what is different, so as to be able to fight the common enemy" (Freire & Faundez, 1989, p. 18).

Let us stop for a moment and recognize that just as we all face limit situations in our world and within ourselves, Freire, too, faced such issues in his private and public life. In 1964, after launching the most successful national literacy campaign Brazil had ever known, he was imprisoned and exiled by the right-wing military dictatorship that had overthrown the democratically elected government of Joao Goulart. Freire remained in exile for almost

16 years. But despite the pain and hardships he and his family experienced, Freire's work as an educator and cultural worker continued unabated. In reminiscences of those years, I recall most the sense that Freire clearly understood domination and exploitation as a worldwide phenomenon. As such, he recognized that within the political struggle for a socialist democracy, a myriad of legitimate political projects existed that, regardless of location, were unequivocally linked by their purpose and commitment to economic and cultural democracy. On a more personal level, he spoke of enduring the pain and suffering of exile, while at the same time not reducing his life to grieving alone. "I do not live only in the past. Rather, I exist in the present, where I prepare myself for the possible" (Freire, 1998, p. 67). Hence, Freire's experience of exile was as much a time of facing a multitude of fears, sorrows, and doubts within unfamiliar contexts as it was a time for remaking himself anew and restoring the dreams that had been shattered.

As Freire's work became more prominent within the United States, he also grappled with a variety of issues that both challenged and concerned him. For almost three decades, feminists across the country fiercely critiqued the sexism of his language. In some arenas, Marxist scholars criticized him brutally for his failure to provide a systematic analysis of class, capitalism, and schooling. To the dismay of many scholars, educators, and organizers of color, Freire seemed at times unwilling (or unable) to engage, with greater depth and specificity, the perverse nature of racism and its particular historical formations within the United States. Neither could he easily accept, from a historical materialist perspective, the legitimacy of the Chicano movement and its emphasis on a mythological homeland, Atzlan. Along the same lines, Freire also questioned the uncompromising resistance or refusal of many radical educators of color to assume the national identity of "American"—an act that he believed fundamentally weakened our position and limited our material struggle for social and economic justice. Beyond these issues, he also harbored serious concerns over what he perceived as the splintered nature of the critical pedagogy movement in the United States. Yet, most of these issues were seldom engaged substantively in public, but rather were the fodder of private dialogues and solitary reflections.

Given this history, it is a real tribute to Freire, that in *Pedagogy of the Heart* (or *Under the Shade of the Mango Tree*—its original title), written shortly before his death, Freire demonstrated signs of change and deepening in his thinking about many of these issues. For example, the language in the book finally reflected an inclusiveness of women when making general references, which had been missing in his earlier writings. He spoke to the issue of capitalism more boldly than ever before and considered the nature of globalization and its meaning for radical educators. He also addressed issues of diversity and racism, acknowledging openly that, "[w]e cannot reduce all prejudice to a classist explanation, but we may not overlook it in understanding the different kinds of discrimination" (p. 86). And more forcefully than ever, he spoke to the necessity of moving beyond our reconcilable differences so that we might forge an effective attack against the wiles of advanced capitalism in the world.

THE CAPACITY TO ALWAYS BEGIN ANEW

This capacity to always begin anew, to make, to reconstruct, and to not spoil, to refuse to bureaucratize the mind, to understand and to live as a process—live to become—is something that always accompanied me throughout life. This is an indispensable quality of a good teacher. (Freire, 1993, p. 98)

The examples above are shared not to diminish, in any way, Freire's contribution or the memory of his work, but rather to remember him within his totality as a human being, with many of the conflicts and contradictions that confront us all, and yet with an expansive ability for sustained reflection, inquiry, and dialogue. But most important, he had an incredible capacity to reconstruct and *begin always anew.* For Freire, there was no question that he, others, and the world were always in a state of becoming, of transforming, and reinventing ourselves as part of our human historical process. This belief served as the foundation for his unrelenting search for freedom and his unwavering hope in the future. In the tradition of Marx, he believed that we both make and are made by our world. And as such, all human beings are the makers of history. In Freire's view, knowledge could not be divorced from historical continuity. Like us, "history is a process of being limited and conditioned by the knowledge that we produce. Nothing that we engender, live, think, and make explicit takes place outside of time and history" (Freire, 1998, p. 32). And more important, educators had to recognize that "it was when the majorities are denied their right to participate in history as subjects that they become dominated and alienated" (Freire, 1970, p. 125).

In light of this, Freire was convinced that this historical process needed to take place within schools and communities, anchored in relationships of solidarity. Freire urged critical educators to build communities of solidarity as a form of *networking,* to help us in problematizing the debilitating conditions of globalized economic inequality and in confronting the devastating impact of neoliberal economic and social policies on the world's population. Freire believed that teachers, students, parents, and others could reproduce skills and knowledge through networks formed around schools and adult education, youth organizations, and religious organizations that have a common democratic interest to enhance individual and collective life. More important, through *praxis*—the authentic union of action and reflection—these education networks could enter into the re-making of a new culture of capital, both as sites for the integration of disassociated workers and for the development of critical consciousness (or *conscientização*), ultimately shaping the future of local and national politics, and hence, altering the nature of the global economy. Freire's notion of establishing critical networks is a particularly compelling thought considering the current political struggles in California for the protection of immigrant rights, affirmative action, and bilingual education.

In many ways, the idea of critical networks is linked directly with the struggle for democracy and an expanded notion of citizenship. Freire urged us to strive for *intimacy with democracy,* living actively with democratic principles and deepening them so that they could come to have real meaning in our everyday life. Inherent in this relationship with democracy was a form of citizenship that could not be obtained by chance. It represented a construction that was always in a state of becoming and required that we fight to obtain it. Further, it demanded *commitment, political clarity, coherence, and decision* on our part. Moreover, Freire insisted that:

> No one constructs a serious democracy, which implies radically changing the societal structures, reorienting the politics of production and development, reinventing power, doing justice to everyone, and abolishing the unjust and immoral gains of the all-powerful, without previously and simultaneously working for these democratic preferences and these ethical demands. (Freire, 1989, p. 67)

Freire also repeatedly associated the work of educators with an unwavering faith in the oppressed, who, too, were always in a state of becoming anew. "Never has there been a deeper need for progressive men and women—serious, radical, engaged in the struggle for transforming society, to give testimony of their respect for the people" (Freire, 1997, p. 84). Freire consistently identified this respect for and commitment to marginalized people as an integral ingredient to the cultivation of dialogue in the classroom. "Dialogue requires an intense faith in [others], faith in their power to make and remake, to create and re-create, faith in [their] vocation to be more fully human (which is not the privilege of an elite but the birthright of all)" (Freire, 1970, p. 79). Moreover, he insisted that true dialogue could not exist in the absence of love and humility. But for Freire, dialogue also implied a critical posture as well as a preoccupation with the meanings that students used to mediate their world. He believed it was impossible to teach without educators knowing what took place in their students' world. "They need to know the universe of their dreams, the language with which they skillfully defend themselves from the aggressiveness of their world, what they know independently of the school, and how they know it" (Freire, 1998, p. 73). Through such knowledge, teachers could support students in reflecting on their lives and making individual and collective decisions for transforming their world. As such, dialogue, through reflection and action, could never be reduced to blind action, deprived of intention and purpose.

INDISPENSABLE QUALITIES OF PROGRESSIVE TEACHERS

> *It is impossible to teach without the courage to try a thousand times before giving up. In short, it is impossible to teach without a forged, invented, and well-thought-out capacity to love. (Freire, 1998, p. 3)*

In *Teachers as Cultural Workers,* Freire (1998) wrote *Letters to Those Who Dare to Teach.* Again, he brings us back to an ethics of love and challenges us to reconsider our practice in new ways and to rethink our pedagogical commitment. Freire argued that the task of a teacher, who is always learning, must be both joyful and rigorous. He firmly believed that teaching for liberation required seriousness and discipline as well as scientific, physical, and emotional preparation. Freire stressed often that teaching was a task that required a love for the very act of teaching. For only through such love could the political project of teaching possibly become transformative and liberating. For Freire, it could never be enough to teach only with critical reason. He fervently argued that we must dare to do all things with feeling, dreams, wishes, fear, doubts, and passion.

> We must dare so as never to dichotomize cognition and emotion. We must dare so that we can continue to teach for a long time under conditions that we know well: low salaries, lack of respect, and the ever-present risk of becoming prey to cynicism. We must dare to learn how to dare in order to say no to the bureaucratization of the mind to which we are exposed every day. We must dare so that we can continue to do so even when it is so much more materially advantageous to stop daring. (Freire, 1998, p. 3)

To be a progressive teacher who dares to teach requires, in Freire's eyes, a set of very particular and indispensable qualities. He believed these qualities could protect radical teachers from falling into the trappings of *avant-gardism,* by helping them become more conscious of their language, their use of authority in the classroom, and their teaching strategies. Through striving to develop these qualities, teachers could also come to understand that they cannot liberate anyone, but rather that they were in a strategic position to invite their students to liberate themselves, as they learned to read their world and transform their present realities.

Unlike the traditional pedagogical emphasis on specific teaching methodologies, particular classroom curricula, and the use of standardized texts and materials, Freire's *indispensable qualities* focus on those human values that expand a teacher's critical and emotional capacity to enter into effective learning-teaching relationships with their students. Freire begins with a *humility* grounded in courage, self-confidence, self-respect, and respect for others. In many ways, he believed that humility is the quality that allows us to listen beyond our differences, and as such represents a cornerstone in developing our intimacy with democracy. Freire associated humility with the *dialectical* ability to live an *insecure security,* which means a human existence that did not require absolute answers or solutions to a problem but rather that, even in the certainty of the moment, could remain open to new ways, new ideas, and new dreams. This anti-authoritarian position also works to prevent teachers from squelching expressions of resistance in their students—resistance that, in fact, is not only meaningful, but necessary to their process of empowerment. Inherent in this quality of humility also is the ability of teachers to build their capacity to express a *lovingness* rooted in their commitment to consistently reflect on their practice and to consider the consequences of their thoughts, words, and actions within the classroom and beyond.

In keeping with his consistent emphasis on the necessity of confronting our fears, Freire identified courage as another indispensable quality of educators. Courage here implies a virtue that is born and nourished by our consistent willingness to challenge and overcome our fears in the interest of democratic action—an action that holds both personal and social consequences. Freire believed that as teachers become clearer about their choices and political dreams, courage sustains our struggle to confront those myths, fueled by the dominant ideology, that fragment and distort our practice. Key to this process is our critical ability to both accept and control our fear.

> When we are faced with concrete fears, such as that of losing our jobs or of not being promoted, we feel the need to set certain limits to our fear. before anything else, we begin to recognize that fear is a manifestation of our being alive. I do not hide my fears. But I must not allow my fears to immobilize me. Instead, I must control them, for it is in the very exercise of this control that my necessary courage is shared. (Freire, 1998, p. 41)

Tolerance is another of the indispensable qualities on Freire's list. Without this virtue, he contends, no authentic democratic experience can be actualized in the classroom or our own lives. But it is important to note that tolerance "does not mean acquiescing to the intolerable; it does not mean covering up disrespect; it does not mean coddling the aggressor or disguising aggression" (Freire, 1998, p. 43). Freire adamantly stressed that tolerance is neither about *playing the game,* nor a civilized gesture of hypocrisy, nor a coexistence with the unbearable. Instead, the critical expression of tolerance is founded on the basic human principles of respect, discipline, dignity, and ethical responsibility.

Finally, Freire assigned *decisiveness, security,* the *tension between patience and impatience,* and the *joy of living* to the set of indispensable qualities. He wholeheartedly believed that the ability to make decisions, despite the possibility of rupture, is an essential strength of our work as progressive educators. He argued that teachers who lack this quality often resort to irresponsible practices of permissiveness in their teaching, a condition that is as damaging to students as the abuse of teacher authority. Further, a lack of confidence was often linked to indecision, although security (or confidence), on the other hand, stems from a sense of competence, political clarity, and ethical integrity.

The ability of teachers to practice their pedagogy within the *dialectical tension of patience and impatience* represented for Freire a significant leap in an educator's development. This virtue allows teachers to both feel the urgency of the difficult conditions they are facing within schools and at the same time respond with thoughtful and reflective tactics and strategies, rather than *blind activism*. Key to understanding this concept is recognizing the problematics of those who espouse an ethic of *absolute patience* on one hand, and those who manifest an *uncontainable impatience* on the other. Both can impair our ability to participate pedagogically in effective ways.

At no time is the ability to cultivate a *dialectical* understanding of the world more necessary than when we as educators are asked to live within the tension of two seemingly contradictory concepts of responses. This is to say, living an *impatient patience* or *insecure security* is predicated on our willingness and ability to grapple with the complexity and ambiguity of the present, despite a heightened level of tension we may experience. And, as such, to respond in coherence with our democratic dream, rather than to seek prescribed formulas or quick-fix recipes to alleviate the tension, potentially is a creative and liberating force in our lives. This dialectical competence also implies a *verbal parsimony,* which helps us to rarely lose control over our words or exceed the limits of considered, yet energetic, discourse—a quality that Freire consistently demonstrated over the years during his participation in difficult dialogues.

Freire placed great significance on our ability to live joyfully despite the multitude of external forces that constantly challenge our humanity. The indispensable quality of *teaching with a joy of living* personifies most the ultimate purpose in both Freire's work and life. In retrospect, I am filled with wonderful memories of Freire—the beauty of his language, the twinkle in his eyes, his thoughtful and respectful manner, the movement of his hands when he spoke, his lively enthusiasm when contemplating new ideas, and his candid expressions of love and gratitude. In his words and his deed, Freire persistently invited teachers to fully embrace life, rather than to surrender our existence to the stifling forces of economic and social injustice.

> By completely giving myself to life rather than to death—without meaning either to deny death or to mythicize life—I can free myself to surrender to the joy of living, without having to hide the reasons for sadness in life, which prepares me to stimulate and champion joy in the school. (Freire, 1998, p. 45)

Although Freire does not explicitly speak of activism in his *Letters to Those Who Dare to Teach* (1998), his theoretical work was never disassociated from his activism. Moreover, he argued tirelessly for the inseparability of political consciousness and political action in our teaching and in our lives. Hence, teachers as intellectuals, cultural workers, and community activists must "aspire to become an association of truly serious and coherent people, those who work to shorten more and more the distance between what they say and what they do" (Freire, 1997, p. 83). The transformation of schools can only take place when teachers, working in solidarity, take ownership and struggle to radically change the political and economic structures of power that defile our revolutionary dreams.

Thus I can see no alternative for educators to unity within the diversity of their interests in defending their rights. Such rights include the right to freedom in teaching, the right to speak, the right to better conditions for pedagogical work, the right to paid sabbaticals for continuing education, the right to be coherent, the right to criticize the authorities without fear of retaliation . . . and to not have to lie to survive. (Freire, 1998, p. 46)

REFERENCES

Carnoy, M. (1997). Foreword to *Pedagogy of the heart* by P. Freire. New York: Continuum.

Dowbor, L. (1997). Preface to *Pedagogy of the heart* by P. Freire. New York: Continuum.

Freire, P. (1970). *Pedagogy of the oppressed.* New York: Seabury.

Freire, P. (July, 1987). *People of Color Caucus Dialogue.* Critical Pedagogy Conference, University of California, Irvine, CA.

Freire, P. (1993). *Pedagogy of the city.* New York: Continuum.

Freire, P. (1997). *Pedagogy of the heart.* New York: Continuum.

Freire, P. (1998). *Teachers as cultural workers: Letters to those who dare to teach.* Boulder, CO: Westview.

Freire, P., and Betto, F. (1985). *Essa escola chamada vida.* São Paulo: Atica.

Freire, P., and Faundez, A. (1989). *Learning to question: A pedagogy of liberation.* New York: Continuum.

Macedo, D., and Araujo Freire, A. (1998). Foreword to *Teachers as cultural workers: Letters to those who dare to teach* by P. Freire. Boulder, CO: Westview.

Shor, I., and Freire, P. (1987). *A pedagogy for liberation.* South Hadley, Mass.: Bergin & Garvey.

Suggested Readings
for Future Study

TEACHING FOR SOCIAL TRANSFORMATION

Allman, P. (2001). *Revolutionary social transformation: Democratic hopes, politic possibilities and critical education.* Westport, Conn: Bergin & Garvey.

Apple, M., and Christian-Smith, L. eds. (1991). *The politics of the textbook.* New York: Routledge.

Ayers, W. (1998). *Teaching for social justice: A democracy and education reader.* New York: New Press.

Beyer, L., and Apple, M. (1998). *The curriculum: Problems, politics and possibilities.* Albany: SUNY Press.

Freire, P. (1973). *Education for critical consciousness.* New York: Continuum.

Freire, P. (1985). *The politics of education.* South Hadley, Mass.: Bergin & Garvey.

Freire, P. (1996). *Pedagogy of hope.* New York: Continuum.

Freire, P. (1998). *Pedagogy of freedom: Ethics, democracy, and civic courage.* Lanham, Md.: Rowman and Littlefield.

Forester, J., ed. (1985). *Critical theory and public life.* Cambridge, Mass.: MIT Press.

Giroux, H. (1997). *Pedagogy and the politics of hope: Theory, culture and schooling.* Boulder, Colo.: Westview.

Giroux, H. (1988). *Schooling and the struggle for public life: Critical pedagogy in the modern age.* Minneapolis: University of Minnesota Press.

Giroux, H. (1994). *Disturbing pleasures: Learning popular culture.* New York: Routledge.

Giroux, H. (1989). *Popular Culture: Schooling and everyday life.* Westport, Conn.: Bergin & Garvey.

Giroux, H. (1988). *Teachers as intellectuals: Toward a critical pedagogy of learning.* South Hadley, Mass.: Bergin & Garvey.

Greene, M. (2000). *Releasing the imagination: Essays on education, the arts and social change.* New York: Jossey-Bass.

Holtz, H., and associates (1988). *Education and the American dream: Conservative, liberals and radical debate the future of education.* MA: Bergin & Garvey.

Kohl, H. (1998). *The discipline of hope: Learning from a lifetime of teaching.* New York: The New Press.

McDonnell, L., Timpane, P. M., and Benjamin, R., eds. (2000). *Rediscovering the democratic purposes of education.* Kansas: University Press of Kansas.

O'Cadiz, M., Wong, P., and Torres, C. (1998). *Education and democracy: Paulo Freire, social movements and educational reform in São Paulo.* Boulder, Colo.: Westview.

Purpel, D. (1989). *The moral and spiritual crisis in education: A curriculum for justice and compassion in education.* South Hadley, Mass.: Bergin & Garvey.

Shor, I., and Freire, P. (1987). *A pedagogy for liberation: Dialogues on transforming education.* South Hadley, Mass.: Bergin & Garvey.

Tierney, W. (1993). *Building communities of difference: Higher education in the twenty-first century.* Westport, Conn.: Bergin & Garvey.

About the Editors

Antonia Darder is Professor of Educational Policy Studies at the University of Illinois, Urbana-Champaign.

Marta Baltodano is Assistant Professor of education and Assistant Coordinator of the bilingual, bicultural program at Loyola Marymount University in Los Angeles.

Rodolfo D. Torres is Associate Professor of education, political science, urban and regional planning and a member of the Focused Program in Labor Studies at the University of California, Irvine.

Permissions

McLaren, Peter, "Revolutionary Pedagogy in Post-Revolutionary Times: Rethinking the Political Economy of Critical Education" *Educational Theory*, vol. 48, no. 4, Fall 1998.

Elenes, C. Alejandra, "Reclaiming the Borderlands: Chicana/o Identity, Difference, and Critical Pedagogy," *Educational Theory*, vol. 47, no. 3, Summer 1997.

Haymes, Stephen Nathan, "Toward a Pedagogy of Place for Black Urban Struggle" reprinted by permission from *Race, Culture, and the City: A Pedagogy for Black Urban Struggle* by Stephen Nathan Haymes (ed.), the State University of New York Press, ©1995, State University of New York. All rights reserved.

hooks, bell, "Reflections on Race and Sex" from bell hooks, *Yearning: Race, Gender, and Cultural Politics*, © 1990 by bell hooks. Reprinted with permission from South End Press.

Darder, Antonia & Torres, Rodolfo D., "Shattering the 'Race' Lens: Toward a Critical Theory of Racism" from *Critical Ethnicity*, Robert Tai & Mary Kentatta (eds.) ©1999 Rowman & Littlefield.

Weiler, Kathleen. "Feminist Analyses of Gender and Schooling" from *Women Teaching for Change*, Kathleen Weiler. ©1987 by Bergin & Garvey. Reproduced with permission of Greenwood Publishing Group, Inc., Westport, CT.

Fine, Michelle, "Sexuality, Schooling, and Adolescent Females: The Missing Discourse of Desire" *Harvard Educational Review*, 58 (1), 1988, pp. 29–53. ©1988 by the President and Fellows of Harvard College. All rights reserved.

Unks, Gerald, "Thinking About the Gay Teen" from Gerald Unks, *The Gay Teen*, ©1999 by Routledge. Reprinted with permission from Routledge, a member of Taylor & Francis Books.

Gore, Jennifer, "What We Can Do for You! What *Can* "We" Do for "You"?: Struggling over Empowerment in Critical and Feminist Pedagogy" from *Educational Foundations* 4(3), 1990, pp. 5–26.

Freire, Paulo and Macedo, Donald, "Rethinking Literacy: A Dialogue" from *Literacy: Reading the Word and the World*, by Paulo Freire and Donaldo Macedo, ©1987 by Bergen & Garvey. Reproduced with permission of Greenwood Publishing Group, Inc., Westport, CT.

Peterson, Robert E., "Teaching How to Read the World and Change It: Critical Pedagogy in the Intermediate Grades" from *Literacy As Praxis: Culture, Language, and Pedagogy*, edited by Catherine Walsh, ©1991 by Ablex. Reprinted with permission of Greenwood Publishing Group, Inc., Westport, CT.

Delpit, Lisa, "Language Diversity and Learning," ©1990 by the National Council of Teachers of English. Reprinted with permission.

INDEX